T0312172

APPLIED METHODS
FOR TRADE POLICY ANALYSIS

Applied Methods for Trade Policy Analysis provides a comprehensive introduction to the applied economic modeling of trade policies. The book introduces the reader to trade policy concepts, welfare measurement, accounting frameworks, and both partial and general equilibrium modeling approaches. It first covers these topics at a basic level and then introduces the reader to a number of more advanced topics: imperfect competition, dynamic modeling, labor market structure, and environmental modeling. Economics graduate students, professors, and policymakers will find the collection to be an important reference tool.

APPLIED METHODS
FOR TRADE POLICY ANALYSIS

A Handbook

Edited by

JOSEPH F. FRANCOIS
Erasmus University,
World Trade Organization,
and the Centre for
Economic Policy Research

KENNETH A. REINERT
Kalamazoo College

CAMBRIDGE
UNIVERSITY PRESS

CAMBRIDGE UNIVERSITY PRESS
Cambridge, New York, Melbourne, Madrid, Cape Town, Singapore, São Paulo

Cambridge University Press
The Edinburgh Building, Cambridge CB2 8RU, UK

Published in the United States of America by Cambridge University Press, New York

www.cambridge.org
Information on this title: www.cambridge.org/9780521580038

First published 1997

A catalogue record for this publication is available from the British Library

Library of Congress Cataloguing in Publication data
Applied methods for trade policy analysis : a handbook / edited by
Joseph F. Francois, Kenneth A. Reinert.
p.   cm.
ISBN 0-521-58003-X (hardback). – ISBN 0-521-58997-5 (pbk.)
1. Commercial policy – Econometric models.   I. Francois, Joseph F.
II. Reinert, Kenneth A.
HF1411.A67   1997
382'.3 – dc20   96-30246
                                                              CIP

ISBN 978-0-521-58003-8 hardback
ISBN 978-0-521-58997-0 paperback

Transferred to digital printing 2007

Contents

Tables

Figures

Acknowledgements

We wish to thank our families for their support and patience during this project, particularly while we worked together in Geneva during October and November of 1994. To Gelaye, Mary-Lynne, Brendan, Conor, Alison, and Susan, *merci*. We would also like to acknowledge a Faculty Development Grant from Kalamazoo College, which supported this work. Finally, thanks are due to our friends and colleagues who endured many of the birth pains associated with this project.

List of Contributors

Bruce A. Blonigen, *University of Oregon*

Shantayanan Devarajan, *The World Bank*

Joseph E. Flynn, *U.S. International Trade Commission*

Joseph F. Francois, *Erasmus University, World Trade Organization, and Centre for Economic Policy Research*

Delfin S. Go, *The World Bank*

H. Keith Hall, *U.S. International Trade Commission*

Thomas W. Hertel, *Purdue University*

Elena Ianchovichina, *Purdue University*

Christian Keuschnigg, *Institute for Advanced Studies, Vienna*

Farida C. Khan, *University of Wisconsin-Parkside*

Wilhelm Kohler, *University of Essen Linz*

Samuel Laird, *World Trade Organization*

Hiro Lee, *Nagoya University*

Jeffrey D. Lewis, *The World Bank*

Andréa M. Maechler, *University of California, Santa Cruz*

William J. Martin, *The World Bank*

Bradley J. McDonald, *World Trade Organization*

Håkan Nordström, *World Trade Organization and Centre for Economic Policy Research*

Kenneth A. Reinert, *Kalamazoo College*

Sherman Robinson, *International Food Policy Research Institute and University of California, Berkeley*

David W. Roland-Holst, *Mills College, OECD Development Centre, and Centre for Economic Policy Research*

Vernon O. Roningen, *U.S. Department of Agriculture*

Clinton R. Shiells, *International Monetary Fund*

Pekka Sinko, *Government Institute for Economic Research, Finland*

Karen E. Thierfelder, *U.S. Naval Academy*

A Note to Readers

The chapters in this book employ numerical partial or general equilibrium models to illustrate concepts covered in the chapters. Many of these chapter models, along with additional stylized models that extend these concepts or that otherwise integrate the concepts from a number of chapters, have been made available over the Internet for classroom use and/or for application. The address for the home page is

http://www.intereconomics.com/handbook

In addition to model files, the home page for this book provides information on modeling software, data, and related sites on the internet.

This book includes references to commercial software packages, including GAMS, EXCEL, QUATTRO, GEMPACK, and GAUSS. These are registered trademarks, and the software is copyrighted and available commercially.

The views expressed herein are those of the authors and should not be attributed in any way to the institutions with which they are affiliated.

This book is dedicated to
Eileen and Frank Francois
Rosemarie and Robert Reinert

PART I

Introduction

1

Applied Methods for Trade Policy Analysis:
An Overview

Joseph F. Francois and Kenneth A. Reinert

After receiving their respective Ph.D.s, the authors of this chapter both set off to work at the U.S. International Trade Commission (USITC) in Washington. In our graduate studies, we had been steeped in mainstream international economics and, consequently, naively thought of ourselves as knowing at least the basics of what was necessary for working in an applied policy environment. Our delusions proved to be short-lived. Within a few weeks of our arrival at the USITC, it became apparent that there was a broad set of tools required for our jobs that were rather different from those emphasized in academia. There was also a need to temper these tools with a sense of policy relevance. Within months of our arrival, we needed to become versed in the nuances of imperfect substitutes models, trade data nomenclature, social accounting matrices, computable general equilibrium modeling, and a host of other concepts and methods. While the standard trade models continued to provide intuition in many areas, our day-to-day professional work was often in another realm entirely. In many cases, the applied work provided new and useful insight into the significance of various theoretical issues.

The purpose of this book is to assist others in their own professional journey from standard trade theory to applied trade analysis in a policy environment. Our objective is to make life easier for the graduate student working on an applied trade topic, the government or international organization economist engaged in the quantitative analysis of trade policy, or the policy analyst trying to understand what in the world trade economists are talking about in their reports. Our success in assisting such individuals in this bridging process will justify the book's existence.

The objective of this chapter is to provide a detailed overview of the objectives of the book, and a suggested strategy for its use. Our first task is to give the reader an idea of what it is that distinguishes applied trade policy analysis from theoretical trade policy analysis. We do not mean to convey the notion that the two types are unconnected, nor even that the delineation between the two is clear-cut. It can be difficult to tell when one has moved from "numbers with theory" to "theory with numbers." However, we recommend that you keep such a delineation in mind. This is discussed in Section I of the chapter. Our second task is to identify and describe some of the basic frameworks of applied trade policy analysis, the foundation concepts of the field. We take up this task in Section II. Building on these basic frameworks, we move on to a set of standard applications to which these methods can be applied; the description of these applications is provided in Section III. Section IV delves into a number of important extensions to the standard applications, all of which are important and active areas of research in their own right. Finally, in Section V we turn briefly to the issue of behavioral parameters. This book is devoted to applied analysis, centred on the collection, organization, and analysis of data through the construction of applied static and dynamic models. Such research depends not only on available production and trade statistics, but also on available parameter estimates. In our view, the econometric estimation of behavioral elasticities is a very important but relatively undervalued area of study. We conclude in Section VI with some final comments on model transparency.

I What Is Applied Trade Policy Analysis?

What distinguishes applied trade policy analysis from theoretical trade policy analysis? There is no clear line of division between theoretical and applied models, but rather a continuum from "theory" to "theory with numbers" to "numbers with theory." Nevertheless, we feel that there are a set of characteristics that *tend* to distinguish applied trade policy analysis from theoretical trade policy analysis. These include (i) a *detailed policy orientation*; (ii) the formulation of models that are not merely local approximations from non-distorted base equilibria but that, in contrast, provide sensible results for *nonlocal changes in policy parameters from distorted base equilibria*; (iii) a concern for *accurate and current data* as the foundation of the modeling exercise; and (iv) *model structure determined by the data*, rather than selective use of data to fit a theoretical structure. For example, data on two-way trade often precludes homogeneous goods models, dictating instead the inclusion of *product differentiation* at the country and/or firm level in the formulation of the model.

I.1 Detailed Policy Orientation

First, let us say a few words about what we mean by "detailed policy orientation." Many theoretical models consider trade policies, especially *ad valorem* tariffs, in the process of considering the properties of the model. The term "detailed policy orientation" as we use it here means more than a simple, theoretical consideration of *ad valorem* tariffs. It involves an analytical commitment to the sectoral and institutional details of a policy as well as a commitment to be engaged in the policymaking process with all the inherent frustrations. A concern for sectoral detail forces the researcher into the realms of trade data nomenclatures, input–output relationships, and industrial classification schemes. A concern for institutional detail requires attention to the way in which a trade measure is implemented. How are quotas allocated? Is there evidence of quota rent sharing? How do quotas and tariffs interact? Are there supporting domestic policies which must be addressed? Finally, engagement in a policymaking process requires a sensitivity to the types of information that are relevant to policymakers, a willingness to engage the public in lay explanations of models and results, and the patience to endure what often appear to the economist as mundane concerns of policymakers and the public.[1] The move from theoretical analysis to applied analysis often involves a change of professional mode from economist to public servant. The applied trade policy economist must wear more than one hat. Occasionally, when wearing the public service hat, we are asked to go beyond (or even contradict) the insights offered by formal analysis and condone purely political judgements on matters of policy. At this point, the hat should be hung back up on the rack.[2]

I.2 Nonlocal Changes from Distorted Base Equilibria

Most static applied trade policy analysis makes use of a procedure of economic analysis known as *comparative statics*. Even "dynamic" models often involve either the comparison of steady-state equilibria (comparative statics with time subscripts) or fake dynamics involving a sequence of static

---

1 An applied trade policy modeller was presenting the basic features of a sectorally detailed CGE trade model to a top trade official. The official's first question was "Does the model have an orange sector in it?" Reply: "I am afraid not, sir, oranges are included in the fruit sector." The official was disappointed.

2 An academic trade economist was presenting the basic features of a partial-equilibrium trade policy model for use in import relief cases to a senior U.S. trade official. At the conclusion of the presentation, the official commented, "That is all well and good, and I will certainly use it as long as it will allow me to vote the way I want to."

equilibria. Under this approach, an initial or base equilibrium is compared to an equilibrium in which some exogenous variable, such as a trade policy variable, has been changed. In most theoretical models, the economy starts off in a nondistorted state with no tariffs, quotas, or other taxes present. From this initial, nondistorted equilibrium, an infinitesimal tariff is introduced and a new, counterfactual equilibrium is solved for using the linear approximation of differential calculus. In applied trade policy analysis, the comparative static framework is used with two differences. First, the initial or base equilibrium has built into it the relevant set of distortions due to trade policy or other government interventions. This allows for second-best welfare effects of changes in trade policies. Second, changes in trade policies are those actually under consideration. They are, therefore, nonlocal.

As a consequence of the presence of distortions in the base equilibrium, the removal of small tariffs can reduce rather than improve welfare by reallocating economic activity into other distorted sectors. Since the model is analysing a second-best world, it is not always the case that trade liberalization improves welfare. As a consequence of the nonlocal policy parameters introduced into the analysis, the functional forms chosen to describe economic behaviour matter. The economy moves far enough away from the initial equilibrium for the functional forms used to determine where the economy lands. For example, in partial equilibrium models, linear versus constant elasticity functional forms can make a big difference when considering the effects of large tariffs or quotas.

I.3 Accurate and Current Data

In trade policy analysis based on the comparative static procedure described, three things determine the result of a policy simulation: the functional forms used to describe the behaviour of the model (model structure), the base data used to describe the initial equilibrium, and the behavioural elasticities used in the functional forms. Even if the analyst chooses functional forms with care, the share and elasticity parameters of these functional forms must be filled in accurately. The share parameters are calibrated from a data set describing the initial equilibrium. In a partial equilibrium model, this data set may be quite simple. In a general equilibrium model, it may be quite complex. In either case, if we want to provide results of some merit, care must be taken to make the base data accurate. That said, policymakers are often very much concerned with the currency of model results. It will be of little use to have a base data set a decade old, ideally, it will be up to date. Unfortunately, there is sometimes a trade-off between accuracy and currency of data. When there is, professional judgement must be used. The last elements of the model, behavioural elasticities, are also important. Their magnitude will determine both qualitative and quantitative results of models. Unfortunately, in our view, while the field of economics is obsessed with functional forms, it does not reward research into either the estimation of base data sets or behavioral elasticities for trade policy modeling. This is part of our field's bias toward theoretical as opposed to applied modeling.

Model Structure and Data Structure Finally, we turn to the trade-off between data structure and model structure. Consider product differentiation. The classical theoretical trade models assume that imports and domestic competing goods are *perfect* substitutes in demand. In this case, the model (i) describes interindustry trade only and (ii) cannot support a number of goods that exceed the number of factors.[3] Both of these characteristics prove to be severe limitations for applied work. To get around the second limitation, it is possible to specify a specific factor for each sector. With the additional factor of labour, then the number of factors exceeds the number of sectors by one, and ten, twenty, or thirty sector models become a possibility. This, however, still does not address the first limitation. Even at high levels of disaggregation, there are both imports *and* exports in the trade data for most sectors of any economy; intraindustry trade is a widespread phenomenon. A perfect substitutes model cannot explain this and therefore resorts to explaining net imports or net exports in any sector. In essence, this sweeps the two-way trade observed in the trade data under an analytical rug, in both partial and general equilibrium frameworks. Applied homogeneous goods models, while consistent with theory, are usually inconsistent with the observed world.

One alternative to all of these difficulties is simply to recognize that imports and domestic competing goods are *imperfect* substitutes in demand. This represents product differentiation by country of origin. This idea was originally proposed by Armington (1969), who used a constant elasticity of substitution (CES) functional form to describe preferences among imports from various countries. Consequently, the combination of product differentiation by country of origin and a CES functional form for preferences has become known as the *Armington assumption*. Product differentiation by country of origin has been incorporated into both partial and general equilibrium frameworks. In the partial equilibrium framework, this assumption

---

3 This result goes back to Samuelson (1953).

was utilized early on by Baldwin and Lewis (1978) and Baldwin, Mutti, and Richardson (1980). It was incorporated into a U.S. International Trade Commission Staff Study by Rousslang and Suomela (1985) which was widely circulated. In general equilibrium frameworks, the Armington assumption was used by Dervis, de Melo, and Robinson (1982); Whalley (1985); and de Melo and Robinson (1989).

The Armington assumption has been the centre of controversy.[4] Out of this controversy, a second alternative to the perfect substitutes assumption that recognizes the existence of product differentiation at the level of the firm has emerged. Appropriately, this approach is known as firm-level product differentiation. This approach has at least two origins. The first of these is the introduction of monopolistic competition into international trade theory, beginning with Krugman (1979, 1980) and Ethier (1979, 1982). The second is the incorporation of firm-level product differentiation into a model of the Canada–United States free trade agreement (CAFTA) by Brown and Stern (1989). The motivation of Brown and Stern was to minimize terms-of-trade effects inherent in the Armington structure. Norman (1990) has argued that the firm-level product differentiation approach is preferable to the country of origin or Armington approach because it locates product differentiation on the supply side. The limitation of the firm-level product differentiation approach is that the absence of firm-level data makes econometric estimation of elasticities difficult. This point has been emphasized by Winters (1990). Another limitation is that, as in the case of homogeneous goods models, models of pure firm-level product differentiation can yield indeterminate production patterns, when the number of goods exceeds the number of factors. In practice, therefore, models with firm-level product differentiation often incorporate product weights that are sector- and region-specific (see Brown, 1994). The result is that the spirit of Armington is often preserved in imperfect competition models, even when the formal Armington assumption is dropped.[5]

II Getting Started: Basic Frameworks

Suppose that you have been recently hired as an economist in the Trade Ministry of your country. Suppose further that your supervisor has given you a few weeks to sharpen your skills in the field of applied trade policy analysis

---

4 An overview of this controversy is provided in Francois and Shiells (1994).
5 It is possible to calibrate the demand elasticity for firm-level product differentiation from an elasticity of scale for the sector in question. The latter, though, are in short supply. For more on this see Chapter 11.

in preparation for an upcoming project. Where should you begin? We want
to suggest that you put aside for these few weeks your trade textbooks and
take a look at Part II of this book. Here we cover a number of subjects which
we think will be of more immediate use to you.[6]

In the classroom, we use a policy parameter *t*, an *ad valorem* tariff, to
introduce commercial policies into our models. In your Trade Ministry,
however, when you begin your first project, you will in all probability en-
counter a proliferation of commercial policies structured according to, perhaps, a number of different nomenclatures. No doubt, when mired in the
intricacies of these commercial policies, you will long for the simple *t* parameter of the graduate texts. To ease the difficulty, Chapter 2 takes up the
subject of quantifying commercial policies. It is only appropriate that a
volume on trade policy analysis begin with the policies themselves.

Chapter 2 considers tariffs, sometimes referred to as nominal protection.
The bulk of the chapter, though, deals with nontariff measures or NTMs.
The chapter analyses the qualitative effects of these trade measures and
their measurement. It also identifies sources of data on trade measures.
Appendix 2.1 presents the UNCTAD nomenclature of trade control measures, and Appendix 2.2 provides a glossary of NTMs. The chapter is not
exhaustive; if it were, it would fill the entire volume. Therefore, the reader
must utilize it, and its excellent set of references, as an *entrée* into the
literature on commercial policies.

In standard trade theory, we consider a move from autarky to free trade
and, under certain conditions, show that welfare under free trade must be at
least as great as welfare under autarky.[7] In your new role as trade economist,
this will be unsatisfactory for two reasons. First, second-best considerations
and terms of trade effects make welfare declines as a result of movements
toward free trade a logical possibility. Second, even if welfare increases as a
result of a movement towards free trade, the burning question will be, How
much? In one way or another, you will have to quantify welfare effects. This
brings us to Chapter 3.

Chapter 3 identifies three commonly used approaches to general equilibrium welfare evaluation in distorted open economies. These are the balance
of trade function approach based on compensation measures, the direct
evaluation approach using a money metric, and Marshallian surplus
measures. The balance of trade function yields measures of the compensation required to maintain utility at a specified level. The equivalent variation

6 Other useful references which address commercial policy *theory* are Vousden (1990) and Helpman and
  Krugman (1989).
7 Dixit and Norman (1980, Chapter 3).

version of this measure provides a money metric of welfare change. The money metric approach is different from the compensation approach in the presence of distortions and is shown to be identical with a modified version of the balance of trade function derived from the public finance literature. Diagrammatic surplus measures are derived by using Taylor series expansions to provide intuition about the source of welfare gains or losses from changes in trade policies or terms of trade.

In trade theory, once we have shown that the movement from autarky to trade cannot reduce welfare, we then turn to a set of comparative static experiments in which we consider the effects of transfers, factor supply changes, technological change, and trade policies on the endogenous variables of the system.[8] When using the linear approximation of total differentiation, there appear in the system a number of parameters that reflect the initial values of variables. The size of these initial values determines the quantitative and sometimes the qualitative results of the comparative static exercises. In applied trade models, we usually solve models in level form rather than using linearization methods.[9] Nevertheless, the system still has a (large) number of parameters reflecting initial values of variables. Since we are very concerned with the quality of both qualitative and quantitative results in applied trade policy modeling, establishing these initial values is of prime importance. In the literature on computable or applied general equilibrium modeling, these initial values are entered into the model by *calibrating* the model to what is known as a *benchmark equilibrium dataset*.[10] The benchmark equilibrium dataset serves as a description of the economy in the initial equilibrium before any policy changes have been made. How does one construct such a dataset? Recently, it has become standard practice to construct them in the form of a *social accounting matrix* or SAM, originally developed to analyze income distribution issues in developing counties.[11] Chapter 4 of this volume is an introduction to the concept of SAMs and their use as benchmark equilibrium datasets. It has circulated in recent years through a number of international organizations and has proved helpful in a number of applications.

Chapter 4 begins in a very straightforward way with simple macroeconomic SAMs which are related to familiar macroeconomic accounting identities. It then moves, step by step, to more complicated SAMs by adding institutional accounts and sectoral detail. The chapter lays out a basic meth-

8 Dixit and Norman (1980, Chapter 5).
9 On the issue of linearization versus level solution, see Hertel, Horride, and Pearson (1992).
10 On calibration and benchmark equilibrium datasets, see Shoven and Whalley (1984) and Shoven and Whalley (1992, Chapter 5).
11 See Pyatt and Round (1985).

odology for SAM construction and consolidation which should help to simplify this tedious process for you. It then begins to describe the relationship between SAMs and general equilibrium analysis of trade policy by addressing three topics: flexible aggregation, calibration, and closure. In the case of flexible aggregation, the authors make a case for maintaining a sectorally detailed SAM which is aggregated in a different fashion for each trade policy that comes under scrutiny. This methodology is taken up in Chapter 7 (discussed later).

While international trade theory is fundamentally a general equilibrium affair, there are many circumstances in which single market or partial equilibrium modeling is both appropriate and desirable. For example, there are many highly detailed trade policies applying to specific products which will be a small portion of standard industrial classifications of the economy in question. In this case, it is simply not possible to construct a SAM for a general equilibrium model. An antidumping case on Chinese candles or Korean baseball uniforms is best addressed in a partial equilibrium framework. The partial equilibrium models of trade that we learned as undergraduates are only the starting point for the models used by applied trade policy analysts today, not in the least because of their perfect substitutes assumption. A whole menu of alternative models, solvable on spreadsheets, are utilized on a daily basis around the world. Chapter 5 provides an introduction to such models.

Chapter 5 outlines, in detail, methodological approaches for constructing simple partial equilibrium trade models. Emphasis is placed on quantifying the effects of tariffs and nontariff measures on trade, production, and national income. The chapter begins with perfect substitute models and then continues with imperfect substitute models. It takes you through the modeling of both tariffs and quotas and numerically illustrates several important concepts, including linearization errors and the implications of underlying distortions for second-best policy options. Despite its partial equilibrium emphasis, welfare measures are explicitly linked to their general equilibrium counterparts, making clear what assumptions are being made when measuring welfare in partial equilibrium. Importantly, the chapter introduces you to the implementation of applied models using spreadsheet software.

As stated in Section I, product differentiation plays an important role in distinguishing applied trade policy analysis from its theoretical counterpart. For many years, a barrier to making the intellectual transition from theoretical to applied models has been the complex model structure introduced by incorporating product differentiation in applied general equilibrium trade models. It is a long leap from a simple Jones or Dixit–Norman style model to the blizzard of goods and prices within a computable general equilibrium (CGE) model. How can you make this leap in the few weeks you have at your Ministry? The answer to this question is, by focusing on a model with a minimum of sectoral detail. This is exactly what is done in Chapter 6.

Chapter 6 introduces a basic applied trade policy model with one country, two producing sectors, and three goods, a model the authors therefore call the 1–2–3 model. The chapter begins with a simple analytical version of the model and relates it to the seminal papers of Salter (1959) and Swan (1960) and the whole issue of nontradables. As you will see, however, from an empirical point of view, their approach to nontradables is more satisfactory than the standard theoretical approach of Komiya (1967) and Ethier (1972) since it does not define nontradability on a sectoral basis. The importance of this approach is obvious when you examine trade data that includes service sectors: There are few sectors which do not show at least some amount of trade. The chapter uses the analytical model to assess the impacts of a number of economic changes which will help give you some intuition for its properties. Next, it adds a government and investment sector to the model to bring it closer to models actually used in trade policy analysis. It then explains how to implement this more realistic model in a spreadsheet framework and conducts a revenue-neutral tariff reform experiment as an illustrative policy experiment. Along the way, you will be introduced to the constant elasticity of substitution and constant elasticity of transformation functional forms widely used in CGE modeling.

Your first few weeks of orientation in your new position have passed. Having assimilated the material of Part II, you will face your first trade policy assignment. However, you now have a number of basic analytical frameworks from which to draw, and you will not be at a loss in making the transition from theory-based analysis to applied policy analysis. What might your first application of these frameworks look like? Part III provides a few alternatives.

III Putting the Basics to Work: Standard Applications

You have just returned from a meeting with your supervisor and other Ministry colleagues, and at this meeting you were given your first assignment. It is likely that you will be working on a project involving a specific set of policies in a specific set of products or sectors. Perhaps a trade delegate is considering offering a specific tariff concession at the World Trade Organization (WTO), or perhaps a domestic industry has successfully lobbied for a quota in a particular sector. Chapter 7 will lead you through an approach to your assignment in a general equilibrium context. In the chapter, the flexible aggregation approach advocated in Chapter 4 is utilized. The chapter makes use of a 487-sector SAM of the United States, using three different aggregations of it to analyze a sectoral tariff, domestic and foreign allocated quotas, and an import prohibition. Along the way, the chapter will introduce you to the specification of a CGE model and describe the modeling of tariffs and quotas. The simulations described will give you an idea of the types of results that can be obtained from general equilibrium models and some of the general equilibrium considerations involved. An Appendix will introduce you to the linear expenditure system which is often used to model household demand in CGE models.

It is possible that your first assignment concerns commodities so narrowly defined that it will not be possible for you to utilize a general equilibrium framework. Or it may be that the time frame of your assignment precludes the construction of a CGE model. Then you may need to resort to partial equilibrium analysis. This does not prevent you from accounting for some basic interactions among the markets or regions involved. Building on Chapter 5, Chapter 8 will introduce you to the procedures involved in specifying and solving multiproduct, multiregion partial equilibrium models. Such models have proved particularly relevant for modeling agricultural policies.

In some instances, your assignment will not only require a general equilibrium point of view, but will be inherently global. For instance, you might be asked to assess the impact of a round of global trade negotiations on developing countries. Since the policy involved is both multisectoral and multilateral, proper analysis requires global modeling. Not long ago, the limits of computer technology would effectively prevent such an endeavour. With current computing technology, however, it is now possible to construct and solve large global general equilibrium models on a personal computer. Chapter 9 of this volume describes the process involved in global modeling. Emphasis is placed on the important differences between macro closure rules employed in single-region models and multiregion models.

Standard trade theory, via the Stolper–Samuelson (1941) Theorem and its Ricardo–Viner equivalents (Ruffin and Jones, 1977), provides information on the effects of tariffs on the returns to primary factors. In most applied general equilibrium trade models, changes in primary factor returns then help to determine the welfare of a single, representative household. Ironically, one early strand of CGE models (e.g., Adelman and Robinson, 1978) as well as the early SAM literature (e.g., Stone, 1985) was developed precisely to analyze income distribution in *multihousehold* contexts. With few exceptions, multihousehold concerns have not been a priority in applied policy research. While this might be appropriate in many developed country applications, it is hardly appropriate in many developing country applications, especially given the present concerns with the impacts of structural adjustment policies on poverty. In light of the above, Chapter 10 takes up the question of household disaggregation in applied general equilibrium trade models. Following a survey of the literature on income distribution and trade policy analysis, the chapter turns to two methodological issues: household classification and measurement of distributional impacts. A CGE trade model for Bangladesh is specified, and the model is used to assess the impacts of trade liberalization on income distribution. Appendix 10.3 provides a brief guide to various income distribution measures.

IV Getting Fancy: Extensions

Imagine now that you have been in your position at the Ministry for a year or two. You are now very comfortable with both the foundation methods of applied trade policy analysis and their application. Most likely, somewhere in your work you have been struck by a problem that lies beyond the standard applications of your models. Perhaps this concerned an issue of labour markets, imperfect competition, or an externality question. Part IV takes up some of these matters. This last section of the book goes significantly beyond Parts II and III in its level of difficulty. The material of this section is also currently under discussion in both academic and policy communities. Finally, these extensions are more information-intensive than the standard applications. For these reasons, you should proceed cautiously when incorporating the material of Part IV into your policy analysis at the Trade Ministry.

In the last decade, international trade theory has incorporated a number of elements from industrial organization to analyze the determinants of trade under imperfect competition. Sometimes referred to as the new international trade theory, these developments have contributed to the understanding of intraindustry trade and multinational corporations.[12] In the applied trade policy literature, there simultaneously developed a concern for the role of economies of scale in measuring the cost of protection (e.g., Dixon, 1978). These two sets of concerns came together in a paper by Harris (1984), who argued that the inclusion of scale economies in a general equilibrium model of trade liberalization can substantially affect the quantitative

---

12 Grossman (1992) collects a number of key papers in this area.

results of liberalization experiments.[13] These matters are taken up in Chapter 11.

Chapter 11 takes a broad view of alternatives available in specifying applied trade policy models with imperfect competition. Beginning with a brief explanation of the potential procompetitive effects of trade policy reform, the chapter then considers alternative approaches to specifying and calibrating firm-level costs. It considers market power in both homogeneous goods models and heterogeneous goods models. In the latter case, it contrasts country-level (Armington) and firm-level product differentiation. Some of the key concepts are illustrated with a multiregion CGE model focused on Korea. This model is an extension of the one used in Chapter 9.

As indicated in Section II, most of international trade theory employs the comparative static framework. The term "static" in this context generally refers to the fact that no attention is given to the path along which the economy travels from one equilibrium to another. The term, however, has at least two other meanings. First, by static we might indicate that economic or policy changes have no effect on the accumulation of capital and the associated change in production possibilities. Second, static might mean that economic or policy changes have no effect on the *rate* of growth. A sizable theoretical literature exists on trade and capital accumulation (e.g., Smith, 1976, 1977; Baldwin, 1992). With regard to the impacts of economic and policy changes on growth rates, a relatively recent branch of trade theory has grown from the contributions of Romer (1987) and Lucas (1988).[14] The incorporation of capital accumulation and growth effects into numerical models is relatively new.[15] However, numerical models in which trade policy affects capital accumulation and production possibilities do exist.

Chapter 12 is devoted to the analysis of trade and investment linkages in steady state. Emphasis is placed on capital market closure rules that relate trade policy to investment effects. Following a brief overview of theoretical linkages between trade and investment, an application that examines the investment-related effects of the Uruguay Round is offered. Chapter 12 is devoted to steady-state comparisons (comparative statics with time subscripts) and ignores the explicit modeling of adjustment paths. In contrast, Chapter 13 provides an introduction to the issues surrounding the dynamic effects of commercial policy, including time paths. It shows that incorporating intertemporal optimization into applied general equilibrium trade models can allow one to describe the growth effects often attributed to liberali-

---

13 See, however, the concerns raised in Section V.
14 For a review of this literature, see Francois and Shiells (1993).
15 For a review of the issues involved, see Kehoe (1994).

zation efforts and to evaluate them in welfare terms. The chapter develops a dynamic general equilibrium model calibrated to Austrian data. The model features overlapping generations with lifetime uncertainty. Investment and savings are determined by intertemporal optimization under perfect foresight. The chapter discusses the calibration of dynamic parameters and applies the model to a number of trade policy exercises.

In your experience at the Trade Ministry, it probably will have become apparent that a primary concern of both trade policy officials and the public is employment. It is often a long distance from such concerns to standard trade theory. Most trade theory models specify labour markets that operate in a perfectly functioning manner with no institutional rigidities. Traditionally, labour market rigidities have been brought into trade theory via wage differentials (e.g., Bhagwati and Srinivasan, 1971), generalized sticky wages (e.g., Brecher, 1974), and sector-specific sticky wages (e.g., Harris and Todaro, 1970). More recently, a number of new approaches to the labour market have been generated from the macroeconomic field of New Keynesian Economics. Efficiency wage, insider–outsider, and implicit contract models are but a few of the new ideas of this literature.[16] At a more basic level, employment data often preclude the treatment of labour as homogeneous. Like trade data, employment data also raise the issue of heterogeneity in relevant markets. Chapters 14 and 15 are devoted to modeling employment in general equilibrium. The chapters will introduce you to some of the possibilities for and implications of incorporating these New Keynesian ideas about labour markets into general equilibrium trade models.

While the relation of trade to employment is a concern with a long history, that of trade and the environment is a concern both recent and intense. When the employment and environment issues coalesce on a particular trade matter, such as the North American Free Trade Area, policy analysis becomes highly politicized. Politics aside, though, the microeconomics of trade and the microeconomics of externalities and depletable resources are fully compatible.[17] It is, for example, quite clear that environmental externalities can yield consequences for the efficiency gains from trade.

Chapter 16 begins with the recognition that the transfer of environmental effects among countries is embodied in trade patterns. It takes up the case of the trade relationship between Japan and Indonesia. In this chapter, you will see how it is possible to make use of environmental satellite accounts, in

16 For a collection of central articles in this field, see Mankiw and Romer (1991).
17 For a collection of papers on the analysis of trade and the environment, see Anderson and Blackhurst (1992).

addition to the SAM framework developed in Chapter 4, in calibrating a general equilibrium trade model with multieffluent components. You will also be introduced to a measure of embodied effluent trade, which can help to establish the extent to which environmental costs have been transferred from one country to another. In this particular case, there is a negative link between trade and the environment for Indonesia, and a variety of policies are examined for mitigation of the pollution intensity of Indonesian production.

Our hope is that Part IV will have, at the least, demonstrated to you the wide array of extensions to standard trade policy modeling which are possible. This should allow you to develop your own research program at the Trade Ministry in light of the issues that appear to be most important in that context.

V Parameterization

Over a decade ago, Dale Jorgenson (1984) made the following statement:

The development of computational methods for solving nonlinear general equilibrium models . . . has been the focus of much recent research. By comparison the development of econometric methods for estimating the unknown parameters describing technology and preferences in such models has been neglected. (p. 139)

In our view, the state of affairs described by Jorgenson is as much a reality today as it was a decade ago. Our own explanation for this phenomenon is that the profession of economics in general and international trade in particular does not value "nut and bolt" empirical work to the extent it values new twists on old theoretical insights. That said, we do want to familiarize you with the econometric literature that does exist and is most relevant to your mission at the Ministry.

To begin, we will describe the ideal approach, represented by Jorgenson's modeling efforts. Jorgenson has constructed a dynamic model of the United States economy which has been applied to trade as well as other issues (Ho and Jorgenson, 1994). The methodology used for estimating the behavioural parameters of this model is presented in Jorgenson (1984). Jorgenson develops a time series of SAMs and then estimates the behavioural parameters of his model from them on the basis of translog functional forms. Without commenting on the translog function itself, it is clear that the time series of SAMs approach has advantages. It represents a consistency extended across time which the single SAM imposes across sectors and institutions. One drawback to the approach is that it is intensive in research resources. A second drawback is that it locks in a particular sectoring scheme, precluding the flexible aggregation approach described in Section II. For these reasons, most trade policy analysts have chosen to focus on the most crucial components of their model for econometric estimation, taking the remainder of their behavioral parameters from the literature. Further, in the estimation of the crucial parameters, the analysts typically construct time series of the relevant variables only, rather than of the entire SAM.

What is the most crucial parameter for trade policy modeling? If a small sample of available studies reveals a preference of modellers, it seems that emphasis is placed on the magnitude of elasticities of substitution between imports and domestic competing goods. This is because these elasticities are the nexus between trade policies on the import side and the domestic economy; an early study that estimated these elasticities was Alaouze, Marsden, and Zeitsch (1977). A more recent series of studies began with Shiells, Stern, and Deardorff (1986); these authors estimated the elasticity of substitution or Armington elasticity between imports and domestic competing goods for the United States, accounting for the simultaneity of the import demand and supply. Reinert and Roland-Holst (1992) also focused on the United States and explicitly utilized the CES functional form for preferences, the Armington assumption. This was also done in the context of the North American Free Trade Area by Shiells and Reinert (1993) and Reinert and Shiells (1992). These authors also employed the Armington assumption but disaggregated U.S. imports into those from Canada, Mexico, and the rest of the world. A summary table of Armington elasticities from Reinert and Roland-Holst is provided in the Appendix to Chapter 5.

Alston et al. (1990) compared the CES functional form with the Almost Ideal Demand System (AIDS) of Deaton and Muellbauer (1980). In the context of some specific agricultural commodities, these authors found that the elasticity of substitution between imports and domestic competing goods in the United States was substantially higher in the AIDS estimation. Shiells, Roland-Holst, and Reinert (1993) estimated an AIDS system for U.S. imports from Canada, Mexico, and the rest of the world but encountered regularity problems. A general equilibrium trade model of United States–Mexico free trade which employs the AIDS import demand formulation can be found in Burfisher et al. (1994).

As stated in Section IV, trade under imperfect competition has become increasingly important during the last decade or so. A part of this importance reflects a concern for the role of scale economies in determining the effects of trade policies. In calibrating a trade model with scale economies, it is necessary to incorporate some information on the extent to which scale economies actually exist. Failure to incorporate high-quality information on scale economies can lead to misleading policy simulations.

Scale economies are typically measured by using what are known as cost disadvantage ratios. The cost disadvantage ratio is related to the scale efficiency parameter, S, which measures the extent to which the average cost (AC) curve lies above the marginal cost (MC) curve: $S=AC/MC$. The cost disadvantage ratio is then defined as $CDR=1-(1/S)=1-(MC/AC)$. If MC is assumed to be constant, $CDR=FC/TC$, where FC denotes fixed cost and TC denotes total costs. De Melo and Tarr (1992) discuss the means by which the CDR is used to calibrate a general equilibrium trade model with scale economies; their estimates of CDRs for the U.S. automobile and steel industries are based on selected industry studies.

For more sectorally comprehensive models, Harris (1986) reports scale efficiency parameters for Canada "based on reported econometric values from the literature" (p. 236). Sobarzo (1994) reports scale efficiency parameters for Mexico. Haaland and Tollefsen (1994) report information on returns to scale for a four-region (European Union, European Free Trade Agency [EFTA], United States, Japan) trade model. Pratten (1988) conducts a survey of engineering estimates of minimum efficient scale by industry for the European Union. Francois, McDonald, and Nordström (1995) and Harrison, Rutherford, and Tarr (1995) utilize figures from Pratten to calibrate CDRs in models of the Uruguay Round. Francois et al. also provide sensitivity testing of their results for both Armington and scale elasticities. In models of trade based on monopolistic competition, the scale elasticity plays a similar theoretical role to the substitution elasticity in Armington models. Not surprisingly, therefore, depending on model specification, the range of numerical results is highly sensitive to both sets of parameters. If one follows the chain of references in various studies, it turns out that most scale elasticity estimates can be traced to a small family of engineering studies centred on the 1960s and 1970s. This leaves us somewhat uneasy about the robustness of scale-based estimates.

A further elaboration on the theme of scale economies is based on the new growth theories, which emphasize trade- and production-based dynamic externalities. Yang (1993) has examined the Uruguay Round in a model of trade-based externalities, while Keuschnigg (1995) emphasizes innovation-based externalities. The literature on imperfect competition points, in reduced form, to factors that suggest static, external scale economies on a regional and global basis. The new growth literature highlights a number of factors that, in reduced form, point to a similar set of dynamic externalities. As for static scale effects, the incorporation of dynamic scale effects in numerical models, in a credible matter, must be built on solid empirical evidence of such dynamic externalities. In our view, recent advances in trade theory, related to both imperfect competition and trade-related growth mechanisms, strengthen the need for empirical research aimed at parameter estimation.

VI Some Final Comments on Transparency

It is important to keep in mind that the methods covered in this book are not economic forecast tools. Rather, they represent extensions of other forms of economic analysis, including theory, statistical description, qualitative analysis, and even simple insight. All models, applied and theoretical, are incomplete by definition. They are deliberately simple representations of a complex world, designed to let us focus on possible interactions in a subset of important elements. The advantage applied modeling offers is that we are able to combine real world data with formal theory as part of the mix of inductive and deductive reasoning that makes up economic analysis. In the process of policy analysis, the construction and use of models will both influence, and be influenced by, these other approaches to economic method. Having said this, the reader should also be aware that the results of numerical analysis can take on a life of their own when released into a policy environment. Very rough guesses can be marketed as precise estimates, packaged with interpretations unanticipated or unintended by the original analysts. In such a situation, the limitations of the original analysis are easily (and sometimes deliberately) forgotten. For this reason, it is very important that the nature of the analytic exercise be kept in mind, and be transmitted (as often as necessary) to the relevant policy audience. Transparency is critical.

References

Adelman, I. and S. Robinson. 1978. *Income Distribution Policy in Developing Countries: A Case Study of Korea*. Stanford, California: Stanford University Press.

Alaouze, C.M., J.S. Marsden, and J. Zeitsch. 1977. "Estimates of the elasticity of substitution between imported and domestically produced commodities at the four digit ASIC level." IMPACT Project Working Paper No. 0-11, Melbourne, Australia.

Alston, J.M., C.A. Carter, R. Green, and D. Pick. 1990. "Whither Armington trade models?" *American Journal of Agricultural Economics* 72:455–467.

Anderson, K. and R. Blackhurst, eds. 1992. *The Greening of World Trade Issues*. New York: Harvester Wheatsheaf.

Armington, P.S. 1969. "A theory of demand for products distinguished by place of production." *IMF Staff Papers* 16:159–177.

Baldwin, R.E. 1992. "Measurable dynamic gains from trade." *Journal of Political Economy* 100:162–174.

Baldwin, R.E. and W.E. Lewis. 1978. "U.S. tariff effects on trade and employment in detailed SIC industries." In *The Impact of International Trade and Investment on Employment*, edited by W.G. Dewald. Washington, D.C.: Bureau of International Labor Affairs, U.S. Department of Labor.

Baldwin, R.E., J.H. Mutti, and J.D. Richardson. 1980. "Welfare effects on the United States of a significant multilateral tariff reduction." *Journal of International Economics* 10:405–423.

Bhagwati, J. and T.N. Srinivasan. 1971. "The theory of wage differentials: Production response and factor price equalization." *Journal of International Economics* 1:19–35.

Brecher, R. 1974. "Minimum wage rates and the pure theory of international trade." *Quarterly Journal of International Economics* 88:98–116.

Brown, D. 1994. "Properties of applied general equilibrium trade models with monopolistic competition and foreign direct investment." In *Modelling Trade Policy: AGE Models of North American Free Trade*, edited by J. Francois and C. Shiells. Cambridge: Cambridge University Press.

Brown, D.K. and R.M. Stern. 1989. "U.S.–Canada bilateral tariff elimination: The role of product differentiation and market structure." In *Trade Policies for Competitiveness*, edited by R.C. Feenstra. Chicago: University of Chicago Press.

Burfisher, M.E., S. Robinson and K.E. Thierfelder. 1994. "Wage changes in a U.S.–Mexico free trade area: Migration versus Stolper–Samuelson effects." In *Modelling Trade Policy: Applied General Equilibrium Assessments of North American Free Trade*, edited by J. Francois and C. Shiells. Cambridge: Cambridge University Press.

Deaton, A. and J. Muellbauer. 1980. "An almost ideal demand system." *American Economic Review* 70:312–326.

De Melo, J. and S. Robinson. 1989. "Product differentiation and the treatment of foreign trade in computable general equilibrium models of small economies." *Journal of International Economics* 27:47–67.

De Melo, J. and D. Tarr. 1992. *A General Equilibrium Analysis of U.S. Foreign Trade Policy*. Cambridge, Massachusetts: MIT Press.

Dervis, K., J. de Melo, and S. Robinson. 1982. *General Equilibrium Models for Development Policy*. Cambridge: Cambridge University Press.

Dixit, A.K. and V. Norman. 1980. *Theory of International Trade*. Cambridge: Cambridge University Press.

Dixon, P.B. 1978. "Economies of scale, commodity disaggregation and the costs of protection." *Australian Economic Papers* 17:63–80.

Ethier, W. 1972. "Nontraded goods and the Heckscher–Ohlin model." *International Economic Review* 13:132–147.

Ethier, W. 1979. "International decreasing costs and world trade." *Journal of International Economics* 9:1–24.

Ethier, W. 1982. "National and international returns to scale in the modern theory of international trade." *American Economic Review* 72:950–959.

Francois, J.F. and C.R. Shiells. 1993. *The Dynamic Effects of Trade Liberalization: A Survey*. Washington, D.C.: U.S. International Trade Commission.

Francois, J.F. and C.R. Shiells. 1994. "Applied general equilibrium models of North American free trade." In *Modelling Trade Policy: Applied General Equilibrium Assessments of North American Free Trade*, edited by J. Francois and C. Shiells. Cambridge: Cambridge University Press.

Francois, J.F., B. McDonald, and H. Nordström. 1995. "Assessing the Uruguay Round." Paper 6, World Bank Conference, *The Uruguay Round and the Developing Economies*, January.

Grossman, G.M., ed. 1992. *Imperfect Competition and International Trade*. Cambridge, Massachusetts: MIT Press.

Haaland, J.I. and T.C. Tollefsen. 1994. "The Uruguay Round and trade in manufactures and services: General equilibrium simulations of production, trade and welfare effects of liberalization." Center for Economic Policy Research Discussion Paper No. 1008.

Harris, J.R. and M.P. Todaro. 1970. "Migration, unemployment and development: A two-sector analysis." *American Economic Review* 60:126–142.

Harris, R.G. 1984. "Applied general equilibrium analysis of small open economies with scale economies and imperfect competition." *American Economic Review* 74:1016–1031.

Harris, R.G. 1986. "Market structure and trade liberalization: A general equilibrium assessment." In *General Equilibrium Trade Policy Modelling*, edited by T.N. Srinivasan and J. Whalley. Cambridge, Massachusetts: MIT Press.

Harrison, G., T. Rutherford, and D. Tarr. 1994. "Quantifying the Uruguay Round." Paper 7, World Bank Conference, *The Uruguay Round and the Developing Economies*, January.

Helpman, E. and P.R. Krugman. 1989. *Trade Policy and Market Structure*. Cambridge, Massachusetts: MIT Press.

Hertel, T., J. Horride, and K. Pearson. 1992. "Mending the family tree: A reconciliation of the linearized and levels schools of AGE modelling." *Economic Modelling* 9:385–407.

Ho, M.S. and D.W. Jorgenson. 1994. "Trade policy and U.S. economic growth.' *Journal of Policy Modelling* 16:119–146.

Jorgenson, D.W. 1984. "Econometric methods for applied general equilibrium analysis." In *Applied General Equilibrium Analysis*, edited by H.E. Scarf and J.B. Shoven. Cambridge: Cambridge University Press.

Kehoe, T.J. 1994. "Towards a dynamic general equilibrium model of North American trade." In *Modelling Trade Policy: Applied General Equilibrium Assessments of North American Free Trade*, edited by J.F. Francois and C.R. Shiells. Cambridge: Cambridge University Press.

Keuschnigg, C. 1995. "Trade policy modelling with innovation-based growth models." Vienna: Institut für Höhere Studien, mimeo.

Komiya, R. "Non-traded goods and the pure theory of international trade." *International Economic Review* 8:132–152.

Krugman, P.R. 1979. "Increasing returns, monopolistic competition, and international trade." *Journal of International Economics* 9:469–480.

Krugman, P.R. 1980. "Scale economies, product differentiation, and the pattern of trade." *American Economic Review* 70:950–959.

Krugman. P.R. and E. Helpman. 1989. *Trade Policy and Market Structure*. Cambridge, Massachusetts: MIT Press.

Lucas, R.E. 1988. "On the mechanics of economic development." *Journal of Monetary Economics* 22:3–42.

Mankiw, N.G. and D. Romer, eds. 1991. *New Keynesian Economics* (two volumes). Cambridge, Massachusetts: MIT Press.

Norman, V.D. 1990. "Assessing trade and welfare effects of trade liberalization: A comparison of alternative approaches to CGE modelling with imperfect competition." *European Economic Review* 34:725–745.

Pratten. 1988. "A survey on the economies of scale." In *Studies on the Economics of Integration*. Luxembourg: Commission of the European Communities.

Pyatt, G. and J.I. Round, eds. 1985. *Social Accounting Matrices: A Basis for Planning*. Washington, D.C.: The World Bank.

Reinert, K.A. and D.W. Roland-Holst. 1992. "Armington elasticities for United States manufacturing sectors." *Journal of Policy Modelling* 14:631–639.

Reinert, K.A. and C.R. Shiells. 1992. *Estimated Elasticities of Substitution for Analysis of a North American Free Trade Area*. Washington, D.C.: U.S. International Trade Commission.

Romer, P.M. 1987. "Growth based on increasing returns due to specialization." *American Economic Review* 77:56–62.

Rousslang, D. and S. Parker. 1984. "Cross-price elasticities of U.S. import demand." *Review of Economics and Statistics* 66:518–523.

Rousslang, D.J. and J. Suomela. 1985. *Calculating the Consumer and Net Welfare Costs of Import Relief*. Washington, D.C.: U.S. International Trade Commission.

Ruffin, R. and R. Jones. 1977. "Protection and real wages: The neoclassical ambiguity." *Journal of Economic Theory* 14:337–348.

Salter, W. 1959. "Internal and external balance: The role of price and expenditure effects." *Economic Record* 35:226–238.

Samuelson, P.A. 1953. "Prices of Factors and Goods in General Equilibrium." *Review of Economic Studies* 21:1–20.

Shiells, C.R. and K.A. Reinert. 1993. "Armington models and terms-of-trade effects: Some econometric evidence for North America." *Canadian Journal of Economics* 26:299–316.

Shiells, C.R., D.W. Roland-Holst, and K.A. Reinert. 1993. "Modelling a North American free trade area: Estimation of flexible functional forms." *Weltwirtschaftliches Archiv* 129:55–77.

Shiells, C.R., R.M. Stern, and A.V. Deardorff. 1986. "Estimates of the elasticities of substitution between imports and home goods for the United States." *Weltwirtschaftliches Archiv* 122:497–519.

Shoven, J.B. and J. Whalley. 1984. "Applied general equilibrium models of taxation and international trade: An introduction and survey." *Journal of Economic Literature* 22:1007–1051.

Shoven, J.B. and J. Whalley. 1992. *Applying General Equilibrium*. Cambridge: Cambridge University Press.

Smith, M.A.M. 1976. "Trade, growth and consumption in alternative models of capital accumulation." *Journal of International Economics* 6:385–388.

Smith, M.A.M. 1977. "Capital accumulation in the open two-sector economy.' *Economic Journal* 87:273–282.

Sobarzo, H.E. 1994. "The gains for Mexico from a North American free trade agreement: An applied general equilibrium assessment." In *Modelling Trade Policy: Applied General Equilibrium Assessments of North American Free*

Trade, edited by J.F. Francois and C.R. Shiells. Cambridge: Cambridge University Press.

Stolper, W. and P.A. Samuelson. 1941. "Protection and real wages." *Review of Economic Studies* 9:58–73.

Stone, R. 1985. "The disaggregation of the household sector in the national accounts." In *Social Accounting Matrices: A Basis for Planning*, edited by G. Pyatt and J. Round. Washington, D.C.: The World Bank.

Swan, T. 1960. "Economic control in a dependent economy." *Economic Record* 36:51–66.

Vousden, N. 1990. *The Economics of Trade Protection*. Cambridge: Cambridge University Press.

Whalley, J. 1985. *Trade Liberalization Among Major World Trading Areas*. Cambridge: Cambridge University Press.

Winters, A. 1990. "Assessing trade and welfare effects of trade liberalization." *European Economic Review* 34:748–751.

Yang, Y. (1994), "Trade liberalization with externalities: A general equilibrium assessment of the Uruguay Round." Australian National University, mimeo.

Young, L. and J. Romero. "International investment and the positive theory of international trade." *Journal of International Economics* 29:333–349.

PART II
Basic Frameworks

2

Quantifying Commercial Policies

Samuel Laird

I Introduction

Most of this chapter is concerned with the measurement of non-tariff measures (NTMs) for use in the models that are discussed elsewhere in the book. However, first there is a brief discussion on problems related to the use of tariff information. Second, NTMs are defined and classified. Third, we look at the effects of NTMs and methods to compute those effects. This includes a review of the inventory approach, under which NTMs are catalogued; modeling approaches; tariff equivalents; subsidy equivalents; the Trade Restrictiveness Index (TRI) and effective protection. Finally, there is also a brief discussion on sources of data on NTMs.

This chapter is a brief introduction to the subject and is not meant to be a comprehensive literature survey. However, the references should be of assistance to those who wish to delve further into the science (or art!) of commercial policy measurement. To steer readers, the most useful starting place would be Baldwin (1970a) and Corden (1971). More recent material is to be found in Laird and Yeats (1990), Feenstra (1988a), Vousden (1990) and Helpman and Krugman (1989). Agriculture has an NTM measurement industry of its own; starting places are Krueger, Schiff and Valdes (1988); Goldin and Knudsen (1990); OECD (1994); and Webb, Lopez and Penn (1990). A new body of literature, in the nascent stage, concerns the Trade Restrictiveness Index, developed by Anderson and Neary (1994a), mainly designed to measure changes in welfare resulting from policy changes over time.

Helpful advice for this chapter was received from Malcolm Bosworth, Clem Boonekamp, L. Alan Winters, Alexander Yeats and the editors.

II Tariffs

There are a number of issues related to customs tariffs which are important for modellers who have to process these basic data before proceeding to the modeling work itself. These issues concern classification (and linkages to other classifications by means of concordances), types of tariff duty, differential rates of duty applied to different countries or groups of countries, other exceptions to the normal rate, and bindings.

II.1 Classifications and Tariff Averages

Customs tariffs are usually published in book form indicating the percentage of customs duty to be charged on goods being imported. Today, these are typically classified according to national tariff classifications, sometimes containing as many as 13 digits, and are based on the 6-digit Harmonized Commodity Coding and Classification System (HS), although in some countries they are still based on the earlier 4-digit Customs Co-Operation Council Nomenclature (CCCN) of the Brussels-based Customs Co-Operation Council.[1] Import statistics are typically collected under these classifications in the first instance, since they are first processed by customs officers.

Tariff classifications are commodity (product) classifications, under which commodities are grouped together through different stages of processing. This is slightly different from the commodity classification used for international trade statistics by the United Nations, the Standard International Trade Classification (SITC), under which the most basic, unprocessed commodities appear first, and later divisions contain commodities which are progressively more processed. These differences mean that there is not a perfect concordance between the highly detailed customs classifications and the full 5-digit SITC, and the issue has not been resolved with the HS system, where the concordance is more or less correct on a many-to-one basis only with the current revision, Revision 3, of the SITC at the 4-digit level. While import statistics shown under the SITC classification are derived from import statistics collected under customs classifications, export statistics are typically produced directly under the SITC classification.[2]

---

1 The prior classification was the Brussels Tariff Nomenclature (BTN).

2 This is not a chapter about trade data, but economists should be aware that there are also re-exports, under which goods are exported to other countries without further processing; e.g., Hong Kong re-exports many goods to and from China. While the UN allows for such a category, it is not clear how well published data capture this fact. There are also problems with the recording of trade from free trade zones. For example, in the past Mexico excluded exports from the maquiladoras from its trade data, while the United States included such trade in its imports from Mexico, leading to a differential in the reported trade of the two countries of as much as 60 percent in some years. Thus, apart from timing, and transport and insurance costs, imports and exports data do not always match.

The main problem that faces modellers is the need to concord tariff (and trade) data to industrial statistics under industrial or input–output classifications. These data, covering value added, value of output, employment, etc., are typically recorded on an industry basis, in which establishments are classified to an "industry" according to their principal activities. Thus, a furniture factory making wooden furniture could be classified to the furniture industry (defined to include only wooden furniture, where the main activities are sawing, dressing, assembling and finishing operations), while a factory which makes mainly plastic furniture would be classified to the plastics industry, where a wide variety of plastic products are extruded or moulded by using quite different techniques. There are concordances between commodity and industrial classifications, showing more or less what is made in what industry, but these do not exist on a one-to-one basis or even a completely clean, many-to-one basis mainly because of the different concepts just described. In general, industrial classifications are broader than commodity classifications, so that existing concordances work only roughly on a many-to-one basis; because of the conceptual problems, they are particularly suspect for certain sectors and certain countries, but there is no uniform pattern.

Most modeling discussed elsewhere in this book will require the precomputation of tariff averages for each sector covered by the model, and the modeller will need to decide how to compute these averages and to take account of the differences in classification. If simple averages are used, the process is straightforward: One assigns (concords) a set of tariff lines to each industry, adds up the corresponding rates and divides by the number of lines.

If it is desired to use some kind of weighting, problems arise. For example, own import weights, which can be obtained from the trade data collected at the tariff line level by customs authorities, contain inherent downward biases, since the imports used as weights are affected by the tariff and any other trade measures in place. (Moreover, tariff classifications are sometimes changed from year to year, so that the most recent tariff information may need to be concorded to trade data for an earlier year.) Some economists have also used global trade weights, to approximate "free trade" weights, but tariffs are usually set at the national level, which is more detailed than the internationally agreed classifications, so it is necessary to use simple averages up to the point at which the global weights can be computed. This technique does not overcome the problem that some important sectors, e.g., textiles and clothing, iron and steel, automobiles, are protected in a number of countries, so that the global weights are also downward-biased.

If it is desired to use domestic output (i.e., turnover) weights, then it may again be necessary to make simple averages of the tariff lines which are concorded to the lowest level of the industrial classification, and use output weights only from that point. (Value added in domestic industries is normally used to weight effective tariff protection; see later discussion.)

The issue of weighting, including related aggregation biases, is not new; it was discussed in a number of papers collected by Grubel and Johnson (1971). Corden (1966) argued that the basic concept against which to measure aggregation bias was the uniform ad valorem tariff which would be needed to maintain a constant value of imports if existing tariffs were removed. The same issue was one of the main motivations for the work on the TRI, which aims to compute an average corresponding to a uniform tariff which would maintain the same level of welfare, as discussed later. Basevi (1971) argues that the best averaging procedure depends on what one wants to measure – effective protection, production or trade effects, balance of payments effects or welfare effects – and discusses appropriate techniques to reduce aggregation bias, focusing largely on effective protection. However, he concludes that aggregation is "a formidable and often hopeless problem" as applied to the measurement of protection, commending a case study approach at the detailed level, while preserving the general equilibrium nature of the analysis by taking account of macroeconomic variables.[3]

II.2 Types of Tariff Duty and Customs Valuation

Another aspect of tariff averaging is that there are a number of different types of tariff duty in use. Fortunately, the easiest to use is the most common, the ad valorem tariff, under which the rate is expressed as a percentage of the value of the goods. The value of the good is typically the free-on-board (f.o.b.) value, but in some cases the cost, insurance and freight (c.i.f.) value is used, increasing the incidence of the tariff on an f.o.b. basis and providing greater protection against exporters with higher transport costs (a kind of double jeopardy). In many developing countries, the value for duty is not the transaction value but some kind of constructed or reference price (to compensate for underinvoicing or simply to provide surer protection for goods with fluctuating world prices or to counter dumping). However, under the single undertaking of the Uruguay Round, all countries,

---

3 Laird and Yeats (1987a) proposed using computed free trade weights to prevent the inherent bias associated with actual trade weights. They used a partial equilibrium model together with information on tariffs and the ad valorem equivalent of non-tariff measures to compute what trade would have been under free trade and then used such weights to compute estimates of tariff escalation in developing countries.

subject to a phase-in period, will in the future be subject to the General Agreement on Tariffs and Trade (GATT) Customs Valuation Code, which places greater emphasis on the use of transaction values as the basis for customs valuation.

In addition to ad valorem tariffs, two other types of tariff have been very common in the past, mainly for agricultural products and chemicals. These are specific duties and variable levies. Specific duties are fixed as a value for a physical unit, e.g., US$6 per pound or SFR10.50 per dozen. Variable levies are duties typically fixed to bring the price of an imported commodity up to a domestic support price for the commodity (as discussed later). Under the Uruguay Round agreement, unbound variable levies are to be eliminated, though duties may still be adjusted subject to bindings, and specific duties may continue to be used. In order to compute the ad valorem equivalent of specific duties, it is necessary to know the import price. For some commodities it may be possible to compute the unit value of imports and use this as a substitute for the import price, but there are obvious risks to this approach. For variable levies, it is necessary to know the import and domestic support prices. The ad valorem equivalent of both specific duties and variable levies varies inversely with international prices, and it may be necessary to compute some average across a "representative period."

Other, less frequently used types of duty are composite rates, alternative rates and seasonal rates. Composite rates can be a combination of specific and ad valorem rates, for example, US$6 a pound plus 15 percent. An alternative rate might be 15 percent or, if higher, US$3 a pound. Seasonal rates are rates which are increased or decreased at certain times of the year, usually in accordance with the growing season in the importing country.

II.3 Differential Rates

Today, many countries accord different tariff treatment to different foreign countries or groups of foreign countries. The highest rates are sometimes called "general" rates, which, for example, the United States accords to the Commonwealth of Independent States (CIS). Most countries have eliminated the general rate and their highest rate is the most favoured nation (MFN) rate, accorded to other World Trade Organization (WTO) members (formerly GATT contracting parties), unless even more favourable treatment has been agreed.

Laird and Yeats (1987b) show that MFN rates are often the worst tariff treatment, being inferior to a range of preferences under free trade areas or customs unions, such as the North American Free Trade Area (NAFTA) or the European Union, the Generalized System of Preferences (GSP), and the U.S. Caribbean Basin Initiative. The European Union also has special preferences for former colonies (Lomé Convention preferences for African, Caribbean and Pacific [ACP] countries), Mediterranean countries, and least developed countries, under what has sometimes been called its "pyramid of preferences." Earlier preferences such as among members of the British Commonwealth still exist, although they are of less importance today. There are also preferences under the Global System of Tariff Preferences among Developing Countries (GSTP).

A complication is that not all trade in a single tariff item from any one country necessarily attracts the same rate of duty. For example, preferential rates under GSP may only be available up to a certain value or volume of trade, beyond which point the full MFN rate is applied. In some cases, that level is not reached, but in others trade is taking place at different rates. This can also occur because the exporting country does not provide the necessary documentation to allow the granting of the preference. The United States is exceptional in showing in its trade statistics for each partner for each tariff item the trade under each tariff treatment.

Where a product from one country is further processed in another country, the rate to be applied depends on whether the tariff classification changes, in which case typically the rate is that applying to the last country of export. If such transformation does not take place and different rates apply to each country, then the appropriate rate will depend on the rules of origin of the relevant trade agreement(s). In some cases, where the importing country supplies materials to the exporting country, tariffs are only applied to the value added abroad.

The issue for the modeller is related to what is being studied. If one is looking at welfare effects in one country, then what may be needed is some kind of average tariff against the world. However, in a global model with a variety of trade flows, consideration may be given to applying the correct rate for each group of partner countries, and allowing for trade flows to be diverted as the differentials in tariff treatment are altered. Needless to say, this is essential in looking at the effects of a free trade area or customs union.

II.4 Exceptions

In many countries, the tariffs which are normally applied can be waived or reimbursed. This may be because the goods are not produced or are currently in short supply in the importing country or because they are destined for use in a sector favoured by the government, e.g., a designated key or strategic industry or an export industry (end use provisions). In these cases the duty collected expressed as a percentage of the value of imports will bear little resemblance to the ad valorem rate shown in customs schedules. Alternatively, the duty may be paid and recorded to the tariff item, but reimbursed on export directly from the public treasury.

II.5 Bindings

In the GATT/WTO system, countries negotiate tariff bindings with principal suppliers and apply the bound rates on an m.f.n. basis. This means they cannot increase such tariffs without compensating the principal suppliers. However, for a number of countries, the bindings only cover part of their trade. In respect to individual items, they can even be so narrowly defined as to cover only part of the item. In addition, the tariffs which are currently applied may be lower than the bound rates, e.g., because of autonomous liberalization. In the Uruguay Round, many developing countries negotiated to lower their ceiling bindings, which were often extended to all trade, but these levels remain above currently applied m.f.n. rates. While this means that no increase in trade should be expected to arise directly from such a change, greater security of access is achieved by ensuring rates cannot be increased above their bound levels.[4] This could be important for certain types of modeling where expectations or probabilities of change matter or where it is desired to simulate increases in protection.

II.6 Other Taxes and Charges

Tariff surcharges are sometimes applied to the whole of trade for balance of payments reasons, or, under escape clause provisions, to some products, as with anti-dumping duties or countervailing measures. These are typically not recorded in tariff schedules or published in easily accessible forms. Even in the case of surcharges, they are sometimes applied unevenly across sectors.

A number of additional taxes are sometimes applied to imports (and exports), ostensibly as charges for services. These include statistical taxes, consular fees for documentation, stamp taxes, port charges, and customs user fees. These may be ad valorem charges against the value of imports or directly related to the cost of the service, where this is genuinely a user fee.

---

4 Of course, NTMs or tariff surcharges could be introduced under GATT's balance of payments provisions or other forms of safeguard action could still be used.

A number of domestic taxes, such as value added or sales taxes, are typically levied at the frontier against imports. In principle, these are supposed to be levied at the same rate as against domestic goods under Article III of the GATT, but this is not always the case. Moreover, even where the rate is the same, they may not be applied on the commodity at precisely the same stage or they may be applied on a cumulative basis so that again the GATT-required equivalence is not achieved.

III Non-tariff Measures

The term "non-tariff measures" is defined to include export restraints and production and export subsidies, or measures with similar effect, not just import restraints. This is the term most widely used in GATT and the United Nations Commission on Trade and Development (UNCTAD), although textbooks generally prefer the terms "barriers" and "distortions."[5] Perhaps the most theoretically satisfying definition is that of Baldwin (1970a), who defines "non-tariff distortion" as "any measure (public or private) that causes internationally traded goods and services, or resources devoted to the production of these goods and services, to be allocated in such a way as to reduce potential real world income." Practically, the introduction of the concept of potential real world income means that very often it is difficult to be sure what is a distortion without undertaking complex, even impossible, calculations. However, it sets the correct framework in which to judge the relative importance of NTMs.

There is a large variety of non-tariff measures. UNCTAD (1994) uses a classification of over 100 trade measures – including tariffs with a discretionary or variable component. This is reproduced in Appendix 2.1. This classification does not include any measures applied to production or to exports.

Following Laird and Vossenaar (1991), NTMs may be broadly classified according to intent or immediate impact of the measures (i.e., the motives or objectives; see the list that follows). They identify five such categories, of which (iv) has been adapted to cover restrictions as well as subsidies:

i   *Measures to control the volume of imports.* Prohibitions and quantitative restrictions (QRs) on imports as well as export restraint agreements

---

5 The reason why the Geneva agencies have adopted the term "measures" is to prevent some of the measurement and judgmental problems associated with the terms "distortions" and "barriers." As UNCTAD has explained it, "measures" encompasses all trade policy instruments, even though their restrictiveness or effects, if any, may vary between countries applying the measures or at different points of time in a specific country; e.g., if the world price of a product rises above the domestic support price, then a variable levy would not be applied although the mechanism remains in force. A quota may be greater than import demand, implying no restrictiveness.

(ERAs). Licenses are often used to administer QRs. ERAs consist of voluntary export restraints (VERs) (covering, inter alia, measures employed for the administration of bilateral agreements under the Multi-Fibre Arrangement) and Orderly Marketing Agreements (OMAs).

ii *Measures to control the price of imported goods.* These include the use of reference or trigger price mechanisms, variable levies, anti-dumping duties, countervailing measures, etc. Tariff-type measures such as tariff quotas and seasonal tariffs also are usually intended to increase import prices under given circumstances. Voluntary export price restraints fall under this broad category of intent.

iii *Monitoring measures including price and volume investigations and surveillance.* Such practices are often associated with charges by domestic interests of unfair trading practices by exporters, e.g., dumping and subsidization. Licenses are sometimes used as a monitoring tool. If seen as such, they may also lead to export restraints: They may have a harassment or "chilling" effect on trade.

iv *Production and export measures.* Subsidies may be directly applied to output or value added, or they may be indirectly applied, i.e., paid to material or other inputs to the production process. They may arise from payments or the non-collection of taxes that would otherwise be due. Restrictions by mean of taxes or prohibitions may also be imposed on production or exports.

v *Technical barriers.* Barriers imposed at the frontier are used to apply various standards for health and safety reasons to imported products to ensure that they conform to the same standards as those required by law for domestically produced goods. They may lead to the prohibition of non-complying imports or oblige cost-increasing production improvements.

It is inevitable that there is a certain arbitrariness in such a classification. For example, most measures, including technical barriers, have price and quantity effects, as discussed in the next section. A glossary of individual non-tariff measures, derived from Laird and Yeats (1990) and based on the five broad classes of NTMs, is included in Appendix 2.2.

OECD (1994), dealing only with agriculture, lists some 150 measures or bodies administering country-specific schemes. In the UNCTAD classification these would be classified to its more limited, but still extensive, list of individual measures, since many are simply national descriptions for a widely used basic measure.

Typically, the objectives or motives for using NTMs range from the long-term desire to promote certain social and economic objectives, including broad economic, industrial or regional development, to shorter-term purposes such as balance of payments (BOP) support or action to protect a specific sector from import surges or from dumped or subsidized imports. Price or volume control measures or subsidies have been used extensively in the past for industrial development reasons by developed and developing countries.

In any type of liberalization simulation, it may be important to look realistically at the likelihood of such measures being removed. It is unlikely that governments will remove permanent controls on technical barriers to trade or on trade in arms, drugs, pornography, etc., although technical barriers may become more harmonized. However, support for industrial development can be attained in more open economies supported by improved macroeconomic management and realistic exchange rates. Governments also seem attached to support for specific sectors (sometimes in key political constituencies) by means of hidden subsidies through government procurement and technology development (e.g., aircraft), but so far international disciplines on the use of such measures remain relatively weak. As a consequence, even after the Uruguay Round, there are still important peaks in sectoral protection in most countries, sometimes in the same sector across countries, e.g., textiles and clothing.

It is important to realize that GATT (including the GATT 1994, negotiated in the Uruguay Round) does not ban the use of all NTMs. Laird and Vossenaar (1991) argue that after the Preamble and first three articles of the GATT – which deal with the overall objectives of the GATT, most favoured nation (MFN) treatment, tariff reductions, and national treatment – one enters the realm of exceptions and sets of rules which deal at least as much with how and when protection may be imposed, especially by means of non-tariff measures, as they do with liberalization. The Tokyo Round and Uruguay Round Codes are a further extension of this idea, embodying higher levels of rights and obligations for Code members, although the Uruguay Round results should see a reduction in the use of some important NTMs, e.g., ERAs, the Multi Fibre Arrangement (MFA), export subsidies, and farm production support.[6]

---

6 In the Tokyo Round, membership of all codes was optional; in the Uruguay Round, all WTO members are bound by all except the Plurilateral Agreements, covering Trade in Civil Aircraft, Government Procurement, the International Dairy Agreement and the International Bovine Meat Agreement.

IV Quantifying the Effects of Trade Measures

The main focuses of this section are the identification of the effects of trade measures and the question of how these effects can be measured. There is an extensive literature in the field.[7] Here, we concentrate on some of the key effects, with a view to identifying some of the political economic factors surrounding the use of trade measures, and then we go on to examine the measurement question only in relation to these effects.

With some exceptions, the main thrust of the presentation is the traditional perfect competition case, in a partial equilibrium framework, mainly for ease of exposition. For those who wish to pursue issues such as economies of scale, etc., in depth it would be advisable to consult, in particular, Helpman and Krugman (1989) and references therein.

IV.1 Effects of Trade Measures

Trade measures have many different effects. These include price and quantity effects on trade and production, as well as employment, and welfare effects. These occur both in the country applying them as well as in other countries directly and indirectly affected by them. In the analysis which follows we concentrate on the price, production, trade, consumption, revenue and redistribution effects, using simple diagrams. First, we look briefly at the partial equilibrium basis of tariffs; this is also a useful point of reference for the subsequent discussion on NTMs. Then, drawing on the broad classification in the previous section, we look at the major types of NTMs, in terms of the means by which they operate: measures which operate on the prices of imports, measures which operate on the volume of imports, production measures, and export measures. The main departure from this focus relates to linking schemes and technical barriers, which can operate either way. We assume infinitely elastic world supply (the small country assumption) to simplify the presentation, but it is clearly necessary to consider the case of upward sloping world supply curves in many real world situations.[8]

Tariffs The standard partial equilibrium trade diagram is given in Figure 2.1. Domestic demand and supply are given by *Dd* and *Sd*, respectively. As

---

7 See, for example, Baldwin (1970a) for one of the earlier and most useful broad treatments of the subject, Bhagwati (1988) for a critique of some of the more recent developments, Laird and Yeats (1990) for a survey of recent studies of the effects of NTMs, and other studies cited in the References.

8 See Corden (1971) for other cases.

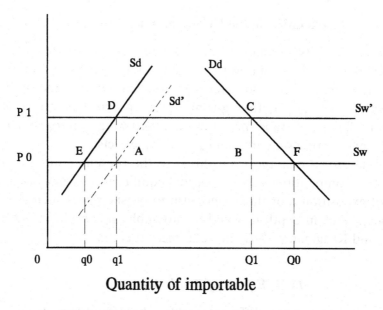

Figure 2.1. *Price and quantity effects of a tariff*

noted, world supply (*Sw*) is assumed to be completely elastic (otherwise it would slope up to the right), and the initial domestic price is *P0*. Domestic producers supply $Oq0$ and imports are $q0Q0$. (The lower supply curve is discussed later in relation to production subsidies.)

Starting with an import *tariff* as a point of reference, if an ad valorem tariff is imposed, the main effects are that the consumer pays the tax to the government, whose revenues increase correspondingly, while domestic producers can produce more and capture a larger share of the domestic market, while charging a higher price. Domestic consumption and imports both decline. On the diagram, the import supply curve and prices facing domestic consumers increase to *Sw'* and *P1* (equal to $P0(1+t)$), respectively. Domestic consumption and imports decline to $0Q1$ and $q1Q1$, respectively. The tariff revenue, *ABCD*, goes to the government of the importing country. This identifies the production effect, the consumption effect, the import effect, the revenue effect and the redistribution effect (the transfer from consumers to producers). Two other effects may also be identified: first, the triangle *EAD* represents the additional cost of producing the extra output locally, also called the deadweight production loss (the area between the price lines and above Sd is known as producer surplus); second, the triangle *BFC* is the deadweight loss in consumer surplus.

In the case of a *tariff quota*, after imports reach a certain level, the tariff rate increases. Whether or not any imports take place at the higher level depends on import demand. If they do, then there is a kink in the supply of imports and these may appear on the domestic market at different prices during the year or they will be averaged by the importer/distributor.

The most common textbook deviation from the assumption of perfectly competitive markets concerns the so-called optimum tariff.[9] In the preceding case, it was assumed that the importer is a price taker. However, where the importing country is sufficiently large to have monopsony power, it can influence world prices and, therefore, faces an upward-sloping world supply curve. The optimum depends on the relative slopes of the domestic demand and foreign supply curves: the more elastic the foreign supply curve, the lower the optimum tariff, and vice versa; however, the optimum cannot be set at prohibitive levels. Moreover, while there is an increase in welfare for the large importing country there is a reduction in global welfare relative to free trade.

For the modeller, the main implication of the case of the increasing world supply curve, that we have just discussed, is that the price wedge in the protected situation does not represent the potential fall in the domestic price that might be expected to occur in a move to free trade; rather, the price wedge is composed of a change in world and domestic prices relative to the free trade situation.

Other Measures Operating Directly on Import Prices A number of *price increasing NTMs* operate analytically exactly like tariffs by pushing up the supply price of the importable faced by the domestic consumer. They include *anti-dumping duties*[10] and *countervailing measures*, which typically increase prices by a fixed percentage, while *standards, marketing and labeling requirements; additional import charges; voluntary export price restraints;* etc., may cause fixed unit or percentage price increases. *Variable levies, minimum prices, reference prices*, etc., operate to push up the world price as perceived by importers to a predetermined, fixed or periodically revised level. Even if free world prices are declining, this fixed import price level is maintained. This means that the protective effects have increased,

---

9 See, for example, Kindleberger and Lindert (1978).

10 Anti-dumping duties are treated as NTMs for a number of reasons. Although they can be expressed in percentage terms (like some other NTMs), they are not scheduled tariffs. There are complex, often discretionary, procedures for their administration which overwhelmingly favour domestic producers and which have been shown to have an adverse effect on imports (see later discussion). There is also the question as to what extent true or predatory dumping exists, as distinct from normal, commercial variations in price fixing behaviour.

but this increase in protection is not immediately apparent to consumers as prices and quantities remain fixed as before. The benefits of falling world prices are simply not passed on to the consumer. On the other hand, if world prices increase above the prevailing reference price, then the actual world and domestic prices allocate trade and production.

Government procurement practices may vary, but, in general, they apply a fixed notional percentage increase to the price of importable goods before deciding on whether the imported goods are cheaper than the domestic goods.[11] If domestic production is relatively high cost, this means the government will pay a higher price for domestically produced goods and purchase more of them than in the absence of this practice. However, the private sector will continue to buy at the world price. Thus, there are segregated markets with price discrimination between them.[12] This is also true if there is a tariff as well as a domestic preference, although this can be offset if government agencies and state-owned enterprises are exempt from payment of duty. In the aggregate, there is an average implicit tariff which is lower than the notional rate of preference to the extent that the private sector is also a purchaser in the market for the importable good. This implicit tariff is what would be taken into account in estimating the effects of removal of government procurement preferences. In the aggregate, it increases production and decreases consumption. Consumers (government agencies, etc.) pay more, but the transfer is directly from the government to the producer because of the higher price. This has to be financed from taxation.

Measures Operating on Import Volumes With respect to quantitative restrictions, operating directly on the import quantity, it is sometimes possible to design an *import quota* or a voluntary export restraint (*VER*) (which can be a genuine export restraint, as discussed later) in such a way that domestic sectoral production, consumption and imports are identical to those under a tariff. However, the "revenue" or "quota rent," generated by sales at the higher prices that are made possible under a quota, goes to domestic importers or to foreign suppliers, depending on to whom the quota is allocated. In the case of a VER the rent goes to foreign suppliers, unless partly captured by an import tariff. With import and export quotas, the governments of the importing and exporting countries, respectively, may use auctions to capture the rents which would otherwise be passed on to the private sector.

---

11 The preference may be "absolute" so that domestic suppliers will charge as much as domestic competition or what the market will bear.
12 Domestic producers supplying the government and the private market will allocate their output to each market in such a way that their marginal revenue is equalized in each market.

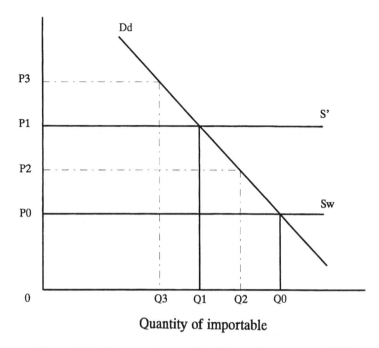

Figure 2.2. *Price and quantity effects of a quota or VER*

If an import quota, or indeed a VER, is set equal to $q1Q1$ in Figure 2.1, then domestic production, consumption and imports are identical to those under tariff t. However, the revenue, $ABCD$, goes to domestic importers or to foreign suppliers, depending on to whom the quota is allocated. In the case of a VER, the revenue goes to foreign suppliers, except where the importing country uses a tariff in conjunction with the quota to capture part of the rent (as in the case of the MFA). Governments in the importing and exporting countries may use auctions to capture quota rents in respect of import and export quotas. For example, if the import quota is allocated to a foreign country, rather than to import or export firms, then the foreign government can capture the quota rents by auction.

The effects of a quota depend on whether the tariff or the quota is the binding constraint. For example, in Figure 2.2, under free trade the domestic and world prices are $P0$ and imports are $Q0$. If a tariff t is imposed such that $P1=P0(1+t)$, then import demand drops to $Q1$. If quota is imposed to limit imports to $Q2$, then, in the absence of any tariff, the domestic price of imports will only rise to $P2$. In the presence of tariff t, the tariff is the binding constraint so that $P1$ and $Q1$ prevail. If a quota is imposed to limit imports to $Q3$, then the domestic price of imports will rise to $P3$. The quota becomes the binding constraint.

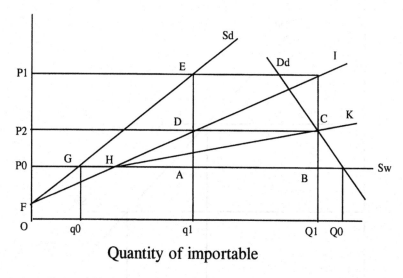

Figure 2.3. *Price and quantity effects of linking schemes*

Among the more important complications, which are all too common in practice, are what Corden (1971) calls *linking schemes*. These include *local content schemes* as well as *export performance requirements*. Figure 2.3 provides an example, where, as in previous diagrams, *P0* and *Q0* represent the domestic price and production under free trade. In *mixing schemes* a government determines that there is to be a fixed share of imports in domestic consumption, e.g., milk, or coal. In the case of a local content scheme, such as has often been used for automobiles in a number of developed and developing countries, auto assemblers are the "consumers" required to use a fixed percentage of local components in the assembly process. However, imports above this amount may be allowed, including by non-assemblers (although this is often excluded in practice), at a higher tariff, so that a local content scheme can operate like a tariff quota.

In Figure 2.3, the line *FHI* is the locus of points obtained by adding horizontally to the domestic supply curve, *Sd*, the percentage of imports permitted for a given amount of domestic production in the ratio determined by the government. In the case of automobiles, this might be the percentage of domestic components required to be used by auto assemblers, e.g., 60 percent or some other percentage fixed by the government. The average cost to the consumer or, in the auto case, of components to assemblers – in effect the supply curve that they face – is given by *FGHK*, determining the average price, as in the mixing case. Demand up to *q0* is met by domestic supply (*FG*), while imports meet the excess demand up to *H* at price $P0$. Above H, the price facing consumers is the average of the below quota price $P0$ and the above quota price lying on the combined supply curve, FHI; this is HK, the locus of average prices for consumption above H. With the specific demand curve Dd, the effect of establishing the ratio is to push up the price received by domestic suppliers to $P1$, while imports at the quota remain at $P0$, giving the average price of $P2$.[13] Domestic production of the local good in the mixing case, or the component in the auto local content case, increases from $0q0$ to $0q1$, while imports decline from $q0Q0$ to $q1Q1$.

The operation of a local content scheme is rarely implemented by fixing absolute percentages for all levels of production. Often there is a tariff on components, from which the assembler is exempt if he meets the local content requirement. This tariff sets a limit or ceiling on the implicit tax on components associated with the local content scheme. Again, the government might set a tariff on assembled (cbu) automobiles for which imports are only possible if the assemblers meet the local content requirement. This tariff would need to be at least as high as the implicit user tax or their own production would be adversely affected (since the local content scheme shifts upward the supply curve for components facing the assemblers).[14]

Production Measures The government may introduce a *subsidy* to domestic producers of importables of a fixed price per unit, such as to cause a downward shift on the domestic producers' supply schedule, Sd', so that it passes through A in Figure 2.1. This would produce the same increase in domestic production as under the tariff t, but domestic consumption and prices to consumers would remain unchanged while imports would decline to $q1Q0$ (instead of $q1Q1$ under the tariff). This would prevent the loss of consumer surplus. The cost to the government, $q0q1AE$, would need to be met from taxation.

Under the Uruguay Round agreement, production subsidies for agriculture will, to a degree, be delinked from the quantity produced, so that in effect subsidies to farmers become income-support schemes, with a diminishing value for each additional unit of production. Additionally, many forms of direct and indirect assistance to industry operate as subsidies. These are noted in the glossary in Appendix 2.2.

---

13 Corden (1971) calls this increase in the average price, $P2P0$, relative to the free trade price, $P0$, the implicit user tax or implicit tariff on components.

14 The supply curve facing assemblers is the vertical sum of the supply curve for components plus the supply of what Corden calls the value-added product, which is the value added in the assembly industry by factors such as labour, capital and natural resources.

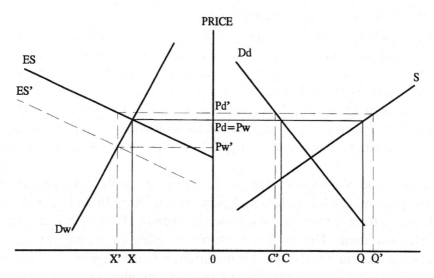

Figure 2.4. *Price and quantity effects of export subsidies*

Typically, the trade economist needs to worry less about direct taxation, since this is normally applied at an equivalent level at the frontier to imports. If applied in a discriminatory manner, which is not uncommon either because the rate is different or it is charged at a different stage in the delivery, then such taxes can work as a tariffs. There are also distortionary effects from unequal taxation across sectors, so that even with non-discriminatory taxation, the trade profile varies under different rates and forms of domestic taxation.

Export Measures Turning from importables to exports, the principal instruments in use are export subsidies or measures having similar effect, such as subsidized credit, etc.[15] The effects of an *export subsidy* are to reduce the export price and increase exports, while increasing domestic prices and reducing supplies to the domestic market. This is shown in Figure 2.4.[16] On the right of the diagram is the interaction of domestic supply and demand. On the left is the interaction of excess domestic supplies available for the world market and the excess demand by the rest of the world, *ES* and *Dw*, respectively. At the world and domestic price, $Pw=Pd$, domestic production

---

15 In recent years, developing countries have largely dropped export subsidies under tighter fiscal management policies, and have turned to tax rebates, duty drawbacks, etc., to offset the anti-export bias of import protection. This is also to prevent the effects of anti-dumping duties and countervailing measures. However, export subsidies are still widely used by developed countries, especially to dispose of agricultural surpluses. These are to be cut back under the Uruguay Round Agreement.
16 I am grateful to Kym Anderson for this point.

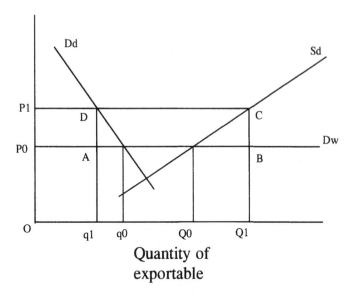

Figure 2.5. *Price and quantity effects of export performance requirements*

is $0Q$, domestic consumption is $0C$, and the amount available for export is CQ ($=0X$). If the exporting country then introduces an export subsidy, this has the effect of lowering the excess supply from ES to ES', driving the export price down to Pw' and exports up to $0X'$, while domestic prices are bid up to Pd', causing production to rise to $0Q'$ and consumption to drop to $0C'$.

Export taxes and export restrictions, in use in both developed and developing countries, can be shown diagrammatically as in Figure 2.4, but with the opposite effects.[17] The export supply curve, ES, would shift upward, driving the export price up and exports down. Domestic prices would be bid down, causing production to fall and domestic consumption to rise. These taxes can be used to exploit a monopoly position on world markets, which effectively gets the foreigner to pay the tax. This is the equivalent of the so-called optimal tariff on imports. They are sometimes used to increase the availability of low-priced supplies to domestic processing industries, e.g., restraints on the export of hides and skins, oil seeds, logs. However, they have also been used at times to drive down food prices on domestic markets as a welfare measure (e.g., in Argentina).

The case of an *export performance requirement* is essentially the reverse of the local content scheme. In Figure 2.5, the foreign demand curve, *Dw*, is

---

17 See GATT (1992) on Argentina for an exposition of the effects of Argentina's export taxes on oil seeds.

assumed to be infinitely elastic, implying the country plays only a small part in the world market for the product. The domestic demand curve is Dd, and the supply curve is Sd, so that the quantity consumed locally is $q0$, while $q0Q0$ is exported. If the government sets a ratio of domestic production to be exported, say $q1Q1$ to $0q1$, then the domestic price rises to $P1$ while domestic demand declines to $q1$. Exports are $q1Q1$ at world prices. This could take the form of a self-financing scheme if domestic consumption were taxed and the proceeds used to subsidize exports. It could even be possible to export an importable if a sufficiently high production or export subsidy were available, with or without tariffs on imports, as exists for wheat in the United States, or automobiles in a number of countries (although product differentiation is also a factor).

Takacs (1992) presents an analysis of the Philippines' local content plan for automobiles, which also incorporates an export balancing (compensatory export) requirement. She provides a mathematical and graphical presentation and goes on to compute consumer losses, efficiency losses in consumption and assembly, transfers to components and assembly and tariff revenues for actual and alternative protection regimes. Takacs also cites other quantitative studies as well as other basic theoretical studies, notably Grossman (1981) and Mussa (1984).

Some Complications It should be noted that analyzing NTMs is not quite the same as analyzing tariffs (Bhagwati, 1965). For example, with identical goods a domestic monopolist will behave as a perfect competitor under a non-prohibitive tariff, albeit at a higher price. However, a quota allows the domestic firm to act as a monopolist within the limits of the quota. It can also be shown that with monopoly behaviour a quota which restricts imports by the same amount as a tariff will raise the domestic price by more than the tariff.

Another difficulty is to distinguish the effects of tariffs from those of NTMs where both exist concurrently. A tariff and an NTM affecting the same product may or may not be additive. Typically, price NTMs work very much as additional tariffs and can simply be added to the tariff to obtain the total price effect from trade intervention. However, as noted earlier, if both a tariff and a quota are applied to the same product, the size of the price effect depends on whether the tariff or the quota is the binding constraint. Thus, if a quota is very large, then only the tariff will matter. (An implication is that a quota can be expanded gradually until the tariff becomes the binding constraint, at which point the quota can be eliminated without any further effects.)

Most NTMs are discriminatory, having differential effects as between foreign trading partners. Examples of these are the MFA, VERs, quotas, minimum prices, and anti-dumping and countervailing duty actions. This means that there may be considerable variations in the effects of NTMs on different overseas suppliers. To identify these effects, it is necessary to look beyond the effects in the importing market alone (the main focus of many NTM studies).

In respect of the MFA, computations are also complicated by the fact that not all MFA quotas are filled. For example, Erzan and Holmes (1990) show that in the period 1986–88 the utilization rates of U.S. quotas for major exporters such as Hong Kong was above 90 percent while quota utilization was much lower for Latin American and Caribbean countries, albeit with wide variations between countries and sectors. Thus, while MFA quotas may constitute the binding constraint for major exports to the United States, it is the tariff which matters more for smaller exporters, although they undoubtedly benefit to some extent from trade diversion away from the major exporters.

Beyond the impact of NTMs on products directly affected, there is, as indicated earlier, now clear evidence from a number of studies (Messerlin, 1988; Dinopoulos and Kreinin, 1988) that the "chilling" or harassment effect of VERs and anti-dumping duties goes far beyond the products and countries immediately affected. Thus, Dinopoulos and Kreinin show that European automobile exporters adjusted the prices for the U.S. market in the wake of the introduction of the Japanese automobile VER; i.e., they genuinely, voluntarily restrained trade to capture the higher rent available in the U.S. market. Messerlin shows the dramatic reduction of imports under anti-dumping investigations, with further reductions in the event of positive findings.

As for tariffs, an issue which may be relevant is the appropriate weighting of estimates of tariffs or tariff equivalents of NTM for individual products to compute economywide or sectorwide statistics. As indicated previously, import weighting can lead to seriously downward-biased results, while simple averages are subject to vagaries in the original statistical classification. Domestic output or value added weights may be more appropriate.

Finally, exchange rates matter – since they operate as a tariff cum export subsidy – and real exchange rates matter more. In many cases fluctuations in nominal exchange rates have by far exceeded tariff levels (hence, the concern expressed by countries eliminating QRs about potentially disruptive effects of trade flows under tariff-only regimes). Real exchange rates (RERs), of course, take account of relative price movements between pairs of countries as well as nominal rates. Their relationship with trade flows is endogenous and complex, because they are also partly determined by financial flows that may at times be strongly linked to interest rate differentials. In some countries the linkage between RERs and trade is very strong (Argentina, Brazil, Chile, etc.), while in other cases the linkage is more tenuous (e.g., the United States). As a footnote, in two countries with uniform tariffs of different levels, export subsidies of equivalent levels to their tariffs and market-set exchange rates, the level of access for imports is to all intents and purposes the same.

For a discussion of multiple exchange rates, which have become much less common in recent years, see Corden (1971).

Effects on Resource Allocation, Exports In addition to the effects of import restrictions on market access, it is also possible to analyze the effects of NTMs in terms of what has been the World Bank's main concern in trade policy lending over the years, namely, the effects on domestic resource allocation. In essence, protection for one sector is a tax on all other sectors, and the net effect of this is to introduce inefficiencies which reduce overall economic welfare. This is one of the reasons for focusing on calculations of effective rates of protection (discussed later) and of the domestic resource costs of NTMs.

Considerable emphasis has also been given, particularly when it comes to persuading governments of the benefits of trade liberalization, to the effects of import orientation on export performance. Here the evidence is now overwhelming that a country's own import barriers constitute a significant tax on its own exports (Clements and Sjaastad, 1984). This is obviously one of the driving concerns behind the recent adoption of outward-oriented strategies by various countries in Latin America and the consequent, significant improvements in their export performance. No doubt they were at least partly influenced by the East Asian success stories.[18]

If there is a concern about the economywide effects of protection and the interaction of protection in more than one sector, then, despite the additional data demands and conceptual questions, it becomes necessary to adopt a more comprehensive approach, looking at the effects of all trade barriers, tariffs and NTMs, throughout an economy in a consistent frame-

---

18 There are, however, important differences: in recent years, Latin American countries have adopted a more neutral outward oriented strategy, whereas, at least initially, East Asian countries adopted export promotion strategies, coupled with import-substitution. East Asian countries used export subsidies, whereas in Latin America the emphasis has been on getting rid of obstacles to exports. Also, a number of East Asian countries did some industrial targeting, although these were not all success stories.

work. This broader approach would lead to estimates of the economywide effects of trade intervention, including on employment. For this, a general equilibrium model is needed to trace out the various indirect price, output and employment effects. This is an important theme of later chapters.

When trade liberalization is taking place across the board, as in the case of the Uruguay Round or a Free Trade Agreement (FTA), such a comprehensive approach is desirable. However, measurement and computational complexity are greater than with simpler methods. Multisector models for this purpose are typically simulation models, as described elsewhere in this book, in which information on NTMs is obtained from partial equilibrium studies.

IV.2 Measurement

There are different methodologies for identifying the importance of trade measures or computing their effects. We look first at the inventory approach for summarizing information on the presence of NTMs, including quasi NTMs. This is followed by a brief discussion of the modeling approaches. Their importance is that they provide a more rigorous analytical framework for analysis of welfare, price, production and trade effects. Most modeling work today focuses on complex simulation models, such as those discussed in other chapters. For this chapter, we follow Deardorff and Stern (1985) and Baldwin (1989), concentrating on four measures of price effects: tariff equivalents, subsidy equivalent, the Trade Restrictiveness Index, and effective protection.

The Inventory Approach Considerable efforts have been made in developing the inventory approach to NTMs,[19] which allows estimates of the extent of trade covered by NTMs or their frequency of application in specific sectors or against individual countries or groups of countries. This has been based on the UNCTAD Data Base on Trade Control Measures (which has undergone several name changes, in part as a result of merging different data bases within UNCTAD), now available on compact disc–read only memory (CD-ROM) (discussed later). In this data base, data is collected by tariff item on the application of a range of NTMs against imports. Other information includes the country or countries affected and the dates of entry into force and termination of each measure. As indicated previously, information is stored on NTMs under more than 100 different categories. However, data is not collected on domestic support measures or export-related

---

19 See various UNCTAD studies in the References, as well as Laird and Yeats (1990).

measures. The main source of the information on NTMs in the data base is GATT notifications and government publications, such as customs tariffs, laws, regulations, etc.

The data base has its usefulness as an inventory of import measures in use by importing countries, including changes in their use and in countries affected. In the context of the present book, it has certain limitations, but there are some possibilities for using the trade coverage and frequency coverage ratios, including, for example, in the computation of the Trade Restrictiveness Index.

The percentage of trade subject to NTMs for an exporting country j at a desired level of product aggregation is given by the trade coverage ratio

$$C_{jt} = \left[\frac{\Sigma(D_{it} \cdot V_{iT})}{(\Sigma V_{iT})} \right] \cdot 100 \qquad (2.1)$$

where, if an NTM is applied to the tariff line item i, the dummy variable D_i takes the value of one and zero otherwise; V_i is the value of imports in item i; t is the year of measurement of the NTM; and T is the year of the import weights.[20] A problem for interpretation of this measure arises from the endogeneity of the import value weights. At the extreme, if an NTM is so restrictive that it precludes all imports of item i from country j, the weight V will be zero and, in consequence, the trade coverage ratio will be downward-biased. Similarly the coverage ratios will not indicate the extent to which NTMs have reduced the value of the affected import items, so they will reduce the weight of restricted items in the total value of a country's imports. It would be a refinement to use import weights from the world as a whole, as a proxy for free trade weights, but, as noted in the discussion on tariff weighting, many important items in trade are subject to import restrictions in a wide range of countries.

Another procedure, which avoids the problem of endogeneity of the weights, is the frequency or transaction index. This approach accounts only for the presence or absence of an NTM, without indicating the value of imports covered. Thus, it is not affected by the restraining effect of NTMs (as long as they do not completely preclude imports from an exporting country).[21] The frequency index shows the percentage of import transactions covered by a selected group of NTMs for an exporting country. It is calculated as

---

20 It is normal to use fixed year weights, so that movement in the ratio is related to changes in the application of measures against countries or products, rather than because of changes in the value of trade under different items, similar to the construction of a fixed basket of groceries in computing price indices. If current weights are used then in the formula $t=T$.

21 If imports from some countries are excluded, this ratio will also have a downward bias. In this case the ratio could be computed only for tariff items.

$$F_{jt} = \left[\frac{\Sigma(D_{it} \cdot M_{it})}{\Sigma M_{it}} \right] \cdot 100 \qquad (2.2)$$

where D_i once again reflects the presence of an NTM on the tariff line item, M_i indicates whether there are imports from the exporting country j of good i (also a dummy variable) and t is the year of measurement of the NTM.

Unlike the coverage index, however, the frequency index does not reflect the relative value of the affected products and, thus, cannot give any indication of the importance of the NTMs to an exporter overall, or, relatively, among export items.

Despite the weaknesses of the trade coverage and frequency ratios, it is possible that within some limits between 0 and 100 percent coverage they do give an indication of trade restrictiveness. This opens up several possibilities for using trade coverage or frequency ratios in econometric studies of trade flows. For example, they could be used as explanatory variables in models explaining bilateral trade flows at an aggregate level or disaggregated to a desired level of sectors. However, in such work it is important to recall that NTMs are often imposed in response to sudden changes in trade flows, which in turn respond to the inhibitory effect of the NTM, and the model has to take account of this endogeneity.

An example of an approach using NTMs as explanatory variables in cross-sectoral, cross-country analysis of OECD imports for a single year is Leamer (1990), in a research project partly financed by the World Bank and using the UNCTAD Data Base.[22]

Another approach which could prove promising is to use trade or frequency coverage ratios in a gravity model.[23]

Modeling Approaches A more comprehensive approach to quantifying the effects of trade barriers may lead to empirical measurement, sometimes on a single-industry partial equilibrium basis, looking at one country or the world, e.g., recent studies on the effects of protection in motor vehicles, textiles and clothing, iron and steel, various agricultural products. Such studies can be used to infer the price wedge, using information on observed changes in volumes together with relevant demand and supply elasticities. For example, Francois, Nelson and Palmeter (1996) survey model-based

---

22 There have been further studies using Leamer's data base, by former students. While these make advances on Leamer's work, they are also limited in not taking account of the endogeneity of NTMs in an inter-temporal context. See, for example, Harrigan (1993).

23 This is not the place to go into the debate on the gravity model. For those who wish to pursue this literature a useful starting place might be Bergstrand (1985). Ana Revenga at the World Bank and the present author explored this approach in unpublished work.

estimation of procurement barriers. There have also been single-country CGE studies focusing on the effects of trade intervention in a particular industry, such as textiles and clothing (de Melo and Tarr, 1992).

Models designed to capture the quantity effects of trade measures, and derive a price effect, may also use cross-country or cross-commodity regression techniques within a model designed to explain trade (Leamer and Stern, 1970). Thus, such models typically include some variation on the Heckscher–Ohlin comparative advantage framework. As examples, Baldwin (1970b) ran cross-commodity regressions for the United States, while Leamer (1974) used cross-country analysis for each commodity. Tinbergen (1962) included trade resistance variables in a gravity model. Clearly, it is more useful to include NTMs explicitly in such models, even if only as dummy variables, rather than regarding them as the reason for unexplained errors in the estimation, as is sometimes done in gravity models. Moreover, it is necessary to be mindful of the endogenous nature of NTMs: They may restrict imports, but they are also sometimes imposed as a response to political pressures which arise, in part, because of import competition.

Laird and Yeats (1990), Feenstra (1988a), Hufbauer and Schott (1992) and USITC (1989, 1990 and 1992a) contain surveys or collections of recent studies, including a variety of models to study the effects of non-tariff measures. Feenstra (1988a) includes several studies based on the testing of propositions from a non-competitive trade model, as well as the hypothesis that quality upgrading takes place under quota constraints. Helpman and Krugman (1989) discuss the problems of quantification in imperfect competition models, noting that there are relatively few such studies. Quantification under imperfect competition is covered in more depth in Chapter 10.

Two particularly useful surveys of U.S. import restraints, which include surveys of modeling work as well as estimates by USITC staff, are USITC (1989), covering manufacturing, and USITC (1990), covering agricultural products and natural resources.

Trade models such as these provide considerable insights into the operation of the sector or sectors being studied. However, they are also a valuable source of information on price wedges to be used as inputs into both partial and general equilibrium simulation models, such as are discussed elsewhere in this book.

Apart from the modeling of trade barriers in specific sectors, the less comprehensive approaches discussed later also cast light on some of the key effects of NTMs and what might be expected if they were removed.

The Tariff Equivalent or Price Wedge For simulation modeling, an important input is the price effect or "price wedge" associated with each NTM – often called the "tariff equivalent" of the NTM. This is the difference between the free world price of a product and the domestic price, which is protected by an NTM.

If world prices are genuinely free – not influenced by widespread use of subsidies – then they can be obtained from customs invoices or from commodity markets. These can then be compared directly with the domestic ex-factory or wholesale prices of identical products. Sometimes it is necessary to identify representative products and find comparable domestic products and imports. It also may be necessary to compute an average over a selected group of products and over a period of time. Sometimes wholesale prices or constructed ex-factory prices in different countries are compared, adjusting for transport costs to compute the price wedge between the country with the lowest wholesale price and the importing country under study.

The price wedge technique is used frequently by World Bank economists and has also been used in published studies by Roningen and Yeats (1976), Baldwin (1975) and Bhagwati and Srinivasan (1975). Roningen and Yeats obtained access to the raw data stored by *Business International*, which publishes comparative information on the cost of living in major cities of the world. The most extensive set of computations of this nature was done in the tariffication of existing import restrictions on agricultural trade for the Uruguay Round.[24] However, in this case the work was done by each government in respect of its own measures, according to a set of mutually agreed procedures, essentially comparing the c.i.f. price of imports with the ex-factory price of identical locally produced goods.

The work of computing the price wedge is much easier for governments than for academic economists. Governments have access to customs invoices and routinely compile information on prices overseas for use in verifying customs declarations. In some cases, they use the services of pre-shipment inspection agencies such as SGS or Veritas, which have widespread international networks collecting such information. Thus, provided no breach of confidentiality is involved, this information can sometimes also be obtained for third-country markets even when there are no direct imports into the market applying the NTM. However, it would then be necessary to compute the cost of delivery to that market – information which can be derived from shipping companies or invoices for similar goods. Price comparisons were

---

24 These are now available in published schedule from GATT, and, at the time of writing, it was intended to release them on diskette in Lotus format.

made by Eurostat for use by the Commission of the European Communities (1988) in estimating the effects of removing barriers between members states of the European Union in 1992.

Observation of the price wedge is relatively straightforward when imports and domestically produced goods are perfect substitutes. However, calculations are often complex for manufactured goods because of the great range and heterogeneity of products. Obviously, the idea is to match items as closely as possible, but it is possible using econometric techniques to normalize differences in the characteristics and qualities of differentiated products. In this respect, a considerable amount of work has been based on the use of hedonic price indices, a technique pioneered by Griliches (1970).[25] However, this has principally been used in work on consumer price indices as well as demand analysis. A recent application is the analysis of protection of differentiated products by Feenstra (1988b) in respect to the U.S. market for U.S. made and Japanese made compact trucks.

The price wedge can sometimes be obtained directly if an auctioning system is used for allocation of import quotas, as has been done at times in Australia (Takacs, 1988),[26] or for allocation of export quotas, as is done in Hong Kong for textiles and clothing exports (Hamilton, 1986). Hamilton also constructs export licence prices from the marginal costs of exporters using relative wage data adjusted for labour productivity. In the Hamilton study there was little difference between the constructed "price" data and the available information on licence prices, while Krishna, Martin and Tan (1992) find substantial differences in the case of Indonesia.

As noted earlier, it might also be possible to use an econometric model of an industry to compute the price wedge on the basis of observed changes in the volume of production and trade together with relevant supply and demand elasticities.

Even if we can calculate the price wedge between domestic and "world" prices associated with an NTM in one market, this does not necessarily give us the basis for computing how any one trading partner will be affected by the removal of certain NTMs. This is because of the discriminatory effects of a number of the NTMs, as noted earlier. Thus, exporting countries, attempting to assess what they will gain from the elimination of other countries' NTMs, need to take bilateral price differentials into account (not to mention

---

25 In the 1970s this technique was regularly used by the Australian Industries Assistance Commission to calculate price differences between foreign and domestically produced manufactures such as domestic appliances and automobiles.
26 One of the first experiments in quota auctioning in Australia – for automobiles in the mid-1970s – was brought quickly to a conclusion as the government became embarrassed at the size of the quota rents.

the substitutability between their own and competitors' exports in the importing market).

Another factor to take into account is the variability of prices, particularly commodity prices, in international markets. With variable levies and reference prices the domestic price of the import remains fixed even when there are fluctuations in world prices. Thus, in markets using such devices the price wedge itself is constantly varying for a number of products.

For a number of products, particularly commodities, governmental intervention is so widespread that the "world price" cannot be observed from transaction values. In these circumstances, there is little alternative to developing a model to attempt to isolate "free world prices" from prices influenced by production and export subsidies (or, indeed, export taxes), as well as import barriers such as variable levies, and quotas. One of the problems is estimating the supply response to changes in world prices by countries which are currently food importers. Fortunately, much work has been done in the area of commodities, as we shall see in the following section.

A further complication is that exporters have been observed to change the quality mix of their product when subject to import restraints expressed in volume terms. This is the importance of the work by Feenstra (1988b), noted earlier.

Subsidy Equivalents The concept of the Producer Subsidy Equivalent (PSE) has come to be used extensively in recent years, following extensive work by the OECD.[27] It is a concise way of measuring the transfers that are a result of government policies to producers. It can be measured (i) by tracing the direct and indirect government expenditures to producers or (ii) by imputing the effects of policies by calculating the difference between actual domestic prices and what they would have been in the absence of trade interventions. Its advantage over nominal protection, such as is given by the price wedge discussed, is that it captures both the transfers from government expenditures as well as the transfers from price distortions.

PSEs can be expressed in different ways. The total *PSE* is simply the value of transfers to producers:

$$\text{Total } PSE\ (PSE) = Q(Pd - Pw \cdot X) + D + I \qquad (2.3)$$

where:

Q = quantity produced
Pd = the producer price in domestic currency units

27 See OECD (1987), the country studies published in the same year, and OECD (1994).

Pw = world price in world currency units
X = exchange conversion factor
D = direct government payments, net of any levies on production
I = indirect transfers through policies such as input subsidies, marketing assistance or exchange rate distortions.

The unit *PSE* is the total *PSE* per tonne or unit of production:

$$\text{Unit } PSE\ (PSEu) = \frac{PSE}{Q} \qquad (2.4)$$

The percentage *PSE* is the total *PSE* expressed as a percentage of the total value of production, valued at domestic prices, and adjusted for direct payments and levies:

$$\text{Percentage } PSE = \left[\frac{PSE}{(Q \cdot Pd + D)} \right] \cdot 100 \qquad (2.5)$$

Another way of expressing the *PSE* is the nominal assistance coefficient (NAC). The NAC for production is the ratio of the border price plus the unit *PSE* to the border price. In essence, it is the price wedge on the production side created by the agricultural policies in use.

$$NAC = \frac{(Pw \cdot X + PSEu)}{Pw \cdot X} \qquad (2.6)$$

It should be noted that changes in world prices, exchange rates or domestic production can change the *PSE* even when government policies remain unchanged. Also, since indirect transfers appear only in the numerator, the *PSE* can be altered by shifting transfers from indirect programs to price support programs or direct payments (Webb, Lopez and Penn, 1990). A negative *PSE* implies that the producer is being taxed as a result of the combination of policies operating in the sector, while a positive *PSE* implies the producer is being supported or assisted by the intervention.

The U.S. Department of Agriculture's Economic Research Service computes and regularly publishes PSEs as well as Consumer Subsidy Equivalents (CSEs) for many agricultural commodities in a wide range of developed and developing countries; see, for example, Webb, Lopez and Penn (1990). Comparable data series are also published by the OECD.

It is important to note that these numbers can vary considerably from year to year for the reasons given. Also, the estimates only take account of exchange rate adjustments in the case of the developing countries, where they often dominate the calculations and can cause the *PSE* to swing wildly over time. There may also be quality differences which reduce the comparability of the data.

A related concept, the CSE, is the value of transfers, resulting from government intervention, from domestic consumers to producers and to taxpayers (e.g., through tariff revenue paid on competing imports). It measures the net implicit tax imposed on consumers by agricultural support measures and any consumer subsidies. A negative CSE implies consumers are being taxed by the policies operating in the sector. A NAC for consumption measures the extent to which consumers are paying more than they would in the absence of government intervention.

The Trade Restrictiveness Index The Trade Restrictiveness Index (TRI), developed by Anderson and Neary (1991), is defined as the "uniform tariff equivalent of the consumption and production distortions." It is a combination of the "consistent PSE" and "consistent CSE," which are defined as the uniform subsidy rates that are equivalent in trade restrictiveness (indexed by welfare loss) to the actual differentiated subsidy or tax structure. It is mainly used to measure change in the restrictiveness of trade policy over time for a single economy or sector of an economy, that is, comparing two distorted situations rather than comparing against the free trade benchmark.[28] Thus, it has important potential for the assessment of progress in the liberalization of an economy, e.g., under World Bank SALs. However, it will be of less interest to modellers seeking to introduce the price wedge into large-scale simulation models. Indeed, in Anderson and Neary (1994b) it is used essentially as a weighting technique (using welfare loss as weights) for averaging license prices for textile exports computed by using the method established by Hamilton (1986). They show important differences from import-weighted averages, which are subject to downward biases, as noted earlier.

The most recent and comprehensive description is Anderson and Neary (1994a) and its most recent application is Anderson and Neary (1994b). In general, the TRI is also more applicable to small variations, for example, "short" periods or in respect of "small" changes in quotas. Anderson and Neary (1994a) note that their alternative, hybrid index, covering goods that are both tariff-constrained and quota-constrained, is difficult to interpret if one wishes to make comparisons across countries or periods in which the mix of goods that are subject to tariffs and quotas differs across the sample. To some extent, this can be avoided by using the tariff equivalents of quota-constrained goods, in which case the resulting index is "a uniform tariff and a tariff-equivalent surcharge factor." The choice between the two forms of the TRI depends essentially on the availability of data.

---

28 In Anderson and Neary (1994b) it is also used to compare the restrictiveness of the U.S. MFA scheme on different exports to that market.

Anderson (1993) provides a manual for use of the TRI in an Excel spreadsheet. This uses actual tariff rates and trade for individual products within an economy or sector of an economy as well as other economywide data. NTMs can be introduced as dummy variables or, in the case of quota-constrained goods, as tariff equivalents of the quotas, as in the textile study by Anderson and Neary (1994b).

Anderson and Neary (1994a) list most of the applied studies carried out using the TRI methodology. These are now quite diverse. For example, one early partial equilibrium application was by Anderson and Bannister (1992) in respect of domestic price policies in Mexican agriculture. General equilibrium applications are discussed in Anderson, Neary and Safadi (1992).

Effective Protection Tariff equivalent and subsidy equivalents do not give a comprehensive view of the trade and production effects of the protective structure of a country. For example, an ad valorem tariff of, say, 20 percent on automobiles does not give an idea of the extent to which protection generates changes in the value added in automotive assembly. For this it is necessary to look at the combined effect of tariffs (and any other restrictions or forms of assistance) on automobiles as well as such protection on the materials and parts used in the production process – steel, rubber, plastics, glass, etc., as well as engines, gearboxes, brake assemblies, electrical components, etc. The combined effect of protection on inputs and outputs can be summed up in the concept of the effective rate of protection (ERP, normally referring to tariffs only) or the effective rate of assistance (ERA, intended to encompass all NTMs, including domestic supports).

The concept of the ERP was developed by Balassa (1965) and Corden (1966) to measure the increase in value added in an industry under protection relative to what value added would be under free trade. In other words effective rates measure assistance to value added in an industry. Mathematically, the effective rate can be expressed in different ways, of which one such expression is

$$g = \frac{(df - x \cdot dm)}{(1 - x)} \tag{2.7}$$

where:

g = effective rate of protection
df = nominal rate on finished good (output of a production process)
dm = nominal rate on inputs to a production process
x = free trade materials/output ratio

As can be seen from the formula, the exact level of effective protection or assistance depends on the rate of protection on the output of a process (whether for final consumption or intermediate goods), the average rate of protection on the inputs of materials and parts, and the extent of value added in the industry at unassisted prices (the free trade material/output ratio or the technical coefficient). Protection may be defined to cover all forms of government intervention, including tariffs, other protection against imports and domestic subsidies, etc., although sometimes only tariff protection is included.

If protection on the finished good is equal to the average protection on the inputs, then the effective rate will be the same as that level of protection. However, if protection is higher on the finished good than on the inputs, then the effective rate will be higher than the protection of the finished good, and value added will also be higher than when the rates were identical. On the other hand if protection is lower on the finished good than on the inputs, then the effective rate will be lower than that on the finished goods, and, correspondingly, value added will also be lower.

Effective rates can also be negative. For example, for a given rate of duty on outputs (df), which is lower than a given rate of duty on the inputs (dm), then as the free trade material/output ratio (x) rises, the effective rate declines and becomes negative, i.e., when $df < (x \cdot dm)$.[29] However, analysts more often take the average effective rate (the free trade value added weighted effective rates applicable to all sectors) as the main point of reference in discussions about resource allocation. If the effective rate for a sector is lower than average, it means that sector is implicitly being taxed to support sectors with higher than average effective rates, and vice versa. This is because highly protected sectors (in terms of effective rates) are able to bid up wages, land and other inputs, thus affecting the costs of other sectors. This does not necessarily mean higher profits for the protected sector, since typically higher protection becomes factored into costs such as land and buildings or lost through economic inefficiency (X-inefficiency). Nor is it a prescription for increasing lower rates to the average, because a non-zero average still implies the implicit taxation of the non-traded sector.

29 The free trade materials/output ratio is computed by adjusting the materials/output ratio under protection for the effects of the existing protection structure. Thus, the unit values of the input and output are divided by $(1+dm)$ and $(1+df)$, respectively, i.e., $x = x' \cdot ((1+df)/(1+dm))$, where x' is the materials/output ratio under protection. Also, note that x can be greater than unity because of this adjustment, implying that the denominator in the effective rate formula is negative and, hence, effective rates may also become negative. In addition, while tariffs must be positive, nominal protection on inputs or outputs can be negative if the net effect of all forms of assistance and taxes is negative. It should also be noted that in effective rate calculations no allowance is made for any shift between materials, or between materials and other factors of production, as a result of relative price variations in the free trade situation vis-à-vis the protected situation.

It should also be noted that the level of the effective rate is highly sensitive to the materials/output ratio, increasing asymptotically to infinity as this ratio increases, i.e., as value added in the industry declines.

Despite their limitations, effective rates have become a standard tool of analysis since the late 1960s, being used by governments to assess the implications of sectoral levels of protection for the efficiency of resource allocation within their own countries. The measure has become a standard analytical tool of the World Bank in most studies associated with trade or structural adjustment lending. The World Bank has also developed standard specialized personal computer (PC) software, SINTIA-ER, using survey data, and SINTIA-IO, using input–output tables, for the purpose of making effective rate calculations, but these have not been published. The concept is currently under examination at OECD with the view to its introduction as a routine tool of analysis of OECD countries' economies, although initial work is focusing on more basic questions, such as trying to obtain up-to-date tariff information, including ad valorem equivalents of specific tariffs, while NTM work is at present following the inventory approach using UNCTAD data.

However, like many statistical tools, the effective rate suffers from a number of shortcomings. It is a partial equilibrium rather than a general equilibrium measure. It assumes that there is no change in technology in shifting between actual and world prices. It assumes that there is perfect substitutability between domestic and foreign goods, whereas most modern trade models assume imperfect substitutability – the so-called "Armington assumption."

There are also problems, such as those we have been discussing, on how to measure NTMs – because this is a summary measure in which price wedges are used as an input, not an alternative technique. In the end, effective rates do not solve the question of measurement of NTMs, but they take more factors into account in assessing their effects.

The difference between the percentage PSE and the ERP/ERA relates to the forms of intervention and the value base or denominator in the computations. First, since PSE estimation has been focused on agriculture, these estimates do not comprehensively include the taxation or subsidy effect of intervention in relation to intermediate inputs produced in other sectors of the economy, whereas effective rates of assistance can be computed to take all forms of intervention into account. Second, PSEs relate assistance to the gross value of output (i.e., under existing intervention), whereas effective rates are based on free trade levels of value added (or the free trade input–

output ratio as shown in the formula). Thus, the effective rate is a more comprehensive summary measure, albeit subject to the limiting, underlying assumptions.

The relationship between effective rates and the results of CGE models is not self-evident. Effective rates measure the value added under protection, while a CGE model can be used to compute changes in value added under a simulation of free trade; that is, in principle, they can do the same thing. However, in various studies, including by the author, there are mixed results as to the pattern of protection, even using a rank correlation of industries according to the change in value added in moving to free trade. The issue is specifically addressed in Devarajan and Sussangkarn (1992), who examine the importance of the assumption of perfect substitutability between imported and domestic goods under the ERP and the assumption of imperfect substitutability under modern CGE models. In essence they show that "the standard method for calculating ERPs can be seriously misleading if domestic and foreign goods are imperfect substitutes." For elasticity assumptions from around 10 to infinity the results of the two methods are similar, except in some cases where the import share in domestic supply is very small (which makes an important difference to the CGE results while having no importance for the standard ERP computations), or when world prices cannot be taken as fixed.

V Sources of Data

Apart from the individual studies and collections or reviews of studies previously cited, it is important to mention several key sources of data. The most comprehensive collection of publicly available information is the UNCTAD Trade Control Measures database, reproduced in CD-ROM in the UNCTAD Trade Analysis and Information System (TRAINS) – see UNCTAD (1993). This contains, inter alia, information on tariffs, GSP, NTMs (but not ad valorem equivalents of NTMs) and trade for most OECD countries and some thirty developing countries. It is available with a retrieval system and certain basic analytical tools on a CD-ROM from UNCTAD.

Another source of publicly available information is the data base produced and periodically updated by the Global Trade Analysis Project (GTAP), a consortium of national and international agencies based at Purdue University. This is available for alumni of the GTAP training course at reduced cost. It has been compiled from information at the U.S.

Department of Agriculture (USDA), WTO, World Bank, OECD, and other sources. The advantage of this database is its explicit linkage of protection data to inter-industry production structure data.

A new publicly available source of information on the tariff equivalent of agricultural NTMs is contained in the published Uruguay Round schedules for major developed and developing countries. This information is available in bound volumes as well as Lotus *.WK3 spreadsheet files from the WTO Secretariat.

The OECD agricultural studies, cited in this chapter, contain detailed information on the operation of agricultural policies, including PSEs and CSEs for OECD countries. USDA's Economic Research Service (ERS) has also published PSEs and CSEs for developed and some developing countries. The data used in USDA's SWOPSIM partial equilibrium model of world agricultural trade is also available to researchers.

For information on tariffs and the operation of trade policies in some forty countries, the WTO has published reports under its Trade Policy Review Mechanism (TPRM). Trade policy studies are also available for about ten countries under the World Bank–UNDP Trade Expansion Project, including details of the operation of specific measures in certain cases. World Bank studies for official use only cover most developing countries and are available in grey cover format. Government officials can usually consult these at their Finance Ministries or equivalents.

The WTO Integrated Data Base, available for official use only, contains highly detailed information on tariffs, including preferences and bindings, and is intended to contain information on currently applicable quantitative restrictions at the four-digit HS level for most GATT contracting parties (WTO members). This is now available on CD-ROM, albeit limited at the moment to official use. This data base, with periodic updates based on TPRM reports and tariff notifications, will eventually be distributed more broadly by the WTO.

For those with a particular interest in the U.S. economy, USITC (1989) for manufacturing and USITC (1990) for agricultural products and natural resources are invaluable. The USITC import restraint studies are subject to periodic update.

VI Concluding Remarks

Most researchers using this book are likely to be economists who wish to learn and apply the simulation models that are discussed in other chapters. For them the most important issue discussed in this chapter would have been the computation of the price wedge associated with the use of NTMs, despite its limitations. This is because partial and general equilibrium simulation models are driven by the price changes that follow international trade. However, as discussed, there are other rewarding approaches to NTM analysis. It is hoped that the discussion has been sufficiently general to allow the application of the approaches described to NTMs other than those specifically identified, because one important lesson from the study of NTMs is that the inventiveness of protectionists is unbounded.

Appendix 2.1

Table 2A.1. *UNCTAD coding system of trade control measures*

Code	Description
1000	**TARIFF MEASURES**
1100	STATUTORY CUSTOMS DUTIES
1200	MFN DUTIES
1300	GATT CEILING DUTIES
1400	TARIFF QUOTA DUTIES
1410	Low duties
1420	High duties
1500	SEASONAL DUTIES
1510	Low duties
1520	High duties
1600	TEMPORARY REDUCED DUTIES
1700	TEMPORARY INCREASED DUTIES
1710	Retaliatory duties
1720	Urgency and safeguard duties
1900	PREFERENTIAL DUTIES UNDER TRADE AGREEMENTS
1910	Interregional agreements
1920	Regional and sub-regional agreements
1930	Bilateral agreements
2000	**PARA-TARIFF MEASURES**
2100	CUSTOMS SURCHARGES
2200	ADDITIONAL TAXES AND CHARGES
2210	Tax on foreign exchange transactions
2220	Stamp tax
2230	Import licence fee
2240	Consular invoice fee
2250	Statistical tax
2260	Tax on transport facilities
2270	Taxes and charges for sensitive product categories
2290	Additional charges n.e.s.
2300	INTERNAL TAXES AND CHARGES LEVIED ON IMPORTS
2310	General sales taxes
2320	Excise taxes
2370	Taxes and charges for sensitive product categories
2390	Internal taxes and charges levied on imports n.e.s.
2400	DECREED CUSTOMS VALUATION
2900	PARA-TARIFF MEASURES N.E.S.

Table 2A.1. *(cont.)*

Code	Description
3000	**PRICE CONTROL MEASURES**
3100	ADMINISTRATIVE PRICING
3110	Minimum import prices
3190	Administrative pricing n.e.s.
3200	VOLUNTARY EXPORT PRICE RESTRAINT
3300	VARIABLE CHARGES
3310	Variable levies
3320	Variable components
3330	Compensatory elements
3340	Flexible import fees
3390	Variable charges n.e.s.
3400	ANTI-DUMPING MEASURES
3410	Anti-dumping investigations
3420	Anti-dumping duties
3430	Price undertakings
3500	COUNTERVAILING MEASURES
3510	Countervailing investigations
3520	Countervailing duties
3530	Price undertakings
3900	PRICE CONTROL MEASURES N.E.S.
4000	**FINANCE MEASURES**
4100	ADVANCE PAYMENT REQUIREMENTS
4110	Advance import deposit
4120	Cash margin requirement
4130	Advance payment of customs duties
4170	Refundable deposits for sensitive product categories
4190	Advance payment requirements n.e.s.
4200	MULTIPLE EXCHANGE RATES
4300	RESTRICTIVE OFFICIAL FOREIGN EXCHANGE ALLOCATION
4310	Prohibition of foreign exchange allocation
4320	Bank authorization
4390	Restrictive official foreign exchange allocation n.e.s.
4500	REGULATIONS CONCERNING TERMS OF PAYMENT FOR IMPORTS
4600	TRANSFER DELAYS, QUEUING
4900	FINANCE MEASURES N.E.S.
5000	**AUTOMATIC LICENSING MEASURES**
5100	AUTOMATIC LICENCE
5200	IMPORT MONITORING
5210	Retrospective surveillance
5220	Prior surveillance
5270	Prior surveillance for sensitive product categories
5700	SURRENDER REQUIREMENT
5900	AUTOMATIC LICENSING MEASURES N.E.S.
6000	**QUANTITY CONTROL MEASURES**
6100	NON-AUTOMATIC LICENSING
6110	Licence with no specific ex-ante criteria
6120	Licence for selected purchasers
6130	Licence for specified use
6131	Linked with export trade
6132	For purposes other than exports
6140	Licence linked with local production
6141	Purchase of local goods

Table 2A.1. *(cont.)*

Code	Description
6142	Local content requirement
6143	Barter or counter trade
6150	Licence linked with non-official foreign exchange
6151	External foreign exchange
6152	Importers' own foreign exchange
6160	Licence combined with or replaced by special import authorization
6170	Prior authorization for sensitive product categories
6190	Non-automatic licensing n.e.s.
6200	QUOTAS
6210	Global quotas
6211	Unallocated
6212	Allocated to exporting countries
6220	Bilateral quotas
6230	Seasonal quotas
6240	Quotas linked with export performance
6250	Quotas linked with purchase of local goods
6270	Quotas for sensitive product categories
6290	Quotas n.e.s.
6300	PROHIBITIONS
6310	Total prohibition
6320	Suspension of issuance of licences
6330	Seasonal prohibition
6340	Temporary prohibition
6350	Import diversification
6360	Prohibition on the basis of origin (embargo)
6370	Prohibition for sensitive product categories
6390	Prohibitions n.e.s.
6600	EXPORT RESTRAINT ARRANGEMENTS
6610	Voluntary export restraint arrangements
6620	Orderly marketing arrangements
6630	Multi-fibre arrangement (MFA)
6631	Quota agreement
6632	Consultation agreement
6633	Administrative co-operation agreement
6640	Export restraint arrangements on textiles outside MFA
6641	Quota agreement
6642	Consultation agreement
6643	Administrative co-operation agreement
6690	Export restraint arrangements n.e.s.
6700	ENTERPRISE-SPECIFIC RESTRICTIONS
6710	Selective approval of importers
6720	Enterprise-specific quota
6790	Enterprise-specific restrictions n.e.s.
6900	QUANTITY CONTROL MEASURES N.E.S.
7000	**MONOPOLISTIC MEASURES**
7100	SINGLE CHANNEL FOR IMPORTS
7110	State trading administration
7120	Sole importing agency
7200	COMPULSORY NATIONAL SERVICES
7210	Compulsory national insurance
7220	Compulsory national transport
7900	MONOPOLISTIC MEASURES N.E.S.

Table 2A.1. *(cont.)*

Code	Description
8000	**TECHNICAL MEASURES**
8100	TECHNICAL REGULATIONS
8110	Product characteristics requirements
8120	Marking requirements
8130	Labelling requirements
8140	Packaging requirements
8150	Testing, inspection and quarantine requirements
8190	Technical regulations n.e.s.
8200	PRE-SHIPMENT INSPECTION
8300	SPECIAL CUSTOMS FORMALITIES
8900	TECHNICAL MEASURES N.E.S.

Source: UNCTAD (1994), which contains notes on certain measures as well as a set of working definitions for trade control measures.

Appendix 2.2

A Glossary of Non-tariff Measures

The following list of the main types of non-tariff measures is adapted from Laird and Yeats (1990) to fit in with the broad classification according to intent by Laird and Vossenaar (1991) given in Section III of this chapter. It has also been extended to cover measures affecting exports.

Measures to Control the Volume of Imports

A wide range of measures are used to control the volume of imports. These include prohibitions, various types of quotas or quantitative restrictions (QRs), non-automatic licensing, import authorizations, voluntary exports restraints, including under the Multi-Fibre Arrangement (MFA), orderly marketing arrangements, and state trading or sole import monopolies.

Prohibitions can apply in general or under special circumstances, e.g., conditional prohibitions. Typically prohibitions apply to arms and munitions as well as other military equipment (unless imported by the armed forces), drugs (except where imported by health authorities or for scientific purposes), pornographic materials, and certain plants or animals (including endangered species, under international conventions). If certain standards or other technical regulations are not fulfilled, imports may be prohibited (technical barriers, discussed later).

Quotas are restrictions on the quantity or value of imports of specific products. They are determined for a specific period and modified periodically. They may be imposed for a limited period as a trade remedy or safeguard action against a surge in imports, e.g., under Article XIX of the GATT. They are sometimes set on a first-come, first-served basis, but more often they are allocated in respect of existing trading partners in proportion to their historic market share. They may be allocated to importing companies, again in relation to historic share in imports, or to foreign governments or companies. If foreign governments receive the quotas, they may allocate them to companies in their country on the basis of historic market share or sell the quotas, including by auction.

Quotas may be applied globally (to all countries), plurilaterally (to a group of countries) or bilaterally (to a single trading partner). They may also be applied at certain times of the year (seasonal quotas), usually during the growing season for protected agricultural products.

Non-automatic licensing is usually the means for administering a quota or a conditional prohibition, and, in such cases, is a condition for importation. However, sometimes quotas are not determined in advance; in these cases, the non-automatic licence may be a means of rationing foreign exchange, or of determining whether certain conditions for import have been met, e.g., export performance requirements. Non-automatic licensing may be relatively restrictive or discretionary, or it may be relatively liberal, often depending on the economic circumstances in the importing country. Import authorizations, usually for a ministry, government agency, etc., are a form of non-automatic import licensing, typically used to administer conditional prohibitions.

Voluntary export restraints (VERs), technically banned under the Uruguay Round Agreement, are usually informal export restraint arrangements (ERAs) between an exporter and an importer whereby the former agrees to limit, for a certain period, the exports of certain goods to the market of the imports to prevent the imposition of import quotas. These are often industry-to-industry arrangements, but governments can be involved on a more or less formal basis. Where governments are formally involved, these are sometimes categorized as organized marketing arrangements (OMAs), although the use of this term seems to have become less frequent.

Textiles and clothing imports by most industrial countries have operated under various restraints for more than 30 years. In its current form, the main instrument is the Multi-Fibre Arrangement (MFA), which is scheduled to be phased out over ten years as part of the Uruguay Round agreement. Essentially, it is a series of bilateral VERs applying to some one hundred or so textile and clothing sectors; the sectors need not be comprehensive, being specified for each affected trading partner. Textile and clothing exporters which are not members of the MFA, e.g., Eastern European countries and China, are covered by similar restrictions, textile restraint agreements.

State trading and import monopolies are procedures whereby a government agency has the exclusive right to trade or has granted this right to a private monopolist. Only that agency or company can determine the level of imports, although it may in practice operate strictly as an independent operator.

Measures to Control the Price of Imported Goods

Measures to control the price of imported goods can be sub-divided into tariff-type or para-tariff measures and price NTMs.

Tariff-Type Measures

These include tariff surcharges, seasonal tariffs, tariff quotas, additional charges, domestic charges levied on imports, variable levies, anti-dumping duties and countervailing duties.

Tariff quotas operate as a limit or a quota on the quantity or value of imports of specific products allowed, for a given period, under the normal tariff, whereas higher rates are charges on imports which exceed the quota. These are sometimes called tariff rate quotas. They are to be applied extensively in the agricultural sector for a range of commodities for which existing restrictions on imports have been "tariffied" under the Uruguay Round Agreement on Agriculture.

Local content plans can work like tariff quotas. In return for achieving a certain degree of local content, producers, such as automobile assemblers, are allowed to import a certain amount or quota of equivalent finished goods at lower or even duty-free prices. Imports above the quota attract the normal, higher rate. An important effect is protection of the domestic components industry, as discussed in the main text. These are now officially banned under the Uruguay Round TRIMs Agreement, following a phase-out period.

Variable levies are special charges imposed on imports of certain goods in order to raise their price to a domestic target price. No levy is imposed when the international price exceeds the domestic support price. They are widely applied to the agricultural sector by the European Union, but are to be eliminated under the Uruguay Round agreement. For an analysis, see Sampson and Yeats (1977).

Anti-dumping duties are levied on certain goods originating in a specific trading partner or specific trading partners to offset the effect of dumping. Such duties may be enterprise-specific or may be applied on a nationwide basis. These have become one of the most widely used measures in recent years. For a discussion, see Finger (1993).

Countervailing measures are special charges on certain goods to offset the effect of any bounty or subsidy granted directly or indirectly on the manufacture, production or export of these goods.

Other Price NTMs

Other price measures include minimum prices, voluntary export price restraints, government procurement procedures, and certain other procedures which increase the costs of imports.

Minimum prices set a decreed target or reference price for an imported good, like the domestic support price used for many agricultural products. Actual import prices below the minimum price may trigger action in the form of compensatory duties or price investigations. A duty which is set to equalize the import price and the minimum or target price is a variable levy. However, where the target price or reference price is the means to determine the value for duty (customs valuation), the "normal" rate is levied on the reference price, not the actual transaction value.

Voluntary export price restraints are an undertaking by an exporter, accepted by the authorities in the importing country, to take actions which neutralize price effects of subsidies and/or dumping to avoid the imposition of countervailing measures.

Government procurement procedures typically involve a price preference for domestic goods. The price preference is computed to determine the outcome of public tenders for the supply of goods or services to government agencies.

Other measures which increase the cost of imports include advance deposit requirements (without interest payments), special regulations on foreign exchange and the use of credit for imports, and special entry procedures, such as the requirement that a fixed share or all of trade be carried by the national fleet or that imports be effected through special ports.

Monitoring Measures, Including Price and Volume Investigations

Monitoring measures include automatic licensing, import surveillance, price surveillance and investigations, and anti-dumping and countervailing investigations. These are sometimes considered to have a harassing or "chilling" effect on imports. It has been shown by Messerlin (1988) that anti-dumping investigations themselves may provoke a reduction in imports.

Automatic licensing and import surveillance are typically used together to track the level of imports. One reason for such action may be concerns about possible import surges, which could trigger safeguard actions.

In some countries, including the United States, there is a separation of two components of an anti-dumping or countervailing investigation. First, there is an investigation as to whether dumping or subsidization is taking place. Only if this is resolved in the affirmative is there an investigation as to whether or not there is injury to the domestic industry. Standards of injury are defined in the relevant GATT codes. Dumping investigations often involve the use of constructed prices, and the methodology applied in some cases has been widely criticized (Finger, 1993).

Production and Export Measures

Production and export measures consist of measures to assist or to control production or exports. The main measures of concern are production and export subsidies and export prohibitions and taxes.

Subsidies, sometimes called bounties (although the latter term is often reserved for inputs), which may be used to assist domestic production, are most common in the agricultural sector, but they have also been a widely used tool of industrial policy in developed and developing countries. For a general treatment, see Hufbauer and Erb (1984). There are many different schemes operating under a wide range of names – see, in particular, OECD (1994) for a catalogue of measures in the agricultural sector. Subsidies can be applied directly to production or, indirectly, to inputs into production. They can also be applied in respect of services, such as finance or transport, used in production or marketing. They are sometimes applied only in certain regions, to assist regional development. They may take the form of financial support or as waivers of taxes or charges that would otherwise be due. In the Uruguay Round one of the important issues was the de-linking of subsidies from the level of production to a form of income support for farmers.

Subsidies may also be applied directly to exports. An Illustrative List of Export Subsidies is attached to the Uruguay Round Code on Subsidies and Countervailing Measures; see GATT (1994). Remission of import charges on imported inputs must be precisely computed to prevent its being considered a subsidy. Various tax breaks applied only to exports are considered to be subsidies.

Export performance requirements are a means of linking certain import concessions (reduced tariffs) or investment tax breaks to the export of a fixed share of domestic production.

Exports may be prohibited, e.g., in support of UN resolutions, or because the products are deemed dangerous or constitute a security risk. However, they are often prohibited to provide materials, such as raw or tanned hides, vegetable oil seeds or cake, or lumber, to processors. The export restriction usually also drives down the domestic price so that processors also obtain their inputs below world prices. Export prohibitions (and taxes) have more recently been invoked as necessary to conserve natural resources, such as rare tropical timbers, but if domestic access is not restrained, the effect may be to encourage technically inefficient processing with little or no effect on conservation. Export taxes are also used to attempt to exploit market power by capturing the economic rents from a dominant supplier position. Such rents can attract expansion by competitors, resulting in their elimination and loss of market power.

Technical Barriers

Technical regulations and standards to be met by products for sale on the domestic market, applying, in principle, equally to domestic and imported goods include health, sanitary, phytosanitary and safety regulations, as well as marking and packaging requirements.

Such measures may be applied to individual items or to samples from shipments. Type approval may be granted for imports from certain suppliers, obviating the need for individual testing. Sometimes a certificate of compliance with international standards or national standards of the United States or member states of the European Union, issued by approved agencies, is acceptable to other countries.

Technical barriers may increase the price of imports or cause non-complying imports to be prohibited.

References

Anderson, J.E. 1993. "Measuring trade restrictiveness in a simple CGE model, with appendix: A manual for using the TRI spreadsheet model." Boston College, Department of Economics; Boston, Massachusetts.

Anderson, J.E. and G. Bannister. 1992. "The trade restrictiveness index: An application to Mexican agriculture." PPR WPS No. 874, International Economics Department, World Bank, Washington, D.C.

Anderson, J.E. and J.P. Neary. 1991. "A new approach to evaluating trade policy." World Bank Working Paper, World Bank, Washington, D.C.

Anderson, J.E. and J.P. Neary. 1994a. "Measuring the restrictiveness of trade policy." *World Bank Economic Review* 8:151–169.

Anderson, J.E. and J.P. Neary. 1994b. "The trade restrictiveness of the Multi-Fibre Arrangement." *World Bank Economic Review* 8:170–189.

Anderson, J.E., J.P. Neary, and R. Safadi. 1992. "The trade restrictiveness index: General equilibrium applications." International Economics Department, World Bank, Washington, D.C., mimeo.

Balassa, B. 1965. "Tariff protection in industrial countries: An evaluation." *Journal of Political Economy* 73:675–594.

Baldwin, R. 1970a. *Non-tariff distortions in international trade*. Washington, D.C.: Brookings Institution.

Baldwin, R. 1970b. "Determinants of the commodity structure of U.S. trade." *American Economic Review* 61:126–146.

Baldwin, R. 1975. *Foreign Trade Régimes and Economic Development: The Philippines*. New York: NBER.

Baldwin, R. 1989. "Measuring nontariff trade policies." NBER Working Paper No. 2978.

Basevi, G. 1971. "Aggregation problems in measurement of effective protection." In *Effective Tariff Protection*, edited by Herbert G. Grubel and Harry G. Johnson. Geneva: GATT and Graduate Institute of International Studies.

Bergstrand, J.H. 1985. "The gravity equation in international trade: Some microeconomic foundations and empirical evidence." *Review of Economics and Statistics* 67:474–481.

Bhagwati, J. 1965. "On the equivalence of tariffs and quotas." In *Trade, Growth and the Balance of Payments: Essays in Honor of Gottfried Haberler*, edited by R.E. Baldwin et al. Amsterdam: North-Holland.

Bhagwati, J. 1988. *Protectionism*. Cambridge, Massachusetts: MIT Press.

Bhagwati, J. and T.N. Srinivasan. 1975. *Foreign Trade Régimes and Economic Development: India*. New York: NBER.

Brandão, A.S.P. and W. Martin. 1993. "Implications of agricultural trade liberalization for the developing countries." WPS 1116, World Bank, Washington, D.C.

Brenton, P.A. and L. Alan Winters. 1993. "Voluntary export restraints and rationing: U.K. leather footwear imports from Eastern Europe." *Journal of International Economics* 34:289–308.

Choksi, A. and D. Papageorgiou, eds. 1986. *Economic Liberalization in Developing Countries*. New York: Basil Blackwell.

Clements, K. and L.A. Sjaastad. 1984. "How protection taxes exporters." Thames Essay No. 39, Trade Policy Research Centre, London.

Commission of the European Communities. 1988. *European Economy: The Economics of 1992*. Luxembourg: Office for the Official Publications of the European Communities.

Corden, W.M. 1966. "The structure of a tariff system and the effective tariff rate." *Journal of Political Economy* 74:221–237.

Corden, W.M. 1971. *The Theory of Protection*. Oxford: Clarendon Press.

Deardorff, A.V. and R. Stern. 1985. "Methods of measurement of non-tariff barriers." UNCTAD, United Nations, Geneva (Document No. UNCTAD/ST/MD/28).

Deardorff, A.V. and R. Stern. 1986. *The Michigan Model of World Production and Trade*. Cambridge, Massachusetts: MIT Press.

De Melo, J. and D. Tarr. 1992. *A General Equilibrium Analysis of U.S. Foreign Trade Policy*. Cambridge, Massachusetts: MIT Press.

Devarajan, S. and C. Sussangkarn. 1992. "Effective rates of protection when domestic and foreign goods are imperfect substitutes: The case of Thailand." *Review of Economics and Statistics* 74:701–711.

Dinopoulos, E. and M.E. Kreinin. 1988. "Effects of the U.S.–Japanese auto VER on European prices and on U.S. welfare." *Review of Economics and Statistics* 70:484–491.

Erzan, R. J. Goto, and P. Holmes. 1989. "Effects of the multi-fibre arrangement on developing countries' trade: An empirical investigation." PPR Working Paper No. 297, International Economics Department, World Bank, Washington, D.C.

Erzan, R. and P. Holmes. 1990. "An evaluation of the main elements in the leading proposals to phase out the Multi-Fibre Arrangement." PPR Working Paper No. 483, International Economics Department, World Bank, Washington, D.C.

Feenstra, R.C., ed. 1988a. *Empirical Methods for International Trade.* Cambridge, Massachusetts: MIT Press.

Feenstra, R.C. 1988b. "Gains from trade in differentiated products: Japanese compact trucks." In *Empirical Methods for International Trade*, edited by Robert C. Feenstra. Cambridge, Massachusetts: MIT Press.

Finger, J.M. 1993. *Antidumping: How it works and who gets hurt.* Ann Arbor: University of Michigan Press.

Finger, J.M. and A. Olechowski. 1987. *The Uruguay Round: A Handbook for the Multilateral Trade Negotiations.* Washington, D.C.: World Bank.

Francois, J., B. McDonald, and H. Nordström. 1994. "The Uruguay Round: A global general equilibrium assessment." Paper presented at Challenges and Opportunities for East-Asian Trade, National Centre for Development Studies, Canberra, Australia, July 13–14.

Francois, J. and C.R. Shiells. 1994. *Modeling Trade Policy.* Cambridge: Cambridge University Press.

Francois, J., H.D. Nelson, and N.D. Palmeter. 1996. "Government procurement: A post Uruguay Round perspective." CEPR discussion paper. June.

GATT. 1992. *Trade Policy Review of Argentina.* Geneva.

GATT. 1994. *The Results of the Uruguay Round of Multilateral Trade Negotiations: The Legal Texts.* Geneva: GATT Secretariat.

Goldin, I. and O. Knudsen. 1990. *Agricultural Trade Liberalization: Implications for Developing Countries.* Paris and Washington, D.C.: OECD and World Bank.

Goldin, I., O. Knudsen, and D. van der Mehnsbrugghe. 1993. *Trade Liberalization: Global Economic Implications.* Paris and Washington, D.C.: OECD and World Bank.

Griliches, Z. 1970. "Hedonic prices for automobiles: An econometric analysis of quality change." In *Economic Statistics and Econometrics*, edited by Arnold Zellner. Amsterdam: North Holland.

Grossman, G.M. 1981. "The theory of domestic content protection and content preference." *Quarterly Journal of Economics* 96:583–603.

Grubel, H.G. and H.G. Johnson, eds. 1971. *Effective Tariff Protection.* Geneva: GATT and Graduate Institute of International Studies.

Hamilton, C.B. 1986. "Restrictiveness and international transmission of the 'new' protectionism." Seminar Paper No. 367, Institute for International Economic Studies, Stockholm.

Hamilton, C.B., ed. 1990. *Textile Trade and Developing Countries: Eliminating the MFA in the 1990s*. Washington, D.C.: World Bank.

Harrigan, J. 1993. "OECD imports and trade barriers in 1983." *Journal of International Economics* 35:91–111.

Helpman, E. and P.R. Krugman. 1989. *Trade Policy and Market Structure*. Cambridge, Massachusetts: MIT Press.

Hufbauer, G.C. and J. Shelton Erb. 1984. *Subsidies in International Trade*. Washington, D.C.: Institute for International Economics.

Hufbauer, G.C. and J.J. Schott. 1992. *North American Free Trade: Issues and Recommendations*. Washington, D.C.: Institute for International Economics.

International Monetary Fund. 1992. *Exchange Arrangements and Exchange Restrictions, Annual Report*. Washington, D.C.

Jones, R.W. and A.O. Krueger, eds. 1990. *The Political Economy of International Trade*. Cambridge: Basil Blackwell.

Kindleberger, C.P. and P.H. Lindert. 1978. *International Economics*. Homewood, Illinois: Irwin.

Krishna, K., W. Martin, and L.-H. Tan. 1992. "Imputing licence prices: Limitations of a cost-based approach." Pennsylvania State University, Department of Economics, mimeo.

Krueger, A.O. 1986. "Problems of liberalization." In *Economic Liberalization in Developing Countries*, edited by Armeane Choksi and Demetrios Papageorgiou. New York: Basil Blackwell.

Krueger, A., M. Schiff, and A. Valdes. 1988. "Agricultural incentives in developing countries: Measuring the effects of sectoral and economy-wide policies." *World Bank Economic Review* 2:255–271.

Kume, H. and G. Piani. 1991. "The politics of tariff protection in Brazil." CTT, Rio de Janeiro, mimeo.

Laird, S. and R. Vossenar. 1991. "Porqué nos preocupan las bareras no arancelarias?" *Informacion Comercial Española* 31–54.

Laird, S. and A. Yeats. 1987a. "Empirical evidence concerning the magnitude and effects of developing country tariff escalation." *Developing Economies* 35:99–122.

Laird, S. and A. Yeats. 1987b. "Tariff cutting formulas and complications." In *The Uruguay Round: A Handbook for the Multilateral Trade Negotiations*, edited by J. Michael Finger and Andrzej Olechowski. Washington, D.C.: World Bank.

Laird, S. and A. Yeats. 1990. *Quantitative Methods for Trade Barrier Analysis*. London: Macmillan.

Leamer, E. 1974. "The commodity composition of international trade: An empirical analysis." *Oxford Economic Papers* 26:350–374.

Leamer, E. 1990. "The structure and effects of tariff and non-tariff barriers in 1983." In *The Political Economy of International Trade*, edited by Ronald W. Jones and Anne O. Krueger. Cambridge: Basil Blackwell.

Leamer, E. and R.M. Stern. 1970. *Quantitative International Economics*. Boston: Allyn and Bacon.

Messerlin, P. 1988. "Antidumping laws and developing countries." PPR WPS No. 16, International Economics Department. World Bank, Washington, D.C.

Michaely, M. 1977. *Theory of Commercial Policy*. Oxford: Philip Allan Publishers.

Mussa, M. 1984. "The Economics of Content Protection." NBER Working Paper No. 1457.

OECD. 1987. *National Policies and Agricultural Trade*. Paris.

OECD. 1993. *Assessing the Effects of the Uruguay Round*, Trade Policy Issues No 2. Paris.

OECD. 1994. *Agricultural Policies, Markets and Trade: Monitoring and Outlook 1994*. Paris.

Papageorgiou, D., M. Michaely, and A. Choksi, eds. 1991. *Liberalizing Foreign Trade*. Oxford: Basil Blackwell.

Roningen, V. and A. Yeats. 1976. "Nontariff distortions of international trade: Some preliminary empirical evidence." *Weltwirtschaftliches Archiv* 122: 613–625.

Sampson, G. and A. Yeats. 1977. "An evaluation of the common agricultural policy as a barrier facing agricultural exports to the European Economic Community." *American Journal of Agricultural Economics* 59:99–106.

Schott, J.J., eds. 1989. *Free Trade Areas and U.S. Trade Policy*. Washington, D.C.: Institute for International Economics.

Stoeckel, A., D. Pierce, and G. Banks. 1990. *Western Trading Blocks: Game, Set or Match for Asia–Pacific and the World Economy*. Canberra: Centre for International Economics.

Takacs, W. 1988. "Auctioning import quota licenses: An economic analysis." Seminar Paper No. 390, Institute for International Economic Studies, Stockholm.

Takacs, W. 1992. "How import protection affects the Philippines' motor vehicle industry." Policy Research WPS 1035, World Bank, Washington, D.C.

Tinbergen, J. 1962. *Shaping the World Economy: Suggestions for an International Economic Policy*. New York: Twentieth Century Fund.

UNCTAD. 1986. "Problems of protectionism and structural adjustment." Introduction and Part I. "Restrictions on trade and structural adjustment." Geneva: United Nations.

UNCTAD. 1993. *A Users' Manual for TRAINS (Trade Analysis and Information System)*. UNCTAD/DMS/1. Geneva: United Nations.

UNCTAD. 1994. *Directory of Import Régimes, Part I Monitoring Import Régimes*. UNCTAD/DMS/2(PART I)./Rev. 1. New York: United Nations.

United States International Trade Commission. 1989. *The Economic Effects of Significant U.S. Import Restraints. Phase I. Manufacturing*. USITC Publication 2222. Washington, D.C.: USITC.

United States International Trade Commission. 1990. *The Economic Effects of Significant U.S. Import Restraints. Phase II. Agricultural Products and Natural Resources*, USITC Publication 2314. Washington, D.C.: USITC.

United States International Trade Commission. 1992a. *Economy-Wide Modelling of the Economic Implications of a FTA with Mexico and a NAFTA with Canada and Mexico*. USITC Publication 2516. Washington, D.C.: USITC.

United States International Trade Commission. 1992b. *U.S. Market Access in Latin America: Recent Liberalization Measures and Remaining Barriers (with a Special Case Study on Chile)*. USITC Publication 2521. Washington, D.C.: USITC.

United States Trade Representative. 1992. *National Trade Estimate Report on Foreign Trade Barriers*. Washington, D.C.: USTR.

Vousden, N. 1990. *The Economics of Trade Protection.* Cambridge: Cambridge University Press.

Webb, A.J., M. Lopez, and R. Penn. 1990. *Estimates of Producer and Consumer Equivalents: Government Intervention in Agriculture, 1982–87.* Statistical Bulletin No. 803, Economic Research Service. Washington, D.C.: United States Department of Agriculture.

Whalley, J. 1985. *Trade Liberalization among Major World Trading Areas.* Cambridge, Massachusetts: MIT Press.

3

Measuring Welfare Changes with Distortions

William J. Martin

Virtually all policy reform occurs in the presence of major, continuing distortions. Unfortunately, we know from theory that recommendations for policy change must take into account the presence of these distortions, and from applied research (e.g., Loo and Tower, 1990) that continuing distortions may dramatically alter the measured welfare effects of policy changes. Fortunately, developments in economic theory and modeling have expanded our ability to evaluate the sign and magnitude of welfare effects of policy changes in the presence of distortions, so that the theory of the second best can be a practical guide to policy, rather than simply a *caveat* on policy recommendations.

Where a formal model of the economy is available, three distinct approaches to the evaluation of welfare change in distorted open economies are now in use. The first, most common in theoretical analyses, is the Balance of Trade Function approach (e.g., Anderson and Neary, 1992; Lloyd and Schweinberger,[1] 1988, p. 293). The second involves evaluating the welfare effects of a shock using an expenditure function or utility function embedded in a general equilibrium model (e.g., Dixit, 1975; Clarete and Whalley, 1988). The third approach uses consumer and producer surplus measures and changes in tax and tariff revenue collections (Loo and Tower, 1990).

Each of the three approaches considered has the advantage of allowing the evaluation of discrete policy changes, rather than being restricted to marginal effects. Each approach has particular advantages and disadvantages. The Balance of Trade Function approach is exact, has a strong theoretical basis, and provides a useful decomposition of welfare changes into producer, consumer and government revenue changes but requires knowl-

---

1 Lloyd and Schweinberger describe this measure as a *Distorted Trade Expenditure Function*.

edge of the complete structure of the economy and does not automatically provide many insights into the source of the welfare change. The direct evaluation of welfare changes is exact and very convenient where a general equilibrium model is available but provides no insights into the source of measured welfare gains. Surplus based measures are not exact, but rather are second order approximations, and frequently lack theoretical precision when complexities such as interacting distortions are considered. However, surplus measures can provide valuable insights into the source and interpretation of measured welfare changes.

Recent work in the Public Finance literature has demonstrated that the welfare effects of taxation may be very sensitive to seemingly minor changes in the specification used to measure changes in welfare (Fullerton, 1991). In particular, whether tax revenue collections are based upon actual Marshallian levels of demand or hypothetical Hicksian levels of demand may substantially change the estimated marginal welfare cost of taxation. Anderson and Martin (1995) show that the effects of marginal tax or tariff changes in highly distorted economies may be sensitive to the choice of measure, but there are no policy implications from this choice, and good reasons exist to prefer welfare measures based on the Equivalent Variation calculated with compensation.

In this chapter, the relationships among the three types of welfare measures for distorted open economies are examined. The primary objective is to identify a set of measures which combine a rigorous theoretical basis with internal consistency and which allow an intuitive basis for understanding numerical results obtained from applied models.

In the next section, the Balance of Trade Function is introduced and its interpretation as a welfare measure discussed. Then, in the third section, attention is focussed on the use of direct, money metric measures of welfare change in applied general equilibrium models, including the relationship between these measures and the compensation measures based on the Balance of Trade Function. In the fourth section, a second order Taylor Series expansion is used to derive graphical measures which show the linkage between the formal general equilibrium techniques and graphical measures, and provide an intuitive basis for understanding the formal measures. Conclusions and recommendations are presented in the final section.

I The Balance of Trade Function Approach

The Balance of Trade Function for distorted economies can be derived from the income-expenditure condition

$$e(p,w,u) - r(p,w,v) - (p - p^*)z_p(p,w,v,u) - f = 0 \qquad (3.1)$$

where p is a vector of (distorted) domestic commodity prices; p^* is a vector of world commodity prices; w is a vector of factor prices endogenous to the economy but determined outside this equation; v is a vector of the economy's resource endowments; u is the level of consumer utility; e is the expenditure[2] required to achieve consumer utility level u at domestic price vector p; r is the revenue at domestic prices attainable with the given resource vector;[3] f is the net financial inflow from abroad (e.g., transfers, returns from factors owned overseas and borrowings) available to the economy; and $z_p(p,v,w,u) = e_p(p,w,v,u) - r_p(p,v)$ is the vector of (compensated) net imports or exports[4] where the subscript p denotes the first derivative of the corresponding function with respect to domestic prices. In this equation, as in subsequent equations, bold type is used to represent vector valued variables.

The vector $(p-p^*)$ in equation (3.1) can be interpreted as the tariffs or tariff equivalents of the prevailing trade distortions in the economy. The product $(p-p^*)z_p$ in equation (3.1) therefore refers to the tariff revenues, or quota rents, accruing to residents of the country under consideration. While these revenues impose a cost on domestic consumers, they accrue as revenues to the government or domestic holders of quotas and hence must be added to the revenue obtained from production when evaluating the country's net expenditure position. Throughout this chapter, we assume that these revenues are costlessly redistributed to the representative consumer.

In addition to border distortions, domestic distortions such as taxes can readily be introduced into the formulation. To incorporate domestic consumption taxes requires distinguishing between domestic producer and consumer prices and accounting for the revenues arising from these price differentials times the quantities consumed.[5] Similarly, taxes levied on producers require a distinction between the prices paid for output and the price received by producers together with incorporation of the revenues arising from such taxes. Factor taxation can be introduced by distinguishing be-

---

2 For this approach to be applied, particular functional forms for the expenditure and revenue functions must be specified. Some of the options available, and references to detailed treatments of these options, are given in the Appendix to this chapter.

3 Note that this function is not a Gross National Product function since GNP includes factor income flows from abroad and excludes revenues accruing domestically to factors owned by non-residents. It also differs from Gross Domestic Product at market prices which include tariff revenues as well as revenues from production (United Nations, 1968, p. 233).

4 Net imports are indicated by a positive value and net exports by a negative value.

5 A model containing a consumption tax would result in a balance of trade function of the form $B = e(p^c, u) - r(p, v) - (p^c - p) \cdot e_p$, where p^c is the distorted consumer price and p is the undistorted price.

tween the cost of factors to purchasers and the return to their owners, and accounting for the revenues raised. Loss or dissipation of rents from any of these taxes can also be introduced by reducing the redistributed tariff or tax revenues by a fixed proportion (e.g., Anderson, 1991). The approach can also be generalized, following Dixit (1975), to incorporate imperfect competition, which introduces a distortion between price and marginal cost, and a consequent transfer of profits.[6] For simplicity, the discussion in this chapter will consider only tariff distortions, but the measures used can readily be generalized to include a wide range of distortions such as those analyzed by Clarete and Whalley (1988).

In the income-expenditure condition given by equation (3.1), the level of utility is endogenous, while the prices, the resource endowment vector and foreign financial inflows are exogenous. The Balance of Trade Function for distorted economies utilized by Anderson and Neary (1992) can be derived from the income expenditure condition by reclassifying the level of utility as exogenous and introducing a new variable, B, to measure the hypothetical additional financial inflow required to maintain a specified level of utility.

$$B^i\left(p, p^*, w, v, u^i\right) = z\left(p, w, v, u^i\right) - \left(p - p^*\right)z_p\left(p, v, u^i\right) - f \qquad (3.2)$$

where $z = e - r$; u^i is the level of utility fixed exogenously at the initial level for a Hicksian Compensating Variation measure or at the final level for a Hicksian Equivalent Variation measure, and B^i is the welfare measure obtained with utility fixed at level u^i.

An important distinction needs to be drawn between the Balance of Trade Function and the related behavioral system. The values of the quantity variables implicit in the Balance of Trade Function are based on the compensated functions and hence may differ from those observed in the behavioral system. Another important distinction is in the classification of these variables between endogenous and exogenous. Many of the price variables may be endogenous in the behavioral model (e.g., the price of nontraded goods in a national model, or the price of traded goods in a global model) but exogenous when evaluating the Balance of Trade Function.

The Compensating Variation measure of welfare change resulting from a change in world prices from p_0^* to p_1^* is given by the change in B^0, at the

---

6 In the case of imperfectly competitive production, the vector of outputs cannot be subsumed within a revenue function, but must be determined within a model containing a complete specification of structural features such as the nature of conjectures and the implied mark-up rule. Given such a model, a suitable Balance of Trade Function for welfare evaluation in a model with competitively supplied inputs would be $B = e(p, w, u) - (p - c_x(x, w)) \cdot x$ where x is a vector of outputs supplied subject under imperfectly competitive conditions, w is a vector of prices of competitively supplied inputs, and $(p - c_x(x, w)) \cdot x$ is pure profits accruing to the representative consumer.

initial utility level u_0, between the initial world price p_0^* and the final world price p_1^*:

$$B_1^0 - B_0^0 = B\left(p_1, w_1, p_1^*, v, u^0\right) - B\left(p_0, w_0, p_0^*, v, u^0\right)$$

$$= B\left(p_1, w_1, p_1^*, v, u^0\right) \tag{3.3}$$

since $B(p_0, w_0, p_0^*, v, u^0) = 0$ by equation (3.1).

The Equivalent Variation measure, $B_1^1 - B_0^1$, is given by evaluating the function B at the utility level u_1 corresponding to the utility level attainable, given the available factor endowment vector, at world price vector p_1^*. This measure is defined in equation (3.4).

$$B_1^1 - B_0^1 = B\left(p_1, w_1, p_1^*, v, u^1\right) - B\left(p_0, w_0, p_0^*, v, u^1\right)$$

$$= -B\left(p_0, w_0, p_0^*, v, u^1\right) \tag{3.4}$$

since $B(p_1, w_1, p_1^*, v, u^1) = 0$ by equation (3.1).

Corresponding measures of the effects of tariff changes can be obtained by examining the response of B^i to changes in the domestic price vector, p, without changing the world price vector, p^*.

Fixing the utility level in both the consumer expenditure function and the tariff revenue terms of equation (3.2) when moving from the income-expenditure condition to the definition of the welfare measure is consistent with the Diamond–McFadden measures frequently used in evaluating the welfare effects of taxation (Diamond and McFadden, 1974; Auerbach 1985, p. 70). Consistent with the interpretation of these measures, the Compensating Variation measure for an increase in tariffs can be interpreted as the magnitude of the transfer which must come from outside the economy in order to compensate for the welfare losses caused by the tariff increase. The Equivalent Variation measure indicates the reduction in the external transfer which would be equivalent in its effect to the tariff increase. While compensation is typically only hypothetical, its effects on consumption levels and hence on tariff revenues are included along with changes in actual revenues under the Balance of Trade Function approach outlined above.

Both the Compensating Variation and the Equivalent Variation measures provide direct, exact measures of compensation required to maintain a specified level of utility in the face of changes in world prices, tariff rates, factor endowments or the financial inflow available to the economy. As is shown in Anderson and Martin (1995), the Equivalent Variation measure has a potentially important advantage in that it provides a money metric measure of changes in utility as well as a compensation measure. If we consider the final level of utility to be endogenous, it is clear from the second line of equation (3.4) that the Equivalent Variation maps changes in utility into changes in a money measure of welfare change, thus providing a money metric measure of welfare change. The Compensating Variation measure does not have this desirable property.

II Direct Welfare Evaluation

For numerical general equilibrium models, a popular approach to welfare evaluation involves the direct evaluation of changes in a money metric of welfare change derived by using an expenditure or utility function embedded within the model. Under this approach, the Hicksian Equivalent Variation measure is defined in the manner defined in many standard theoretical treatments (see, for example, Just, Hueth and Schmitz, 1982, p. 370) as

$$H = e(p_0, u_0) - e(p_0, u_1)$$

The Hicksian Compensating Variation is similarly defined, except that final period prices are used in the evaluation of the expenditure function.

Where the demand equations of the model have been derived from an underlying expenditure function, this is straightforward in practice. Even where the demand equations have not been derived from an explicit function, it may still be possible to evaluate the expenditure function exactly, particularly if the demand equations have been derived from a primal utility function. Most of the utility functions which yield tractable demand systems (e.g., the Cobb–Douglas and the Constant Elasticity of Substitution) also yield simple expenditure functions. Burniaux and van der Mensbrugghe (1991) present the expenditure function for the commonly used Linear Expenditure demand system[7] allowing direct evaluation of changes when preferences are expressed using this commonly used functional form.

In the absence of distortions, money metric measures of welfare change are identical to the corresponding compensation measures and it is frequently assumed that this is universally the case. Although the Hicksian measures of Compensating and Equivalent Variation were originally defined in terms of compensation required to maintain the initial or the final level of utility in response to a shock to prices, or to other factors such as

---

7 An interpretation of this system is given in the Appendix to Chapter 7 of this volume.

technology changes (see Martin and Alston, 1994), they are frequently defined in textbooks in terms of the amount of money which would be equivalent to a particular change in prices (see, for example, Varian, 1984, p. 264).

In the presence of distortions, the equivalence between the money metric measures and the compensation measures breaks down. The money metric measures of welfare change are different from the compensation measures. They turn out to be identical to the modified compensation measures advocated by Mayshar (1990) and Ballard (1990) in the taxation literature.

The Mayshar–Ballard approach can be extended from the closed economy case to the open economy using a modification of the Balance of Trade Function. In the modified measure, the utility level is exogenously fixed in the consumer expenditure function but not in the tax revenue term. The revenue change used is the actual change in revenues, rather than the change in revenues with consumers compensated to maintain their utility at a fixed level.

The modified Balance of Trade Function measure which results when the hypothetical tariff revenues are replaced by the actual revenues is denoted H and defined as

$$H\left(p, p^*, w, v, u^i\right) = z\left(p, w, v, u^i\right) - \left(p - p^*\right)m\left(p, v, w, h\right) - f \qquad (3.5)$$

where $m(p, w, v, h)$ is the import demand function evaluated at the level of utility, h, determined from the income-expenditure condition,[8] and not at the exogenous value of u^i.

To simplify the demonstration of equivalence between the money metrics and the Mayshar–Ballard measures, it is convenient to drop the w and v terms, which illustrate the generality of the approach but are not needed for this purpose, to define z^j to represent $z(p_j, u^i)$ and to represent the vector of tariff rates $(p - p^*)$ by a vector t. An Equivalent Variation version of the welfare effect of a tariff change which changes the domestic price vector from p_0 to p_1 can then be written

$$H_1^1 - H_0^1 = z\left(p_1, u^1\right) - z\left(p_0, u^1\right) - t_1 m\left(p_1, u^1\right) + t_0 m\left(p_0, u^0\right) - f_1 + f_0 \qquad (3.6)$$

where the utility levels in the tariff revenue terms have been determined endogenously at these levels, rather than being specified exogenously as under the standard Balance of Trade Function approach.

---

8 That is, at the value $h = \{u | B(p, w, v, u) = 0\}$.

Using the income-expenditure condition (3.1), equation (3.6) can be simplified to

$$
\begin{aligned}
H_1^1 - H_0^1 &= z^1 - z\left(\boldsymbol{p_0}, u^1\right) - \left(z^1 - z^0\right) \\
&= z\left(\boldsymbol{p_0}, u^0\right) - z\left(\boldsymbol{p_0}, u^1\right) \\
&= e\left(\boldsymbol{p_0}, u^0\right) - e\left(\boldsymbol{p_0}, u^1\right)
\end{aligned}
\tag{3.7}
$$

which is a direct money metric measure of the welfare consequences of the change, evaluated at initial prices, such as might be calculated within an applied general equilibrium model.

If a Compensating Variation measure is used, the corresponding measure of welfare change is

$$
H_1^0 - H_0^0 = e\left(\boldsymbol{p_1}, u^0\right) - e\left(\boldsymbol{p_1}, u^1\right)
\tag{3.8}
$$

The correspondence between the modified Balance of Trade Function and the direct, money metric approach to measuring welfare effects is fortunate in that it reduces the apparent proliferation of distinct measures of welfare change. However, it does raise a question about the best measure to use in applied work.

Anderson and Martin (1995) obtain additional insights into the reason for the continuing difference between compensation measures and the money metric measures by considering small changes in, say, the price vector $\boldsymbol{p}$. The resulting compensation measure is obtained by differentiating equation (3.2) to yield

$$
dB = -\left(\boldsymbol{p} - \boldsymbol{p}^*\right) z_{pp} d\boldsymbol{p}
\tag{3.9}
$$

This implies that the welfare impact of a small change in a trade distortion is given by the change in the volume of trade multiplied by the magnitude of the distortion. Intuitively, $(\boldsymbol{p} - \boldsymbol{p}^*)$ is the difference between the marginal value of the good to consumers and producers in the economy, p, and its opportunity cost to the economy, p^*, and hence represents the gain to the economy from an additional unit of trade.

As demonstrated by Anderson and Martin (1995), the corresponding money metric expression, obtained by differentiating equation (3.1) in p and u, is:

$$
e_u du = -\left[\frac{1}{\left(1 - \left(\boldsymbol{p} - \boldsymbol{p}^*\right) c_y\right)}\right]\left(\boldsymbol{p} - \boldsymbol{p}^*\right) z_{pp} d\boldsymbol{p}
\tag{3.10}
$$

where c_y is the vector of income effects on consumer demands.

Equation (3.10) is simply equation (3.9) premultiplied by the conversion factor in square brackets. This conversion factor adjusts for the fact that changes in welfare have income effects, and that these income effects induce changes in tariff revenues. Because the level of utility changes under this approach, whereas it does not under the Balance of Trade Function approach, the marginal welfare impact of a tariff change must reflect these income effects.

The decision about the appropriate measure to be applied will depend to some degree on the objectives of the analyst. If the compensation interpretation is important, and particularly if actual compensation is envisaged, then the compensation-based measures have strong appeal. If a money metric measure of welfare change is required, then three measures qualify for consideration: the Equivalent Variation measure based on the compensation approach and the two money metric measures.

In practice, the choice between the two measures is almost certain not to have significant policy implications if both taxation and spending decisions are considered together. If the evaluated burden of a tax or tariff change is larger using one measure, the benefits of any corresponding spending will be correspondingly larger. Overall, therefore, the choice of measure is not fundamentally important as long as the same methodology is applied consistently to both the benefits and costs of any decision.

If benefit and cost estimates are not made together, the compensation approach has a very important practical advantage over the direct evaluation approach. An estimated welfare cost of one dollar obtained using the compensation approach can be compared directly with a subsequently estimated benefit of one dollar. Using the money metric approach, it is necessary to ensure that both benefits and costs are pre-multiplied by the same common factor, as is evident from a comparison of equations (3.9) and (3.10). If a measure of the marginal cost of taxation based on the money metric measure is provided (see, for example, Fullerton, 1991), there seems a serious risk that subsequent users, who do not have access to the underlying model, will erroneously compare this measure with the unadjusted benefits arising from a government project.

III Graphical Surplus Measures

Graphical measures can be useful for estimating the welfare effects of changes in a single price, and are invaluable as an aid to interpreting the results obtained from a numerical model. In simple cases, the Marshallian intuition of evaluating consumer willingness to pay can allow the identification of the relevant triangles under demand curves and above supply curves, and of revenue collections, and provide powerful insights into the sources of welfare changes (see Loo and Tower, 1990, for an illustration of the advantages of this approach). However, once revenue changes and interacting distortions are introduced and changes in related, distorted markets are introduced, it becomes very difficult to identify the appropriate areas to be evaluated and the graphical surplus measures lose their tractability. Even in simple cases, the applicability of the Marshallian measures is limited by the fact that they merely approximate any welfare change resulting from changes in consumer prices.

What seems to be needed is a measure which combines the insights into the sources of benefits which can be provided by the graphical surplus approach together with the general applicability of the Balance of Trade Function approach. Fortunately, a set of graphical measures can be derived from the Balance of Trade Function quite readily using second-order Taylor Series approximations. For the compensation-based measures these diagrams involve only compensated demand functions and are relatively simple. For the money metric measures, the corresponding diagrams are more complex since they involve areas under compensated demand curves combined with tariff revenue changes evaluated by using Marshallian demand curves.

In the remainder of this section, graphical measures of the welfare effects of particular price changes are derived by applying a second-order Taylor Series approximation to the (compensated) Balance of Trade Function and interpreting the resulting expressions.

III.1 Effects of a Single Tariff Change

For a small economy, a change in a single tariff corresponds to a change in the domestic price, p, but not the international price, p^*. Applying a second-order Taylor Series Approximation, and ignoring third derivatives,[9] the Compensating Variation for a tariff increase which raises domestic prices from p_0 to p_1 is given by

$$B_1^0 - B_0^0 = -(p_0 - p^*)z_{pp}^0(p_1 - p_0) - \frac{1}{2}(p_1 - p_0)z_{pp}^0(p_1 - p_0) \quad (3.11)$$

where each subscript p denotes the derivative of the relevant function with respect to a particular price and z_{pp}^0 indicates the derivative of the import

---

9 Even "flexible" functional forms for profit or expenditure functions are typically only quadratic approximations, implying that their third derivatives will vanish.

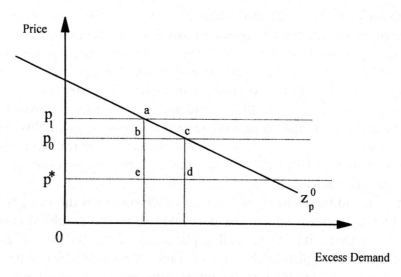

Figure 3.1. *Welfare effects of a single tariff increase*

demand function with respect to the domestic price evaluated at the initial utility level.

The first term on the right-hand side of equation (3.11) represents a hypothetical decrease in revenue (at the initial tariff rate) resulting from the decrease in import volume as the tariff level rises. It has welfare significance because it measures the difference between the value of the good in the country and its cost to the economy (at the initial tariff level) times the induced change in the volume of imports. The second term is a Harberger-type welfare triangle capturing the efficiency losses associated with incremental increases in the tariff rate.

The second-order approximation provided by equation (3.11) is represented graphically for a single tariff increase in Figure 3.1, assuming there are no distortions in any other related markets. The compensated excess demand function $z_p(p, u_0)$ represents the economy's excess demand at varying price levels given the specified level of utility. The world price level is $p*$ and the domestic price level rises from p_0 to p_1 in response to the tariff increase. The welfare loss is represented by the two areas, *abc* and *bcde*, which correspond to an efficiency loss associated with reductions in the volume of imports and the induced revenue loss resulting from the initial tariff distortion, respectively.

The area *bcde* in Figure 3.1 is the reduction in tariff revenue at the initial tariff rate and corresponds to the first term in equation (3.11). This component of welfare loss is first-order and, in the diagram, is clearly larger the greater is the initial tariff distortion. The presence of this term fundamentally distinguishes the second-best welfare evaluation undertaken from approaches to analysis of welfare change which do not take into account the presence of initial distortions when evaluating the implications of changes in the presence of distortions.

In terms of policy interpretation, Figure 3.1 highlights an important difference between the second-best welfare measures used in this chapter and measures using the welfare triangles derived from models where only moves to or from a zero tariff are considered. The gains from a tariff reduction that lowers domestic prices from p_1 to p_0 are given by abc plus $bcde$. Clearly, this implies that the gains from a given degree of liberalization are greater for the initial increment of liberalization than for subsequent price declines of the same magnitude. This front-end loading of welfare gains has important policy implications.

III.2 A World Price Change

The Taylor Series expansion of the net expenditure function can also be used to obtain a simple but useful expression for the welfare effects of world price changes. In this case, the change in the Compensating Variation based measure for a world price increase is considered. The relationship corresponding with equation (3.11) is

$$B_1^0 - B_0^0 = \left[z_p - \left(p - p^* \right) z_{pp} \right] \left(p_1^* - p_0^* \right) + \frac{1}{2} \left(p_1^* - p_0^* \right) z_{pp} \left(p_1^* - p_0^* \right)$$

$$(3.12)$$

If the initial tariff level were zero, equation (3.12) would contain only two terms. The first term, $z_p(p_1^*-p_0^*)$, would measure the terms of trade loss resulting from an increase in the world prices of this imported good. The second, quadratic term on the far right would measure the extent to which that loss is diminished by the substitution of domestically produced goods for more expensive imported goods, or the diversion of goods previously exported to domestic markets. In this first-best case, the welfare effects of a change in world prices depend most heavily on the sign of the first-order z_p term, that is, on whether the goods whose price changes are imports or exports.

With an initial nonzero tariff, the second term within the square brackets must also be considered. This term is the change in the trade vector induced by the complete set of trade distortions applying in the country. The sum of

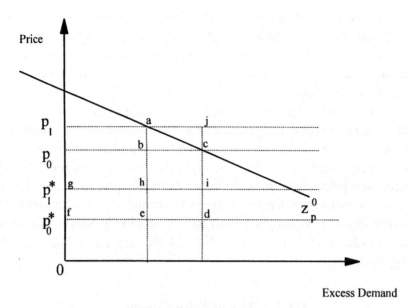

Figure 3.2. *Welfare effects of an increase in world prices*

the two terms is, as noted by Tyers and Falvey (1989), the pattern of trade which would have prevailed in the absence of the trade distortions, that is, the pattern of trade which would be expected on the basis of comparative advantage. This result is consistent with Tyers and Falvey's (1989) conclusion for a marginal change in prices: that the critical influence on the marginal welfare effect is not whether a country is a net exporter (importer) of products whose price rises (falls), but whether that country *would be* a net exporter (importer) in the absence of distortions. The discrete approach used here highlights a qualification to this rule not evident from a purely marginal analysis. For a sufficiently small net import position at initial prices, the second-order welfare consequences of a price rise may outweigh the first-order revenue effect. This would be the case when, for example, a country moves from a net importing position at initial prices to a net exporting position for a particular commodity.[10]

As an aid to understanding, the welfare effects of a rise in the world price of a particular imported good from p_0^* to p_1^* are illustrated in Figure 3.2. The compensating variation for this price increase can usefully be identified with the three areas *abc*, *ajih* and *gidf*. The area *abc* represents the welfare triangle associated with replacement of imported commodities with now

10 I am grateful to Rod Tyers for this interpretation.

cheaper domestically produced goods, and corresponds to the quadratic term in equation (3.11). The area *ajih* (=*bcde*) represents the loss of tariff revenues resulting from reduced import volumes, that is, the term $(p-p^*)z_{pp}(p_0^*-p_1^*)$ in equation (3.11). Intuitively, this area has welfare significance because imports are already below their optimal level, and further reduction has a markedly adverse welfare impact. The area *gidf* is the income loss resulting from the terms of trade decline brought about by the rise in world prices, as represented by $z_p(p_1^*-p_0^*)$.

The two areas *ajih* and *gidf* both reflect welfare losses, and hence have the same positive sign. The area *abc* (=*ajc*) reflects an efficiency gain, and hence is opposite in sign to *ajih* and *gidf*. The total welfare loss from the increase in the world price of this importable can be seen as (*abc+bcde+ghef*), an area which is immediately recognizable in terms of the areas conventionally measured using the traditional graphical approach with compensated functions. The Taylor Series approach does, however, allow a considerable increase in confidence that the resulting welfare measure is soundly based and provides a basis for its extension to the real-world case of multiple distortions and multiple policy changes.

III.3 Effects of Distortions in Related Markets

The examples considered thus far have involved changes in policies or in world prices in the presence of a single distortion. The approach can, however, readily be extended to deal with situations involving distortions in related markets. This is done simply by taking into account the presence of any non-zero elements in the $(p-p^*)$ vector together with the relevant cross-price effects implicit in equations (3.11) and (3.12).

If a change in the domestic price of good 1 affects the excess demand for a related good, say good 2, then equation (3.11) allows the effect of this change on welfare to be evaluated. If the price of good 1 increases and goods 1 and 2 are substitutes, the resulting shift in the excess demand for good 2 is depicted in Figure 3.3. With a positive distortion in the import market for this good, the increase in demand will have a favorable welfare effect measured by $(p-p^*)\cdot(m_1-m_0)$. The welfare gain in the related market is thus measured by the change in tariff revenue in that market. The underlying source of the gain is the fact that additional imports of the good have a higher value in the economy than their marginal cost, and this shock causes the volume of these imports to expand. The approach can readily be generalized to deal with distortions in more than one related market.

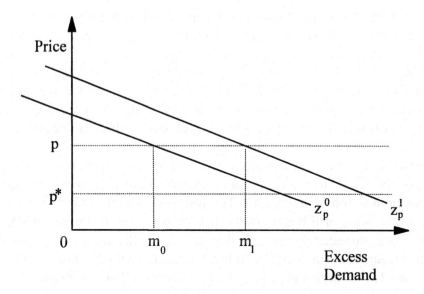

Figure 3.3. *Effects of a tariff increase in a related market*

This experiment highlights the importance of the relationship between distortions in related markets for determining the welfare consequences of liberalization. Since the gains in one market from partial tariff liberalization can be offset by welfare losses in distorted markets for close substitutes, it is important to consider the relative magnitude of the initial distortions when designing liberalization experiments. Clearly, the overall gains are likely to be larger when tariffs are reduced in markets with higher initial rates of protection than their close substitutes. This experiment provides an intuitive rationale for "concertina" rules of tariff reform where tariff reductions are concentrated on goods with the highest tariffs.

IV Conclusions

In this chapter, three broad approaches to the measurement of welfare change in applied modeling work were considered. The first class of measures is based directly on the original concept of the compensation needed to maintain a particular level of utility. The second class is based on the use of a money metric of welfare change. The final class of measures is based on graphical surplus approaches.

The two versions of compensation measure, the Equivalent and Compensating Variations, provide well-defined money measures of welfare change.

The Equivalent Variation measure has the advantage of providing a money metric of utility change. While providing exact, and powerful, measures of welfare change, neither provides much insight into the source of any welfare gains or losses.

Direct, or money metric, measures are frequently used to assign money values to the changes in utility levels. These measures are shown to be identical to currently popular modified versions of the Balance of Trade Function using actual rather than compensated tariff revenues.

The choice between measures depends to some degree upon the problem at hand. If both benefits and costs are evaluated together, the outcome will not be affected. However, if benefits and costs are to be evaluated independently, the compensation measures have a clear practical advantage. With the money metric measures, there is a major risk of erroneous decisions from comparing benefit and cost measures which have different conversion factors and hence are not directly comparable.

In the final section of the chapter, graphical measures derived from the compensation-based measures of welfare change were used to provide insights into the sources of welfare change. For simple experiments involving tariff changes and world price changes, it was possible to obtain insights into the sources of welfare change even in the presence of multiple distortions. The results highlighted the nature of the second-best gains from partial liberalization in ways which are likely to be useful to analysts and practical policy advisers.

Appendix 3.1

Functional Forms for Empirical Expenditure and Revenue Functions

In order to apply the balance of trade approach, it is necessary to specify a particular functional form for the expenditure and revenue functions. Functional forms used to represent expenditure systems in applied general equilibrium analysis include the Cobb–Douglas, Constant Elasticity of Substitution (CES), Linear Expenditure System (LES), Constant Difference of Elasticities (CDE), and Almost Ideal Demand System (AIDS). These functional forms range from the very simple Cobb–Douglas, which imposes an elasticity of substitution of unity and unit income elasticities, to the AIDS model, which is much more flexible but requires a great deal more information on parameter values.

A detailed discussion of the use of the Cobb–Douglas demand system in applied general equilibrium models is given in Dixon, Parmenter, Sutton and Vincent (1982). A succinct analysis of the use and interpretation of CES demand systems for import demands is given in Armington (1969) while Shoven and Whalley (1992) discuss the use of this functional form for systems of consumer demand equations.

The expenditure function underlying the Linear Expenditure System is derived by Burniaux and van der Mensbrugghe (1991) and De Melo and Tarr (1992, p. 61) as a basis for assessments of welfare effects. Also see Chapter 7 of this volume. The properties of the CDE function and its use in applied general equilibrium models are discussed in detail by Hertel, Peterson, Preckel, Surry and Tsigas (1991). A definitive treatment of the AIDS model is in Deaton and Muellbauer (1980).

Some applied general equilibrium models do specify their supply side by beginning with a revenue function and differentiating to obtain output supply and input demand functions. Anderson (1994) does this by using the Constant Elasticity of Transformation (CET) formulation, while Martin and Alston (1994) use a quadratic profit function. A more common approach for applied general equilibrium models is to specify the production technology in terms of multiple stages involving demands for intermediate inputs and primary factors conditional on industry output levels, and a production (see Dervis et al., 1982) or a cost function (Dixon et al., 1980) approach to determining the level of output. Given such a production specification, the maximum revenue obtainable given a particular resource endowment can be calculated by evaluating the revenue generated by the production system.

References

Anderson, J.E. 1991. "The theory of protection." In *Surveys of International Trade*, edited by D. Greenaway and L.A. Winters. Oxford: Basil Blackwell.

Anderson, J.E. 1994. "Trade restrictiveness benchmarks." World Bank, Mimeo.

Anderson, J.E. and W.J. Martin. 1995. "The welfare analysis of fiscal policy: A simple unified account." Boston College, Mimeo.

Anderson, J.E. and J.P. Neary. 1992. "Trade reform with quotas, partial rent retention, and tariffs." *Econometrica* 60:57–76.

Armington, P. 1969. "A theory of demand for products distinguished by place of production." *IMF Staff Papers* 16:179–201.

Auerbach, A. 1985. "The theory of excess burden and optimal taxation." In *Handbook of Public Economics*, Vol. 1, edited by A. Auerbach and M. Feldstein. Amsterdam: North-Holland.

Ballard, C. 1990. "Marginal welfare cost calculations." *Journal of Public Economics* 41:263–277.

Burniaux, J.M. and D. van der Mensbrugghe. 1991. *The RUNS Model: A Rural–Urban North–South General Equilibrium Model for Agricultural Policy Analysis.* Paris: OECD Development Centre, Technical Paper No. 33.

Clarete, R. and J. Whalley. 1988. "Interactions between trade policies and domestic distortions in a small open developing economy." *Journal of International Economics* 24:345–358.

Deaton, A. and J. Muellbauer. 1980. "An almost ideal demand system." *American Economic Review* 70:312–326.

De Melo, J. and D. Tarr. 1992. *A General Equilibrium Analysis of U.S. Foreign Trade Policy.* Cambridge, Massachusetts: MIT Press.

Dervis, K., J. de Melo, and S. Robinson. 1982. *General Equilibrium Models for Development Policy.* New York: Cambridge University Press.

Diamond, P. and D. McFadden. 1974. "Some uses of the expenditure function in public finance." *Journal of Public Finance* 3:3–21.

Dixit, A. 1975. "Welfare effects of tax and price changes." *Journal of Public Economics* 4:103–123.

Dixon, P., B. Parmenter, J. Sutton, and D. Vincent. 1982. *ORANI: A Multisectoral Model of the Australian Economy*. Amsterdam: North-Holland.

Fullerton, D. 1991. "Reconciling recent estimates of the marginal welfare cost of taxation." *American Economic Review* 81:302–308.

Hertel, T., P. Peterson, P. Preckel, Y. Surry, and M. Tsigas. 1991. "Implicit additivity as a strategy for restricting the parameter space in CGE models." *Economic and Financial Computing* 1:265–289.

Just, R.E., D.L. Hueth, and A. Schmitz. 1982. *Applied Welfare Economics and Public Policy*. Englewood Cliffs, New Jersey: Prentice-Hall.

Kay, J. 1980. "The deadweight loss from a tax system." *Journal of Public Economics* 13:111–119.

Lloyd, P. and A. Schweinberger. 1988. "Trade expenditure functions and the gains from trade." *Journal of International Economics* 24:275–297.

Loo, T. and E. Tower. 1990. "Agricultural liberalization, welfare, revenue and nutrition in developing countries." In *Agricultural Trade Liberalization: Implications for Developing Countries*, edited by I. Goldin and O. Knudsen. Paris: OECD and World Bank.

Martin, W.J. and J.M Alston. 1994. "A dual approach to evaluating research benefits in the presence of distortions." *American Journal of Agricultural Economics* 76:26–35.

Mayshar, J. 1990. "On measures of excess burden and their application." *Journal of Public Economics* 43:263–289.

Shoven, J. and J. Whalley. 1984. "Applied general equilibrium models of taxation and international trade: An introduction and survey." *Journal of Economic Literature* 22:1007–1051.

Shoven, J. and J. Whalley. 1992. *Applying General Equilibrium*. Cambridge: Cambridge University Press.

Tyers, R. and R. Falvey. 1989. "Border price changes and domestic welfare in the presence of subsidized exports." *Oxford Economic Papers* 41:434–451.

United Nations. 1968. *A System of National Accounts*. New York.

Varian, H.R. 1984. *Microeconomic Analysis*. New York: Norton.

Vousden, N. 1990. *The Economics of Trade Protection*. Cambridge: Cambridge University Press.

4

Social Accounting Matrices

Kenneth A. Reinert and David W. Roland-Holst

I Introduction

The theory of international trade is a general equilibrium affair: offer curves, Edgeworth–Bowley box diagrams, and Travis boxes are frequently used tools. For a long time, however, applied trade policy analysis was restricted to partial equilibrium techniques.[1] This was primarily due to constraints on data and computation for general equilibrium calibration and simulation. Nonlinear simulation software is now readily available, and general equilibrium techniques are often applied to trade policy problems. Surveys of these applications can be found in Shoven and Whalley (1984) and de Melo (1988).

Computable general equilibrium (CGE) models are calibrated to what are known as benchmark equilibrium datasets. The calibration process computes intercept and share parameters for the model's mathematical functions, given assumed or estimated values of behavioral elasticities, to reproduce the observed data as an equilibrium solution of the model. While much attention is devoted to the assumed or estimated behavioral elasticities, the calibrated intercept and share parameters are at least as important. Regardless of the quality of elasticity estimates, comparative static results have little empirical significance if they are not evaluated with respect to observed economic conditions.

A consistent and convenient means of compiling a benchmark equilibrium dataset is the social accounting matrix (SAM). This data framework has been extensively applied to developing countries under promotion by the World Bank and has been more recently applied to developed countries.[2] A SAM for 1984 underlies the CGE model of the United States

---

1 A modern presentation of these techniques is presented in Chapter 5 by Francois and Hall.
2 Applications to developing countries are reviewed in Pyatt and Round (1985). Hanson and Robinson (1991) and Reinert and Roland-Holst (1992) apply the SAM framework to the United States. Reinert, Roland-Holst, and Shiells (1993) apply the SAM framework to North America.

developed by de Melo and Tarr (1992). The CGE model in use at the U.S. International Trade Commission is currently based on a SAM updated biannually (Reinert and Roland-Holst, 1991). The analysis of the North American Free Trade Area conducted by Roland-Holst, Reinert, and Shiells (1994) is based on a three-country SAM for the region. The initial GATT assessment of the Uruguay Round was based on a SAM for nine regions of the world economy (Francois et al., 1994). These nonexhaustive examples indicate that SAMs are rapidly becoming the standard data construct for CGE models of trade policy.

This chapter will provide the reader with an introduction to SAMs, beginning in Section II with simple macroeconomic SAMs and moving on to SAMs with sectoral detail. Section III shows how SAMs are constructed for trade policy modeling. Section IV discusses the relationship between SAMs and CGE trade policy models. Finally, concluding comments are presented in Section V.

II What Is a SAM?

Economic accounting is based on a fundamental principle of economics: For every income or receipt there is a corresponding expenditure or outlay.[3] This principle underlies the double-entry accounting procedures that make up the macroeconomic accounts of any country. A SAM is a form of *single-entry accounting*. SAMs also embody the fundamental principle, but they record transactions between accounts in a square tableau or matrix format.[4] The transactors or accounts constitute the dimension of the square matrix. By convention, incomes or receipts are shown in the rows of the SAM while expenditures or outlays are shown in the columns. The utility of SAMs is that they can provide a *comprehensive* and *consistent* record of the interrelationships of an economy at the level of individual production sectors, factors, and general public and foreign institutions. They can be used to disaggregate the macroeconomic accounts, and they can reconcile these with the economy's input–output accounts.

Traditionally, the database for models with sectoral detail was the input–output accounting tableau, which captures linkages through flows of intermediate inputs. Although it provides sectoral disaggregation, an input–output model does not include enough institutional detail to provide a

---

3 Pyatt (1988), p. 329. The title of this section is taken from King (1985). The interested reader is referred to this source for further introductory material.

4 United Nations Statistical Office (1968) shows that national accounts can be presented in four ways: standard double-entry accounts, balance statements, matrices, and equations.

framework for considering the full impact of policy on the economy. The input–output accounts can be extended to capture income and expenditure flows between other institutions, such as households, government, and the rest of the world, in a SAM. Indeed, the development of SAMs was motivated in part by the desire for a unified framework that reconciled the input–output accounts with macroeconomic accounts. The SAM thus provides detail and an economywide policy perspective in a fully consistent accounting framework.

Algebraically, a SAM may be represented as a square matrix:

$$\mathbf{T} = \left\{ t_{ij} \right\} \tag{4.1}$$

where t_{ij} is the value of the transaction with income accruing to account i from expenditure by account j.

Nominal flows cross the SAM from columns to rows. For transactions involving goods and services, there are corresponding real flows crossing the SAM from rows to columns. For financial transactions, there are corresponding flows of assets from rows to columns. For pure transfers, there are only the nominal flows from column accounts to row accounts.

The fundamental law of economics ensures that the corresponding row and column totals of a SAM, the income and expenditure for each account, must be equal. That is:

$$\sum_j t_{kj} = \sum_i t_{ik} \qquad \text{for all } k \tag{4.2}$$

As a consequence of this, SAMs satisfy a variant of Walras's Law. If all accounts but one balance, then the last account must also balance.[5] This property hints at the relationship between SAMs and neoclassical general equilibrium models.

Let us first consider a closed economy where economic activity is divided into three main types: production, consumption, and accumulation.[6] The representative accounts for this economy are presented in Table 4.1. Production receives its revenue from selling consumption goods in transaction t_{12} and investment goods in transaction t_{13}. The revenue from these sales passes to the consumption account as income paid to the factors of production in transaction t_{21}. The consumption-account income is spent in two ways. Part of it goes to purchase consumption goods in transaction t_{12}, and part is saved in transaction t_{32}. Savings is channeled to investment goods demand

5 Robinson (1989), p. 903.
6 The accumulation account is also known as the capital account. It can be thought of as a loanable funds market. This simple economy is addressed in Stone (1981, Chapter 1).

Table 4.1. *A closed-economy SAM*

Receipts	Expenditures			Totals
	1	2	3	
1. Production	-	C	I	Demand
2. Consumption	Y	-	-	Income
3. Accumulation	-	S	-	Savings
Totals	Supply	Expenditure	Investment	

Variables:

$t_{12} = C = $ consumption

$t_{13} = I = $ investment

$t_{21} = Y = $ income

$t_{32} = S = $ savings

Accounting Identities:

1. $Y = C + I$ (GNP)

2. $C + S = Y$ (Domestic Income)

3. $I = S$ (Saving-Investment)

in transaction t_{13}, closing the macroeconomic system of income-expenditure flows.

The accounts of Table 4.1 reflect a functional classification. We next introduce an institutional classification. First, production and consumption accounts are redefined as the institutions "suppliers" and "households," respectively. Second, the government sector is included as an institution. Third, the economy is opened to the rest of the world. The resulting new accounts are set forth in Table 4.2.[7] Suppliers receive revenue by selling final consumption goods to households (transaction t_{12}) and government (transaction t_{13}), investment goods to the capital account (transaction t_{14}), and export goods to the rest of the world (transaction t_{15}). Revenue from production is

7 This five-account economy is addressed in Robinson and Roland-Holst (1988).

Table 4.2. *An open-economy SAM with a government sector*

Receipts	Expenditures 1	2	3	4	5	Totals
1. Suppliers	-	C	G	I	E	Demand
2. Households	Y	-	-	-	-	Income
3. Government	-	T	-	-	-	Receipts
4. Capital Accnt.	-	S_h	S_g	-	S_f	Savings
5. Rest of World	M	-	-	-	-	Imports
Total	Supply	Expend- diture	Expend- diture	Invest- ment	Foreign Exchange	

Additional Variables:

$t_{42} = S_h$ = private savings $t_{32} = T$ = tax payments

$t_{43} = S_g$ = government savings $t_{15} = E$ = exports

$t_{45} = S_f$ = foreign savings $t_{51} = M$ = imports

$t_{13} = G$ = government spending

Accounting Identities:

1. $Y + M = C + G + I + E$ (GNP)

2. $C + T + S_h = Y$ (Income)

3. $G + S_g = T$ (Government Budget)

4. $I = S_h + S_g + S_f$ (Saving-Investment)

5. $E + S_f = M$ (Trade Balance)

spent on value added (transaction t_{21}) and imports from the rest of the world
(transaction t_{51}). Household outlays take the form of consumption expenditures (transaction t_{12}), tax payments (transaction t_{32}), and private domestic
savings (transaction t_{42}). Government outlays take the form of consumption
goods (transaction t_{13}) and government savings (transaction t_{43}). Inflows
from the rest of the world take the form of export demand (transaction t_{15})
and foreign savings (transaction t_{45}). Foreign savings is the negative of the
trade balance.

Actual SAMs typically include more detail than Table 4.2 in part because of a more detailed specification of the production side of the economy. The "suppliers" account of Table 4.2 is usually replaced with four accounts: activities, commodities, factors, and enterprises. The activities accounts buy intermediate inputs and hire factor services to produce commodities, generating value added in the process.[8] The goods sold by activities should be valued at producer prices in the SAM. The commodities accounts combine domestic supply with imports.[9] Commodities should be valued at purchaser prices in the SAM. Factors are a set of accounts for the expenditures and receipts of the factors of production: labor, land, and capital. Enterprises collect gross profits and government transfers and distribute them to other accounts.[10]

The new set of accounts is presented in Table 4.3. We describe the accounts from the receipts side and leave the reader to look at them from the expenditure side. Activities' receipts consist of payments at producer prices for the sales of goods to the commodity accounts (transaction t_{12}).[11] In an actual SAM, there would be many commodity and activity accounts (i.e., cell t_{12} would be a matrix). In the terminology of the input–output accounts, t_{12} is the "make table."[12] Commodities' receipts fall under five accounts. The first of these, transaction t_{21}, is from activities where commodities receive payments in purchaser prices for the sales of intermediate goods.[13] Input–output accounting refers to t_{21} as the "use table."[14] Transactions t_{25}, t_{26}, t_{27}, and t_{28} are

8 The United Nations' System of National Accounts (SNA) defines activity accounts as follows: "Production accounts of industries, producers of government services, producers of private non-profit services to households, and the domestic service of households, in respect of their gross output of goods and services and their intermediate consumption, primary inputs and indirect taxes *less* subsidies" (United Nations Statistical Office, 1968, p. 230).

9 The SNA defines commodity accounts as follows: "Accounts relating to the supply of commodities from domestic production and imports and their disposition to intermediate and final uses" (United Nations Statistical Office, 1968, p. 231). Hanson and Robinson (1988) describe the commodity account as "a giant department store" which "buys goods from domestic producers and foreigners (imports) down the column and sells them to demanders (including exports) along the row" (p. 218).

10 Hanson and Robinson (1991) describe the difference between activities and enterprises as follows: "(A)ctivities are aggregations of establishments within a sector. They purchase inputs on factor and product markets and sell output on product markets. They are different from enterprises which collect gross capital income and distribute it to other institutions. The distinction provides a framework for capturing an establishment-firm dichotomy, which exists in both data and theory" (p. 228).

11 "Producers' values are equal to the accumulation of factor costs, including the factor costs of the distribution and transport services embodied in inputs, and all indirect taxes" (United Nations Statistical Office, 1968, p. 54).

12 "The make table shows the value of each commodity produced by each industry.... The value of the primary product is shown in the diagonal cell.... The secondary products of the industry (products primary to other industries) are shown in the other cells along the row" (United States Department of Commerce, 1984, pp. 49–50). In terms of the vocabulary of this chapter, we can replace the word "industry" in this statement with "activity."

13 "Purchasers' values are equal to producers' values plus the trade and transport margins appropriate to the purchaser in question" (United Nations Statistical Office, 1968, p. 54).

14 "The use table shows the value of each commodity used by each industry" (United States Department of Commerce, 1984, p. 48).

Table 4.3. *A more detailed SAM*

Receipts \ Expenditures	1 Activities	2 Commodities	3 Factors	4 Enterprises	5 Households	6 Government	7 Capital Acct.	8 Rest of World	9 Total
1. Activities		gross outputs (make table)							total sales
2. Commodities	intermediate demand (use table)				household consumption	government consumption	investment	exports	aggregate demand
3. Factors	value added (net of taxes on activities)							factor service exports	factor income
4. Enterprises			gross profits			transfers			enterprise income
5. Households			wages	distributed profits		transfers		foreign remittances	household income
6. Government	indirect taxes	tariffs	factor taxes	enterprise taxes	direct taxes				government income
7. Capital acct.				retained earnings	household savings	government savings		capital transfers from abroad*	total savings
8. Rest of World		imports	factor service imports	transfers abroad	transfers abroad	transfers abroad	capital transfers abroad		foreign exchange payments
9. Total	total costs	aggregate supply	factor expenditure	enterprise expenditure	household expenditure	government expenditure	total investment	foreign exchange receipts	

*Includes increase in reserves.

commodity receipts from sales (again at purchaser prices) of consumption goods to households and the government, of investment goods to the capital account, and of exports to the rest of the world. Factor receipts (transaction t_{31}) record the value-added payments from the activities accounts and factor-service exports (transaction t_{38}) from the rest of the world.[15]

Now consider the receipts of institutions. Enterprises receive payments from two sources. The first is gross profits from the factors account, transaction t_{43}; the second is transfers from the government account (t_{46}). Households receive payments from four sources; the first is wages from the factors account (t_{53}). The second and third are from other institutional accounts: distributed profits from enterprises (t_{54}) and transfers from the government (t_{56}). The fourth source is foreign remittances (t_{58}). The government receives payments from the first five accounts: indirect taxes from activities (t_{61}), tariffs from commodities (t_{62}), factor taxes (t_{63}), enterprise taxes (t_{64}), and direct taxes from households (t_{65}).

The capital account receives payments in the form of domestic and foreign savings. Transaction t_{74} comprises the retained earnings of enterprises, while t_{75} and t_{76} represent the savings of households and the government, respectively. Capital transfers from abroad, including any increase in reserves, are received from the rest of the world in transaction t_{78}.

Lastly, there are the receipts of the rest of the world. The first of these is import payments from the domestic commodity account, transaction t_{82}. The second is factor-service imports (t_{83}).[16] Finally, the rest-of-the-world account receives three types of transfers: transfers abroad from persons (t_{86}) and government (t_{85}) and capital transfers abroad (t_{87}).

To illustrate an actual macroeconomic SAM, we next consider a SAM of the United States based on the 1989 National Income and Product Accounts (NIPA). This macroeconomic SAM has twelve accounting categories. Accounts 1 and 2 are the activity and commodity accounts, respectively. There are two factor accounts: labor (account 3) and property (account 4). Gross national product or value added is allocated between accounts 2 and 3 in accordance with the conventions adopted by the Department of Commerce in their input–output accounts (U.S. Department of Commerce, 1984). That is, charges against GNP are broken up into three types: (1) compensation of employees, which is received by labor; (2) profit-type income, net interest, and capital consumption allowances, which are received by property;[17] and (3) indirect business taxes, which are received by government.

---

15 Factor-service exports consist of a flow of profits into the country in question from its foreign investments.
16 Factor-service imports consist of a flow of profits from the country in question to foreign investors.
17 Profit-type income consists of proprietors' income, rental income of persons, corporate profits, and business transfer payments, less (subsidies less current surplus of government enterprises).

Account 5 is the enterprise account. Accounts 6 and 7 are the household and government accounts, respectively. Account 8 is the capital account, which closes the system of income-expenditure flows. Account 9 is the rest-of-the-world account (ROW), which records international transactions. Account 10 collects tariffs and distributes them to the government. Accounts 11 and 12 are the errors account and the total account, respectively.

To construct the macroeconomic SAM requires a mapping between the NIPA account items and the twelve SAM accounts. The mapping used is detailed in Reinert and Roland-Holst (1992), and its implementation for the year 1989 is presented in Table 4.4.[18] The mapping is designed so that factor-service imports (transaction t_{94}) and factor-service exports (transaction t_{49}) are broken out of net output. We assume that all factor-service payments are for capital. In contrast to typical practice, we define gross domestic product (GDP) to be net of imports valued at market prices rather than border prices. Therefore, the \$5,145,736 transaction t_{12} represents the typically defined GDP *less* customs duties. We do this because it is government, not activities, that engages in tariff collection.

Property income is passed on to enterprises (t_{54}) and to the rest of the world in the form of factor-service imports (t_{94}), whereas some of labor income is passed to the government in the form of social insurance contributions (t_{73}). Enterprise income is distributed among households (t_{65}), government (t_{75}), and the capital account (t_{85}). Household income is distributed between commodities (t_{26}), enterprises (t_{56}), government (t_{76}), the capital account (t_{86}), and the rest of the world (personal transfer payments in t_{96}). Government receipts are spent on commodities (t_{27}) and transfers to enterprises (t_{57}) to households (t_{67}), and to the rest of the world (interest and transfer payments to foreigners in t_{97}). Capital account expenditures are divided between commodities (t_{28}) and the government deficit. This last item, \$87,832 million (\$87.8 billion) in transaction t_{78}, represents a net deficit for federal, state, and local governments combined. The rest of the world makes payments to the commodities account for exports of goods and non-factor services (t_{29}), to the property account for factor-service exports (t_{49}), and to the capital account in the form of net foreign investment (t_{89}). The tariff account makes payments to the government ($t_{7,10}$).

SAMs which are actually used to calibrate CGE trade policy models have a sectoral structure instead of just a single sector as in macroeconomic SAMs such as the one presented in Table 4.4. To give the reader a sense of what a multi-sector SAM looks like, Table 4.5 presents a 1989 SAM for the United

---

18 The mapping is an adaptation of that presented in Hanson and Robinson (1991).

Table 4.4. A macro SAM for the United States, 1989 (millions of dollars)

Receipts	1 Activ.	2 Commod.	3 Labor	4 Prop.	5 Enter.	6 Hsehld.	7 Govt.	8 Capital	9 ROW	10 Tariff	11 Error	12 Total
1. Activities	0	5,145,736	0	0	0	0	0	0	0	0	0	5,145,736
2. Commodities	0	0	0	0	0	3,450,085	1,025,579	771,232	490,991	0	0	5,737,887
3. Labor	3,079,017	0	0	0	0	0	0	0	0	0	0	3,079,017
4. Property	1,687,273	0	0	0	0	0	0	0	135,235	0	0	1,822,508
5. Enterprises	0	0	0	1,724,858	0	102,175	93,057	0	0	0	0	1,920,090
6. Households	0	0	2,602,254	0	1,177,548	0	604,472	0	0	0	0	4,384,274
7. Government	396,494	0	476,763	0	135,092	658,754	0	87,832	0	17,481	0	1,772,416
8. Capital acct.	0	0	0	0	607,450	171,834	0	0	96,828	0	-17,048	859,064
9. Rest of World	0	574,670	0	97,650	0	1,426	49,308	0	0	0	0	723,054
10. Tariffs	0	17,481	0	0	0	0	0	0	0	0	0	17,481
11. Errors and Omissions	-17,048	0	0	0	0	0	0	0	0	0	0	-17,048
12. Total	5,145,736	5,737,887	3,079,017	1,822,508	1,920,090	4,384,274	1,772,416	859,064	723,054	17,481	-17,048	

Table 4.5. *A 1989 SAM with sectoral detail for the United States (millions of dollars)*

	1 agforfsh	2 mining	3 construct	4 ndurmfg	5 durmfg	6 trcomut	7 trade	8 fininsre	9 services
1 agforfsh	38,126	8	1,601	99,351	3,915	54	2,068	5,758	7,323
2 mining	91	12,581	2,415	94,532	9,239	30,424	1	32	38
3 construct	1,838	6,256	817	12,092	14,977	31,392	11,435	48,436	36,287
4 ndurmfg	28,226	1,790	31,129	380,908	94,362	31,703	26,253	12,765	171,496
5 durmfg	3,368	4,519	164,147	53,692	554,616	16,832	8,019	3,197	68,872
6 trcomut	3,965	2,094	16,987	74,988	67,178	89,804	55,069	23,890	100,551
7 trade	9,122	1,980	114,570	77,008	96,320	20,121	26,271	14,077	78,059
8 fininsre	7,301	4,639	6,425	19,202	25,768	14,058	54,642	186,314	92,169
9 services	2,326	3,000	66,338	83,685	88,934	34,296	165,043	90,875	287,060
10 labor	35,840	18,361	206,728	227,430	448,031	219,985	395,520	217,032	1,310,090
11 property	65,927	46,332	33,356	152,053	73,094	218,134	155,628	567,000	375,748
12 enterprise	0	0	0	0	0	0	0	0	0
13 household	0	0	0	0	0	0	0	0	0
14 government	8,472	10,109	7,624	28,363	19,242	37,254	135,160	117,844	32,427
15 capaccount	0	0	0	0	0	0	0	0	0
16 row	11,115	41,593	0	123,195	304,973	51,908	0	4,202	37,683
17 rowtaxes	169	212	0	8,860	8,240	0	0	0	0
18 error	-406	-276	-912	-1,502	-1,990	-1,751	-2,528	-3,322	-4,360

	10 labor	11 property	12 enterprise	13 household	14 govt.	15 capaccnt.	16 row	17 rowtaxes	18 error
1 agforfsh	0	0	0	24,532	9,261	-4,660	28,143	0	0
2 mining	0	0	0	307	827	-4,495	7,208	0	0
3 construct	0	0	0	0	124,985	362,709	0	0	0
4 ndurmfg	0	0	0	496,358	53,700	8,858	96,307	0	0
5 durmfg	0	0	0	228,777	139,146	323,428	238,286	0	0
6 trcomut	0	0	0	249,367	44,338	10,919	55,067	0	0
7 trade	0	0	0	518,776	15,675	60,601	0	0	0
8 fininsre	0	0	0	834,059	17,544	13,804	12,173	0	0
9 services	0	0	0	1,097,910	620,103	68	53,807	0	0
10 labor	0	0	0	0	0	0	0	0	0
11 property	0	0	0	0	0	0	135,235	0	0
12 enterprise	2,602,254	1,724,858	0	102,175	93,057	0	0	0	0
13 household	476,763	0	1,177,548	658,754	604,472	0	0	0	0
14 government	0	0	135,092	0	0	87,832	0	17,481	0
15 capaccount	0	0	607,450	171,834	0	0	96,828	0	-17,048
16 row	0	97,650	0	1,426	49,308	0	0	0	0
17 rowtaxes	0	0	0	0	0	0	0	0	0
18 error	0	0	0	0	0	0	0	0	0

note: Key to sectors: agforfsh–agriculture, forestry, and fishing; mining–mining and mineral resources; construct–construction; ndurmfg–nondurable manufacturing; durmfg–durable manufacturing; trcomut–transportation, communication, and utilities; trade–wholesale and retail trade; fininsre–finance, insurance, and real estate; services–personal, business, and public services; labor–labor value added; property–property value added; enterprise–enterprise; household–household final demand; government–government final demand; capaccount–savings and investment; row–rest of the world; rowtaxes–rest of the world taxes (tariffs).

States in which the economy has been divided into nine broad sectors. The reader will find that the transaction values in rows and columns 3–11 of Table 4.4 are repeated in rows and columns 10–18 of Table 4.5. The activity and commodity accounts of Table 4.4 (rows and columns 1 and 2) have been replaced by a set of nine commodity accounts.[19] Let us look at columns 1–9. Rows 1–9 of these columns give the interindustry transactions matrix. Rows 10 and 11 give the value added payments. Row 14 records the indirect business tax payments of each sector. Row 16 records imports, and Row 17 records tariff collections. Finally, Row 18 is a sectoral distribution of the macroeconomic accounting error.

Next, let us look at rows 1–9 of columns 13–16 in Table 4.5. In column 13, these rows give sectoral household expenditures. In columns 14 and 15, these give government and investment (including inventories) demand, respectively. Finally column 16 gives sectoral export demands.

In most countries, the United States included, the data which go into a SAM such as that presented in Table 4.5 come from a number of sources: macroeconomic accounts, input–output accounts, trade data, etc. The process of combining these data, which may not all be from the same year, into a consistent and balanced SAM is neither fully a science nor merely an art. The next section gives the reader some idea of how this process works.

III SAM Construction

Building a SAM of any size can be a tedious exercise. However, while there are few rewards in SAM construction *per se*, we have found the process well worth the effort in its contribution to trade policy analysis. This section will outline some general procedures we have used in SAM construction with the hope of minimizing difficulties for others embarking on similar efforts.[20]

Construction of a SAM begins with the transformation of the country's macroeconomic accounts into a macroeconomic tableau such as that presented in Table 4.4. This macroeconomic SAM provides control totals for each submatrix of the detailed SAM, as well as scalar interinstitutional transfers. The most recent year for which the macroeconomic data are available sets a limit on the choice of a base year. For a multi-country SAM, macroeconomic SAMs must be constructed for each of the member countries. Next, the individual macroeconomic SAMs must be joined into a single

19 Activity accounts are removed by using a procedure described in Section III.
20 The interested reader also may want to consult Keuning and de Ruijter (1988). Reinert and Roland-Holst (1992) describe the construction of a U.S. social accounting matrix for trade policy analysis in some detail, and Reinert, Roland-Holst, and Shiells (1993) describe the construction of a multi-country social accounting matrix of North America.

macroeconomic SAM. This involves converting the macroeconomic SAMs into a single currency using exchange rates, including trade flows among the member countries, and subtracting these from the respective rest-of-the-world accounts. Finally, factor-service flows and capital flows among the member countries might be added, with appropriate subtractions made from the respective rest-of-the-world acounts.

To construct the detailed accounts, the practitioner will need input–output tables for the country or countries in question and a host of other data sources to be mentioned later. It is typically the case that recent data are at a higher level of sectoral aggregation than less recent data. For example, detailed input–output accounts might be available five years prior to the chosen base period. To deal with this problem, we generally use the most recent data first for broad sectoral aggregates and then estimate more detailed sectoral transactions using shares from the less recent data. Often this procedure will evolve into a cascade of data steps progressing from high levels of aggregation and recent data to progressive disaggregation with less recent data, the latter being used in share form. While tedious, this approach attempts to make the SAM as timely as possible given the available data.

Construction of sectoral accounts can begin with activity output data, perhaps disaggregated to the required degree by the cascade procedure just described. To obtain commodity output data, the make matrix from the input–output accounts can be row normalized and premultiplied by a row vector of the activity outputs. The make matrix can then be updated to the base year by using a matrix balancing method, such as the RAS procedure, with activity and commodity output vectors as control totals.[21]

For the value-added submatrix, sectoral control totals are needed and may have to be estimated by a cascade procedure. The sectoral totals can be allocated among labor income, property income, and indirect business taxes based on shares from the input–output data. Finally, the value-added submatrix is balanced to the macro-SAM control totals by using the RAS procedure.

To estimate the import and export submatrices, control totals for both are taken from the macroeconomic SAM. Data on imports and exports for the base (or nearest) year should be available from the country's customs agency.[22] The resulting totals of imports and exports are unlikely to agree

---

21 Matrix balancing methods, including the RAS procedure, are discussed in the Appendix.
22 Customs agencies generally only collect data on merchandise trade. For an attempt to incorporate service trade data into a SAM of the United States, see the Appendix of Dighe, Francois, and Reinert (1994).

with the control totals taken from the macroeconomic SAM. Such discrepancies can be allocated among the sectors in proportion to their shares in the resulting totals.

Final demand submatrices can contain four types of vectors: household demand vectors, government demand vectors, investment demand vectors, and export demand vectors. In a trade model, it will be necessary to have separate export demand.[23] The simplest way to deal with domestic final demand is to aggregate the household, government, and investment final demands into a single vector.[24] Alternatively, one can maintain separate household, government, and investment accounts.[25] The former approach avoids a number of macroeconomic closure issues discussed in Section IV, but the latter is more complete and consistent with national income accounting conventions. For the purposes of this section, we assume the various final demand vectors are maintained.[26]

A dated final demand submatrix will be available from the input–output accounts. The export vector will be updated as described. The household, government, and investment vectors can be simply updated, using control totals from the macroeconomic SAM and shares from the dated vectors. Alternatively, more recent data on sectoral final demand by institution can be used if they are available. One wrinkle arises from those commodities without intermediate deliveries. In these cases, total final demand must be set equal to estimated commodity supply. In practice, the construction of the final demand submatrix can be difficult and may require ingenuity and selective matrix balancing.

The last step is to update the use matrix to the base year. For the row control vector, the estimated vector of commodity output, plus the import vectors, and less the final demand vectors will be used. For the column control vector, the activity output vector, less the value-added and error vectors, will be used. With these control vectors, the use matrix can be updated by using the RAS procedure.

---

23 Multi-country SAMs have more than one export demand vector, whereas a single-country SAM would have only one.

24 This is the approach taken by de Melo and Tarr (1992).

25 This was the approach taken by Reinert and Roland-Holst (1991).

26 One can go further in detailing final demand vectors. The disaggregation of the household final demand vector into income levels and the mapping of labor and property income into these household types would provide the opportunity to explore the relationship between trade policies and the household distribution of income. This disaggregation of the household sector is at the heart of the original purpose of the SAM framework (see Stone, 1985) but has not been applied very often in trade policy modeling. For exceptions, see Chapter 10 of this volume by Khan. See also Hanson and Reinert (1994).

Most trade policy applications of SAMs require that the make and use matrices be consolidated into a transactions matrix. There are two possible approaches: to eliminate the commodity accounts or to eliminate the activity accounts. The following example consolidates via elimination of activity accounts. We then explain why the resulting SAM may be more suitable for trade policy analysis than one obtained by elimination of commodity accounts.

Consider a simple case with two activity accounts $(A1, A2)$, two commodity accounts $(C1, C2)$, a demand account (D), and a rest-of-the-world account (R). We partition the SAM with the accounts to be retained $(C1, C2, D, R)$ in the upper-left-hand corner:

	C1	C2	D	R	A1	A2
C1:	0	0	F_1	E_1	U_{11}	U_{12}
C2:	0	0	F_2	E_2	U_{21}	U_{22}
D:	0	0	0	0	V_1	V_2
R:	I_1	I_2	0	0	0	0
A1:	M_{11}	M_{12}	0	0	0	0
A2:	M_{21}	M_{22}	0	0	0	0

The use matrix has coefficients U_{ij}, and the make matrix has coefficients M_{ji}. Final demands are F_i, and the value added values are V_j. Imports and exports are I_i and E_i, respectively.

As Pyatt (1985) demonstrates, the consolidated accounts may be expressed in matrix form:[27]

$$T = \begin{bmatrix} 0 & 0 & F_1 & E_1 \\ 0 & 0 & F_2 & E_2 \\ 0 & 0 & 0 & 0 \\ I_1 & I_2 & 0 & 0 \end{bmatrix} + \begin{bmatrix} \underline{U}_{11} & \underline{U}_{12} \\ \underline{U}_{21} & \underline{U}_{22} \\ \underline{V}_1 & \underline{V}_2 \\ 0 & 0 \end{bmatrix} \begin{bmatrix} M_{11} & M_{12} & 0 & 0 \\ M_{21} & M_{22} & 0 & 0 \end{bmatrix} \tag{4.3}$$

where the underbars denote column-sum normalized coefficients.

As can be seen from this expression, the trade accounts are preserved in their original form by commodity. This is *not* the case for the elimination of the commodity accounts under which the imports (including tariffs) and exports are apportioned. Therefore, elimination of activity accounts facilitates interpretation for trade policy analysis.

---

27 It can be shown that the use of the Pyatt apportionment method to eliminate either the commodity or the activity accounts implies the assumption of activity technology. On the distinction between commodity and activity technologies, see United Nations Statistical Office (1968, p. 39).

IV SAMs and the General Equilibrium Analysis of
Trade Policy

By themselves, SAMs are insufficient to allow the analyst properly to assess the impacts of changes in trade policies. This limitation has been clearly expressed by Thorbecke (1985):

The SAM is clearly an essential tool in diagnosing the initial situation and in organizing data in a systematic way with respect to accounts and the classification and interrelationship of variables appearing in these accounts. At the same time, by itself, the SAM is nothing more than a snapshot in time, yielding base-year information in a consistent way among a whole set of variables. If the SAM is to be used for policy rather than purely diagnostic purposes, it has to be coupled with a conceptual framework that contains the behavioral and technical relationships among variables within and among sets of accounts or modules. In other words, the SAM as a data framework is a large-scale identity which, to come alive, should be linked to a model of the causal relationships among variables. (p. 207)

An exhaustive description of the transition from SAM to CGE model is beyond the scope of this chapter. Instead, we will touch on a few issues which the practitioner may face in moving from the one to the other. These issues are flexible aggregation, calibration, and closure.

IV.1 Flexible Aggregation

By its nature, trade policy often is directed at detailed sectors. Import quotas on cheese, export taxes on coffee, and high tariffs on machine tools are the focal points of commercial policies. It is often important, then, to have very detailed accounts to assess these policies. Unfortunately, implementing a CGE model at such a level of disaggregation would be difficult numerically and would generate vast amounts of information extraneous to the issue at hand. These considerations have led us to advocate a "flexible aggregation" approach to using SAMs for trade policy analysis. The base SAM is estimated for as many sectors as possible to address a broad spectrum of detailed industry issues. For a particular application, however, those detailed sectors which do not bear on the current problem are aggregated into fewer broad sectors (e.g., one-digit SITC).

The role of the SAM and flexible aggregation in supporting CGE modeling of trade policy is represented in Figure 4.1. The fully disaggregated base SAM is denoted as *SAM* I in this figure, and the initial exogenous behavioral parameter estimates are denoted *EPE* I. The aggregation procedure takes the information in this disaggregated data base and creates a

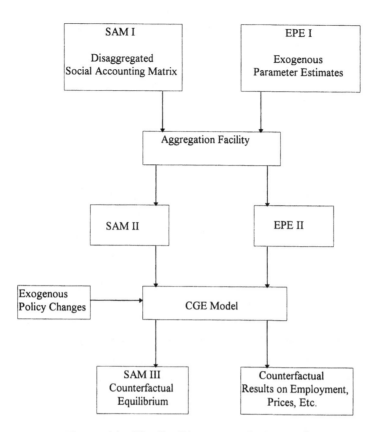

Figure 4.1. *The flexible aggregation procedure*

second SAM and corresponding parameter set at the level of aggregation specified for a given analysis. The resulting aggregates are labeled *SAM* II and *EPE* II in the figure. *SAM* II composes the benchmark equilibrium data set to calibrate the CGE model. The analyst introduces an exogenous, counterfactual policy change, such as a tariff cut, and the behavioral model simulates the response of the economy to such a policy change. This results in a counterfactual equilibrium which can be expressed as a new SAM, denoted *SAM* III. In this way, *the modeling exercise begins and ends with a SAM.* At the third stage, the model also produces a large volume of subsidiary counterfactual results on changes in employment, trade, production, etc.

Consider an example. Flynn and Reinert (1993) undertook a study of the U.S. dairy quotas. Their CGE model was structured around five detailed dairy sectors and nine aggregate sectors for a total of fourteen model sectors. The detailed dairy sectors were dairy farm products, butter, cheese, con-

Table 4.6. A 1989 SAM for the analysis of the U.S. dairy quotas (millions of dollars)

	1 dairyfarms	2 butter	3 cheese	4 condevap	5 fldmilk	6 agforfish	7 mining	8 construct	9 ndurmfg	10 durmfg	11 trcomut
1 dairyfarms	0	669	3,769	2,372	10,194	400	0	0	1,155	7	0
2 butter	0	29	19	10	80	0	0	0	498	0	8
3 cheese	0	15	2,411	54	85	0	0	0	78	3	1
4 condevap	0	38	60	321	349	0	0	0	1,266	0	0
5 fldmilk	0	669	479	428	1,249	0	0	0	467	1	0
6 agforfish	3,992	0	21	6	1,005	33,685	8	1,602	80,167	3,914	6
7 mining	0	0	2	0	0	90	12,585	2,420	94,613	9,262	54
8 construct	103	8	277	39	179	1,700	6,144	803	11,377	14,741	30,416
9 ndurmfg	4,129	134	998	503	2,603	24,021	1,787	31,122	367,569	94,391	30,812
10 durmfg	117	29	124	248	273	3,223	4,485	163,170	52,640	551,637	31,610
11 trcomut	389	40	263	142	444	3,564	2,089	16,982	73,996	67,197	16,695
12 trade	405	187	795	286	761	8,675	1,972	114,328	74,734	96,172	89,580
13 fininsre	362	16	64	63	267	6,916	4,628	6,421	18,759	25,768	20,034
14 services	71	41	270	100	673	2,246	2,992	66,288	82,447	88,917	14,019
15 labor	1,790	363	1,572	534	2,466	34,020	18,361	207,063	222,621	449,018	34,194
16 property	6,779	172	1,201	802	4,248	59,105	46,340	33,415	145,738	73,268	219,857
17 enterprise	0	0	0	0	0	0	0	0	0	0	218,046
18 household	0	0	0	0	0	0	0	0	0	0	0
19 government	531	20	60	19	189	7899	10,068	7,605	27,975	19,207	37084
20 capaccount	0	0	0	0	0	0	0	0	0	0	0
21 row	0	2	353	22	13	11,088	41,524	0	122,670	305,141	51,792
22 rowtaxes	0	0	34	0	0	168	211	0	8,818	8,247	0

	12 trade	13 fininsre	14 services	15 labor	16 property	17 enterprise	18 household	19 government	20 capaccount	21 row	22 rowtaxes
1 dairyfarms	0	0	0	0	0	0	103	0	0	0	0
2 butter	1	0	830	0	0	0	561	348	0	50	0
3 cheese	3	0	1,255	0	0	0	8,506	330	0	31	0
4 condevap	1	0	463	0	0	0	2,592	436	0	424	0
5 fldmilk	2	0	1,827	0	0	0	18,150	1,768	0	37	0
6 agforfsh	2,065	5,749	7,316	0	0	0	24,491	9,298	-4,804	28,231	0
7 mining	0	31	37	0	0	0	307	831	-4,637	7,236	0
8 construct	11,220	47,520	35,618	0	0	0	0	123,296	367,381	0	0
9 ndurmfg	26,170	12,727	166,712	0	0	0	467,106	50,957	9,118	95,931	0
10 durmfg	7,951	3,169	68,315	0	0	0	227,727	138,713	331,045	237,334	0
11 trcomut	54,911	23,819	100,305	0	0	0	249,636	44,451	11,239	55,159	0
12 trade	26,148	14,010	77,726	0	0	0	518,389	15,686	62,268	0	0
13 fininsre	54,470	185,717	91,918	0	0	0	834,724	17,584	14,205	12,190	0
14 services	164,492	90,567	286,225	0	0	0	1,098,576	621,397	70	53,871	0
15 labor	395,141	216,811	1,309,394	0	0	0	0	0	0	0	0
16 property	155,506	566,524	375,614	0	1,724,729	0	0	0	0	135,744	0
17 enterprise	0	0	0	0	0	0	0	0	0	0	0
18 household	0	0	0	2,602,196	0	1,177,398	0	93,190	0	0	0
19 government	134,493	117,257	32,280	476,820	0	135,094	102,170	604,679	90,225	0	17,481
20 capaccount	0	0	0	0	0	607,597	658,100	0	0	96,811	0
21 row	0	4,191	37,600	0	97,778	0	171,702	0	0	0	0
22 rowtaxes	0	0	0	0	0	0	1,427	49,447	0	0	0

densed and evaporated milk, and fluid milk. The nine aggregate sectors were broad groups utilized in the U.S. National Income and Product Accounts. The resulting SAM is presented in Table 4.6. Unlike the SAM in Table 4.5, the SAM in Table 4.6 has no error account. Since modeling an error account makes little economic sense, this account was removed and the matrix rebalanced. Therefore, the inter-institutional transactions in Table 4.6 will differ slightly from those in Table 4.5.

Row 1 of columns 2–5 in Table 4.6 illustrates the relevance of SAMs to trade policy analysis. The dairy farm sector is an important upstream supplier to the butter, cheese, condensed and evaporated milk, and cream sectors, all of which are protected by quotas. In fact, these quotas are in place to protect labor and property incomes in the dairy farm sector via these input–output relationships. The flexible aggregation approach allows the practitioner to focus on such detailed linkages without confusing the model with an unwieldy number of sectors.

IV.2 Calibration

As we stated in the introduction, the term "calibration" refers to the process of calculating intercept and share parameters of a CGE model's mathematical functions (given exogenously specified behavioral elasticities) so that the model will replicate the base year SAM as an equilibrium solution. Nearly every transaction in the SAM is used to calibrate a model function, calculate a policy parameter, or define a model constraint. Consider Table 4.6 as an example. The upper-left-hand submatrix formed by accounts 1–14 contains 196 transactions which will be involved in calibrating (typically fixed) input–output coefficients. Rows 15 and 16 of columns 1–4 contain value-added transactions which will be used to calibrate value-added functions such as Cobb–Douglas or constant elasticity of substitution (CES). Row 19 of columns 1–14 gives the indirect business tax collections which will be used to calculate *ad valorem* indirect business tax rates. Row 21 of columns 1–14 gives imports. These will be used in the calibration of (typically CES) import aggregation functions.[28] The tariff collections given in row 22 of columns 1–14 will be used to calibrate *ad valorem* tariff equivalents.

Final demand vectors are given in rows 1–14 of columns 18–21. The transactions in column 18 will be used in calibrating a household demand

---

28 See de Melo and Robinson (1989) and Chapter 6 of this volume by Devarajan, Go, Lewis, Robinson, and Sinko.

function such as a Cobb–Douglas, CES, or Linear Expenditure System (LES). The transactions in column 21 give export demands and will be used to calibrate export aggregation functions such as constant elasticity of trans-formation (CET).[29] Columns 19 and 20 give government and investment demands. The way these transactions are dealt with involves questions of macro closure discussed later.

The remaining submatrix defined by accounts 15–22 contains inter-institutional transactions. Foreign remittances, which transactions $t_{16,21}$ less transactions $t_{21,16}$ and comprise $t_{21,18}$, enter into the balance of payments constraint. Transaction $t_{20,21}$ is foreign savings, which also is an element of the balance of trade constraint as well as the savings–investment balance. Transaction $t_{21,19}$ is government lending and enters both the balance of payments and government budget constraints. The government deficit is represented in transactions $t_{19,20}$ and enters the government budget con-straint and the savings–investment balance. Transactions $t_{17,19}$ and $t_{18,19}$ are government transfers, which enter the government budget constraint and the income equations. Private savings is given by the sum of transactions $t_{20,17}$ and $t_{20,18}$. This will be used to calculate a savings rate. Factor tax collections given in transactions $t_{19,15}$ and $t_{19,17}$ are used to calculate factor tax rates. The income tax rate will be calculated by transaction $t_{19,18}$.

The remaining interinstitutional transactions ($t_{17,16}$, $t_{17,18}$, $t_{18,15}$, $t_{18,17}$, and $t_{19,22}$) will not be directly used. The first four of these will be implicit in the model structure and the last (total tariff revenue) will be calculated as a sum of sectoral tariff collections.

IV. 3 *Closure*

The term "closure" refers to prescribing which variables are endogenous and exogenous in a general equilibrium system. For example, in a system of linear equations based on a SAM, closure is simply the choice of which accounts are to be the exogenous accounts and which are to be endogenous accounts.[30] A number of different closure issues must be addressed in build-ing a CGE model, and we discuss only a few of them here, concentrating on those most closely related to the SAM.[31] Before proceeding, it will be helpful to say a word about the specification of a numéraire. A convenient numéraire is a weighted average index of the model's prices or a GDP deflator. This variable is then fixed exogenously, and the exchange rate of

29 Again, see de Melo and Robinson (1989) and Chapter 6 of this volume.
30 See Robinson (1989).
31 Other closure issues are discussed in Chapter 7 of this volume by Blonigen, Flynn, and Reinert.

the model behaves as a real exchange rate.[32] In what follows, we assume that such a specification has been implemented.

In the preceding calibration section, we mentioned that a foreign savings variable is given an initial value from the SAM. In one type of foreign sector closure, this variable is made exogenous and the real exchange rate is endogenous. Changes in the real exchange rate ensure that the base period current account position is maintained. Alternatively, this foreign savings variable can be made endogenous and the real exchange rate would then be held fixed exogenously. In this latter case, however, welfare calculations are difficult to interpret, since foreign exchange (a basic resource) in the hands of the economy in question will change. We also mentioned a government deficit variable. Typically, one fixes government demand in each sector in real terms, and the government deficit is thereby endogenous. This is a neoclassical approach. Alternatively, one could take a more structuralist view and fix this or other magnitudes in nominal terms.[33]

Perhaps the most important closure issue from a macroeconomic viewpoint is how the savings–investment balance is achieved. Private savings, foreign savings, and government savings all enter into this balance. A straightforward closure which facilitates welfare analysis based on the household sector account is one in which government and investment demands are fixed in each sector in real terms.[34] The numéraire price index is fixed. Foreign savings is fixed in terms of the foreign currency, and the household savings rate is fixed. The government transfer variable is specified as endogenous and maintains the savings–investment balance. This approach has been used by Devarajan and Rodrik (1991) and Flynn and Reinert (1993), among others. A savings-driven closure described by Robinson (1989, 1991) involves investment determined by savings. In this case, real investment demands are endogenous, and welfare changes cannot be properly measured on the basis of the household sector alone. This specification brings intertemporal considerations into any welfare analysis. Finally, alternative "structuralist" closures are available and are discussed in some detail by Taylor (1990).

---

32 We use the term "exchange rate" to refer to a conversion factor that translates world prices of imported or exported goods into domestic prices. See de Melo and Robinson (1989) and de Melo and Tarr (1992).

33 As Taylor (1990) states, "A . . . distinctive feature of structuralist models is that they are *not* set up in 'real' terms (i.e. with only relative prices). Rather, they explicitly include prices and income flows in nominal or money terms" (p. 4). For neoclassical models, homogeneity of degree zero can be checked by exogenously increasing the numéraire variable by a small amount. All prices and variables expressed in terms of prices (nominal magnitudes) should increase by the same proportionate amount. Real quantities should not change at all. See Condon, Dahl, and Devarajan (1986).

34 In a static trade-policy model, investment demand merely maintains accounting balance since it does not augment the capital stock.

A number of these closure issues can be avoided by aggregating the household, government, and investment accounts into a single final demand account (e.g., de Melo and Tarr, 1992). Turning to the accounting identities presented at the bottom of Table 4.2, the government budget and savings–investment balances are no longer operative. However, there will be an endogenous intra-institutional transfer from the final demand account to itself.

V Concluding Comments

The workhorse of the trade theorist is the $2\times2\times2$ Heckscher–Ohlin–Samuelson model. Unfortunately for the trade policy analyst, this simple model offers little guidance to the effects of real-world policy changes. This has been stated quite clearly by two notable trade theorists, Dixit and Norman (1980):

We should stress . . . that one should avoid drawing general conclusions from the two-good results. The moral . . . is that one cannot say much about the general equilibrium effects of changes in parameters without knowing the exact values of the parameters and the exact characteristics of demand and supply functions. If the theory is to be applied, therefore, it should be done by putting numerical values into the general formulae; not by applying qualitative results from the two-good case directly. (pp. 127–128)

If trade policy analysts are to provide accurate assessments of trade policy changes, they must "put numerical values in the general formulae" as carefully as they can. In our view, the SAM framework helps the analyst to do just that. It represents a comprehensive and consistent framework for developing databases for rigorous economic methods like applied general equilibrium analysis. Finally, it helps in the reconciliation of the numerous data sources to complete the detailed picture of economywide activity.

Appendix 4.1

SAM Balancing

One of the objectives of the Cambridge Growth Project was to estimate a detailed SAM of the United Kingdom for the year 1960. A transactions matrix was only available for 1954, so Stone (1962) suggested a procedure to update the matrix to 1960. This "RAS" method takes its name from the notation used in Stone's original equations. The RAS method estimated a transactions matrix for the year 1960 by starting with the 1954 transactions matrix, expressing it in 1960 prices, and adjusting rows and columns iteratively so that they add up to the 1960 totals.[35]

---

35 See Bacharach (1970, Chapter 3).

Let R_0 be a known, initial matrix of transactions and let R be the unobservable transaction matrix for the year we desire to estimate. Let p be a vector whose elements are the ratios of desired period prices to initial period prices. Let $\langle z \rangle$ denote the diagonal matrix having vector z on its main diagonal. The R matrix in desired period prices then takes the form[36]

$$R_0^* = \langle p \rangle R_0 \langle p \rangle^{-1} \tag{A4.1}$$

The next step is to calculate a column vector of intermediate outputs for the desired year as the difference between gross outputs and final demands. Stone and Brown (1965) denote this vector u. The row vector v of intermediate inputs for the desired year is the difference between gross outputs and value added.

The following constraints must be satisfied:

$$Ri = u \tag{A4.2}$$

$$i'R = v \tag{A4.3}$$

where i is the conformal unit column vector. Equation A4.2 states that the rows of the new transaction matrix must sum to the observed row totals. Equation A4.3 states that the columns must sum to the observed column totals.

The problem is then to adjust R_0^* to obtain an estimate of R. The RAS algorithm proceeds as follows:[37]

Step 0 $\left(\text{Initialization}\right)$: Set $k = 0$ and $R^k = R_0^*$.

Step 1 $\left(\text{Row Scaling}\right)$:

Define $\rho^k = \langle u \rangle \left(R^k i \right)^{-1}$

and update R^k as $\acute{R} \leftarrow \langle \rho^k \rangle R^k$

Step 2 $\left(\text{Column Scaling}\right)$:

Define $\sigma^k = \left(i' \acute{R} \right)^{-1} \langle v \rangle$

and define R^{k+1} by $R^{k+1} = \acute{R} \langle \sigma^k \rangle$

Step 3: Replace $k \leftarrow k + 1$ and return to Step 1.

The algebraic RAS has a number of limitations. First, it cannot handle negative matrix elements. While this is not a problem for balancing the transactions matrix, it could be a problem for balancing other components of a SAM. Second, it is necessary to rescale the problem if any negative row or column totals appear. This rarely arises in practical work, however. Finally, the method assumes that the elements of the matrix are identically uniformly distributed random variables. This

36 The reader might multiply out a 2×2 example to elucidate this adjustment.
37 See Stone and Brown (1965) and Schneider and Zenios (1990).

may not always be the case if one is less certain about some elements of the matrix than others. It is this consideration that has led to research in new matrix balancing techniques.

Byron (1978) proposed the estimation of R by the minimizing of a constrained quadratic loss function. Let r_0^* denote the column vector created from the row vectorization of the nonzero elements of R_0^*. Similarly, the column vector created from the row vectorization of estimates of the nonzero elements of R is denoted by r. Now re-express (A4.2) and (A4.3) as

$$Gr - h = 0 \tag{A4.4}$$

The objective will be for the estimates r to be as close to r_0^* as possible in a quadratic loss sense subject to the constraints in (A4.4). This can be accomplished by using the following constrained quadratic loss function:

$$Z = \frac{1}{2}\left(r - r_0^*\right)' V^{-1}\left(r - r_0^*\right) + \lambda'\left(Gr - h\right) \tag{A4.5}$$

The term λ is a vector of Lagrange multipliers. The diagonal matrix V consists of weights that indicate the degree of certainty (variance) in the original r_0^*. The less the certainty, the less important are the differences between the estimated element and the original element. Byron proposes a conjugate gradient algorithm for minimizing (A4.5).

References

Bacharach, M.O.L. 1970. *Biproportionate Matrices and Input–Output Change.* Cambridge: Cambridge University Press.

Byron, R. 1978. "The estimation of large social accounting matrices." *Journal of the Royal Statistical Society*, Series A 141:359–367.

Condon, T., H. Dahl, and S. Devarajan. 1986. "Implementing a computable general equilibrium model in GAMS: The Cameroon model." Development Research Department, Discussion Paper No. 290, World Bank.

De Melo, J. 1988. "Computable general equilibrium models for trade policy analysis in developing countries: A survey." *Journal of Policy Modeling* 10:469–503.

De Melo, J. and S. Robinson. 1989. "Product differentiation and the treatment of foreign trade in computable general equilibrium models of small economies." *Journal of International Economics* 27:47–67.

De Melo, J. and D. Tarr. 1992. *A General Equilibrium Analysis of U.S. Foreign Trade Policy.* Cambridge, Massachusetts: MIT Press.

Devarajan, S. and D. Rodrik. 1991. "Pro-competitive effects of trade reform: Results for a CGE model of Cameroon." *European Economic Review* 35:1157–1184.

Dighe, R.S., J.F. Francois, and K.A. Reinert. 1994. "The role of services in U.S. production and trade: An analysis of social accounting data for the 1980s." In *The Service Productivity and Quality Challenge*, edited by P.T. Harker. Boston: Kluwer.

Dixit, A. and V. Norman. 1980. *Theory of International Trade.* Cambridge: Cambridge University Press.

Flynn, J.E. and K.A. Reinert. 1993. "The welfare and resource allocation implications of the U.S. dairy quotas." *International Economic Journal* 7:91–108.

Francois, J.F., B. McDonald, and H. Nordström. 1994. "The Uruguay Round: A global general equilibrium assessment." Paper presented at the Challenges of East Asian Trade Conference, Canberra, Australia.

Hanson, K.A. and K.A. Reinert. 1994. "The MFA and household welfare in the United States: A general equilibrium analysis." Working Paper 94-02, Department of Economics, Kalamazoo College, Kalamazoo, Michigan.

Hanson, K.A. and S. Robinson. 1991. "Data, linkages, and models: U.S. national income and product accounts in the framework of a social accounting matrix." *Economic Systems Research* 3:215–232.

Keuning, S.J. and W.A. de Ruijter. 1988. "Guidelines to the construction of a social accounting matrix." *Review of Income and Wealth* 34:71–100.

King, B.B. 1985. "What is a SAM?" In *Social Accounting Matrices: A Basis for Planning,* edited by G. Pyatt and J. Round. Washington, D.C.: The World Bank.

Pyatt, G. 1985. "Commodity balances and national accounts: A SAM perspective." *Review of Income and Wealth* 31:155–169.

Pyatt, G. 1988. "A SAM approach to modeling." *Journal of Policy Modeling* 10:327–352.

Pyatt, G. and J. Round, eds. 1985. *Social Accounting Matrices: A Basis for Planning.* Washington, D.C.: The World Bank.

Reinert, K.A. and D.W. Roland-Holst. 1991. *An Introduction to the ITC Computable General Equilibrium Model.* USITC Publication 2433. Washington, D.C.: U.S. International Trade Commission.

Reinert, K.A. and D.W. Roland-Holst. 1992. "A detailed social accounting matrix for the United States, 1988." *Economic Systems Research* 4:173–187.

Reinert, K.A., D.W. Roland-Holst, and C.R. Shiells. 1993. "Social accounts and the structure of the North American economy." *Economics Systems Research* 5:295–326.

Robinson, S. 1989. "Multisectoral models." In *Handbook of Development Economics,* Vol. II, edited by H.B. Chenery and T.N. Srinivasan. Amsterdam: Elsevier.

Robinson, S. 1991. "Macroeconomics, financial variables, and computable general equilibrium models." *World Development* 19:1509–1525.

Robinson, S. and D.W. Roland-Holst. 1988. "Macroeconomic structure and computable general equilibrium models." *Journal of Policy Modeling* 10:353–375.

Roland-Holst, D.W., K.A. Reinert, and C.R. Shiells. 1994. "A general equilibrium analysis of North American economic integration." In *Modeling Trade Policy: Applied General Equilibrium Assessments of North American Free Trade.* Cambridge: Cambridge University Press.

Schneider, M.H. and S.A. Zenios. 1990. "A comparative study of algorithms for matrix balancing." *Operations Research* 38:439–455.

Shoven, J.B. and J. Whalley. 1984. "Applied general-equilibrium models of taxation and international trade: An introduction and survey." *Journal of Economic Literature* 22:1007–1051.

Stone, R. 1962. *A Computable Model of Economic Growth. A Programme for Growth 1*. Cambridge: Chapman and Hall.

Stone, R. 1981. *Aspects of Economic and Social Modelling.* Geneva: Librairie Druz.

Stone, R. 1985. "The disaggregation of the household sector in the national accounts." In *Social Accounting Matrices: A Basis for Planning*, edited by G. Pyatt and J. Round. Washington, D.C.: The World Bank.

Stone, R. and A. Brown. 1965. "Behavioural and technical change in economic models." In *Problems in Economic Development*, edited by E.A.G. Robinson. London: Macmillan.

Taylor, L. 1990. "Structuralist CGE models." In *Socially Relevant Policy Analysis: Structuralist Computable General Equilibrium Models for the Developing World*, edited by L. Taylor. Cambridge, Massachusetts: MIT Press.

Thorbecke, E. 1985. "The social accounting matrix and consistency-type planning models." In *Social Accounting Matrices: A Basis for Planning*, edited by G. Pyatt and J. Round. Washington, D.C.: The World Bank.

United Nations Statistical Office. 1968. *A System of National Accounts*. New York: United Nations.

United States Department of Commerce. 1984. "The input–output structure of the U.S. economy, 1977." *Survey of Current Business* 64:42–84.

5

Partial Equilibrium Modeling

Joseph F. Francois and H. Keith Hall

I Introduction

By definition, partial equilibrium models do not take into account many of the factors emphasized in general equilibrium trade theory. While this is the root of the practical limitations of applied partial equilibrium modeling, it is also the source of its basic advantage. By focusing on a very limited set of factors, such as a few prices and policy variables, applied partial equilibrium models allow for relatively rapid and transparent analysis of a wide range of commercial policy issues. As long as the limitations of the approach are kept in mind, useful insights can often be drawn under time and data constraints that preclude more complex forms of analysis. In many circumstances, in fact, it may be difficult to justify devoting otherwise scarce resources to more complex and less transparent models, when they may yield only marginal extensions of the basic insights drawn from simpler approaches. In other situations, such as econometric exercises, it may simply be impossible to introduce general equilibrium constraints to the relevant market equations.

Our primary objective in this chapter is to present basic techniques for a relatively simple, partial equilibrium approach to comparative static analysis of commercial policy. However, while our ultimate goal is partial equilibrium analysis, we start by grounding the modeling framework in standard general equilibrium trade theory. Our intent is to use trade theoretic concepts as a reference point, both to offer general equilibrium interpretations for "'partial" equilibrium measures related to welfare and to make explicit what limitations we adopt when we choose this type of approach. Standard partial equilibrium welfare measures are linked explicitly in this chapter to the framework for welfare measurement developed in Chapter 3. Throughout this chapter, we ignore issues related to externalities and imperfect competition. These issues are covered in later chapters, particularly those dealing with imperfect competition, dynamics, employment, and the environment. Multi-market extensions of the basic framework developed here are offered in Chapter 8.

A number of variations on the theme of applied partial equilibrium modeling are covered in this chapter. They serve to illustrate not only different approaches to modeling competition between imports and domestic goods (i.e., perfect and imperfect substitute models), but the implications of different solution strategies, including both linear and non-linear specifications. Both sets of issues are revisited in later chapters on more complex models. The chapter is organized as follows: We first explore formal linkages between general equilibrium trade theory and simple partial equilibrium models. We then develop a simple perfect substitutes model and an imperfect substitutes (Armington) model. Both model types are implemented on spreadsheets. Finally, an application in which the analysis of U.S. protection of the steel industry is contrasted under alternative approaches is offered.

II Tariffs, Imports, and Welfare

II.1 Income and Expenditures in an Open Economy

Consider a country trading with the rest of the world, facing a set of world prices P^*. Making standard assumptions, we can then specify a national income or GDP function as follows:

$$GDP = R(v, P) + \tau \tag{5.1}$$

where v is the national resource base, P represents internal prices and τ represents tariff revenue.[1] With tariffs t we then also have

$$P = P^*(1+t) \tag{5.2}$$

We assume that we are able to specify a single measure of national welfare W in terms of prices and income. We therefore are going to abstract away from issues of income distribution (see Chapter 10). We define the expenditure function in terms of prices P and welfare W. The expenditure function relates national expenditures to welfare and prices and represents the minimum level of expenditure necessary, at internal prices P, to achieve welfare level W. Formally, we have the following condition:

1 The approach followed here follows Dixit and Norman (1980). See Dixit and Norman for a discussion of the properties of national revenue and expenditure functions, and the assumptions typically made to keep them well behaved.

$$GDP = E(P,W) \tag{5.3}$$

Combining equations (5.1) and (5.3) relates national income to expenditures. This is simply the dual expression of the more familiar condition that the value of national income (plus any transfers) will equal the total value of final expenditures and represents the national budget constraint.

$$R(v,P) + \tau = E(P,W) \tag{5.4}$$

We can extend the basic system further. In particular, from Hotelling's Lemma, we know that domestic output of good X^1 will be

$$X^1(P,v) = \frac{\partial R}{\partial P^1} = R_{p^1} \tag{5.5}$$

At the same time, domestic demand for goods x can be derived, again in equilibrium, from equation (5.3).

$$C^1(P,W) = E_{p^1} \tag{5.6}$$

Combining equations (5.5) and (5.6), we have import demand, defined in general equilibrium as the difference between consumption and domestic production:

$$M^{D1} = E_{p^1} - R_{p^1} \tag{5.7}$$

Equation (5.7) tells us that, properly defined, an import demand function represents the reduced form, general equilibrium excess demand for that good. In Figure 5.1, we have represented this with the curve M^{D1}, which plots import demand as a function of changes in internal prices for the good. As developed, the curve represents the reduced form response of import demand to changes in prices in the import market. To close the system, we have drawn import supply as the curve M^{S1}.

Tariffs

Next, consider the role of tariffs in this framework. We can show (Dixit and Norman 1980, Chapter 4) that, when we introduce a tariff on good 1 from a free trade equilibrium, the marginal welfare effects of the tariff can be represented by the following equation:

$$E_W dW = t \cdot dM - M \cdot dP^*$$
$$= t^1 \cdot dM^1 - M^1 \cdot dP^{1*} \tag{5.8}$$

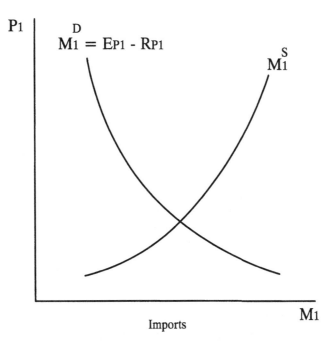

Figure 5.1. *Import market equilibrium*

The term $E_w dW$ provides a measure, at world prices, of the welfare/ income effect of the tariff. Technically, it refers to the equivalent variation for small tariff changes around the region of the free trade equilibrium.[2] At free trade prices and income, it measures the additional income gain or loss necessary to achieve a change in welfare equivalent to that realized by the introduction of the tariff from free trade. The first term on the right side of equation (5.8) measures the cost of consumption distortions to intermediate and final consumers, while the second measures terms of trade effects.

For a large tariff T_1, the welfare impact of the tariff may be approximated from the condition represented by equation (5.8), where we treat the introduction of the tariff in "small," incremental steps. This is by no means an exact measure, though it is a common one, with deep theoretical roots in linearization through differential calculus. In particular, this approach yields a total welfare effect ΔW measured as follows:

$$\Delta W = \int_0^{T^1} \left[t^1 \cdot \frac{dM}{dt^1} \right] dt^1 - \int_0^{T^1} \left[M(t^1) \cdot \frac{dP^*}{dt^1} \right] dt^1 \tag{5.9}$$

2 See Martin in Chapter 3 for a fuller discussion of alternative welfare measures under general equilibrium.

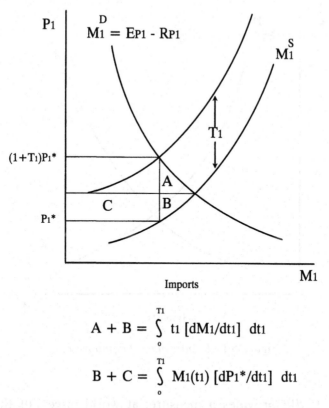

$$A + B = \int_0^{T_1} t_1 \, [dM_1/dt_1] \, dt_1$$

$$B + C = \int_0^{T_1} M_1(t_1) \, [dP_1^*/dt_1] \, dt_1$$

Figure 5.2. *Welfare and distributional effects of a tariff*

This has been represented in Figure 5.2, where

$$\int_0^{T^1} \left[t^1 \cdot \frac{dM^1}{dt^1} \right] dt^1 = A + B \qquad (5.10)$$

and

$$\int_0^{T^1} \left[M^1(t^1) \cdot \frac{dP^{1*}}{dt^1} \right] dt^1 = B + C \qquad (5.11)$$

Geometrically, the welfare impact of a tariff is defined, for very small changes in a tariff, by the total of areas $(C + B) = (A + B) = (C - A)$. For the case of real changes in tariffs, which in general are not infinitesimally small, the areas C and A are often assumed to serve as a reasonable approximation of welfare changes. For a small country, where world prices are assumed to be fixed, the second term in equation (5.8), which reflects terms of trade effects, will be zero, and the welfare impact of a tariff is then measured directly by area A in the second panel of Figure 5.2.

II.2 Welfare Triangles

The area A is commonly referred to as a welfare triangle. While we have grounded it in general equilibrium theory, in application the full general equilibrium definition of import demand found in equation (5.7) is usually replaced by a much simpler specification:

$$M^{D1} = M^{D1}\left(P^1, P^{S_1}\right) \qquad (5.12)$$

In equation (5.12), P^{S_1} represents a price index for close substitute products for the import i. In some cases, P^{S1} may also be dropped from the import demand equation. Given equation (5.12), and an appropriate import supply function M^{S1}, we can specify the complete equilibrium in a single market as follows:

$$M^{D1}\left(P^1\right) = M^{S1}\left(P^1\right) \qquad (5.13)$$

Geometrically, the equilibrium condition still looks like Figure 5.2. The welfare effect of a tariff can be still be addressed by using the areas A and C as simple metrics. Rather than solving for exact areas, however, a further abstraction is often adopted, wherein we recognize that the area A is approximately equal to a triangle defined as follows:

$$A \approx \frac{1}{2} \cdot \left(M^1 - M^{1'}\right)\left(\left(P^{1*\prime} + T^1\right) - P^{1*}\right) \qquad (5.14)$$

Even as such a model is expanded to include related domestic sectors, a basic sense of the welfare effects of a single tariff often can still be captured by equation (5.14) and related terms-of-trade effects in the primary market. As we introduce related markets, changes in tariffs and imports in those markets can also be used as a proxy for the secondary effects of changes in the primary market (see Chapter 3).

Equation (5.14) can also be derived from the balance of trade function (see Chapter 3). Returning to equations (5.3) and (5.4), and ignoring any net transfers, the balance of trade function for a small country is defined as

$$B = z\left(p, W, v\right) - \left(\frac{\partial z}{\partial P}\right)\left(P - P^*\right)$$
$$= z - z_P\left(P - P^*\right) \qquad (5.15)$$

where we have defined $z(\cdot) = e(\cdot) - R(\cdot)$, and where external prices are fixed. The second term simply represents tariff revenues t. When considering the effect of discrete changes in the level of protection on the balance of trade function from a free-trade equilibrium, the second term can be dropped. Recall from Chapter 3 that the change in the balance of trade function provides a money measure of the change in welfare resulting from a tariff change. Using a second-order Taylor Series expansion (and ignoring third derivatives), we can approximate the discrete change in B for an arbitrary change in the tariff rate through a variation of equation (3.11):

$$\Delta B \approx z_P \Delta P - z_{PP}\left(P - P^*\right)\Delta P$$

$$- z_P \Delta P - \left(\frac{1}{2}\right) z_{PP}\left(\Delta P\right)^2 \qquad (5.16)$$

$$\approx \left(\frac{1}{2}\right)\left(\frac{\partial M^{D1}}{\partial P_1}\right)\Delta P_1^2$$

Equation (5.16) involves several simplifications. First, we have assumed that we start from an initial free trade equilibrium, so that $(P-P^*)=0$. We have also ignored secondary cross-price effects, so that the term z_P collapses to the net import function in equation (5.7).

Note that, defining the elasticity of demand as $\eta=(\Delta M/\Delta P)(P/M)$, and defining quantities so that $P=1$, equation (5.14) (and identically equation [5.16]) can be respecified as follows:[3]

$$C \approx \Delta B \approx -\left(\frac{1}{2}\right)\eta M_0^{D1}\left(\Delta P_1\right)^2 \qquad (5.17)$$

where M_0^{D1} is demand given free trade in the market for good 1.

At this point, it is worth summarizing some of the steps we have taken in moving from general equilibrium theory to partial equilibrium application. Our derivation of both equations (5.8) and (5.17) has followed from the assumption that we can ignore cross-price effects in other markets. In addition, in adopting specific functional forms for import demand and export supply functions that are only defined over certain key prices (as developed later), we are deliberately *not* modeling explicit linkages between the sector(s) modeled and the rest of the economy. In principle, the import demand function reflects underlying economywide linkages, which determine the local elasticity of the import demand function. In practice, however, such linkages are effectively sterilized when we turn to model implementation.

---

3 For further discussion of welfare measurement in partial equilibrium trade models, see Rousslang and Suomela (1984).

III A Perfect Substitutes Model

We now turn to two alternative approaches to implementing a partial equilibrium model. The differences between the two relate to the specification of linkages between imports in a particular market and competing domestic production. We start with the assumption of homogenous goods. In particular, we initially assume that imports are perfect substitutes for domestic production.

III.1 The Model

Assuming that elasticities are constant, we define the import and domestic market as follows:

$$\text{Domestic demand:} \quad Q^D = Q^D(P) = K^D(P)^{\eta^D} \tag{5.18}$$

$$\text{Domestic supply:} \quad Q^S = Q^S(P) = K^S(P)^{\varepsilon^S} \tag{5.19}$$

$$\text{Import demand:} \quad M^D = Q^D(P) - Q^S(P) \tag{5.20}$$

$$\text{Import supply:} \quad M^S = M^S(P*) = K^{MS}(P*)^{\varepsilon^{MS}} \tag{5.21}$$

$$\text{Price equation:} \quad P*(1+t+w) = P \tag{5.22}$$

where t represents a tariff wedge, and w represents a quota price wedge. The terms K^D, K^S, and K^{MS} are constants, while the exponential terms ε are elasticities. We have assumed quota rights held by exporters (such as a voluntary export restraint), with tariffs applied in addition to the quota price wedge.

If we are willing to accept a linear approximation, we can derive the following alternative specification in log form:

$$\text{Import Supply:} \quad \ln(M^S) = \ln(K^{MS}) + \varepsilon^{MS}\ln(P)$$
$$-\varepsilon^{MS}\ln(1+t+w) \tag{5.23}$$

$$\text{Import Demand:} \quad \ln(M^D) = \ln(K^{MD}) + \eta^{MD}\ln(P)$$

$$\text{where} \quad \eta^{MD} = \left[\frac{\left(\eta^D K^D - \varepsilon^S K^S\right)}{K^{MD}}\right] \tag{5.24}$$

Domestic Demand: $\ln(Q^D) = \ln(K^D) + \eta^D \ln(P)$ (5.25)

Domestic Supply: $\ln(Q^S) = \ln(K^S) + \varepsilon^S \ln(P)$ (5.26)

Note that, while we have specified the log-linear system in levels, the price and quantity system can also (identically) be specified in terms of differences, where ε^i measures relevant elasticities with respect to price. Without specifying particular functional forms, the linear system can then serve as a "locally general" linear approximation for more general functional forms for import supply and demand. In particular, when $g=g(P)$ and we define the elasticity $\eta^{gp}=(dg/dP)(P/g)$, then for small changes $\eta^{gp}=(d\ln(g)/d\ln(P))$, and hence $d\ln(g)=\eta^{gp}d\ln(P)$. Complex models, even general equilibrium models, are sometimes solved by using this type of linearization.[4] The advantage is that, for small policy changes around the region of an initial equilibrium, estimates can be obtained as part of a simple linear programming problem. An important shortcoming of this approach, even in single-market models, is the linearization error that can be introduced with large policy shocks.

From the non-linear system defined by equations (5.18)–(5.22), we can solve the system for price P, yielding the following non-linear equation:

$$K^{MS}(P)^{\varepsilon^{MS}}(1+t+w)^{-\varepsilon^{MS}} + K^S(P)^{\varepsilon^S} - K^D(P)^{\eta^D} = 0 \qquad (5.27)$$

Alternatively, we can solve equations (5.23)–(5.26) directly for the log of price P, yielding the following:

$$\ln(P) = \left[\varepsilon^{MS} - \eta^{MD}\right]^{-1}\left[\ln(K^{MD}) - \ln(K^{MS}) + \varepsilon^{MS}\ln(1+t+w)\right] \quad (5.28)$$

From either of these, a solution for the full system of equations can be obtained by first solving for the internal import price and then using the solution for price to solve for quantities. While the log-linear solution offers certain advantages related to generality and computational complexity, when compared to specific functional forms, such as constant elasticity demand and supply functions, linearization can include substantial linearization error. This is particularly true with large policy shocks.

Table 5.1 presents a spreadsheet implementation of the model, in both linear and non-linear form. The implications of linearization can be seen by comparison of the linear and non-linear results in the table, which can diverge dramatically as policy shocks increase. Corresponding to Table

---

4 For example, the SALTER/GTAP model, a large multi-region general equilibrium model, can be solved as a linearized system. See Hertel (1996).

Table 5.1. *A perfect substitutes model*

A	A	B	C	D	E	F	G	H
1		**Inputs**					**corrosion resistant steel**	

3	6373		Benchmark sales of the domestic industry
4	7800		Benchmark total sales (domestic origin and imported)
6	3		Es: Elasticity of domestic supply
7	1.5		Ed: Elasticity of demand
8	15		Ems: Elasticity of import supply
10	10.30%		Initial tariff
11	10.30%		New tariff
13	0.00%		Initial foreign-held quota price wedge
14	27.60%		Final foreign-held quota price wedge

(Solve)

Calibrated values

6.4E+03	Ks : domestic supply constant term
7.8E+03	Kd: total demand constant term
6.2E+03	Kms: import supply constant term
1.4E+03	Kmd: import demand constant term
1.4E+03	Md: Import demand
2.2E+01	Emd: elasticity of import demand

Counterfactual equilibrium price

1.096	Linear domestic price solution:
1.043	Non-linear domestic price solution
-9.0E-08	non-linear optimization constraint (excess supply)
0.961	Free trade price (linear)
0.951	Free-trade price (nonlinear)
1.0E-07	non-linear free trade constraint

Welfare and Output Comparisons

	linear	nonlinear
National income effects: old regime		
welfare triangle	-38.83	-36.67
terms-of-trade effect	133.26	133.26
quota rent transfers	0.00	0.00
Total national income effect	94.43	96.58
National income effects: new regime		
welfare triangle	-226.10	-131.99
terms-of-trade effect	16.53	15.73
quota rent transfers	-12.03	-11.45
Total national income effect	-221.61	-127.71
Net welfare effect	-316.04	-224.29
percent change in border price of imports	9.59%	4.29%
percent change in internal price	9.59%	4.29%
percent change in imports	-96.15%	-96.34%
percent change in domestic output	31.60%	13.44%
old tariff revenues	$133.26	$133.26
new tariff revenues	$4.49	$4.27

note: Border prices are f.o.b., and measure prices prior to the application of the quota premium. Terms-of-trade effects are also prior to quota rent deductions.

5.1, Appendix Table 5A.1 presents the programming structure of the spreadsheet, including cell references and formulas. In the spreadsheet, the system is first calibrated, meaning that the constant terms in the various equations are derived from the benchmark equilibrium data. We have employed a common normalization, which involves defining quantities so that price is equal to 1. This means that, when calibrating the model, most of the relevant constant terms are simply equal to initial benchmark dollar values. Welfare comparisons involve using welfare triangles – see equation (5.17) – and the corresponding terms-of-trade effect term. Quotas imply some transfer of rents, which are also included in the calculations. The spreadsheet uses the "Solve" option of Quattro Pro, a commercially available spreadsheet package. Other commercial spreadsheets offer similar utilities for solving a non-linear equation, or for solving a simple system of equations subject to a set of constraints. An alternative would be to use the non-linear optimizer, which is also included with most spreadsheet packages, where equation (5.27) defines the objective function. Other options involve programming the model in a non-linear optimization package, such as GAMS/MINOS or GAMS/MPSGE (Rutherford 1994a,b).

In structuring the spreadsheet, we have assumed that quotas are binding and can be modeled as export taxes. Tariffs and quota premiums are applied additively to world prices. This means that, when tariffs are used to recapture quota rents fully, one simply replaces the binding quota with an equally binding tariff. In general, attention must be paid to whether or not a quota is the binding constraint, and the extent to which tariffs recapture quota rents.

III.2 Welfare Calculations in a Second-Best World

Recall from our discussion of equations (5.8) and (5.17) that we assumed that we were starting from an undistorted equilibrium. In the presence of an initial distortion, the welfare impact of a new tariff or quota is complicated by the existence of the initial distortion. This is illustrated in Figure 5.3. In the figure, we assume an initial tariff for a small country at t_1, such that the internal price is $P=(1+t_1)P^*$, where P^* is world price. If we introduce an additional tariff t_2, so that $P=(1+t_1+t_2)$, the welfare impact will include the welfare triangle A. However, the new tariff also magnifies the impact of the initial distortion, resulting in additional welfare loss B. This highlights an important point. In many instances, it is difficult to justify comparing one tariff to another in isolation from related trade policies in the same market. To account for this, the spreadsheet in Table 5.1 calculates the welfare

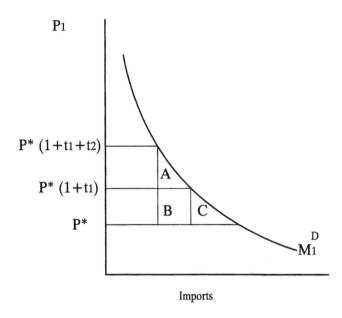

Figure 5.3. *The incremental effect of a tariff with an existing distortion*

implications of the benchmark regime relative to free trade and compares it
to the counterfactual regime's implications relative to free trade. In terms of
Figure 5.3, we compare triangle C, derived from tariff t_1, to triangle
$(A+B+C)$, derived from tariff (t_1+t_2). Hence, in Table 5.1, the welfare
equations in the spreadsheet are based on these calculations with reference
to a non-distorted trade equilibrium and reflect a comparison of compensating variations for free trade options. Of course, it is not necessary to include
these calculations within the spreadsheet itself. As an alternative, one could
simply calculate and compare the welfare implications of various regimes,
including the status quo, relative to free trade. With relatively large
spreadsheet models, such an approach may allow more flexibility in implementing other aspects of the model.

In the world of second best, underlying distortions can carry very important implications for policy initiatives. In the presence of a quota, for example, a tariff may improve welfare by re-capturing quota rents. This is illustrated in Table 5.2, which reports simulation results, for a set of hypothetical
import data, when a new 10 percent tariff or an equally restrictive voluntary
export restraint is introduced. The trade flow data and elasticities are the
same in all examples. The only difference is the initial underlying protection.
For the new tariff, note that when the tariff replaces an existing voluntary

Table 5.2. *Impact of a new 10 percent tariff*

perfect substitutes model

	Case 1	Case 2	Case 3	Case 4	Case 5
Benchmark data					
Benchmark sales of the domestic industry	1000.00	1000.00	1000.00	1000.00	1000.00
Benchmark total sales	2000.00	2000.00	2000.00	2000.00	2000.00
Es: Elasticity of domestic supply	3.00	3.00	3.00	3.00	3.00
Ed: Elasticity of demand	2.00	2.00	2.00	2.00	2.00
Ems: Elasticity of import supply	10.00	10.00	10.00	10.00	10.00
Initial tariff	0.00	0.10	0.00	0.10	0.50
New tariff	0.10	0.20	0.10	0.20	0.60
Initial foreign-held quota price wedge	0.00	0.00	0.10	0.10	0.00
Final foreign-held quota price wedge	0.00	0.00	0.00	0.00	0.00
Counterfactual simulation results					
National income effects: old regime					
welfare triangle	0.00	-12.29	-12.29	-48.38	-271.93
terms-of-trade effect	0.00	90.91	90.91	166.67	333.33
quota rent transfers	0.00	0.00	-90.91	-83.33	0.00
Total national income effect	0.00	78.62	-12.29	34.96	61.40
National income effects: new regime					
welfare triangle	-15.52	-52.26	-12.29	-48.38	-376.94
terms-of-trade effect	39.01	77.01	90.91	166.67	211.70
quota rent transfers	0.00	0.00	0.00	0.00	0.00
Total national income effect	23.49	24.76	78.62	118.29	-165.24
Net welfare effect	23.49	-53.86	90.91	83.33	-226.64
percent change in border price of imports	-4.34%	-3.93%	-9.09%	-8.33%	-2.84%
percent change in internal price	5.22%	4.80%	-0.00%	-0.00%	3.63%
percent change in imports	-59.43%	-56.10%	-0.00%	-0.00%	-45.65%
percent change in domestic output	16.50%	15.11%	-0.00%	-0.00%	11.30%
old tariff revenues	0.00	90.91	0.00	83.33	333.33
new tariff revenues	39.01	77.01	90.91	166.67	211.70

Case 1: No initial underlying protection.
Case 2: Initial 10% tariff.
Case 3: Quota-rent recapture, no initial tariffs.
Case 4: Quota rent recapture, with initial tariff.
Case 5: Initial 50% tariff.

export restraint, the tariff improves welfare for the importer by capturing quota rents. In the example, when the initial equilibrium involves free trade, a small tariff improves welfare through terms-of-trade effects. However, when there is already a large initial tariff, the effect of the new 10 percent tariff is to reduce welfare. Because of quota rent transfers, the new "equivalent" quota carries more adverse welfare implications than the new tariff.[5]

The interaction of existing distortions illustrated in the table highlights the importance of underlying distortions. When working in a single-market model, we are limited to the interaction of various distortions within the market being examined. At the same time, there may be other distortions that, while significant and related to the present market, carry important implications for equilibria in other markets. This may justify movement away from a single-market model, and toward a multi-market partial equilibrium model (Chapter 8) or a simple general equilibrium model (Chapter 6). At a minimum, these issues must be taken into account when the modeling framework is first chosen.

IV Armington Models

A common alternative to the perfect substitutes model involves more complex specification of the markets for related products. Two tacks are often followed here. One involves the analysis of upstream and downstream markets; the other involves the analysis of competing products. Upstream and downstream linkages are explored in later chapters, both in partial and in general equilibrium. We focus in this section on horizontal linkages between markets.

We follow Armington (1969) in assuming well behaved preferences over a weakly separable product category that comprises similar, but not identical products. These imperfect substitutes are differentiated by their country of origin. The first version of the model is a log-linear version with constant own and cross-price elasticities of demand. This type of approach is relatively standard, and is followed in a number of spreadsheet-based partial equilibrium models, including the CADIC dumping model (Boltuck, 1991) and the COMPAS model (Francois and Hall, 1993). The second version of the model is specified as a non-linear system with a constant elasticity of substitution between products.

IV.1 A Log-Linear Specification

We start with an n good model, separating the product category into market segments by country of origin: domestic products (good 1) and imports (goods $2 \ldots n$). Further, all price elasticities of demand are assumed con-

---

5 One compelling reason for shifting from single-market models to multi-market models (partial or general equilibrium) is the type of policy interaction demonstrated in Table 5.2. Other policy variables, such as consumption or factor income taxes, can carry similar, though more complex, implications.

stant as in the preceding perfect substitutes model and may therefore be represented in log-linear form as follows:

Price Equation: $\qquad P_i = P_i^*(1 + t_i + w_i), \qquad i \neq 1$ $\hfill$ (5.29)

Domestic Supply: $\qquad \ln(Q_1^S) = K_1^S + \varepsilon_1^S \ln(P_1)$ $\hfill$ (5.30)

Import Supply: $\qquad \ln(Q_i^S) = K_i^S + \varepsilon_i^S \ln(P_i^*), \qquad i \neq 1$ $\hfill$ (5.31)

Domestic Demand: $\qquad \ln(Q_1^D) = K_1^D + N_1 \ln(P_1) + \sum_{j \neq 1} N_{1j} \ln(P_j)$ $\hfill$ (5.32)

Import Demand: $\qquad \ln(Q_i^D) = K_i^D + N_i \ln(P_i) + \sum_{j \neq 1} N_{ij} \ln(P_j), \qquad i \neq 1$

$\hfill$ (5.33)

where each K is a constant and N_{ij} is the total price j elasticity of demand for product i.

Separability For the price elasticities of demand to be constant, we assume that demand for each product within the industry is a function of industry prices and total expenditure alone:

$$Q_i^D = D_i(P_i, P_{j,j \neq 1}, y)$$ $\hfill$ (5.34)

where y is total industry expenditure. In individual consumer theory, this would result from the assumption of weakly separable preferences.[6] Differentiating with respect to price j we get

$$\frac{dD_i}{dP_j} = \frac{\partial D_i}{\partial P_j} + \frac{\partial D_i}{\partial y}\frac{\partial y}{\partial P_j}$$ $\hfill$ (5.35)

This can be rearranged to describe total price elasticity of demand as a function of the partial price elasticity of demand holding industry expenditures fixed:

$$N_{ij} = \eta_{ij} + \eta_{iy}\eta_{yj}$$ $\hfill$ (5.36)

where N_{ij} is the total price elasticity of demand, η_{ij} is the partial price j elasticity of demand for product i (holding y fixed), η_{iy} is the industry

---

6 Note that there is no utility function from which log-linear demand functions can be generally derived for all commodities. See Green (1978).

expenditure elasticity of demand for product i, and η_{yj} is the price j elasticity of industry expenditure.

With well behaved preferences, we can convert the partial price elasticities of demand into substitution elasticities using the Slutsky decomposition of partial demand

$$\eta_{ij} = \eta_{ij}^* - \theta_j \eta_{iy} \tag{5.37}$$

(where η_{ij}^* is the compensated partial price j elasticity of demand for product i and θ_j is the product j share of industry expenditures) and conditional Allen elasticities of substitution[7] to get

$$N_{ij} = \theta_j \sigma_{ij} + \eta_{iy} \left(\eta_{yj} - \theta_j \right) \tag{5.38}$$

From the zero homogeneity property of Hicksian demand (see Henderson and Quandt, 1980, p. 33) we can use the fact that

$$\sum_j \eta_{ij}^* = 0$$

to substitute

$$-\sum_{j \neq 1} \eta_{ij}^*$$

for η_{ii} to obtain

$$N_{ii} = -\left(\sum_{j \neq i} \theta_j \sigma_{ij} \right) + \eta_{iy} \left(\eta_{yi} - \theta_i \right) \tag{5.39}$$

Two-Stage Budgeting Equation (5.39) can be further simplified with the additional assumption of homothetic preferences for industry expenditures, which, along with the assumption of weak separability, is sufficient for two-stage budgeting (see Shiells et al., 1986). We can therefore define price and quantity indexes P and $Q(P)$ over all prices P_i from the first stage utility maximization problem, and substitute them into the definition of the price j elasticity of industry expenditures as follows:

$$\eta_{yj} \equiv \frac{\partial y}{\partial P_j} \frac{P_j}{y}$$

$$= \frac{\partial (PQ)}{\partial P_j} \frac{P_j}{y} = \left(\frac{\partial P}{\partial P_j} Q + \frac{\partial Q}{\partial P} \frac{\partial P}{\partial P_j} P \right) \frac{P_j}{y} \tag{5.40}$$

---

7 Allen elasticities are defined as $\sigma_{ij} = \eta_{ij}/\theta_j$.

Homotheticity of preferences implies that income elasticity of demand for every product is 1 (again see Shiells et al.), so that if we define NA as the aggregate demand elasticity for products in the industry with respect to industry price index P, Shepard's Lemma leads to

$$\frac{\partial P}{\partial P_j} = \frac{Q_j}{Q} \tag{5.41}$$

which can be substituted into the previous equation to obtain

$$\eta_{yj} = \theta_j \left(1 + NA\right) \tag{5.42}$$

Both results can be substituted into (5.37) and (5.38) to obtain

$$N_{ij} = \theta_j \left(\sigma_{ij} + NA\right) \quad \text{for } i \neq j \tag{5.43}$$

$$N_{ii} = \theta_i NA - \sum_{j \neq i} \theta_j \sigma_{ij} \tag{5.44}$$

Constant Industry Expenditures Alternatively, rather than adding the assumption of homothetic preferences for industry expenditures we could assume that industry expenditures are fixed ($\eta_{yj}=0$) and obtain the following:

$$N_{ij} = \theta_j \left(\sigma_{ij} - \eta_{iy}\right) \quad \text{for } i \neq j \tag{5.45}$$

$$N_{ii} = -\theta_i \eta_{iy} - \sum_{j \neq i} \theta_j \sigma_{ij} \tag{4.46}$$

Implementation Working with either equations (5.43)–(5.44) or alternatively equations (5.45)–(5.46), the elasticity parameters in equations (5.29)–(5.33) can be calculated from a relatively small number of parameters: the elasticity of substitution σ, the composite demand elasticity NA, and market share data. If we scale quantities so that prices are unity, then the constant terms are simply equal to market revenues.

A warning is called for here. Examination of equation (5.43) should make it apparent that theory suggests an important relationship between composite demand elasticities and low-tier substitution elasticities. In particular, if the lower-tier substitution elasticity is *smaller* than the upper-tier composite demand elasticity NA, then "competing" goods will be net complements instead of net substitutes. Basically, with relatively low substitution elasticities, the composite price effects related to trade liberalization will dominate cross-price effects. Hence, while there may be some substitution away from the domestic product and toward imports, the net effect of a tariff reduction will be an increase in demand for the domestic product caused by increased expenditures on the category. This result is the "Henning conundrum," which refers to cases where models yield increased demand for domestic goods when tariffs on competing imports are reduced. Equation (5.43) identifies a constraint (the Henning conundrum constraint) sufficient to rule out such results, particularly $\sigma > |NA|$.

IV.2 A Non-Linear Specification

As an alternative, we can also specify an Armington model as a system of non-linear equations. We first define the Armington composite good, q, as a CES composite of the domestic good $X1$, and of imports Xi from countries $i=2 \ldots n$.

$$q = \left[\sum_{i=1}^{n} \alpha_i X_i^{\rho} \right]^{1/\rho} \tag{5.47}$$

In calibrating the model, we again scale quantities so that internal prices are all unity in the benchmark. This includes the price for the Armington composite good q. The price index for the composite good can be shown to equal

$$P = \left[\sum_{i=1}^{n} \alpha_i^{\sigma} P_i^{1-\sigma} \right]^{1-1/\rho} \tag{5.48}$$

At the same time, from the first-order conditions, the demand for good Xi can be shown to equal

$$x_i = \left[\frac{\alpha_i}{P_i} \right]^{\sigma} \left[\sum_{i=1}^{n} \alpha_i P_i^{1-\sigma} \right]^{-1} Y$$

$$= \left[\frac{\alpha_i}{P_i} \right]^{\sigma} P^{\sigma-1} Y, \qquad \text{where } \rho = 1 - \left(\frac{1}{\sigma} \right) \tag{5.49}$$

Combined with supply equations, these terms can be used to define a simple non-linear system in terms of prices. In particular, if we specify supply as a function with constant supply elasticity ε_{si}, then excess demand conditions in each market are defined as follows:

$$\left[\frac{\alpha_i}{P_i} \right]^{\sigma} P^{\sigma-1} Y - K_{si} P_i^{\varepsilon_{si}} = 0 \tag{5.50}$$

At the same time, the composite price equation can be re-written as follows:

$$\left[\sum_{i=1}^{n} \alpha_i^\sigma P_i^{1-\sigma} \right]^{1-1/\rho} - P = 0 \tag{5.51}$$

Finally, if we define demand for the composite good as

$$q = k_A P^{NA} \tag{5.52}$$

where NA is the elasticity of demand for the composite good, then we can specify excess demand for the composite good as follows: Note that, in equation (5.53), $Y=Pq$.

$$k_A P^{NA+1} - Y = 0 \tag{5.53}$$

Equations (5.50), (5.51), and (5.53) define a system of $(n+2)$ equations and $(n+2)$ unknowns. The system can be solved for prices, and solution prices can then used to solve for quantities and welfare measures.

Tariffs or other price-based measures of import protection can be added to the system through the import supply functions. This requires a slight modification of equation (5.50), as follows:

$$\left[\frac{\alpha_j}{P_j} \right]^\sigma P^{\sigma-1} Y - K_{si} \left(\frac{P_j}{(1+t_j)} \right)^{\varepsilon_{sj}} = 0 \qquad for\ j = 2 \ldots n \tag{5.54}$$

Table 5.3 presents a spreadsheet implementation of a non-linear Armington model with two import sources. The programming structure of the spreadsheet is detailed in Appendix Table 5A.2. Calibration is based on unit price normalization, so that all constants are equal to benchmark expenditures. The model is solved by using a spreadsheet-based non-linear solver provided with Quattro Pro (this feature is now common to most commercial spreadsheets). The non-linear solver is used to solve for the price of the composite good – equation (5.52) – subject to the constraint that all excess demands must equal zero (equations (5.50)–(5.51), and (5.54)). As constructed, the spreadsheet model must first be benchmarked, by means of a macro routine that sets initial guess values for the counterfactual value of variables on the basis of benchmark equilibrium values.

In Table 5.3, welfare measures are calculated on the basis of changes in trade policy regarding imports from country 2. This includes comparison of welfare triangles and terms-of-trade effects for the benchmark and counterfactual equilibrium, both with respect to a free trade equilibrium. As described in Chapter 3, the measure of the welfare effect of induced changes in

Table 5.3. *A non-linear imperfect substitutes (Armington) model*

C	A	B	C	D	E	F	G	H	I	J
1		**Inputs**				**corrosion resistant steel**				
2										
3		1716		Benchmark sales of X1 (i.e. domestic) industry						
4		228		Benchmark sales of country 2 imports						
5		56		Benchmark sales of country 3 imports						
6		2000		Benchmark total sales (domestic origin and imported)						
7										
8		1.5		NA: Composite elasticity of demand				(RE)CALIBRATE		
9		3		Es1: Elasticity of domestic supply						
10		15		Es2: Elasticity of country 2 import supply						
11		15		Es3: Elasticity of country 3 import supply						
12		3.08		σ: Elasticity of substitution				SOLVE		
13										
14		10.30%		t2,0: Initial tariff on country 2 imports						
15		10.30%		t3,0: Initial tariff on country 3 imports						
16		10.30%		t2,1: Final tariff on country 2 imports						
17		10.30%		t3,1: Final tariff on country 3 imports						
18										
19		0.00%		w2,0: Initial export tax/quota price wedge on country 2 imports						
20		0.00%		w3,0: Initial export tax/quota price wedge on country 3 imports						
21		55.70%		w2,1: Final export tax/quota price wedge on country 2 imports						
22		0.00%		w3,1: Final export tax/quota price wedge on country 3 imports						

Calibrated values

1.72E+03	Ks1 : domestic supply constant term	1.00	P1: calibrated domestic product market
9.92E+02	Ks2 : country 2 import supply constant term	1.00	P2: calibrated internal price for good 2
2.44E+02	Ks3 : country 3 import supply constant term	1.00	P3: calibrated internal price for good 3
2.00E+03	KD : composite demand constant term	0.91	P2*: calibrated country 2 border price
0.95	ω1: CES weight for domestic good	0.91	P3*: calibrated country 3 border price
0.49	ω2: CES weight for country 2 import	1.00	PA: calibrated composite good price
0.31	ω3: CES weight for country 3 import		

Counterfactual solution values

counterfactual	free-trade in X2		internal prices and Y	
Excess demands	excess demands		free trade in X2	counterfactual
5.3E-10	1.4E-10	P1: domestic product market	1.00	1.01
2.7E-07	7.0E-08	P2: good 2 market	0.92	1.41
2.0E-11	5.1E-12	P3: good 3 market	1.00	1.00
3.3E-12	3.7E-13	PA: composite good price	0.99	1.04
-2.3E-10	-6.2E-11	Y: total expenditure	2013.07	1962.55

Results

National income effects of policy change in market for X2:

	old regime	new regime	change
welfare triangle	-32.55	-155.74	-123.19
terms-of-trade effects	3.24	6.10	2.86
quota rent transfers	0.00	-39.84	-39.84
secondary effects for X3	*	0.27	0.27
Net welfare effect			-159.90

Price, quantity and tariff revenue effects of policy change in X2 market:

percent change in internal price of domestic good	0.99%
percent change in shipments of domestic good	2.99%
percent change in border price of good 2	-6.42%
percent change in internal price of good 2	40.84%
percent change in imports of good 2	-63.03%
percent change in border price of good 3	0.33%
percent change in internal price of good 3	0.33%
percent change in imports of good 3	5.08%
Change in tariff revenue	
tariffs in market for X2	-13.92
tariffs in market for X3	0.28
total change in tariff revenue	-13.64

note: Border prices are measured f.o.b., and are net of quota markups.

demand for imports of good 3 is based on induced changes in tariff revenue in the import market for good 3.

V An Application to U.S. Steel Protection

We turn to an applied example, focusing on U.S. steel imports. Since the early 1980s, U.S. steel imports have been subjected to a variety of import restraints (USITC, 1993a). In 1984, negotiations began on voluntary export restraints (VERs) on steel. Agreement was eventually reached with nineteen countries (including Portugal and Spain) and the European Community; these are listed in Table 5.4. The VER negotiations followed an episode where the U.S. steel industry threatened to file literally hundreds of antidumping and countervailing duty complaints. These involved the threat of massive litigation over alleged unfair pricing of imports. These unfair trade cases were terminated when the series of bilateral VERs were imposed. Because these quotas were "voluntary," they escaped GATT strictures on most favored nation (MFN) treatment and discriminatory protection. With exchange rate changes, the binding effects of these quotas were gradually eroded, and by the end of the 1980s, they had largely ceased to be binding. In 1989, the president announced his intention to phase out the VERs by March 31, 1992. With the loss of protection through quotas, the U.S. steel industry again pursued antidumping and countervailing duty actions. The result this time was not new VERs, but rather the imposition of antidumping and countervailing duty orders. Table 5.4 provides a comparison of the VERs and their subsequent replacement with antidumping and countervailing duties. This episode, with the transition from bilateral quotas to bilateral tariffs, offers an opportunity to compare and contrast the implications of importer and exporter administered protection.

Table 5.5 presents data on U.S. import trade in steel and existing tariffs in 1992. The results of the dumping investigations are also presented, as a set of trade-weighted tariffs. Simulation results are also presented in Table 5.6, under alternative assumptions about model structure and about the policy options undertaken. In particular, we have modeled the actual imposition of antidumping and countervailing duties, and the alternative imposition of identical restraints. Because we model quotas as an export tax, export quotas or price undertakings are operationally identical in this type of model.[8]

---

8 An alternative approach involves the explicit modeling of quotas, initially specified as slack constraints on imports. The constraint can then be tightened until it is binding. Under this type of approach, the import quantity is exogenously specified, while the resulting quota price wedge or export tax equivalent is endogenous. This can be done with a slack-complementarity solver, like GAMS/MPSGE (Rutherford, 1994a,b).

Table 5.4. *The expiration of VERs and the imposition of antidumping and countervailing duties*

Country	VER on exports of certain steel products 1984-92	Anti-dumping duty orders on certain flat-rolled steel products, 1993	Countervailing duty orders on certain flat-rolled steel products, 1993	Antidumping and/or countervailing orders on flat-rolled steel, 1993
Australia	yes	yes	no	yes
Austria	yes	no	no	no
Brazil	yes	yes	yes	yes
China	yes	no	no	no
Czechoslovakia	yes	no	no	no
European Community	yes	yes	yes	yes
Finland	yes	yes	no	yes
German Democratic Republic	yes	no	no	no
Hungary	yes	no	no	no
Japan	yes	no	no	no
Korea, Republic of	yes	yes	yes	yes
Mexico	yes	yes	yes	yes
Poland	yes	yes	no	yes
Romania	yes	yes	no	yes
Trinidad and Tobago	yes	no	no	no
Venezuela	yes	no	no	no
Yugoslavia	yes	no	no	no

Source: GATT secretariat (1994), Table IV.4.

Table 5.5. *Flat rolled steel products, 1992: summary of U.S. antidumping and countervailing duty actions*

	Plate	Hot-rolled	Cold-rolled	Corrosion resistant
Benchmark sales of domestic industry, 1992	1,716	13,369	10,318	6,373
Benchmark total sales (domestic and foreign)	2,000	14,500	11,300	7,800
Initial tariff on imports				
subject imports	0.103	0.103	0.103	0.103
non-subject imports	0.103	0.103	0.103	0.103
Benchmark subject imports, c.i.f.	228	1,021	884	1,308
Benchmark non-subject imports, c.i.f.	56	110	98	120
Trade weighted AD/CVD duties				
weighted by all imports	0.447	0.000	0.063	0.276
weighted by subject imports	0.557	0.000	0.070	0.302

note: imports are in millions of dollars for 1992, valued at internal market prices
Final duties were published in July 1993. See USITC (1993).

Table 5.6. *Comparison of tariffs and quotas*

national income effects, millions of dollars

	imports as perfect substitutes		imports as imperfect substitutes	
	tariffs	quotas	tariffs	quotas
cut-to-length steel plate	-42.3	-43.4	-120.6	-159.9
cold-rolled products	-49.5	-73.1	-72.32	-120.9
corrosion resistant product	-212.8	-224.3	-401.5	-596.5
Total	-304.6	-340.8	-594.42	-877.3

import effects, percent

	imports as perfect substitutes	imports as imperfect substitutes	
		subject imports	non-subject imports
cut-to-length steel plate	-99.4	-63	5.1
cold-rolled products	-56.1	-13.9	0.7
corrosion resistant products	-96.3	-43.4	5

note: Trade and domestic production data are all from Table 5.5. Application examples are shown in Tables 5.1 and 5.3, including the elasticities used. A substitution elasticity of 3.08 is used in the Armington model, based on Reinert and Roland-Holst (1992).

The implications of alternative model structures are highlighted in Table 5.6. The results are calculated by using the non-linear models presented in Tables 5.1 and 5.3. For a given policy shock, the largest trade impacts are realized in the perfect substitutes model. In contrast, the largest welfare impacts are identified under the imperfect substitutes model. As suggested by the relative trade impact, as we move to an imperfect substitutes framework, the impact of protection on the domestic industry is substantially less. This is because the degree of competition between imports and the domestic like product has been limited by the degree of substitution, which is now less than infinite.

While not highlighted in Table 5.6, it is important to recognize that the results generated by Armington models are particularly sensitive to the value of the parameter σ. This should be apparent from our earlier discussion of equation (5.43) and the Henning conundrum constraint. This can also be seen by comparing the results when $\sigma=3$ (the right set of results in Table 5.6) with the results when $\sigma\to\infty$ (the left set of results). We have drawn our Armington parameters from Reinert and Roland-Holst (1992). Other sources of estimates include Shiells and Reinert (1993) and Shiells, Deardorff, and Stern (1986). Estimates from Reinert and Roland-Holst are reproduced in Appendix Table 5A.3. The sensitivity of Armington parameters to the substitution elasticity carries over to large, general equilibrium models as well. In general equilibrium, the implications are more complex and carry over to the factor market and economywide terms-of-trade effects of trade liberalization. However, the roots of this central role for the substitution elasticity can be identified even in a simple partial equilibrium setting.

There are some qualitative results that are largely invariant to model structure. In particular, the imposition of tariffs is welfare superior, for the United States, to the imposition of identical protection through quotas or a price undertaking. This is because the latter involves the transfer of some of the rents generated by protection to the exporter. This also illustrates why, politically, export restraints are easier to agree on with an exporter than import restraints. Such rents offer partial "compensation" for reduced market access. When threatened with high, discriminatory tariffs (such as antidumping duties), an exporter may prefer to impose protection itself. Depending on the size of the rents at stake, an exporter may even prefer such "voluntary" restraints to free trade.

While not developed here, the welfare implications of alternative policy instruments can vary with extensions to the analytical framework employed in Table 5.6. For example, if we assume that domestic firms have market power, the imposition of a quota will have different implications for domestic production than a tariff (see Chapter 11). With quotas and a domestic monopolist, for example, protection may actually lead to a reduction in domestic production, as the monopolist raises his prices to take advantage of the protection offered by the quota.[9] Alternatively, shifts in the terms of trade due to exchange rate swings may also cause tariffs to carry different welfare implications than quotas.

VI Extensions

In this chapter, we have presented basic techniques for relatively simple, partial equilibrium modeling of commercial policy. The techniques are quite

---

9 See Chapters 2 and 10 for further discussion. Also see Krugman and Helpman (1989, Chapter 3) for a comparison of tariffs and quotas when protected domestic firms have market power.

flexible, and can be applied relatively quickly, and with a limited amount of information on trade flows and relevant parameter values. At the same time, the limitations of this type of analysis must also be taken into account. While the simplicity of these models implies relative transparency when compared to more complex models, such simplicity also limits the scope of the analysis.

The welfare measures we offer emphasize the trade-off between domestic distortions in consumption and terms-of-trade effects. However, these are not likely to be the only variables in an inherently political objective function. National income effects may, in fact, enter relatively far down the list of relevant factors considered by trade officials. More "immediate" trade and production effects may, for various reasons, be ranked higher. Still, as our applied example of U.S. steel protection illustrates, the tools developed here can identify options that help to minimize costs when protection is to be chosen from a range of policy instruments. These tools may also allow some exploration of the distributional implications, production effects, and terms-of-trade effects of various policy options.

The basic framework developed here can be extended in a number of directions, while still offering relative simplicity and transparency. The example of vertical market linkages and multi-region models is covered in Chapter 8. The basic framework developed here is also employed in the suite of spreadsheets that constitute the COMPAS model (Francois and Hall, 1993) for assessment of trade remedies. As long as limitations are kept in mind, this type of approach can also be employed for assessment of the welfare and production effects of trade regimes. Examples include research on U.S. import protection (USITC, 1989), the MFA (Martin and Suphachalasai, 1990; Cline, 1987), and the European Union's single market program (Commission of the European Communities, 1988).

Appendix 5.1

Table 5A.1. *Spreadsheet structure for Table 5.1*

A:B3:	6373
A:B4:	7800
A:B6:	3
A:B7:	1.5
A:B8:	15
A:B10:	0.103
A:B11:	0.103
A:B13:	0
A:B14:	0.276
A:B19:	(B3)
A:B20:	(B4)
A:B21:	(((1+B10+B13))^B8)*B23
A:B22:	(B23)
A:B23:	(B4-B3)
A:B24:	-(-(B7*B20)-(B6*B19))/(B22)
A:B29:	@EXP((1/($B$8+$B$24))*(@LN($B$22)-@LN($B$21)+($B$8*@LN((1+$B$11+$B$14)))))
A:B30:	1.0429239642158
A:C31:	($B$21*($B$30^$B$8)*(((1+$B$11+$B$14))^(-$B$8)))+(($B$19)*($B$30^$B$6))-($B$20*($B$30^(-$B$7)))
	))
A:B32:	@EXP((1/($B$8+$B$24))*(@LN($B$22)-@LN($B$21)+($B$8*@LN((1)))))
A:B33:	0.95108669942967
A:C34:	($B$21*($B$33^$B$8)*(((1))^(-$B$8)))+(($B$19)*($B$33^$B$6))-($B$20*($B$33^(-$B$7)))
A:F40:	((($B$21*($B$32^$B$8))-$B$23))*($B$32-1)*0.5
A:G40:	((($B$21*($B$33^$B$8))-$B$23))*($B$33-1)*0.5
A:F41:	(((1+B10+B13)-1)/((1+B10+B13)))*B23
A:G41:	(((1+B10+B13)-1)/((1+B10+B13)))*B23
A:F42:	-(B13/((1+B10+B13)))*B23
A:G42:	-(B13/((1+B10+B13)))*B23
A:F43:	@SUM(F40..F42)
A:G43:	@SUM(G40..G42)
A:F46:	((($B$21*($B$32^$B$8))-($B$23*(1+$F$55))))*($B$32-$B$29)*0.5
A:G46:	((($B$21*($B$33^$B$8))-($B$23*(1+$G$55))))*($B$33-$B$30)*0.5
A:F47:	(B29/((1+B11+B14)))*((1+B11+B14)-1)*(1+F55)*B23
A:G47:	(B30/((1+B11+B14)))*((1+B11+B14)-1)*(1+F55)*B23
A:F48:	-(B29/((1+B11+B14)))*(B14)*(1+F55)*B23
A:G48:	-(B30/((1+B11+B14)))*(B14)*(1+F55)*B23
A:F49:	@SUM(F46..F48)
A:G49:	@SUM(G46..G48)
A:F51:	(F49-F43)
A:G51:	(G49-G43)
A:F53:	((($B$29/(1+$B$11))-(1/(1+$B$10)))*(1+$B$10))
A:G53:	((($B$30/(1+$B$11))-(1/(1+$B$10)))*(1+$B$10))
A:F54:	($B$29-1)
A:G54:	($B$30-1)
A:F55:	(($B$21*($B$29/((1+$B$11+$B$14))^$B$8))-$B$23)/$B$23
A:G55:	(($B$21*($B$30/((1+$B$11+$B$14))^$B$8))-$B$23)/$B$23
A:F56:	(($B$19*($B$29^$B$6))-$B$3)/$B$3
A:G56:	(($B$19*($B$30^$B$6))-$B$3)/$B$3
A:F58:	(F41+F42)
A:G58:	(G41+G42)
A:F59:	(F47+F48)
A:G59:	(G47+G48)
A:A64:	'SOLVE MACRO
A:A65:	'{SolveFor.Formula_Cell A:C31}
A:A66:	'{SolveFor.Variable_Cell A:B30}
A:A67:	'{SolveFor.Target_Value 0}
A:A68:	'{SolveFor.Max_Iters 10}
A:A69:	'{SolveFor.Accuracy 5E-06}
A:A70:	'{SolveFor.Go}
A:A71:	'{SolveFor.Formula_Cell A:C34}
A:A72:	'{SolveFor.Variable_Cell A:B33}
A:A73:	'{SolveFor.Target_Value 0}
A:A74:	'{SolveFor.Max_Iters 10}
A:A75:	'{SolveFor.Accuracy 5E-06}
A:A76:	'{SolveFor.Go}

note: Quota rents are included in calculation of "gross" terms-of-trade effects. These are then backed out of net welfare calculations.

C:B3:	1716
C:B4:	228
C:B5:	56
C:B6:	@SUM(B3..B5)
C:B8:	1.5
C:B9:	3
C:B10:	15
C:B11:	15
C:B12:	3.08
C:B14:	0.103
C:B15:	0.103
C:B16:	0.103
C:B17:	0.103
C:B19:	0
C:B20:	0
C:B21:	0.557
C:B22:	0
C:A27:	(B3)
C:A28:	(B4)*(((1+B14+B19))^(B10))
C:A29:	(B5)*(((1+B15+B20))^(B11))
C:A30:	(B6)
C:A31:	(B3/A$30)^(1/B$12)
C:A32:	(B4/A$30)^(1/B$12)
C:A33:	(B5/A$30)^(1/B$12)
C:G27:	1
C:G28:	(1+B14+B19)*G30
C:G29:	(1+B15+B20)*G31
C:G30:	(1/((1+B14+B19)))
C:G31:	(1/((1+B15+B20)))
C:G32:	(((A31^B12)+((A32^B12)+((A33^B12))^(-1/(B12-1)))
C:A39:	(((A31/I39)^(B$12))*(I$43)*(I$42^(B$12-1)))-(A27*(I39^B9))
C:A40:	(((A32/I40)^(B$12))*(I$43)*(I$42^(B$12-1)))-(A28*(((I40/((1+B16+B21)))^B10)))
C:A41:	(((A33/I41)^(B$12))*(I$43)*(I$42^(B$12-1)))-(A29*(((I41/((1+B17+B22)))^B11)))
C:A42:	(((A31^(B$12))*(I39^(1-B$12))+((A32^(B$12))*(I40^(1-B$12))+((A33)^(B$12))*(I41^(1-B$12)))^(1/(1-B12))-I42
C:A43:	(A30)*(I42^(-B8+1))-I43
C:C39:	(((A31/H39)^(B$12))*(H$43)*(H$42^(B$12-1)))-(A27*(H39^B9))
C:C40:	(((A32/H40)^(B$12))*(H$43)*(H$42^(B$12-1)))-(A28*(((H40/((1)*(1)))^B10)))
C:C41:	(((A33/H41)^(B$12))*(H$43)*(H$42^(B$12-1)))-(A29*(((H41/((1+B17+B22)))^B11)))
C:C42:	(((A31^(B$12))*(H39^(1-B$12))+((A32^(B$12))*(H40^(1-B$12))+((A33)^(B$12))*(H41^(1-B$12)))^(1/(1-B12))-H42
C:C43:	(A30)*(H42^(-B8+1))-H43
C:H39:	0.996621077741846
C:H40:	0.920837680437056
C:H41:	0.998862448733529
C:H42:	0.987059999394282
C:H43:	2013.06695303149
C:I39:	1.00987375148887
C:I40:	1.408393924513B1
C:I41:	1.00330955595646
C:I42:	1.03853269183699
C:I43:	1962.54629206507
C:G49:	(((B4)-(((A32/H40)^(B$12))*(H$43)*(H$42^(B$12-1))))*(1/H40))*0.5
C:G50:	(H40-G30)*B4
C:G51:	-((1/(1+B19+B14)))*B19*B4
C:G52:	^*
C:H49:	(((B4*(1+I63))-(((A32/H40)^(B$12))*(H$43)*(H$42^(B$12-1))))*(I40/H40))*0.5
C:H50:	(H40-(I40/(1+B21+B16)))*(1+I63)*B4
C:H51:	-(I40/(1+B21+B16))*B21*B4*(1+I63)
C:H52:	(G31*(1+I67)*B5*B17)+H71-(B5*G31*B15)
C:I49:	(H49-G49)
C:I50:	(H50-G50)
C:I51:	(H51-G51)
C:I52:	(H52-G52)
C:I53:	@SUM(I49..I52)
C:I58:	(I39-1)
C:I59:	((((A31/I39)^(B$12))*(I$43)*(I$42^(B$12-1)))-B3)/B3
C:I61:	((I40/((1+B16+B21)))-G30)/G30
C:I62:	(I40-1)
C:I63:	((((A32/I40)^(B$12))*(I$43)*(I$42^(B$12-1)))-B4)/B4
C:I65:	((I41/((1+B17+B22)))-G31)/G31
C:I66:	(I41-1)
C:I67:	((((A33/I41)^(B$12))*(I$43)*(I$42^(B$12-1)))-B5)/B5
C:I70:	((1+I61)*G30*(1+I63)*B4*B16)-(B4*G30*B14)
C:I71:	((1+I65)*G31*(1+I67)*B5*B17)-(B5*G31*B15)
C:I72:	@SUM(I70..I71)

Table 5A.2. *(cont.)*

C:N1:	'(RE)CALIBRATE MACRO
C:N2:	'{HLine -5}
C:N3:	'{VLine 24}
C:N4:	'{SelectBlock g27..g29}
C:N5:	'{EditCopy}
C:N6:	'{SelectBlock H39..H41}
C:N7:	'{PasteSpecial "",Values,"",""}
C:N8:	'{SelectBlock I39..I41}
C:N9:	'{PasteSpecial "",Values,"",""}
C:N10:	'{SelectBlock g32..g32}
C:N11:	'{EditCopy}
C:N12:	'{SelectBlock H42..H42}
C:N13:	'{PasteSpecial "",Values,"",""}
C:N14:	'{SelectBlock I42..I42}
C:N15:	'{PasteSpecial "",Values,"",""}
C:N16:	'{SelectBlock a30..a30}
C:N17:	'{EditCopy}
C:N18:	'{SelectBlock H43..H43}
C:N19:	'{PasteSpecial "",Values,"",""}
C:N20:	'{SelectBlock I43..I43}
C:N21:	'{PasteSpecial "",Values,"",""}
C:N22:	'{SelectBlock A1..A1}
C:R1:	'SOLVE MACRO
C:R2:	'{Optimizer.Reset}
C:R3:	'{Optimizer.Solution_Cell A42}
C:R4:	'{Optimizer.Solution_Goal "Target Value:"}
C:R5:	'{Optimizer.Variable_Cells I39..I43}
C:R6:	'{Optimizer.Add 1,"A39..A39","=","0"}
C:R7:	'{Optimizer.Add 2,"A40..A40","=","0"}
C:R8:	'{Optimizer.Add 3,"A41..A41","=","0"}
C:R9:	'{Optimizer.Add 4,"A43..A43","=","0"}
C:R10:	'{Optimizer.Solve}
C:R11:	'{Optimizer.Reset}
C:R12:	'{Optimizer.Solution_Cell C42}
C:R13:	'{Optimizer.Solution_Goal "Target Value:"}
C:R14:	'{Optimizer.Variable_Cells H39..H43}
C:R15:	'{Optimizer.Add 1,"C39..C39","=","0"}
C:R16:	'{Optimizer.Add 2,"C40..C40","=","0"}
C:R17:	'{Optimizer.Add 3,"C41..C41","=","0"}
C:R18:	'{Optimizer.Add 4,"C43..C43","=","0"}
C:R19:	'{Optimizer.Solve}
C:R20:	'{SelectBlock A1..A1}

note: Quota rents are included in calculation of "gross" terms-of-trade effects. These are then backed out of net welfare calculations.

Table 5A.3. *Estimated elasticities of substitution between imports and domestic competing goods (based on U.S. imports)*

Sector No.	Elasticity	t-statistic		Sector Name
1	1.22	1.63		Iron and ferroalloy ores mining
4	0.16	0.23		Coal mining
5	0.31	2.3	*	Crude petroleum and natural gas
6	0.97	17.84	*	Stone, sand, and gravel
8	1.13	1.78		Chemical and fertilizer mineral mining
9	1.68	3.3	*	Meat packing plants and prepared meats
11	1	33.92	*	Creamery butter
12	1.99	6.74	*	Cheese, natural and processed
15	0.67	3.1	*	Fluid milk
17	1.16	2.84	*	Flour and other grain mill products
18	0.35	8.04	*	Cereals and flour
19	1.88	7.9	*	Dog, cat, and other pet food
20	1.26	6.24	*	Prepared feeds, n.e.c.
21	0.59	1.67		Wet corn milling
22	1.11	7.68	*	Bread, cake, cookies, and crackers
24	0.13	6.57	*	Chocolate and other confectionary products
25	0.02	0.8		Malt and malt beverages
26	3.49	6.95	*	Wine, brandy, and brandy spirits
27	0.15	8.46	*	Distilled liquor, except brandy
28	1.49	4.75	*	Soft drinks, flavorings, and syrups
29	0.93	2.82	*	Vegetable oil mills
30	0.06	0.14		Animal and marine fats and oils
32	1.85	4.12	*	Shortening and cooking oils
33	0.27	5.16	*	Sea foods, ice, and pasta
34	0.69	1.52		Cigarettes
35	0.15	3.28	*	Cigars
36	0.99	6.21	*	Tobacco
37	0.54	3.96	*	Yarn, thread, and broadwoven fabric mills
38	0.82	7.41	*	Narrow fabric mills
39	1.21	2.55	*	Floor coverings
40	0.57	1.91		Felt, lace and other textile goods
41	2.53	9.8	*	Hosiery
43	0.45	3.55	*	Apparel made from purchased materials
44	2.18	3.74	*	Housefurnish., textile bags, canvas
45	0.64	2.6	*	Logging camps and logging contractors
46	0.58	0.64		Sawmills
47	1.73	8.53	*	Hardwood dimension and flooring mills
48	0.06	2.1	*	Millwork, wood kitchens and cabinets
50	1.02	20.13	*	Wood pallets, skids, and containers
52	0.49	9.92	*	Wood preserving and particleboard
53	0.05	0.91		Household furniture
56	0.97	16.6	*	Paper mills, except building papers
57	1.5	6.92	*	Paperboard mills

Table 5A.3. *(cont.)*

Sector No.	Elasticity	t-statistic		Sector Name
59	1.42	8.19	*	Sanitary paper products
60	0.97	1		Building paper and board mills
61	1.68	10.15	*	Paper coating and glazing
62	1.48	4.57	*	Paperboard containers and boxes
63	0.98	9.26	*	Newspapers
64	1	43.12	*	Periodicals, books, and greeting cards
65	0.8	11.48	*	Printing
66	0.48	4.17	*	Industrial inorganic and organic chemicals
67	0.31	3.62	*	Agricultural chemicals
68	0.96	18.73	*	Chemical preparations
69	1.71	11.55	*	Plastics materials and resins
70	0.87	4.47	*	Synthetic rubber
71	0.66	2.31	*	Organic fibers
72	1.09	6.49	*	Drugs
73	0.58	1.44		Soap, detergents, and sanitation goods
76	0.4	1.53		Paving mixtures, blocks, asphalt felts
77	0.02	0.34		Tires and inner tubes
78	0.29	4.32	*	Rubber and plastics footwear
79	0.01	0.14		Other rubber products
80	1.46	1.71	*	Miscellaneous plastics products
81	1.07	1.89	*	Leather tanning and finishing
83	1.27	14.85	*	Other leather goods
84	0.36	11.95	*	Glass and glass products, exc. containers
85	0.23	1.13		Glass containers
86	1.09	12.73	*	Cement, hydraulic
87	1.04	28.48	*	Brick and structural clay tile
88	0.88	24.13	*	Ceramic wall and floor tile
90	0.84	8.94	*	Ceramic plumbing and electrical supplies
91	1.45	7.38	*	China and earthenware products
93	0.82	16.13	*	Stone and nonmetalic mineral products
94	0.76	7.75	*	Primary steel
95	3.08	4.06	*	Iron and steel foundries
96	0.69	2.17	*	Metal heat treating and primary metal
97	0.91	0.98		Primary copper
103	0.16	1.3		Other nonfer. rolling, drawing, insulating
106	1.03	2.76	*	Metal barrels, drums and pails
107	0.45	1.47		Metal plumbing fixtures, heating equipment
108	0.74	6.26	*	Fabricated metal work
109	1.07	2.34	*	Fabricated plate work (boiler shops)
110	0.22	2.34	*	Screw machine products and bolts, etc.
111	1.17	23.65	*	Forgings and stampings
112	0.2	0.48		Cutlery
113	0.22	8.87	*	Hand tools
115	0.24	2.75	*	Other fabricated metal products
116	0.3	1.25		Pipe, valves, and pipe fittings
117	0.99	21.77	*	Turbines and turbine generator sets
118	0.3	17.75	*	Internal combustion engines, n.e.c.
119	1.06	11.08	*	Farm and garden machinery and equipment
120	0.97	7.6	*	Construction, mining, oil field machinery

Sector No.	Elasticity	t-statistic		Sector Name
121	0.94	10.79	*	Elevators, conveyors, cranes
122	0.79	8.01	*	Machine tools and power driven hand tools
123	0.69	7.05	*	Special industry machinery
124	0.26	2.77	*	Pumps, compressors, blowers, fans, furnaces
125	0.83	10.89	*	Ball and roller bearings transmiss. equip.
127	0.85	5.6	*	Electrical computing equipment
128	1.22	9.67	*	Service industry machines
129	0.2	2.13	*	Transformers, switchgear and switchboard
130	0.72	3.3	*	Electrical industrial apparatus
131	2.69	2.6	*	Household cooking equipment
132	1.13	5.91	*	Household refrigerator and freezers
133	1.01	19.66	*	Household laundry equipment
134	1.97	11.77	*	Electric housewares and fans
135	1.99	3.92	*	Household vacuum cleaners
136	0.09	1.12		Sewing machines, household appliances
137	0.82	3.59	*	Electric lamps, lighting, wiring devices
138	1.41	3.52	*	Radio, TV, phonograph records and tapes
139	0.63	4.18	*	Telephone and telegraph apparatus
140	1.42	16.54	*	Radio and TV communication equipment
141	0.62	9.8	*	Electron tubes
143	2.65	11.6	*	Storage batteries
144	0.36	5.99	*	Electrical equipment and supplies
145	1.16	12.02	*	Motor vehicles parts and accessories
146	0.76	3.3	*	Aircraft
147	0.62	3.24	*	Aircraft and missile equipment, n.e.c.
149	0.3	2.47	*	Boat building and repairing
150	0.92	5.07	*	Railroad equipment
151	1.73	6.3	*	Motorcycles, bicycles, and parts
153	0.65	2.31	*	Transportation equipment, n.e.c.
155	0.89	1.64		Ordnance and accessories
157	0.89	22.52	*	Engineering, scientific, optical equipment
158	1.05	18.18	*	Measuring devices, environmental controls
159	0.66	2.61	*	Surgical, medical and dental equipment
160	0.28	2.26	*	Watches, clocks, and ophthalmic goods
162	0.14	4.13	*	Jewelry, musical instruments, toys

* Indicates that the estimated elasticity is statistically significant
at the 5 percent level.

Source: Kenneth A. Reinert and David W. Roland-Holst (with permission),
"Disaggregated Armington Elasticities for the Mining and Manufacturing Sectors"
Journal of Policy Modeling, 4:5, 1992.

References

Armington, P. 1969. "A theory of demand for products distinguished by place of origin." *IMF Staff Papers* 16:159–178.

Boltuck, R. 1991. "Assessing the effects on the domestic industry of price dumping." In *Policy Implications of Antidumping Measures*, edited by P.K.M. Tharakan. Amsterdam: North-Holland.

Cline, W. 1987. *The Future of World Trade in Textiles and Apparel*. Washington, D.C.: Institute of International Economics.

Commission of the European Communities. 1988. *European Economy: The Economics of 1992*. Luxembourg: Office for the Official Publications of the European Communities.

Dixit, A.K. and V. Norman. 1980. *Theory of International Trade*. Cambridge: Cambridge University Press.

Francois. J.F. and K.H. Hall. 1993. "COMPAS: Commercial Policy Analysis System." Washington, D.C.: U.S. International Trade Commission.

General Agreement on Tariffs and Trade. 1994. *Trade Policy Review: United States*, Vol. I. Geneva.

Green, H.A. John. 1978. *Consumer Theory*. New York: Academic Press.

Henderson, J.M. and R.E. Quandt. 1980. *Microeconomic Theory: A Mathematical Approach*. New York: McGraw-Hill.

Hertel, T.W. ed. 1996. *Global Trade Analysis: Modelling and Applications*. Cambridge: Cambridge University Press.

Krugman, P.R. and E. Helpman. 1989. *Trade Policy and Market Structure*. Cambridge, Massachusetts: MIT Press.

Martin, W. and S. Suphachalasai. 1990. "Effects of the Multi-Fibre Arrangement on developing country exporters: A simple theoretical framework." In *Textiles Trade and the Developing Countries*, edited by C.B. Hamilton. Washington, D.C.: World Bank.

Reinert, K.A. and D.W. Roland-Holst. 1992. "Disaggregated Armington elasticities for the mining and manufacturing sectors." *Journal of Policy Modelling* 14:631–639.

Rousslang, D.J. and J. Suomela. 1985. *Calculating the Consumer and Net Welfare Costs of Import Relief*. Washington, D.C.: U.S. International Trade Commission.

Rutherford, T. 1994a. "Applied General Equilibrium Modelling with MSPGE as a GAMS Subsystem." University of Colorado, Mimeo.

Rutherford, T. 1994b. "Extensions of GAMS for Complementarity Problems Arising in Applied Economic Analysis." University of Colorado, Mimeo.

Shiells, C.R., A. Deardorff and R. Stern. 1986. "Estimates of the elasticities of substitution between imports and home goods for the United States." *Weltwirtschaftliches Archiv* 122:497–519.

Shiells, C.R. and K.A. Reinert. 1993. "Armington models and terms-of-trade effects: Some econometric evidence for North America." *Canadian Journal of Economics* 26:299–316.

U.S. International Trade Commission. 1989. *The Economic Effects of Significant U.S. Import Restraints, Phase I*. USITC Publication 2222, Washington, D.C.

U.S. International Trade Commission. 1993a. *The Economic Effects of Significant U.S. Import Restraints*. USITC Publication 2699, Washington, D.C.

U.S. International Trade Commission. 1993b. "Flat-rolled carbon steel products from 16 countries injure the U.S. industry, says ITC." USITC Office of Public Affairs document 93-077, Washington, D.C.

6

Simple General Equilibrium Modeling

*Shantayanan Devarajan, Delfin S. Go, Jeffrey D. Lewis,
Sherman Robinson, and Pekka Sinko*

I Introduction

This chapter describes how to specify, solve, and draw policy lessons
from small, two-sector, general equilibrium models of open, developing
economies.[1] In the last two decades, changes in the external environment
and economic policies have been instrumental in determining the performance of these economies. The relationship between external shocks and
policy responses is complex; this chapter provides a starting point for its
analysis.

Two-sector models provide a good starting point because of the nature of
the external shocks faced by these countries and the policy responses they
elicit. These models capture the essential mechanisms by which external
shocks and economic policies ripple through the economy. By and large, the
shocks have involved the external sector: terms-of-trade shocks, such as the
fourfold increase in the price of oil in 1973–74 or the decline in primary
commodity prices in the mid-1980s; or cutbacks in foreign capital inflows.
The policy responses most commonly proposed (usually by international
agencies) have also been targeted at the external sector: (1) depreciating the
real exchange rate to adjust to an adverse terms-of-trade shock or to a
cutback in foreign borrowing and (2) reducing distortionary taxes (some of
which are trade taxes) to enhance economic efficiency and make the
economy more competitive in world markets.

A "minimalist" model that captures the shocks and policies mentioned
should therefore emphasize the external sector of the economy. Moreover,
many of the problems – and solutions – are related to the relationship
between the external sector and the rest of the economy. The model thus

---

1 This chapter is derived extensively from two previous papers: Devarajan, Lewis, and Robinson (1990)
and Go and Sinko (1993).

should have at least two productive sectors: one producing tradable goods and the other producing non-tradables. If an economy produces only traded goods, concepts like real devaluation are meaningless. Such a country will not be able to affect its international competitiveness since all of its domestic prices are determined by world prices. If a country produced only nontraded goods, it would have been immune to most of the shocks reverberating around the world economy since 1973. Within the category of tradable goods, it is also useful to distinguish importables and exports. Such a characterization enables us to look at terms-of-trade shocks as well as the impact of policy instruments such as import tariffs and export subsidies.

The minimalist model that incorporates these features, while small, captures a rich array of issues. We can examine the impact of an increase in the price of oil (or other import and/or export prices). In addition, this model enables us to look at the use of trade and fiscal policy instruments: export subsidies, import tariffs, and domestic indirect taxes. The implications of increases or decreases in foreign capital inflows can also be studied with this framework.

While the minimalist model captures, in a stylized manner, features characteristic of developing countries, it also yields policy results that cut against the grain of received wisdom. For example, it is not always appropriate to depreciate the real exchange rate in response to an adverse international terms-of-trade shock; reducing import tariffs may not always stimulate exports; unifying tariff rates need not increase efficiency; and an infusion of foreign capital does not necessarily benefit the nontradable sector (in contrast to the results from "Dutch disease" models).

A major advantage of small models is their simplicity. They make transparent the mechanisms by which an external shock or policy change affects the economy. In addition, the example presented in this chapter can be solved analytically – either graphically or algebraically. It also can be solved numerically by using the most widely available, personal computer– (PC)-based spreadsheet programs; hence, it is not necessary to learn a new, difficult programming language in order to get started. The presentation will introduce the approach used to solve larger, multisector models. Finally, these minimalist two-sector models behave in a similar fashion to more complex multisector models, so we can anticipate some of the results obtained from multisector models, such as those presented in some of the ensuing chapters of this volume.

The plan of the chapter is as follows: In Section II, we present the simplest two-sector models. We specify the equations and discuss some modeling issues. We then analyze the impact of terms-of-trade shocks and changes in foreign capital inflows. In Section III, we describe an easy way of implementing the framework and use it to discuss some policy issues. The conclusion, Section IV, draws together the main points of the chapter.

II Two-Sector, Three-Good Model

The basic model refers to one country with two producing sectors and three goods; hence, we call it the "1–2–3 model." For the time being, we ignore factor markets. The two commodities that the country produces are (1) an export good, E, which is sold to foreigners and is not demanded domestically, and (2) a domestic good, D, which is only sold domestically. The third good is an import, M, which is not produced domestically. There is one consumer who receives all income. The country is small in world markets, facing fixed world prices for exports and imports.

The equation system is presented in Table 6.1. The model has three actors: a producer, a household, and the rest of the world. Equation 6.1 defines the domestic production possibility frontier, which gives the maximum achievable combinations of E and D that the economy can supply. The function is assumed to be concave and will be specified as a constant elasticity of transformation (CET) function with transformation elasticity Ω. The constant $\overline{X}$ defines aggregate production and is fixed. Since there are no intermediate inputs, $\overline{X}$ also corresponds to real GDP. The assumption that $\overline{X}$ is fixed is equivalent to assuming full employment of all primary factor inputs. Equation (6.4) gives the efficient ratio of exports to domestic output (E/D) as a function of relative prices. Equation (6.9) defines the price of the composite commodity and is the cost-function dual to the first-order condition, equation (6.4). The composite good price P^x corresponds to the GDP deflator.

Equation (6.2) defines a composite commodity made up of D and M which is consumed by the single consumer. In multisector models, we extend this treatment to many sectors, assuming that imports and domestic goods in the same sector are imperfect substitutes, an approach which has come to be called the Armington assumption.[2] Following this treatment, we assume the composite commodity is given by a constant elasticity of substitution (CES) aggregation function of M and D, with substitution elasticity σ. Consumers maximize utility, which is equivalent to maximizing Q in this model, and equation (6.5) gives the desired ratio of M to D as a function of relative prices.[3] Equation (6.10) defines the price of the composite commodity. It is

2 See Armington (1969).
3 In the multisector models, we add expenditure functions with many goods based on utility maximization at two levels. First, allocate expenditure among goods. Second, decide on sectoral import ratios. In the 1–2–3 model, the CES function defining Q can be treated as a utility function directly.

Table 6.1. *The basic 1–2–3 CGE model*

Flows	Prices
(6.1) $\bar{X} = G(E, D^S; \Omega)$	(6.7) $P^m = R \cdot pw^m$
(6.2) $Q^S = F(M, D^D; \sigma)$	(6.8) $P^e = R \cdot pw^e$
(6.3) $Q^D = \dfrac{Y}{P^q}$	(6.9) $P^x = g_1(P^e, P^d)$
(6.4) $\dfrac{E}{D^S} = g_2(P^e, P^d)$	(6.10) $P^q = f_1(P^m, P^d)$
(6.5) $\dfrac{M}{D^D} = f_2(P^m, P^d)$	(6.11) $R \equiv 1$
(6.6) $Y = P^x \cdot \bar{X} + R \cdot \bar{B}$	Equilibrium Conditions
	(6.12) $D^D - D^S = 0$
	(6.13) $Q^D - Q^S = 0$
	(6.14) $pw^m \cdot M - pw^e \cdot E = \bar{B}$

Identities

(6.15) $P^x \cdot \bar{X} \equiv P^e \cdot E + P^d \cdot D^S$

(6.16) $P^q \cdot Q^S \equiv P^m \cdot M + P^d \cdot D^D$

(6.17) $Y \equiv P^q \cdot Q^D$

Endogenous Variables

E: Export good

M: Import good

D^S: Supply of domestic good

D^D: Demand for domestic good

Q^S: Supply of composite good

Q^D: Demand for composite good

Y: Total income

P^e: Domestic price of export good

P^m: Domestic price of import good

P^d: Domestic price of domestic good

P^x: Price of aggregate output

P^q: Price of composite good

R: Exchange rate

Exogenous Variables

pw^e: World price of export good

pw^m: World price of import good

$\bar{B}$: Balance of trade

σ: Import substitution elasticity

Ω: Export transformation elasticity

---

the cost-function dual to the first-order conditions underlying equation (6.5). The price P^q corresponds to an aggregate consumer price or cost-of-living index.

Equation (6.6) determines household income. Equation (6.3) defines household demand for the composite good. Note that all income is spent on the single composite good. Equation (6.3) stands in for the more complex system of expenditure equations found in multisector models and reflects an important property of all complete expenditure systems: The value of the goods demanded must equal aggregate expenditure.

In Table 6.1, the price equations define relationships among seven prices. There are fixed world prices for E and M; domestic prices for E and M; the price of the domestic good D; and prices for the two composite commodities, X and Q. Equations (6.1) and (6.2) are linearly homogeneous, as are the corresponding dual price equations, (6.9) and (6.10). Equations (6.3) to (6.5) are homogeneous of degree zero in prices – doubling all prices, for example, leaves real demand and the desired export and import ratios unchanged.[4] Since only relative prices matter, it is necessary to define a numéraire price; in equation (6.11), this is specified to be the exchange rate R.

Equations (6.12), (6.13), and (6.14) define the market-clearing equilibrium conditions. Supply must equal demand for D and Q, and the balance of trade constraint must be satisfied. The complete model has fourteen equations and thirteen endogenous variables. The three equilibrium conditions, however, are not all independent. Any one of them can be dropped and the resulting model is fully determined.

To prove that the three equilibrium conditions are not independent, it suffices to show that the model satisfies Walras's Law. Such a model is "closed" in that there are no leakages of funds into or out of the economy. First note the three identities – (6.15), (6.16), and (6.17) – that the model satisfies. The first two arise from the homogeneity assumptions and the third from the fact that, in any system of expenditure equations, the value of purchases must equal total expenditure.[5] Multiplying equations (6.12) and (6.13) by their respective prices, the sum of equations (6.12), (6.13), and (6.14) equals zero as an identity (moving $\overline{B}$ in equation [6.14] to the left side). Given these identities, simple substitution will show that if equations (6.12) and (6.13) hold, then so must (6.14).

The 1–2–3 model is different from the standard neoclassical trade model with all goods tradable and all tradables perfect substitutes with domestic goods. The standard model, long a staple of trade theory, yields wildly implausible results in empirical applications.[6] Empirical models that reflect these assumptions embody "the law of one price," which states that domestic relative prices of tradables are set by world prices. Such models tend to yield

---

4 For the demand equation, one must show that nominal income doubles when all prices double, including the exchange rate. Tracing the elements in equation (6.6), it is easy to demonstrate that nominal income goes up proportionately with prices.

5 In this model equation (6.3) and identity (6.17) are the same. In a multisector model, as noted, identity (iii) is a necessary property of any system of expenditure equations.

6 Empirical problems with this specification have been a thorn in the side of modelers since the early days of linear programming models. For a survey, see Taylor (1975).

extreme specialization in production and unrealistic swings in domestic relative prices in response to changes in trade policy or world prices. Empirical evidence indicates that changes in the prices of imports and exports are only partially transmitted to the prices of domestic goods. In addition, such models cannot exhibit two-way trade in any sector ("cross-hauling"), which is often observed at fine levels of disaggregation.

Recognizing these problems, Salter (1959) and Swan (1960) specified a two-sector model distinguishing "tradables" (including both imports and exports) and "nontradables." Their approach represented an advance and the papers started an active theoretical literature. However, they had little impact on empirical work. Even in an input–output table with over five hundred sectors, there are very few sectors which are purely non-traded; i.e., with no exports or imports. So defined, non-traded goods are a very small share of GDP; and, in models with ten to thirty sectors, there would be at most only one or two non-traded sectors. Furthermore, the link between domestic and world prices in the Salter–Swan model does not depend on the trade share, only on whether or not the sector is tradable. If a good is tradable, regardless of how small is the trade share, the domestic price will be set by the world price.

The picture is quite different in the 1–2–3 model with imperfect substitutability and transformability. All domestically produced goods that are not exported (D in Table 6.1) are effectively treated as non-tradables (or, better, as "semi-tradables"). The share of non-tradables in GDP now equals 1 minus the export share, which is a very large number, and all sectors are treated symmetrically. In effect, the specification in the 1–2–3 model extends and generalizes the Salter–Swan model, making it empirically relevant.

De Melo and Robinson (1985) show, in a partial equilibrium framework, that the link between domestic and world prices, assuming imperfect substitutability at the sectoral level, depends critically on the trade shares, for both exports and imports, as well as on elasticity values. For given substitution and transformation elasticities, the domestic price is more closely linked to the world price in a given sector the greater are export and import shares. In multisector models, the effect of this specification is a realistic insulation of the domestic price system from changes in world prices. The links are there, but they are not nearly as strong as in the standard neoclassical trade model. Also, the model naturally accommodates two-way trade, since exports, imports, and domestic goods in the same sector are all distinct.

Given that each sector has seven associated prices, the model provides for a lot of product differentiation. The assumption of imperfect substitutability on the import side has been widely used in empirical models.[7] Note that it is equally important to specify imperfect transformability on the export side. Without imperfect transformability, the law of one price would still hold for all sectors with exports. In the 1–2–3 model, both import demand and export supply depend on relative prices.[8]

De Melo and Robinson (1989) analyze the properties of this model in some detail and argue that it is a good stylization of most recent single-country, trade-focused, computable general equilibrium (CGE) models. Product differentiation on both the import and export sides is very appealing for applied models, especially at the levels of aggregation typically used. The specification is a faithful extension of the Salter–Swan model and gives rise to normally shaped offer curves. The exchange rate is a well-defined relative price. If the domestic good is chosen as the numéraire commodity, setting P^d equal to 1, then the exchange rate variable R corresponds to the real exchange rate of neoclassical trade theory: the relative price of tradables (E and M) to non-tradables (D). Trade theory models (and our characterization in Table 6.1) often set R to 1, with P^d then defining the real exchange rate. For other choices of numéraire, R is a monotonic function of the real exchange rate.[9]

The 1–2–3 model can also be seen as a simple programming model. This formulation is given in Table 6.2 and is shown graphically in Figure 6.1. The presentation emphasizes the fact that a single-consumer general equilibrium model can be represented by a programming model that maximizes consumer utility, which is equivalent to social welfare.[10] In this model, the shadow prices of the constraint equations correspond to market prices in the CGE model.[11] We will use the graphical apparatus to analyze the impact of

---

7 The CES formulation for the import-aggregation function has been criticized on econometric grounds (see Alston et al., 1990, for an example). It is certainly a restrictive form. For example, it constrains the income elasticity of demand for imports to be one in every sector. Rather than completely rejecting approaches that rely on imperfect substitutability, this criticism would seem to suggest that it is time to explore the many alternative functional forms that are available. For example, Hanson, Robinson, and Tokarick (1993) estimate sectoral import demand functions based on the almost ideal demand system (AIDS) formulation. They find that sectoral expenditure elasticities of import demand are generally much greater than one in the United States, results consistent with estimates from macroeconometric models. Factors other than relative prices appear to affect trade shares, and it is important to study what they might be and how they operate. Alston and Green (1990) also estimated the AIDS import formulation. A related paper is Shiells, Roland-Holst, and Reinert (1993).

8 Dervis, de Melo, and Robinson (1982) specify a logistic export supply function in place of equation (6.4) in Table 6.1. Their logistic function is locally equivalent to the function that is derived from the CET specification.

9 Dervis, de Melo, and Robinson (1982), Chapter 6, discuss this relationship in detail.

10 Ginsburgh and Waelbroeck (1981) discuss, in detail, the general case where a multiconsumer CGE model can be represented by a programming model maximizing a Negishi social welfare function. See also Ginsburgh and Robinson (1984) for a brief survey of the technique applied to CGE models.

11 In the programming model, we implicitly choose Q as the numéraire good, with $P^q \equiv 1$. In the graphical analysis, we set $R \equiv 1$.

Table 6.2. *The 1–2–3 model as a programming problem*

Maximize $Q = F(M, D^D; \sigma)$	(absorption)	
with respect to: M, E, D^D, D^s		
subject to:		
		Shadow Price
(6.18) $G(E, D^s; \Omega) \leq \bar{X}$	(technology)	$\lambda^x = P^x/P^q$
(6.19) $pw^m \cdot M \leq pw^e \cdot E + \bar{B}$	(balance of trade)	$\lambda^b = R/P^q$
(6.20) $D^D \leq D^s$	(domestic supply and demand)	$\lambda^d = P^d/P^q$

where Constraints 6.18 to 6.20 correspond to Equations 6.1, 6.14, and 6.12 in Table 6.1.

---

two shocks: an increase in foreign capital inflow and a change in the international terms of trade.[12] We will also use this programming-model formulation, including endogenous prices and tax instruments, to derive optimal policy rules under second-best conditions.

The transformation function (equation [6.1] in Table 6.1 and constraint [6.18] in Table 6.2) can be depicted in the fourth (southeast) quadrant of the four-quadrant diagram in Figure 6.1. For any given price ratio P^d/P^e, the point of tangency with the transformation frontier determines the amounts of the domestic and exported good that are produced. Assume, for the moment, that foreign capital inflow $\bar{B}$ is zero. Then, constraint 6.19, the balance-of-trade constraint, is a straight line through the origin, as depicted in the first quadrant of Figure 6.1. If we assume for convenience that all world prices are equal to 1, then the slope of the line is 1. For a given level of E produced, the balance-of-trade constraint determines how much of the imported good the country can buy. Intuitively, with no capital inflows ($\bar{B}=0$), the only source of foreign exchange is exports. The second quadrant shows the "consumption possibility frontier," which represents the combinations of the domestic and imported goods that the consumer can buy, given the production technology as reflected in the transformation frontier and the balance of trade constraint. When world prices are equal and trade is balanced, the consumption possibility frontier is the mirror image of the transformation frontier. Equation (6.2) in Table 6.1 defines "absorption," which

---

12 The discussion follows de Melo and Robinson (1989).

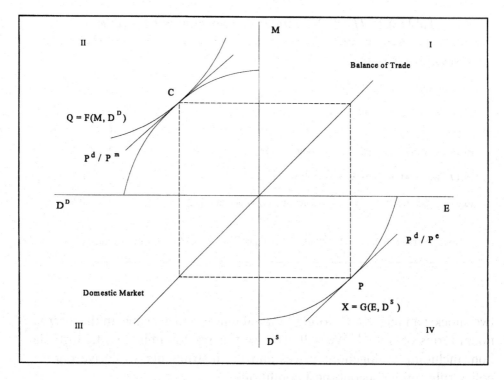

Figure 6.1. *The 1–2–3 programming model*

is maximized in the programming problem. The tangency between the "iso-absorption" (or indifference) curves and the consumption possibility frontier will determine the amount of D and M the consumer will demand, at price ratio P^d/P^m. The economy produces at point P and consumes at point C.

Now consider what would happen if foreign capital inflow increased from its initial level of zero to some value $(\overline{B}>0)$. For example, the country gains additional access to world capital markets or receives some foreign aid. Alternatively, there is a primary resource boom in a country where the resource is effectively an enclave, so that the only direct effect is the repatriation of export earnings.[13] In all of these cases, we would expect domestic prices to rise relative to world prices and the tradable sector to contract relative to the non-tradable sector. In short, the country would contract "Dutch disease." That this is indeed the case can be seen by examining Figure 6.2. The direct effect is to shift the balance of trade line up by $\overline{B}$. This

13 See Benjamin and Devarajan (1985) or Benjamin, Devarajan, and Weiner (1989).

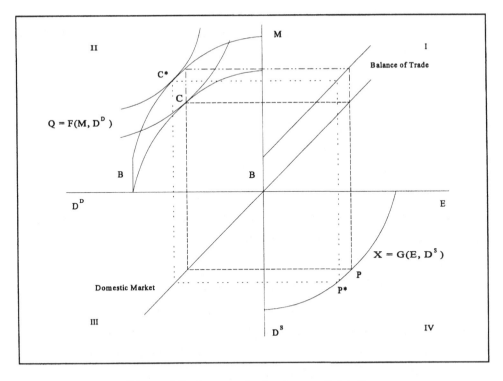

Figure 6.2. *Increase in foreign capital inflow*

shift, in turn, will shift the consumption possibility frontier up vertically by the same $\overline{B}$. The new equilibrium point will depend on the nature of the import aggregation function (the consumer's utility function). In Figure 6.2, the consumption point moves from C to C^*, with increased demand for both D and M and an increase in the price of the domestic good, P^d. On the production side, the relative price has shifted in favor of the domestic good and against the export – an appreciation of the real exchange rate.

Will the real exchange rate always appreciate? Consider two polar extremes, which bracket the range of possible equilibria. Suppose the elasticity of substitution between imports and domestic goods is nearly infinite, so that the indifference curves are almost flat. In this case, the new equilibrium will lie directly above the initial one (point C), since the two consumption possibility curves are vertically parallel. The amount of D consumed will not change and all the extra foreign exchange will go toward purchasing imports. By contrast, suppose the elasticity of substitution between M and D is zero, so the indifference curves are L-shaped. In this case (assuming homotheticity of the utility function), the new equilibrium will lie on a ray radiating from the origin and going through the initial equilibrium. In this new equilibrium, there is more of both D and M consumed, and the price ratio has risen. Since P^m is fixed by hypothesis, P^d must have increased – a real appreciation. The two cases bound the range of possible outcomes. The real exchange rate will appreciate or, in the extreme case, stay unchanged. Production of D will either remain constant or rise and production of E, the tradable good in this economy, will either stay constant or decline. The range of intermediate possibilities describes the standard view of the Dutch disease.

Consider now an adverse terms-of-trade shock represented by an increase in the world price of the imported good. The results are shown in Figure 6.3. The direct effect is to move the balance of trade line, although this time it is a clockwise rotation rather than a translation (we assume that initially $\overline{B}=0$). For the same amount of exports, the country can now buy fewer imports. The consumption possibility frontier is also rotated inward. The new consumption point is shown at C^*, with less consumption of both imports and domestic goods. On the production side, the new equilibrium is P^*. Exports have increased in order to generate foreign exchange to pay for more expensive imports, and P^e/P^d has also increased to attract resources away for D and into E. There has been a real depreciation of the exchange rate.

Will there always be a real depreciation when there is an adverse shock in the international terms of trade? Not necessarily. The characteristics of the new equilibrium depend crucially on the value of σ, the elasticity of substitution between imports and domestic goods in the import aggregation function.

Consider the extremes of $\sigma=0$ and $\sigma=\infty$. In the first case, as in Figure 6.3, there will be a reduction in the amount of domestic good produced (and consumed) and a depreciation of the real exchange rate. In the second case, however, flat indifference curves will have to be tangent to the new consumption possibility frontier to the left of the old consumption point (C), since the rotation flattened the curve. At the new point, output of D rises and the real exchange rate appreciates. When $\sigma=1$, there is no change in either the real exchange rate or the production structure of the economy. The intuition behind this somewhat unusual result is as follows:[14] When the price of imports rises in an economy, there are two effects: an income effect (as the consumer's real income is now lower) and a substitution effect (as domestic goods now become more attractive). The resulting

---

14 We derive the result analytically later.

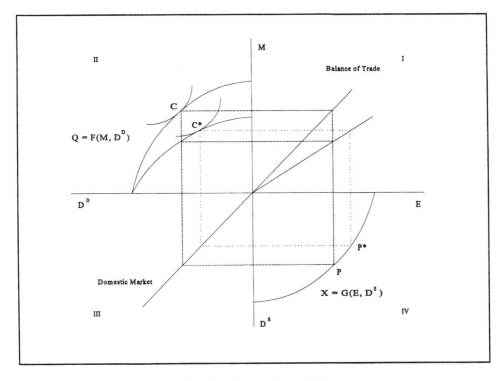

Figure 6.3. *Change in world prices*

equilibrium will depend on which effect dominates. When $\sigma < 1$, the income effect dominates. The economy contracts output of the domestic good and expands that of the export commodity. In order to pay for the needed, non-substitutable import, the real exchange rate depreciates. However, when $\sigma > 1$, the substitution effect dominates. The response of the economy is to contract exports (and hence also imports) and produce more of the domestic substitute.

For most developing countries, it is likely that $\sigma < 1$, so that the standard policy advice to depreciate the real exchange rate in the wake of an adverse terms-of-trade shock is correct. For developed economies, one might well expect substitution elasticities to be high. In this case, the responses to a terms-of-trade shock are a real revaluation, substitution of domestic goods for the more expensive (and non-critical) import, and a contraction in the aggregate volume of trade. In all countries, one would expect substitution elasticities to be higher in the long run. The long-run effect of the real exchange rate will thus differ, and may be of opposite sign, from the short-run effect.

The relationship between the response of the economy to the terms-of-trade shock and the elasticity of substitution can also be seen by solving the model algebraically. By considering only small changes to the initial equilibrium, we can linearize the model and obtain approximate analytical solutions. We follow this procedure to analyze the impact of a terms-of-trade shock.[15]

Let a "^" above a variable denote its log-differential. That is, $\hat{z}=d(\ln z)=dz/z$. Log-differentiate equations (6.4), (6.5), and (6.14) in Table 6.1, assuming an exogenous change in the world price of the import. The results are

$$\hat{E} - \hat{D} = \Omega \cdot \hat{P}^d$$

$$\hat{M} - \hat{D} = \sigma\left(\hat{P}^d - \hat{p}w^m\right)$$

$$\hat{M} + \hat{p}w^m = \hat{E}$$

Eliminating $\hat{M}$, $\hat{D}$, and $\hat{E}$ and solving for $\hat{P}^d$ yields

$$\hat{P}^d = \frac{\sigma-1}{\sigma+\Omega}\hat{p}w^m$$

Thus, whether P^d increases or decreases in response to a terms-of-trade shock depends on the sign of $(\sigma-1)$, confirming the graphical analysis discussed. Figure 6.4 illustrates the impact of a 10 percent import price shock on P^d under varying trade elasticities, $0<\sigma<2$ and $0<\Omega<2$. Note that the direction of change in P^d will determine how the rest of the economy will adjust in this counterfactual experiment. If P^d falls (the real exchange rate depreciates), exports will rise and production of the domestic good will fall.

Our analysis with the 1–2–3 model has yielded several lessons. First, the bare bones of multisector general equilibrium models are contained in this small model. Second, and perhaps more surprisingly, this two-sector model is able to shed light on some issues of direct concern to developing countries. For example, the appreciation of the real exchange rate from a foreign capital inflow, widely understood intuitively and derived from more complex models, can be portrayed in this simple model. In addition, results from this small model challenge a standard policy dictum: Always depreciate the real exchange rate when there is an adverse terms-of-trade shock. The model

---

15 De Melo and Robinson (1989) derive the closed-form solution for the country's offer curve in the 1–2–3 model. A more complete discussion and mathematical derivation are given in Devarajan, Lewis, and Robinson (1993).

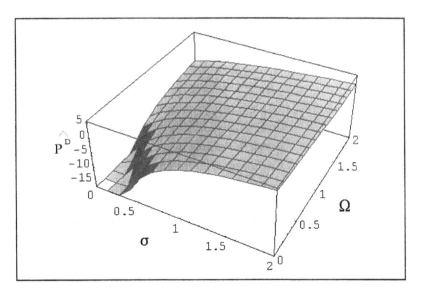

Figure 6.4. *Import price shock, trade elasticities, and domestic prices*

shows the conditions under which this policy advice should and should not be followed.

Of course, many aspects of the economy are left out of the small model. In particular, there are no government, factor markets, and intermediate goods; the framework is also static. Devarajan, Lewis, and Robinson (1990) discuss several extensions and modeling issues in a one-period setting; Devarajan and Go (1993) present a dynamic version of the 1–2–3 framework in which producer and consumer decisions are both intra- and intertemporally consistent. All these extensions require that the model be solved numerically. We turn therefore to the numerical implementation of the 1–2–3 model, extending the basic 1–2–3 model to include the government sector in order to look at policy instruments such as taxes.

III Numerical Implementation

As a means of evaluating economic policy or external shocks, general equilibrium analysis has several known advantages over the partial approach and its numerical implementation has become increasingly the preferred tool of investigation.[16] So far, however, CGE models are cumbersome to build,

---

16 Robinson (1989) contains a survey of CGE applications to developing countries.

requiring extensive data, model calibration, and the learning of a new and often difficult programming language. For that reason, the partial approach still dominates practical applications because of its simplicity. In the field of public finance, for example, it is a relatively simple affair for non-specialists to deal with tax ratios, the projections of collection rates of taxes and their corresponding bases, and, if necessary, to augment the analysis with estimations of tax elasticities.[17] Moreover, since only ratios of taxes to GDP are used, the partial approach has the further advantage of requiring the least information and offering a quick way of looking at the revenue significance of taxes. Nevertheless, using fixed ratios and assuming zero elasticities ignore the feedback into other markets and the division of the tax burden; it limits the investigation and leads to an incomplete picture. General equilibrium analysis avoids these limitations, but the problem has been to find an easy and convenient way of doing it.

Fortunately, the simplicity of the 1–2–3 model and the availability of more powerful Windows-based spreadsheet tools for the desktop PC, like *Microsoft Excel for Windows* (Excel hereafter),[18] provide appealing and tempting alternatives for CGE modeling. These tools have built-in graphics, easy integration with other Windows applications, and convenient access to interesting add-in programs. Being much easier to learn and use, they make CGE analysis more accessible to economists who are otherwise discouraged by unwieldy programming. A model based on a popular spreadsheet program can also become an effective vehicle for illustrative and educational purposes. While Excel is one example and hardly the only software suitable for economic modeling, the robustness and flexibility of its solver function, which is quite capable of finding numerical solutions of systems of linear and non-linear equations and inequalities, as well as its user-friendliness and wide distribution make it a particularly attractive tool for potential CGE modelers.

In what follows, we describe a stepwise procedure to implement the 1–2–3 model using Excel.[19] We also run a few policy simulations by applying the model to one small open economy, Sri Lanka.

III.1 The 1–2–3 Model with Government and Investment

In the previous section, the discussion of the 1–2–3 model focused on the relative price of traded goods relative to the price of domestic goods and

17 See Prest (1962) and Chelliah and Chand (1974) for a discussion of such an approach.
18 *Microsoft Excel* and *Windows* are trademarks of Microsoft Corporation.
19 The discussion of Excel procedures is compatible with version 5 or later, such as version 5 under Windows 3.1 or version 7 under Windows 95. We also include in the notes, where applicable, how to implement the same procedures in the previous version of Excel.

how this real exchange rate adjusts in response to exogenous shocks. In order to apply the framework to a particular country, however, it has to be modified to fit real data and to handle policy issues. For example, the real exchange rate is not an instrument, which the government directly controls. Rather, most governments use taxes and subsidies as well as expenditure policy to adjust their economies. Nor did the previous section touch on the equality of savings and investment, which is important in bringing about macroeconomic balance or equilibrium. Table 6.3 presents an extended version of the 1–2–3 model to include government revenue and expenditure and also savings and investment. We make sure that the modifications introduced will conform to data that are commonly available (see calibration later). In the new setup, four tax instruments are included: an import tariff t^m, an export subsidy t^e, an indirect tax on domestic sales t^s, and a direct tax rate t^y. In addition, savings and investment are included. The single household saves a fixed fraction of its income. Public savings (budgetary deficit or surplus) is the balance of tax revenue plus foreign grants and government expenditures (all exogenous) such as government consumption and transfers to households. The current account balance, taken to represent foreign savings, is the residual of imports less exports at world prices, adjusted for grants and remittances from abroad. Output is fixed for reasons cited in Section II. Foreign savings is also presently fixed, so that the model is savings-driven; aggregate investment adjusts to aggregate savings.[20] In sum, we have twenty equations and nineteen endogenous variables. By Walras's Law, however, one of the equations, say the savings–investment identity, is implied by the others and may be dropped.

III.2 Defining Model Components

Building the 1–2–3 framework in Excel requires the usual modeling steps: (1) declaration of parameters and variables, (2) data entry, (3) assignment of initial values to variables and parameters, and (4) specification of equations. In addition, the model has to be precisely defined as a collection of equations; in some cases, it may require an objective function to be optimized. Finally, the solver is called on to conduct numerical simulations.

A suitable way to arrange the 1–2–3 model in an Excel worksheet is to assign separate columns or blocks for parameters, variables, and equations.

---

20 In the alternative investment-driven closure, aggregate investment is fixed and savings adjust through foreign savings (endogenous). For a discussion of alternative macroclosures, see the original work of Sen (1963) or the surveys by Rattso (1982) and Robinson (1989).

Table 6.3. *The 1–2–3 model with government and investment*

Real Flows	**Prices**
(6.21) $\bar{X} = G(E, D^s; \Omega)$	(6.30) $P^m = (1 + t^m) \cdot R \cdot pw^m$
(6..22) $Q^s = F(M, D^D; \sigma)$	(6.31) $P^e = (1 + t^e) \cdot R \cdot pw^e$
(6.23) $Q^D = C + Z + \bar{G}$	(6.32) $P^t = (1 + t^t) \cdot P^q$
(6.24) $E/D^s = g_2(P^e, P^d)$	(6.33) $P^x = g_1(P^e, P^d)$
(6.25) $M/D^D = f_2(P^m, P^t)$	(6.34) $P^q = f_1(P^m, P^t)$
Nominal Flows	(6.35) $R = 1$
(6.26) $T = t^m \cdot R \cdot pw^m \cdot M$	**Equilibrium Conditions**
$\quad + t^e \cdot P^q \cdot Q^D$	(6.36) $D^D - D^s = 0$
$\quad + t^y \cdot Y$	(6.37) $Q^D - Q^s = 0$
$\quad - t^e \cdot R \cdot pw^e \cdot E$	(6.38) $pw^m \cdot M - pw^e \cdot E - ft - re = \bar{B}$
(6.27) $Y = P^x \cdot \bar{X} + tr \cdot P^q + re \cdot R$	(6.39) $P^t \cdot Z - S = 0$
(6.28) $S = \bar{s} \cdot Y + R \cdot \bar{B} + S^g$	(6.40) $T - P^q \cdot \bar{G} - tr \cdot P^q - ft \cdot R - S^g = 0$
(6.29) $C \cdot P^t = (1 - \bar{s} - t^y) \cdot Y$	

Accounting Identities

(6.41) $P^x \cdot \bar{X} \equiv P^e \cdot E + P^d \cdot D^s$

(6.42) $P^q \cdot Q^s \equiv P^m \cdot M + P^t \cdot D^D$

Endogenous Variables:	**Exogenous Variables:**
E: Export good	pw^m: World price of import good
M: Import good	pw^e: World price of export good
D^s: Supply of domestic good	t^m: Tariff rate
D^D: Demand for domestic good	t^e: Export subsidy rate
Q^s: Supply of composite good	t^t: sales/excise/value-added tax rate
Q^D: Demand for composite good	t^y: direct tax rate
P^e: Domestic price of export good	tr: government transfers
P^m: Domestic price of import good	ft: foreign transfers to government
P^d: Producer price of domestic good	re: foreign remittances to private sector
P^t: Sales price of composite good	$\bar{s}$: Average savings rate
P^x: Price of aggregate output	$\underline{X}$: Aggregate output
P^q: Price of composite good	$\underline{G}$: Real government demand
R: Exchange rate	B: Balance of trade
T: Tax revenue	Ω: Export transformation elasticity
S^g: Government savings	σ: Import substitution elasticity
Y: Total income	
C: Aggregate consumption	
S: Aggregate savings	
Z: Aggregate real investment	

Separate columns are assigned for the base year and simulation values of variables. Labels and explanations for parameters, variables, and equations are easily provided in the adjacent left column to improve readability. We also assign a block for the dataset with both initial and calibrated values displayed. Thus, we are able to arrange all necessary ingredients conveniently on a single worksheet.

III.3 *Variables and Parameters*

Table 6.4 is an example of how to organize the parameters and variables in an Excel-based model. We separate out from the rest of the exogenous variables the parameters related to the trade elasticities; the trade elasticities are generally defined at the outset of an experiment, and parameters such as the share and scale values of the CES and CET functions are calibrated just once for both the base case and the current simulation (see the calibration section later). Column A provides a brief description of each parameter and column B lists the corresponding numerical value. The exogenous variables (described in column C) specify the external or policy shocks introduced in a particular experiment – their magnitudes are defined in column E while their base-year values are presented in column D. Likewise, the endogenous variables are listed in columns F to I. New values are computed for the endogenous variables during a simulation and entered in column H as *Current*. Column I, *Cur/Base*, provides simple indices of change of the endogenous variables.

A useful feature in Excel is the capability to define names for various model parts. This is done by using the *Name* command and *Define* option under the *Insert* menu.[21] The cell in *B6* of Table 6.4, for example, can be called by its parameter name, *st*; hence, we can refer to parameters, variables, or equations by using their defined or algebraic names instead of cell locations. By doing this, we make the model specifications easier to read and mistakes easier to detect. To keep track of these names, it is advisable to write them out in explanation cells adjacent to the corresponding parameters, variables, and equations. In the example shown in Table 6.4, we write a short description and put in parentheses the Excel label or name. Base year and current values of variables are distinguished by using the normal convention – in the case of export good *E*, for example, the base year level is labeled as *E0* while *E* is retained for the simulated level.

---

21 Prior to version 5 of Excel, this is done by using the *Define Name* command in the *Formula* menu.

Table 6.4. *List of parameters and variables in the Excel-based 1–2–3 model*

	A	B	C	D	E	F	G	H	I
3									
4	Parameters		Exogenous Variables	Base Year	Current	Endogenous Variables	Base Year	Current	Cur/Base
5									
6	Elasticity for CET (st)	0.60	World Price of Imports (wm)	0.89	0.89	Export Good (E)	0.33	0.33	1.00
7	Elasticity for CES/Q (sq)	0.60	World Price of Exports (we)	1.01	1.01	Import Good (M)	0.50	0.50	1.00
8						Supply of Domestic Good (Ds)	0.67	0.67	1.00
9	Scale for CET (at)	2.22	Import Tariffs (tm)	0.13	0.13	Demand of Domestic Good (Dd)	0.67	0.67	1.00
10	Share for CET (bt)	0.77	Export Duties (te)	0.01	0.01	Supply of Composite Good (Qs)	1.18	1.18	1.00
11	Rho for CET (rt)	2.67	Indirect Taxes (ts)	0.08	0.08	Demand of Composite Good (Qd)	1.18	1.18	1.00
12			Direct Taxes (ty)	0.03	0.03				
13	Scale for CES/Q (aq)	1.97	Savings rate (sy)	0.17	0.17	Tax Revenue (TAX)	0.20	0.40	2.00
14	Share for CES/Q (bq)	0.38	Govt. Consumption (G)	0.10	0.10	Total Income (Y)	1.13	2.26	2.00
15	Rho for CES/Q (rq)	0.67	Govt. Transfers (tr)	0.12	0.12	Aggregate Savings (S)	0.27	0.53	2.00
16			Foreign Grants (ft)	0.02	0.02	Consumption (Cn)	0.83	0.83	1.00
17			Net Priv Remittances (re)	0.01	0.01				
18			Foreign Saving (B)	0.08	0.08	Import Price (Pm)	1.00	2.00	2.00
19			Output (X)	1.00	1.00	Export Price (Pe)	1.00	2.00	2.00
20						Sales Price (Pt)	1.08	2.17	2.00
21						Price of Supply (Pq)	1.00	2.00	2.00
22						Price of Output (Px)	1.00	2.00	2.00
23						Price of Dom. Good (Pd)	1.00	2.00	1.00
24						Exchange Rate (Er)	1.00	2.00	2.00
25									
26						Investment (Z)	0.25	0.25	1.00
27						Government Savings (Sg)	-0.01	-0.02	1.00
28						Walras Law (Z-S)	0.00	0.00	
29									

III.4 Equations

The organization of the equations of our model is illustrated in Table 6.5. The equations are numbered and listed (in column J of Table 6.5) in the same order as Table 6.3. Column K of Table 6.5 lists the equation descriptions and the Excel names in parentheses. The corresponding mathematical expressions are entered in column L. In the normal mode the formulas are hidden in the background and only the current numerical values are evident. The formulas are easily displayed by using the *Options* command on the *Tools* menu, selecting (or clicking) the *View* tab, and choosing *Formulas* in the *Window Options* box.[22]

In a spreadsheet like Excel, a formula is typically entered into a cell by writing out just the right-hand side of an equation as shown in Table 6.5. To complete the equation, each of these mathematical expressions has to be matched and set equal to a variable defined as indicated earlier (see the Solver section).

The complicated expressions in column L of Table 6.5 require some explanations. Equations (6.21) and (6.22), called *CETEQ* and *ARMG* in Excel, are the right-hand expressions of the CET and Armington (CES) functions in the 1–2–3 model, which usually take the following algebraic form:

$$Y = \overline{A} \left[\delta \cdot X_1^\rho + (1-\delta) \cdot X_2^\rho \right]^{1/\rho}$$

where the CES substitution elasticity σ and CET transformation elasticity Ω are given by $\sigma = 1/(1-\rho)$; $-\infty < \rho < +1$ in the CES case and $\Omega = 1/(\rho-1)$; $1 < \rho < +\infty$ in the CET case. In the Excel implementation, the share parameter δ is labeled as *bt* or *bq*, the exponent ρ as *rt* or *rq*, and the elasticities as *st* or *sq*. Equation (6.24), *EDRAT*, is the right-hand side of the export supply function or the first-order condition of the CET function:

$$\frac{E}{D} = \left[\frac{(1-\delta_t) \cdot P^e}{\delta_t \cdot P^d} \right]^\Omega$$

while equation (6.25) (*MDRAT*) in Table 6.5 is the corresponding case (import demand function)

$$\frac{M}{D} = \left[\frac{\delta_q \cdot P^d}{(1-\delta_q) \cdot P^m} \right]^\sigma$$

---

22 In earlier versions of Excel, the equations are easily unveiled by pulling down the *Options* menu and selecting *Formula* among the *Display* options.

Table 6.5. *List of equations in the Excel-based 1–2–3 model*

	J	K	L
3			
4	Eq.#	Equations	
5		*Real Flows*	
6	6.21	CET Transformation (CETEQ)	= at*(bt*E^(rt) + (1-bt)*Ds^(rt))^(1/rt)
7	6.22	Supply of Goods (ARMG)	= aq*(bq*M^(-rq) + (1-bq)*Dd^(-rq))^(-1/rq)
8	6.23	Domestic Demand (DEM)	= Cn + Z + G
9	6.24	E/D Ratio (EDRAT)	= ((Pe/Pd)/(bt/(1-bt)))^(1/(rt-1))
10	6.25	M/D Ratio (MDRAT)	= ((Pd/Pm)*(bq/(1-bq)))^(1/(1 + rq))
11		*Nominal Flows*	
12	6.26	Revenue Equation (TAXEQ)	= tm*wm*Er*M + te*Pe*E + ts*Pq*Qd + ty*Y
13	6.27	Total Income Equation (INC)	= Px*X + tr*Pq + re*Er
14	6.28	Savings Equation (SAV)	= sy*Y + Er*B + Sg
15	6.29	Consumption Function (CONS)	= Y*(1-ty-sy)/Pt
16		*Prices*	
17	6.30	Import Price Equation (PMEQ)	= Er*wm*(1 + tm)
18	6.31	Export Price Equation (PEEQ)	= Er*we/(1 + te)
19	6.32	Sales Price Equation (PTEQ)	= Pq*(1 + ts)
20	6.33	Output Price Equation (PXEQ)	= (Pe*E + Pd*Ds)/X
21	6.34	Supply Price Equation (PQEQ)	= (Pm*M + Pd*Dd)/Qs
22	6.35	Numeraire (REQ)	= 1
23		*Equilibrium Conditions*	
24	6.36	Domestic Good Market (DEQ)	= Dd - Ds
25	6.37	Composite Good Market (QEQ)	= Qd -Qs
26	6.38	Current Account Balance (CABAL)	= wm*M - we*E -ft - re
27	6.39	Government Budget (GBUD)	= Tax - G*Pt - tr*Pq + ft*Er
28			

The dual price equations, equations (6.33) (*PXEQ*) and (6.34) (*PQEQ*), can take the following form:

$$P = \overline{A}^{-1} \left[\delta^{1/(1-\rho)} P_1^{\rho/(\rho-1)} + (1-\delta)^{1/(1-\rho)} P_2^{\rho/(1-\rho)} \right]^{\rho-1/\rho}$$

$$P^q = \frac{P^m \cdot M + P^d \cdot D}{Q}$$

However, in practice, it is often convenient to replace the dual price equations with the expenditure identities, invoking Euler's theorem for linearly homogeneous functions:

$$P^x = \frac{P^e \cdot E + P^d \cdot D}{X}$$

In the 1–2–3 model, the dual price equations embody the same information as the CET export transformation and CES import aggregation functions. In

Table 6.6. *Data in the Excel-based 1–2–3 model*

	M	N	O	P	Q	R	S	T
3								
4		Data - Sri Lanka, 1991						
5			Rs Billion	Output = 1			Rs Billion	Output = 1
6		National Accounts			3	Fiscal Account		
7	1	Output (Value Added)	324.69	1.00		Revenue	76.18	0.23
8		Wages	163.32	0.50		NonTax	8.02	0.02
9						Current Expenditure	83.76	0.26
10		GDP at market prices	375.34	1.16		Goods & Services	35.58	0.11
11		Private Consumption	291.69	0.90		Interest Payments	22.07	0.07
12		Public Consumption	35.58	0.11		Transfers & Subsidies	26.10	0.08
13		Investment	86.38	0.27		Capital Expenditure	35.77	0.11
14		Exports	106.39	0.33		Fiscal Balance	-43.35	-0.13
15		Imports	144.7	0.45				
16								
17		Tax Revenue			4	Balance of Payments		
18	2	Sales & Excise Tax	32.03	0.10		Exports - Imports	-38.32	-0.12
19		Import Tariffs	18.62	0.06		Net Profits & Dividends	-0.78	0.00
20		Export Duties	1.14	0.00		Interest Payments	-8.82	-0.03
21		Payroll Tax	0.00	0.00		Net Private Transfers	11.60	0.04
22		Personal Income Tax	3.54	0.01		Net Official Transfers	7.90	0.02
23		Capital Income Tax	12.84	0.04		Current Account Balance	-28.42	-0.09
24		Total	68.16	0.21				
25						External Debt	260.50	0.80
26						Debt Service Payments	20.21	0.06
27								

some applications, it is convenient to include the dual price equations, but drop the CET and CES functions.

III.5 Calibration

Another convenient feature of the 1–2–3 framework is its modest data requirements. Data from national income, fiscal, and balance-of-payments accounts, those normally released by national governments, are sufficient. To carry out the model, we used the 1991 data for Sri Lanka (Table 6.6). The original data were measured in billions of rupees. In the calibration, all data were scaled and indexed with respect to output, which is set to 1.00 in the base year (note columns P and T).

Tables 6.7 and 6.8 show the calibration of parameters and variables. The values of the parameters and variables are linked to the data in Table 6.6 so that model calibration is automatically done whenever the elasticities or base year data are changed. In Table 6.7, the calibration of the exponents, *rt*

Table 6.7. *Calibration of parameters in the Excel-based 1–2–3 model*

	A	B
	A	B
3		
4	Parameters	
5		
6	Elasticity for CET (st)	0.6
7	Elasticity for CES/Q (sq)	0.6
8		
9	Scale for CET (at)	= X0/(bt*E0^(rt) + (1-bt)*Ds0^(rt))^(1/rt)
10	Share for CET (bt)	= 1/(1 + (Pd0/Pe0)*(E0/Ds0)^(rt-1))
11	Rho for CET (rt)	= 1/st + 1
12		
13	Scale for CES/Q (aq)	= Qs0/(bq*M0^(-rq) + (1-bq)*Dd0^(-rq))^(-1/rq)
14	Share for CES/Q (bq)	= ((Pm0/Pd0)*(M0/Dd0)^(1+rq))/(1 + (Pm0/Pd0)*(M0/Dd0)^(1+rq))
15	Rho for CES/Q (rq)	= 1/sq -1
16		

and rq, of the CET and CES functions (in cells *B11* and *B15*) follows the discussion of the preceding equations. Given the base-year values of the exports *E0*, imports *M0*, and domestic good *Ds0* or *Dd0*, the share parameters bt and bq are calculated by using the formulas in cells *B10* and *B14*; these are derived from the input demand functions of CET and CES functions (see preceding equation section), respectively. The scale parameters at and aq are computed from the CET and CES functions directly in cells *B9* and *B13*, respectively. An alternative procedure for calibration is to fix the variables and ask Excel to solve for parameter values that satisfy the base-year equilibrium. Thus, one need not derive explicit formulas for the parameters, a useful property when dealing with more complicated functional forms.[23]

III.6 Solving the Model

Excel's solver is capable of solving a system of non-linear equations. The first step is to delineate parts of the worksheet that make up the model and specify the problem for Excel's solver. This is done by selecting the *Solver* command from the *Tools* menu in Excel.[24] A *Solver Parameters* dialog box will appear on the screen (Figure 6.5). As in the General Algebraic Modeling System (GAMS),[25] another numerical modeling software, Excel

23 However, calibration needs to be repeated every time that elasticities or base-year data are altered.
24 Prior to version 5, this is done by selecting the *Solver* command from the *Formula* menu in Excel.
25 See Brooke, Kendrick, and Meeraus (1988).

Table 6.8. *Calibration of variables in the Excel-based 1-2-3 model*

	C	D	E	F	G
3					
4	Exogenous Variables	Base Year	Current	Endogenous Variables	Base Year
5					
6	World Price of Imports (wm)	=PmO/ErO/(1 + tmO)	=wmO	Export Good (E)	=P14
7	World Price of Exports (we)	=PeO*(1 + teO)/ErO	=weO	Import Good (M)	=P15 + P19
8				Supply of Domestic Good (Ds)	=1-EO
9	Import Tariffs (tm)	=O19/O15	=tmO	Demand of Domestic Good (Dd)	=DsO
10	Export Duties (te)	=O20/O14	=teO	Supply of Composite Good (Qs)	=MO + DdO
11	Indirect Taxes (ts)	=P18/QsO	=tsO	Demand of Composite Good (Qd)	=QsO
12	Direct Taxes (ty)	=SUM(P21,P23)/YO	=tyO		
13				Tax Revenue (TAX)	=tmO*wmO*MO*ErO + teO*PeO*EO + tsO*PqO*QdO + tyO*YO
14	Savings rate (sy)	=(YO - CnO*PqO*(1 + tsO) - ty*YO)/YO	=syO	Total Income (Y)	=PxO*XO + trO*PqO + reO*ErO
15	Govt. Consumption (G)	=P12/(1 + tsO)/PqO	=GO	Aggregate Savings (S)	=syO*YO + ErO*BO + SgO
16	Govt. Transfers (tr)	=(T11 + T12-T8)/PqO	=trO	Consumption (Cn)	=P11/PtO
17	Foreign Grants (ft)	=T22/ErO	=ftO		
18	Net Priv Remittances (re)	=SUM(T19:T21)/ErO	=reO	Import Price (Pm)	=1
19	Foreign Saving (B)	=wmO*MO - weO*EO - ftO - reO)/ErO	=BO	Export Price (Pe)	=1
20	Output (X)	=1	=XO	Sales Price (Pt)	=PqO*(1 + tsO)
21				Price of Supply (Pq)	=1
22				Price of Output (Px)	=1
23				Price of Dom. Good (Pd)	=1
24				Exchange Rate (Er)	=1
25					
26				Investment (Z)	=P13/PtO
27				Government Savings (Sg)	=TaxO - GO*PtO - trO*PqO + ftO*ErO
28				Walras Law (Z-S)	=ZO*PtO- SO
29					

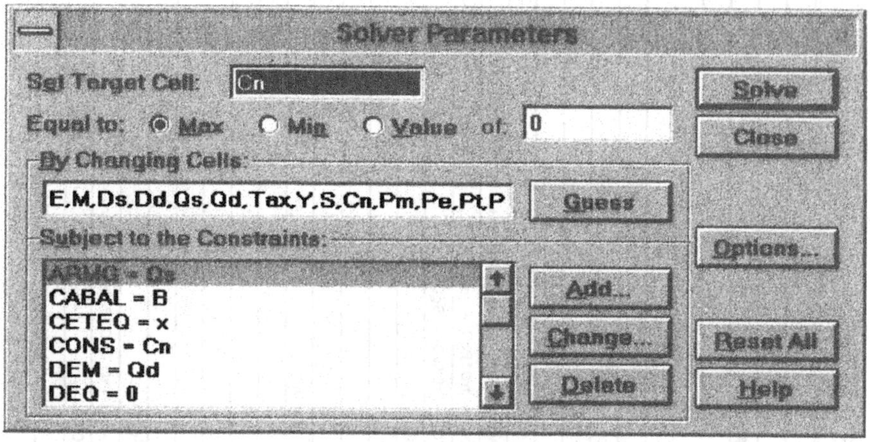

Figure 6.5. *Excel's solver*

solves the model as an optimization or programming problem. In the *Set Target Cell* space, at the top of the dialog box, the name of the variable that is being maximized (max option) or minimized (min option) in the objective function may be entered. We select the consumption variable *CN* in this case, but this has no effect in a CGE application since there will be as many variables and equations. The space may also be left empty. The "optimal" solution is found *By Changing Cells*, where all the endogenous variables in the model are entered using their names or cell locations, and *Subject to the Constraints*, where all equations and non-negativity constraints of the model are listed. The *Add* option in the dialog box allows us to specify the equations and constraints one at a time. For example, the line highlighted in Figure 6.5 matches the mathematical expression of the Armington function to total supply (ARMG=Q), which corresponds to the first equation of our model when arranged alphabetically.

The *Options* command in the *Solver Parameters* menu controls the solution process. The *Options* command lets one adjust the maximum iteration time and tolerance level as well as choose the appropriate search method. In the model, we used the Newton solution algorithm, which proved out to be robust and fast. Average time for solving simulations with a 486/33 PC was around 10 seconds.

The model is run by choosing the *Solve* command. The solver starts iterating and the number of trial solutions appears in the lower-left part of the worksheet. Once a solution that satisfies all the constraints has been found, the Solver stops and displays a dialog box to show the results. A variety of ways for reporting the outputs are possible. One can now choose between displaying the solution values on the worksheet and restoring the original values (initial guesses) of variables. Also, one may choose the option that produces both the original values and solution values. If there is no shock and the model is correctly calibrated, one should find a solution where all the variables equal their base-year values within the fixed tolerance.[26] For example, 0.33, the base-year value of $E0$ (export good) in cell $G6$ in Table 6.4, is entered as the initial guess or current value for the variable E in cell $H6$. It is important to enter some feasible initial guesses for current values of variables before starting the solver. An empty cell is interpreted as zero, which is frequently an infeasible value for a variable.

III.7 Simulations

To test the model, we conduct two experiments. The first is a trivial case – we double the nominal exchange rate, which is our numéraire. This is done by changing the right-hand side of equation 6.35 from 1.0 to 2.0 as shown in cell $L22$ in Table 6.5. After the experiment is run, the results are shown as the current values of the variables in column H of Table 6.4. As expected, all prices and incomes double while all quantities remain the same.

Next, we look at one important tax policy issue in developing countries – the fiscal/revenue implications of a tariff reform. Tariffs are a significant source of public revenue in many developing countries. In Sri Lanka, about 28 percent of tax revenue came from import duties in 1991. Therefore, the potential revenue losses of a tariff reduction in any attempted trade liberalization has to be offset by other revenue sources so as to prevent the balance of external payments from deteriorating.[27] In the experiment, we set the tariff collection rate to 0.05 (down from 0.13 in the base year) and ask by how much the domestic indirect taxes need to be raised to maintain the current account deficit from deteriorating, while keeping the same level of productive investment in the economy. To do this, we simply replace investment Z with the sales tax ts in the variable list and run the 1–2–3e model again. To attain the preceding policy objective, we find that sales and excise taxes need to be raised by about 33 percent (from the current rate of 0.08 to

---

26 A good a way of testing the model is to maximize and minimize the objective variable, which should produce identical solutions in a general equilibrium framework.
27 Greenaway and Milner (1991) and Mitra (1992) discuss the substitution of the domestic and trade taxes in greater detail.

Table 6.9. *Coordinated tariff and tax reform*

	F	G	H	I
3				
4	Endogenous Variables	Base Year	Current	Cur/Base
5				
6	Export Good (E)	0.33	0.33	1.02
7	Import Good (M)	0.50	0.51	1.01
8	Supply of Domestic Good (Ds)	0.67	0.67	0.99
9	Demand of Domestic Good (Dd)	0.67	0.67	0.99
10	Supply of Composite Good (Qs)	1.18	1.18	1.00
11	Demand of Composite Good (Qd)	1.18	1.18	1.00
12				
13	Tax Revenue (TAX)	0.20	0.19	0.95
14	Total Income (Y)	1.13	0.10	0.97
15	Aggregate Savings (S)	0.27	0.26	0.98
16	Consumption (Cn)	0.83	0.83	1.00
17				
18	Import Price (Pm)	1.00	0.93	0.93
19	Export Price (Pe)	1.00	1.00	1.00
20	Sales Price (Pt)	1.08	1.05	0.97
21	Price of Supply (Pq)	1.00	0.95	0.95
22	Price of Output (Px)	1.00	0.97	0.97
23	Price of Dom. Good (Pd)	1.00	0.96	0.96
24	Exchange Rate (Er)	1.00	1.00	1.00
25	Indirect Taxes (ts)	0.08	0.11	1.33
26	Investment (Z)	0.25	0.25	1.00
27	Government Savings (Sg)	-0.01	-0.01	1.10

0.11 in cells *G25* and *H25*, respectively, in Table 6.9). This figure of course depends on, among other factors, the degree of substitution possibilities between imports and domestic goods. Because of the "automatic" calibration embedded in the worksheet, it would be straightforward to test the sensitivity of the results on alternate values of critical parameters by just entering new estimates to the corresponding cells.

IV Conclusion

This chapter shows how two-sector models can be used to derive policy lessons about adjustment in developing countries. Starting from a small, one-country, two-sector, three-good (1–2–3) model, we show how the effects of a foreign capital inflow and terms-of-trade shock may be analyzed. In particular, we derive the assumptions underlying the conventional policy recommendation of exchange rate depreciation in response to adverse shocks.

We also implemented the model by using a popular spreadsheet software, Excel, and by using widely available data. While Excel is not suitable for all types of tax or CGE models and certainly other programs, such as GAMS, offer greater capability and indexing ease (e.g., over sectors or time), it is simple to use and a great way to get started. Add-in programs also extend its potential in new directions; for example, it is possible to add the element of uncertainty over critical parameters (e.g., trade elasticities) or exogenous shocks (e.g., the collapse of an export market like the CMEA trade) by performing risk analysis and Monte Carlo simulations.[28]

The models in this chapter present a stylized picture of how developing economies function. They are useful for qualitative analysis. However, policymakers are also concerned with the magnitude of the response to their initiatives. Furthermore, they require models that incorporate the more distinctive structural and institutional features of their economies. The lessons drawn from this chapter will facilitate the interpretation of results from more complex models, since these are essentially multisectoral analogues of the small models developed here.

References

Alston, J.M., C.A. Carter, R. Green, and D. Pick. 1990. "Whither Armington trade models?" *American Journal of Agricultural Economics* 72:455–467.

Alston, J.M. and R. Green. 1990. "Elasticities in AIDS models." *American Journal of Agricultural Economics* 72:442–445.

Armington, P. 1969. "A theory of demand for products distinguished by place of production." *IMF Staff Papers* 16:159–176.

Benjamin, N. and S. Devarajan. 1985. "Oil revenues and the Cameroon economy." In *The Political Economy of Cameroon*, edited by I.W. Zartman and M. Schatzberg. New York: Praeger.

Benjamin, N., S. Devarajan, and R. Weiner. 1989. "The 'Dutch disease' in a developing country: Oil reserves in Cameroon." *Journal of Development Economics* 30:71–92.

Brooke, A., D. Kendrick, and A. Meeraus. 1988. *GAMS: A User's Guide.* Redwood, California: Scientific Press.

Chelliah, R. and S. Chand. 1974. "A note on techniques of adjusting tax revenue series for discretionary changes." International Monetary Fund Working Paper, FAD-74-1.

De Melo, J. and S. Robinson. 1985. "Product differentiation and trade dependence of the domestic price system in computable general equilibrium trade models." In *International Trade and Exchange Rates in the Late Eighties*, edited by Theo Peeters, Peter Praet, and Paul Reding. Amsterdam: North-Holland.

---

28 See, for example, Go (1994).

De Melo, J. and S. Robinson. 1989. "Product differentiation and the treatment of foreign trade in computable general equilibrium models of small economies." *Journal of International Economics* 27:47–67.

Dervis, K., J. de Melo, and S. Robinson. 1982. *General Equilibrium Models for Development Policy.* Cambridge: Cambridge University Press.

Devarajan, S. and D.S. Go. 1993. "The simplest dynamic general equilibrium model of an open economy." Paper presented at the 4th International Computable General Equilibrium Modeling Conference, University of Waterloo, Canada, October 28–30, processed.

Devarajan, S. and J.D. Lewis. 1991. "Structural adjustment and economic reform in Indonesia: Model-based policies versus rules of thumb." In *Reforming Economic Systems in Developing Countries*, edited by D. Perkins and M. Roemer. Cambridge, Massachusetts: Harvard University Press.

Devarajan, S., J.D. Lewis, and S. Robinson. 1990. "Policy lessons from trade-focused, two-sector models." *Journal of Policy Modeling* 12:625–657.

Devarajan, S., J.D. Lewis, and S. Robinson. 1993. "External shocks, purchasing power parity and the equilibrium real exchange rate." *World Bank Economic Review* 7:45–63.

Ginsburgh, V. and S. Robinson. 1984. "Equilibrium and prices in multisector models." In *Economic Structure and Performance*, edited by M. Syrquin, L. Taylor, and L. Westphal. New York: Academic Press.

Ginsburgh, V. and J. Waelbroeck. 1981. *Activity Analysis and General Equilibrium Modeling.* Amsterdam: North-Holland.

Go, D.S. 1994. "Revenue uncertainty and the choice of tax instrument during the transition in Eastern Europe." World Bank Policy Research Working Paper No. 1330.

Go, D.S. and Pekka Sinko. 1993. "A simple tax model of Sri Lanka." Paper presented at the 4th International Computable General Equilibrium Modeling Conference, University of Waterloo, Canada, October 28–30.

Greenaway, D. and C. Milner. 1991. "Fiscal dependence on trade taxes and trade policy reform." *The Journal of Development Studies* 27:95–132.

Hanson, K., S. Robinson, and S. Tokarick. 1993. "U.S. adjustment in the 1990's: A CGE analysis of alternative trade strategies." *International Economic Journal* 7:27–49.

Microsoft Excel User's Guide. 1993. Bedmond, Washington: Microsoft Corporation.

Mitra, P. 1992. "The coordinated reform of tariffs and indirect taxes." *World Bank Research Observer* 7:195–218.

Prest, A. 1962. "The sensitivity of tax yield of personal income tax in the United Kingdom." *Economic Journal* 72:576–596.

Rattso, J. 1982. "Different macroclosures of the original Johansen model and their impact on policy evaluation." *Journal of Policy Modeling* 4:85–97.

Robinson, S. 1989. "Multisectoral models." In *Handbook of Development Economics*, Vol. II, edited by Hollis Chenery and T.N. Srinivasan. Amsterdam: North-Holland.

Salter, W. 1959. "Internal and external balance: the role of price and expenditure effects." *Economic Record* 35:226–238.

Sen, A.K. 1963. "Neo-Classical and Neo-Keynesian theories of distribution." *Economic Record* 39:53–66.

Shiells, C.R., D.W. Roland-Holst, and K.A. Reinert. 1993. "Modeling a North American free trade area: Estimation of flexible functional forms." *Weltwirtschaftliches Archiv* 129:55–77.

Swan, T. 1960. "Economic control in a dependent economy." *Economic Record* 36:51–66.

Taylor, Lance. 1975. "Theoretical foundations and technical implications." In *Economy-Wide Models of Development Planning*, edited by C.R. Blitzer, P.B. Clark, and L. Taylor. London: Oxford University Press.

PART III

Standard Applications

7

Sector-Focused General Equilibrium Modeling

Bruce A. Blonigen, Joseph E. Flynn, and Kenneth A. Reinert

I Introduction

Computable general equilibrium (CGE) models have become a useful tool in analyzing a number of varied trade policy issues.[1] These models have been used to study the economic effects of trade policies, such as tariffs and non-tariff barriers (NTBs), in a variety of settings. Some are multi-country models that focus on analyzing the effects of global trade policies or policy changes, such as the latest Uruguay Round agreements. Others focus on analyzing commercial policies of a single country, where depending on whether the country is a developed or developing economy, the modeled trade issues and policies can be quite diverse.

This chapter builds on the methodology developed in Part II and describes how it can be applied to analyze detailed and sector-specific commercial policies in a general equilibrium framework. More specifically, we utilize the flexible aggregation procedure introduced in Chapter 4 by Reinert and Roland-Holst to analyze tariffs and quotas in a single-country model of the United States.[2] We utilize a social accounting matrix (SAM) with a high degree of sectoral disaggregation: 487 industrial sectors. We aggregate it in various ways specific to the commercial policies under consideration. This allows for very exact modeling of commerecal policies that are targeted at high levels of disaggregation and for credible analysis of the commercial policies' effects on the protected sectors' upstream suppliers and downstream industrial consumers.

Section II of the chapter will motivate and outline the flexible aggregation approach to commercial policy analysis. Section III will then present the

---

1 See Shoven and Whalley (1984), Srinivasen and Whalley (1986), and de Melo (1988) for surveys of the CGE trade model literature.
2 The model we use is similar to one routinely in use at the U.S. International Trade Commission, which was constructed by Ken Reinert and David Roland-Holst.

specification of the model, with how traded goods are handled and how commercial policies are incorporated into the model presented in particular detail. Section IV discusses how to analyze detailed commercial policies and gives examples of analyzing the effects of a tariff (using nonrubber footwear as an example), a quota (using the dairy sector as an example), and an outright prohibition of imports (using the Jones Act restrictions on cabotage by foreign vessels as an example). Section V presents the conclusions of the chapter. An Appendix provides for the interested reader some details on the Linear Expenditure System used in the model.

II The Flexible Aggregation Approach

Trade policy is formulated, negotiated, and implemented at a high level of disaggregation. Not surprisingly, then, policymakers are particularly concerned with receiving information on the effects of existing or proposed trade policies on output and employment at a very disaggregated level. With these considerations in mind, the 1991 SAM and behavioral parameter dataset underlying the model used here are disaggregated to 487 sectors. The data for this social accounting matrix (SAM) are based on the input–output tables of U.S. industrial production published by the Bureau of Economic Analysis (BEA) and the national income and product accounts (NIPA), also published by BEA. The input–output tables detail the transactions among the industrial sectors in the economy. The NIPA data details the macroeconomic interactions of various agents in the economy: the production sector as a whole, households (treated as one entity in this model), government, and the rest of the world (also treated as one entity). Trade data from the U.S. Department of Labor are also used.[3]

Also supporting the model is a set of behavioral parameters that are used in the functional forms specified by the model to represent economic behavior. These parameters are in the form of elasticities and are either estimated or gathered from published sources.[4] The parameters necessary for the model will become obvious in the next section, which specifies the economic interactions modeled and their exact functional forms.

The high level of sectoral disaggregation allows a very detailed analysis of commercial policies. This is important since commercial policies are in general targeted at a highly disaggregated level. The advantages from modeling

---

3 Construction of the SAM followed Reinert and Roland-Holst (1988). For information on SAM construction in general, see Chapter 4 of this volume by Reinert and Roland-Holst.
4 These parameters are described in more detail in Reinert and Roland-Holst (1991).

an industrial sector individually, rather than deriving the results from a model which includes the individual sector in a much more aggregate sector, should be obvious. The process of disentangling focus sector effects from a more aggregate sector calls for assumptions and judgements by the researcher that are better left for the data to decide: by constructing the model and the SAM at a level disaggregated enough to isolate the sector of interest before the analysis is conducted.

The high level of disaggregation has another important advantage as well: It allows credible analysis of effects on sectors that are upstream or downstream from the sector of interest. These upstream and downstream relationships are very important economically, but often hard to analyze (especially in an economywide CGE model) because they are only discernible at a very disaggregated level. For example, suppose a CGE model has very aggregate sectors, with durable and nondurable manufacturing constituting two of these sectors. The cross-trading that most likely goes on between these two sectors in both directions makes it virtually impossible to designate whether one of them is upstream or downstream from the other. There may be many individual pairs of industries within these aggregate sectors that have definite upstream–downstream relationships, but once these many interactions are aggregated there is no discernible upstream–downstream designation possible. At the level of disaggregation of the model used here, however, the designation of upstream–downstream relationships between sectors is often quite clear, allowing analysis to uncover distinct effects in sectors related to the sector of interest.

Of course, implementing a model with close to 500 industrial sectors can be both unwieldy and costly. Therefore, for policy analysis, the many sectors that have little or no direct economic interaction with the sector of interest are aggregated into nine large reference sectors.[5] This flexible aggregation facility discussed in Chapter 4 of this volume by Reinert and Roland-Holst allows construction of a model that is unique to the detailed commercial policy under consideration because it isolates not only the sector of interest, but its closely related upstream suppliers and downstream industrial consumers as well. Yet, the aggregation of nonrelated sectors makes the model compact enough to allow for efficient computation.

---

5 These sectors are (1) agriculture, forestry, and fisheries (AGFORFSH); (2) mining (MINING); (3) construction (CONSTRUCT); (4) nondurable manufacturing (NDURMFG); (5) durable manufacturing (DURMFG); (6) transportation, communications, and utilities (TRCOMUT); (7) wholesale and retail trade (TRADE); (8) finance, insurance, and real estate (FININSRE); (9) other services (SERVICES).

III Generalized Model Specification

In this section, we provide detail on the structure of a standard single-country, multi-sector CGE model. It can be considered as a multi-sectoral extension of the model developed in Chapter 6 by Devarajan, Go, Lewis, Robinson, and Sinko. The model outlined here will be combined with three different flexible aggregations of the 487-sector SAM described to yield three different sectorally focused models in Section IV. The specification of the general model is divided into nine components: final demand behavior, production technology, factor supplies and demands, treatment of traded goods, domestic prices, domestic market equilibrium, income and government revenue, foreign sector closure, and macro closure. Where appropriate, equations are indexed over sectors *i*. The model views each of these sector as consisting of *three* goods, where imports and exports in each sector are imperfect substitutes for their domestic counterparts.[6] Imports combine with the domestic substitute to form a composite consumption (intermediate and final) good, and domestic output is supplied to both the domestic market and the export market.

To simplify the presentation, we have removed indirect business taxes, the income tax, the labor tax, the capital tax, government foreign borrowing, and household remittances from the system. No saving–investment balance equation appears in the equations since this is satisfied by Walras's Law. Following an explanation of the model specification, we detail how commercial policies are incorporated into the model.

III.1 Final Demand Behavior

The model considers three separate components of domestic final demand: household consumption, government demand, and investment demand. The consumption behavior of households is given in equation (7.1):

$$P_i^Q C_i = P_i^Q \mu_i + s_i \left[(1 - mps)Y - \sum_h P_h^Q \mu_h \right] \quad \forall i \quad (7.1)$$

where C_i represents household demand for composite consumption good i, P_i^Q denotes the domestic purchaser price of the composite consumption good i, s_i is the marginal budget share for composite good i, mps is the marginal propensity to save, Y is domestic income, and μ_i is the subsistence minimum for composite consumption good i. The functional form is a linear

---

6 See Chapter 6 of this volume by Devarajan, Go, Lewis, Robinson, and Sinko.

expenditure system (LES).[7] The LES is a generalization of the Cobb–Douglas utility function in which the origin is translated to a point in the positive quadrant. While the income expansion paths are linear, the displaced origin allows preferences to be nonhomothetic. That is, income elasticities of demand can differ from unity.

Government and investment spending in each sector (and overall) is held constant in real terms:

$$I_i = is_i I \qquad \forall i \qquad\qquad (7.2)$$

$$G_i = gs_i G \qquad \forall i \qquad\qquad (7.3)$$

where I and G are total investment and government demand, respectively, and is_i and gs_i are the share of the total investment and government demand each sector receives. This specification avoids questions concerning the substitution between present and future consumption which would make static welfare comparisons difficult.

III.2 Production Technology

Production technology is modeled by using a constant elasticity of substitution (CES) value added function specified as[8]

$$X_i = a_i \left(b_i L_i^{(\phi_i - 1)/\phi_i} + (1 - b_i) K_i^{(\phi_i - 1)/\phi_i} \right)^{\phi_i/(\phi_i - 1)} \qquad \forall i \qquad\qquad (7.4)$$

where X_i denotes gross domestic output for sector i, L_i is labor used in sector i, K_i is capital used in sector i, and ϕ_i is the elasticity of substitution between labor and capital for sector i. The parameter ϕ_i is exogenous and is estimated outside the model. a_i and b_i are the respective intercept and share parameters that allow the CES production function to be calibrated for each sector i. A Leontief (fixed coefficients) function is assumed between value added and intermediate products as well as between various intermediates:

$$D_i = \sum_h io_{ih} X_h \qquad \forall i \qquad\qquad (7.5)$$

where D_i is the intermediate demand for composite consumption good i, X_h is the gross domestic output of sector h, and io_{ih} is the input–output coefficient between sectors i and h. The input–output coefficients are determined by calibration to the SAM.

---

7 For an introduction to the LES, see the Appendix to this chapter.
8 For an introduction to CES production functions, see Chapter 9 of Layard and Walters (1978) and Chapter 9 of Silberberg (1990).

III.3 Factor Supplies and Demands

Factor demands are derived from the CES production function:

$$L_i = a_i^{(\phi_i-1)} X_i \left(\frac{b_i P_i^V}{w} \right)^{\phi_i} \qquad \forall i \tag{7.6}$$

$$K_i = a_i^{(\phi_i-1)} X_i \left[\frac{(1-b)_i P_i^V}{r} \right]^{\phi_i} \qquad \forall i \tag{7.7}$$

where P_i^V is the value added price in sector i, w is the economywide wage rate, and r is the economywide rental rate on capital.

While the total capital stock is fixed in the model, we specify a variable labor supply function using a nested linear expenditure system as in de Melo and Tarr (1992) and the Appendix to this chapter:

$$L = L_0 - \left(\frac{\lambda_l}{w} \right) \frac{\left[(1-mps)Y - P^{LES}\Gamma \right]}{(1-\lambda_l)} \tag{7.8}$$

$$P^{LES} = \frac{\left[(1-mps)Y - \sum_i P_i^Q \Gamma_i \right]}{\prod_i (C_i - \Gamma_i)^{\lambda_i}} \tag{7.9}$$

where L_0 is maximum labor supply, λ_l is the marginal budget share for leisure, λ_i is the marginal budget share of composition good i, P^{LES} is the *LES* aggregate price index, Γ_i is the *LES* subsistence minimum for composition good i, and Γ is the aggregate *LES* subsistence minimum. This represents just one possible labor market closure. One alternative is to fix L and maintain a flexible w. Another alternative is to fix w and allow L to vary.

III.4 Treatment of Traded Goods

The treatment of traded goods is the most important component of the model specification. As mentioned, the model views each sector as consisting of three goods, where imports and exports in each industry category are imperfect substitutes for their domestic counterparts.[9] On the import side,

---

9 The treatment of traded goods follows de Melo and Robinson (1989). See also Chapter 6 of this volume by Devarajan, Go, Lewis, Robinson, and Sinko for an explanation of this approach.

the model treats foreign and domestic commodities as imperfect substitutes in domestic use. Therefore, the import composition of domestic demand is influenced by the ratio of domestic and import prices, as well as by any administrative quantity restrictions. The model aggregates imports and their domestic counterparts into an aggregate good for each sector, Q_i, using a *CES* aggregation:

$$Q_i = \alpha_i \left[\beta_i M_i^{(\sigma_i-1)/\sigma_i} + (1-\beta_i) S_i^{(\sigma_i-1)/\sigma_i} \right]^{\sigma_i/(\sigma_i-1)} \qquad \forall i \qquad (7.10)$$

$$\left(\frac{M_i}{S_i} \right) = \left[\left(\frac{\beta_i}{(1-\beta_i)} \right) \left(\frac{P_i^S}{P_i^M} \right) \right]^{\sigma_i} \qquad \forall i \qquad (7.11)$$

Equation (7.10) is the aggregation relation in which Q_i denotes the composite good for domestic consumption in sector i, M_i is the imports of sector i, S_i is the domestic supply in sector i, α_i and β_i are the respective intercept and share parameters in this CES product aggregation function for each sector i, and σ_i is the elasticity of substitution between imports and domestic competing goods in sector i.[10] Equation (7.11) is the tangency condition in which P_i^S is the sector i's price of the domestic good and P_i^M is sector i's domestic price of imports.

The use of the CES functional form for aggregation implies that preferences with respect to imports and domestic goods within a sector are homothetic, while preferences between sectors are not. For a given level of demand for a product category, determined by the specification of the three components of final demand, the shares of imports and domestic goods are determined in response to relative prices.

On the export side, the model assumes that domestic firms allocate their output between domestic and foreign markets according to a transformation function which depends on the ratio of domestic and foreign prices. Therefore, the export composition of domestic supply is influenced by the ratio of domestic and export prices. The functional form used is a constant elasticity of transformation (CET) as indicated in the following equations:[11]

$$X_i = \gamma_i \left[\delta_i E_i^{(\tau_i+1)/\tau_i} + (1-\delta_i) S_i^{(\tau_i+1)/\tau_i} \right]^{\tau_i/(\tau_i+1)} \qquad \forall i \qquad (7.12)$$

---

10 This is often referred to as the "Armington" elasticity (Armington, 1969).
11 The original reference to this functional form is Powell and Gruen (1968). See also Chapter 6 of this volume by Devarajan, Go, Lewis, Robinson, and Sinko.

$$\left(\frac{E_i}{S_i}\right) = \left[\left(\frac{(1-\delta_i)}{\delta_i}\right)\left(\frac{P_i^E}{P_i^S}\right)\right]^{\tau_i} \qquad \forall i \qquad (7.13)$$

Equation (7.12) is the allocation relation in which S_i is domestic supply in sector i, E_i is exports of sector i, τ is the elasticity of transformation between domestic supply and exports, and γ_i and δ_i are the respective intercept and share parameters used to calibrate the model for each sector i. Equation (7.13) is the tangency condition in which P_i^E is the domestic price of exports in sector i. The shares of domestic supply and exports are determined in response to relative prices.

III.5 Domestic Prices

We next turn to the equations for domestic prices, including those of import and export goods. These are given in the following five equations:

$$P_i^X X_i = P_i^S S_i + P_i^E E_i \qquad \forall i \qquad (7.14)$$

$$P_i^Q Q_i = P_i^S S_i + P_i^M M_i \qquad \forall i \qquad (7.15)$$

$$P_i^V = P_i^X - \sum_h io_{hi} P_h^Q \qquad \forall i \qquad (7.16)$$

$$P_i^M = (1+t_i)(1+\rho_i) er PW_i^M \qquad \forall i \qquad (7.17)$$

$$P_i^E = er PW_i^E \qquad \forall i \qquad (7.18)$$

where t_i is the tariff rate on imports in sector i, ρ_i is the quota premium rate in sector i, PW_i^M is the world price of the import good in sector i, PW_i^E is the world price of the export good in sector i, and er is the exchange rate (U.S. dollars per unit of foreign currency).

III.6 Domestic Market Equilibrium

Three equations are required for domestic market equilibrium, one for the commodity market and two others for the factor markets:

$$Q_i = D_i + C_i + G_i + I_i \qquad \forall i \qquad (7.19)$$

$$\sum_i K_i = K \qquad (7.20)$$

$$\sum_i L_i = L \qquad (7.21)$$

III.7 Income and Government Revenue

Income and government revenue are summarized by the following six equations:

$$R_T = \frac{\sum_i t_i P_i^M M_i}{\left(1 + t_i\right)} \tag{7.22}$$

$$R_Q = \sum_i \rho_i er PW_i^M M_i \tag{7.23}$$

$$Y = Y_L + Y_K + GT + R_Q \tag{7.24}$$

$$\sum_i P_i^Q G_i + GS + GT = R_T \tag{7.25}$$

$$S = mps Y + GS + er FS \tag{7.26}$$

$$I = \sum_i P_i^Q I_i \tag{7.27}$$

Equations (7.22) and (7.23) represent tariff revenue (R_T) and domestically captured quota rents (R_Q), respectively. Equation (7.24) defines income, which is the sum of labor income ($Y_L = wL$), capital income ($Y_K = rK$), government transfer payments (GT), and domestically captured quota rents. The government budget constraint is captured in equation (7.25), where GS is government savings. Finally, total investment and savings are defined in equations (7.26) and (7.27), respectively, where FS is foreign savings. As indicated, by Walras's Law we leave out any savings–investment balance equation.

III.8 Foreign Sector Closure

To characterize the foreign sector we specify the following balance of payments equation:

$$\sum_i PW_i^M M_i + \frac{R_Q}{er} = \sum_i PW_i^E E_i + FS \tag{7.28}$$

With foreign savings (FS) held constant, the balance of payments is maintained in equation (7.28) via changes in the exchange rate, er. An alternative foreign sector closure is to fix the exchange rate and allow foreign savings to vary. The closure used here better supports welfare analysis, however. With a numéraire price index held fixed (see the section Macro Closure), the exchange rate behaves as a real exchange rate.

III.9 Macro Closure

Because the model is SAM-based, a macroeconomic closure must be specified. A numéraire price index is held fixed, as suggested by de Melo and Robinson (1989) and de Melo and Tarr (1992). Government and investment demands by sector are fixed in real terms as described. As in Devarajan and Rodrik (1991), real government transfers adjust to maintain the savings–investment balance. The model is homogeneous of degree zero in prices.

III.10 Commercial Policies

Given the model specification, we now examine how commercial policies are incorporated into it. There are two types of trade policies that are typically examined in a CGE framework from an importing country's viewpoint: tariffs and quantitative restrictions on imports such as quotas, voluntary restraint agreements (VRAs), and voluntary export restraints (VERs).[12,13] Tariffs are fairly straightforward, whereas quotas involve a number of issues that must be considered in order to model them correctly.

Tariffs To simplify and standardize the analysis, tariffs are specified as the average Most Favored Nation (MFN) *ad valorem* tariff equivalent and calculated on a dutiable value basis.[14] This *ad valorem* tariff rate gives the percentage by which the domestic U.S. price exceeds the world price. In other words we have the following relationship:

$$P_d = e(1+t)P_W \Rightarrow P_W = \frac{P_d}{e(1+t)} \qquad (7.29)$$

where P_d is the domestic price of the imported good in the sector, P_W is the world price of the import good, e is the exchange rate (units of local currency per unit of foreign currency), and t is the *ad valorem* tariff rate. Figure 7.1

12 We will not directly address commercial policies that affect the export side, such as export subsidies. Methods analogous to those outlined here may be appropriate for modeling these effects, since subsidies are simply negative taxes.

13 Quotas and other quantitative restrictions, such as VERs and VRAs, have similar effects in the market. Consequently, the term "quota" will be used to represent all types of quantitative restrictions. See Chapter 2 of this volume by Laird on the entire spectrum of protective measures.

14 Average *ad valorem* tariff rates on a dutiable value basis are calculated by dividing the estimated duties collected for a sector by the value of imports in that sector that are subject to duties.

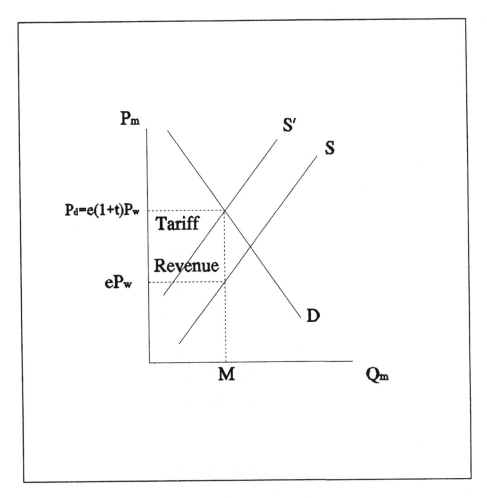

Figure 7.1. *Tariff only*

shows the initial situation using a supply and demand graph for the import good. In Figure 7.1, D represents the U.S. demand of the foreign good, whereas S represents foreign supply of the good. The tariff introduces a schedule of "market" supply prices, S', which lies above S.[15] In other words, the tariff creates a gap between what U.S. consumers must pay for the import good versus what the rest of the world receives for its sale. For a given initial level of observed imports M the tariff revenue can be easily calculated:

$$\text{Tariff Revenue} = \left[e(1+t)P_W - eP_W\right]M$$
$$= etP_W M \qquad (7.30)$$

15 On the distinction between "basic" and "market" prices, see Layard and Walters (1978, p. 85).

Substituting in for the initial P_W and simplifying

$$\text{Tariff Revenue} = \frac{tP_d}{(1+t)} M \qquad (7.31)$$

In this way, the tariff revenue is expressed as a function solely of the *ad valorem* tariff rate, the domestic price, and the initial level of imports – all of which are observable.[16] Thus, these expressions can be used to calibrate the model and derive an expression for the initial world price.

Quotas Modeling quotas raises a number of issues that are not encountered with tariffs. First, the researcher must consider whether the quota is "binding" on imports, i.e., whether current imports are actually restricted by the quotas in place. If foreign producers are exporting significantly less than the quota allows, it is likely that there will be no difference between the world price and the domestic price;[17] hence, the quota causes no distortion and there is no economic effect to estimate. It is important to note, however, that quotas may be considered binding even if they are not fully utilized. Because of informational constraints or other considerations, foreign exporters may not completely utilize the entire quota, even though it restricts their deliveries to the domestic market.[18] Determining the utilization level that signals whether a quota is binding or not is an empirical question unique to each quota, based on the characteristics of the industry and the quota arrangement.[19]

Notwithstanding the question of whether the quota is binding or not, it is more difficult to model a market distortion caused by a quota than by a tariff. We can identify the restricted quantity of imports, but there is often no certain way of knowing what the level of imports would be if the quota were not in place. For this reason, we focus our attention on the *price* distortion the quota causes. We can observe what the domestic price of a good is with the quota in place, but we also may have an idea of what the price would be without the quota – the world price of the good. We can then calculate the percentage by which the domestic price is above the world price, yielding a "tariff equivalent" of the quota. This method is often referred to as the

---

16 In the model, the initial domestic price (P_d) is set to unity in the base solution. The world price will therefore be less than unity.

17 The domestic price may include a tariff.

18 For example, in many of the bilateral agreements under the Multi-Fibre Arrangement (MFA), flexibility is allowed by "swing," "carry-forward," and "carry-over" provisions. This makes the utilization rate less effective in determining whether the quota was binding.

19 See Chapter 2 of this volume by Laird.

price-gap method of estimating a tariff-equivalent of a quota.[20] Since this measure is analogous to an *ad valorem* tariff rate, it also simplifies the modeling.

The final significant issue involving quotas concerns who is able to appropriate the rents that accrue from the quota – foreign exporters or domestic importers.[21] This is not always easy to measure and depends on a number of factors including the respective market structures of the foreign exporters and domestic importers. But the issue is not always a small matter when determining the welfare and resource allocation effects to an economy of removing a quota. If the domestic importers effectively receive the quota rents, elimination of the quota results in a transfer of the rents from domestic importers to domestic consumers, representing no net welfare change to the economy as a whole from this transfer. However, if foreign producers capture the quota rents, removal of the quota leads to a transfer of those rents to the economy, resulting in a welfare gain and, in general, a reallocation of resources toward domestic goods.

In the presence of a tariff, the analysis varies according to who captures the quota rents as well. The difference hinges on the fact that when foreign exporters hold the import rights, the price at the border (i.e., the foreign export price P_{fe}) already embodies the quota premium, and the tariff is simply placed on top of this distorted border price. On the other hand, when the domestic importers hold the import rights, the price at the border is still free of distortion (i.e., the foreign export price is equal to the foreign producer price P_{fp}),[22] and thus, the tariff and quota premium are imposed simultaneously.

Specifically, consider the case where the domestic importers hold the import rights, as shown in Figure 7.2. As in Figure 7.1, S and D represent supply and demand for U.S. imports of a certain commodity. Identical to the case of a tariff by itself, the imposition of the tariff introduces a schedule of "market" supply prices S'. In this case, importers bear the full burden of the tariff, so the price at which they purchase the good rises above the world price. In other words, the tariff taxes a portion of the quota rents away from domestic importers. Following a rule of thumb expressed by Corden (1971), if the margin between the demand and supply price produced by the quota

---

20 For a detailed discussion of tariff equivalents of quotas and of the price gap method, see USITC (1990a), Baldwin (1989), and Deardorff and Stern (1985). Also see Chapter 2 of this volume by Laird.

21 In standard terminology, the rents accrue to whoever (the domestic importers or foreign exporters) holds the import rights.

22 In order to keep the analysis that follows comparable to the tariff case, we note that P_{fp} is equivalent to P_W, which we called the world price in analysis of a tariff only. This will be accounted for in Figures 7.2 and 7.3.

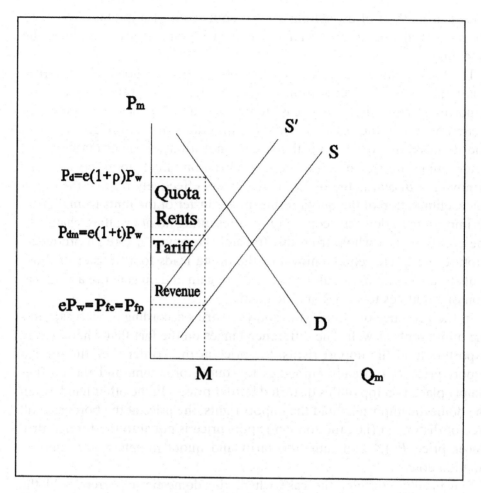

Figure 7.2. *Domestic-held quota*

in the absence of the tariff is greater than the tariff, then it is the quota that sets the domestic price; if the tariff is higher, it sets P_d. In Figure 7.2, we have graphed the case where the quota premium is larger than the *ad valorem* tariff rate.

As with the tariff-only case, we can use these relationships to calculate the initial tariff revenue, quota rents, and world price. Given the implied relationship between the domestic and world price in Figure 7.2, we express the world price as

$$P_W = \frac{P_d}{e(1+\rho)} \qquad (7.32)$$

Tariff revenue is calculated in the normal fashion taking the difference between P_{dm} and the world price in Figure 7.2 multiplied by the initial level of imports M. After substituting the world price expression into this calculation we get

$$\text{Tariff Revenue} = \frac{tP_d}{(1+\rho)} M \qquad (7.33)$$

Tariff revenue in this case is different from that in the tariff-only case because it is now a function of the *ad valorem* tariff equivalent rate of the quota ρ as well as the tariff rate t. In similar fashion, we calculate the quota rents accruing to the domestic importers.

$$\text{Quota Rents} = \left[e(1+\rho)P_W - e(1+t)P_W\right]M$$
$$= e(\rho - t)P_W M \qquad (7.34)$$

Appropriate simplification and substitution of the world price expression yield

$$\text{Quota Rents} = \frac{\rho}{(1+\rho)} M - \text{Tariff Revenues} \qquad (7.35)$$

In our second case of interest foreign exporters hold the import rights, as depicted in Figure 7.3. The imposition of the tariff introduces a schedule of market import demand prices D'. Foreign exporters bear the full burden of the tariff, so the foreign export price P_{fe} falls below the domestic price. But since the quota premium is already embedded in the border price, the tariff rate is applied on top of this border price. A given tariff rate generates more revenue in this second case than in the former, where importers held the licenses, since it is applied to a larger, premium-inclusive import volume. Another important point, illustrated by Figure 7.3, is that tariffs can be used to recover foreign quota rents. This is called rent recapture. The recapture of quota rents can greatly complicate the political economy and welfare effects of trade liberalization involving tariffs and quotas.

Since the quota rents are captured by foreign exporters and the tariff is simply calculated from the border price, the analysis is quite similar to when there is only a tariff. Referring to Figure 7.3, we calculate tariff revenue as

$$\text{Tariff Revenue} = (P_d - P_{fe})M = \left[e(1+t)(1+\rho)P_W - e(1+\rho)P_W\right]M$$
$$= et(1+\rho)P_W M \qquad (7.36)$$

Substituting for the world price implied by the expression for the domestic price and simplifying we obtain the following function of the tariff rate, domestic price and initial level of imports:

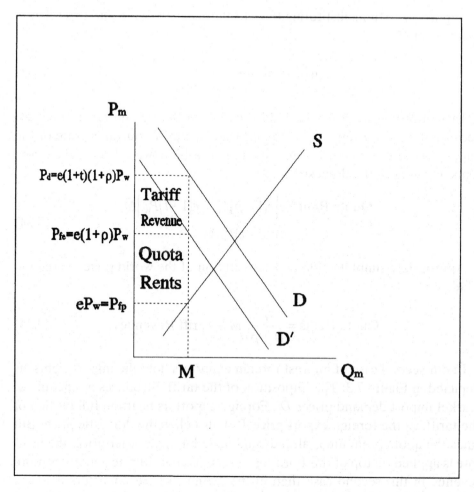

Figure 7.3. *Foreign-held quota*

$$\text{Tariff Revenue} = \frac{tP_d}{(1+t)}M \qquad (7.37)$$

Since the tariff revenue is independent of the quota, we obtain the identical expression for the tariff revenue as in the tariff-only case represented in Figure 7.1. The expression for the quota rents received by the foreign exporters is derived in identical fashion as the tariff revenue in this case by taking the difference between P_{fe} and the world price (translated into dollars) eP_W and multiplying this by the level of observed initial imports. After substitution and simplification

$$\text{Foreign Quota Rents} = \frac{\rho P_d}{(1+t)(1+\rho)} M \qquad (7.38)$$

IV Applications

In analyzing the economic effects of commercial policies, the standard CGE methodology is a counterfactual experiment: It asks what would have happened in the base year of study (here, 1991) if the commercial policies were removed and all other domestic policies (fiscal and monetary) as well as foreign conditions (economic behavior in foreign countries) remained the same. The analysis thus emphasizes the effects of the commercial policy in isolation from other factors. Since the analysis does not incorporate expected future changes in these other factors, it is not a forecast. Finally, the CGE model is static and does not incorporate dynamic features. These conceptual issues are important for a researcher to keep in mind when interpreting and presenting results from a CGE model.[23]

An important step before the policy experiment can be conducted is to calibrate the model to the base year behavioral parameters and data of the model. It is necessary that the commercial policies of interest are included in this base model during the calibration process.[24] With the calibrated model in hand, counterfactual experiments of commercial policies can be simulated.

To examine the effect of a specific commercial policy, an *ad valorem* tariff and/or an *ad valorem* tariff equivalent (in the case of quotas and specific tariffs) is set equal to zero and the model is solved again.[25] Changes in prices, output, and employment generated from this policy experiment and the base model represent the economic effects of the commercial policy. In addition to changes in prices, output, and employment, economists are often concerned with the overall welfare effect on an economy from a change in the commercial policy. As is the case with many other models, the CGE model uses an equivalent variation (EV) measurement as its basic indicator of welfare effects.[26] With government and investment spending held constant in real terms in this model, the EV measure can be calculated solely through the household sector. Specifically, we calculate the amount of income that would have to be given to the household sector in the base model (with the

---

23 For a contrast to the comparative static approach, see Chapter 13 of this volume by Keuschnigg and Kohler.

24 The calibration process is described in Shoven and Whalley (1984, 1993).

25 In the case of quotas, it also must be decided whether the quota rents are held by domestic importers, foreign exporters, or a combination of both.

26 See Chapter 3 of this volume by Martin on the measurement of welfare.

commercial policy in place) to reach the level of overall economic welfare achievable with liberalization.

With this general methodology in mind, we present three specific examples of estimating effects of commercial policies. Our first example examines liberalization of a tariff in the U.S. nonrubber footwear industry. The flexible aggregation facility allows us to isolate the effects not only on the nonrubber footwear sector, but on its main upstream suppliers as well.

A second example examines quotas in the U.S. dairy industry. Analysis of these quotas is complicated by the fact that they operate in conjunction with domestic price support programs. Our analysis is unique in two ways. First, the highly disaggregated SAM allows us to model four separate dairy sectors in a CGE framework; this in turn permits a better fit of the detailed commercial policies specific to each of these four sectors. Second, we are able to model the upstream sector, dairy farms, separately from the protected sectors, allowing analysis of the quota in conjunction with the price support programs.

A final example examines the elimination of the restriction on maritime transport between U.S. ports by foreign vessels.[27] These restrictions, often called Jones Act restrictions, are considered to be important not only for the water transportation sector of the U.S. economy, but also for its upstream sector, shipbuilding. Again, our flexible aggregation facility allows us to examine the important upstream and downstream effects of elimination of these restrictions.

IV.1 Nonrubber Footwear

Nonrubber footwear includes leather and vinyl shoes, boots, and sandals; slippers of all materials; and some athletic shoes. Rates of duty on nonrubber footwear range from free to 15%, and with the exception of disposable footwear, are not eligible for duty-free treatment under the Generalized System of Preferences (GSP) or the Caribbean Basin Economic Recovery Act (CBERA). On the basis of dutiable value, we estimate an average Most Favored Nation (MFN) *ad valorem* tariff rate of 10.7% for the base year 1991.

To create an aggregated SAM and behavioral parameter data set specific to nonrubber footwear analysis, we identify from the detailed SAM the sectors that are major upstream suppliers and downstream industrial consumers. For nonrubber footwear we find two major upstream suppliers: (1)

---

27 Transportation of goods between domestic ports is often called "cabotage."

boot and shoe cut stock and (2) leather tanning and finishing. These two sectors supplied nonrubber footwear with approximately $250 million and $500 million in intermediate inputs, respectively. The next closest sectors contributed less than $50 million. Downstream, no significant industrial consumers of nonrubber footwear were identified, since final goods in this sector are mainly for retail. Therefore, all other sectors were aggregated into nine different reference sectors, which represent the rest of the U.S. economy. We are left with a model that separately identifies our sector of interest, its two major upstream consumers, and the rest of the U.S. economy. The aggregated SAM is presented in Table 7.1.

The economic effects of the tariff on nonrubber footwear are estimated by setting the tariff rate on this sector to zero. Detailed economic effects of tariff removal in this sector are presented in Table 7.2. Direct effects on the nonrubber footwear sector are a $110 million fall in output and almost 1,400 fewer full-time equivalent workers (FTEs). Both figures represent a 2 percent decline from original levels. The effect of liberalization on imports is larger, with an increase in imports of $455 million, almost a 6.0 percent increase. Both upstream sectors are negatively affected as expected, with leather tanning and finishing experiencing a $17 million loss and almost 100 fewer FTEs. Trade effects for the upstream sectors are small, each $6 million or less.

The model also estimates that the U.S. economy experiences a welfare gain of $170 million from tariff removal in the nonrubber footwear sector using the equivalent variation measure described. A large contribution to this welfare gain is the 6.0 percent fall in the overall price of nonrubber footwear enjoyed by consumers.

By design, the sectors the remainder of the U.S. economy comprises have few direct linkages to the nonrubber footwear sector. As a result, they experience negligible effects in percentage terms from the liberalization of the tariff on nonrubber footwear, although the dollar amounts appear significant because the sectors are so large in terms of the total industrial output each one represents. In general, these sectors experience output and employment gains from the removal of the tariff on nonrubber footwear. This reflects a shift of resources out of the footwear sector. It illustrates the factor allocation effects of commercial policy.

Because there are few direct linkages between the nonrubber footwear sector and the sectors that compose the rest of the economy, these aggregate sectors experience economic effects mainly through the economywide changes generated by the commercial policy change. These effects are related to changes in the exchange rate, consumer spending, and the price of

Table 7.1. Nonrubber footwear SAM, 1991

	footwear	leathrtan	shoestock	agforfsh	mining	construct	ndurmfg	durmfg	trcomut	trade
footwear	1886	0	0	0	0	0	4	3	0	0
leathrtan	742	294	42	0	0	0	1490	239	0	0
shoestock	358	0	18	0	0	0	2	2	0	0
agforfsh	0	0	0	40374	8	1171	108204	4209	58	2183
mining	0	0	0	101	13488	2382	104296	10288	33032	1
construct	12	6	1	1778	6867	591	13448	15023	34567	12285
ndurmfg	453	20	64	29138	2011	28159	416068	97493	35818	28276
durmfg	65	1210	10	3849	5697	164349	62275	615003	20629	9160
trcomut	58	14	7	4058	2393	13030	84632	69082	99531	59467
trade	99	138	13	10058	2387	98631	91451	101605	25299	31899
fininsre	71	251	2	6419	5207	4566	21077	24033	15024	57346
services	165	25	11	2386	3516	60367	95467	90420	38081	176657
labor	1049	120	76	39508	20221	227369	248811	492349	242405	435926
property	547	362	38	69985	49136	35328	160050	77351	231469	165178
enterprise	0	514	0	0	0	0	0	0	0	0
household	0	0	0	0	0	0	0	0	0	0
government	17	0	2	9861	11756	8854	32933	22328	43348	157301
capaccount	0	9	0	0	0	0	0	0	0	0
row	7083	589	424	12249	45630	0	121826	312033	67830	0
rowtaxes	635	14	14	165	188	0	8043	8131	0	0

	fininsre	services	labor	property	enterprse	househld	governmnt	capaccnt	row	rowtaxes
footwear	0	0	0	0	0	10871	57	-18	439	0
leathrtan	0	3	0	0	0	0	1	-8	763	0
shoestock	0	190	0	0	0	0	16	-0	137	0
agforfsh	6811	9155	0	0	0	27558	9430	-4206	24974	0
mining	38	46	0	0	0	344	842	-4054	7696	0
construct	54857	41898	0	0	0	0	129733	333717	0	0
ndurmfg	14822	192265	0	0	0	547625	54696	8034	113942	0
durmfg	4279	82788	0	0	0	258846	142711	294030	275890	0
trcomut	27489	115794	0	0	0	280594	45224	9872	75723	0
trade	20707	97590	0	0	0	584782	16017	54888	0	0
fininsre	214021	102300	0	0	0	938956	17903	12487	15524	0
services	105359	328078	0	0	0	1236071	673733	62	83674	0
labor	239217	1443545	0	0	0	0	0	0	0	0
property	601828	398701	0	1807251	0	0	0	0	142905	0
enterprise	0	0	0	0	1184387	0	0	0	0	0
household	0	0	2861660	0	0	0	90371	0	0	0
government	137157	37729	529176	0	124160	620527	787493	187714	0	17190
capaccount	0	0	0	0	701578	199928	0	0	-8990	0
row	8377	44086	0	125779	0	14934	-28166	0	0	0
rowtaxes	0	0	0	0	0	0	0	0	0	0

note: Key to sectors: footwear–nonrubber footwear; leathrtan–leather tanning and finishing; shoestock–boot and shoe cut stock; agforfsh–agriculture, forestry, and fishing; mining–mining and mineral resources; construct–construction; ndurmfg–nondurable manufacturing; durmfg–durable manufacturing; trcomut–transportation, communication, and utilities; trade–wholesale and retail trade; fininsre–finance, insurance, and real estate; services–personal, business, and public services; labor–labor value added; property–property value added; enterprise–enterprise; household–household final demand; government–government final demand; capaccount–savings and investment; row–rest of the world; rowtaxes–rest of the world taxes (tariffs).

Table 7.2. *Nonrubber footwear: economic effects of tariff removal, 1991*

Sector	Employment		Output		Imports		Exports	
	Number[a]	Percent[b]	Dollar[c]	Percent[b]	Dollar[c]	Percent[b]	Dollar[c]	Percent[b]
Liberalized sector:								
Nonrubber footwear	-1,472	-2.0	-110	-2.0	455	5.9	10	2.3
Upstream sectors:								
Boot and shoe cut stock	-39	-1.1	-3	-1.1	-6	-1.2	-1	-1.0
Leather tanning and finishing	-94	-0.6	-17	-0.6	-4	-0.6	-4	-0.6
Rest of the economy:								
Agforfish	391	0.0	51	0.0	-2	0.0	37	0.1
Mining	94	0.0	14	0.0	-2	0.0	3	0.0
Construct	39	0.0	2	0.0	([d])	([d])	([d])	([d])
Ndurmfg	331	0.0	43	0.0	-36	0.0	25	0.0
Durmfg	1,675	0.0	253	0.0	-85	0.0	106	0.0
Trcomut	402	0.0	52	0.0	-22	0.0	35	0.0
Trade	-227	0.0	-25	0.0	([d])	([d])	([d])	([d])
Fininsre	-169	0.0	-71	0.0	-3	0.0	5	0.0
Services	-181	0.0	-31	0.0	-16	0.0	33	0.0

[a] Full-time equivalents.
[b] Changes less than one-tenth of one percent are reported as 0.0.
[c] In millions of dollars in base year prices. Changes less than $500,000 are reported as 0.
[d] Nontradeable sector.

production inputs in the model caused by the commercial policy change. In this experiment, the exchange rate depreciates slightly. This raises both import and export prices in the domestic currency. On the export side, this tends to move firms along the CET frontier away from domestic supply toward exports. On the import side, this tends to move firms along the CES composite good isoquant away from imports and toward domestic goods. This helps to explain why exports increase and imports decrease in the nine sectors of the rest of the economy.

IV.2 Dairy

Regulation of the U.S. dairy industry evolved from legislation enacted in the 1930s, 40s, and 50s. In particular, the Agricultural Marketing Agreement Act of 1937 provided for federal milk-marketing orders, the Agricultural Act of 1949 established the dairy price support program, and the Defense Production Act of 1950 established import quotas on most dairy products. In addition, there are tariffs on imports as well, but it is the dairy programs that play a major role in determining the prices and production of U.S. dairy products.[28] The quotas were put in place to prevent imports from interfering with the price support program for milk and products derived from milk. These quotas limit the importation of dairy products equal to a quantity of approximately 2 percent of the equivalent of U.S. production of milk. In recent years, the U.S. dairy quotas have been substantially filled (nearly 99 percent).[29] Thus, we can be quite certain that the quotas are binding.[30]

Accurate modeling of the economic effects of the dairy quotas requires consideration of several issues. First, as discussed, it is important to identify whether the quotas are domestically held, foreign-held, or some combination of both. Given the level of disaggregation of our SAM we are able to separate the dairy industry into four separate sectors: butter, cheese, dry/condensed milk products, and cream. Of these four dairy sectors, the quotas for butter and cheese require USDA licenses that are allocated to qualified domestic importers. This would lead one to believe that the quota rents accrue to these firms. However, recent research on the cheese quotas by Hornig, Boisvert, and Blandford (1990a,b) indicates that the export side of the cheese market is highly concentrated, resulting in market power for both the importers and exporters. They estimate that in 1980 the quotas gener-

---

28 For a detailed history of the U.S. dairy programs, see USITC (1990b).
29 See Warren (1992).
30 For a more complete discussion of the U.S. dairy quotas and a CGE analysis of their effects, see Flynn and Reinert (1993).

ated rents of about $41 million for importers and $52 million for exporters. On the basis of this work, the quota rents are split on a 50/50 basis between domestic importers and foreign exporters for both the butter and cheese sectors. The quotas for the dry/condensed milk products and cream sectors are administered by the U.S. Customs Service on a first-come, first-served basis. Consequently, it is assumed that foreign exporters capture all of the quota rents in these two sectors because the import side is unconcentrated and the foreign exporters benefit from higher prices for their products.

A second issue that must be considered is how the U.S. federal marketing orders and price support programs interact with the import quotas. Since milk is a perishable product and is expensive to transport in liquid form, the U.S. government, through the Commodity Credit Corporation (CCC), supports the farm price of raw milk indirectly by purchasing butter, cheddar cheese, and nonfat dry milk from dairy processors at specified prices. The price of milk produced under sanitary conditions that qualify it for fluid consumption is regulated directly by the Federal Milk Marketing Order Program. This program regulates the price of consumption grade milk. The minimum prices set by the marketing orders are based on the average price of raw milk in Minnesota and Wisconsin (the M–W price), which, in turn, is indirectly supported by CCC purchases of surplus dairy products. In general, prices for consumption grade milk used for manufactured products are set at or near the M–W price, while prices for consumption grade milk destined for the fluid market are set higher by fixed differentials unique to each federal order. Thus, the milk-marketing orders extend the support price of raw grade milk to all milk prices.

If the dairy quotas were eliminated, the CCC would substantially increase its purchases of dairy products to maintain the M–W price of raw milk. In essence, the M–W price would become the world price for raw milk, supported by U.S. government purchases. Consequently, effectively modeling the impact of the U.S. dairy quotas requires suspension of CCC purchases. Thus, we reduce the amount of government demand in these dairy sectors by the amount of CCC purchases in the base year, 1991. This also implies that the milk-marketing orders are suspended so that the price of raw milk can move freely in the market.

It can be argued that the liberalization scenario described is politically unlikely, since suspension of both the import quotas and price support programs would have a significantly adverse impact on farmers' incomes. Therefore, we divide our policy experiments into two cases. In the first case, we assume that the U.S. government provides an *ad valorem* production subsidy to dairy farmers sufficient to maintain dairy farm output at the base period level, despite the elimination of the import quotas and price support programs. In this way, we are able to maintain farm incomes, hold dairy production constant, and allow processors and final consumers to benefit from lower prices for milk and other dairy products. This subsidy is a first-best policy option for a production level objective.[31] Again, our level of disaggregation in the SAM allows us to model this scenario in a straightforward fashion, since we can separately identify the dairy farm sector, which is upstream to the sectors we are liberalizing (butter, cheese, dry/condensed milk products and cream). With the dairy farm sector explicitly identified, it is quite easy to solve for the endogenous production subsidy that keeps the dairy farm sector's output constant in the face of the liberalization. In the second case, we allow dairy farm output and income to move freely as the import quotas are removed.[32]

To model the U.S. dairy quotas, we use the price-gap method to estimate equivalent *ad valorem* tariff rates for the four sectors. U.S.D.A. collects both domestic and world price data for whole milk powder, butter, and cheese. These three price series serve as a basis for the estimates of the tariff equivalents of the U.S. dairy quotas used in the CGE model. The butter and cheese sectors have a straightforward application of the price-gap method because data exist for both domestic and world prices.[33] For the other two sectors, dry/condensed milk products and cream, the price gap for whole milk powder is used as a proxy because these sectors contain primarily milk and cream products, which have a high butterfat content, and because world price data for these sectors are not available. The 1991 tariff equivalents are butter, 26.9 percent; cheese, 35.4 percent; dry/condensed milk products, 60.3 percent; and cream, 60.3 percent.[34]

The overall effects of the two quota removal simulations are presented in Table 7.3. The first line presents the equivalent variation welfare gains. As expected, welfare gains are larger in the case of no market distortions ($847 million) relative to the case with production subsidies ($711 million). The second line of Table 7.3 reports the total production subsidy required to

---

31 See Bhagwati (1971). Alternatively, we could have held farm incomes constant. Our choice to hold output constant was due to modeling ease and the explicit link to the trade theory literature.

32 Given the well known subsidization practices of certain dairy producing countries, we assume in both cases that removal of the U.S. dairy quotas will not result in countervailing duty actions under Title VII of the Tariff Act of 1930.

33 The world price data U.S.D.A. collects in the cheese sector are prices for cheddar cheese. Consequently, a tariff equivalent for cheddar cheese is used as a proxy for the cheese sector, although there are many different types of cheeses.

34 In 1991, the average world price (including transportation costs to the United States) for butter was $0.78/1b, for cheddar cheese $0.92/lb, and for dry whole milk $0.71/lb. In 1991, the average U.S. price for butter was $0.99/lb, for cheddar cheese $1.24/lb, and dry whole milk $1.14/lb. These pricing data are from *Dairy Market Statistics* and *World Dairy Situation* published by USDA.

Table 7.3. *Overall effects of removing the U.S. dairy quotas*

Item	Case I (subsidy)	Case II (no subsidy)
Equivalent Variation (millions of dollars)	711	847
Total Subsidy (millions of dollars)	2,168	-
Real Exchange Rate (percent change)	0.00	0.01
Real Wage Rate (percent change)	0.00	0.03
Wage/Rental Ratio (percent change)	0.00	0.01
Labor Supply (full-time equivalents)	1,580	-1,561

keep dairy farm production levels constant in the face of quota removal and elimination of CCC expenditures in case I. This production subsidy amounts to approximately $2.2 billion, a substantial amount, given current U.S. fiscal difficulties. The real exchange rate effects of quota removal are small, ranging from 0.00 to 0.01 percent depreciation. These reflect the net of relative price effects (toward depreciation) as well as quota rent recapture effects (toward appreciation). The real wage and wage–rental ratio increase slightly in case II, suggesting slight shift of factor incomes toward wages. Finally, the last line of Table 7.3 reports labor supply effects. Under case II, the labor supply falls because the increased income resulting from liberalization causes increased consumption of leisure. In case I, labor is drawn back into production by the subsidy, which is less welfare improving than in case II.

Table 7.4 presents the domestic output and employment effects of removing the U.S. dairy quotas. Standard economic theory suggests that domestic output and employment should fall with the elimination of the dairy quotas. However, under case I domestic output and employment *increase* in the cheese and cream sectors. This general equilibrium result is due to the fall in the domestic price of dairy-farm output, stimulating cheese and cream pro-

Table 7.4. *Domestic output and employment effects of removing the U.S. dairy quotas*

Sector	Employment				Output			
	Case I		Case II		Case I		Case II	
	Number[a]	Percent[b]	Number[a]	Percent[b]	Dollar[c]	Percent[b]	Dollar[c]	Percent[b]
Liberalized Sectors:								
Butter	-337	-13.0	-357	-13.8	-344	-13.1	-365	-13.8
Cheese	108	0.4	-505	-1.9	56	0.4	-260	-1.9
Dry/condensed milk products	-624	-3.8	-886	-5.4	-246	-3.8	-348	-5.4
Cream	1,327	1.5	-447	-0.5	408	1.5	-136	-0.5
Upstream Sector:								
Dairyfarms	0	0.0	-1,245	-1.8	0	0.0	-365	-1.8
Rest of the Economy:								
Agforfsh	561	0.0	-771	-0.1	73	0.0	94	0.0
Mining	59	0.0	-43	0.0	9	0.0	0	0.0
Construct	22	0.0	-67	0.0	1	0.0	-2	0.0
Ndurmfg	888	0.0	-757	0.0	156	0.0	-98	0.0
Durmfg	-3	0.0	882	0.0	-4	0.0	153	0.0
Trcomut	-27	0.0	168	0.0	-8	0.0	44	0.0
Trade	-960	0.0	-732	0.0	-67	0.0	-23	0.0
Fininsre	-149	0.0	412	0.0	-51	0.0	167	0.0
Services	713	0.0	2,787	0.0	31	0.0	209	0.0

[a] Full-time equivalents.
[b] Changes less than one-tenth of one percent are reported as 0.0.
[c] In millions of dollars in base year prices. Changes less than $500,000 are reported as 0.

Table 7.5. Trade effects of removing the U.S. dairy quotas

Sector	Imports				Exports			
	Case I		Case II		Case I		Case II	
	Dollar[a]	Percent[b]	Dollar[a]	Percent[b]	Dollar[a]	Percent[b]	Dollar[a]	Percent[b]
Liberalized sectors:								
Butter	0	7.5	0	12.0	-4	-9.3	-5	-13.8
Cheese	189	50.0	217	57.5	1	2.1	-1	-1.6
Dry/condensed milk products	18	56.9	20	63.7	-4	-1.1	-19	-4.7
Cream	3	36.4	3	38.1	3	5.8	0	-0.5
Upstream sector:								
Dairyfarms	(c)	(c)	(c)	(c)	(c)	(c)	(c)	(c)
Rest of the economy:								
Agforfsh	1	0.0	-8	-0.1	32	0.1	1	0.0
Mining	4	0.0	-3	0.0	0	0.0	1	0.0
Construct	(c)	(c)	(c)	(c)	(c)	(c)	(c)	(c)
Ndurmfg	-20	0.0	-26	0.0	30	0.0	0	0.0
Durmfg	-8	0.0	-12	0.0	3	0.0	46	0.0
Trcomut	0	0.0	-7	0.0	-1	0.0	15	0.1
Trade	(c)	(c)	(c)	(c)	(c)	(c)	(c)	(c)
Fininsre	0	0.0	0	0.0	-1	0.0	4	0.1
Services	-3	0.0	-2	0.0	9	0.0	18	0.1

[a] In millions of dollars in base year prices. Changes less than $500,000 are reported as 0.
[b] Changes less than one-tenth of one percent are reported as 0.0.
[c] Nontradeable sector.

duction.[35] The fall in the domestic price of dairy-farm output is, in turn, due to reduced demand from the other dairy sectors in the face of constant (subsidized) output. These positive output effects are not present under case II.

Case II obviously represents the worst case for the dairy industry as a whole. The butter sector is the hardest hit with domestic output falling by 13.1 percent. Output in the dairy farm sector itself falls by 1.8 percent. In addition, output in the cheese, dry/condensed milk products, and cream sectors falls by 5.4, 1.9, and 0.5 percent, respectively. In percentage terms, output changes for the rest of the U.S. economy are very small. Because of the size of these sectors, however, the implied employment effects can be large. For example, service employment increases by almost 3,000 FTEs under case II. Of note, too, is that employment in the agriculture, forestry and fisheries sector declines, despite output gains. This general equilibrium result occurs because sectors engage in substitution of capital for labor, as a result of the higher wage-rental ratio induced by liberalization.

The trade effects of dairy quota removal are presented in Table 7.5. The removal of the quotas causes imports of the protected items to increase.[36] The increases in imports are greater without the subsidy (case II). In dollar terms, cheese imports increase by the largest amount, $189 to $217 million. In percentage terms, both cheese and dry/condensed milk products experience a 50 percent increase in import penetration in both cases. Import changes in the rest of the U.S. economy are very small in percentage terms and driven by the changes in the real exchange rate.

Dairy product export results can be understood in light of two effects. The first consists of expansions or contractions of the CET frontier, which we call domestic output effects. The second consists of movements along the CET frontier, which we call relative price effects. Under case I, domestic outputs fall, except in the cream sector. However, domestic prices fall relative to export prices to such an extent that domestic supply tends to be diverted to export markets. In most cases, domestic output effects outweigh relative price effects, and exports contract slightly.

IV.3 Jones Act Restrictions

The United States protects U.S. vessels from import competition in the U.S. domestic maritime market by the Merchant Marine Act of 1920, commonly

---

35 Examination of the 1991 SAM reveals that the fluid milk sector is more intensive in raw milk inputs than the other dairy sectors.
36 The increase in butter imports was less than $500,000 in both cases and thus recorded as zero.

referred to as the Jones Act, and in foreign trade mainly through a collection of preference cargo requirements.[37] In addition, there are numerous other restrictions that apply to (1) foreign ownership of U.S. registered ships; (2) citizenship of U.S. crews on U.S.-flag ships; and (3) dredging, towing, or salvaging operations in the United States by foreign vessels. With the exception of the Jones Act, most of the restrictions listed are too complex to quantify; therefore, this analysis provides a quantitative assessment only of the economic costs of Jones Act restrictions on domestic shipping.

The current cabotage prohibition on foreign vessels is covered in section 27 of the Merchant Marine Act of 1920, which states that no merchandise transported by water between U.S. ports is to be carried "in any other vessel than a vessel built in and documented under the laws of the United States and owned by persons who are citizens of the United States."[38] Therefore, the act effectively reserves U.S. maritime cabotage for ships that are registered and built in the United States and that are owned and crewed, predominantly, by U.S. citizens. This protection is meant to protect U.S. shipyards. U.S. ships tend to be priced at 100 percent or more above those made in foreign ports (USITC, 1993). Generally, ships operating in trades that are protected by the Jones Act are prohibited from receiving the operating and construction subsidies that are made to U.S.-flag ships.[39]

In value terms, cargo trade covered by the Jones Act in 1990, which includes oceanborne, lakewise, and inland shipping, amounted to approximately $6.4 billion. Of this amount, oceanborne cargo accounted for about 47 percent of the value of total shipments. The Jones Act also prevents foreign cruise vessels from transporting passengers between U.S. ports and restricts foreign access to U.S. river and canal traffic.

The dominant share of Jones Act cargo consists of liquid-bulk shipments of petroleum and petroleum-based products. By law, Alaska North Slope oil is effectively restricted to Jones Act trade. It cannot be exported, and it

---

37 In addition to the Jones Act, there are two other statutes that reserve transport of certain types of U.S. domestic cargo to U.S.-flag vessels. The Export Administration Act, 50 U.S.C., app., 2406(d), prohibits the export of Alaskan oil and, in effect, reserves this cargo for U.S.-flag vessels. In addition, section 4 of the Outercontinental Shelf Lands Act of Aug. 7, 1953, 43 U.S.C. 1333 and 1346, reserves the supply of offshore drill rigs and other exploration activities to U.S.-flag vessels.

38 46 U.S.C. 883.

39 Numerous exemptions to the Jones Act exist. In terms of the volume of cargo affected, the largest general exemption applies to merchandise that is transported between the U.S. Virgin Islands and other U.S. ports. This cargo may be carried by foreign-flag carriers. Another general exemption applies to foreign-built U.S.-flag ships. These foreign-built vessels are allowed to carry cargo between Guam, other U.S. Pacific possessions, and U.S. ports. In addition, under a wide variety of circumstances, individual waivers to the act are also granted to foreign and U.S. vessels that are not protected by the act.

cannot be transported by foreign ships to domestic markets.[40] As a result of this restriction, petroleum and petroleum products account for approximately 90 percent of the volume, in ton-miles, of oceanborne freight carried by Jones Act carriers.

In many ways, estimation of the Jones Act restrictions can proceed in analogous fashion to analyzing a quota. The restriction can be thought of as a quota specifying zero imports. This causes a price distortion between the domestic price and world price that can be estimated with an *ad valorem* tariff-equivalent rate. In particular, we calculate the tariff-equivalent of this restraint as the output-weighted average price gap between the U.S. and world prices for shipping services for the two main types of cargo transported: "wet cargo," which consists mostly of petroleum bulk cargos, and "dry cargo," which consists of liner and non-liquid bulk cargos.[41] Because of the Gulf War, 1991 tanker freight rates were artificially high, and after the war, shipping rates gradually "returned to more normal levels." Consequently, pricing data for 1992 are used because they are more representative estimates of the price difference between U.S. and world shipping rates.

The tariff equivalent estimated for the Jones Act restrictions is a weighted average of wet and dry cargo tariff equivalents. The wet cargo tariff equivalent is weighted by the portion of cabotage trade in crude petroleum, 90 percent. The dry cargo tariff equivalent is weighted by its portion of cabotage trade, 10 percent. The tariff equivalent for wet cargo, 147 percent, was based on the weighted average of two price gaps. The first price gap, 105 percent, is the difference between the average U.S. price for shipping Alaskan North Slope (ANS) crude petroleum to the U.S. West Coast, $0.00447/ton-mile, and the average world price for a comparable tanker shipment transported an equal distance, $0.00218/ton-mile. This gap is weighted by the portion of ANS shipments to the U.S. West Coast, 85 percent. The second price gap, 384 percent, is the difference between the average U.S. price for ANS tanker shipments to the U.S. Gulf Coast, $0.00423/ton-mile, and the average world price for a comparable tanker shipment transported an equal distance, $0.00087/ton-mile. This gap is weighted by the portion of ANS shipments to the U.S. Gulf Coast, 15 percent. The tariff equivalent for dry cargo, 10 percent, is based on estimates

---

40 These restrictions are found in the Export Administration Act and the Trans-Alaska Authorization Act of 1973.

41 Cabotage output was measured in terms of ton-miles, i.e., the number of ton-miles for wet and dry cargo in the U.S. domestic market. The dry cargo premium was taken from previous estimates used in USITC (1991a). U.S. and world prices for transporting "wet," or petroleum, cargo were obtained from the state of Alaska and Drewry Shipping Consultants (1992).

reported by Whitehurst (1985). The overall tariff equivalent estimated for this analysis is 133 percent.

One problem in application relates to estimating import demand conditions when there are no imports. To account for this, the model differs slightly from the one detailed in Section III. In particular, cabotage services are modeled as perfect substitutes. Conceptually, this is motivated by our price gap analysis, which is based on direct price comparisons. Operationally, it is motivated by the difficulty of calibrating an Armington-type CES demand function to zero import shares.[42] Liberalization involves setting the domestic price to the world price. In general, with prohibitive protection and inactive import markets, an alternative approach involves specifying for the inactive import market exactly how unproductive the import activity is. The slack market would then become active once profitability was restored through policy changes. This requires specifying slack constraints and implies a mix of equality and inequality constraints imposed on the theoretical model (see Rutherford, 1994a,b).

Only a limited number of studies have attempted to assess the economic costs of the Jones Act. The Congressional Budget Office (1984) found that the cost to the U.S. economy resulting from the Jones Act equaled $1.3 billion in 1983. White (1988) estimated that the Jones Act imposed an additional $2 billion in costs in 1984. Francois, Arce, Reinert, and Flynn (1996) estimate a cost of $3.0 billion in 1989 based on a general equilibrium analysis. Finally, using a partial equilibrium analysis, the USITC (1991a) found that the cost to the U.S. economy in 1989 ranged from $3.6 billion to $9.8 billion.

Our Jones Act SAM divides the U.S. economy into fifteen sectors in addition to the nine aggregate sectors that account for the rest of the U.S. economy. The highlighted sectors include the cabotage and water transportation sectors, which are directly affected by the Jones Act, and those sectors that have significant upstream or downstream linkages to cabotage services or to petroleum and refined petroleum products, as well as to other competing transportation sectors.

Table 7.6 presents the domestic employment, output, and trade effects of opening the cabotage sector to foreign competition. Removal of the Jones Act reduces the domestic price of cabotage port services, causing a modest increase in domestic output of these services of $396 million, or 5 percent.[43] In contrast, the oceanborne Jones Act fleet shuts down completely, with

---

42 See Francois, Arce, Reinert, and Flynn (1994) for more model details.
43 The cabotage sector includes not only cabotage trade (Jones Act fleet), but also other port services associated with cabotage trade.

Table 7.6. *Jones Act: economic effects of liberalization, 1991*

Sector	Employment Number[a]	Employment Percent[b]	Output Dollar[c]	Output Percent[b]	Imports Dollar[c]	Imports Percent[b]	Exports Dollar[c]	Exports Percent[b]
Liberalized sectors:								
Cabotage[d]	-11905	-100.0	396	4.6	3594	(f)	(e)	(e)
Water	12790	8.5	3983	8.5	12	0.1	1841	10.6
Upstream sectors:								
Management/consulting services	-780	-0.1	-58	-0.1	0	0.0	-2	-0.1
Maintenance and repair	-666	0.0	-75	0.0	(e)	(e)	(e)	(e)
Shipbuilding	-350	-0.1	-27	-0.2	0	-0.1	-2	-0.1
Downstream sectors:								
Chemicals	5	0.0	31	0.0	2	0.0	7	0.0
Electric utilities	83	0.0	58	0.0	0	0.0	0	0.0
Logging, sawmills, and millwork	-118	0.0	-8	0.0	1	0.0	-5	-0.1
Petroleum refining products	182	0.1	230	0.1	-9	-0.1	37	0.5
Plastics	25	0.0	14	0.0	0	0.0	4	0.0
Steel and steel products	-28	0.0	-3	0.0	-5	0.0	1	0.0
Competing sectors:								
Air transportation	256	0.0	45	0.0	2	0.0	22	0.1
Pipelines	9	0.1	7	0.1	(e)	(e)	1	0.1
Railroads	21	0.0	4	0.0	1	0.1	0	0.0
Trucking	16	0.0	11	0.0	1	0.0	(e)	(e)
Rest of the U.S. economy:								
Agforfsh	-200	0.0	16	0.0	4	0.0	-20	-0.1
Mining	312	0.0	88	0.1	42	0.1	3	0.0
New construct	-188	0.0	0.0	0.0	(e)	(e)	(e)	(e)
Ndurmfg	732	0.0	267	0.0	41	0.0	12	0.0
Durmfg	-1475	0.0	-139	0.0	119	0.0	-87	0.0
Other trcomut	-537	0.0	-43	0.0	8	0.0	-7	0.0
Trade	1956	0.0	238	0.0	(e)	(e)	(e)	(e)
Financial services	-372	0.0	10	0.0	5	0.1	5	0.0
Real estate and other services	3278	0.0	774	0.0	32	0.1	-5	0.0

[a] Full-time equivalents.
[b] Changes less than one-tenth of one percent are reported as 0.0.
[c] In millions of dollars in base year prices. Changes less than $500,000 are reported as 0.
[d] The change in domestic output for the cabotage sector is the change in the total value of cabotage services. It represents composite cabotage services, which are produced using both domestic and imported water transportation services, as well as other water sector services. Hence, composite output rises as domestic employment falls in the Jones Act fleet. Changes in employment reflect oceanborne cabotage services only.
[e] Nontradeable sector.
[f] Not applicable since base level imports are zero.

employment declining by 11,905 FTEs and imports into the cabotage sector increasing by $3.6 billion. The change in domestic output for the cabotage sector represents composite cabotage services, which are produced by using both domestic and imported water transportation services, as well as other water sector services. Hence, composite output rises as domestic employ-ment falls in the Jones Act fleet. Changes in employment reflect deep water cabotage services and the increase in imports provided by the foreign-flag carriers that enter into U.S. cabotage trade and replace the Jones Act fleet.

The increased shipping activity across the entire water sector increases output in the sector by approximately $4 billion (8.5 percent). In addition, employment in the water sector also experiences a gain in employment of 12,790 FTEs (8.5 percent). Imports in the water sector increase by a small amount, $12 million (0.1 percent), whereas exports in the water sector increase by approximately $2 billion, or 10.6 percent.[44]

The results of the model also suggest that the Jones Act provides indirect protection to its upstream sectors: shipbuilding, maintenance and repair, and management/consulting services. Indeed, one of the arguments in favor of the Jones Act is that it helps to maintain the existence of domestic shipyards. The model indicates that the Jones Act protected approximately 1,016 FTEs in shipyards (shipbuilding, maintenance and repair), while ensuring an addi-tional $102 million of domestic activity in these sectors.[45] Aside from the cabotage and water sectors, changes in output, employment, and trade in the remaining sectors were small in percentage terms, in most cases measuring less than 0.2 percent.

The economywide effect of removing the Jones Act is an economic wel-fare gain to the U.S. economy of approximately $3.1 billion. This figure can also be interpreted as the annual reduction in real national income imposed by the Jones Act. A primary reason for the large gain in welfare is a decline in the price of shipping services formerly prohibited by the Jones Act of approximately 57 percent. In addition, prices fall in the rest of the water sector by 4 percent. Across the economy, liberalization results in a negligible gain in both employment and output.

V Concluding Comments

Commercial policies are a detailed affair, with tariff nomenclatures involv-ing thousands rather than hundreds of lines. This characteristic has not always been well recognized by trade economists, however. The modeling approach described in this chapter recognizes the detailed nature of com-

---

44 The water sector includes all other services related to non–Jones Act activity such as international traffic between U.S. and foreign ports, dock and port services incidental to international traffic, dock workers' services, tugboat services, and other water transportation services.
45 These figures are obtained by summing the estimates for the two upstream sectors: shipbuilding and maintenance and repair.

mercial policy. It adopts the flexible aggregation approach described in Chapter 4 by Reinert and Roland-Holst. This allows the construction of policy-specific SAMs and the tailoring of a general model to commercial policies in specific sectors. The results, in our view, are encouraging. Flexible aggregation modeling has become part of routine policy analysis at agencies such as the U.S. International Trade Commission. Such institutionalization of modeling approaches is an important measure of success for applied trade policy modeling.

Appendix 7.1

The Linear Expenditure System

Many computable general equilibrium (CGE) models rely on the Cobb–Douglas and Constant Elasticity of Substitution (CES) functional forms for both production and household consumption. The limitation of using these functional forms for consumption, however, is that they imply unitary income elasticities of demand. Some CGE practitioners feel that this fails to account for the way changes in income affect the structural adjustment of the economy to policy changes and exogenous shocks. One easily implemented demand system that does not imply unitary income elasticities is the Linear Expenditure System (LES), introduced by Stone (1954). More recent explanations can be found in Chapter 5 of Layard and Walters (1978); Chapter 3 of Deaton and Muellbauer (1980); Appendix A.5 of Dervis, de Melo, and Robinson (1982); and Silberberg (1990, Chapter 11). The LES maintains straight Engel curves, but these curves begin at points in the positive quadrant of the demand space rather than at the origin: hence the deviation from unitary income elasticities. We will consider two versions of the LES here: the standard LES and an LES with leisure.

Standard LES

Let x_i be the demand for good i, p_i its price, and y money income. The LES is derived by maximizing the Stone–Geary direct utility function subject to the budget constraint

$$\text{max}: u(x_1, \ldots, x_n) = \prod_i (x_i - \gamma_i)^{\alpha_i}$$

$$\text{s.t.} \sum_i p_i x_i = y \tag{A7.1}$$

where $0 < \alpha_i < 1$ and $\Sigma_i \alpha_i = 1$.

As Silberberg (1990) shows, the resulting Marshallian demand functions are

$$x_i = \gamma_i + \left(\frac{\alpha_i}{p_i}\right)\left(y - \sum_j p_j \gamma_j\right), \quad i = 1, \ldots, n \tag{A7.2}$$

Now, let us give some interpretation to the components of the LES. The γ_i are subsistence requirements, which are met before the preference structure comes into play. The value $\Sigma_j P_j \gamma_j$ is a "floor" expenditure defined by the prices and subsistence requirements. The excess of total spending over the floor expenditure $(y - \Sigma_j P_j \gamma_j)$ is referred to as "supernumerary income." The supernumerary income is directed to commodities in line with the marginal budget shares, α_i.

Substituting the Marshallian demand functions into the direct utility function gives the indirect utility function[46]

$$v(p,y) = \prod_i \left[\left(\frac{\alpha_i}{p_i} \right) \left(y - \sum_j P_j \gamma_j \right) \right]^{\alpha_i}$$

which can be rewritten as

$$v(p,y) = \alpha \frac{\left(y - \sum_j P_j \gamma_j \right)}{\prod_i p_i^{\alpha_i}} \tag{A7.3}$$

where

$$\alpha = \prod_i \alpha_i^{\alpha_i}$$

This indirect utility function can be interpreted in terms of real expenditure. The supernumerary income is deflated by the price index (Deaton and Muellbauer 1980, p. 65):

$$\prod_i p_i^{\alpha_i}$$

Inverting the indirect utility function gives the expenditure function[47]

$$e(p,u) = \left(\frac{v}{\alpha} \right) \prod_i p_i^{\alpha_i} + \sum_j P_j \gamma_j \tag{A7.4}$$

The indirect compensation function (Varian, 1984, p. 124) is given by

$$\mu\left(p^0; p^1, y^1 \right) = e\left(p^0; v\left(p^1, y^1 \right) \right)$$

This function measures how much money one would need at prices p^0 to be as well off as one would be facing prices p^1 and having income y^1.

For the LES, we have

$$\mu\left(p^0; p^1, y^1 \right) = \left[\frac{\left(y^1 - \sum_j p_j^1 \gamma_j \right)}{\prod_i p_i^{1^{\alpha_i}}} \right] \prod_i p_i^{0^{\alpha_i}} + \sum_j p_j^0 \gamma_j \tag{A7.5}$$

---

46 See Deaton and Muellbauer (1980, p. 38) and Varian (1984, p. 116).
47 See Deaton and Muellbauer (1980, p. 38) and Varian (1984, p. 122).

We can use the indirect compensation function to measure the equivalent variation (EV) welfare change from position (p^0, y^0) to (p^1, y^1). This is given as (Varian 1984, p. 264)

$$EV = \mu\left(p^0; p^1, y^1\right) - y^0 \tag{A7.6}$$

The EV measure "uses the status-quo prices as the base and asks what income change at the current prices would be *equivalent* to the proposed change" (Varian, 1984, p. 264).

Implementation of the LES utilizes a parameter known as the "Frisch parameter" (Frisch, 1959). The Frisch parameter measures the expenditure elasticity of the marginal utility of expenditure, and in the LES it is given by (see Dervis et al., 1982, p. 483)

$$\phi = -\frac{y}{y - \sum_j p_j \gamma_j} \tag{A7.7}$$

In calibration, the marginal budget shares are calculated from the average budget shares as follows:

$$\alpha_i = \eta_i \beta_i \tag{A7.8}$$

where η_i is the income elasticity of commodity i and β_i is the average budget share.

The subsistence minima are related to the other parameters as follows:

$$\gamma_i = x_i + \frac{\alpha_i y}{p_i \phi} \tag{A7.9}$$

The Engel aggregation condition (see Deaton and Muellbauer, 1980, p. 16) requires that

$$\sum_i \beta_i \eta_i = 1$$

Since the η_i are taken from the literature, this condition may not hold. Therefore, the income elasticities are adjusted so that the Engel aggregation condition holds, using the following scaling procedure:

$$\theta = \sum_i \left(\frac{\eta_i p_i x_i}{y}\right); \qquad \eta_i = \frac{\eta_i}{\theta} \tag{A7.10}$$

LES with Leisure

The model used in this chapter is based on a nested LES with a work–leisure choice. This formulation goes back to Abbot and Ashenfelter (1976), who made use of a LES with the form

$$u = \alpha_0 \log(x_0 - \gamma_0) + \sum_i \alpha_i \log(x_i - \gamma_i)$$

where x_0 is leisure.

De Melo and Tarr (1992, Chapter 6) point out that this form implies that

$$\sum_i \gamma_i < 1$$

which will violate Walras's Law in a CGE model. These authors adopt a nested Stone–Geary utility function:

$$u(x_0, x_1, \ldots, x_n) = (x_0 - \gamma_0)^{\alpha_0} \left[\prod_i (x_i - \gamma_i)^{\alpha_i} \right]^{\alpha} \qquad (A7.11)$$

where $\alpha_0 + \alpha = 1$. This utility function is weakly separable between leisure and commodities (Deaton and Muellbauer, 1980, p. 127).

Let us define the aggregate commodity x by

$$(x - \gamma) = \prod_i (x_i - \gamma_i)^{\alpha_i} \qquad (A7.12)$$

where γ is the aggregate subsistence requirement.

Then the first-stage maximization problem is

$$\text{max}: \ u(x_0, x) = (x_0 - \gamma_0)^{\alpha_0} (x - \gamma)^{\alpha}$$
$$\text{s.t.}: \ wx_0 + px = Y \qquad (A7.13)$$

where w is the wage, Y is "full income," and p is an aggregate price index. If y^* is unearned income and T is the time endowment, then $Y = y^* + wT$, and the labor supply is $l = T - x_0$.

The resulting demand functions are (Deaton and Muellbauer 1980, p. 95)

$$x_0 = \gamma_0 + \left(\frac{\alpha_0}{w} \right)(Y - w\gamma_0 - p\gamma) \qquad (A7.14)$$

$$x = \gamma + \left(\frac{\alpha}{p} \right)(Y - w\gamma_0 - p\gamma) \qquad (A7.15)$$

The labor supply function is

$$l = (T - \gamma_0) - \left(\frac{\alpha_0}{w} \right)[Y - w\gamma_0 - p\gamma]$$

Since $T = x_0 + l$, $Y = y + wx_0$ where y is total money income. If we substitute this into the leisure demand function and solve for leisure, we obtain

$$x_0 = \gamma_0 + \left(\frac{\alpha_0}{w} \right)\frac{(y - p\gamma)}{(1 - \alpha_0)}$$

Therefore,

$$l = \left(T - \gamma_0\right) - \left(\frac{\alpha_0}{w}\right)\frac{\left(y - p\gamma\right)}{\left(1 - \alpha_0\right)} \tag{A7.16}$$

The second-stage maximization problem is simply that given in the previous section.

Before turning to the indirect utility function, we need to establish one result. By our definition of the aggregate commodity

$$p\gamma = \sum_i p_i\gamma_i \tag{A7.17}$$

Therefore,

$$y - \sum_i p_i\gamma_i = y - p\gamma \tag{A7.18}$$

Now, we substitute the Marshallian demand function x_0 and x_i, $i=1,\ldots,n$ into the nested direct utility function to obtain

$$v(p,w,y) = \left[\left(\frac{\alpha_0}{w}\right)\frac{\left(y - p\gamma\right)}{\left(1 - \alpha_0\right)}\right]^{\alpha_0}\left\{\prod_i\left[\left(\frac{\alpha_i}{p_i}\right)\left(y - \sum_j p_j\gamma_j\right)\right]^{\alpha_i}\right\}^{\alpha}$$

Given (A7.18), this expression can be rewritten as

$$v(p,w,y) = \left[\left(\frac{\alpha_0}{w}\right)\Big/\left(1 - \alpha_0\right)\right]^{\alpha_0}\left[\frac{\alpha}{\prod_i p_i^{\alpha_i}}\right]^{\left(1 - \alpha_0\right)}\left(y - p\gamma\right) \tag{A7.19}$$

Inverting the indirect utility function gives the expenditure function

$$e(p,w,u) = v\left[\frac{\left(1 - \alpha_0\right)}{\left(\alpha_0/w\right)}\right]^{\alpha_0}\left[\frac{\prod_i p_i^{\alpha_i}}{\alpha}\right]^{\left(1 - \alpha_0\right)} + p\gamma \tag{A7.20}$$

In this case, the indirect compensation function is given by

$$\mu\left(p^0, w^0; p^1, w^1, y^1\right) = \left(\frac{w^0}{w^1}\right)^{\alpha_0}\left(\frac{\prod_i p_i^{0\alpha_i}}{\prod_i p_i^{1\alpha_i}}\right)^{\left(1 - \alpha_0\right)}\left(y^1 - p^1\gamma\right) + p^0\gamma \tag{A7.21}$$

It remains to discuss how α_0 and the aggregates x, γ, and p are obtained in the model calibration. Differentiating equation (A7.16) with respect to income gives

$$\frac{\partial l}{\partial y} = -\frac{\alpha_0}{\left(w\left(1 - \alpha_0\right)\right)}$$

The income elasticity of labor supply is therefore

$$\varepsilon = -\frac{\alpha_0 y}{\left(w(1-\alpha_0)l\right)}$$

We solve this for α_0 as follows:

$$\alpha_0 = -\frac{wl\varepsilon}{\left(y - wl\varepsilon\right)} \tag{A7.22}$$

Given (A7.12), (A7.17), and the requirement that $px=y$, we have

$$p(x-\gamma) = p\prod_i (x_i - \gamma_i)^{\alpha_i} \tag{A7.23}$$

or

$$\left(y - \sum_i p_i\gamma_i\right) = p\prod_i (x_i - \gamma_i)^{\alpha_i}$$

Therefore,

$$p = \frac{\left(y - \sum_i p_i\gamma_i\right)}{\prod_i (x_i - \gamma_i)^{\alpha_i}} \tag{A7.24}$$

From (A7.17), $\gamma = \Sigma_i p_i\gamma_i/p$, or:

$$\gamma = \frac{\left(\sum_i p_i\gamma_i\right)\prod_i (x_i - \gamma_i)^{\alpha_i}}{\left(y - \sum_i p_i\gamma_i\right)} \tag{A7.25}$$

Finally, from (A7.23), we see that

$$x = \prod_i (x_i - \gamma_i)^{\alpha_i} + \gamma \tag{A7.26}$$

References

Abbott, M. and O. Ashenfelter. 1976. "Labor supply, commodity demand, and the allocation of time." *Review of Economic Studies* 43:389–411.

Armington, P.S. 1969. "A theory of demand for products distinguished by place of production." *IMF Staff Papers* 16:159–176.

Baldwin, R. 1989. "Measuring nontariff trade policies." *NBER Working Paper* 2978.

Bhagwati, J. 1971. "The generalized theory of distortions and welfare." In *Trade, Balance of Payments and Growth*, edited by R. Jones, R. Mundell, and J. Vanek. Amsterdam: North-Holland.

Congressional Budget Office. 1984. *U.S. Shipping and Shipbuilding: Trends and Policy Choices*. Washington, D.C.

Corden, W.M. 1971. *The Theory of Protection*. Oxford: Clarendon Press.

Deardorff, A. and R. Stern. 1985. *Methods of Measurement of Non-Tariff Barriers*. UNCTAD/ST/MD/28. Geneva: United Nations Conference on Trade and Development.

Deaton, A. and J. Muellbauer. 1980. *Economics and Consumer Behavior*. Cambridge: Cambridge University Press.

De Melo, J. 1988. "Computable general equilibrium models for trade policy analysis in developing countries: A survey." *Journal of Policy Modeling* 10:469–503.

De Melo, J. and S. Robinson. 1989. "Product differentiation and the treatment of foreign trade in computable general equilibrium models of small economies." *Journal of International Economics* 27:489–497.

De Melo, J. and D. Tarr. 1992. *A General Equilibrium Analysis of U.S. Foreign Trade Policy*. Cambridge, Massachusetts: MIT Press.

Dervis, K., J. de Melo, and S. Robinson. 1982. *General Equilibrium Models for Development Policy*. Cambridge: Cambridge University Press.

Devarajan, S. and D. Rodrik. 1991. "Pro-competitive effects of trade reform: Results from a CGE model of Cameroon." *European Economic Review* 35:1157–1184.

Drewry Shipping Consultants. 1992. *The Tanker Market: Five Year Forecast of Demand, Supply, and Profitability*. London: Drewry.

Fallert, R., D. Blarney, and J. Miller. 1990. *Dairy: Background for 1990 Farm Legislation*. Economic Research Service staff report AGES 9020. Washington, D.C.: USDA.

Flynn, J.E. and K.A. Reinert. 1993. "The welfare and resource allocation implications of the U.S. dairy quotas." *International Economic Journal* 7:91–108.

Francois, J.F., H.M. Arce, K.A. Reinert, and J.E. Flynn. 1996. "Commercial policy and the domestic carrying trade." *Canadian Journal of Economics* 29:181–198.

Frisch, R. 1959. "A complete scheme for computing all direct and cross demand elasticities in a model with many sectors." *Econometrica* 27:177–196.

Hornig, E., R. Boisvert, and D. Blandford. 1990a. "Explaining the distribution of quota rents from U.S. cheese imports." *Australian Journal of Agricultural Economics* 34:1–20.

Hornig, E., R. Boisvert, and D. Blandford. 1990b. "Quota rents and subsidies: The case of U.S. cheese import quotas." *European Review of Agricultural Economics* 17:421–434.

Layard, P.R.G. and A.A. Walters. 1978. *Microeconomic Theory*. New York: McGraw-Hill.

Powell, A.A. and F. Gruen. 1968. "The constant elasticity of transformation production frontier and linear supply system." *International Economic Review* 9:315–328.

Reinert, K.A. and D.W. Roland-Holst. 1991. "Parameter estimates for U.S. trade policy analysis." Unpublished manuscript.

Reinert, K.A. and D.W. Roland-Holst. 1992. "A detailed social accounting matrix for the USA, 1988." *Economic Systems Research* 4:173–187.

Rutherford, T. 1994a. "Applied general equilibrium modeling with MPSGE as a GAMS subsystem." Unpublished paper.

Rutherford, T. 1994b. "Extensions of GAMS for complementarity problems arising in applied economic analysis." Unpublished paper.

Shoven, J.B. and J. Whalley. 1984. "Applied general-equilibrium models of taxation and international trade." *Journal of Economic Literature* 12:1007–1051.

Shoven, J.B. and J. Whalley. 1993. *Applying General Equilibrium.* Cambridge: Cambridge University Press.

Silberberg, E. 1990. *The Structure of Economics.* New York: McGraw-Hill.

Srinivasan, T.N. and J. Whalley, eds. 1986. *General Equilibrium Trade Modeling.* Cambridge, Massachusetts: MIT Press.

Stone, J.R.N. 1954. "Linear expenditure systems and demand analysis: An application to the pattern of British demand." *Economic Journal* 64:511–527.

U.S. International Trade Commission. 1989. *The Economic Effects of Significant U.S. Import Restraints, Phase I: Manufacturing.* USITC Publication 2222. Washington, D.C.

U.S. International Trade Commission. 1990a. *Estimated Tariff Equivalents of U.S. Quotas on Agricultural Imports and Analysis of Competitive Conditions in U.S. Foreign Markets for Sugar, Meat, Peanuts, Cotton, and Dairy Products.* USITC Publication 2276. Washington, D.C.

U.S. International Trade Commission. 1990b. *The Economic Effects of Significant U.S. Import Restraints, Phase II: Agricultural Products and Natural Resources.* USITC Publication 2314. Washington, D.C.

U.S. International Trade Commission. 1991a. *The Economic Effects of U.S. Import Restraints, Phase III: Services.* USITC Publication 2422. Washington, D.C.

U.S. International Trade Commission. 1991b. *An Introduction to the ITC Computable General Equilibrium Model.* USITC Publication 2423. Washington, D.C.

U.S. International Trade Commission. 1993. *The Economic Effects of Significant U.S. Import Restraints.* USITC Publication 2699. Washington, D.C.

Varian, H.R. 1984. *Microeconomic Analysis.* New York: Norton.

Warren, F. 1992. *Industry Trade and Summary: Dairy Produce.* Publication 2477 (AG-3). Washington, D.C.: USITC.

White, L.J. 1988. *International Trade in Ocean Shipping Services: The United States and the World.* Cambridge, Massachusetts: American Enterprise Institute/Ballinger.

Whitehurst, C.H., Jr. 1985. *American Domestic Shipping in American Ships: Jones Act Costs, Benefits, and Options.* Washington, D.C.: American Enterprise Institute.

8

Multi-Market, Multi-Region Partial Equilibrium Modeling

Vernon O. Roningen

I Introduction

Much applied economic modeling focuses on problems concerning selected markets. By definition, a partial equilibrium model includes those markets most immediately relevant to a problem and excludes everything else. If a modeling effort focuses on trade issues, then multiple trading regions may be added. A multi-market, multi-region partial equilibrium model can be small and simple, or large and complex. The model's scope is usually determined by the nature of the analytical problem at hand, the availability of data, the deadline for completion of the analysis, and the cost of construction.

The theory behind partial equilibrium models is the textbook treatment of supply and demand curves. Partial equilibrium models use economic theory to organize data and economic assumptions about markets in a systematic way. The model builder must understand issues concerning data and the measurement of economic parameters as well as the mechanics of computer based model construction. Above all, there must be an understanding of the markets modeled and the economic problem to be analyzed.

This chapter extends concepts developed in Chapter 5, expanding the partial equilibrium framework to multi-market, multi-region partial equilibrium models, like the Static World Policy Simulation framework (SWOPSIM) (Roningen et al., 1991). The "problem oriented" nature of partial equilibrium models is illustrated by their role in the analysis of international agricultural policy reform. A simple partial equilibrium model is expanded, first to two markets, then to two regions. Model analytics are presented in geometric form, then as algebraic equations, and finally as a model constructed in a spreadsheet. The chapter ends with a discussion of some of the choices associated with the construction of multi-market, multi-region partial equilibrium models.

II Historical Background

When problems arise where the economic impact of policy or economic changes must be estimated, partial equilibrium economic models can offer a reasonable, cost-effective way to provide answers. Even simple mathematical models encourage disciplined thinking about economic problems. They also force the modeller to make explicit assumptions about economic behaviour. Too often in informal economic analysis, critical economic assumptions about a problem are overlooked or simply not understood. Therefore, even if the economic impact problem is not completely resolved with the use of a model (as is often the case), the problem itself is much better understood after the modeling exercise. This has been particularly true of agricultural policy analysis in the context of the Uruguay Round.

Two decades ago, D. Gale Johnson described world agricultural markets as being in disarray and documented some of the high levels of agricultural support in major trading nations (Johnson, 1973). Agricultural economists then began a closer examination of the trade impacts of all agricultural policies. In trade negotiations prior to the Uruguay Round, agriculture was discussed but largely excluded from the final agreements that were signed (Hathaway, 1987). This time, major agricultural exporters like the United States, Canada, and Australia insisted that agricultural policy reform be included. The Uruguay Round of trade negotiations provided a new opportunity to open world agricultural markets.

The final Uruguay Round Agreements include steps toward agricultural policy reform. The problem of analysing the impact of this type of international agricultural policy reform gave rise to several modeling efforts. Several multi-market, multi-region partial equilibrium models were assembled and exercised during the early stage of the negotiations. One postmortem of the Uruguay Round credits this data development and modeling work for making negotiations on agriculture possible, if not successful (Meilke and de Gorter, 1994). Studies provided measures of farm support and gave rise to modeling exercises that mapped out alternative global scenarios where farm support, subsidies, and trade barriers did not exist or were reduced to lower levels. In comparison to the disarray surrounding agricultural policies twenty years ago, the public level of understanding about global farm support policies and their impact was much higher after a series of these studies, including partial equilibrium modeling results, had been published.

The analytical problem associated with agricultural policy reform was the estimation of the level and impact of agricultural support. The problem was especially difficult because agricultural support systems around the world were a complicated mix of domestic and border policies, including the extensive use of non-tariff barriers to trade. Nevertheless, by the time the Uruguay Round was formally begun in 1986, preliminary agricultural trade liberalization results from a global partial equilibrium analysis already highlighted the costs of farm support in the developed countries (Tyers and Anderson, 1986). The United States and other Organization for Economic Cooperation and Development (OECD) member countries began an extensive global analysis of agricultural trade liberalization (Dixit et al., 1992). This included a thorough documentation of support for agriculture in OECD countries and the calculation of the impact of removal of that support via multi-market, multi-region partial equilibrium models.

Much of the data required for global agricultural analysis already existed. For example, an extensive set of global commodity supply, utilization, trade, and price data for grains, oilseeds, and livestock has been maintained by the U.S. Foreign Agricultural Service (FAS) for many years. However, prior to the Uruguay Round, comparable and consistent data on agricultural support policies were not readily available. At the urging of agricultural exporters, the OECD undertook a project to calculate comparable measures of agricultural support called Producer Subsidy Equivalents (PSEs) for member countries (OECD, 1987). As explained in Chapter 2, the PSE is a measure of the producer income derived from all forms of agricultural support, including tariffs and quotas (also see Josling, 1981). The creation of the PSE measure made agricultural support comparable across countries and commodities (ERS, 1988) and, combined with existing quantity and price data, provided the basis for policy oriented partial equilibrium modeling of world agricultural markets.

While many multi-region partial equilibrium models for agricultural products had been constructed in the past (Thompson, 1981), the questions posed by the trade negotiations led to a new round of global agricultural policy modeling efforts. Besides measures of agricultural support, the OECD developed a multi-product, multi-region partial equilibrium multilateral trade model for member countries (OECD, 1987). A large multi-market, multi-region global model constructed at the International Institute for Applied Systems Analysis in Vienna (Parikh et al., 1988) was re-focused from the analysis of world food problems to trade liberalization issues. Concurrently, the U.S. Department of Agriculture created a global agricultural trade modeling framework that took advantage of existing global agricultural data and the new information on agricultural support. The resulting SWOPSIM modeling framework was ultimately used by many researchers around the world to build multi-market, multi-region partial equilibrium models for analysis from their particular viewpoint. One SWOPSIM global trade model constructed with twenty-two products and eleven regions was the basis of an early agricultural trade liberalization analysis (Roningen and Dixit, 1989). The SWOPSIM modeling framework was popular because it allowed users to construct models in spreadsheets at a fairly low cost. As computational and modeling capacity improved, estimates of trade liberalization impacts from computable general equilibrium models also became available (Robinson et al., 1989; Stoeckel et al., 1989).

Choices for market and regional coverage in the partial equilibrium modeling exercises focused on the data defining world agricultural markets. Models were multi-region because the major agricultural commodity markets were global in nature. The multiple markets included involved those most important for the world's major agricultural traders. For the United States, for example, the entire range of grain, oilseeds, and livestock products was modeled. The OECD research effort to measure support served as an additional guide to market coverage by calculating support measures for the most important traded commodities (Sullivan et al., 1992). Models typically included significant cross-market relationships in agriculture such as those found in the feed–livestock complex. The mechanisms of agricultural support also influenced the selection of markets modeled. For example, support for the dairy and oilseeds markets in many countries was applied to processed products such as butter, cheese, oils, and meals rather than to the primary products, milk and oilseeds. This meant that a complete study had to model markets for both the primary product and the processed derivatives.

Multi-market, multi-region partial equilibrium modeling in support of agricultural policy reform was focused by the nature of world agricultural markets, the available data and modeling experience for agricultural markets, and the economic theory required to understand agricultural markets. The economic literature associated with the agricultural policy reform effort began with studies that defined the problem by analysing agricultural policies, their history, and their potential impact. At the end of the Uruguay Round, there were many published studies based on partial equilibrium models, which measured the impact of existing agricultural policies and outlined likely impacts of policy reform. Undoubtedly, the knowledge gained from these studies helped global agricultural support move from a situation of disarray closer to one of discipline and reform.

The success of partial equilibrium models in analysing problems like agricultural trade liberalization, coupled with their decreasing cost and increasing ease of use, guarantees them an important future role in the tool bag of the analytical economist. In the economic literature, many partial equilibrium model success stories can be found in other problem areas as well. Since multi-market, multi-region partial equilibrium models are tools built for solving particular economic problems, there is no universal "best" type of model or "right" set of choices that a model builder can make. But some simple examples can illustrate the economic theory and model mechanics involved in most partial equilibrium modeling efforts.

III The Geometry of Multi-Market Models

III.1 A Simple Model

Basic partial equilibrium modeling can be understood with a supply and demand diagram for a simple model for an importing country, as shown in Figure 8.1. The supply schedule shows what producers will produce at a particular price while the demand schedule shows what consumers will purchase. The supply and demand schedules summarize behaviour in the domestic market; the trade price marks what domestic consumers pay for the domestic or imported product. Figure 8.1 also shows how an import tariff can affect prices and quantities in the domestic market by adding a tax on imports. Without a tariff, the market in Figure 8.1 is cleared (domestic supply plus imports equal domestic demand) at price P where producers produce the quantity S and consumers purchase the quantity D, which includes the quantity $(D-S)$ of imports. If an import tariff $(P'-P)$ is imposed, the consumer now has to pay price P' and consumes only D', which includes $(D'-S')$ of imports. At this higher price, producers now sell a greater quantity S' in the domestic market.

Even though the analysis in Figure 8.1 is simple, there are important economic assumptions about the market behind it. Since the figure represents changes that can occur in market equilibrium, the time required for those changes is embedded in the supply and demand schedules themselves. For example, in a short period in response to a price increase, producers can only adjust their variable costs by hiring extra workers or paying overtime. This means that in the short run, price increases are likely to bid up input prices and raise production costs as production increases. A supply schedule

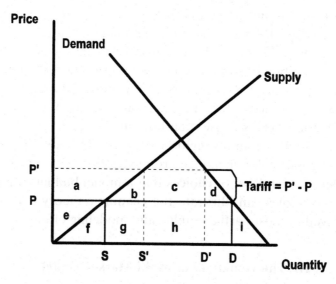

Figure 8.1. *A simple model for an importer*

will be steeper if Figure 8.1 represents market adjustment possibilities for a short period. In the longer run, producers can add plant, machinery, and other capital equipment, which will allow more production without these extra short-run costs, yielding a flatter supply schedule. Similar considerations apply to the demand schedule. If the demand price change in Figure 8.1 occurs over a long time, other markets might produce substitutes for some consumers. This would make the demand schedule more price responsive (flatter). As emphasized in Chapter 5, the parameterization of the supply and demand schedules in Figure 8.1 implicitly defines linkages to parts of the economy not included in the model as well as the period for those linkages to play out.

Figure 8.1 also contains assumptions about the trade market for the product. The quantity of imports is shown as a flat line at the price P (or P' in the case of a tariff). The price of imports does not depend upon the quantity; this assumes that the quantity of imports in this market is small enough so that it does not affect prices elsewhere in world markets. We have also assumed that the consumer accepts the import as a perfect substitute for the domestically produced product. Finally, the schedules in Figure 8.1 contain assumptions about the domestic market's competitive structure. The slopes and position of the schedules would differ if production or consumption were not competitive in nature.

In the domestic market shown in Figure 8.1, changed market conditions cause a new equilibrium to be established (as illustrated by the previous example with an import tariff). This type of model is referred to as a "static" model. The initial conditions, such as the "no tariff" free trade equilibrium in the figure, are the "base period" equilibrium conditions. Analysis consists of calculating the economic changes occurring in a new equilibrium situation and comparing them to those prevailing in the base period.

Many economic changes can be shown when a new equilibrium is established in Figure 8.1. For example, the tariff on imports $(P'-P)$ allows producers to raise the domestic market price to P' while remaining competitive with imports. With the tariff in place, producers gain extra net income (area a) over the extra cost $(b+g)$ of producing S'. The consumer buys less $(D-D')$ but pays more $(a+b+c)$ for the quantity D' consumed. The government collects tariff revenue (area c). Economists speak of a national welfare loss in this situation $(b+d)$. The economy loses the value of area b because extra domestic resources are now needed to produce $(S'-S)$, which used to be imported. These resources are now unavailable for the production of other products. The consumer, with a given income, now chooses to buy less (D') at the higher market price. Some of the consumer's extra expenditure goes to the producer $(a+b)$ and some to the government as tariff revenue (area c). Area d represents the net value of the consumer's loss, being unable to purchase $(D'-D)$ of the commodity at the lower price P. With the tariff, imports fall from $(D-S)$ to $(D'-S')$.

The tariff scenario in Figure 8.1 assumes that the quantity imported by the country imposing the tariff is small enough that its actions will not affect the trade price P. If this assumption is not true, the decrease in import demand would cause the world price P to fall. The government would collect more revenue (area c would increase). All of the calculations based upon a fixed trade price P would change. This alternative situation is especially important when calculating the effect of policy changes of large trading countries like the United States, which can affect world markets by their policy actions.

Producer support mechanisms other than tariffs can also be analysed in Figure 8.1. Other trade and domestic policy mixes, appropriately set, could yield identical results for the quantity of production, consumption, trade, and producer income. For example, if an import quota of $(D'-S')$ were imposed instead of a tariff, the same price and quantity results would occur for the producer and consumer. The extra revenue (area c) from sales of imports at the higher price P' in the domestic market does not accrue to the government but is captured by the importer and/or the foreign exporter.

Another way to support producers at the same income level in Figure 8.1 is for the government to pay the producer a subsidy of $(P'-P)$ per unit of commodity produced. If the payment affected producers' production incentives, S' would still be produced. The consumer now would pay only P and imports would be greater $(D-S')$ than in the tariff or quota example $(D'-S')$. Now the government would have to spend money $(a+b)$ to pay the subsidy to the producer.

A less trade distorting version of a direct government subsidy to the producer would exist if the producer receiving the subsidy were required to limit production. If production were limited by the amount $(S'-S)$, consumers would import the same amount $(D-S)$ as in the free trade situation. This example could be labelled a "trade neutral" policy where there are no trade changes caused by the producer subsidy accompanied by a supply control policy. This variation in policy structure is found, for example, in some U.S. agricultural policies, where crop producers receive direct government payments but are required to limit production.

Factors other than tariff or trade policies can impact the market in Figure 8.1, causing a new equilibrium to be established. For example, a technical improvement in production could lead to more production with the same inputs, shifting the supply schedule to the right. An increase in the production of other products competing for the same resources could require higher prices to maintain production, shifting the supply schedule to the left. An increase in the demand for a product in another market that is a substitute in consumption could shift the demand schedule for the product to the right. The creation of a multi-market model involves the explicit quantification of these important linkages between markets.

III.2 A Two-Market Model

Figure 8.2 illustrates multi-market linkages in a partial equilibrium model with a two-market example where there is no trade. The linkage is a vertical one between a market for a product using an input (product 1) and the input market (product 2) itself. Two products are shown at their equilibrium positions in their two respective markets. The supply and demand schedules for product 1 are in equilibrium at price $P1a$ and quantity $Q1a$ while the schedules for product 2 set the equilibrium price at $P2a$ and the quantity produced and consumed at $Q2a$.

The analysis of a change in the input market impacting both markets can be traced in four steps: In *step 1* an exogenous decrease in input supply shifts the supply curve $(S2a)$ for product 2 to the left $(S2b)$, establishing an initial

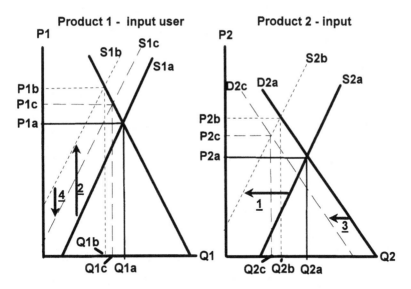

Figure 8.2. *A two-market model with vertical linkages*

higher price (*P2b*) for product 2. Production and consumption of product 2 decrease from *Q2a* to *Q2b*. In *step 2* the higher price for the product 2 raises production costs for product 1, which uses product 2 as an input, shifting the supply schedule for product 1 (*S1a*) upward (*S1b*). Product 1 production and consumption decrease from *Q1a* to *Q1b*. In *step 3* the decrease in production of product 1 causes less demand for input product 2, shifting the demand curve (*D2a*) in the input market to the left (*D2c*). This lowers the price of product 2 from *P2b* to *P2c* and further decreases the equilibrium quantity from *Q2b* to *Q2c*. In *step 4* the lower input price reduces the cost of production of product 1, shifting the supply schedule (*S1b*) back down (*S1c*). This lowers the price of product 1 from *P1b* to *P1c* and increases production and consumption from *Q1b* to *Q1c*. Over an appropriately defined period, the subsequent changes in steps 2–4 would occur simultaneously, leading to the final equilibrium at prices *P1c* and *P2c* and equilibrium quantities at *Q1c* and *Q2c*, respectively. The exogenous decrease in input supply results in the sharing of impacts via price and quantity changes in both the input market and the market of the product that uses the input. Consumers in both markets pay higher prices and consume less.

The situation in Figure 8.2 introduces cross-price and direct cross-quantity linkages between product markets. A cross-price linkage occurs when an increase in the price of input product 2 shifts the supply curve up in the input-using market. A direct cross-quantity linkage occurs when the decrease in the quantity of production of product 1 results in a decrease in demand for input product 2, shifting the demand schedule to the left. The specification of multi-market models involves the addition of cross-market linkages of this type.

As the number of explicitly connected markets grows, graphical analysis becomes impractical. A full analysis of linked multiple markets requires the algebraic specification of supply and demand equations, including their cross-market linkages, and the use of computational methods to iterate to new equilibria simultaneously in all markets.

III.3 A Two-Region Model

When markets in different countries are linked, multi-region models are required. As an illustration of this process, the simple model for an importing region from Figure 8.1 is made part of a two-region trade model in Figure 8.3 by adding the supply and demand schedule for the exporting region (2), which provides all the imports for region 1. In the free trade situation, region 1 imports $(D1 - S1)$, which equals $(S2 - D2)$, the exports of region 2. The explicit linkage added is that the imports of region 1 always must equal the exports of region 2. The free trade price in region 1 is $P1$ while in region 2, the free trade price is $R \cdot P2$, where R is the exchange rate converting region 2's currency to the currency units of region 1.

When region 1 imposes a tariff $(P1' - P1)$, its domestic price increases to P' and its imports decrease to $(D1' - S1')$. Exports of region 2 decline to $(S2' - D2')$ (which equals $D1' - S1'$) at the lower domestic price $R \cdot P2'$. The market conditions are different in regions 1 and 2. In this example, region 2's supply and demand schedules are steeper, requiring a larger price change to clear the market, so the price decline in region 2 is greater than the price increase in region 1. The explicit linkage of these two regions by trade means that any disturbance in the market of one region, such as a demand shift or trade policy change, leads to simultaneous changes in prices, supply, demand, and trade in both regions.

The example in Figure 8.3 assumes that the traded product is a perfect substitute for the domestic product in both countries, leading to trade's being modeled on a "net trade" basis. Depending upon where supply and demand schedules intersect relative to the international price, a region is either an exporter (region 2) or an importer (region 1). More complex models which allow the same product to be exported and imported require a relaxation of the simple assumption that traded and domestic products are perfect substitutes in consumption. (Such a model was developed in Chapter 5.)

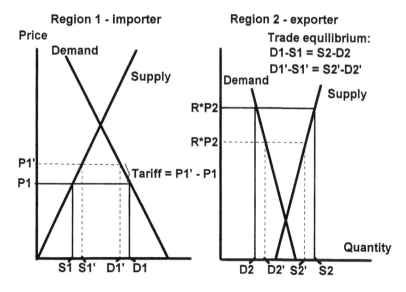

Figure 8.3. *A two-region trade model*

Geometric analysis illustrates important economic relationships in multi-market, multi-region partial equilibrium models. But the specification of larger multi-market, multi-region models with complex relationships requires an algebraic presentation, and computation requires that these be written as a set of simultaneous equations. This process can be illustrated with the creation of a simple two-market, two-region partial equilibrium model, first as a set of equations, and then as an operating model in a spreadsheet.

IV An Applied Partial Equilibrium Model

The simultaneous nature of a multi-market, multi-region model is illustrated with a flowchart of linkages for a simple two-market, two-region trade model in Figure 8.4. Lines and arrows show the direction of the linkages. Each region and market has a set of domestic prices which determine supply and demand quantities. These quantities, in turn, define the net trade for each market in each region. Domestic prices for one market in a region help determine the quantity supplied and demanded not only in that market but also in the other market through cross-market price linkages.

Each market itself is linked across regions through net trade. The sum of net trade for each market has to equal zero in the equilibrium state because world exports equal world imports. If world net trade for a market is not zero, a new world market clearing price is calculated; it, in turn, feeds back

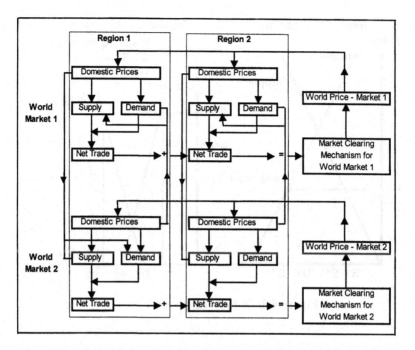

Figure 8.4. *A flowchart for a two-market, two-region partial equilibrium trade model*

into the domestic market price structure for each market. In the model, this process continues until both markets are cleared (world net trade in both markets equals zero). The result of all of these simultaneous cross-market, cross-region linkages is that all markets in all regions are connected. Markets are connected domestically through cross-market effects and internationally through trade and world prices. Trade policies typically affect price linkages between world and domestic prices. Domestic policies affect supply and demand schedules themselves but have cross-region effects as well through trade linkages. More complex models with more markets and regions would have more boxes and linkage arrows. However, their structures are conceptually similar.

IV.1 The Algebra of the Model

An algebraic version of the simple two-market, two-region partial equilibrium model outlined in Figure 8.4 is given in Table 8.1. The algebraic specification of a model requires some mathematical notation to represent model variables. The equations shown in Table 8.1 follow the notation used

Table 8.1. *Equations for a two-market, two-region partial equilibrium trade model*

	Region 1	Region 2
Market 1: Mt		
1.	PMt1 = cPMt1 + WpMt + TariffMt1	PMt2 = cPMt2 + WpMt
2.	SMt1 = cSMt1*(PMt1 ^ .7)*(PCg1^ -.2)	SMt2 = cSMt2*(PMt2^.5)*(PCg2^-.1)
3.	DMt1 = cDMt1*(PMt1^-.6)	DMt2 = cDMt2*(PMt2^-.8)
4.	NtMt1 = SMt1 - DMt1	NtMt2 = SMt2 - DMt2

	Region 1	Region 2
Market 2: Cg		
5.	PCg1 = cPCg1 + WgCg	PCg2 = cPCg2 + WpCg + TariffCg2
6.	SCg1 = cSCg1*(PCg1^.6)	SCg2 = cSCg2*(PCg2^.4)
7.	DCg1 = cDCg1*(PCg1^-.8)*(SMt1^.7)	DCg2 = cDCg2*(PCg2^-.5)*(SMt2^.3)
8.	NtCg1 = SCg1-DCg1	NtCg2 = Scg2 - DCg2

Market Clearing:	Market 1: Mt	Market 2: Cg
World Trade	WtMt = NtMt1 + NtMt2	WtCg = NtCg1 + NtCg2
World Price	WpMt = World Mt price that clears the world Mt market by driving WtMt to 0	WpCg = World Cg price that clears the world Cg market by driving WtCg to 0

The notation for the model equations: P - domestic Price, Wp - World price, Mt - domestic market for Meat, Cg - domestic market for Coarse grains, S - quantity Supplied, D - quantity Demanded, Nt - quantity of Net trade, Wt - World net trade, 1 - region 1, 2 - region 2, c - constant (intercept) term, Tariff - import Tariff. Variables are named by concatenation of these symbols, e.g. PMt1 is the domestic price of meat in region 1. Equation 5 for region 2 (PCg2 = cPCg2 + WpCg + TariffCg2) reads as "the domestic price of coarse grains in the market in region 2 equals a constant term plus the world price of coarse grains plus the tariff on imports of coarse grains into region 2".

for the coding of these same model equations in a spreadsheet (Figure 8.5). Two specific products, meat and coarse grains (i.e., feed grains such as corn, oats, barley), make up the two markets in the model. Constant elasticity functions are assumed by using the following mnemonic symbols: *P*, domestic price; *Wp*, world price; *Mt*, domestic market for meat; *Cg*, domestic market for coarse grains; *S*, quantity supplied; *D*, quantity demanded; *Nt*, quantity of net trade; *Wt*, world net trade; 1, region 1; 2, region 2; *c*, constant (intercept) term; *Tariff*, import tariff. Variables are named by the concatenation of these symbols; e.g., *PMt*1 is the domestic price of meat in region 1. The equation $PMt1 = cMt1 + WpMt + TariffMt1$ translates as "the domestic price of meat in region 1 equals a constant (intercept) term plus the world price of meat plus the import tariff on meat in region 1." Equations are written with elasticities as numbers so that the algebraic model is easy to read. The equation specification in this example is based on that found in the SWOPSIM model (Roningen et al., 1991).

Equations (1) to (4) in Table 8.1 give a simple structure for the meat (Mt) market for regions 1 and 2. The equations in line 1 link the domestic meat price (PMt) to the world meat price ($WpMt$). Region 1 has an import tariff on meat ($TariffMt1$), which is added to the world price of meat, while region 2 has no import tariff. The price linkage, supply, and demand equations each begin with a constant (intercept) term which can be calibrated so that the other terms in the equation reproduce the base period value of the variable that is explained by the equation. Equations calculating the supply of meat are shown in line 2. The quantity of meat supplied depends upon the meat price (PMt). The constant elasticity form has been assumed in Table 8.1, and we have also assumed that the supply price elasticity is 0.7 for region 1 and 0.5 for region 2. The quantity of meat supplied also depends upon the price (cost) of coarse grains (PCg) which are fed to animals as an input to meat production. As shown in the example in Figure 8.2, if feed (input) prices rise and raise production costs, less meat is supplied. This relationship is represented in the meat supply equation by coarse grains price elasticities of –0.2 for region 1 and –0.1 for region 2. The quantity of meat demanded in line 3 depends upon the meat price (PMt): The higher the meat price, the less meat is demanded. Net meat trade ($NtMt$) for each region is calculated in line 4 as the difference between the quantity supplied (SMt) and the quantity demanded (DMt).

Equations in lines 5 through 8 of Table 8.1 specify the markets for coarse grains in regions 1 and 2, respectively. The equation structure is the same as for meat except that now region 2 has an import tariff on coarse grains while region 1 does not. Even though the equations have a similar structure, their elasticities differ and the constant terms can be calibrated to different values. One important difference from the meat equations is in the equation describing the quantity of coarse grains (DCg) demanded in line 7 of Table 8.1. Here the supply of meat (SMt) appears as variable because coarse grains demand is assumed to depend partly upon the amount of meat produced. For region 1, for example, 70 percent of the quantity of coarse grains is assumed to be used for meat production (the elasticity of demand for coarse grains with respect to the quantity of meat supplied is 0.7).

The market clearing equations in Table 8.1 close world markets for meat and coarse grains and provide a mechanism for clearing those markets if they are out of balance. The world trade equations for each market define net world trade as the sum of the net trade for regions 1 and 2. World markets are cleared when $WtMt$ and $WtCg$ are both zero, equating world exports and world imports and ensuring that world supply equals world demand in both markets.

The world (market clearing) price for each market is represented symbolically by the last set of equations. It normally is calculated in an iterative routine that finds the world prices for meat and coarse grains that clear the two world trade markets after an exogenous change is made in a market, e.g., a tariff change. A model is constructed and initialized (by calculating appropriate constant terms) so that world net trade is zero in both markets in the base period. Then, in response to an exogenous change (such as the removal of a tariff), equations in the model are used to recalculate supply, demand, and trade. World net trade is then recalculated, and if it is not balanced, a new world price is chosen and is passed back to domestic prices and markets. New domestic prices are passed to supply and demand equations in both markets. This process continues until the world net trade for each market is zero. In the applied version of this two-market example, an iterative market clearing process occurs. World price changes are calculated in both markets and both markets change simultaneously in each iteration. When world net trade quantities for meat and coarse grains are again zero, the iteration process stops. World trade markets are in their new equilibrium state, and a new model solution has been found.

A simple calculation scheme for finding a new world price can start with the base period equilibrium price and raise it a certain amount if world net trade for the market is negative or lower it if world net trade is positive. Negative world net trade means world imports exceed exports and world demand exceeds world supply. Raising the world price decreases demand in each region and therefore in the world, increases supply in each region and therefore world supply, and makes world net trade less negative. On the other hand, if world net trade is positive, world prices have to be lowered to decrease supply, increase demand, and move world net trade back toward a balanced position.

IV.2 An Application

A spreadsheet containing this simple two-market, two-region partial equilibrium model is shown in Figure 8.5. The model is organized in groups of boxes which reflect mechanical and organizational aspects of model construction. A text box at the top of the spreadsheet gives the notation used for variable names. Components of the model are shown for the two regions side by side. First there are matrices displaying the supply and demand elasticities used. Below are boxes for each region containing the variable names, base period values, the model solution values, and a list of equations that calculate the solution values (in the spreadsheet, the cells showing

Notation for two-market, two region partial equilibrium trade model: Mt - Meat, Cg - Coarse Grains, P - domestic Price, Tariff - import Tariff, Wp - World price, S - quantity Supplied, D - quantity Demanded, Nt - Net trade, Wt - World net trade, 1 - region 1, 2 - region 2, c - constant (intercept) term. Codes are concatenated to make variable names, e.g. SMt1 is the Supply of Meat in region 1.

Model-8

.... Region 1 .... Region 2 ....

Matrix of supply elasticities - region 1

	PMt1	PCg1
Mt	0.7	-0.2
Cg		0.6

Matrix of supply elasticities - region 2

	PMt2	PCg2
Mt	0.5	-0.1
Cg		0.4

Matrix of demand elasticities - region 1

	PMt1	PCt1	SMt1
Mt	-0.6		
Cg		-0.8	0.7

Matrix of demand elasticities - region 2

	PMt2	PCg2	SMt2
Mt	-0.8		
Cg		-0.5	0.3

Variables, values, equations for markets 1, 2 - region 1

	Name	Base	Solution	Equation
	PMt1	2600	2600	= 0 + WpMt + TariffMt1
Market	TariffMt1	600	600	<--Policy variable
1 - Mt	SMt1	30259	30259	= 309.295*PMt1^.7*PCg1^-.2
(Meat)	DMt1	37847	37847	= 4236581*PMt1^-.6
	NtMt1	-7588	-7588	= SMt1-DMt1
	PCg1	100	100	= 0 + WpCg
Market				
2 - Cg	SCg1	208033	208033	= 13126*PCg1^.6
(Coarse	DCg1	170846	170846	= 4966*PCg1^-.8*SMt1^.7
grains)	NtCg1	37187	37187	= SCg1 - DCg1

Variables, values, equations for markets 1, 2 - region 2

Name	Base	Solution	Equation
PMt2	2000	2000	= 0 + WpMt
SMt2	64979	64979	= 2398.099*PMt2^.5*PCg2^-.1
DMt2	57391	57391	= 25099657*PMt2^-.8
NtMt2	7588	7588	= SMt2-DMt2
PCg2	150	150	= 0 + WpCg + TariffCg2
TariffCg2	50	50	<--Policy variable
SCg2	233840	233840	= 31512.46*PCg2^.4
DCg2	271027	271027	= 119461*PCg2^-.5*SMt2^.3
NtCg2	-37187	-37187	= SCg2 - DCg2

Calibrated Constant Terms

Name	Region 1	Name	Region 2
cPMt1	0	cPMt2	0
cSMt1	309.295	cSMt2	2398.099
cDMt1	4236581	cDMt2	25099657
cPCg1	0	cPCg2	0
cSCg1	13126	cSCg2	31512.46
cDCg1	4966	cDCg2	119461

Calibrate Constants   Done

World Market Clearing Mechanism

	Name	Base	Solution	Equation
		Base	Solution	
Market 1	WpMt	2000	2000	WpMt*(1-f*WtMt/C)
Mt	WtMt	0	0	= NtMt1 + NtMt2
Market 2	WpCg	100	100	WpCg*(1-f*WtCg/C)
Cg	WtCg	0	0	= NtCg1 + NtCg2

Solve Model   0   Done

Figure 8.5. *A two-market, two-region partial equilibrium trade model in a spreadsheet (The spreadsheet used here is Excel, version 5. "Excel" is a trademark of Microsoft Corporation.)*

solution values actually contain the equations, but they display the values calculated by those equations). The box at the lower left of the figure displays the constant terms which calibrate the model to the base period data. Finally, a box at the bottom right of Figure 8.5 shows variable names, base and solution values, and equations for the world market clearing mechanism.

Notation for variables and equations enhances model organization and readability. If a spreadsheet is used, the mathematical notation is determined by the spreadsheet itself. The notation shown in the text box concatenates symbols to make up variable names in a systematic way. This makes existing equations easier to read and simplifies the process of adding new ones. For example, under the convention followed here, any variable beginning with an *S* is a supply equation. If a new product is added to a model, a new product code added to an existing symbol such as *S* proves a consistent nomenclature for identification of the supply equation for the new product.

The matrices of supply and demand elasticities are shown as a way of organizing the structure of the model. Although elasticities are embedded in model equations, it is helpful to be able to read them as a summary of the model structure. Furthermore, spreadsheet macro programming techniques can automatically use elasticities from a matrix for the automatic creation of model equations (see Roningen, 1992, for specific applications).

The heart of the model itself is shown in the variable and equation boxes for each region and market. The base period values of the variables are those with the tariffs in place in the model. The solution values in bold print are the same as the base values in Figure 8.5. This is because the model constant terms have been calibrated so that the equations for each variable, with explanatory variables set at their base period values and with the elasticities shown, reproduce the base period values. When tariffs are removed in a model simulation exercise, the solution values will be different from the base period values. The equations shown in Figure 8.5 are the same as those found in Table 8.1 except that constant term symbols have been replaced by the numerical values of the constant terms.

Constant term names and their calibrated values shown in the box highlight the need to calibrate a partial equilibrium model so that it reproduces the conditions of a base period. In the spreadsheet shown in Figure 8.5, the calibrating process is an automated one initiated by clicking a mouse on the "Calibrate Constants" button. This convenience means that if the modeller changes base period values by entering new data, the model can be quickly re-calibrated to fit the new data.

Finally, the box at the bottom of the spreadsheet shows the market clearing equations and structure for the two markets. Spreadsheets can be used to solve simultaneous equation models because they allow repetitive iterations to resolve "circular" linkages between equations in cells. The coding of the solution process depends upon the way a spreadsheet deals with these circular linkages. The spreadsheet in Figure 8.5 is set to a manual calculation mode. Symbolic equations are shown for the calculation of world market clearing prices. The logic of world price calculation is that described for Table 8.1; the world price is increased if world net trade is negative and decreased if it is positive. The actual equations are more complicated, containing some logic expressions which change equations from the base value of the price to new values as iterations proceed. The manual solution process is initiated by clicking a mouse on the "Solve Model" button. This starts a

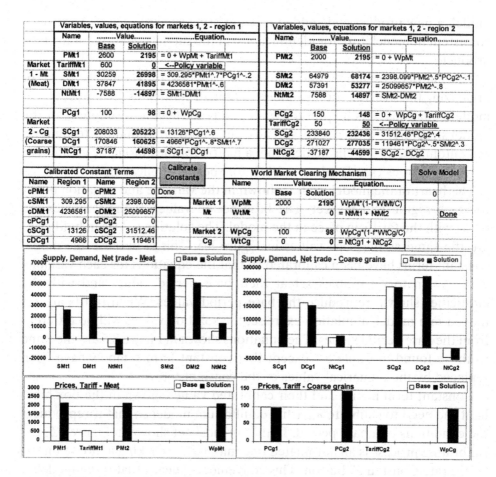

Figure 8.6. *A model solution with meat import tariffs removed*

spreadsheet program which controls the solution process. The term "Done" appears below the button, indicating that the solution process has been completed. When a new solution is reached, the value of world trade in each market is again equal to zero.

When tariffs are removed in the spreadsheet model shown in Figure 8.5, the model can be solved by iterating to a new equilibrium where world markets are again cleared. Figure 8.6 shows the spreadsheet model, including the new equilibrium solution values, when the tariff on meat has been removed (set to zero) in region 1. Charts embedded in the spreadsheet are shown at the bottom of Figure 8.6; they graph the new equilibrium price and quantity values of model variables along with the original base period values. The solution values in regions 1 and 2 no longer equal the base values

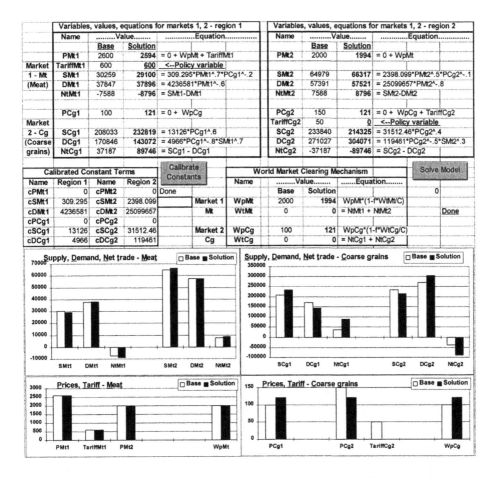

Figure 8.7. *A model solution with coarse grains tariffs removed*

with the exception of the coarse grains tariff in region 2, which has not changed. World trade for meat (*WtMt*) and coarse grains (*WtCg*) is again zero, meaning world markets are in balance even though solution values of variables in the two regions have changed.

The removal of the meat tariff (*TariffMt1*) in region 1 leads to domestic meat market price (*PMt1*) decreases in region 1 and increases (*PMt2*) in region 2. In region 1, the meat supply (*SMt1*) decreases while meat demand (*DMt1*) and imports (*NtMt1*) increase. The increased meat imports in region 1 become the increased exports (*NtMt2*) from region 2 which are made available because of less demand (*DMt2*) and more supply (*SMt2*) brought about by higher meat prices. World meat prices (*WpMt*) rise while those for coarse grains (*WpCg*) fall slightly. Coarse grains supply (*PCg1*) in region 1 and region 2 (*PCg2*) falls because world coarse grains prices fall. The demand for coarse grains (*DCg1*) in region 1 decreases because of decreased meat supply. This frees up more coarse grains for export (*NtCg1*) to accommodate the increased demand for coarse grains (*DCg2*) in region 2 because of increased meat production. The removal of the meat import tariff has led to a decrease in meat supply and an increase in meat demand in region 1 and the reverse in the meat market in region 2.

One of the advantages of spreadsheets for partial equilibrium modeling is shown in Figure 8.6: the ability to display simulation results, including graphs, instantly upon conclusion of a simulation. The value of quick turn-around time of models in the construction and simulation phase should not be underestimated since the value of the modeller's time is the ultimate modeling constraint and can be the greatest modeling construction cost.

Figure 8.7 shows spreadsheet graphs of model variable changes when the coarse grains import tariff in region 2 is removed but the meat import tariff in region 1 is not changed. The coarse grains supply (*SCg2*) decreases in region 2 because of the removal of the import tariff but increases (*SCg1*) in region 1 because of the resulting increase in world price (*WpCg*). Lower coarse grains domestic prices (*PCg2*) in region 2 lead to lower meat supply costs and increased meat supply (*SMt2*). This, in turn, increases coarse grains demand (*DCg2*) and imports (*NtCg2*). Again, a policy change in one market ultimately affects both markets in both regions.

When both the meat import tariff in region 1 and the coarse grains import tariff in region 2 are removed, the results are a complex set of changes in both regions. Now it is useful to compare changes not only to base period values, but to the individual tariff removal scenarios as well. Table 8.2 presents a comparison of the three scenarios for price and quantity variables in the model in terms of changes and percentage changes from base period values. The top part of the table shows changes in prices while the middle part summarizes changes in quantities. In general, the percentage changes in prices and quantities from removing both tariffs are roughly the sum of the percentage changes resulting from each unilateral tariff removal scenario. But this is only a linear approximation of the final results. The table shows that the unilateral tariff removals impact their domestic markets the most in the region removing the tariff. The result of removal of both tariffs is that all markets are significantly affected since each region is removing a tariff.

As Table 8.2 illustrates, even a relatively simple model with only a few variables and equations generates complex results. A comparative table is one way of organizing, presenting and understanding results of multiple model scenarios. Table 8.2 also shows that additional indicators created

Table 8.2. *Changes from three tariff removal scenarios in the two-market, two-region model*

	Remove Meat Tariff in Region 1		Remove Coarse Grains Tariff in Region 2		Remove Meat and Coarse Grains Tariff	
	Change	% Change	Change	% Change	Change	% Change
Meat Tariff (TariffMt1)	-600	-100			-600	-100
C.G. Tariff (TariffCg2)			-50	-100	-50	-100
Meat Price			...Changes in Dollars per Metric Ton...			
Region 1 (PMt1)	-405	-16	-6	0	-413	-16
Region 2 (PMt2)	195	10	-6	0	187	9
World (WpMt)	195	10	-6	0	187	9
Coarse Grains Price						
Region 1 (PCg1)	-2	-2	21	21	19	19
Region 2 (PCg2)	-2	-1	-29	-20	-31	-21
World (WpCg)	-2	-1	21	21	19	19
Meat Supply			...Changes in Thousand Metric Tons...			
Region 1 (SMt1)	-3261	-11	-1159	-4	-4368	-14
Region 2 (SMt2)	3195	5	1338	2	4559	7
Meat Demand						
Region 1 (DMt1)	4048	11	49	0	4144	11
Region 2 (DMt2)	-4114	-7	130	0	-3953	-7
Meat Net Trade						
Region 1 (NtMt1)	-7309		-1208		-8512	
Region 2 (NtMt2)	7309		1208		8512	
Coarse Grains Supply						
Region 1 (SCg1)	-2810	-1	24785	12	22814	11
Region 2 (SCg2)	-1404	-1	-19515	-8	-20727	-9
Coarse Grains Demand						
Region 1 (DCg1)	-10221	-6	-27774	-16	-37508	-22
Region 2 (DCg2)	6008	2	33044	12	39595	15
Coarse Grains Net Trade						
Region 1 (NtCg1)	7411		52559		60322	
Region 2 (NtCg2)	-7411		-52559		-60322	
Meat Values			...Changes in Billions of Dollars...			
Region 1 Supply	-19.4	-25	-3.1	-4	-22.1	-28
Region 2 Supply	19.7	15	2.3	2	22.1	17
Region 1 Demand	-6.4	-7	-.1	0	-6.6	-7
Region 2 Demand	2.2	2	-.1	0	2.1	2
Coarse Grain Values						
Region 1 Supply	-.7	-4	7.3	35	6.7	32
Region 2 Supply	-.7	-2	-9.2	-26	-9.7	-28
Region 1 Demand	-1.4	-8	.2	1	-1.2	-7
Region 2 Demand	.3	2	-4.0	-10	-3.7	-9
Meat, Coarse Grain Value						
Region 1 Total Supply	-20.1		4.2		-15.4	
Region 2 Total Supply	19.0		-6.9		12.4	

Change and % change are calculated relative to the base period value of the variable. Variable names are shown in parentheses in the left column. Variable units of measurement are assumed: price - dollars/metric ton; supply, demand, net trade quantity - thousand metric tons; values - billion dollars. Values are examples of indicators calculated from model solution variables. Many types of other indicators, including economic welfare measures can be calculated from model variables.

from model variables can be helpful in summarizing model results. The bottom third of Table 8.2 shows calculations of changes in market values in the three scenarios, where the values are the result of multiplication of a quantity times a price from a model solution. The values allow comparison and aggregation of scenario results across markets and help bring the economic scale of the impact of the three scenarios into focus. In value terms, the removal of the meat import tariff in region 1 is the most important policy change. This scenario results in the switching of about $19 billion of meat production from region 1 to region 2. The associated changes in the coarse grains markets in both regions are small, relative to changes in the value of meat production in both regions. This scenario results in about a $20 billion loss in meat and coarse grains production in region 1 and a $19 billion production increase (both products) in region 2.

The scenario removing the coarse grains tariff in region 2 yields about a $9 billion decline in coarse grains production in region 2. About $7 billion of coarse grains production value moves to region 1. However, region 2 gains about $2 billion worth of meat production (because of lower feed costs) at the expense of meat production in region 1. In this scenario, total production of meat and coarse grains declines by almost $7 billion in region 2 but increases by about $4 billion in region 1. The results of these unilateral tariff removal scenarios show that protection for the domestic market is at the expense of producers in foreign markets.

The removal of both tariffs reduces the value of meat supplied more in region 1 than the value of the increased coarse grains supply. The final result from the removal of both tariffs is that region 1 loses about $15 billion of production value while region 2 gains $12 billion. This is because the value of meat supply changes in the scenario outweighs the value of coarse grain supply changes. This outcome is better for producers in region 1 than a unilateral removal of its meat tariff. Similar types of calculations can be made in terms of consumer savings and national welfare gains or losses (see Chapters 2 and 5). Depending upon the types of variables included in a partial equilibrium model, many types of useful indicators can be created to help the modeller understand, summarize, compare, and interpret model scenarios.

A multi-market, multi-region partial equilibrium model is useful for analysing complex economic changes. But the changes must be put in perspective and made transparent. The model builder who conducts a study has to tell as clear and compelling an analytical story as possible to the recipients of a study. That is why the preceding types of indicators, graphs, tables, and post-simulation analysis are very important in any partial equilibrium modeling exercise. Good economic studies based on models require effective ways of presentation of the results and conclusions. The ordered thinking that goes into the development and exercise of models as well as the effective presentation of results makes partial equilibrium models important learning as well as analytical tools.

A larger, more complicated model can have more markets and regions, and therefore many more equations and variables. Equations can be of many different forms, e.g., linear or non-linear, like the equations in Figure 8.5. Equations can have many more cross-market linkages if a model has more markets. The equation structure can be different for each market. There can even be direct market linkages across countries. Policy and price structures would likely be more complicated with a larger model. For example, the model outlined in Figure 8.5 did not explicitly include exchange rates or domestic policies affecting coarse grain supply and demand. Alternatively, products produced in each country might be assumed to be different and constitute a separate market by themselves. But in spite of all the possible complexities arising in a multi-market, multi-region partial equilibrium model, the organizational and mechanical structure of such a model would be similar to this two-market, two-region example.

V Extensions

When faced with an analytical problem that can benefit from partial equilibrium modeling, a wide range of choices can be made about model construction. These choices involve trade-offs. For example a larger, more complex model might better capture the economic details of a problem but may cost more to construct or may be more difficult to use. With overly complex partial equilibrium or general equilibrium models, the mechanisms driving the model may be impossible to understand or explain. This can severely limit the usefulness of the model in real policy assessments. In general, the modeling choices made should depend upon the nature of the problem to be analysed, the availability of data and information for analysis, the time available for a modeling exercise, and the cost of model construction.

The assumptions used in a partial equilibrium model should be consistent with the nature of the markets and economic problem modeled. In agricultural markets, for example, many commodities are fairly homogeneous. This is reflected in commodity global data sets which deal with net, rather than gross exports. The assumption of homogeneity is validated by prices in different markets that track each other fairly closely over time. Therefore, at a fairly aggregate level, it is possible and reasonable to construct global agricultural models for policy analysis on a net trade basis (similar to the example in Figure 8.1). Net trade models can deal with policies that a region uses to drive a price wedge between its domestic prices and prices in all other regions. Net trade models are simple because bilateral trade flows between regions are ignored. But if a problem requires an alternative assumption that products are differentiated by region, then a more complex model is needed to provide for both exports and imports of similar products (gross trade) and allocate these trade flows between regions. This means many more equations are needed and a model will become much larger. If, for example, the problem at hand is the analysis of a free trade area where trade policies are modified on a bilateral basis between regions, a net trade model is inadequate and a partial equilibrium modeling system has to allow differentiated markets and bilateral trade flows (Dixit and Roningen, 1989).

Another example where the analytical problem determines modeling choices concerns the issue of static versus dynamic models. A static partial equilibrium model, such as the type presented in Figure 8.5, analyses a one-time change over a period which is built into the specification of the market behaviour in the model. The static model compares the new equilibrium state to the base equilibrium state after all adjustments have occurred and world markets have been cleared. Static models require the calculation of only one solution. A dynamic model, on the other hand, traces out the path of adjustment for each model variable over time and requires a full model solution every period. Dynamic models have to deal with lag structures that capture the path of economic adjustment over time. They also have to deal with formidable problems of model stability. Once solutions to dynamic models are obtained, simulation scenarios have to be compared to a dynamic baseline generated with the model. All in all, dynamic models are more costly to build and operate. So if the problem at hand only requires an estimate of the final impact of an economic change, a static model can usually deliver an answer at a lower cost than a dynamic model. But if the problem at hand is of a forecasting nature or demands an analysis of the path of economic adjustment over time, then the larger costs and complexities of a dynamic model must be dealt with.

If a static model is deemed to be an adequate tool for the analysis of a problem, then care has to be taken with the model parameters so that a reasonable interpretation of the results can be given in a dynamic context. As pointed out in Figure 8.1, a static model assumes an implicit adjustment time when the scenario results are interpreted. A static model also assumes that dynamic factors driving an economy forward over time are not themselves influenced by any shock applied to the model (Roningen, 1993). Dynamic models do have an advantage in that history can be a guide. Time series can be used for model estimation and for the judgment of the acceptability of results (model validation). Fortunately, if partial equilibrium dynamic modeling is required, there are many computer packages available to help the modeller get the job done. Some of the spreadsheet modeling techniques used for constructing static partial equilibrium models can also be applied to the construction of dynamic partial equilibrium models (Roningen, 1992).

The choices for market coverage in a model are important determinants of model size and complexity. At one extreme is the computable general equilibrium model, where detail is focused around the markets of analytical interest, but the rest of the economy is included in the model. At the other extreme is a model of a single market with no cross-market linkages at all. When an economic problem focuses on certain markets, the modeller has to address the question of the interaction of those markets with the rest of the economy. Sometimes secondary markets linked to those being analysed have to be included, requiring a larger and more complex partial equilibrium model. In the case of global agricultural policy reform, for example, early partial equilibrium models concentrated on agricultural markets where data was available and modeling results were needed quickly. But because agriculture is very important in many economies and the linkages between agriculture and other sectors are strong, computable general equilibrium models were also built for the analysis of agricultural policy reform.

Since partial equilibrium modeling is problem focused, its net result should be to clarify and illuminate an economic problem. This means that models and their analytical results should be transparent, not just to the modeller, but also to those using the analysis to make decisions. A modeling package which helps to create and operate a partial equilibrium model does not relieve the economist of the responsibility for learning the economics and mathematics behind the model. "Black box" models created by modeling packages but not fully understood by the user simply do not meet the transparency and credibility goals that underlie the successful application of partial equilibrium analysis to real world problems. Another common modeling mistake is to underestimate the time needed to organize and present the results of a model based analysis effectively. In many cases, because such analysis can also be explained and emphasized graphically in a compelling way for non-economists, policymakers, and students of economics, the education provided to policymakers from a partial equilibrium modeling analysis is as important as the actual analytical results.

Because of their flexibility, relative simplicity, and limited data requirements, partial equilibrium models will continue to be used in policy settings. They are useful problem solving tools for the applied economist. In the problem area of global agricultural policy reform, multi-market, multi-region partial equilibrium models have made important contributions to the public debate and to actual policy formation. However, the Uruguay Round of trade negotiations did not come close to removing all support for agriculture or other sectors of the world economy. As such, there are much trade modeling and analysis left to be done in the future. In addition, environmental issues are becoming very important on the political and trade agenda (Anderson and Blackhurst, 1992). Since environmental problems are often associated with particular production processes or products, partial equilibrium modeling can be a useful analytic tool in this area as well.

References

Anderson, K. and R. Blackhurst, eds. 1992. *The Greening of World Trade Issues.* Ann Arbor: University of Michigan Press.

Dixit, P., B. McDonald, and V. Roningen. 1992. "Supplying quantitative analysis of agriculture in the Uruguay Round." *Atlantic Economic Society Best Paper Proceedings* 2:85–89.

Dixit, P. and V. Roningen. 1989. "Quantitative implications of creating an agricultural free trade area between the U.S. and Canada." *Canadian Journal of Agricultural Economics* 37:1023–1033.

Dixit, P. and V. Roningen. 1990. "Assessing the implications of freer agricultural trade." *Food Policy* 15:67–75.

Economic Research Service, U.S. Department of Agriculture. 1988. *Estimates of Producer and Consumer Subsidy Equivalents: Government Intervention in Agriculture, 1982–1986.* Staff Report No. AGES 880127. Washington, D.C.

Foreign Agricultural Service, U.S. Department of Agriculture (annual). "Production, supply, and utilization database." Washington, D.C.

Hathaway, D. 1987. *Agriculture and the GATT: Rewriting the Rules.* Washington, D.C.: Institute for International Economics.

Houck, J. 1986. *Elements of Agricultural Trade Policies.* Prospect Heights, Illinois: Waveland Press.

Johnson, D. 1973. *World Agriculture in Disarray.* Bungay, England: Chaucer Press.

Josling, T. 1981. *Intervention in Canadian Agriculture: A Comparison of Costs and Benefits Among Sectors.* Palo Alto, California. Food Research Institute, Stanford University.

Meilke, K. and H. de Gorter. 1994. "Challenges in Quantitative Assessment of Multilateral Trade Deals." Paper prepared for the International Agricultural Trade Research Consortium. University of Guelph.

Parikh, K.S., G. Fischer, K. Frohberg, and O. Gulbrandsen. 1988. *Towards Free Trade in Agriculture.* Dordrecht, Netherlands: Martinus Nijhoff.

Organization for Economic Cooperation and Development. 1987. *National Policies and Agricultural Trade*. Paris.

Robinson, S., M. Kilkenny, and I. Adelman. 1989. "The effect of agricultural trade liberalization on the U.S. economy: Projections to 1991." In *Macroeconomic Consequences of Farm Support Policies*, edited by A.B. Stoeckel et al. Durham, North Carolina: Duke University Press.

Roningen, V.O. 1992. *Documentation of the Dynamic World Policy Simulation (DWOPSIM) Model Building Framework*. Staff Report Number AGES 9226. Washington, D.C.: Economic Research Service, U.S. Department of Agriculture.

Roningen, V.O. 1993. *Managing Free Trade for Agriculture*. Washington, D.C.: National Center for Food and Agricultural Policy.

Roningen, V.O. and P. Dixit. 1989. *How Level Is the Playing Field? An Economic Analysis of Agricultural Policy Reforms in Industrial Market Economies*. Foreign Agricultural Economic Report 239. Washington, D.C.: Economic Research Service, U.S. Department of Agriculture.

Roningen, V. O., J. Sullivan, and P. Dixit. 1991. *Documentation of the Static World Policy Simulation (SWOPSIM) Model Building Framework*. Staff Report Number AGES 9151. Washington, D.C.: Economic Research Service, U.S. Department of Agriculture.

Stoeckel, A.B., D. Vincent, and S. Cuthbertson, eds. 1989. *Macroeconomic Consequences of Farm Support Policies*. Durham, North Carolina: Duke University Press.

Sullivan, J., V. Roningen, S. Leetmaa, and D. Gray. 1992. *A 1989 Global Database for the Static World Policy Simulation (SWOPSIM) Modelling Framework*. Staff Report AGES 9215. Washington, D.C.: Economic Research Service, U.S. Department of Agriculture.

Thompson, R. 1981. "A survey of recent U.S. developments in international agricultural trade models." *Bibliographies and Literature of Agriculture*, No. 21. Washington, D.C.: Economic Research Service, U.S. Department of Agriculture.

Tyers, R. and K. Anderson. 1986. "Distortions in world food markets: A quantitative assessment." Unpublished background paper for the World Bank's *World Development Report*. Washington, D.C.

Tyers, R. and K. Anderson. 1992. *Disarray in World Food Markets: A Quantitative Assessment*. Cambridge, England: Cambridge University Press.

9

Multi-Region General Equilibrium Modeling

Thomas W. Hertel, Elena Ianchovichina, and Bradley J. McDonald

I Introduction

This chapter is about the issues that modellers confront in deciding whether to apply single-region or multi-region general equilibrium models and, when multi-region models are used, the inherent differences in data and modeling methods that modellers face. The chapter provides an overview of the key data and conceptual issues involved in moving from single-region to multi-region models, such as the organization of trade and protection data, assumptions about product differentiation, and implications of alternative macroeconomic model closures.

The single-region and multi-region approaches are directly compared for a particular example involving the Uruguay Round. During the course of these negotiations, many countries sought quantitative guidance on the likely impact of the agreement on their economies. Because of limited data and modeling capacity, most of these countries conducted this analysis by using either single-region applied general equilibrium (AGE) models or multi-region partial equilibrium models. In our example, we ask the question, How much additional analytical insight would have been gained by having access to a multi-region model? The answer obviously depends on the country in question. We focus our analysis on Korea, which permits us to draw some tentative conclusions about the value added from multi-region AGE models.

II Conceptual Issues in Multi-Region AGE Models

International trade is the key inter-regional link in multi-region AGE models, even when these models are not explicitly oriented toward trade issues. "Current account" relations between regions overshadow their counterpart "capital account" relations partly because of the issues being studied, but also because the numerical modeling of financial and asset-related international flows is less well-developed.[1] Data on bilateral flows of merchandise trade are also easier to obtain than similar data for capital flows. Finally, many of the existing models were developed to support multi-lateral trade negotiations, which in the past have largely focused on merchandise trade. Within the current account, regional exports and imports of goods (and often services) are usually the only categories considered explicitly. International transfers and flows of investment income, the other components of the current account, rarely receive careful attention, although their values must be present somewhere in the underlying social accounting matrix. Clearly, this is an important area for future research.

II.1 Product Differentiation

Modeling merchandise and services trade in multi-region models involves most of the same choices that one confronts in single-region modeling, plus some additional complications. Perhaps the most important assumptions pertain to the structure of final and intermediate demands for products sourced from the various regions of the model. Are competing products from the various regions assumed to be identical, or are they instead differentiated by their region of origin? If they are assumed to be identical, this aspect of the model is straightforward: Net exports of the product are equal to the excess of production over total domestic use of the product. Any intra-industry trade that exists is "netted out," reducing the apparent importance of trade to the region. Intra-industry trade may be reduced by increasing the sectoral detail of a model, but the detail needed to reduce it to inconsequential levels is unlikely to be achieved in multi-region models.[2] Net trade models can also be hypersensitive to changes in transportation cost and trade policy wedges. Finally, they run the risk of extreme specialization when sector-specific factors of production are not present in the model.

---

1 In AGE modeling, capital account issues are normally considered to be questions of model closure, a topic discussed later. For recent efforts in this area, see Goulder and Eichengreen (1992).

2 The size of a model increases rapidly with the number of regions, especially in the presence of bilateral trade flows, and sectoral detail is computationally and otherwise more expensive in multi-region models. Furthermore, differences in data coverage across countries makes it difficult to develop comparable social accounting data for a narrowly defined industry in more than one country: Industry definitions for input–output tables are not harmonized across countries, while merchandise trade categories of the Harmonized System (HS) are harmonized only to six digits.

II.2 Endogenous Versus Exogenous Differentiation

Once one introduces the idea of product differentiation, the immediate question that arises is, Why are the products differentiated? The traditional approach to modeling product differentiation, due to Armington (1969), is to assume that it is related to exogenous considerations that somehow are linked to the country of origin. For example, as a result of variation in climate and soils, Canadian wheat tends to be differentiated from U.S. wheat. Alternatively, it is sometimes argued that while particular products such as soft wheat are nearly identical regardless of source, the aggregation of soft wheat and hard wheat into a single product, "wheat," means that the composition of wheat produced in different regions varies. One can capture these phenomena by introducing imperfect substitutability among wheat from different sources. Whatever the source of this differentiation, the key assumption in the Armington approach is that it is *exogenous* to the model.[3]

An alternative approach to product differentiation in models of international trade is based on the work of Spence (1976), and of Dixit and Stiglitz (1977), in which products are differentiated by firm. In this case firms incur fixed or overhead costs, such as research and development and product marketing, when producing differentiated goods. In its pure form, firm-level differentiation means that an automobile manufactured by Honda is modeled as being different from one manufactured by Mercedes-Benz, regardless of origin. This *endogenous* differentiation has important implications for the structure of costs and the consequences of trade liberalization. In particular, it is customary to treat the resources associated with differentiation as fixed costs. Coupled with constant returns to scale in production (i.e., fixed marginal costs), this gives rise to declining average total costs. Therefore, any shock that causes individual firms (as opposed to the industry) to increase their output results in positive *scale effects* for the economy, as fixed costs are spread over more units.

Working in the other direction is the *varietal effect* associated with the number of differentiated products on offer. Clearly, firms would not engage in product differentiation if consumers, in aggregate, preferred a single variety, or if variety itself were not somehow valued. In this case, there would be no incentive to deviate from a single variety. Therefore, the pres-

---

3 There is no particular reason why all products and/or all regions need to have the same Armington structure. For example, in the RUNS model (Goldin, Knudsen and van der Mensbrugghe, 1993), trade in industrial products was described by two-stage CES Armington functions. Agricultural products, on the other hand, were not assumed to be differentiated by region of origin and trade in these products was on a net trade basis.

ence of differentiated products implies either heterogeneity among consumers or a demand for variety among at least some consumers. When additional products are added to the marketplace, thereby incurring fixed costs and diluting the sales of existing firms, there is an offsetting gain due to increased variety. In particular, the new products permit individual consumers either to obtain a better match between their preferred variety and those extant in the marketplace or to obtain increased variety in consumption.[4]

Applied models of trade based on consumer-level product differentiation build on theoretical work by Helpman (1981), Krugman (1979, 1980), and Lancaster (1980). An alternative interpretation involves differentiation of intermediate products. In particular, this approach builds on Ethier's (1979, 1982) work on international scale economies related to increased specialization of intermediate goods.[5] Regardless of the particular approach, equilibrium in a setting with firm-level product differentiation generally requires firms to exercise some market power, marking up their price over marginal cost in order to cover the fixed costs of product differentiation. The degree of market power obtained will depend on the number of firms and the heterogeneity of consumers. In particular, as emphasized by Anderson, DePalma, and Thisse (1992), greater heterogeneity implies a smaller elasticity of substitution in the aggregate utility function and thus larger markups. If entry and exit are permitted, the extra revenues obtained via this markup will be precisely exhausted on fixed costs in the zero profits equilibrium.

There is now an extensive body of theoretical literature exploring the properties of trade policy in the presence of endogenous product differentiation (e.g., Krugman, 1979; Helpman and Krugman, 1989; Venables, 1987; Brown, 1991; Francois, 1992, 1994; Hertel, 1994). There is also an emerging body of literature based on empirical analysis using global trade models under different specifications (e.g., Francois et al., 1995; Harrison et al., 1995; Hertel and Lanclos, 1994). Alternative approaches to modeling firm-level differentiation are examined by Francois and Roland-Holst in Chapter 11 of this volume. The introduction of imperfect competition gives rise to several additional mechanisms through which trade policy can influence the economy. Since these models require more data about industry structure, they are also more difficult to implement empirically in the context of a global model. For these reasons, we will restrict our attention in the remainder of this chapter to the Armington, perfect competition specification. This

---

4 See Helpman and Krugman (1985, Chapter 6), for a technical discussion of the love-of-variety and preferred variety approaches.
5 For example, see the technical annex of Francois et al. (1995).

provides a good starting point for the individual interested in multi-region AGE analysis.

II.3 Focus on the Armington Specification

When applied to single-region models, the product-differentiation-by-region-of-origin assumption is implemented by defining a composite product, $C_i = f(D_i, M_i)$ ($i \in I$, where I is the set of all tradeable products), that is an aggregation of domestically produced quantities of product i, D_i, and imported quantities, M_i. This is the end of the story for single-region models, which are not required to distinguish among import sources.[6] In contrast, multi-region models must take this notion a step further and distinguish M_{ir} (imports of i sourced from region r) from M_{is} (imports of i sourced from region s): $C_i = g(D_i, M_{ir}, M_{is}, \ldots)$.[7] Exactly how the Armington distinction is made varies in two key ways: the functional form chosen for the aggregator function, $g(\cdot)$, and whether the Armington aggregation is specific to each agent within a region or instead is simply performed at the border. The approaches used in various model applications are summarized in Table 9.1. We now turn to a discussion of each of these points, in turn.

In specifying import demand, either a single constant elasticity of substitution (CES) aggregator function or a nested CES Armington structure is often employed.[8] Under the nested approach, the composite good C_i is assumed to be a function of the domestic good and a composite of imports sourced from the other regions in the model:

$$C_i = g\Big[D_i, h\big(M_{ir}, M_{is}, \ldots\big)\Big] \tag{9.1}$$

where both the function g (the "top level" nest) and the function h (the "bottom level" nest) are CES functions. This formulation places two main restrictions on the structure of international trade. First, imports are made *separable* from the domestic good: Relative price changes among imports do not affect the quantity demanded of the domestic good, and a change in the price of the domestic good does not affect the relative quantities demanded

---

6 See Dervis, de Melo and Robinson (1982).
7 This notation is meant to indicate that regions r and s are two of an unspecified number of regions in the model other than the importing region under examination here.
8 See, for example, Shoven and Whalley (1992). For econometric evidence regarding the validity of this approach, see Winters (1984). Alternatives to the CES functional form include the almost ideal demand system (AIDS) of Deaton and Muellbauer (1980). In the context of agricultural commodities, Alston et al. (1990) have found that the elasticity of substitution between imports and domestic competing goods in the United States was substantially higher from AIDS estimation than from a CES-based estimation. Burfisher et al. (1994) work with a multi-region general equilibrium trade model which employs the AIDS import demand formulation.

Table 9.1. *Armington structure in selected multi-region CGE model applications*

Model Application	No. of Stages	Functional Form	Location of Armington Aggregation	Export-side Armington ?	Comments
Francois, McDonald and Nordström (1995)	One	CES	At the Border	No	
Jomini, *et al* (1991)	Two	CES	User Specific	No	Disaggregate imports sourced by agent
Lewis, Robinson and Wang (1995)	One	AIDS	At the Border	Yes	
Michigan Model (Deardorff and Stern, 1986)	One	CES	At the Border	Yes	
Roland-Holst, Reinert and Shiells	One	CES	At the Border	Yes	
RUNS Model (Goldin, Knudsen and van der Mensbrugghe, 1993)	Two	CES	At the Border	Yes	Agricultural products are not differentiated by region of origin
Standard GTAP Model (Hertel and Tsigas, 1995)	Two	CES	User specific	No	Composite imports sourced by agent
Whalley (1985), Seven-region model	Two	CES/LES	At the border	No	
Whalley (1985), Four-region model	One	CES/LES	User-Specific	No	Number of agents varies across regions

of the various imported goods.[9] Second, the particular assumption of g and h as CES functions implies not only that the elasticities of substitution at these two levels are constant, but that the elasticity of substitution at the lower level is equal for each pair of imports.[10] Under the non-nested specification, the substitution elasticities are implicitly identical at both levels.

9 As shown by Perroni and Rutherford (1995), it is possible to introduce more complex CES nesting structures in order to allow for nonseparability. The motivation behind their non-separable CES (NCES) form is primarily to allow flexibility in the representation of production technology rather than the international trade structure.

10 A special case of the nested CES Armington structure is that in which the elasticity of substitution among imports (the lower nest) is equal to that between imports and the domestic good (the upper nest). By restricting the elasticity of substitution to be equal among each pair of goods entering the aggregation, the Armington structure can be represented in a single stage function, $C_i = g(D_i, M_{ir}, M_{is}, \ldots)$, where g is a CES function. Of course, if the elasticity of substitution in the lower nest becomes smaller than that in the upper nest, then gross complementarity among imports becomes a possibility. That is, a reduction in one import's price could lead to an increase in the demand for *all* imports.

Modellers have tended to accept these restrictions because the empirical information necessary to exploit a less-restrictive structure is not typically available and because this structure has the virtues of analytical simplicity and computational ease.[11]

Largely on the basis of results of sensitivity analyses of models to changes in the substitution elasticities (σ^D in the top level nest and σ^M in the bottom nest) in CES-based Armington functions, modellers have come to appreciate the extent to which these parameters influenced the model results, particularly because the parameters largely determine terms of trade effects in the two-nest specification. The magnitude of terms of trade effects in Armington AGE models is often considered to be "excessive." These issues have been studied analytically by Brown (1987), who has concluded the following:

1 Terms of trade effects are reduced as σ^M approaches ∞.
2 As σ^D increases in the region making a tariff change, the terms of trade effects of the change are increased. However, as σ^D increases in the other regions, the terms of trade effects of the same tariff change are diminished. Increasing σ^D in all regions has an ambiguous influence on the magnitude of terms of trade effects.

Experience with sensitivity analysis by economists working with multi-region models suggests that the magnitude of the terms of trade effects noted by Brown in fact vary substantially with the substitution elasticities. This is especially troublesome, since there remains considerable uncertainty about the appropriate values of these elasticities.[12] Francois (1996) notes that the body of the Armington-based CGE literature steadfastly suggests gains to all participating countries in practically all regional trading arrangements, in contrast to economic theory on trade diversion. He argues that this may be an artifact of the Armington parameters. In this regard, it is important to conduct systematic sensitivity analysis on these and other parameters. Preckel et al. (1993) have proposed a method of sampling based on Gaussian quadrature that is particularly useful in large-scale, multi-region models where repeated solutions can be very time-consuming.

Of course the ultimate solution to the problem of parametric uncertainty rests in sound econometric work. However, the empirical estimation of Armington elasticities presents several challenges. For example, the product definition used in the estimation may be more narrow, or more broad, than

---

11 The analytical properties of the CES function are summarized in Table 4.9 of Shoven and Whalley (1992).
12 See Shiells and Reinert (1993).

the product definition used in the model; the same problem exists with regard to regional aggregation as well as product aggregation.[13] Another issue is the appropriate time frame for econometric estimation. The use of (appropriately adjusted) quarterly data may be necessary to gain a sufficient sized data set but, for reasons similar to those underlying the "J-curve," quarterly data may generate very inelastic estimates.

Brown's second point indicates the likely importance of region-specific estimates of the top nest substitution elasticity in determining the magnitude of terms of trade effects. Effects will be smaller if this elasticity is small in the region that changes tariffs, but larger if this elasticity is small in other regions. Relative sizes of upper nest elasticities thus help determine the magnitude of terms of trade effects. Nevertheless, when the nested CES Armington approach is used in multi-region models, the substitution elasticities used for a particular product usually are common to all regions in the model. While thorough econometric estimation of these elasticities has been performed by some modeling teams (see Roland-Holst et al., 1994; and the brief discussion in Chapter 1 of this volume), these estimates have typically been for only one region of a multi-region model.

II.4 Import Sourcing by Agent

Regardless of the type of Armington structure used, there are two alternatives in locating the structure within the model. The more common alternative is to use just one Armington function for each good in each region. We refer to this approach as applying the Armington aggregation "at the border." The other alternative is to specify one Armington function for each agent "consuming" each good in each region. We refer to this approach as using user-specific Armington functions. Here the modeller may choose to track *differentiated* imports to the users (more demanding) or, alternatively, to track *aggregated* imports to users.

User-specific Armington functions imply a substantial increase in model size compared to aggregation at the border. The number of potential users equals the number of sectors (which is usually equal to the number of goods) plus the number of final demand agents (typically consumers, government, and investment). This requires $(G+3) \cdot G \cdot R$ Armington functions, one for each good G used in each productive sector in each region R, one for each good privately consumed in each region, one for each good purchased by

---

13 Research into appropriate methods of aggregating econometric estimates obtained for detailed product specifications into the broader product categories common in multi-region AGE models may be very fruitful.

government in each region, and one for investment demand. If *differentiated* imports are tracked to users (e.g., Jomini et al., 1991), data are required on the sourcing of intermediate and final inputs for each user in each region. Such detailed data are not available from the input–output accounts. This has led to a third alternative, a compromise between full-blown sourcing of imports by agent and complete Armington aggregation at the border. Here, *disaggregate* imports are sourced at the border, but *composite* imports are tracked to the individual agents (Hertel and Tsigas, 1996). This matches the level of detail available in some national social accounting matrices, since breakdown of intermediate and final demands according to domestic and imported origins is a common practice in national input–output accounting (e.g., Hambley, 1992).

II.5 Macroeconomic Closure

One of the more contentious aspects of comparative static AGE models is the question of *macroeconomic closure*, a term first coined by Sen (1963) and later applied to AGE modeling by Taylor and Lysy (1979). Dewatripont and Michel (1987) note that there are four popular solutions to the fundamental indeterminacy of investment determination in comparative static models. The first three are non-neoclassical closures in which investment is simply fixed and another source of adjustment is permitted. In the fourth closure investment is permitted to adjust. However, rather than including an independent investment relationship, it simply accommodates any change in savings. Contemporary comparative static multi-region trade models often employ some form of this last closure rule, although variants of the other three are also sometimes adopted as special cases.[14]

In addition to adopting a closure rule with respect to investment, it is also necessary to come to grips with potential changes in the current account. Many multi-region trade models have evolved as a set of single-region models that are linked via bilateral merchandise trade flows (e.g., early versions of the SALTER model, which evolved from the ORANI model of Australia). These models have no *global closure* with respect to savings and investment, but instead impose the macroeconomic closure at the regional level. Here it is common to force domestic savings and investment to move in tandem, by fixing the current account balance. To understand this, it is

---

14 A collection of structuralist single-region AGE models, along with an analytical overview of the features of such models, is found in Taylor (1990). See Chapter 12 of this volume for dynamic extensions of these basic closure options.

useful to recall the following accounting identity, which follows from equating national expenditure from the sources and uses sides:

$$S - I + (T - G) \equiv X + R - M \qquad (9.2)$$

which states that the private sector savings minus investment plus the government budget surplus is identically equal to the current account surplus, where R is international transfer receipts.[15] By fixing the right-hand side of identity (9.2) one also fixes the difference between national savings (including government savings) and investment.

If global savings equals global investment in the initial equilibrium, then the summation over the left-hand side of (9.2) equals zero and the sum of all current account balances (including transfer receipts) must initially be zero (provided *c.i.f./f.o.b.* margins are accounted for in national exports). Furthermore, by fixing the right-hand side of (9.2) on a regional basis, each region's share of savings in the global pool of net savings is fixed. In this way, equality of global savings and investment in the new equilibrium is also assured, in spite of the fact that there is no "global bank" to intermediate formally between savings and investment on a global basis. However, since investment is forced to adjust in line with regional changes in savings, this approach clearly falls within the "neoclassical" closure, as identified by Dewatripont and Michel.

The exogeneity of the current account balance embodies the notion that this balance is a macroeconomic, rather than microeconomic, phenomenon. To a great extent, the causality in identity (9.2) runs from the left side to the right side. It also facilitates analysis by forcing all adjustment to external imbalance entirely onto the current account. If savings does not enter the regional utility function, this is also the right approach to welfare analysis because an arbitrary shift away from savings towards current consumption would otherwise permit an increase in utility to be attained, even in the absence of improvements in efficiency or regional terms of trade.

For some types of experiments, however, modellers may wish to endogenize the balances on the left and right sides of identity (9.2). Some trade policy reforms may, for example, raise returns to capital or lower the price of imported capital goods (see Goulder and Eichengreen, 1992, and Chapters 12 and 13 of this volume). In this case, we would expect an increase in regional investment and, *ceteris paribus*, a deterioration in the current account. In other cases one might wish to explore the implications of, for example, an *exogenous* increase in foreign direct investment, which would

---

15 See, for example, Dornbusch (1980).

also dictate a deterioration in the current account. Once the left-hand side of (9.2) is permitted to adjust, we need a vehicle for ensuring that the global demand for savings equals the global demand for investment in the post-solution equilibrium. This can be ensured through the use of a "global bank" to assemble savings and disburse investment, an approach adopted in the Global Trade Analysis Project (GTAP) model (Hertel and Tsigas, 1996).

For the purpose of illustration, we work in this chapter with the GTAP model. The GTAP model treats savings and investment in an analogous manner to all other goods and services in the model. In particular, savings enters a regional Cobb–Douglas utility function, along with composite private consumption and aggregate government purchases. This reflects an implicit assumption of fixed savings rates. Fixing the savings rate prevents an arbitrary shift of savings in favor of current consumption from generating apparent increases in utility. The resulting behavioral equations are also compatible with a multi-period optimization problem, in which current period savings result in future consumption (Howe, 1975). Thus, from a consumption point of view, savings is treated analogously with other goods in the GTAP model. However, since bilateral information on savings flows is not available, we do not employ an Armington-type specification here. Rather, regional savings are gathered by the global banking sector and treated as a homogeneous good, which serves as numéraire in the model.

The global bank in the GTAP model uses savings to assemble a portfolio of regional investment goods. The size of this portfolio adjusts to accommodate changes in global savings. Therefore, the *global closure* in this model is neoclassical. However, on a regional basis, some adjustment in the portfolio is permitted, thereby adding another dimension to the determination of investment in the model. In particular, the global bank equates *expected* rates of return on investment across regions. This approach breaks the link between domestic investment levels and domestic savings rates, allowing welfare analysis in a static setting that involves shifts in capital flows. Any change in net capital flows is directly linked to a change in investment. This rules out direct linkages between an arbitrary shift in capital flows (foreign savings) and apparent shifts in utility due to shifting budget constraints.

Expected rates of return are an increasing function of current returns and a decreasing function of current period investment, following a specification originally proposed by Dixon et al. (1982):

$$RORE(r) = RORC(r) \left[\frac{KE(r)}{KB(r)} \right]^{-RORFLEX(r)} \tag{9.3}$$

Thus investors behave as if they expect a region's rate-of-return in the next period ($RORE(r)$) to decline with positive additions to the capital stock ($KE(r)$). The rate at which this decline is expected to take place depends on the flexibility parameter $RORFLEX(r) > 0$. Therefore, the elasticity of $RORE(r)$ with respect to $KE(r)$ is equal to $-RORFLEX(r)$. A small value for $RORFLEX(r)$, say $RORFLEX(r) = 0.5$, implies that a 1 percent increase in $KE(r)$ is expected to reduce the rate of return on capital by 0.5 percent. For example, if the current rate of return were 10 percent, the expected rate of return on a net investment equal to 1 percent of $KE(r)$ would be 9.95 percent, i.e., little change. In this case, the supply of new investment is *very* sensitive to the expected rate of return. In order to maintain equal changes in *RORE* across regions, the model will produce large changes in regional investment.

However, a large value for $RORFLEX(r)$, say $RORFLEX(r) = 50$, implies that a 1 percent increase in $KE(r)$ is expected to cut the rate of return on capital in half. In this case the supply of new capital goods is not very sensitive to changes in the expected rate of return. Therefore, equal changes in *RORE* across regions can be accommodated with small changes in regional investment. In other words, if the user believes that the experiment under consideration will not have a great impact on regional investment (or wishes to abstract from such effects) large values of $RORFLEX(r)$ are chosen.

II.6 International Factor Mobility

In a multi-period model, international investment flows in the current period will be accompanied by reverse flows in international factor payments in future periods. However, in a comparative static model (like that considered here), new investment does not come on line, so this aspect need not be considered. However, any global data set must contain (albeit implicitly) such income flows that result from historical transboundary investment. These factor service flows are an important part of the international economy, particularly in the case of certain closely linked countries. For example, increased factor payments in the United States will benefit investors in Canada, and vice versa. Foreign ownership claims on capital income are represented in the models of Whalley (1985) and have been emphasized by researchers such as Markusen and Wigle (1989), who take explicit account of cross-ownership of factors in their analysis of a Canada–United States Free Trade Agreement.[16] Unfortunately, data on bilateral factor service flows are limited and so most global trade models have abstracted from this issue. An exception is provided by recent innovations to the SALTER model (McDougall, 1993).

III Data Issues in Multi-Region AGE Modeling

III.1 MFN Tariffs and the Compositional Effects of Aggregation

When working with single-region models, one faces the question of how to aggregate most favored nation (MFN) tariffs.[17] One approach often used is the weighting of tariffs by import value. With hundreds or perhaps thousands of individual lines in the tariff schedule being combined into one model sector, the compositional effects that can be captured by import weighting are potentially of great importance. It is often noted, though, that weighting by import value can lead to a downward bias in tariff aggregations. Higher tariffs lead to smaller (tariff-exclusive) import values, since imports are themselves a decreasing function of tariffs.[18] This is sometimes used as an argument in favor of another often-used approach, the simple averaging of tariffs, which in effect assumes the identical weight for each tariff line, regardless of its importance in trade. It also sometimes goes unrecognized that, for political economy reasons, past tariff reductions may have been deepest on those items that were more lightly imported. This implies that higher tariffs may remain on items of greater importance to trade and argues against the use of simple averaging.[19]

Uneven tariffs are more distorting than a uniform tariff with the same mean. Regardless of the weighting method used, the averaging process may incorporate tariff variance. This will be particularly desirable when dealing with policies that lead to very uneven protection, either across tariff lines

---

16 International labor mobility may also be important in certain applications. One approach is that of Burfisher et al. (1994). This area of research, however, remains underdeveloped.

17 Further discussion of this issue is contained in Chapter 2 in this volume.

18 By weighting tariffs with the duty-inclusive value of imports, some of this bias might be offset. Ultimately the degree of bias will depend on the price elasticity of import demand.

19 An additional argument in favor of import weighted averaging in the context of AGE modeling is that this method gives an accurate accounting of the tariff revenue. The importance of this accuracy will depend on several factors, including the presence of certain model features (are government revenue sources distinguished?), the size of tariff revenue collections relative to total government revenue or to GDP, and the value of imports that enter the country under other than MFN tariffs (for example, under preferential tariff arrangements).

Table 9.2. *Results of alternative tariff averaging methods*

GTAP Region and GTAP Product Name	Simple Average	Trade-Weighted Average	Bilateral Trade-Weighted Average	
			Low	High
		Per cent		
Indonesia, non-grain crops	17.1	3.9	0.0	24.1
United States, beverages and tobacco	8.0	4.3	0.8	15.8
Australia, textiles	25.4	13.2	4.2	29.4
New Zealand, chemicals, rubber and plastics	14.0	19.8	5.0	36.0

Source: Calculations reported in Gehlhar, et al. (1996) based on tariff data from the GATT Integrated Data Base.

(within a model sector) or across import sources. Magee (1972) proposed an averaging method that incorporates tariff variance. This method was applied in calculations of average anti-dumping duties for the 1994 GTAP database (Gehlhar et al., 1996).

Multi-region modeling adds yet another dimension to the debate over tariff averaging methods. The composition of the imports of a product from one source differs from the composition of imports of the same product from another source. By using the Armington assumption of product differentiation by region of origin, one recognizes this compositional effect in trade flows. It is reasonable to extend this recognition to tariffs as well and to use *bilateral* import-weighted tariffs, with the result that each of the model's bilateral trade flows (potentially $G \cdot R \cdot (R-1)$ of them) has an associated MFN tariff rate.

This is the method by which tariff rates are calculated for the 1994 and subsequent releases of the GTAP database (Gehlhar et al., 1996), a standard data source for multi-region modeling, and one which we work with in this chapter. For calculating the tariff data, data on bilateral imports and applied MFN tariffs were collected at the tariff-line level, where the number of tariff lines exceeded 12,000 for some regions. Results from this exercise indicate that, in many cases, compositional effects lead to tariff averages that vary substantially by source region, sometimes by multiples of 2 or 3. Gehlhar et al. (1996) report four examples, which are summarized in Table 9.2. The first row in this table shows that the simple average of all tariffs on non-grain crops imported into Indonesia is equal to 17.1 percent. This contrasts sharply with the trade-weighted average tariff on this group of products, which is only 3.9 percent, indicating that some of the highest tariffs are on lightly traded products. Also worthy of note is the variation in bilateral tariff rates which results from the differing composition of imports from different sources. These range from a zero bilateral tariff on imports to a 24.4 percent tariff. In sum, applying a simple average tariff to all imports hides a good deal of variation in effective tariff rates by source.[20]

III.2 Discriminatory Tariffs

In reality, much of global movement in merchandise goods does not take place under MFN tariffs. Price-based trade policies other than MFN tariffs include preferential tariffs, minimum import prices, anti-dumping duties and countervailing (anti-subsidy) duties. These policies, typically applied bilater-

---

20 When bilateral weighting is used in the development of the base tariff rates, the same process can be applied to aggregate tariff reductions.

ally, present special challenges in the setting of a multi-region model that may be "aggregated away" in single-region modeling. To date, however, there has been little progress toward a comprehensive treatment of such policies.

In the category of preferential tariffs we include tariff rates applied under regional trade agreements and tariff preferences for developing countries under the Generalized System of Preferences. Because the spread of regional trade agreements is quite recent, these preferential tariffs have not yet been incorporated into the benchmark data for multi-region AGE models. Many models built for the analysis of actual or proposed preferential trade agreements or tariff preferences do introduce preferential rates as the key component of counterfactual simulations (see, for example, particular chapters in Francois and Shiells, 1994; Hertel, 1996). To the extent they existed in the base period of the model from which trade data are taken, however, preferences have rarely, if ever, been recorded in the base data of multi-region AGE models.[21]

Anti-dumping and countervailing duties (AD/CVD) are other important policy instruments that discriminate among import sources.[22] Anti-dumping duties, by far the more prevalent of the two, are common in most major trading countries, with the exception of Japan. As of December 1994, the United States had 277 final anti-dumping duty orders in effect, each order country- and product-specific.[23] In late 1994, the European Union applied final anti-dumping duty orders on some 115 country and product combinations and had 51 price undertakings in effect.[24] In both these major traders, anti-dumping duty margins typically are in the range of 20 to 40 percent – many times the rates of MFN tariffs – and sometimes exceed 100 percent. AD/CVD actions have not yet been fully incorporated into multi-region model databases. To our knowledge, the first step in this direction is the 1994 release of the GTAP database, which incorporates, on a bilateral basis, aggregated anti-dumping duties and price undertakings of the United States, European Union, and Canada (Gehlhar et al., 1996).

The extent to which the neglect of discriminatory policies in multi-region models will distort results is not known, but it can be expected to depend on

21 Some 40 agreements were notified to the GATT between 1989 and 1994.
22 An excellent overview and several case studies are provided in Finger (1993). Staiger and Wollak (1994) establish empirically that anti-dumping actions restrict trade for other reasons in addition to the final orders that may be applied.
23 U.S. Department of Commerce (1994). In addition, according to this report, there were twelve suspension agreements in effect that resulted from anti-dumping actions, and ninety-seven countervailing duty (final) orders in effect. The country and product coverage of anti-dumping and countervailing orders often overlap.
24 Anti-dumping and countervailing duty actions of the European Union are reported in the *Official Journal*, available on CD-ROM.

several factors. One example with the potential to distort results is when preferential tariffs are in place but are neglected in the benchmark data, and counterfactual simulations are run in which MFN tariffs are reduced. In fact, we might expect a reduction in exports by preference-receiving countries as their margin of preference is eroded. If the preferential tariffs are not reflected in the benchmark data, however, the model results can be expected to show an increase in exports by the preference-receiving countries, as well as other exporters.

The neglect of bilateral policies will also lead to what we term "dirty calibration." An example is when imports are influenced by anti-dumping duties, but these duties are neglected in the benchmark protection data and in the calibration process. The calibrated share parameter in the Armington function will then be understated. Because the benchmark equilibrium is inaccurately recorded, dirty calibration will distort the results of all counter-factuals, although the magnitude of such effects has not been studied.[25]

III.3 Non-Tariff Barriers to Trade

Non-tariff trade barriers (NTBs) are, in many cases, administered bilaterally and therefore present many of the same modeling and data challenges discussed in the section on discriminatory tariffs. As with single-region models, however, incorporating NTBs into multi-region AGE models requires additional information on the price-based measure equivalent to the NTB. Typically, these equivalent measures are import tariffs when the NTB is a restraint on imports, and export taxes when the NTB is a restraint on exports. A discussion of NTB measurement issues is provided in Chapter 2.

III.4 International Transportation Margins

One feature of international trade that has been largely neglected in multi-region AGE models is the presence of international transport costs. The difficulty has been one of data availability, since these margins vary by route and commodity and are not directly observed in the international trade data. However, Tsigas et al. (1992) show how these margins may be estimated from pooled times series/cross section bilateral trade data. Indeed, the estimation of these margins is a critical step in the process of reconciling re-

---

25 As pointed out in Chapter 5, the neglect of underlying distortions also can lead to the systematic and substantial underestimation of the welfare benefits attributable to the removal of a particular distortion. The welfare impact of a tariff reduction from 50 percent to 40 percent will exceed that of the elimination of a 10 percent tariff, given the same initial trade values.

ported (*c.i.f.*) imports and (*f.o.b.*) exports. This concept is further refined in Gehlhar et al. (1996), where a trade margins function depending on distance, volume and an input price index is explicitly estimated. The resulting margins are incorporated in the GTAP database. As modeled here, they result in incomplete transmission of *f.o.b.* price changes into *c.i.f.* changes. Furthermore, they open the opportunity for users to explore the implications of changes in technology, policy and market structure that might alter these transport margins.

IV Multi-Region and Single Region Analysis Compared: Korea and the Uruguay Round

We now turn to the analysis of a specific problem in trade policy, namely, the impact of the Uruguay Round Agreement reached under the auspices of the GATT. We approach this problem from the point of view of an individual country and ask how multi-region analysis adds to their understanding of the agreement and its impact on them.

IV.1 Motivation

During the course of the Uruguay Round negotiations, virtually every country involved found itself faced with the question, What will be the impact of this agreement on our national economy? As a result of improvements in software and computing capabilities, as well as a fairly broad base of international expertise, many countries had access to some sort of economywide analysis, often using applied general equilibrium models. However, very few had access to applicable results from a global AGE model. How much more information would they have been able to obtain from such a model? Is it worth the effort associated with acquiring the necessary expertise?

This question is impossible to answer in the abstract. One's conclusion will depend on the relative size of an individual country's offers, as compared to that of its trading partners. It also depends on their size in the various international markets of interest. An extreme case is provided by Taiwan, a country which is not currently a member of the GATT and therefore not directly affected by the agreement. A single-region analysis of the Uruguay Round is not helpful for Taiwan, since all of the "action" occurs in other regions. Yet given its heavy reliance on trade, the welfare of Taiwan clearly depends on what happens to border measures in its partner regions. Without a multi-region model, there is little to say about this issue, other than to take

Table 9.3. *Average pre– and post–Uruguay Round protection levels,*
by importing region

Importing Region	Pre-Round[a] Tariff (%)		Post-Round[a] Tariff (%)		Average Import[b] Price Cuts (%)	
	Food	Mnfcs	Food	Mnfcs	Food	Mnfcs
US & Canada (USC)	11.7	4.3	11.0	2.8	-0.6	-1.4
European Union (EU)	26.5	6.5	26.0	3.9	-0.3	-2.4
Japan (JPN)	87.8	4.9	56.1	2.1	-8.1	-2.7
Korea (KOR)	99.5	16.1	41.1	8.2	-17.9	-6.8
Taiwan (TWN)	0.0[c]	0.0[c]	0.0[c]	0.0[c]	0.0[c]	0.0[c]
Hong Kong(HKG)	0.0[c]	0.0[c]	0.0[c]	0.0[c]	0.0[c]	0.0[c]
China (CHI)	0.0[c]	0.0[c]	0.0[c]	0.0[c]	0.0[c]	0.0[c]
Indonesia (IND)	21.9	14.2	15.5	13.5	-4.2	-0.6
Malaysia (MYS)	87.9	11.0	34.3	7.7	-14.9	-2.9
Philippines (PHL)	86.9	23.9	33.4	21.5	-15.3	-1.8
Thailand (THA)	59.8	36.2	34.5	27.6	-10.8	-5.9
Latin America (LTN)	2.3	17.1	1.5	14.9	-0.5	-1.6
Sub-Saharan Africa (SSA)	15.6	9.5	12.4	9.4	-1.7	-0.1
South Asia (SAS)	-3.5	51.9	-4.3	37.1	-0.7	-9.4
Rest of World (ROW)	15.7	10.6	14.1	9.1	-1.2	-1.3

[a] Source: Hertel et al. (1995). See also Hathaway and Ingco for details on farm and food protection. Nonfood protection levels are based on information from the GATT's Integrated Data Base.
[b] Change in tariff rate divided by the power of the initial tariff rate. This is the average of the disaggregate price cuts, and therefore differs from the price cut computed from the average tariffs.
[c] Taiwan, Hong Kong, and China are not covered by the Integrated Data Base from which these data are derived.

partial results from other analyses and try to relate them to variables in a national model.

The case of Korea is rather different, and for that reason more interesting for purposes of this chapter. Because Korea's offer under the Uruguay Round made deeper cuts in protection than was generally true on average, we expect that a disproportionate amount of the "action" will occur in the domestic economy. What does multi-region analysis contribute in this case? How closely are predictions from the two approaches correlated? What

Table 9.4. *Value of Uruguay Round cuts in import tax on commodities imported to Korea in millions of U.S. dollars (percentage change in power of the import tax in italics)*

	JPN	OAS[c]	NAM	EAZ	ROW	TOTAL
crops	-2	-1537	-1559	-501	-187	-3786
	-1[b]	*-24*	*-24*	*-35*	*-10*	
othagr	-5	-73	-253	-113	-36	-480
	-15	*-15*	*-16*	*-13*	*-16*	
extract	-86	-42	-155	-67	-47	-397
	-7	*-1*	*-4*	*-3*	*0*	
food	-5	-51	-227	-247	-4	-534
	-3	*-4*	*-20*	*-21*	*-1*	
textiles	-38	-26	-8	-22	-24	-118
	-4	*-2*	*-3*	*-5*	*-5*	
apparel	-2	-3	-1	-3	-1	-10
	-5	*-2*	*-10*	*-3*	*-5*	
crp	-315	-59	-268	-202	-68	-912
	-9	*-6*	*-9*	*-9*	*-8*	
metals	-298	-36	-78	-120	-125	-657
	-11	*-4*	*-4*	*-7*	*-6*	
trnseq	-39	-2	-8	-10	-6	-65
	-6	*-1*	*0*	*-2*	*-1*	
macheq	-1001	-396	-821	-331	-87	-2636
	-7	*-11*	*-9*	*-6*	*-6*	
othmnfc	-59	-28	-57	-50	-12	-206
	-6	*-6*	*-9*	*-8*	*-8*	
svces	0	0	0	0	0	0
	0	*0*	*0*	*0*	*0*	
Total	-1850	-2253	-3435	-1666	-597	-9801

[a] Source: Hertel et al. (1995). See also Hathaway and Ingco for details on farm and food protection. Nonfood cuts are based on the GATT's Integrated Data Base.
[b] Change in tariff rate divided by the power of the initial tariff rate. This is the average of the disaggregate price outs, and therefore differs from the price cut computed from the average tariffs.
[c] Taiwan, Hong Kong, and China are not covered by the Integrated Data Base.

explains the sources of discrepancy? We investigate these questions in the subsequent sections.

IV.2 Korea and the Uruguay Round

Table 9.3, taken from Hertel et al. (1995), shows the pre– and post–Uruguay Round levels of protection for non-food manufacturing and farm and food products under the Round. Note that Korean protection prior to the Round

Table 9.5. *Value of the Uruguay Round cuts in the import tax on commodities exported from Korea (percentage change in the power of the import tax in italics)*

	JPN	OAS	NAM	EAZ	ROW	TOTAL
crops	-13	-2	0	0	0	-15
	-2	*-1*	*0*	*0*	*-1*	
othagr	0	-1	0	0	0	-1
	0	*-4*	*0*	*0*	*-1*	
extract	-31	-14	-9	-11	-12	-77
	-1	*-1*	*-2*	*-4*	*-2*	
food	-79	-3	0	0	0	-82
	-10	*-1*	*0*	*0*	*0*	
textiles	-9	-147	-29	-44	-33	-262
	-1	*-3*	*-3*	*-6*	*-1*	
apparel	-84	-1	-51	-28	-11	-175
	-4	*-1*	*-2*	*-2*	*-2*	
crp	-22	-19	-12	-25	-59	-137
	-2	*-1*	*-1*	*-2*	*-4*	
metals	-88	-3	-45	-48	-47	-231
	-4	*0*	*-3*	*-5*	*-4*	
trnseq	-6	0	-14	-5	-19	-44
	-3	*0*	*-1*	*0*	*0*	
macheq	-73	-78	-169	-104	-112	-536
	-3	*-1*	*-2*	*-2*	*-2*	
othmnfc	-38	-12	-112	-86	-44	-296
	-2	*-1*	*-2*	*-3*	*-3*	
svces	0	0	0	0	0	0
	0	*0*	*0*	*0*	*0*	
Total	-443	-280	-441	-351	-337	-1852

[a] Source: Hertel et al. (1995). Hathaway and Ingco for details on farm and food protection. Nonfood cuts are based on the GATT's Integrated Data Base.
[b] Change in tariff rate divided by the power of the initial tariff rate. This is the average of the disaggregate price cuts, and therefore differs from the price cut computed from the average tariffs.
[c] Taiwan, Hong Kong, and China are not covered by the Integrated Data Base.

was quite high, especially for farm and food products, where the average tariff equivalent was almost 100 percent. Even in non-food manufacturing, the average tariff rate was relatively high (16 percent) compared with that of OECD countries and some other Asian economies. The cuts agreed to by Korea under the Round reduce the average tariff on food products (using pre-Round trade flows to weight the tariffs) to 40 percent and that on non-food manufactures by half. The resulting average price cuts, at constant *c.i.f.* prices, amount to 18 percent and 7 percent, respectively.

These cuts in protection can also be broken out by commodity and source, as is done in Table 9.4, which shows the value of cuts offered by Korea under the Round, in 1992 US$. These cuts represent the simple product of the reduction in *ad valorem* equivalent tariff, multiplied by 1992 imports (*c.i.f.* basis). Fully half of the total cuts ($9.8 billion) are in farm and food products (crops, other agriculture and food). A single-region analysis of the Korea cuts would be based on the row totals in this table. By expanding to a multi-region context, these cuts may be sourced by region. When broken out in this way, we see that U.S. and Canadian (NAM) exports are associated with the largest cuts ($3.4 billion).

If we were conducting a one-region analysis of cuts in protection under the Uruguay Round, this is where we would have to stop. There would be no vehicle for organizing the information on other regions' cuts and simulating them endogenously in the model. While these cuts are proportionately smaller than those in Korea, they are still significant in the case of some products. Table 9.5 displays the value of other regions' tariff cuts on products exported by Korea. These cuts are valued (on the basis of pre-Round trade) at almost $2 billion, with about one-fourth of this in machinery and equipment exports. When separated by destination, the value of cuts in Japan and the United States is largest – both are about $440 million.

IV.3 Non-Tariff Barriers Reduced in the Uruguay Round

Up to this point, we have only discussed cuts in import tariffs and the newly established tariff equivalents for farm and food products. However, the Uruguay Round also addressed two other areas relevant to this quantitative analysis. First, countries agreed to cut agricultural export subsidies by 36 percent. The major impact of this for Korea, at this level of aggregation, is an 11 percent increase in the *f.o.b.* price (assuming constant market prices) of crops exported from the EU to Korea. There is also a small increase in the U.S. price of crops sold to Korea. All other changes are negligible.

More significant is the agreement to accelerate quota growth associated with textiles and wearing apparel exports under the Agreement on Textiles and Clothing, eventually abolishing them altogether in 2005. As one of the relatively "older" exporters under this arrangement, Korea exports a relatively large share of its products to the restricted markets. Table 9.6 reports the estimated quota rents on textiles and wearing apparel sales exported from Korea, Other Asia, and the rest of the world (ROW) to those regions containing restricted importers. The quotas on Korea are less binding than the quotas on Other Asian exporters across the board, indicating that

Table 9.6. *Quota rents associated with the MFA ($1,992 million, proportion of exporter's market price in parentheses)*

| | | Destination | | |
| | | Textiles | | Wearing Apparel |
Source	NAM	EAZ	NAM	EAZ
KOR	65.5	45.7	388.9	165.7
	(0.10)	(0.08)	(0.123	(0.19)
OAS	266.3	384.1	3,344.1	2,246.6
	(0.13)	(0.14)	(0.28)	(0.25)
ROW	235.9	873.0	1,665.8	1,805.9
	(0.11)	(0.10)	(0.23)	(0.12)

Source: Hertel et al. (1995).

Korea's comparative advantage has been moving away from this type of export in recent years (Yongzheng et al., 1996).

IV.4 Overview of the Korean Economy

Before turning to the results of the Uruguay Round experiment, it is useful to provide a brief overview of the Korean economy. Table 9.7 provides some summary statistics for Korea as well as several other aggregated regions which are represented in the multi-region data base used later. The top set of entries reports the regional shares in global gross domestic product (GDP). From this it can be seen that the Korean economy is small relative to the world economy, and relative to some of its major trading partners. This means that the feedback effects from changes in the Korean economy, through other economies and back to Korea, are likely to be small. There-fore, a small-open economy representation is likely appropriate for analysis of *Korea-specific* shocks.

The next block of entries in Table 9.7 refers to the composition of final demand, by region. From this, it can be seen that the share of private household consumption in GDP is relatively small in Korea. This is due in large part to the dominant role of investment. Japan has a similar profile of final demand, with slightly lower investment and higher private consumption. North America stands out with 68 percent of GDP expended by private households, and investment equal to only 14 percent of this aggregate.

The final block of entries in Table 9.7 refers to the structure of production in each of these regions. Here, the entries refer to the share of economywide

Table 9.7. *Composition of Korean economy and other regions compared*

	KOR	JPN	OAS	NAM	EAZ	ROW
Share of Global GDP (percent)	1.09	14.50	4.5	30.35	29.89	19.62
Composition of Final Demand (Share of GDP)						
Consumption	0.53	0.57	0.57	0.68	0.62	0.66
Investment	0.36	0.31	0.29	0.14	0.20	0.20
Government	0.11	0.10	0.13	0.19	0.19	0.15
Exports	0.33	0.11	0.47	0.11	0.11[a]	0.20
Imports	-0.33	-0.09	-0.46	-0.12	-0.12[a]	-0.21
Total	1.0	1.0	1.0	1.0	1.0	1.0
Structure of Production (Share of Value-added)						
Food & AGR	0.13	0.05	0.22	0.04	0.08	0.13
N Resources	0.08	0.06	0.14	0.09	0.09	0.13
Textile & APP	0.02	0.01	0.03	0.01	0.01	0.02
O. Manuf	0.18	0.19	0.14	0.12	0.12	0.12
Svces	0.59	0.69	0.47	0.74	0.70	0.60
Total	1.0	1.0	1.0	1.0	1.0	1.0

[a] Excludes intra-EU trade

value added employed in various groupings of sectors. The services sector (including wholesale/retail and transport margins for all consumer goods) is dominant in all of these economies, with the highest share appearing in the United States and Canada (NAM), where it reaches 74 percent. Korea and ROW have a smaller, but still dominant share in this sector (about 60 percent), and Other Asia has only 47 percent of value added in the services and margins activities. Also worthy of note are the relatively small shares of value added devoted to textiles and wearing apparel production. Finally, the share of value added in agriculture and food processing varies considerably across economies. In Korea, this equals 13 percent, which is comparable to Other Asia and ROW. However, in the more industrialized economies, this share is much smaller.

In addition to patterns of final demand and value added, it is important to consider the patterns of import use and export intensity in the Korean economy. Table 9.8 reports the share of imports in composite demand, by commodity and use. The information in this table is based on the 1985 input–

Table 9.8. Share of imports in composite demand at market prices, by use

	Intermediate Uses												Final Demands			Total Uses
	crops	othagr	extract	food	textiles	apparel	crp	metals	trnseq	macheq	othmnfc	svces	Inv	Priv	Gov	
crops	0.06	0.00	0.51	0.40	0.99	0.50	0.99	0.52	0.76	0.67	0.81	0.00	0.01	0.07	0.14	0.41
othagr	0.13	0.84	0.63	0.11	1.00	0.99	0.44	0.79	0.90	0.12	0.64	0.18	0.93	0.40	0.83	0.32
extract	0.00	0.00	0.51	0.21	0.01	0.03	0.48	0.40	0.20	0.26	0.21	0.10	0.01	0.06	0.08	0.28
food	0.00	0.00	0.10	0.26	0.04	0.88	0.58	0.00	0.10	0.03	0.47	0.03	0.26	0.02	0.08	0.07
textiles	0.03	0.01	0.18	0.04	0.17	0.27	0.14	0.05	0.11	0.11	0.06	0.02	0.14	0.04	0.21	0.17
apparel	0.05	0.01	0.18	0.01	0.01	0.79	0.49	0.01	0.38	0.01	0.23	0.01	0.30	0.06	0.60	0.06
crp	0.05	0.00	0.24	0.15	0.14	0.17	0.39	0.18	0.31	0.23	0.23	0.07	0.08	0.03	0.09	0.22
metals	0.19	0.04	0.10	0.08	0.11	0.25	0.09	0.21	0.23	0.24	0.14	0.07	0.23	0.19	0.07	0.18
trnseq	0.00	0.00	0.09	0.00	0.00	0.00	0.01	0.04	0.42	0.19	0.16	0.34	0.17	0.01	0.15	0.22
macheq	0.02	0.02	0.32	0.18	0.40	0.15	0.46	0.45	0.36	0.54	0.28	0.33	0.55	0.15	0.14	.0.47
othmnfc	0.09	0.01	0.08	0.41	0.57	0.54	0.24	0.23	0.39	0.67	0.27	0.41	0.23	0.44	0.65	0.36
svces	0.01	0.01	0.05	0.03	0.02	0.06	0.06	0.02	0.04	0.05	0.04	0.13	0.01	0.03	0.00	0.04
all goods	0.04	0.04	0.39	0.27	0.38	0.27	0.36	0.21	0.27	0.36	0.23	0.13	0.17	0.04	0.00	0.18

Source: GTAP data base, modified to include pre-Uruguay Round protection links.

output table (provided by the Bank of Korea), updated to 1992 macroeconomic and trade data. It is clear that the intensity of imports of any given commodity varies widely by use. For example, the last column of Table 9.8 shows that 22 percent (value-based share) of all chemical, rubber and plastic (CRP) products used in Korea are imported. However, only 3 percent of private household purchases of CRP products are sourced from abroad, while 39 percent of the own-intermediate inputs used by the chemical, rubber and plastics sector are purchased from overseas. This means that a tariff reduction in this sector will have little direct effect on consumer prices. The first-round effect will be predominantly through lower input costs to firms. Furthermore, the intensive use of imported CRP intermediates by the CRP sector itself will somewhat blunt the effect of competition from more competitive imports.

The last row in Table 9.8 reports the average variation in import intensity by use. Here it can be seen that, on average, the firms use imports relatively more than do households. Indeed, the average import intensity of private household consumption is only 4 percent. This stands in sharp contrast to many of the productive sectors, where average import intensities across all intermediate purchases are between 35 and 40 percent in the cases of extractive industries, textiles, chemicals, rubber, and plastics and machinery and equipment. Even investment goods are more heavily imported, with an average intensity of 17 percent. This means that the first round effects of tariff cuts are more likely to be evidenced in terms of reduced costs. Of course, all of this information is lost in the bulk of the multi-region AGE studies, where imports are blended at the border. In this case the implicit intensity in all uses is equal and the value is given by the entries in the final column of Table 9.8.

The strong effect of tariff cuts on firms' variable costs becomes doubly important in models of endogenous product differentiation and entry/exit. This is because the tariff cuts reduce average variable costs relative to the fixed cost of product differentiation. In order to maintain a zero profits equilibrium in the presence of declining average total costs, output per firm must increase. Hertel and Lanclos find that this mechanism gives rise to strong scale effects, which serve to benefit the liberalizing economy substantially.

Table 9.9 reports the size and disposition of estimated 1992 exports from Korea.[26] Korea is shown to be a net exporter of textiles and apparel, transport equipment, other manufactures and services. These are also the sectors

---

26 See Gehlhar et al. (1996) for a discussion of the procedures for estimating these bilateral flows.

Table 9.9. *Korean exports, by commodity (f.o.b. values)*

Commodity	Net Exports	Gross Exports	jpn	oas	nam	eaz	row	Exports/ Output
crops	-2967	498	315	138	13	18	14	0.02
othagr	-1524	55	27	15	2	6	5	0.01
extract	-17911	4194	1911	1285	378	208	412	0.06
food	-1547	1109	514	184	133	160	117	0.02
textiles	5371	8284	571	3895	733	649	2435	0.33
apparel	5127	5391	1741	138	2079	1048	385	0.50
crp	-2979	6159	738	2844	763	768	1047	0.14
metals	-1030	7167	1736	2577	1208	776	869	0.15
trnseq	5381	9148	228	709	2061	1334	4817	0.38
macheq	-5876	22616	1983	6172	7304	3733	3425	0.37
othmnfc	9668	12040	1831	1464	4977	2442	1326	0.70
svces	7906	20323	3987	1789	1756	3039	7593	0.07
Totals	-382	96984	15582	21208	21408	14182	22446	2.76

Source: GTAP data base, modified to include pre-Uruguay Round protection links.

with the highest overall export intensity, as shown in the final column of Table 9.9.[27] Distribution of these exports is relatively even across destination regions, with North America, Other Asia and ROW all showing about $22 billion of total sales.

The distribution of textiles and wearing apparel exports in Table 9.9 is particularly significant in this application, since sales to the United States, Canada and Europe are currently restricted under the Multifiber Agreement. Fifty-eight percent of wearing apparel exports from Korea are destined for the North America (NAM) and Europe, Australia, and New Zealand (EAZ) regions. The average quota rates on these exports (Table 9.6) are 12 percent and 19 percent, respectively. Thus, elimination of the bilateral quotas on wearing apparel will result in a significant loss of rents, which is unlikely to be made up by the increases in *f.o.b.* prices on clothing exported to third countries.[28] In the case of textile products, the share sent to restricted markets is only about 17 percent and the average quota rents are much smaller. As a result, elimination of the Multi-Fibre Arrangement (MFA) as it pertains to textiles is more likely to benefit Korea.

IV.5 General Equilibrium Elasticities of Demand Facing Korea

Having reviewed key features of the multi-region data base, as it pertains to Korea, we may now examine how this data base works in concert with the model structure, parameters and closure. A convenient method for examining the local behavior of any non-linear CGE model (be it single-region or multi-region) is to generate so-called general equilibrium elasticities of demand (Hertel et al., 1996). These elasticities embody the response of all agents (in the neighborhood of the benchmark equilibrium) to a perturbation in the market price of a given commodity. As such, these elasticities capture the impact of factor market interactions, inter-industry and income effects, as well as any special closures used in the model. The qualitative relationships which are revealed greatly facilitate subsequent analysis of policy shocks.

Before turning to these elasticities, we must say something about the GTAP model, which we employ in this section.[29] This is a relatively standard AGE model in which perfectly competitive firms produce subject to con-

---

27 Machinery and equipment also shows a high export intensity, but is a net importer in the aggregate because of a high level of intra-industry trade.
28 See Yongzheng, Martin, and Yanagishima (1996) for a detailed analysis of the welfare impacts of reforming the MFA.
29 The GTAP model is documented in Hertel and Tsigas (1996).

Table 9.10. *Own- and cross-price, general equilibrium elasticities of demand for Korean products (single region elasticities in parentheses)*

	crops	othagr	extract	food	textiles	apparel	crp	metals	trnseq	macheq	othmnfc	svces
crops	-0.761 (-0.764)	-0.02	0.07	-0.15	0.03	0.02	0.01	0.09	0.1	0.18	0.03	0.43
othagr	-0.9	-0.56 (-0.561)	0	-0.63	0.01	0	0	0.09	0.09	0.19	-0.04	0.38
extract	0.08	0	-1.029 (-1.034)	0.01	0.08	0.06	0.05	0.08	0.18	0.3	0.11	0.36
food	-0.13	-0.09	-0.01	-0.553 (-0.554)	-0.03	-0.02	-0.03	0.04	0.03	0.1	-0.12	0.38
textiles	0.11	0.01	0.25	0.04	-2.454 (-2.525)	-0.8	-0.44	0.38	0.43	0.75	-0.28	0.79
apparel	0.15	0.02	0.32	0.07	-1.6	-4.222 (-4.244)	-0.16	0.47	0.53	0.9	0.22	1.01
crp	0.02	0	0.08	-0.01	-0.22	-3.43	-1.096 (-1.106)	0.17	0.18	0.26	-0.1	0.54
metals	0.18	0.03	0.16	0.14	0.28	0.19	0.21	-2.048 (-2.069)	-0.05	0.01	0.32	0.67
trnseq	0.23	0.04	0.43	0.2	0.38	0.27	0.28	-0.1	-4.568 (-4.604)	0.4	0.57	1.06
macheq	0.17	0.03	0.29	0.14	0.28	0.19	0.17	0.01	0.21	-3.178 (-3.206)	0.39	0.82
othmnfc	0.11	-0.01	0.38	-0.25	-0.27	0.19	-0.21	0.54	0.83	1.32	-5.025 (-5.108)	1.31
svces	0.08	0.01	0.05	0.03	0.03	0.01	0.04	0.06	0.07	0.14	0.06	-0.414 (-.405)

Source: GTAP data base and model, using procedures discussed in Hertel et al. (1996).

stant returns to scale technology. As noted, it embodies an Armington structure, with composite imports sourced by agent. As is often done in multi-region models, separability between primary factors and intermediate inputs is assumed, and there is no scope for substitution among composite inputs and value added. The latter is a CES function of land, labor and capital. Final demand is determined by a Cobb–Douglas utility function specified over consumption, government spending and savings. Private purchases are modeled using the non-homothetic, Constant Difference of Elasticities (CDE) implicitly additive expenditure function. Government budget shares are assumed constant via the Cobb–Douglas specification.

Table 9.10 presents the GE elasticities for the commodity aggregation used in the following analysis. In this particular closure, we assume that endowments, technology and *ad valorem* equivalent policy distortions are exogenous, and the global bank's investment portfolio is fixed, i.e., $RORFLEX=\infty$. Each column in the table refers to the change in equilibrium output when the output tax on that particular commodity is raised by enough to cause a 1 percent increase in market price. Thus the GE, own-price elasticity of demand facing the Korean crops sector equals –0.761. Most of this is due to competition from imports, as the own-price elasticity of final demand for crops is very small and there is no scope for substitution among composite intermediate inputs in the model.

Running down the diagonal of Table 9.10, we note that some of these own-price elasticities are greater than 1 in absolute value. This elastic response is attributable to adjustments in export demands. When the export share of output is large (see the last column in Table 9.9), the Armington parameters in other regions come to play an important role in the sectoral own-price elasticity of demand. Indeed, in the case where all of the output is exported and the exporter's share in composite imports in the receiving region is small, then the GE demand elasticity equals the export demand elasticity, which in turn approaches the Armington elasticity in absolute value. This is why the GE demand elasticity for other manufactures is so large. The Armington elasticity of substitution among imports in all regions is equal to 6.7 for Other Manufactures and 70 percent of output is exported. Therefore, roughly $(0.7 \cdot 6.7)/5.025$, or more than 90 percent of the price responsiveness in this sector, is due to export demand.

The cross-price elasticities in Table 9.10 are largely positive in sign. This is because of Korean factor market equilibrium conditions. When the GE demand for Machinery and Equipment falls, output falls as well, releasing resources for use in other sectors, all of which tend to expand. Depending on the size and factor intensity of the contracting sector, and the GE elasticity facing the other sector, the resulting expansion may be quite large. Indeed, in the case of a 1 percent price hike in services, all of the non-food manufacturing sectors in Korea expand by a greater percentage than the services sector contracts. This is because 59 percent of the value added in Korea is in services (Table 9.7), and the manufacturing sectors are generally highly dependent on price responsive exports (Table 9.9).

However, there are some notable negative entries off-diagonal in Table 9.10. For example, crops and other agriculture and crops and food are complementary goods, because of their close inter-industry linkages. Crops products are inputs into the other sectors and when this price rises, so does the price of other agriculture and food, thereby leading to a decline in equilibrium output. These relationships tend to be symmetric, since if it is the price of food products which increases, thereby reducing equilibrium food output, then the demand for intermediate agricultural inputs will fall, thereby leading to a decline in output of those sectors. Other notable complementary relationships in Table 9.10 arise among textiles, wearing apparel and chemicals/rubber/plastics (as a result of the use of synthetic fibers). Other manufacturing is also complementary with a number of sectors.

Table 9.10 also presents information that is pertinent to the question of multi- versus single-region closures. In the GTAP framework, it is possible to create *partial equilibrium closures*.[30] In order to investigate the importance of adjustment in non-Korean regions, for Korean demand elasticities, we reproduced Table 9.10 under a *partial equilibrium* closure in which activity levels, endowment prices, own-commodity prices and expenditures *in the non-Korean regions* are all fixed. The resulting own-price elasticities of demand are given in parentheses in Table 9.10. It is immediately clear that there is little difference between the two: Korea really is a small economy when it comes to global economic adjustments (recall Table 9.7). *Adjustments in other regions to shocks emanating from Korea are simply not large enough to result in significant GE feedbacks to Korea.* This is good news for the single-region modeller. If she/he can accurately implement the trade policy experiment of interest in the single-region model, then the omitted feedback effects are unlikely to be a serious problem. However, the "if" qualification in the previous sentence is an important one, as we will see in the next section.

---

30 Technically, this is done by swapping "slack variables" with complementary variables that are normally endogenous. For example, by endogenizing the income slack variable in GTAP, it is possible to eliminate the equation linking regional income and expenditure. In order to retain equal numbers of endogenous and exogenous variables, it is then possible to fix expenditure in selected regions of the model. In a similar fashion we may drop zero profit conditions and fix activity levels in selected sectors; drop market-clearing relationships and fix the associated prices for tradable commodities; and drop endowment market clearing conditions and fix primary factor prices.

V Results from Uruguay Round Reforms

V.1 Implications for Output and Pattern of Sales

In this section, we discuss the impact on Korea of the Uruguay Round reforms outlined in Tables 9.3–9.6, from two different perspectives. In the first case, we simulate the full package of reforms, taking advantage of the multi-region (MR) data base and modeling framework. We refer to these as the MR solution. These results are reported as the top entry in Table 9.11. In the second case (bottom entry), we implement only the shocks that can be incorporated into our specification of the Korean region of the model.

The single-region (SR) shocks include all of those given in Table 9.4, but none of the shocks in Table 9.5 (other regions' cuts). We implement reform of the MFA in the same manner we would expect a single-region modeller to proceed, namely, by eliminating the Korean export tax equivalents associated with these quotas. In sum, the comparison of numbers in Table 9.11 illustrates the value added of incorporating a better specification of the Uruguay Round experiment. *Both sets of results rely upon the same model and closure.* We could have built a parallel, single-region model, using only information from Korea. However, as we have seen from comparison of the diagonal entries in Table 9.10, the global, GE feedback effects for Korea are small. Therefore, if the two models are specified in an equivalent manner (hardly a trivial task), they should give similar results for a Korea-only shock.

Table 9.11 compares the impact of the MR and SR shocks on output, domestic sales, exports and bilateral trade. Examination of these results shows that some outcomes are quite robust in the face of ignoring the non-Korea shocks associated with the Uruguay Round. For example, SR (lower entry) output changes in crops, extractive industries, other agriculture, food, chemicals, rubber and plastics, transport equipment and services are very close, if not identical, to the MR (upper entry) predictions. However, the proportionate divergences are quite large in the cases of textiles, apparel, metals, machinery and equipment and other manufactures. Here, the policy changes in the rest of the world (Table 9.5 and rows 2 and 3 of Table 9.6) are significant enough to make a difference. For example, the average bilateral import price cuts in the JPN, NAM and EAZ regions on Korean exports of metals products range from 3 to 5 percent. This is enough to stimulate a significant increase in overall metals exports (12 percent from the third column of Table 9.11), as compared to a predicted 3 percent *decrease* in exports under the SR Uruguay Round shocks.

Table 9.11. *Impact of Uruguay Round on Korean output and distribution of sales (percentage change)*

	qo	*qds*	*qxw*	Bilateral Exports				
	Output	Domestic Sales	Total Exports	JPN	OAS	NAM	EAZ	ROW
crops	-8	-8	-7	-20	8	39	35	55
	-8	**-9**	**32**	**32**	**31**	**32**	**32**	**31**
othagr	-1	-2	37	29	55	29	28	36
	-1	**-1**	**29**	**29**	**29**	**30**	**29**	**29**
extract	-1	-1	0	-1	0	3	13	3
	-2	**-2**	**-8**	**-8**	**-8**	**-8**	**-8**	**-8**
food	3	3	35	27	40	39	40	55
	4	**3**	**43**	**44**	**43**	**44**	**43**	**43**
textiles	35	28	51	29	64	63	69	28
	47	**52**	**38**	**32**	**28**	**88**	**78**	**30**
apparel	40	4	77	46	53	104	105	28
	121	**5**	**248**	**23**	**22**	**452**	**371**	**24**
crp	4	3	11	11	10	7	10	16
	4	**4**	**5**	**6**	**5**	**6**	**6**	**6**
metals	-3	-6	12	21	2	13	24	15
	-8	**-9**	**-3**	**-3**	**-3**	**-3**	**-3**	**-3**
trnseq	-3	-2	-4	12	-10	3	-4	-6
	-3	**-2**	**-5**	**-5**	**-5**	**-5**	**-5**	**-5**
macheq	-2	-9	10	16	7	11	7	11
	-6	**-10**	**2**	**2**	**2**	**2**	**2**	**2**
othmnfc	16	3	21	20	22	16	27	25
	10	**6**	**12**	**12**	**12**	**12**	**12**	**12**
svces	0	0	-7	-8	-4	-9	-9	-9
	0	**0**	**-10**	**-11**	**-12**	**-11**	**-11**	**-11**

Source: GTAP model simulation. Note: For each commodity, we first report numbers from the MR solution file. In the second row we report (boldface) numbers from the solution file in which we use SR shocks.

Of course, it is not always the case that the omitted shocks work in the same direction. For example, there are significant tariff cuts on textiles and wearing apparel in the other regions. Taken alone, this should stimulate additional Korean exports. However, from Table 9.11, it can be seen that the increase in exports is much smaller under the MR shocks (top entry). In the case of apparel, the difference is quite striking: MR=77 percent increase, while SR=248 percent increase. What accounts for this difference? To answer this question, we must return to Table 9.6. Here, we see that abolishing the MFA quotas also affects textiles and apparel exports from other Asian countries and ROW. Indeed, the current bilateral quotas are even more binding for some of those flows. Thus, when the MFA is abolished, there is a very strong surge from these regions. As a result, the overall increase in Korean exports is much smaller under the true, MR, Uruguay Round experiment.

V.2 Effects of Alternative Macroeconomic Closures

We turn next to the macroeconomic effects of the Uruguay Round on the Korean economy. Outcomes based on multi-region and single-region shocks are reported in Table 9.12 for a variety of macroeconomic closures. As was the case with Table 9.11, we record the MR shocks in the upper entry, and the SR shocks in the lower entry. Consider first the impact of the MR shocks over alternative closures. In the first column, we have the case where the global bank's portfolio is fixed. In terms of equation (9.3), this means that $RORFLEX=\infty$. That is, expected rates of return on investment across regions are not required to be equated. In the absence of significant changes in regional incomes, we expect little change in net domestic savings and hence global savings. Since this determines global investment in our neoclassical closure of the model, that variable does not change much either. Therefore, the fixed portfolio assumption effectively fixes regional investment as well. Having tied down regional savings and investment, we have also effectively tied down the trade balance, via equation (9.2). Exports increase by about the same amount as imports and the change in the trade balance reported in the second row of Table 9.12 is very small.

However, trade liberalization in Korea has a significant impact on the current rate of return to capital in that region, by boosting production in the relatively capital intensive manufacturing sectors and by lowering the cost of imported investment goods. For this reason, it is interesting to consider the case where the global bank's investment portfolio is responsive to changes in the relative rates of return across regions. Table 9.13 reports changes in current rates of return under the flexible portfolio assumption. The equilibrium value of the Korean RORC (equation [9.3]) rises by more than 6 percent, whereas increases in other regions are generally less than 1 percent. As a result, there is a significant incentive to increase investment in Korea, provided $RORFLEX<\infty$. With domestic savings determined by income, which changes relatively little (see Table 9.12), this increased investment must be diverted from other regions. In the second column of Table 9.12, we report results from the Uruguay Round experiment with $RORFLEX=10$. Here we see that the current account deteriorates by $3.4 million because of the decline in the left-hand side of equation (9.2), as the global bank in-

Table 9.12. *Selected macro variables for Korea under alternative assumptions about regional allocation of global investment (outcomes with single region shocks in parentheses)*

Variable	Fixed Portfolio	Variable Portfolio	
		$\Delta TBAL \neq 0$	$\Delta TBAL = 0$
Export Volume (Δ%)	13	10	13
	(15[*])	(11)	(15)
Trade Balance ($ million)	363	-3412	0
	(921)	(-3763)	(0)
TOT (Δ%)	-1.3	-.6	-1.2
	(-1.0)	(-0.24)	(-0.9)
Utility (Δ%)	1.4	1.9	1.4
	(2.1)	(2.72)	(2.2)
EV ($ million)	3828	5121	3762
	(5760)	(7267)	(5831)

Source: GTAP model simulation.
[*] Parenthetic entries refer to cases where only Korea specific shocks are applied.

creases the allocation of investment to Korea in response to the increased rate of return.

The final column in Table 9.12 illustrates the impact of adopting the macroeconomic closure in which Korea's trade balance is explicitly fixed and Korean savings adjust to equilibrate the system. As can be seen from a comparison of this column with the first, in which the global portfolio is fixed, there is little difference between the two. Therefore, this popular macroeconomic closure (fixed current account balance) may be viewed as a special case of the more general specification in which the global banking sector intermediates between savings and investment and *RORFLEX* is chosen to reflect the degree to which current rates of return on investment across regions are expected to be equalized. Adherents to this macroeconomic view would find the fixed trade balance assumption quite restrictive, and perhaps implausible, at least in the short run, in the case of Korea.

The choice of macroeconomic closure can have strong implications for the terms of trade effects of a policy shock. This is of critical importance as a result of the tendency of terms of trade effects to dominate the welfare picture in CGE models with Armington structures. The third row in Table 9.12 illustrates this point. Since Korean liberalization is significantly greater than that in the other regions (see Tables 9.5 and 9.6), the pressure to increase imports is stronger than the increase in demand for Korean exports.

Table 9.13. *Implications of the Uruguay Round for current rates of return on investment (RORC) using flexible portfolio and variable trade balance (single region shocks in parentheses)*

Region	
KOR	6.37[a]
	(6.79)
JPN	.59
	(0.02)
OAS	2.36
	(-0.11)
NAM	.34
	(0.02)
EAZ	.62
	(0.01)
ROW	.79
	(-0.07)

Source: GTAP model simulation.
[a] Entries are percentage changes in the level of the rate of return NOT percentage point changes. If the initial rate of return is 20 percent per year, then a 6.3 percent change translates into a 1.27 percentage point increase so the new rate of return is 21.27 percent per year.

In order to maintain balance of payments equilibrium in the face of the import surge and a fixed trade balance, *f.o.b.* prices for Korean exports must fall. This leads to a significant deterioration in the terms of trade (1.2 percent from the last column of Table 9.12).

In contrast, when the variable portfolio assumption is introduced, the surge in imports is accompanied by a rise in the rate of return on investment. From equation (9.3), it can be seen that this offsets to some degree (although not entirely) the pressure caused by the increased imports. The trade balance is allowed to worsen and as a result, the necessary decline in *f.o.b.* export prices is less and Korea's terms of trade deteriorate by only half as much. This, in turn, has important consequences for welfare.[31]

The final two rows in Table 9.12 refer to the welfare consequences of the Uruguay Round simulations under alternative macro closures. They indicate that the welfare gain to Korea under the MR shocks is 33 percent greater when the flexible portfolio assumption is employed. This is a direct

---

31 The investment inflow implies a reduction in the current account surplus (or increase in the deficit) and, *ceteris paribus*, reduces the amount by which Korean exports increase in the current period. However, depending on the nature of this increased investment it may well contribute to increased exports in some future period. In this sense one might argue that the terms of trade consequences of liberalization have simply been postponed.

consequence of the dampened decline in the regional terms of trade. This serves to emphasize the extent to which alternative macroeconomic closures can influence the results of applied trade policy analysis.

A comparison of the upper and lower entries in Table 9.12 also permits us to analyze the macroeconomic consequences of using single-region, rather than multi-region, shocks in our analysis of the Uruguay Round and the Korean economy. From this comparison, it is clear that simple use of the single-region shocks leads to a considerable overstatement of the welfare gains due to the Round. In the case of a variable portfolio, the degree of overstatement is more than 40 percent! This difference is largely driven by the overly optimistic analysis of the consequences of abolishing the MFA (see Tables 9.6 and 9.11).

VI Conclusions

The purpose of this chapter has been to discuss conceptual issues as well as data problems associated with multi-region AGE modeling. We have approached this task by comparing multi-region methods and analysis to those employed by single-region trade policy modellers. Key issues that arise when going beyond a single region involve the treatment of import sourcing and global macroeconomic closure. The question of bilateral variation in protection also comes into play. In general, it is a very large task to construct a data base in which bilateral trade, transport and protection values are accurately identified and are matched up with regional input–output information.

Our empirical example, which focuses on Korea's role in the Uruguay Round, seeks to identify the value added obtained by examining this problem in a multi-region context. We find that single-region analysis provides a good approximation to the multi-region outcome for many variables. However, Korean welfare gains from the Round are substantially overstated in the one-region case. This is due to the significance of non-Korean cuts in protection on metal products, machinery and equipment, and other manufactures. Also, the impact of the response of other Asia economies to the elimination of the bilateral quotas on textiles and wearing apparel is quite important for the Korean economy, and can only be captured in a multi-region model.

While there are some significant benefits of the move to global modeling, there clearly are also substantial costs. Because of the sometimes prohibitive expense of assembling a global data base, global trade analysis is only feasible for most researchers if they use an existing data base, such as that provided by the GTAP consortium. This limits the degree of disaggregation of firms and households. Global models are typically also much larger, and therefore considerably more complex to interpret. Furthermore, we find that the multi-region feedback effects of Korea-specific shocks, through the rest of the world and back to Korea, are quite limited. For this reason we argue that the step to multi-region AGE analysis should only be taken if the problem at hand is truly global in scope, as is the case with the Uruguay Round analysis presented here.

In closing, we would like to emphasize the importance of several aspects of multi-region AGE analysis that deserve more attention in the future. In our empirical results, we show the importance of the global, macroeconomic closure for Korea's terms of trade in the wake of the Uruguay Round. In particular, this effect, and hence aggregate welfare in Korea, depend on whether the resulting increase in the expected rate of return on capital generates additional foreign investment. Perhaps the most common closure in static, global AGE analysis, namely, that of a fixed current account, does not permit this type of response. Is this is a reasonable assumption? What alternatives exist, short of moving to a full inter-temporal model?

This paper has not dealt at all with the question of international factor mobility. In the debate over NAFTA, this has proved to be an important part of the analysis (see Francois and Shiells, 1994). More work on this feature of global trade models is very important. Incorporation of imperfect competition in global trade modeling has received somewhat more atten-tion, but this area remains underdeveloped in terms of the data required to support serious calibration of such models to differing types of industry structures across regions and sectors (see Chapter 11). Finally, there remains the challenge of dealing with both the time and regional dimensions in a single model. That is beyond the scope of this chapter, but it is clearly on the long-term agenda for many researchers in this area.[32]

References

Alston, J.M., C.A. Carter, R. Green, and D. Pick. 1990. "Whither Armington trade models?" *American Journal of Agricultural Economics* 72:455–467.
Anderson, S.D., A. de Palma, and J. Thisse. 1992. *Discrete Choice Theory of Product Differentiation*. Cambridge, Massachusetts: MIT Press.
Armington, P.A. 1969. "A theory of demand for products distinguished by place of production." *IMF Staff Papers* 16:159–178.
Brown, D. 1987. "Tariffs, the terms of trade and national product differentiation." *Journal of Policy Modelling* 9:503–526.

---

32 See Chapters 12 and 13 for discussions of dynamic modeling.

Brown, D.B. 1991. "Tariffs and capacity utilization by monopolistically competitive firms." *Journal of International Economics* 30:371–381.

Brown, D. 1994. "Properties of applied general equilibrium trade models with monopolistic competition and foreign direct investment." In *Modelling Trade Policy: Applied General Equilibrium Models of North American Free Trade*, edited by J.F. Francois and C.R. Shiells. Cambridge: Cambridge University Press.

Burfisher, M.E., S. Robinson, and K.E. Thierfelder. 1994. "Wage changes in a U.S.–Mexico free trade area: Migration vs. Stolper–Samuelson effects." In *Modelling Trade Policy: Applied General Equilibrium Models of North American Free Trade*, edited by J.F. Francois and C.R. Shiells. Cambridge: Cambridge University Press.

Deardorff, A. and R. Stern. 1986. *The Michigan Model of World Production and Trade*. Cambridge, Massachusetts: MIT Press.

Deaton, A. and J. Muellbauer. 1980. "An almost ideal demand system." *American Economic Review* 70:312–326.

Dervis, K., J. de Melo, and S. Robinson. 1982. *General Equilibrium Models for Development Policy*. Cambridge: Cambridge University Press.

Dewatripont, M. and G. Michel. 1987. "On closure rules, homogeneity, and dynamics in applied general equilibrium models." *Journal of Development Economics* 26:65–76.

Dixit, A.K. and J.E. Stiglitz. 1977. "Monopolistic competition and optimum product diversity." *American Economic Review* 67:297–308.

Dixon, P.B., B.R. Parameter, J. Sutton, and D.P. Vincent. 1982. *Orani: A Multisectoral Model of the Australian Economy*. Amsterdam: North-Holland.

Dornbusch, R. 1980. *Open Economy Macroeconomics*. New York: Basic Books.

Ethier, W.J. 1979. "Internationally decreasing costs and world trade." *Journal of International Economics* 9:1–24.

Ethier, W.J. 1982. "National and international returns to scale in the modern theory of international trade." *American Economic Review* 72:950–959.

Finger, J.M., ed. 1993. *Antidumping: How It Works and Who Gets Hurt*. Ann Arbor: University of Michigan Press.

Francois, J. 1992. "Optimal commercial policy with international returns to scale." *Canadian Journal of Economics* 23:109–124.

Francois, J. 1994. "Global production and trade: Factor migration and commercial policy with international returns to scale." *International Economic Review* 35:565–581.

Francois, J. 1996. "A note on import substitutability and regional integration." World Trade Organization. Staff working paper RD-96-9.

Francois, J., B. McDonald, and H. Nordstrom. 1994. "The Uruguay Round: A global, general equilibrium assessment." CEPR Discussion Paper No. 1067.

Francois, J., B. McDonald, and H. Nordstrom. 1995. "Assessing the Uruguay Round." Paper No. 6, Developing Economies and the Uruguay Round. Washington, D.C.: World Bank.

Francois, J.F. and C.R. Shiells, eds. 1994. *Modeling Trade Policy: Applied General Equilibrium Assessments of North American Free Trade*. Cambridge: Cambridge University Press.

Gehlhar, M.J., J.K. Binkley, and T.W. Hertel. 1991. "Estimation of Trade Margins for Food Products: An Application of the UN Bilateral Trade Data." NC-194 Occasional Paper Series OP-24.

Gehlhar, M.J., D. Gray, T.W. Hertel, K. Huff, E. Ianchovichina, B.J. MacDonald, R. McDougall, M.E. Tsigas, and R. Wigle. 1996. "Overview of the GTAP data base." In *Global Trade Analysis: Modeling and Applications*, edited by T.W. Hertel. Cambridge: Cambridge University Press.

Goldin, I., O. Knudsen, and D. van der Mensbrugghe. 1993. *Trade Liberalisation: Global Economic Implications*. Paris and Washington: OECD Development Center and World Bank.

Goulder, L.H. and B. Eichengreen. 1992. "Trade liberalization in general equilibrium: Inter-temporal and inter-industry effects." *Canadian Journal of Economics* 25:253–280.

Hambley, J. 1992. "Early stage processing of international trade and input–output data for SALTER." SALTER Working Paper No. 15.

Harrison G., T. Rutherford, and D. Tarr. 1995. "Quantifying the Uruguay Round." Paper presented at the World Bank Conference on Developing Economies and the Uruguay Round, Washington, D.C.

Hathaway, D.E. and M.D. Ingco. 1995. "Agricultural Liberalization and the Uruguay Round." Paper presented at the World Bank Conference on Developing Economies and the Uruguay Round, Washington, D.C.

Helpman, E. 1981. "International trade in the presence of product differentiation, economies of scale and monopolistic competition: A Chamberlin–Heckscher–Ohlin Approach." *Journal of International Economics* 11:305–340.

Helpman, E. and P.R. Krugman 1985. *Market Structure and Foreign Trade*. Cambridge, Massachusetts: MIT Press.

Helpman, E. and P.R. Krugman 1989. *Trade Policy and Market Structure*. Cambridge, Massachusetts: MIT Press.

Hertel, T.W. 1994. "The procompetitive effects of trade policy reform in a small, open economy." *Journal of International Economics* 36:391–411.

Hertel, T.W., ed. 1996. *Global Trade Analysis: Modeling and Applications*. Cambridge: Cambridge University Press.

Hertel, T.W. and D.K. Lanclos. 1994. "Trade policy reform in the presence of product differentiation and imperfect competition: Implications for food processing activity." In *Agricultural Trade and Economic Integration in Europe and in North America*, edited by M. Hartmann, P.M. Schmitz, and H. von Witzke. Kiel: Wissenschaftsverlag Vauk Kiel KG.

Hertel, T.W., D.K. Lanclos, K.R. Pearson, and P.V. Swaminathan. 1996. "Structure of GTAP." In *Global Trade Analysis: Modeling and Applications*, edited by T.W. Hertel. Cambridge: Cambridge University Press.

Hertel, T.W., W. Martin, K. Yanagishima, and B. Dimaranan. 1995. Paper presented at the World Bank Conference on Developing Economies and the Uruguay Round, Washington, D.C.

Hertel, T.W. and M.E. Tsigas. 1996. "Structure of GTAP." In *Global Trade Analysis: Modeling and Applications*, edited by T.W. Hertel. Cambridge: Cambridge University Press.

Howe, H. 1975. "Development of the extended linear expenditure system from simple saving assumptions." *European Economic Review* 6:305–310.

Jomini, P., J.F. Zeitsch, R. McDougall, A. Welsh, S. Brown, J. Hambley, and J. Kelly. 1991. *SALTER: A General Equilibrium Model of the World Economy*. Vol. 1. *Model Structure Database and Parameters*. Canberra: Australian Industry Commission.

Krugman, P.R. 1979. "Increasing returns, monopolistic competition, and international trade." *Journal of International Economics* 9:469–479.

Krugman, P.R. 1980. "Scale economies, product differentiation, and the pattern of trade." *American Economic Review* 70:950–995.

Lancaster, K. 1980. "Intra-industry trade under perfect monopolistic competition." *Journal of International Economics* 10:151–175.

Magee, S. 1972. "The welfare effects of restrictions on U.S. trade." *Brookings Papers on Economic Activity* 3:645–701.

Markusen, J.R. and R.M. Wigle. 1989. "Nash equilibrium tariffs for the United States and Canada: The roles of country size, scale economies and capital mobility." *Journal of Political Economy* 97:368–386.

McDougall, R. 1993. "Incorporating International Capital Mobility into SALTER." Working Paper No. 21. Canberra: Australian Industry Commission.

Perroni, C. and T. Rutherford. 1995. "Regular Flexibility of Nested CES Functions." *European Economic Review* 39:335–343.

Preckel, P.V., E. DeVuyst, D.K. Lanclos, and T.W. Hertel. 1993. "Sensitivity analysis in CGE models using discrete approximating probability distributions (abstract)." *American Journal of Agricultural Economics* 75:1297.

Roland-Holst, D.W., Reinert, K.A., and Shiells, C.R. 1994. "A general equilibrium assessment of North American economic integration." In *Modelling Trade Policy: Applied General Equilibrium Models of North American Free Trade*, edited by J.F. Francois and C.R. Shiells. Cambridge: Cambridge University Press.

Sen, A.K. 1963. "Neo-classical and neo-Keynesian theories of distribution." *Economic Record* 39:54–64.

Shiells, C.R. and K.A. Reinert. 1993. "Armington models and terms-of-trade effects: Some econometric evidence for North America." *Canadian Journal of Economics* 26:299–316.

Shoven and Whalley. 1992. *Applying General Equilibrium*. New York: Cambridge University Press.

Spence, M.E. 1976. "Product selection, fixed costs, and monopolistic competition." *Journal of International Economics* 43:217–236.

Staiger, R. and F. Wollak. 1994. "Measuring industry-specific protection: Antidumping in the United States." *Brookings Papers on Economic Activity* 2:51–103.

Taylor, L. ed. 1990. *Socially Relevant Policy Analysis: Structuralist Computable General Equilibrium Models for the Developing World*. Cambridge, Massachusetts: MIT Press.

Taylor, L. and F.J. Lysy. 1979. "Vanishing income redistributions: Keynesian clues about model surprises in the short run." *Journal of Development Economics* 6:11–29.

Tsigas, M.E., T.W. Hertel, and J.K. Binkley. 1992. "Estimates of systematic reporting biases in trade statistics." *Economic Systems Research* 44:297–310.

U.S. Department of Commerce. 1994. "Antidumping and countervailing duty orders, findings, and suspension agreements currently in effect." Washington, D.C. December.

Venables, A.J. 1987. "Trade and trade policy with differentiated products: A Chamberlinian–Ricardian model." *Economic Journal* 97:700–717.

Whalley, J. 1985. *Trade Liberalisation Among Major World Trading Areas.* Cambridge, Massachusetts: MIT Press.

Winters, L.A. 1984. "Separability and the specification of foreign trade functions." *Journal of International Economics* 17:239–263.

Yongzheng, Y., W. Martin, and K. Yanagishima. 1996. "Structure of GTAP." In *Global Trade Analysis: Modeling and Applications*, edited by T.W. Hertel. Cambridge: Cambridge University Press.

10

Household Disaggregation

Farida C. Khan

I Introduction

What is the effect of import tariff changes on the distribution of income? Or of an exchange rate devaluation on the poorest decile of income earners? Such questions have not been emphasized in the trade policy literature. Trade policy is usually justified from an standpoint of efficiency or protection rather than of how the benefits of such a policy are distributed among households.

This chapter considers the impact of trade policy on the household sector. From a methodological standpoint, the modeling of income distribution within a general equilibrium framework is examined. The purpose is to determine the impact of policy changes on the welfare of households disaggregated by income groups.

The first section provides a summary of the literature on trade policy and income distribution using multisectoral models. *There is no strong consensus on what effect trade policy will have on income distribution*, and inferences depend on which aspect of trade policy is examined and which type of model is constructed.

The second section discusses methodological issues and continues the presentation of existing literature. This section first discusses the basis for household disaggregation and shows how distributional mechanisms are modeled. The manner in which distributional mechanisms are endogenized is also addressed. The final part of this section reviews measures of distribution or welfare used in the literature and how the objective of each study shapes the measure applied.

The third section shows an application of a numerical general equilibrium model to Bangladesh and considers the income distribution outcomes of import tariff and quota removal. This exercise elucidates how a disaggregated household sector can be incorporated into a computable general equilibrium (CGE) model. The welfare impact on each household group is analyzed, and the source of welfare changes is separated into those arising from factor price changes and those from changes in product prices.

II Survey of the Literature

How trade policy affects the distribution of income is not a question that has been posed very often in the economics literature.[1] More generally, issues linking policy and income distribution have rarely been addressed. A policy is justifiable if it meets the Pareto optimum criteria, i.e., if sufficient compensation can be given to maintain the utility of those adversely affected by the policy, the policy is considered to make the society better off.[2] Given that the Pareto criterion is based on an initial distribution of endowments, this criterion does not enable the comparison of two different distributions. This is similar to the problem in consumer theory in that the marginal utility of income cannot be compared between two individuals. Neoclassical economics does not have the grounds for any theoretical argument that says a dollar taken from a rich individual will benefit a poor individual by more or less. Income distribution objectives are seen as contentions regarding slicing up the national pie, as opposed to Pareto improving policies that increase the size of the pie.

II.1 Approaches to Income Distribution

How the pie can be sliced can be seen in different ways: the functional distribution of income, the extended functional distribution of income, and the size distribution of income. Adelman and Robinson (1989) provide a substantive discussion of these concepts and their applications in the economic development literature.

The functional distribution of income refers to the distribution of income among groups classified by their function in productive activity, e.g., capital or labour. The literature on trade theory is replete with the impact of exogenous changes on the functional distribution of income. The well known Stolper–Samuelson Theorem, for instance, describes how the return to labour and capital is altered if the relative price of tradables changes. In

---

1 Refer to Dixit and Norman (1980, p. 25 and pp. 155–159) for discussions on tariffs and income distribution.
2 See Chapters 3 and 5 of Dixit and Norman (1980), which elaborate on the Pareto superiority of one trade regime over another.

its strictest form, the Stolper–Samuelson Theorem states that if the relative price of a capital-intensive good increases, the owners of capital will benefit at the expense of the owners of labour, and the real return to capital will increase.

Because the strict versions of the Stolper–Samuelson Theorem are based on the two-factor capital–labour model, it is able to incorporate only two household groups defined by their functional role. However, weaker versions of these linkages, related to economywide Stolper–Samuelson derivatives, may still hold under alternative theoretical specifications (see Dixit and Norman, 1980). For example, the Jones–Neary Specific Factors model can accommodate more income groups by allowing three or more factors of production into the analysis. At least one of these factors of production is mobile across sectors but the others are sector-specific. The main distributional result of the specific factors model is that the factor specific to that sector which experiences a relative price increase benefits, while the factor specific to the other sectors loses. These losses and gains are unambiguous. The welfare effects on the mobile factor, on the other hand, are ambiguous and dependent on which good the mobile factor is used more intensively to produce and whether owners of the mobile factor have a relative preference (as consumers) for one good versus another.[3]

The extended functional distribution of income identifies income recipients by sector of activity as well as asset ownership. This type of disaggregation of income is done in studies which integrate the assets market into the analytical framework. The models therefore have to be intertemporal and define income distribution over time. Adelman and Robinson (1989) argue that the extended functional distribution of income provides an appropriate framework for analysing policy in developing countries. Their reasoning is that, particularly in these countries, economic pressures on the policy process are determined by the structure of ownership of different forms of wealth.

The size distribution of income is the distribution of income among households classified by income intervals. Such a distribution, even on a very aggregate level, distinguishes between higher and lower income groups. Since the determinants of size distribution include social, political, and cultural factors in addition to economic ones, there is no firm theoretical grounding for an economic analysis of the influences on size distribution. The theoretical literature has tried to incorporate the role of human and

---

3 See Ruffin and Jones (1977) for a detailed exposition of this "neoclassical ambiguity" present in the specific factors model.

non-human capital in determining size distribution.[4] Many of the studies reviewed later endogenize size distribution by showing its link to the functional distribution of income and other factors such as migration and demographics.

II.2 Existing Studies on Income Distribution and Trade Policy

Consideration of the effects of economic policy on the size distribution of income in the public finance literature is primarily restricted to changes in domestic (rather than trade) taxes.[5] While research relating trade to relative wages (i.e., the functional distribution of income) in the Organization for Economic Cooperation and Development (OECD) is an active area of current research, the trade policy literature incorporating assessments of the size distribution of income is quite limited (see, for example, Deardorff and Haveman, 1991). For the OECD economies, changes in trade policies are likely to have far less apparent distributional consequences than changes in domestic taxes. However, while distributional consequences arising from changes in consumer prices, factor prices or employment usually are not primarily due to international trade policy (because of the relatively small foreign sector in the U.S. economy), this has not prevented a heated debate about the linkages between trade policy and the functional distribution of income (see Richardson, 1995).

In contrast to the trade literature, the economic development literature has placed much more emphasis on incorporating the distributional impact of government trade and development policies when evaluating the success of different policy regimes. The issues have been discussed in the broader context of development and income distribution and the notion of the trade-off between growth and equity.[6] Adelman and Robinson's (1978) pioneering book on the effect of policy on income distribution in Korea is a comprehensive piece of work incorporating various institutional and dynamic determinants of income distribution. Another early general equilibrium model of income distribution is Taylor, Bacha, Cardosa, and Lysy's work on Brazil (1980). Both of these studies considered the impact of programs and policies on the size distribution of income as well as the extended functional distribution of income. Both found that the extended functional distribution of

4 For theoretical work on the size distribution of income, see Champerowne (1974) and Becker (1967).
5 In addition to numerous others, two well known studies are those by Ballard et al. (1985) and Pechman (1985).
6 Adelman and Robinson (1989) provide extensive coverage of income distribution issues in the economic development literature.

income is sensitive to policy changes but that the size distribution of income is very stable (Adelman and Robinson, 1988). Research on structural adjustment, trade reform, and income distribution includes Bourguignon, de Melo, and Suwa (1991a,b) and Bourguignon, de Melo, and Morrisson (1991).

The Korea model developed by Adelman and Robinson is one of the first computable general equilibrium models used to analyse economic development policy. Export promotion policy is among the many counterfactual simulations undertaken in this study. The core of the Korea model is neoclassical in that demand for factors is derived from profit maximization, there is factor substitutability in production, and household demand for goods and services is determined through a linear expenditure system. The model also has a dynamic component, with each within-period model being linked together by an intertemporal adjustment model. Also, apart from various structural features such as limited factor mobility and substitution, it includes an assets or loanable funds market which contributes to the intertemporal equilibria.

The study concludes that there is little connection between the functional and size distributions of income. Even though the size distribution is generated from the functional distribution, simulations show that policy changes affect the functional distribution by altering relative prices but are unable to affect the size distribution. The size distribution remained almost the same despite substantial change in the composition of the deciles of income groups by socioeconomic categories. The size distribution changes over time but its path is insensitive to exogenous or policy shocks.

Adelman and Robinson (1978) find that export promotion programs which emphasize labour-intensive industries affect the distribution of income favourably. Subsidies to such export industries are found to increase the income of the bottom decile by 5.1 percent and to reduce the Gini coefficient as well as the percentage of households in poverty.

The Lysy and Taylor model for Brazil (1980) deviates substantially from a standard Walrasian general equilibrium specification. Instead, a Kaldor–Kalecki variant is adopted in which investment is fixed in real terms and either nominal wages or non-wage incomes are fixed. The adjustment mechanism in the model turns out to be the functional distribution of income. The effect of a devaluation is examined and found to increase government savings by reducing export subsidy requirements and increasing tariffs collected. Also, the current account deficit (foreign savings), which is fixed in world prices, is worth more in domestic currency after a devaluation. When saving has risen, effective demand falls and leads to unemployment and lower wages and deflation in this Keynesian type of model. Deflation has a positive effect on income distribution, as indicated by several measures of the size distribution of income, including the Gini coefficient, Theil index, and others. Both the Korea and Brazil models conclude that an outward looking trade regime results in improvements in the distribution of income and increases the proportion of national income earned by the lowest income groups.

De Melo and Robinson (1980) carry out trade policy exercises using Colombian data. They consider three alternative policy regimes – inward looking with a 50 percent tariff on manufacturing, outward looking with a 50 percent subsidy to exports, and production promoting with a direct 50 per-cent value added subsidy to the manufacturing sector. Compared to the free trade base case, the size distribution of income varies little. Some worsening of income distribution is found to occur in the direct subsidy case. This happens because transfers are reduced to finance the subsidy and the rela-tive prices of agricultural goods rise, both of which adversely affect the poorest household groups. In her analysis of the Sri Lankan economy, de Melo (1979) finds that the removal of an existing export tax on agriculture improves the income of workers in this sector in the short run. These workers constitute the lowest income group. However, there is a reversal of these results in the longer run and the income distribution effects are eroded.

Two recent studies examining trade policy effects on different household groups are those by Thorbecke (1991) for Indonesia and McMahon (1991) for Kenya. The Indonesian study is based on a general equilibrium model with financial markets and is used to examine numerous macroeconomic policies such as devaluation of the Indonesian rupiah. Thorbecke (1991) finds that accelerated devaluation benefits medium- and large-size farmers, who produce much of the export crops, but affects real incomes of all other household groups unfavourably. This conclusion seems to stem mostly from short-run considerations because the inflationary pressures of devaluation are expected to lead to capital flight in the long run. Distributional consid-erations for such a long run are not investigated.

McMahon considers various tariff reduction simulations for Kenya. He constructs five different combinations of tariffs on goods by their end use. The beneficiaries of the tariff reduction are found to be rich peasants who export coffee and tea and do not receive any protection in the first place. This group benefits from the lower price of imported consumer goods, as do capital owners in the manufacturing sectors. The groups which are hurt are smallholders in agriculture, who now face competition from imported agricultural products, as well as other lower income groups such as landless rural labourers or workers in the informal sector.

In the context of the OECD countries, recent work has also explored linkages among regional integration, the household distribution of income, and migration incentives. Levy and van Wijnbergen (1994, 1995), for example, have emphasized the impact of agricultural liberalization, under the North American Free Trade Area (NAFTA), on household welfare for several classes of Mexican households. The distributional impact determines the incentives for rural–urban migration. In related work, Burfisher et al. (1994) have explored linkages of the functional distribution of income, weak Stolper–Samuelson relationships, and Mexico–United States migration. The empirical literature on trade and employment also emphasizes, in part, the impact of trade on the functional distribution of income (see Chapter 14 of this volume).

In summary, the previous studies are inconclusive as to how a more open trade regime can affect the distribution of income. In terms of the functional distribution of income, this should not be surprising, as economywide Stolper–Samuelson relationships will vary with underlying theoretical assumptions. At a more general level, the literature reminds us that distributional outcomes depend on the initial protection accorded to the various groups, their functional role in production, their consumption patterns, and the nature and degree of openness examined.

III Methodological Issues

III.1 Household Classification

The manner in which income distribution is modeled ranges from simple exogenous forms to more elaborate and endogenous ones, depending both on data availability and on the questions addressed by the study. Since households represent people in any society, these households could be disaggregated into various types of groups. The groups could be socioeconomic, e.g., small farmers as opposed to larger farmers. Alternatively, the groups could reflect the functional distribution or the size distribution. As long as income and expenditure data can be obtained for the same household classification, any type of group definition is possible. Since most studies draw on household budget surveys for such data, an existing available classification is most commonly used or regrouped to be tailored to questions of interest.

In the Kenya study, sixteen income groups were identified, twelve of these various sizes of landholders in different regions of the country. This type of breakdown could be of particular interest for a regional development model. The labour share, income share, and expenditure data were all available for that particular breakdown. The Indonesia study also grouped households by location and function. Ten groups, composed of agricultural and nonagricultural households, were broken down into urban and rural locations with urban households being disaggregated into occupational categories according to head of household.

If households are defined into K groups denoted by subscript k, then the aggregate consumption row vector C_i consisting of the quantity consumed of each good i must be broken down into the consumption matrix $\{C_{ik}\}$ such that the sum of each column $k \Sigma_k C_{ik} = C_i \forall i$. This is not a problem if national accounts and household expenditure surveys are obtained from the same source and are consistent with each other. If such consistency does not already exist, then one approach may be to use the ratio $C_{ik}/\Sigma_k C_{ik}$ to distribute aggregate consumption C_i over households. Stone (1985) discusses several discrepancies that may be found when undertaking household disaggregation in social accounting matrix (SAM) based models and suggests possible remedies. The issues raised include inconsistency in classifications of goods consumed and produced.

The household surveys also supply income Y_k for each household. Reconciliation of such income information with national income (Y) is also necessary. If it is assumed that all income is redistributed to households then $\Sigma_k Y_k = Y$. The next step is to obtain the source of income for each household. If there are S such sources (subscripted s) comprising wages, transfers, etc., then $Y_k = \Sigma_s Y_{ks}$ where Y_{ks} refers to income of type s received by household group k. The S sources have a relationship to factor incomes and other income sources endogenous to the model. When counterfactual simulations are done, Y_{ks} will change, thus altering total income Y_k of each household group.

The Colombia, Sri Lanka and Brazil studies as well as the National Bureau of Economic Research (NBER) study on U.S. tax policy (Ballard et al., 1985) all make use of the existing link between the functional and size distributions of income in the benchmark. Factor payments are mapped from income data onto the household groupings used. The Brazil study categorizes consumers into socioeconomic classes by region and by level of education. Various surveys are reconciled to map the functional distribution of income into the socioeconomic groups mentioned.

The Colombia study uses sector-specific factors of production and creates six "socioeconomic" income groups around the functional definitions. The size distribution is then determined in two steps. First, the distribution of income within each functional group is assumed to be log normally distributed, the log variance specified exogenously and the group mean income solved for. Second, the overall size distribution of income is computed by aggregating the within group distributions.[7]

The Korea study probably has the most elaborate income distribution specification of all the models. There are fifteen types of households defined by socioeconomic type. The number of workers in each household and their occupational distribution are assumed to remain constant. As in the Colombia model, the distribution of income within each category is assumed to be log normal and the log variance is estimated. The distribution of income (before and after taxes) for households classified by deciles of population is then generated. The technique used allows examination of changes in the composition of these deciles. Because of the inclusion of the money market in this study as well as in the work on Brazil and Indonesia, the extended functional distribution of income is endogenized into the model. Also, there is a dynamic component in that the base run income distribution is assumed to change in conjunction with overall industrialization and growth and the movement of the terms of trade against agriculture.[8] Given this base dynamic path of income distribution, the policy experiments alter this path over time.[9]

III.2 Measurement of Distributional Impact

How can the change in income distribution as a response to various policies be quantified? When policy simulations are carried out, factor prices, transfers, or other endogenous variables may change, thereby altering Y_k, income received by any household k. This will also alter some function $\theta = f(Y_k)$ which represents the distribution of income.

Some studies have used a single measure such as θ while others rely on a discussion of the benefits and gains to each group. Commonly used summary measures indicate whether the policy affects distribution favourably or adversely. Most studies use one or more measures such as the Gini coefficient, the log variance of income, the Theil index, and/or the Atkinson measure. Some of these inequality indicators are applied to the case study in Section IV of this chapter. One shortcoming of these measures is that they are unchanged when there are proportional increases in income for all groups

---

7 The procedure used is described in Dervis, de Melo, and Robinson (1982, Chapter 12).
8 Factors such as rural–urban migration are also incorporated into the dynamic subcomponent of the model.
9 The Kenya model also has a dynamic subcomponent and allows for rural–urban migration as well as the growth of output and investment.

defined, although there may be substantial poverty alleviation. If the poorest groups form the focus of the study, emphasis may be placed on the lower tail of the size distribution. In such cases, reduction in the percentage of people in poverty, mean income of the bottom 10 percent of the population, or expenditure of the poorest group is reported. Sometimes value judgements may be made about the income of rich groups and some studies (de Melo and Robinson, 1980) also look at the impact on the mean income of the top decile of households. If location is used as a basis of household classification, other statistics such as urban to rural expenditure gap (de Melo, 1979) may be reported.

The Indonesian study avoids using a summary statistic and more generally discusses the gains and losses for each household group. Studies that are more Walrasian in flavour use the equivalent variation as an indicator of household welfare. The Ballard study of the United States (1985) and the McMahon study of Kenya (1990) both report changes in equivalent variation of each household group. In the illustration that follows, the equivalent variation of each different household group is examined and welfare changes resulting from changes in factor prices and the prices of consumer goods are distinguished from one another.

IV An Application to Bangladesh

In the following example, the welfare effect of import liberalization is examined for Bangladesh. How eight household groups are affected is analysed, assuming the initial distortion in the trade regime is only from import tariffs and quotas.

The Bangladesh economy has been characterized by numerous deregulation efforts during the last decade. This exercise focuses on the import liberalization that took place within the broader move toward greater market orientation. The initial equilibrium depicted entailed a host of import controls and bans coupled with a high average tariff on most goods, particularly manufactures. The two main imports are cereals and producer goods. Controls were placed on both categories, and tariffs were put on the latter. The effect of tariff and quota removal on resource allocation has been examined in a previous paper (Khan, 1994). The following illustration demonstrates that import liberalization reduces the dispersion of income and benefits poorer households by increasing the demand for labour in the manufacturing sector.

The exercise presumes that the link between the functional and size distributions of income is fixed. The framework moves from an SAM of the economy to a CGE model.[10] The model is disaggregated to six sectors, two each in agriculture (cereals and non-cereals), manufacturing (importables and exportables), and nontradables (construction and services). The general features of the model are discussed next.

IV.1 The Model

Some of the key equations of the model are shown in analytical form in this section; the entire set of equations in their complete functional form is presented in Appendix 10.2. The production structure is depicted in Figure 10.1. The production function is nested Leontief and specifies complementarity between domestic factors DF_i and imported intermediate inputs $\{VM_{ji}\}$ which flow from sector j to i. These domestic factors are a Cobb–Douglas composite of value added VA_i and a composite of domestic intermediates V_i with unitary Allen elasticity of substitution between primary factors and domestically produced raw materials.[11] V_i is a Leontief aggregate over j of $\{VD_{ji}\}$, the flow of domestic intermediate goods from sector j to i. Value added is a constant elasticity of substitution (CES) aggregate of labour L_i and capital K_i. The model has three factors of production – sector-specific capital in agriculture and non-agriculture, and labour, which can move across all sectors (Figure 10.1).

The constant elasticity of transformation (CET) assumption is used for output, which is a composite of sales to the domestic market and abroad. The CET approach is standard in computable general equilibrium models examining trade policy issues.[12]

Household income is obtained from value added, quota rents, and government redistribution of revenue and foreign capital inflow ($\bar{F}$). The specification that $\bar{F}$ is distributed in the same manner as other transfers appeals to the fact that the major share of $\bar{F}$ is foreign grants channelled through public institutions. The nested household utility function is separable at three levels. Utility is first a function of current consumption and saving. Once present consumption is determined, it is divided among the various commodities available in the current period. Current consumption is a Cobb–Douglas aggregate of the consumption of goods classified by sectors of production.

---

10 Refer to Chapter 4 of this volume by Reinert and Roland-Holst on using data from a SAM for CGE modeling.
11 The Allen elasticity of substitution refers to the partial elasticity of substitution between two factors of production in a multi-factoral production function (Allen, 1938).
12 The CET formulation was originally developed by Powell and Gruen (1968).

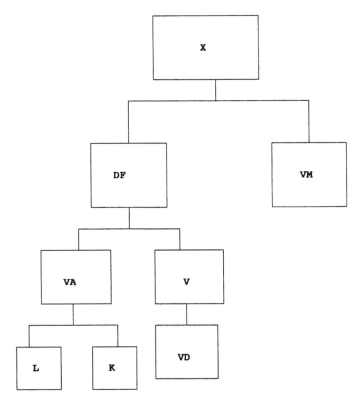

Figure 10.1. *The production structure*

The Armington assumption of product differentiation is applied to each tradable consumer good. Consumption parameters for the different households are calibrated from benchmark data. These include saving and consumption shares as well as shares of total consumption of each good. Substitution between foreign and domestic consumer goods is distinguished across goods but not across the household groups.

Domestic demand and production for domestic supply are set equal to each other, implying that the market for tradables is in equilibrium, given the exogenous trade deficit $\bar{F}$. Tariffs and indirect taxes are included in the analysis. Quotas present on imports are modeled by taking their tariff equivalent.

IV.2 Data and Calibration

The data are based on an input–output table compiled by the Planning Commission in Bangladesh. In addition, foreign trade statistics were used to

Table 10.1. *Aggregation and size of income groups*

Income in Takas per month	Category	Percentage of Total Population
Less than 999	Urban 1	1.5
1000 to 2499	Urban 2	5.77
2500 to 4999	Urban 3	2.97
5000 and above	Urban 4	1.04
Less than 999	Rural 1	21.58
1000 to 2499	Rural 2	50.98
2500 to 4999	Rural 3	13.22
5000 and above	Rural 4	2.897

break down the import vector into final goods and producer or intermediate goods. The household expenditure survey allowed disaggregation of the household sector and, finally, labour force survey figures were used to separate value added into labour and capital.

During the reconciliation of the data, much of the disaggregated information had to be sacrificed in order build a framework that would be consistent and at the same time contain the requisite detail to carry out the exercise. Although input–output data were available for 53 sectors of production, value added for these sectors was not broken down into payments to labour and other factors. Labour and wage information for the economy could be derived for six sectors of production. Given the limited factor use information, six sectors were used in the analysis. Value added was divided into labour and non-labour factoral incomes that could be matched against the sources of income reported in the household survey.

The household expenditure survey showed income and expenditure for income groups by monthly income size for urban and rural areas. The lowest range of income categories used in this study is taka 999 per month (approximately $32 at the official exchange rate in 1981–82) or below. The highest range is taka 5,000 per month ($160) or more.

Table 10.1 shows that rural households constitute 88.69 percent of the total population and urban households make up the remaining 11.31 percent. The two lowest-income rural groups (rural 1 and rural 2) account for just under 73 percent of the entire population.

Table 10.2. *Distribution of income among the household groups (percentage of total income category received)*

Household Groups	Labour Income	Capital Income	Rent Income	Transfers
Urban 1	16	0.4	0.06	0.04
Urban 2	9.6	6	0.7	4.3
Urban 3	8.5	7.8	0.9	6.2
Urban 4	4	7.9	0.08	4.9
Rural 1	15	5.1	5	6.8
Rural 2	46.7	41.4	42.7	30.9
Rural 3	11.3	20.8	32.7	26.1
Rural 4	3.3	10.6	17.1	20.5

Income is acquired from twenty-two different sources. These sources were matched with the definition of income sources used in the model. The correspondence is shown in Appendix Table A10.1. Once the source of factor payments was obtained, a matrix showing the bridge between the functional and size distributions of income (Table 10.1) was established. Table 10.2 shows the distribution of the three types of factor income among households in the model. These include wages and salaries (labour income), return to the agriculture-specific factor (rent income), and income from industry-specific factor (capital income). The pattern in which receipts from transfers are distributed is also shown in Table 10.2. Another source of household income is that from quota rents which arise from import restrictions. In the absence of information on the distribution of this quota income, it is assumed to be distributed in the same proportions across households as profits from non-agricultural activity or capital income.

The percentages of each type of income going to each household grouping were then used as exogenous parameters in the model. Changes in the price of factors affect each household group because of the fixed proportion of income earned from each type of economic activity.

The two forms of direct taxation that are included are personal income taxes and property taxes. Property taxes are taken to be lump sum taxes in the model and income taxes are modeled as proportional taxes, thus departing from any increased institutional ability to expand the scope and collection of such taxes within the dynamic realm of the model. Income taxes are collected only from the two highest income urban groups, according to benchmark information.

Saving and expenditure information is also obtained from the Household Expenditure Survey. When the household income and expenditure data are available by the same classification, the problems of data reconciliation are prevented. However, in a number of studies surveyed such data must be reconciled. The Ballard study reconciles consumption and income data using the RAS procedure.[13] In this study, the distribution of aggregate consumption over the household groups defined was obtained from the household survey. The coefficient obtained was then used to disaggregate consumption data derived from the national income accounts.

IV.3 Simulation Results

The initial benchmark equilibrium is first solved by using a numerical model on General Algebraic Modeling System (GAMS). This initial position is then perturbed under the assumption of import liberalization. The impact on the welfare of the households is examined with a discussion of the source of the welfare changes. The results obtained are shown in Table 10.3 as percentage deviation from the benchmark point.

The welfare impact of a policy change is often measured by using the equivalent variation.[14] The ratio of the equivalent variation to the expenditure function valued at the benchmark prices and income provides the same information as the equivalent variation because both are positive if household welfare increases. Given the homothetic utility function used in this model, the expenditure function is separable in prices and utility and therefore the ratio $\{e[p^0, v(p^1, y^1)] - e[p^0, v(p^0, y^0)]\}/e[p^0, v(p^0, y^0)]$ is simply equal to the percentage change in utility from the initial to the counterfactual equilibrium. Accordingly, the percentage change in utility is the welfare measure reported in Table 10.3.

In addition, well known measures of the size distribution of income such as the Gini coefficient, Theil index, and log variance of income, are shown in Table 10.4, as is the ratio of income received by the poorest quintile of the

---

13 The RAS procedure is based on an updating and reconciliation technique for interindustry flow matrices described in Brown and Stone (1962).
14 The equivalent variation is equal to $e[p^0, v(p^1, y^1)] - e[p^0, v(p^0, y^0)]$ where e is the expenditure function, v is the indirect utility function, p^0, y^0 are the price vectors and income for the initial benchmark and p^1, y^1 are the new prices and income in the counterfactual regime.

Table 10.3. *Welfare impact of import liberalization on households (percentage change in utility from benchmark)*

Household Groups	
Urban 1	9.69
Urban 2	5.31
Urban 3	-3.03
Urban 4	-2.51
Rural 1	15.15
Rural 2	10.16
Rural 3	1.95
Rural 4	-6.24

population.[15] The formulations used for these calculations are reported in Appendix 10.3.

The results are mixed, indicating that income inequality increases slightly with trade liberalization. Table 10.4 shows that the Gini coefficient falls from 0.296 to 0.277 and the Theil index of inequality rises. This implies that the distribution of income becomes more skewed in favour of the rich. However, the income dispersion indicators, the log variance and coefficient of variation of income, both point to a more equal distribution of income across the household categories after trade liberalization. On the other hand, measures specifically aimed at gauging the condition of the poor show that this group gains from trade liberalization. The share of income received by the lowest

---

15 Actually, the share of income received by rural 1 and urban 1, the two poorest household groups, is calculated. These two groups constitute about 22 percent of the population and therefore approximately constitute the poorest quintile of households.

Table 10.4. *Values of selected variables and income distribution measures for the benchmark and counterfactual equilibria (variables measured in domestic currency)*

Variable	Benchmark	Counterfactual case
wage rate	1.0	1.13
return to capital	1.0	1.09
return to land	1.0	1.061
Consumer price of:		
cereals	1.0	0.999
non-cereal agricultural	1.0	0.995
manufactured exportables	1.082	0.765
manufactured importables	1.0	0.922
services & energy	1.005	1.034
Producer price of:		
cereals	1.0	1.042
non-cereal agricultural	1.0	1.052
manufactured exportables	1.0	0.71
manufactured importables	1.0	0.849
construction	1.0	0.801
services & energy	1.0	1.029
Log variance of income	0.2321	0.2246
Share of income of lowest quintile	9.3%	9.95%
Rural/Urban Expenditure	4.55	4.62
Coefficient of Variation	0.996	1.012
Theil Index	.07455	.07665
Gini Coefficient	0.2964	0.2776

quintile rises marginally, suggesting a reduction in poverty. In addition, regional income inequality is reduced as the rural urban expenditure gap falls. In the benchmark average income per household in urban areas is 72 percent higher than that in rural areas. Finally, the equivalent variation measure used in Table 10.3 shows that the welfare of the lower income urban and rural families increases in relation to that of the upper income groups.

Table 10.5. *Share of income category in total income of each household (percentage of total)*

Household Groups	Labour Income	Rent Income	Capital Income	Transfers
Urban 1	69.4	1.5	14.7	8.3
Urban 2	52.1	2.3	25.1	10.1
Urban 3	44.2	2.6	31.3	13.9
Urban 4	32.1	3.5	48.3	17.1
Rural 1	57	10.8	14.9	11.2
Rural 2	36.1	18.8	24.6	10.4
Rural 3	17.7	29.2	25.1	17.8
Rural 4	10	29.5	24.6	26.9

Since some of the summary measures indicate that the lower income households are benefitted by import liberalization and others such as the Gini or Theil indices do not, it is pertinent to ask which indicators are more truly reflective of the impact on the welfare of households. Dervis, de Melo, and Robinson (1982) write that Gini coefficient and log variance are especially sensitive to the lower tail of the income distribution, while the Theil index and the coefficient of variation are more influenced by extreme relative wealth.[16] Because of the controversy surrounding the use of a single statistic to sum up the effect of policy on households, the following discussion will focus on that of the equivalent variation measure and its components. The equivalent variation more adequately reflects the change in satisfaction of households because it takes into account consumer preferences as well as income changes. On the other hand, it must be noted that in this study such preferences are specified a priori because a specific functional form has been chosen to depict these preferences.

16 See Chapter 12, pages 429–431, of their book for this discussion.

Household welfare is affected by factor price changes as well as changes in the price of consumer goods. In order to understand how such price changes affect households, it is necessary to identify the main sources of income and destinations of expenditure for each group. Table 10.5 examines the origin of income for households.[17] This table is particularly useful to see how the welfare of each household is affected by factor price changes, given that the endowments of each factor per household are assumed fixed over the period of the analysis. If the lower income households 1 and 2 are grouped as the poor and the other higher income households as the rich, then Table 10.5 shows that wages form the major source of earnings for all poor households, both urban and rural. Wages are also significant, although less important, for the urban rich, such wages constituting payments to relatively skilled labour. Capital income is important for all households, but more overwhelmingly so for the urban rich and to some extent for the rural rich. Rental income from agricultural activity is of significance for the rural rich, as are transfer payments. Transfers received per capita are higher for rural rich households than any other group. Appendix Table 10A.1 shows that transfers are defined as gifts and charity from all sources. It is interesting that although these transfer payments are designed for the poor groups, the data are able to capture impediments to the "trickling down" of transfers. Rental income from agricultural activity is also of some importance to rural poor households.

Table 10.6 shows the share of consumption of each good in total consumption for each household group. How important the consumer goods price changes are for each household can be determined by these shares (σ_i). Cereal consumption accounts for a large share of total consumption of the poorer group – the value of σ_1 declines as households move into higher income brackets. This is also the case (although to a smaller degree) with σ_2, the share of consumption made up of non-cereal agricultural products. The opposite is true for σ_6. The share of total consumption taken up by services increases as household income rises, especially in the urban areas. Manufactured goods form about the same share of total consumption for all household groups.

Removing import taxes on all tradables lowers the domestic prices of such items[18] and increases consumption and investment expenditure on them. Also, the cost of production in the import-intensive sectors is reduced. These

---

17 It is different from Table 10.2 in that it shows what percentage of total household income is derived from each source (the ratio Y_{ks}/Y_k). Table 10.2 shows what percentage of each type of factoral income is received by each household (the ratio Y_{ks}/Y_s).
18 Note that there are no import tariffs on cereals.

Table 10.6. *Share of consumption of each good in total consumption (percentage of total consumption expenditure)*

Household Groups	σ_1	σ_2	σ_3	σ_4	σ_6
Urban 1	34.2	16.3	0.6	22.2	26.7
Urban 2	28.3	16.4	0.6	24	30.7
Urban 3	18.1	12.3	0.6	22.1	46.9
Urban 4	10.7	9.8	0.7	21.2	57.7
Rural 1	38.8	16.9	0.6	22.3	21.4
Rural 2	36.7	17.3	0.7	23	22.4
Rural 3	29.9	14.1	0.6	22	33.3
Rural 4	21.7	11	0.6	23.7	43

import-intensive sectors (primarily manufacturing and construction) expand, drawing resources away from grain production and services. This increases the demand for factors, particularly those in the expanding sectors. Table 10.4 shows that all factor prices rise. Wage earners gain the most, followed by owners of capital. Even though capital is sector-specific in the industries which expand, the expanding sectors are also labour-intensive, particularly manufactured exportables. This is why wages increase more than the return to capital.

These factor price changes benefit the poor household groups and the urban rich. The poor households gain relatively because of the increase in wages. The urban rich gain both because wages increase and because the return to industrial capital is raised. Since the rent from land rises relatively less, the rural rich benefit proportionately less from factor markets. Transfer income is also an important source of income for the rural rich group. This type of income is now cut back because of the loss in government tariff revenue, further reducing the welfare of these households.

With the exception of services, prices of all consumer items and investment goods fall, compared to the initial equilibrium. Purchaser prices of
manufactured goods fall substantially. It should be noted that although the
price of manufactured exportables falls most, these goods are not significantly consumed by households. Table 10.6 shows that these items constitute
no more than 6 to 7 percent of most household budgets. This table also
indicates that most households spend about the same share of their budget
on manufactured goods overall, so that price changes of these goods affect
all groups about uniformly. Food prices fall marginally while the price of
services, which rich households spend most of their income on, rises. The
poorer households therefore gain, while the higher income households
which allocate a larger share of their budget to services lose.

The distributional effects may be summarized as follows: A liberalized
import regime leads to welfare gains for poor households (both rural and
urban) both because of factor price increases and because of product price
reductions. Because the rural poor make up such a sizable portion of households, the rural–urban expenditure gap is also reduced. The welfare of the
higher income households is reduced, particularly that of the rural landown-
ers, whose net income is diminished because government transfers have
fallen, as has the price of land relative to other factors.

In this particular context, an open trade regime benefits poor households
and reduces the dispersion of income because consumer goods prices fall
and the demand for the factors that poorer households own is increased.
These conclusions would not necessarily hold under a different type of initial
trade regime. The exercise therefore affirms the desirability of examining
existing links among households, expenditure, and income in order better to
understand what effect trade policy might have on different household
groups.

Appendix 10.1

Table 10A.1. *Reconciliation of income source with model definition*

Bureau of Statistics Income Definition:	Model Definition
Wages and salary Benefits Professional salary Additional profit above salary Pension Gratuity and Provident Fund	Labour income
Real agricultural income Land rent earned	Sector specific rental income in agriculture
Commercial/industrial income Interest income Profit Imputed rent Rent from house owned Income from working capital	Sector specific capital income in industry
Gifts/charity (cash and kind)	Transfers

Appendix 10.2

Equations of the Model

Equations

Production Equations

$$X_i = \min\left(\frac{1}{ad_i} \cdot DF_i, \frac{1}{am_{ji}} \cdot VM_{ji}\right) \quad i,j = 1 \text{ to } 6 \qquad (A10.1)$$

$$DF_i = \tau_i\left[VA_i^\kappa V_i^{1-\kappa}\right] \quad i = 1 \text{ to } 6 \qquad (A10.2)$$

$$V_i = \min\left(\frac{1}{a_{ji}} V_{ji}\right) \quad j,i = 1, \,..6 \qquad (A10.3)$$

$$VA_i = \gamma_i\left[\chi_i K_i^{(\sigma_i-1)/\sigma_i} + (1-\chi_i)L_i^{(\sigma_i-1)/\sigma_i}\right]^{\sigma_i/(1-\sigma_i)} \quad i = 1 \text{ to } 6 \qquad (A10.4)$$

$$\overline{L} = \sum L_i \qquad i = 1 \text{ to } 6 \tag{A10.5}$$

$$\overline{K_A} = K_1 + K_2 \tag{A10.6}$$

$$\overline{K_M} = \sum_i K_i \qquad i = 3 \text{ to } 6 \tag{A10.7}$$

$$r_i = \frac{P_{vi}}{a_{vi}(\gamma_i)^{(\sigma_i-1)/\sigma_i}} (\chi_i) \left(\frac{VA_i}{K_i}\right)^{1/\sigma_i} \qquad r_1 = r_2 \neq r_3 = r_4 = r_5 = r_6 \tag{A10.8}$$

$$w_i = \frac{P_{vi}}{a_{vi}(\gamma_i)^{(\sigma_i-1)/\sigma_i}} (\chi_i) \left(\frac{VA_i}{Li}\right)^{1/\sigma_i} \qquad i = 1 \text{ to } 6 \tag{A10.9}$$

$$P_{xi} \cdot X_i = P_{vi} \cdot VA_i + \sum_j P_j^c \cdot V_{ji} + \sum_j P_k^M \cdot VM_{ki} \qquad i, j = 1 \text{ to } 6, \qquad k = 1 \text{ to } 4 \tag{A10.10}$$

$$X_i = AP_i \left[\phi_i E_i^{(\pi_i-1)/\pi_i} + (1-\phi_i) XD_i^{(\pi_i-1)/\pi_i} \right]^{\pi_i/(1-\pi_i)} \qquad i = 1 \text{ to } 4 \tag{A10.11}$$

$$\frac{XD_i}{E_i} = \frac{(1-\phi_i)}{\phi_i} \left(\frac{P_{di}}{P_i^e}\right)^{\pi_i} \qquad i = 1 \text{ to } 4 \tag{A10.12}$$

$$P_{xi} X_i = P_i XD_i + P_i^e E_1 \qquad i = 1 \text{ to } 4 \tag{A10.13}$$

Income

$$Y_h(1-t_h) = l_h(w\overline{L}) + ka_h(\overline{K_A}) + km_h(\overline{K_M}) + tr_h(\overline{F} + Grev) + km_h(QY) - PROPT_h \tag{A10.14}$$

$$GREV = \sum tp_i \cdot X_i + \sum\sum tm_j(VM_{ji}) + \sum tm_j M_j + tm_4 \cdot I_m \qquad i = 1 \text{ to } 6, \qquad j = 1 \text{ to } 4 \tag{A10.15}$$

$$QY = (tm_j - tf_j)(VM_{ji} + M_j) + (tm_4 - tf_4)I_M \qquad i = 1 \text{ to } 6, \qquad j = 1 \text{ to } 4 \tag{A10.16}$$

$$\overline{F} = \sum P_{mi}^* \cdot M_i + \sum\sum P_{mi}^* \cdot VM_{ij} - \sum P_{ei}^* \cdot E_i + P_{m4}^* \cdot I_m \qquad i = 1 \text{ to } 4, \qquad j = 1 \text{ to } 6 \tag{A10.17}$$

Demand

$$S_h = \frac{(1-\alpha_h)Y_h}{P_S} \tag{A10.18}$$

$$C_{ih} = \frac{\lambda_{ih}\alpha_h Y_h}{P_{ai}} \qquad i = 1 \text{ to } 4 \tag{A10.19}$$

$$C_{ih} = \frac{\lambda_{ih}\alpha_h Y_h}{P_i^c} \qquad i = 5,6 \tag{A10.20}$$

$$P_{ai} \cdot C_i = P_i^c \cdot CD_i + P_i^m \cdot M_i \qquad i = 1 \ to \ 4 \tag{A10.21}$$

$$C_i = AC_i \left[\mu_i M_i^{(\rho_i-1)/\rho_i} + (1-\mu_i) CD_i^{(\rho_i-1)/\rho_i} \right]^{\rho_i/(1-\rho_i)} \qquad i = 1 \ to \ 4 \tag{A10.22}$$

$$\frac{CD_i}{M_i} = \left[\frac{(1-\mu_i)}{\mu_i} \left(\frac{P_i^m}{P_i^c} \right) \right]^{\rho_i} \qquad i = 1, \ to \ 4 \tag{A10.23}$$

$$I = I_4 + I_5 + I_m \tag{A10.24}$$

$$I_4 = \overline{I_4} \tag{A10.25}$$

$$I_M = \beta \left[\sum_i PX_i X_i + \sum_j PD_j X_j \right] \qquad i = 3 \ to \ 4, \qquad j = 5 \ to \ 6 \tag{A10.26}$$

Product Market Equilibrium

$$XD_i = CD_i + \sum_j Vij \qquad i = 1 \ to \ 3, \qquad j = 1 \ to \ 6 \tag{A10.27}$$

$$XD_4 = CD_4 + I_4 + \sum_j V_{4j} \qquad j = 1 \ to \ 6 \tag{A10.28}$$

$$XD_5 = C_5 + I_5 + \sum_j V_{5j} \qquad j = 1 \ to \ 6 \tag{A10.29}$$

$$XD_6 = C_6 + \sum_j V_{6j} \qquad j = 1 \ to \ 6 \tag{A10.30}$$

Prices

$$P_i^c = P_i(1 + tp_i) \qquad i = 1 \ to \ 6 \tag{A10.31}$$

$$P_i^m = P_{mi}^*(1 + tm_i) \qquad i = 1 \ to \ 4 \tag{A10.32}$$

$$P_i^e = P_{ei}^* \qquad i = 1 \ to \ 4 \tag{A10.33}$$

Endogenous Variables

C_{ih} = consumption demand for composite good
CD_i = consumption demand for domestic production
DF_i = domestic inputs by sector of use
E_i = exports
I_i = investment by domestic sector of origin
I_m = purchase capital goods from abroad
I = total investment in the economy
K_i = sectoral capital stock
L_i = sectoral labour input

M_i = imports for final consumption
P_i^e = price of exports
P_i^m = price of imports
P_{di} = producer price of domestically sold domestic goods
P_S = price of the investment or saving good
P_{xi} = Armington supply composite price
P_i^c = purchaser price of domestic goods
P_{ai} = Armington consumption composite price
r_i = sectoral rental rate
S_h = saving
VA_i = value added
V_{ij} = flow of intermediates from sector i to j
Vj = composite of domestic intermediates used in sector j
VM_{ij} = imported intermediate inputs in production
w_i = wage rate
X_i = production at home sold domestically and abroad
XD_i = domestic production sold locally
Y_h = income
QY = quota income

Exogenous Variables and Parameters

a_{ij} = ratio of domestic intermediates from sector i to total domestic intermediates used in sector j
ad_j = ratio of domestic factors to output
am_{ij} = ratio of imported intermediate input to output
AC_i = scale parameter in Armington demand function
$\bar{F}$ = foreign transfers
$GREV$ = government revenue from domestic and trade taxes
I_4 = lump sum inventory investment
$\bar{K}_M$ = total capital available for the modern sectors
ka_h = share of agricultural-specific income received by household h
km_h = share of modern sector capital income received by household h
$\bar{K}_A$ = total capital available for agriculture
$\bar{L}$ = total supply of labour
l_h = share of wage income received by household h
$PROPT_h$ = lump sum property taxes paid by household h
P_{mi}^* = world price of imports
P_{ei}^* = world price of exports
tf_i = official tariff rate
tm_i = tariff rate inclusive of quota premium
tp_i = indirect tax rate
tr_h = share of transfers received by household h
α_h = share of income devoted to consumption by household h
λ_{ih} = share of good i in total consumption expenditure by household h
μ_i = share of imports in total consumption of good i

ρ_i = elasticity of substitution between consumption of domestic good and imported good, in sector i

π_i = elasticity of transformation between selling domestic goods at home and abroad

ϕ_i = share of exports in total domestic production

τ_i = scale parameter in domestic input aggregation

κ_i = share parameter in domestic input aggregation

γ_i = scale parameter in value added function

χ_i = share parameter in value added function

σ_i = elasticity of substitution between capital and labour

Appendix 10.3

Income Distribution Measures

The income distribution measures applied in this chapter were calculated by using the following formulas. All formulas are computed by using income after taxes and transfers. Average income of households in category h is written as y_h while θy_h refers to the income share of the hth household group.

The coefficient of variation is σ/μ, where σ and μ are, respectively, the standard deviation and the mean of y_h. The log variance of income is the variance of the logarithm of y_h. The Gini coefficient is formulated following Mangahas (1974) as

$$G = 1 - 2\sum_h \left[\frac{1}{2}\left(f'_h - f'_{h-1}\right)\left(\theta y'_h - \theta y'_{h-1}\right) + \left(f'_h - f'_{h-1}\right)\theta y'_{h-1} \right] \qquad \text{(A10.34)}$$

where f'_h is the cumulated population share of the household groups one through h and $\theta y'_h$ is the cumulated income share. $G=1$ denotes that there is complete equality or that income shares correspond to population shares.

The Theil index of inequality is measured as

$$\log H - \sum_h \theta y_h \log \frac{1}{\theta y_h} \qquad \text{(A10.35)}$$

where θy_h is the share of income received by the hth household group.

References

Adelman, I. and S. Robinson. 1978. *Income Distribution Policy in Developing Countries: A Case Study of Korea*. Oxford: Oxford University Press.

Adelman, I. and S. Robinson. 1988. "Macroeconomic adjustment and income distribution: Alternative models applied to two economies." *Journal of Development Economics* 29:23–44.

Adelman, I. and S. Robinson. 1989. "Income distribution and development." In *Handbook of Development Economics*, Vol. II, edited by H. Chenery and T.N. Srinivasan. Amsterdam: Elsevier Science.

Allen, R.G.D. 1938. *Mathematical Analysis for Economists*. London: Macmillan.

Ballard, C.L., D. Fullerton, J.B. Shoven, and J. Whalley. 1985. *A General Equilibrium Model for Tax Policy Evaluation*. Chicago: University of Chicago Press.

Becker, G. 1967. *Human Capital and the Personal Distribution of Income*. Ann Arbor: University of Michigan Press.

Bourguignon, F., J. de Melo, and C. Morrisson. 1991. "Poverty and income distribution during adjustment: Issues and evidence from the OECD Project." *World Development* 19:1485–1508.

Bourguignon, F., J. de Melo, and A. Suwa. 1991a. "Modelling the effects of adjustment programs on income distribution." *World Development* 19:1527–1544.

Bourguignon, F., J. de Melo, and A. Suwa. 1991b. "Distributional effects of adjustment policies: Simulations for archetype economies in Africa and Latin America." *World Bank Economic Review* 5:339–366.

Brooke, A., D. Kendrick, and A. Meeraus. 1988. *GAMS: A User's Guide*. San Francisco: Scientific Press.

Brown, J.A.C. and R. Stone. 1962. "Output and investment for exponential growth in consumption." *Review of Economic Studies* 29:241–245.

Burfisher, M.E., S. Robinson, and K.E. Thierfelder. 1994. "Wage changes in a U.S.–Mexico Free Trade Area: Migration versus Stolper–Samuelson effects." In *Modelling Trade Policy: Applied General Equilibrium Assessments of North American Free Trade*, edited by J.F. Francois and C.R. Shiells. Cambridge: Cambridge University Press.

Champerowne, D. 1974. "A comparison of measures of inequality of income distribution." *Economic Journal* 84:787–816.

Deardorff, A.V. and J.D. Haveman. 1991. "The effects of U.S. trade laws on poverty in America." University of Michigan, Mimeo.

De Melo, M. 1979. "Agricultural policies and development: A socioeconomic investigation applied to Sri Lanka." *Journal of Policy Modelling* 1:1–21.

De Melo, J. and S. Robinson. 1980. "The impact of trade policies on income distribution in a planning model for Colombia." *Journal of Policy Modelling* 2:81–100.

Dervis, K., J. de Melo, and S. Robinson. 1982. *General Equilibrium Models for Development Policy*. Cambridge: Cambridge University Press.

Dixit, A.K. and V. Norman. 1980. *Theory of International Trade*. Cambridge: Cambridge University Press.

Government of Bangladesh. 1986. *Bangladesh Household Expenditure Survey 1981–82*. Dhaka: Bangladesh Bureau of Statistics.

Government of Bangladesh. 1987. *Foreign Trade Statistics of Bangladesh 1976–77 to 1983–84*, Vol. III. Dhaka: Bangladesh Bureau of Statistics.

Government of Bangladesh. 1988. "The input output structure of Bangladesh economy – 1981/82." Draft Mimeo. Dhaka: Planning Commission.

Jorgensen, D.W. 1984. *Aggregate Consumer Behavior and the Measurement of Inequality: An Econometric Approach to General Equilibrium Analysis*. Nankang, Taipei: Institute of Economics, Academia Sinica.

Khan, F.C. 1994. "Import liberalization in a developing country with import intensive industry: The case of Bangladesh." *International Economic Journal* 8:77–90.

Kehoe, T.J. and J. Serra-Puche. 1983. "A computable general equilibrium model with endogenous unemployment: An analysis of the 1980 fiscal reform in Mexico." *Journal of Public Economics* 22:1–26.

Krueger, A.O. 1977. *Growth, Distortions and Pattern of Trade Among Many Countries*. Princeton Studies in International Finance. No.4. Princeton, New Jersey: Princeton University.

Levy, S. and S. van Wijnbergen. 1994. "Agriculture in the Mexico–U.S. Free Trade Agreement: A general equilibrium assessment." In *Modelling Trade Policy: Applied General Equilibrium Assessments of North American Free Trade*, edited by J.F. Francois and C.R. Shiells. Cambridge: Cambridge University Press.

Levy, S. and S. van Wijnbergen. 1995. "Transition problems in economic reform: Agriculture in the North American Free Trade Agreement." *American Economic Review* 85(4):738–754.

Lysy, F. and L. Taylor. 1980. "A computable general equilibrium model for the functional distribution of income: Experiments for Brazil, 1959–71." In *Models of Growth and Distribution for Brazil*, edited by L. Taylor, E. Bacha, E. Cardoso, and F. Lysy. Oxford: Oxford University Press.

Mangahas, M. 1974. *A Note on Decomposition of the Gini Ratio Across Regions*. Discussion Paper No. 74–2. Institute of Economic Development and Research, School of Economics. Manila: University of Philippines.

McMahon, G. 1990. "Tariff policy, income distribution, and long-run structural adjustment in a dual economy: A numerical analysis." *Journal of Public Economics* 42:105–123.

Narayana, N.S.S., K.S. Parikh, and T.N. Srinivasan. 1991. *Agriculture, Growth and Redistribution of Income: Policy Analysis with a General Equilibrium Model of India*. Amsterdam: North-Holland.

Pechman, J.A. 1985. *Who Paid the Taxes 1966–1985?* Washington D.C.: Brookings Institution.

Powell, A.A. and F. Gruen. 1968. "The constant elasticity of transformation production frontier and linear supply system." *International Economic Review* 9:315–328.

Richardson, D. 1995. "Income inequality and trade: How to think. What to conclude." *The Journal of Economic Perspectives* 9:33–54.

Ruffin, R. and R. Jones. 1977. "Protection and real wages: The neoclassical ambiguity." *Journal of Economic Theory* 14:337–348.

Srinivasan, T.N. and J. Whalley, eds. 1986. *General Equilibrium Trade Policy Modelling*. Cambridge, Massachusetts: M.I.T. Press.

Stone, R. 1985. "The disaggregation of the household sector in the national accounts." In *Social Accounting Matrices: A Basis for Planning*, edited by G. Pyatt and J.I. Round. Washington D.C.: World Bank.

Taylor, L., E. Bacha, E.A. Cardoso, and F.J. Lysy. 1980. *Models of Growth and Distribution for Brazil*. Oxford: Oxford University Press.

Theil, H. 1967. *Economics and Information Theory*. Chicago: North-Holland.

Thorbecke, E. 1991. "Adjustment, growth and income distribution in Indonesia." *World Development* 19:1595–1614.

PART IV
Extensions

11

Scale Economies and Imperfect Competition

Joseph F. Francois and David W. Roland-Holst

I Introduction

The links between trade policy and competition have received intense scrutiny in recent years. Current interest in the policy community follows a long period during which many of the basic tenets of modern industrial organization theory were integrated into the core of mainstream trade theory. A number of empirical studies of commercial policy have attempted to incorporate theoretical insights from this literature into numerical assessments of commercial policy. These include studies of regional integration in North America and Europe (Venables and Smith, 1986, 1989; Cox and Harris, 1985; Francois and Shiells, 1994), studies of national trade policies (de Melo and Tarr, 1992), studies of multi-lateral liberalization (Francois et al., 1994; Haaland and Tollefson, 1994), and sector-focused commercial policy studies (Dixit, 1988; Baldwin and Krugman, 1988a,b).

Over roughly the same period during which trade and industrial organization theory were being integrated, developing countries were grappling with the very real consequences of dramatic changes in their trade orientation and domestic economic structure. Since 1980, developing countries have passed through stabilization and adjustment experiences which rival those of the Organization for Economic Cooperation and Development (OECD) countries at any time since the Second World War. For the most part, closer examination of the vivid and diverse lessons of this experience by mainstream trade economists has just begun.[1] It is therefore somewhat ironic that the new school of trade theorists has until recently focused its attention on developed countries, since nowhere has the link between trade and industry structure and conduct been more apparent in recent times than in developing countries.

---

1 See Roberts and Tybout (1990), Devarajan and Rodrik (1988a,b), Rodrik (1988), and de Melo (1988) for more on the perspective from development studies.

In this chapter, we examine a variety of alternative specifications of market structure in applied trade models. After a brief discourse on the concept of procompetitive effects of trade, we turn to an overview of conventions for specifying scale economies. We then set out a menu of specifications for market structure and conduct. While these approaches can be, and have been, employed in both partial and general equilibrium models, we limit ourselves here to general equilibrium examples. These examples are drawn from numerical assessments of the Uruguay Round, under alternative specifications of market structure. For the numerical examples, we work with a modified version of the same Korea-focused multi-region general equilibrium model employed in Chapters 9 and 12.

II The Procompetitive Effects of Trade Policy

When we depart from the perfect competition paradigm, variations in industry structure and market structure greatly complicate formal analysis of the gains from trade. These complications relate to potential shifts in the cost of production, rising and falling profit margins, new product introduction, increased competitive pressure on domestic producers, and changes in the parameters underlying strategic decisions. The interaction of these effects with trade and trade policy can be quite complex, though the minimum conditions for welfare gains are generally linked to changes in industry output (see Markusen et al., 1995). While the specifics vary by model type, the gains from trade that are directly linked to conditions of scale economies and/or imperfect competition are grouped under a common label – *procompetitive effects.*

Markusen et al. offer the relatively simple example of procompetitive effects for a small country in which one sector is monopolistic. This is represented in Figure 11.1, where sector X is assumed to be monopolized. Under autarky, the monopolist sets prices that do not reflect the social rate of transformation. Introduction of trade will have two sets of effects. First, the threat of imports may be sufficient to force the monopolist to price competitively. This is the procompetitive effect in this example, and it is reflected in expanded output from X_0 to X_1. It moves the economy from welfare W_0 to W_1. Note that it is not necessary that any trade actually occur. Rather, it is the potential for entry by foreign suppliers that leads to this effect. Second, traditional gains from trade imply a further welfare shift to W_2. Under more complex specifications of market power and industry structure, procompetitive effects may relate to increased scale economies and

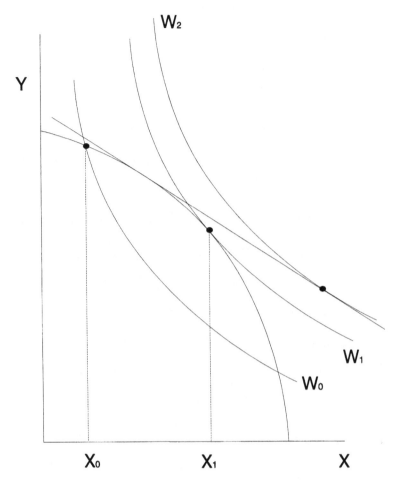

Figure 11.1. *Procompetitive effects with a domestic monopoly*

falling costs, increased product variety, or increased total profits (measured as the gap between social cost and price).

In addition to complicating the welfare calculus underlying the gains from trade relative to autarky, imperfect competition also complicates the inter-action of production incentives, welfare, and commercial policy. At the most basic level, tariffs alter the competitive position of domestic firms relative to foreign firms, as reflected in the demand conditions they face. Just as impor-tant, different types of protection have different effects on the competitive position of domestic firms (Bhagwati, 1965). In other words, instruments that are "equivalent" under perfect competition can lead to disparate effects under imperfect competition. An important direction for research relates to the interaction between the types of trade policy instrument surveyed in Chapter 2, and the mechanics of scale economies and competitive market structures explored in this chapter. While the literature on quotas is relatively extensive (see Anderson 1988), our understanding of the more exotic instruments, like domestic content requirements, product standards, and contingent protection triggered by threshold market shares, is limited at best. This is made even more difficult by the almost infinite scope for creating derivative commercial policy instruments out of combinations of these individual instruments. At a general level, we refer the reader to Markusen and Venables (1988), Grossman (1991), Helpman and Krugman (1989), and Markusen et al. (1995) as good starting points on abstract treatment of commercial policy under these conditions. For more concrete examples involving applied studies of specific industries, see Baldwin and Krugman (1988a,b), Dixit (1988), Feenstra (1988), and de Melo and Tarr (1992). On a regional basis, Cox and Harris (1985) and Francois and Shiells (1994) focus on economic integration in North America, Venables and Smith (1986, 1991) and Haaland and Wooton (1991) examine economic integration in Europe, and Lee and Roland-Holst (1995) examine economic integration in the Pacific Basin. For multi-lateral liberalization, recent studies include Haaland and Tollefson (1994) and Francois et al. (1994, 1995).

To highlight how important the interactions between imperfect competition and choice of commercial policy instruments can be, we close this section with a simple example involving tariffs and quotas. Consider a small country, with a monopolist producing good X, subject to the cost schedule MC in Figure 11.2. This good is also available on the world market at price P^*. If we introduce a tariff at t which is less than the prohibitive tariff, the domestic monopolist then faces the marginal revenue schedule $P_t = P^*(1+t)$ and will produce at point E_t. Imports will be at level M_t, and price will be at P_t. Next, assume the government replaces the import tariff with a quota allowing for the same level of imports as under the tariff. The relevant demand schedule for the domestic firm is then represented by the heavy line in the figure, which maps residual demand. Under the quota, the monopolist then faces the marginal revenue schedule MR. The result is that he will restrict output to Xq, charging price Pq. Basically, with the quota, the domestic monopolist has more market power, as a result of a less elastic demand curve than under the "equivalent" tariff. Helpman and Krugman (1989) offer a generalization of this point, showing that the basic insight is relatively robust and follows even within frameworks incorporating declin-

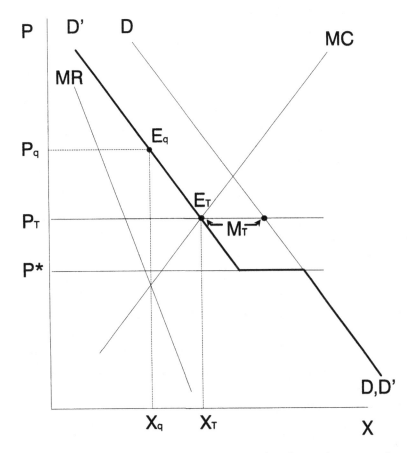

Figure 11.2. *Tariffs versus quotas with a domestic monopoly*

ing marginal costs, imports that are imperfect substitutes for domestic goods, non-cooperative oligopoly, and collusive oligopoly. In the extreme, quotas even at the full free trade level of imports can induce anti-competitive behaviour and reductions in output by a domestic monopolist. We may therefore expect liberalization of quantitative restrictions to induce greater procompetitive effects than tariff liberalization.

III Firm-Level Costs

In empirical models, the cost structure of firms, and hence of industry, follows from the choice of modeling technique and the observed data to which it is calibrated. One aspect which has received intense scrutiny in recent years is returns to scale. Beginning with a study by Harris (1984), a large literature on empirical modeling arose to evaluate trade liberalization under various specifications of returns to scale.[2] This new empirical research initiative was abetted by the intense parallel interest among trade theorists in applying concepts from industrial organization to trade theory.[3] Both strains of work on firm-level scale economies confirm a basic conclusion of the earlier literature on trade with industrywide scale economies – the results of empirical and theoretical work grounded in classical trade theory can be contradicted, in magnitude and/or direction, when scale economies or diseconomies play a significant role in the adjustment process.

Constant returns to scale (CRTS) is an attractive property in terms of flexibility and parsimony. It facilitates practical data gathering, calibration, and interpretation of results. However, there is strong empirical evidence against this assumption. In the real world, factors are heterogeneous in quality and mobility, and changes in the level of output often involve changes in average cost, even for relatively simple production processes (Westerbrook and Tybout, 1990). While there may be uncertainty about the precise magnitude, scale economies are a fact of life and appear to be pervasive even in mature industries with diverse firm populations. For these reasons, a re-appraisal of insights drawn from CRTS-based empirical results is probably justified.

The most common departure from CRTS incorporates unrealized economies of scale in production. Increasing returns to scale (IRTS), where average cost falls as output rises, often takes the form of a monotonically decreasingly average cost function, calibrated to some simple notion of a fixed cost intercept. In other words, one assumes that marginal costs are governed by the preferred CRTS production function (usually constant elasticity of substitution [CES]), but that some subset of inputs are committed *a priori* to production and their costs must be covered regardless of the output level. The total cost function may be homothetic (i.e., fixed costs involve the same mix of inputs as marginal costs), or alternatively fixed costs may be assumed to involve a different set of inputs. In either case, average costs are given by a reciprocal function of the form

$$AC = \frac{FC}{X} + MC \tag{11.1}$$

---

2 See de Melo and Tarr (1992) for methodological discussion, Roland-Holst, Reinert, and Shiells (1994) and Francois et al. (1995) for more recent applications.
3 See, e.g., Helpman and Krugman (1985) for examples from this literature.

As an alternative, scale economies can also be specified as deriving from costs that enter multiplicatively, with an average cost function like the following:

$$AC = X^{\theta-1} f(\omega) \qquad where \ 0 < \theta < 1 \qquad (11.2)$$

where ω is the input price vector, and $f(\omega)$ represents the cost function for a homogenous bundle of primary and intermediate inputs. In later discussion, we shall index the bundle of inputs by the variable Z. This type of reduced form structure can be derived, for example, from scale economies due to returns from specialization (i.e., an increased division of labour) inside firms (Francois, 1990). In reduced form, it can also represent returns to specialization on an industrywide basis of intermediate inputs, resulting in industrywide scale effects (Markusen, 1990).

With scale economies as in equation (11.1) (i.e., with fixed costs), the cost disadvantage ratio (CDR), as defined later, will vary with the scale of output. Alternatively, with a cost function like (11.2), the CDR remains fixed. The properties of the two cost functions are illustrated in Figure 11.3.

Under either approach, one "only" needs to calibrate the cost function from engineering estimates of the distance between average and marginal cost. With fixed costs, this also requires some idea about how to impute fixed cost to initial factor and/or intermediate use. In practice, it has become customary to appeal to the concept of a cost disadvantage ratio. This measure of unrealized scale economies is generally defined as

$$CDR = \frac{AC - MC}{AC} \qquad (11.3)$$

At the margin, output elasticities are equal to $(1/(1-CDR))$.

In practice, calibration of either (11.1) or (11.2) can be problematic. At a conceptual level, estimated CDRs may be based on one level of "typical" production, while the benchmark dataset we are working with corresponds to another. If we model scale economies with fixed costs and variable CDRs (i.e., equation [11.1]), then the CDR estimates can be inappropriate and even misleading. At a more basic level, the pattern of citations in the empirical literature employing scale economies is circular and converges on a set of engineering studies on scale elasticities, many of which are surveyed by Pratten (1988), and many of which date from the 1950s, 1960s, and early 1970s. Given technical change over this period, including the introduction of numerically controlled machinery, computerization of central offices, and

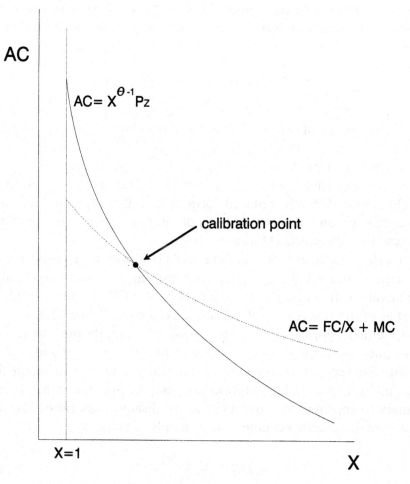

Figure 11.3. *Increasing returns with fixed costs and fixed CDRs*

the shift toward white-collar workers and away from production workers in the OECD countries, these estimates appear somewhat stale. Clearly, this is an important area for future research.

IV Market Power and Homogeneous Goods

IV.1 Perfect Competition

The standard starting point for market structure in applied trade models, and our reference point for the discussion in this section, is a competitive industry that can be described in terms of a representative firm facing

perfectly competitive factor markets and behaving competitively in its relevant output markets. Under these assumptions, the representative firm
takes price as given, and the cost structure of the industry then determines
output at a given price. Formally, we have

$$P = MC \qquad (11.4)$$

With competitive markets, real or threatened entry forces economic profits
to zero. Demand for primary and intermediate inputs then depends on the
specific cost structure that is assumed:

$$P = AC \qquad (11.5)$$

If we assume constant instead of increasing returns, then equation
(11.5) holds by definition. Otherwise, we can motivate equation (11.5) by
contestability.

IV.2 Monopoly

Our first departure from the competitive paradigm is the case of monopoly.
The monopoly specification is a straightforward extension of perfect competition. In terms of equations (11.4) and (11.5), we still have a representative
firm in the sector under consideration. The difference lies in the firm's
pricing behaviour. In particular, the monopolist does not take price as given,
but rather takes advantage of her ability to manipulate price by limiting
supply. This means that the pricing equation (11.4) is then replaced by the
following equation:

$$\frac{P - MC}{P} = \frac{1}{\varepsilon} \qquad (11.6)$$

where the market elasticity of demand is given by

$$\varepsilon = -\frac{\partial Q}{\partial P} \frac{P}{Q} \qquad (11.7)$$

The relationship of price to average cost depends on our assumptions
about the cost and competitive structure of the industry. For example, with
contestability and scale economies, entry may still force economic profits to
zero, such that the monopolist prices according to equations (11.6) and
(11.5). This is the approach taken in models with monopolistic competition.
Alternatively, we may instead have price determined by equation (11.6) in
isolation from (11.5), such that demand quantities at the monopoly price

also then determine average cost. Equation (11.5) is then replaced by a definition of economic profits:

$$\pi = (P - AC)Q \tag{11.8}$$

IV.3 Homogeneous Products and Oligopoly

Between the perfect competition and monopoly paradigms lies a continuum of possible firm distributions. When the number of firms is small enough for them to influence one another, complex strategies can arise. We will not pretend to cover the full spectrum of oligopoly theory in this chapter. Instead, we offer a set of representative specifications which indicate the decisive role that firm interactions can play in determining price, quantity, efficiency and welfare.

One vehicle often used to explore oligopoly interactions is the so-called Cournot conjectural variations model. Under this approach, we assume that each firm produces a homogeneous product, faces downward sloping demand and adjusts output to maximize profits, with a common market price as the equilibrating variable. We further assume that firms anticipate or conjecture the output responses of their competitors. Consider an industry populated by n identical firms producing collective output $Q = nQ_i$. When the ith firm changes its output, its conjecture with respect to the change in industry output is represented by

$$\Omega_i = \frac{dQ}{dQ_i} \tag{11.9}$$

which equals a common value Ω under the assumption of identical firms. Combined with a representative profit function

$$\Pi_i = PQ_i - TC_i \tag{11.10}$$

this yields the first-order condition

$$\frac{d\Pi_i}{dQ_i} = P + Q_i \frac{dP}{dQ} \frac{dQ}{dQ_i} - \frac{dTC_i}{dQ_i} = P - \frac{Q_i}{n\varepsilon} \frac{P}{Q_i} \Omega - MC = 0 \tag{11.11}$$

and also the oligopoly pricing rule

$$\frac{P - MC}{P} = \frac{\Omega}{n\varepsilon} \tag{11.12}$$

The preceding expression encompasses a variety of relevant cases. The classic Cournot specification corresponds to $(\Omega/n) = (1/n)$, where each firm believes that the others will not change their output, and industry output changes coincide with its own. Price–cost margins vary inversely with the number of firms and the market elasticity of demand, as logic would dictate. In the extreme cases, a value of $\Omega=0$ corresponds to perfectly competitive, average cost pricing, while $\Omega=n$ is equivalent to a perfectly collusive or monopolistic market. The range of outcomes between these extremes, as measured by $1\geq(\Omega/n)\geq0$, can provide some insight into the significance of varying degrees of market power.

IV.4 Market Entry and Exit

In the previous section, we defined Cournot interactions with respect to a fixed number of incumbent firms, implying barriers to entry (and exit). When we allow for the possibility of market entry and exit, then the number of firms (n) becomes endogenous, and the competitive climate in the industry under consideration varies accordingly.

Note that the price–cost margins in equation (11.12) vary with the number of firms. In particular, margins shrink with an increase in the number of firms. This is the first effect of entry. In addition, a major effect of entry and exit relates, under increasing returns, to firm-level scale economies. Entry and exit can alter the average scale of firm operations, other factors equal, and in the increasing and decreasing returns cases this can have aggregate efficiency effects.

The ultimate scope for entry, exit, or realization of scale economies in particular industries is an empirical question. In the present context, entry and exit are basically model closure problems, taking the form of limiting rules for incumbent profits, prices, or some other indicator of the return on existing operations. In general, these rules should provide an explicit link between profits and entry. We will briefly discuss two illustrative cases. One stylized approach involves assuming that there is no actual entry or exit, but that the threat of entry forces incumbent firms to limit profits. In this case, the scale of individual (representative) firm operations varies proportionately with industry output, and changes in scale economies are easy to predict. An alternative is to allow firm numbers to be endogenous and linked to profitability, while also specifying a secondary rule linking incumbent pricing to the number of firms. It is then actual entry and exit that acts as an explicit constraint on profitability. For example, endogenous Cournot conjectures of the form

$$\Omega = \frac{\Omega_0 n_0}{n} \tag{11.13}$$

imply that firms perceive their markets as becoming more competitive when the number of firms increases.

IV.5 Dynamic Interactions

While the conjectural variation approach to Cournot competition allows us to specify a set of equilibria ranging from competition to monopoly, it has been criticized by a number of authors as being an unrealistic and rather naive approach to dynamic market interactions.[4] In recent years, significant advances have been made in the theory of repeated games. It may be that, when incorporated into applied models, these theoretical approaches yield more realistic approaches to simulating market dynamics. The repeated game approach can be appealing not only because it explicitly considers the sequential and historical aspects of competition, but also because it opens up a richer universe of strategic opportunities and solution concepts. At the same time, depending on the context of the modeling exercise, one must be careful not to hang too much significance on the benefits of such methods. It is not always clear what is gained when complex, firm-level interactions are explicitly modeled for a heterogeneous sector such as "other machinery" or "transport equipment" that is clearly a collection of firms and industries (such as bicycles, automobiles, and airplanes) that are only related directly through statistical aggregation. Even at the level of only a few firms (like automobiles or mid-sized aircraft), lack of data may mean that we have replaced conjectural variations with conjectural data manufacturing.

Repeated games can yield tacit collusion (Tirole, 1988; Shapiro, 1989). The simple Cournot strategy, for example, emerges as the Nash equilibrium for a repeated game. However, this strategy does not maximize profits for the industry as a whole or for individual firms. The same is true of Bertrand competition. Under both price and quantity competition, we can construct repeated games that yield sustained collusion with higher profits. Use of repeated game frameworks may therefore allow for modeling of cases where trade liberalization, through its effect on relevant variables, can induce changes in the incentives for collusion (with reversion from collusion to Cournot equilibria, for example).

V Heterogeneous Goods

We turn next to market power in models that explicitly incorporate heterogeneous goods, emphasizing specifications involving two or more regions. In

4 See, e.g., Shapiro (1989).

the first case, a class of heterogeneous goods is assumed to be differentiated by country of origin. This is the Armington assumption, which was first introduced in Chapter 5. The second specification is based on firm-level product differentiation.

V.1 Market Power in Armington Models

In Armington models, goods are differentiated by country of origin, and the similarity of goods from different regions is measured by the elasticity of substitution. Formally, within a particular region r, we assume that demand goods j from different regions are aggregated into a composite good $Q_{j,r}$ according to the following CES function:

$$Q_{j,r} = \left[\sum_{i=1}^{R} \alpha_{j,i,r} X_{j,i,r}^{\rho_j} \right]^{1/\rho_j} \tag{11.14}$$

In equation (11.14), $X_{j,i,R}$ is the quantity of X_j from region i consumed in region r. The elasticity of substitution between varieties from different regions is then equal to σ_j, where $\sigma_j = 1/(1 - \rho_j)$. For tractability, we focus here on the non-nested case, where σ_j is identical across regions, and is equal to the degree of substitution between imports, as a class of goods, and domestic goods.[5] Within a region, the price index for the composite good $q_{j,r}$ can be derived from equation (11.14):

$$P_{j,r} = \left[\sum_{i=1}^{R} \alpha_{i,r}^{\sigma_j} P_{i,r}^{1-\sigma_j} \right]^{1-1/\rho_j} \tag{11.15}$$

At the same time, from the first-order conditions, the demand for good $X_{j,i,r}$ can then be shown to equal

$$X_{j,i,r} = \left[\frac{\alpha_{j,i,r}}{P_{j,i,r}} \right]^{\sigma_j} \left[\sum_{i=1}^{R} \alpha_{j,i,r}^{\sigma_j} P_{j,i,r}^{1-\sigma_j} \right]^{-1} E_{j,r}$$

$$= \left[\frac{\alpha_{j,i,r}}{P_{j,i,r}} \right]^{\sigma_j} P_{j,r}^{\sigma_j-1} E_{j,r} \tag{11.16}$$

---

5 A variation on this approach involves nesting the Armington structure, so that imports from different sources are first aggregated, and the composite good then competes with domestic goods in a second Armington aggregation function. This is discussed in Chapter 9. In the present context, this would involve another set of equations for each region, though the discussion would be qualitatively similar.

where E_j represents economywide expenditures in region r on the sector j Armington composite. From equation (11.16) (and fixing cross-prices), the elasticity of demand for a given variety of good X_j, produced in region i and sold in region r, will then equal

$$\varepsilon_{j,i,r} = \sigma_j + (1-\sigma_j) \left[\sum_{k=1}^{R} \left(\frac{\alpha_{j,k,r}}{\alpha_{j,i,r}} \right)^{\sigma_j} \left(\frac{P_{j,kr}}{P_{j,i,r}} \right)^{1-\sigma_j} \right]^{-1} \tag{11.17}$$

The last term in square brackets measures market share.

Monopoly At this stage, there are a number of ways to introduce imperfectly competitive behaviour. For example, for a monopolist in each region that can price discriminate between regional markets, the regional elasticity of demand (and hence the relevant mark-up of price over marginal cost) is determined in each market by equation (11.17). This implies, potentially, $n \cdot R^2$ sets of elasticity and price markup equations for an n sector, R region model. In models where different sources of demand can potentially source imported inputs in different proportions (like the SALTER and GTAP models), we then have a potential for $(n+k) \cdot n \cdot R^2$ elasticity and markup equations, where k is the number of final demand sources in each region. Hence, in large multi-region models, full regional price discrimination for each product in each region can add a great deal of numerical complexity to the model.

A greatly simplifying assumption involves assuming a monopolist that does not price discriminate, but instead charges a single markup. From equation (11.17), the aggregate elasticity of demand for a given variety will then be determined by a combination of σ_j and a weighting of $(1-\sigma_j)$ determined by regional market shares. One option is to assume that each firm forms a conjecture about the value of this weighting parameter, represented by ζ.[6] If each firm assumes that $\zeta_{j,i}$ is fixed, this means it forms a conjecture about the elasticity of demand based on $\zeta_{j,i}$ and σ_j. For a monopolist in region i producing j, we then have

$$\varepsilon_{j,i} = \sigma + (1-\sigma)\zeta_{j,i} \tag{11.18}$$

---

6 Clearly, this raises the question of how to calibrate ζ, and the relative advantages and disadvantages of endogenizing ξ. In the numeric examples in this chapter, we could have employed estimates of the reduced form elasticity of demand in general equilibrium, based on perturbations of price and as reported in Chapter 9, to calibrate $\varepsilon_{j,R}$, on the basis of the assumption that firms correctly know the marginal elasticity of demand, and assuming that this value is constant in counterfactual simulations. We have chosen instead to simplify the demand structure slightly, and to calculate these share parameters directly.

Instead of assuming that ζ is fixed (at least for relevant equilibria), we can also specify an explicit definition based on equation (11.17). For each sector, we must then add the equations necessary to endogenize ζ.

$$\zeta_{j,i} = \sum_{r=1}^{R} \frac{X_{j,i,r}}{X_{j,i}} \left(\sum_{k=1}^{R} \left(\frac{\alpha_{j,k,r}}{\alpha_{j,i,r}} \right)^{\sigma_j} \left(\frac{P_{j,kr}}{P_{j,i,r}} \right)^{1-\sigma_j} \right)^{-1} \tag{11.19}$$

This is less complex in implementation than it appears, as equation (11.19) is simply a quantity weighting of regional market shares.

There are trade-offs between the complexity of the model and the degree of discriminatory power allowed for monopolists. If we expect significant procompetitive effects related to changes in perceived market power in particular markets, through changes in either $\varepsilon_{j,i,r}$ or $\zeta_{j,i}$, then we should explicitly specify relative market power in those markets that are at least partially segmented through tariffs, transport costs, or other trade barriers.

Equations (11.17), (11.18), and (11.19) are based on a non-nested CES structure for aggregation of imports and domestic production. A common alternative Armington specification involves nested CES functions, where the lower tier is defined over all imports, and the upper tier is then defined over a composite import and the competing domestic good. In this case, equation (11.17) is replaced by the following:

$$\varepsilon_{j,i,r} \mid_{i \neq r} = \left[\sigma_j^M \left(\theta_{j,r}^D \left(\frac{\sigma_j^D}{\sigma_j^M} \right) + \sum_{k=1}^{R} \theta_{j,k,r}^M \right) + \left(1 - \sigma_j^M \right) \theta_{j,i,r}^M \right]$$

$$\cdot \left[\theta_{j,r}^D \left(\frac{\sigma_j^D}{\sigma_j^M} \right) + \sum_{k=1}^{R} \theta_{j,k,r}^M + \left[\theta_{j,r}^D \phi_{j,i,r}^M \left(\left(\frac{\sigma_j^D}{\sigma_j^M} \right) - 1 \right) \right] \right]^{-1} \tag{11.17'}$$

$$\text{and} \quad \varepsilon_{j,i,r} \mid_{i=r} = \sigma_j^D + \left(1 - \sigma_j^D \right) \theta_{j,r}^D$$

where σ^D and σ^M are the upper- and lower-tier substitution elasticities, θ^M measures market shares for imports by source at the upper tier, θ^D measures market share for the domestic good at the upper tier, and ϕ^M measures the market share of imports at the lower tier. The reader can verify that, with a non-nested specification, where $\sigma^D = \sigma^M$, this collapses to equation (11.17). With a non-discriminating monopolist, equation (11.18) will still involve a quantity weighting of regional demand elasticities.

Oligopoly If we start with the non-discriminatory case of market power, then extending our model from monopoly to oligopoly is relatively straight-forward. We keep the simplifying assumption, introduced earlier, that under oligopoly firms are identical. The key difference is that they now produce a regionally homogeneous product. Demand for a regional product is down-ward sloping, as defined by equation (11.17). We further assume that firms adjust output to maximize profits, with a common market price as the equilibrating variable, and that firms anticipate or conjecture the output responses of their competitors. This leaves us with a variation of the basic oligopoly pricing rule

$$\frac{P - MC}{P} = \frac{\Omega}{n\varepsilon} = \frac{\Omega}{n}\left[\sigma + (1-\sigma)\zeta\right]^{-1} \tag{11.20}$$

V.2 Firm-Level Product Differentiation

Next, we turn to firm-level product differentiation. This approach builds on the theoretical foundations laid by Ethier (1982) and Krugman (1979, 1980). Arguments for following this approach, where differentiation occurs at the firm level, have been offered by Norman (1990) and Brown (1987). The numeric properties of this type of model have been explored in a highly stylized model by Brown (1994). Theoretical properties of the type of model developed here, which explicitly allows for firms having different market shares in the various markets in which they operate, have been examined by Venables (1987).

General Specification of Monopolistic Competition Formally, within a region r, we assume that demand for differentiated intermediate products belonging to sector j can be derived from the following CES function, which is now indexed over firms or varieties instead of over re-gions. We have

$$Q_{j,r} = \left[\sum_{i=1}^{n} \alpha_{j,i,r} x_{j,i,r}^{\rho_j}\right]^{1/\rho_j} \tag{11.21}$$

where $\alpha_{j,i,r}$ is the demand share preference parameter, $x_{j,i,r}$ is demand for variety i of product j in region r, and $\sigma_j = 1/(1-\rho_j)$ is the elasticity of substitu-tion between any two varieties of the good. Note that we can interpret Q as the output of a constant returns assembly process, where the resulting composite product enters consumption and/or production.[7] Equation (11.21) could therefore be interpreted as representing an assembly function embedded in the production technology of firms that use intermediates in production of final goods, and alternatively as representing a CES aggregator implicit in consumer utility functions. In the literature, both cases are specified with the same functional form. Because most industrial trade involves intermediates, we lean toward the former interpretation. While we have technically dropped the Armington assumption by allowing firms to differentiate products, the vector of α parameters still provides a partial geographic anchor for production.[8]

In each region, industry j is assumed to be monopolistically competitive. This means that individual firms produce unique varieties of good j, and hence are monopolists within their chosen market niche. Given the demand for variety, reflected in equation (11.21), the demand for each variety is less than perfectly elastic. However, while firms are thus able to price as monopolists, free entry drives their economic profits to zero, so that pricing is at average cost. The joint assumptions of average cost pricing and monopoly pricing imply the following conditions for each firm f_i in region i:

$$P_{f,i} = AC_{f,i} \tag{11.22}$$

$$\frac{P_{f,i} - MC_{f,i}}{P_{f,i}} = \frac{1}{\varepsilon_{f,i}} \tag{11.23}$$

7 An approach sometimes followed involves monopolistic competition within regions, with trade only involving composite goods. Trade then is not based on firm-level differentiation (i.e., monopolistic competition), and firms in different regions do not "compete" directly in the sense emphasized by Ethier (1982), Krugman (1980), and Helpman and Krugman (1985). Rather, trade is then based on the Armington assumption regarding regional composite goods, as discussed in Chapter 9. The basic difference between this approach and the one developed in the text is the relaxation of the linkage between upper tier substitution elasticities and measures of market power for regional firms. We leave it to the reader to verify, from equations (11.35) and (11.40), that this implies a model exhibiting, in reduced form, external scale economies at the regional level.

8 The Armington assumption, or more generally allowing for region-specific differentiation, ensures uniqueness of production equilibria with v factors and $n > v$ goods. Numerically, such models exhibit properties of models with sector-specific factors of production. Otherwise, we would need explicitly to adopt a specific-factor specification, or in some other way ensure that the number of goods did not exceed the number of factors, in order to solve for unique production and trade patterns for a given set of prices. With inter-sectoral mobility of capital and labour, and more than two goods, if we assumed differentiation was only at the firm level, and that all firm output entered the CES aggregator identically regardless of origin (i.e., with identical weights), free trade production patterns with two-way trade, at least in an integrated equilibrium, would be indeterminate. See Dixit and Norman (1980, pp. 56–59). In general, the introduction of scale economies raises the likelihood of multiple equilibria.

We assume firms treat the prices of other firms or varieties as given (i.e., Bertrand behaviour). The elasticity of demand *for each firm* f_i will then be defined by the following conditions:

$$\varepsilon_{j,f_i} = \sigma_j + (1 - \sigma_j)\zeta_{j,f_i} \tag{11.25}$$

$$\zeta_{j,f_i} = \sum_{r=1}^{R} \frac{x_{j,f,r}}{x_{j,f_i}} \left(\sum_{k=1}^{n} \left(\frac{\alpha_{j,k,r}}{\alpha_{j,f_i,r}} \right)^{\sigma_j} \left(\frac{P_{j,k,r}}{P_{j,f,r}} \right)^{1-\sigma_j} \right)^{-1} \tag{11.24}$$

In a fully symmetric equilibrium, $\zeta = n^{-1}$. Under more general conditions, it is a quantity weighted measure of market share. To close the system for regional production, we index total resource costs for sector j in region i with a resource index, designated Z. In a Ricardian framework, Z is simply labour employed in production. In multiple input models, Z indexes the overall level of activity, measured on the input side. Because we have assumed homothetic cost functions, Z will move in proportion to changes in all inputs. Full employment of resources hired by firms in the sector j in region i then implies the following condition:

$$Z_{j,i} = \sum_{f=1}^{n_i} TC_{j,i,f} \tag{11.26}$$

In models with regionally symmetric firms (so that $Z_{j,i} = n_{j,i} \times TC_{j,i}$), equations (11.22)–(11.26), together with the definition of $AC = AC(x)$, define a subsystem that determines six sets of variables: x, ε, ζ, P, n, and the cost disadvantage ratio $CDR = (1 - MC/AC)$.

These equilibrium conditions are represented graphically in Figure 11.4. The full employment of resources at level Z in the regional sector implies, from equation (11.26), possible combinations of n and x mapped as the curve *FF*. At the same time, demand for variety, combined with zero profit pricing (equations [11.22] and [11.23]), imply demand-side preference for scale and variety mapped as the curve *ZZ*. Equilibrium is at point E_0. Holding the rest of the economy-wide system constant, expansion of the sector means the *FF* curve shifts out, yielding a new combination of scale and variety and point E_1. The exact pattern of shifts in n and x depends on the assumptions we make about the cost structure of firms, and about the competitive conditions of the sector. It may also be affected by general equilibrium effects.

Some Simplifications: Variety Scaling To simplify the system of equations somewhat, symmetry can be imposed on the cost structure of firms within a region. Regional symmetry means that, in equilibrium, regional firms will

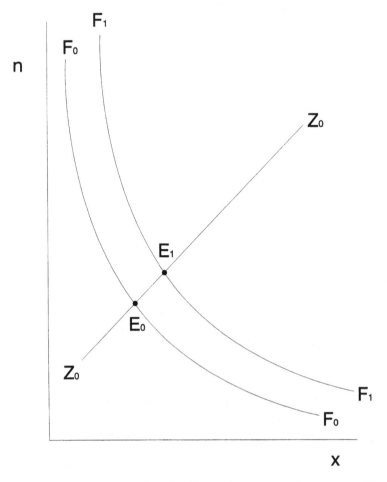

Figure 11.4. *Variety and scale effects with monopolistic competition*

produce the same quantity of output and charge the same price. Under variety scaling, we further assume that the CES weights applied to goods produced by sector j firms from region i, when consumed in a particular region r, are equal. This means we can rewrite equation (11.8) as follows:

$$Q_{j,r} = \left[\sum_{i=1}^{R} n_{j,i} \alpha_{j,i,r} \bar{x}_{j,i,r}^{\rho_j} \right]^{1/\rho_j} \tag{11.27}$$

where $\bar{x}$ is the identical consumption in region r of each variety produced in region i. Upon inspection of equations (11.27) and (11.14), it should be evident that the Armington assumption and firm-level product differentiation, in practice, bear a number of similarities. The primary difference is that, in equation (11.27), the CES weights are now endogenous, as they include both variety scaling effects and the base CES weights. We can make a further modification to equation (11.27). Noting that total quantities are $X_{j,i,r}=n_{j,r}\times\bar{x}$, we then have

$$Q_{j,r} = \left[\sum_{i=1}^{R}\gamma_{j,i,r}\tilde{x}_{j,i,r}^{\rho_j}\right]^{1/\rho_j}$$

$$\gamma_{j,i,r} = \alpha_{j,i,r}n_{j,i0}^{1-\rho_j}$$

$$\tilde{x}_{j,i,r} = \left(\frac{n_{j,i}}{n_{j,i0}}\right)^{(1-\rho_j)/\rho_j} X_{j,i,r} \qquad (11.28)$$

where $\tilde{x}_{j,i}$ is variety-scale output, and where $n_{j,i0}$ is the benchmark number of firms. Note that $\tilde{x}_{j,i}=X_{j,i}$ in the benchmark.

When we specify the system of equations for monopolistic competition using a variation of equation (11.22), the final set of equations for producing sector j composite commodities is then almost identical to that employed in standard, non-nested Armington models. The key difference is that the relevant CES weights are endogenized through $\tilde{x}_{j,i}$, as defined by equation (11.28). In fully symmetric equilibria, the reader should be able to verify that complete firm exit from particular regions is possible, since the regional CES weights are simply equal to the number of firms, which collapse to zero with full exit. Depending on the specification of the structure of monopolistically competitive markets, as detailed later, the combination of output and variety scaling can then be specified as part of the regional production function for $\tilde{x}_{j,i}$.

Scale Economies from Fixed Costs We will focus on two particular specifications of increasing returns. The first is a variation of equation (11.1), in which we assume that the cost function, while exhibiting increasing returns due to fixed costs, is still homothetic. In particular, for a firm in region i, we have

$$C(x_{j,i}) = (\alpha_{j,i} + \beta_{j,i}x_{j,i})P_{z_{j,i}} \qquad (11.29)$$

where $\alpha_{r,i}$ and $\beta_{r,i}$ represent fixed and marginal costs, and $P_{z_{j,i}}$ represents the price for a bundle of primary and intermediate inputs $Z_{j,i}$, where the production technology for $Z_{j,i}$ is assumed to exhibit constant returns to scale.

Substituting equation (11.29) into (11.22), (11.23), and (11.26), the system of equations (11.22) through (11.26), along with the definition of average cost, can be used to define general conditions for equilibrium in a monopolistically competitive industry. Starting from equations (11.22) and (11.23), the elasticity of demand can be related directly to the cost disadvantage ratio:

$$\frac{AC - MC}{AC} = \frac{\alpha_{j,i}}{\alpha_{j,i} + \beta_{j,i}x_{j,i}} = \frac{1}{\varepsilon_{j,i}} \tag{11.30}$$

The remainder of the system is as follows:

$$\varepsilon_{j,i} = \sigma_j + (1 - \sigma_j)\zeta_{j,i} \tag{11.31}$$

$$\zeta_{j,i} = \sum_{r=1}^{R} \frac{\tilde{x}_{j,i,r}}{\tilde{x}_{j,i}} \left[\sum_{k=1}^{R} n_{j,k} \left(\frac{\alpha_{j,k,r}}{\alpha_{j,i,r}} \right)^{\sigma_j} \left(\frac{P_{j,k,r}}{P_{j,i,r}} \right)^{1-\sigma_j} \right]^{-1} \tag{11.32}$$

$$Z_{j,i} = n_{j,i}(\alpha_{j,i} + \beta_{j,i}x_{j,i}) \tag{11.33}$$

Given the resources allocated to sector j in region i, as measured by the index $Z_{j,i}$, equations (11.30) through (11.33) define a subsystem of four equations and four unknowns: $n_{j,i}$, $x_{j,i}$, $\zeta_{j,i}$, and $\varepsilon_{j,i}$. In addition, the value of $\tilde{x}_{j,i}$ is then determined by equation (11.28), while producer price is set at average cost. Note that the price terms in equation (11.32) are internal prices and will hence reflect trade barriers and other policy and trade cost aspects of the general equilibrium system, implying still more equations linking producer and consumer prices.

A special case of this specification involves "large group" monopolistic competition. In large group specifications, we assume that n is arbitrarily large, such that $\zeta_{j,i}$ is effectively zero, and hence, through equations (11.30) and (11.31), the elasticity of demand and the scale of individual firms are also fixed. In this case, changes in the size of an industry involve entry and exit of identically sized firms. The full set of equations then collapses to the following single equation:

$$\tilde{x}_{j,i} = \left(\frac{Z_{j,i1}}{Z_{j,i0}} \right)^{(1-\rho_j)/\rho_j} X_{j,i} \tag{11.34}$$

Here, $X_{j,i}$ is produced subject to constant returns to scale, given entry and exit of identical firms of fixed size, which follows from our assumptions about the cost function for $Z_{j,i}$. At the same time, changes in variety are directly proportional to changes in $Z_{j,i}$.

It can be shown that proportional changes in $\tilde{x}_{j,i}$ as defined by equation (11.28) relate to proportional changes in $Z_{j,i}$:

$$\hat{x}_{j,i} = \left(\frac{\sigma_j}{(\sigma_j - 1)}\right)\hat{Z}_{j,i} + \left(\frac{(\sigma_j - \varepsilon_{j,i})\zeta_{j,i}}{(\sigma_j - 1)(1 - \zeta_{j,i})}\right)CDR\hat{\zeta}_{j,i} \qquad (11.35)$$

In equation (11.35), a ^ denotes a percentage change. What does this equation tell us? The first term is clearly positive and relates to the impact of increased resources on the general activity level of the sector, given its structure. The second term relates to changes in the condition of competition. Controlling for changes in market share for the entire regional industry, changes in $\zeta_{j,i}$ are proportional to changes in the inverse number of firms in the industry. Hence, we expect the last term to have a negative sign, but also to become smaller in absolute value as the sector expands. In particular, as the sector expands, the value $(\sigma - \varepsilon)$ converges on zero, as does $\zeta_{j,i}$, so that this last term becomes less important. This follows from the procompetitive effects of sector expansion. As the sector expands, new entrants intensify competition, forcing existing firms down their cost curves and squeezing the markup of price over marginal cost. As the sector becomes increasingly competitive, the marginal benefits of devoting more resources to the sector are greater, until at the limit the output elasticity for variety-scaled output converges on $(1/\rho)$. This is the large group case identified in equation (11.39), where $(\sigma = \varepsilon)$, such that the second term vanishes.

Scale Economies with Fixed Scale Effects We close this section with an alternative specification of monopolistic competition, in which cost functions for individual firms take the form of equation (11.2):

$$C(x_{j,i}) = (x_{j,i})^{\theta_{j,i}} P_{z_{j,i}} \qquad \text{where } 0 < \theta_{j,i} < 1 \qquad (11.36)$$

With costs described by equation (11.36), the cost disadvantage ratio is constant. From equations (11.22) through (11.25), this requires entry and exit such that the parameter $\zeta_{j,i}$ remains constant. This ensures that monopoly pricing is consistent with zero profits. Hence, the relevant subsystem of equations will be the following, along with equation (11.28):

$$(1 - \theta_{j,i})^{-1} = \sigma_j + (1 - \sigma_j)\overline{\zeta}_{j,i} \qquad (11.37)$$

$$\overline{\zeta}_{j,i} = \sum_{r=1}^{R} \frac{\tilde{X}_{j,i,r}}{\tilde{X}_{j,i}} \left(\sum_{k=1}^{R} n_k \left(\frac{\alpha_{j,k,r}}{\alpha_{j,i,r}}\right)^{\sigma_j} \left(\frac{P_{j,k,r}}{P_{j,i,r}}\right)^{1-\sigma_j}\right)^{-1} \qquad (11.38)$$

$$Z_{j,i} = n_{j,i}(x_{j,i})^{\theta_{j,i}} \qquad (11.39)$$

In purely symmetric equilibria, where firms are identical across regions, this specification yields a fixed number of firms, with sector expansion characterized strictly by expansion of existing firms. In this case, we have $\zeta = (1/n)$. Given estimated cost disadvantage ratios, equation (11.37) can therefore be used to calibrate the value of σ.

We can again show that changes in $\tilde{x}_{j,i}$ relate to proportional changes in $Z_{j,i}$:

$$\hat{\tilde{x}}_{j,i} = \left(\frac{\sigma_j}{(\sigma_j - 1)}\right)\hat{Z}_{j,i} - \left(\frac{(\sigma_j - \varepsilon_{j,i})}{(\sigma_j - 1)(\varepsilon_{j,i} - 1)}\right)\hat{n}_{j,i} \qquad (11.40)$$

Equation (11.40) is quite similar to equation (11.35). The difference is that the second term, which is again negative, now relates to the entry of additional firms. In a framework that now emphasizes output scaling, entry reduces the cost benefits of increased scale somewhat (the first term), though this is moderated by the varietal benefits of entry, which are incorporated in the first term. In symmetric equilibria or under the large group assumption, the second term is zero.

In the large group case, equations (11.35) and (11.40) are identical. Hence, while the large group specification, with fixed costs, yields pure variety scaling, the fixed CDR specification yields output scaling. These two mechanisms both imply the same reduced functional form, though the underlying story is different. In both cases, the output elasticity of variety-scale output is $1/(1 - CDR)$. In terms of Figure 11.5, these two cases correspond to curves Z_A and Z_B.

VI An Application to Korea

We now turn to a specific application involving scale economies and imperfect competition. The basic model we work with is the Korea-focused multi-region general equilibrium introduced in Chapter 9. We will limit ourselves to the Uruguay Round scenario, involving multilateral liberalization. While the model is basically the same, some modifications have been introduced for the present application. First, the current account balance is held constant in all simulations. In addition, the nested Armington structure employed in Chapter 9 has been changed to a non-nested structure. Finally, as described later, the assumption of constant returns to scale (CRTS) and perfect competition is replaced by various specifications of increasing returns to scale (IRTS) and imperfect competition.

Table 11.1 presents the trade and scale elasticities employed in the numerical assessments. The trade substitution elasticities are identical to the upper tier substitution elasticities employed earlier, in Chapter 9, in the

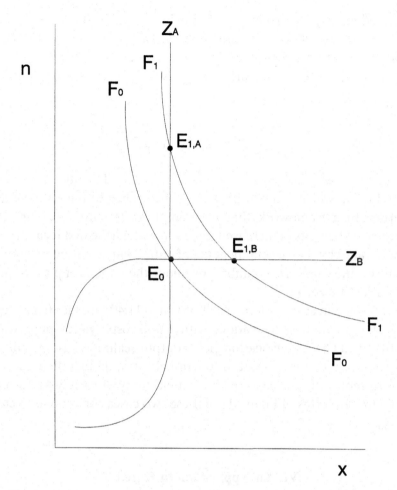

Figure 11.5. *Pure variety and pure output scaling under "large group" monopolistic competition*

nested specification. The CDR estimates are taken from various sources (primarily Pratten, 1988).

When specifying oligopolistic competition, we limit ourselves to the Korean manufacturing sector. In this case, we work with Cournot conjectural variations, as defined earlier in the chapter, assuming two values for (Ω/n), $(\Omega/n)=0.2$ and 0.5. These values are consistent with classic Cournot competition with five firms and two firms, respectively. In general, with Cournot competition and identical firms, the markup of price over average cost is defined as follows:

Table 11.1. *Trade and scale elasticities*

	trade substitution elasticity	CDR
crops	2.20	*
other agriculture	2.79	*
extraction	2.37	.05
processed food	2.38	.15
textiles	2.20	.14
apparel	4.40	.00
chemicals, rubber, and plastics	1.90	.14
metals	2.80	.14
transport equipment	5.20	.15
machinery and equipment	2.80	.12
other manufacturing	3.41	.15
services	1.94	*

$$P_{j,i} = AC_{j,i}\left(1 - CDR_{j,i}\right)\left(1 - \left(\frac{\Omega_{ji}}{\left(n_{j,i}\varepsilon_{j,i}\right)}\right)\right)^{-1} \qquad (11.41)$$

Upon inspection of equation (11.41), it should be clear that, with scale economies, Cournot behaviour can be inconsistent with positive profits. In particular, with a large enough CDR or highly elastic demand, pricing such that $MR=MC$ will imply setting $P<AC$.

Table 11.2 presents estimated oligopoly markups for Korean industry, based on equation (11.41), and derived from the benchmark 1992 dataset. These markups are a function of market shares, and of the substitution elasticities presented in Table 11.1. In some cases, like processed food, home market shares, and hence the implicit markups, are a direct result of import protection. This becomes evident when we examine the output effects of

Table 11.2. *Estimated oligopoly markups in Korea (percentage over average cost)*

	Ω/n = .2	Ω/n = .5
crops	*	*
other agriculture	*	*
extractions	*	*
processed food	21.69	81.20
textiles	15.17	48.77
apparel	7.79	24.33
chemicals, rubber, and plastics	18.31	62.77
metals	14.82	47.32
transport equipment	6.73	14.97
machinery and equipment	10.05	29.19
other manufacturing	7.44	20.79
services	*	*

trade liberalization, which exhibit significant procompetitive features for these same sectors.

Table 11.3 presents estimated output effects in Korea under alternative assumptions about Korean industry. The first set of simulation results involves CRTS and perfect competition and serves as a reference experiment. The next two columns in the table correspond to IRTS and average cost pricing. The second column involves scale economies with fixed costs, while the third involves scale economies and fixed CDRs. The estimated effects are almost identical, implying that the choice of specification of scale economies is not very important in the present experiment. Note that for a number of industrial sectors, output effects are almost double their values under CRTS, indicating the potential importance of scale effects when evaluating trade liberalization.

Table 11.3. *Scale economies, Cournot competition, and output effects in Korea (percentage changes)*

	CRTS perfect competition	IRTS AC pricing fixed costs	IRTS AC pricing fixed CDRs	CRTS Cournot $\Omega/n=0.2$	CRTS Cournot $\Omega/n=0.5$	IRTS Cournot $\Omega/n=0.5$
crops	-7.2	-7.5	-7.5	-6.9	-7.2	-7.5
other agriculture	-1.8	-1.8	-1.8	-0.4	-1.5	-0.5
extractions	-0.3	-0.9	-0.9	-0.1	-0.8	-1.4
processed food	2.8	3.7	3.8	4.4	3.5	5.9
textiles	25.2	39.8	40.4	32.6	33.2	48.5
apparel	33.8	72.5	74.9	41.5	41.4	64.3
chemicals, rubber, and plastics	2.4	3.5	3.5	5.0	7.0	9.1
metals	-2.5	-6.7	-6.7	-0.1	4.3	2.1
transport equipment	-0.8	-4.2	-4.7	1.4	7.1	-2.4
machinery and equipment	-1.7	-5.9	-5.9	-0.3	5.5	2.1
other manufacturing	10.8	19.7	21.4	13.6	17.6	26.0
services	0.1	-0.1	-0.1	0.4	1.2	0.8

We next turn to Cournot behaviour, as reported in columns 4, 5, and 6 of Table 11.3. The first two of these sets of results involve CRTS. Evidence of the procompetitive effects of trade liberalization can be seen if we compare these results with those in the first column. Recall from Table 11.2 that some sectors, like processed food and chemicals, had particularly high estimates of price over average cost markups. Because trade liberalization erodes the market power derived from protection, these markups are reduced and output increased in Cournot sectors. The result in some sectors, like chemicals and processed foods, is output effects roughly twice as great as those estimated under CRTS and perfect competition. Finally, the last column of the table combines Cournot behaviour with increasing returns. The result, across a broad range of sectors, is substantially greater output effects than those reported in the other columns. This follows from the effects of reduced market power, combined with the output boost that follows from falling average costs. Taken together, the result of IRTS and Cournot is that several manufacturing sectors expand by roughly twice the amount estimated in the benchmark experiment.

The welfare effects reported in Table 11.4 correspond to the same specifications employed in Table 11.3. Recall that we only introduce Cournot behaviour in Korea, and not surprisingly, the greatest variation in welfare results relates to Korea. In particular, the introduction of Cournot behaviour in isolation from scale economies, or IRTS in isolation from imperfectly competitive behaviour, implies a significant magnification of the estimated welfare gains for Korea. In particular, while our benchmark case involves a 0.6 percent increase in welfare, this is basically increased by a factor of 3 in columns 2 through 5. Column 6 presents estimates where we have introduced both scale economies and Cournot behaviour. Here, welfare increases by 3.2 percent, as compared to 0.6 percent in the benchmark and 1.5 to 1.9 percent in columns 2 through 5.

Finally, Table 11.5 contrasts the implications of scale economies under national product differentiation (the Armington assumption) with scale economies under firm-level product differentiation (large group monopolistic competition). While the result is a magnification of estimated benefits for Korea (4.6 percent versus 1.9 percent in columns 3 and 2), this is not true for all regions. For the region "Other Asia," welfare gains are greater with national product differentiation. For all other regions excluding ROW, firm-level product differentiation clearly implies greater procompetitive benefits than those estimated under Armington preferences.

Table 11.4. *Welfare effects (percentage) with regionally homogeneous goods, scale economies, and Cournot competition*

	CRTS perfect competition	IRTS AC pricing fixed costs	IRTS AC pricing fixed CDRs	CRTS Cournot $\Omega/n=0.2$	CRTS Cournot $\Omega/n=0.5$	IRTS Cournot $\Omega/n=0.5$
Korea	0.6	1.7	1.9	1.6	1.5	3.2
Japan	0.4	0.4	0.4	0.3	0.3	0.4
Other Asia	0.9	1.6	1.7	1.0	1.1	0.9
North America	0.2	0.1	0.2	0.2	0.2	0.2
Europe and Australasia	0.2	0.1	0.1	0.2	0.2	0.2
ROW	-0.1	-0.1	-0.1	-0.1	-0.1	-0.1

Table 11.5. *Welfare effects (percentage) with scale economies and average cost pricing – regional versus firm-level differentiation*

	CRTS perfect competition	IRTS regional differentiation	IRTS firm-level differentiation
Korea	0.6	1.9	4.6
Japan	0.4	0.4	0.8
Other Asia	0.9	1.7	1.0
North America	0.2	0.2	0.3
Europe and Australasia	0.2	0.1	0.2
ROW	-0.1	-0.1	-0.1

VII Summary and Closing Remarks

This chapter has been concerned with relationships among trade policy, imperfect competition, and industry performance. Our basic goal has been to provide an overview of linkages between trade policy and competitive behaviour, including the presentation of a menu of relatively standard specifications of imperfect competition and scale economies. As a now extensive body of applied research demonstrates, these linkages can easily dominate, in sign and/or magnitude, the production and welfare effects estimated under the perfect competition paradigm.

The empirical literature confirms a basic finding of the new trade theories, suggesting that there may be small potential gains from mild unilateral protection. However, these numerically estimated gains, like their theoretical counterparts, are often the product of single-market or partial equilibrium modeling exercises. Dixit and Grossman (1984) have rightly objected to drawing policy conclusions from this type of single-market framework for a simple reason. In general equilibrium, it is impossible to subsidize or effectively protect the entire economy. Targeting expansion of some increasing returns sectors implies targeting contraction of others. In addition, as Helpman and Krugman (1989, Chapter 8) have noted, while there may be small gains from *unilateral* protection, the apparent costs of *mutual* protection are magnified when scale economies and imperfect competition enter the picture.[9] A corollary of this last point is that bilateral and multi-lateral

9 This follows, in part, from effects related to market segmentation. To the extent that trade liberalization reduces market fragmentation, we can expect a reduction in firm markups (Baldwin and Venables, 1995).

trade liberalization tend to imply much greater welfare gains, once allowance is made for imperfect competition and scale economies, than analyses based on perfect competition and constant returns to scale would otherwise imply.[10]

As an illustration, we have offered a set of Korea-focused Uruguay Round simulation results. These results highlight rather starkly the role that imperfect competition can play in assessments of trade liberalization. While our estimates are of course sensitive to the assumptions we make, the pattern of the results demonstrates that the procompetitive effects of trade liberalization, including falling market power and expanded output in imperfectly competitive sectors, may be some of the most substantial effects following from trade liberalization. At a minimum, it is clear that the constant returns, perfect competition paradigm suppresses a number of potentially powerful mechanisms linking trade policy with industry performance.

References

Anderson, J.E. 1988. *The Relative Inefficiency of Quotas*. Cambridge, Massachusetts: MIT Press.

Baldwin, R.E. and P. Krugman. 1988a. "Industrial policy and international competition in wide-bodied jet aircraft." In *Trade Policy Issues and Empirical Analysis*, edited by R.E. Baldwin. Chicago: University of Chicago Press.

Baldwin, R.E. and P. Krugman. 1988b. "Market access and international competition: A simulation study of 16K random access memories." In *Empirical Methods for International Trade*, edited by R.C. Feenstra. Cambridge: MIT Press.

Baldwin, R.E. and A.J. Venables 1995. "Regional economic integration." In *Handbook of International Economics*, Vol. III, edited by G.M. Grossman and K. Rogoff. Amsterdam: North-Holland/Elsevier.

Bhagwati, J.N. 1965. "On the equivalence of tariffs and quotas." In *Trade, Growth, and the Balance of Payments: Essays in Honor of Gottfried Haberler*, edited by R.E. Baldwin. Chicago: Rand McNally.

Brown, D. 1994. "Properties of applied general equilibrium trade models with monopolistic competition and foreign direct investment." In *Modelling Trade Policy: AGE Models of North American Free Trade*, edited by J.F. Francois and C.R. Shiells. Cambridge: Cambridge University Press.

Brown, D.K. 1987. "Tariffs, the terms of trade and national product differentiation." *Journal of Policy Modeling* 9:503–526.

---

10 To quote Venables and Smith, "It seems unlikely, to say the least, that in a world in which all countries pursue restrictive trade policies the potential benefits of scale economies will actually be realized. One of the reasons we have institutions such as the GATT is to discourage this type of beggar-thy-neighbour policies. The fact that our analysis indicates that there may be significant potential gains from policy intervention should not be taken as establishing a case for nationalistic trade restrictions but as providing a strong rationale for negotiated reductions in trade barriers" (Venables and Smith, 1986, p. 660).

Cox, D. and R. Harris. 1985. "Trade liberalization and industrial organization: Some estimates for Canada." *Journal of Political Economy* 93:115–145.

De Melo, J. and D. Tarr. 1992. *A General Equilibrium Analysis of U.S. Foreign Trade Policy*. Cambridge, Massachusetts: MIT Press.

Devarajan, S. and D. Rodrik. 1988a. "Trade liberalization in developing countries: Do imperfect competition and scale economies matter?" *American Economic Review* 78:283–287.

Devarajan, S. and D. Rodrik. 1988b. "Pro-competitive effects of trade reform: Results from a CGE model of Cameroon." Working Paper, Harvard University.

Dixit, A. 1988. "Optimal trade policy and industrial policies for the U.S. automobile industry." In *Empirical Methods for International Trade*, edited by R.C. Feenstra. Cambridge: MIT Press.

Dixit, A. and G. Grossman. 1984. "International Trade Policy with Several Oligopolistic Industries." Discussion Paper in Economics No. 71, Woodrow Wilson School, Princeton University.

Dixit, A. and V. Norman. 1980. *Theory of International Trade*. Cambridge: Cambridge University Press.

Eaton, J. and G.M. Grossman. 1986. "Optimal trade and industrial policy under oligopoly." *Quarterly Journal of Economics* 101:383–406.

Ethier, W. 1982. "National and international returns to scale in the modern theory of international trade." *American Economic Review* 72:950–959.

Feenstra, R.C. 1988. "Gains from trade in differentiated products: Japanese compact trucks." In *Empirical Methods for International Trade*, edited by R.C. Feenstra. Cambridge, Massachusetts: MIT Press.

Francois, J.F. 1990. "Trade in producer services and returns to specialization under monopolistic competition." *Canadian Journal of Economics* 21:100–109.

Francois, J.F. 1992. "Optimal commercial policy with international returns to scale." *Canadian Journal of Economics* 23:109–124.

Francois, J.F., B. McDonald, and H. Nordström. 1994. "The Uruguay round: A global general equilibrium assessment." Centre for Economic Policy Research Discussion Paper 1067.

Francois, J.F., B. McDonald, and H. Nordström. 1995. "Assessing the Uruguay Round." In *The Uruguay Round and the Developing Countries*, edited by W. Martin and A. Winters. World Bank Discussion Paper 201.

Francois, J.F. and C.R. Shiells, 1994. *Modelling Trade Policy: AGE Assessments of North American Free Trade*. Cambridge: Cambridge University Press.

Grossman, G.M. 1991. *Imperfect Competition and International Trade*. Cambridge, Massachusetts: MIT Press.

Haaland, J. and T.C. Tollefsen. 1994. "The Uruguay Round and trade in manufactures and services: General equilibrium simulations of production, trade and welfare effects of liberalization." Center for Economic Policy Research Discussion Paper 1008.

Haaland, J. and I. Wooton. 1991. "Market Integration, Competition, and Welfare." Center for Economic Policy Research Discussion Paper No. 547.

Harris, R. 1984. "Applied general equilibrium analysis of small open economies with scale economies and imperfect competition." *American Economic Review* 74:1016–1033.

Helpman, E. and P. Krugman. 1985. *Market Structure and Foreign Trade*. Cambridge, Massachusetts: MIT Press.

Helpman, E. and P. Krugman. 1989. *Trade Policy and Market Structure.*
    Cambridge, Massachusetts: MIT Press.
Krugman, P.R. 1979. "Increasing returns, monopolistic competition, and
    international trade." *Journal of International Economics* 9:469–480.
Krugman, P.R. 1980. "Scale economies, product differentiation, and the pattern
    of trade." *American Economic Review* 70:950–959.
Lee, H. and D.W. Roland-Holst. 1995. "Trade liberalization and employment
    linkages in the Pacific Basin." *Developing Economies* 33:155–184.
Markusen, J.R. 1990. "Micro-foundations of external scale economies." *Canadian
    Journal of Economics* 23:285–508.
Markusen, J.R., J.R. Melvin, W.H. Kaempfer, and K.E. Maskus. 1995.
    International Trade: Theory and Evidence. London: McGraw-Hill.
Markusen, J.R. and A.J. Venables. 1988. "Trade policy with increasing returns
    and imperfect competition: Contradictory results from competing
    assumptions." *Journal of International Economics* 24:299–316.
Norman, V.D. 1990. "Assessing trade and welfare effects of trade liberalization:
    A comparison of alternative approaches to CGE modelling with imperfect
    competition." *European Economic Review* 34:725–745.
Pratten. 1988. "A survey on the economies of scale." In *Studies on the Economics
    of Integration.* Luxembourg: Commission of the European Communities.
Roberts, M.J. and J.R. Tybout. 1990. "Size rationalization and trade exposure in
    developing countries." Working Paper, Department of Economics,
    Georgetown University.
Rodrik, D. 1988. "Imperfect competition, scale economies and trade policy in
    developing countries." In *Trade Policy Issues and Empirical Analysis*, edited
    by R. Baldwin. Chicago: University of Chicago Press.
Roland-Holst, D.W., Reinert, K.A., and C.R. Shiells. 1994. "A general
    equilibrium analysis of North American integration." In *Modelling Trade
    Policy: AGE Models of North American Free Trade,* edited by J.F. Francois
    and C.R. Shiells. Cambridge: Cambridge University Press.
Shapiro, C. 1989. "Theories of oligopoly behaviour." In *Handbook of Industrial
    Organization*, edited by R. Schmalansee and R. Willig. Amsterdam:
    North-Holland.
Smith, A. and A.J. Venables. 1988. "Completing the internal market in the
    European Community." *European Economic Review* 32:1501–1525.
Tirole, J. 1988. *The Theory of Industrial Organization.* Cambridge: MIT Press.
Venables, A. 1987. "Trade and trade policy with differentiated products: A
    Chamberlinian–Ricardian model." *Economic Journal* 97:700–717.
Venables, A. and Smith, A. 1986. "Trade and industrial policy under imperfect
    competition." *Economic Policy* 1:622–672.
Venables, A. and Smith, A. 1991. "Completing the internal market in the
    European Community: Some industry simulations." *European Economic
    Review* 32:1501–1525.
Westerbrook, M.D. and J.R. Tybout. 1990. "Using large imperfect panels to
    estimate returns to scale in LDC manufacturing." Working Paper,
    Department of Economics, Georgetown University.

12

Capital Accumulation in Applied Trade Models

Joseph F. Francois, Bradley J. McDonald, and Håkan Nordström

I Introduction

Trade theory suggests that the more efficient utilization of productive resources following trade liberalization will lead to a one-time (static) increase
in gross domestic product (GDP). Depending on country size and the nature
of competition, terms-of-trade effects and scale effects may magnify or even
reverse the sign of these static efficiency gains. On top of the static impact,
growth theory suggests the potential for a medium-run growth effect as
static gains induce changes in savings and investment patterns. These effects
are referred to by Baldwin and Venables (1995) as *accumulation effects*. The
magnitude and direction of such effects depend on the assumed underlying
savings behaviour (fixed savings, fixed time discount factors, overlapping
generations, etc). These medium-run effects are different from the long-run,
permanent growth effects emphasized in the new growth literature. They are
grounded firmly in the capital accumulation mechanisms highlighted in classical growth theory and are not dependent on the dynamic externalities
featured in the new growth theory. In this chapter, capital accumulation
effects are explored in a general equilibrium context. Emphasis is placed on
comparison of steady states. The explicit modeling of optimization-based
transition dynamics is covered in Chapter 13.[1]

II Trade and Growth: Some Background

The gains from trade in static, perfectly competitive models stem from the
increased efficiency of resource allocation and improved consumption pos-

---

[1] For developing countries, which are by definition far from steady state, transitional effects can greatly
magnify the welfare implications of trade policy changes. See Francois, Nordström, and Shiells
(1996).

sibilities. In static models with imperfect competition, additional gains from trade may result from increasing returns to scale, as firms realize internal scale economies, and from increased product and input variety for consumers and producers, respectively. Such static gains imply a one-time change in the amount of aggregate output but not its growth rate. These effects are at the core of the welfare insights drawn from basic trade theory. Yet, numerical estimates of the static efficiency gains from trade liberalization tend to be relatively small as a percentage of GDP. For example, static assessments of the Tokyo Round and Uruguay Round typically pointed to income gains of less than 1 percent of base GDP. This is not consistent with cross-country studies of trade and income, which suggest linkages between trade policy and incomes much stronger than those identified in numerical studies of the static efficiency effects of trade policy.

The endogeneity of the capital stock has potentially important implications for the income and resource allocation effects of trade and trade policy. In particular, while the core static models of trade theory assume fixed endowments, these same models highlight the effect of trade on incomes and factor earnings. To the extent that investment hinges on income levels and expected returns, the medium- and long-term results of changes in trading conditions will include induced shifts in the capital stock. Such effects have been explored in the theoretical literature linking trade to classical growth theory (Samuelson, 1975; Smith, 1976, 1977; Srinivasan and Bhagwati, 1980). Similarly, the more recent literature on endogenous growth and trade highlights dynamic linkages among trade policy, investment, and steady-state growth (Baldwin 1989; Grossman and Helpman, 1991, 1995). The formal analysis of these processes can, of course, be complicated still further by the introduction of full or partial mobility of physical, human, and knowledge capital between trading regions, in addition to the endogeneity of the underlying available capital stock.

The empirical literature on the dynamic effects of trade policy and integration can be divided into two broad groups. The first group of studies is concerned with the modeling of current regional and global integration efforts. This includes work on the North American Free Trade Agreement (Francois and Shiells, 1994), the European Community's economic integration program (Baldwin, 1992), and the Uruguay Round (Goldin et al., 1993; Francois et al., 1994, 1995). This literature is devoted largely to the assessment of policy options and highlights estimates of the likely effects of changes in current trade regimes. The studies in the second set are historical in nature. Some assess how growth rates have been affected by past trade liberalization efforts, such as multi-lateral efforts in the post–World War II period. Others assess recent government intervention in specific dynamic, innovation-intensive industries, such as semiconductors and aircraft (Baldwin and Krugman, 1988a,b).

Among the historical studies, Reynolds (1983) asserts that economic growth in the industrial countries was the single most important factor generating growth in the Third World in the post-1945 period. In this context, one role for trade has been to provide a link for developing countries to innovation in the industrial countries. The empirical importance of the underlying policy regime, including trade policy, has also been highlighted in a number of studies. For example, Barro (1991) offers evidence that market distortions, particularly with respect to investment goods, are negatively correlated with growth rates. Barro also finds a positive relationship between human capital levels and growth rates. High levels of human capital investment are positively related to low fertility rates and high rates of physical investment. De Melo and Panagariya (1992) have concluded that, for developed countries that engaged in both regional integration arrangements and multi-lateral arrangements (i.e., the General Agreement on Tariffs and Trade), it was multi-lateral arrangements, not regional ones, that provided liberalization-related contributions to the acceleration of growth rates in the post-1945 period. Like Barro, de Melo and Panagariya also find that education is significant when explaining growth in developing countries.

Harrison (1993) draws together a variety of "openness" measures to test the robustness of the empirical findings in the trade and growth literature. The statistical significance of openness indexes points to a positive relationship between low trade distortions and growth. Harrison also investigates the direction of causality between openness and growth. It runs in both directions. Periods of high growth seem to provide an impetus for more open markets (which seems natural because it alleviates adjustment problems and reduces the resistance to change), while more open markets in turn are conducive to growth. Levine and Renelt (1992) also test the robustness of cross-country regression studies. Testing the robustness of coefficient estimates with respect to alteration in the set of explanatory variables, they were able to identify two "robust" correlations: first, a positive correlation between growth and the share of investment in GDP, and second, a positive correlation between the share of investment in GDP and the share of trade in GDP. As pointed out by Levine and Renelt, "the results suggest an important two-link chain between trade and growth through investment" (1992, p. 955).

III Accumulation Effects: Basic Theory

III.1 Income and Investment

To illustrate the capital accumulation effects of trade policy, we will follow Baldwin (1992) and start with a simple neoclassical model of economic growth. The first element is a regional "production function" linking output (Y_t) at time t to the amount of capital (K_t) and labour (L_t) employed

$$Y_t = AK_t^a L_t^{1-a}; \qquad 0 < a < 1 \qquad (12.1)$$

where A is an overall productivity parameter, and a and $1-a$ are the elasticity of output with respect to capital and labour, respectively. The relation between the stock of capital and output is plotted as YY in Figure 12.1. Note the curvature of YY, reflecting diminishing return to capital when the labour force is held constant.

To determine GDP growth, we must first determine how the capital stock grows over time via savings and investment. For a given flow of investment, the capital stock evolves over time according to the formula

$$K_{t+1} = (1-d)K_t + I_t; \qquad 0 < d < 1 \qquad (12.2)$$

where d is the fraction of the capital stock that depreciates each year (as a result of wear and tear), and I_t is the flow of current investment. Equation (12.2) states that the capital stock next period is equal to the sum of (non-depreciated) capital carried over from this period and current investment. The capital stock will be higher next period if today's investment is sufficiently large to replace worn out capital as well as to add new units to the stock.

To complete the model, we specify how much of current output is set aside for savings and investment. For the moment, we adopt the classical assumption that consumers save a fixed share (s) of income

$$S_t = sY_t \qquad (12.3)$$

where S_t is total saving. Ignoring international capital flows for the moment, knowing savings means we also know investment. Furthermore, since savings depends on income that in turn depends on the capital stock, savings depends (indirectly) on the stock of capital. (Of course, the savings investment link need not hold exactly for individual countries that can borrow abroad to finance their investment.) Assuming savings is proportionate to

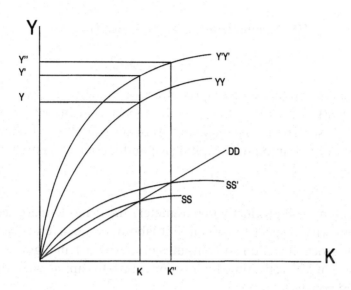

Figure 12.1. *Output and the capital stock*

income, the savings function is plotted as *SS* in Figure 12.1. The final relation plotted in Figure 12.1 is $DD=dK_t$, the amount of investment needed to replace worn-out capital in each period. The capital stock will grow over time if savings and investment are larger than the rate at which capital depreciates $(SS>DD)$, it will be constant if savings and investment are just sufficient to replace depreciated capital $(SS=DD)$, and it will fall otherwise $(SS<DD)$.

Starting from a low capital stock with high returns on investment, income will grow over time as capital is accumulated through savings and investment. However, in the absence of technical progress, this process will eventually come to an end because of the diminishing returns of adding more capital per worker. Growth in per capita income will stop at the point where savings is just enough to replace depreciated capital. The "steady-state" capital stock and output are marked in the figure by *K* and *Y*, respectively.

Now, consider the impact of trade liberalization. Assume that the region we are modeling is initially in a steady state. Further assume that trade liberalization enhances the efficiency of capital and labour, by moving resources into sectors where they are more valuable on the margin. In Figure 12.1, this is represented by an increase in the economywide productivity parameter *A*, which shifts out the production function from *YY* to *Y'Y'* for any given level of capital and labour. That is, the same amount of labour and capital can now produce more than before, as illustrated by the difference between Y' and Y in the figure. This is the short-run or static gain. Part of the additional income will be saved and invested in new capital, which in turn yields an additional income gain. (Note the positive difference between $S'S'$ and DD for the initial capital stock K, implying positive net investments.) The economy will, over time, move up to a new higher steady-state capital stock and corresponding higher output market in the figure by K'' and Y''', respectively.

Decomposing the total income gain into static and induced (medium-run) gains we have

$$\frac{(Y''-Y')}{Y}=\frac{(Y'-Y)}{Y}+\frac{(Y''-Y')}{Y} \tag{12.4}$$

where the first part is the static income gain and the second part is the induced (medium-run) gain. After some mathematical manipulations, one can show that the induced marginal gain is simply a multiple of the marginal static gain.

$$\frac{(Y''-Y')}{Y}=\left(\frac{a}{1-a}\right)\frac{(Y'-Y)}{Y} \tag{12.5}$$

That is, for each percentage increase in static income one gets an additional fraction in induced income gain over the medium run. This is sometimes referred to as the Baldwin multiplier effect of trade liberalization. (Of course, *any* policy change that improves productivity will induce higher incomes with a savings–investment linkage.) As a first-order approximation, the multiplier can be applied to static income effects to estimate medium-run income effects. For marginally small shocks, equation (12.5) holds exactly with both fixed or endogenous savings rate specifications. For discrete (i.e., large) policy changes, the distinction becomes important and equation (12.5) may prove misleading, as income effects are not likely to be neutral with respect to relative factor returns. Note that, if we interpret a as the output elasticity of capital, then equation (12.5) relates not only to equation (12.1) but more generally to marginal shocks to any linear homogenous GDP function.

The size of the induced income gain depends on the curvature of the YY schedule, which in turn depends on the elasticity of output with respect to capital, measured by the parameter a in the production function. The larger the output capital elasticity, the less curvature of the YY schedule, and the larger the induced gain in income. This may differ from country to country and there exists, as far as we know, no single, precise aggregate estimate for the world as a whole. However, a general perception is that *a* is in the range 0.25 to 0.4. This suggests a medium-run growth bonus in the range of one-third to two-thirds of initial efficiency gains.

III.2 Factor Returns and Investment

So far, we have discussed capital accumulation effects with reference to an aggregate GDP function and a fixed savings rate. We can demonstrate that our results also hold when savings rates are endogenous, and the real return to capital is fixed in steady state.[2] However, a number of complicating factors should also be kept in mind. We have shown that accumulation effects can compound initial output and welfare effects over the medium run and can magnify income gains or losses. However, how much these "accumulation effects" will supplement static effects depends on a number of factors. These include the marginal product of capital and underlying savings behaviour, sectoral interactions, and terms-of-trade effects. Results will also depend on the pattern of underlying distortions embedded in the GDP function. Whether or not the savings rate is fixed, or alternatively whether it responds to changes in the expected return to savings and investment, can have important implications.

Beyond aggregate effects, allowing the capital stock to be endogenously determined can also lead to a magnification of trade and production effects at the sectoral level. Consider, for example, the effect of an exogenous, neutral shock to the GDP function (in the previous section, we described the effects of trade liberalization in terms of such a shock to the national GDP function). We assume a small, two-good economy, producing goods $X1$ and $X2$. Good $X2$ is relatively capital intensive. The two goods are combined, through a linear homogenous aggregation function, into a composite good that can be either consumed or saved/invested. In Figure 12.2, the production possibility frontier for such an economy in steady state is represented by AB. Production is initially at point 1, and the world price line is tangent to point 1. In the figure, the GDP shock is represented by the outward shift of

---

2 To see that, for equation (12.1), a fixed savings rate or interest rate implies the same closure rule, consider the following: Under a fixed savings rate, a change in steady-state GDP will be matched by a proportionate change in steady-state investment. In particular, we have $sY = I = -\delta K$, where δ is the rate of capital depreciation. Hence, when comparing steady-state incomes Y_0 and Y_1, we can relate them to the underlying capital stocks as follows: $Y_1/Y_0 = K_1/K_0$. Alternatively, consider a fixed real interest rate. Since, with a Cobb–Douglas GDP function, the share of income allocated to capital is fixed at a, we have $\rho K = aY$. Hence, when comparing steady-state incomes Y_0 and Y_1, we can again relate them to the underlying capital stock as follows: $Y_1/Y_0 = K_1/K_0$. This equality breaks down with alternative GDP functions. See Francois, McDonald, and Nordström (1996) for a formal demonstration of this point.

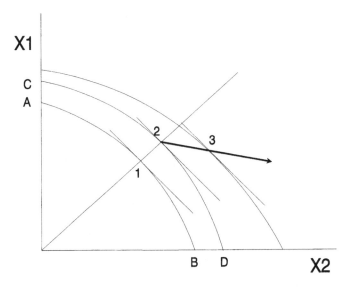

Figure 12.2. *Output expansion in a two-sector model following a neutral productivity shock*

the PPF to *CD*. Ignoring tariffs, such a shock would move the trade equilibrium from a point like 1 to a point like 2.

The shift from point 1 to point 2 is not the end of the story, however. The GDP shock has increased real income, and also the rental price of capital (and hence the relative return to investment). Under a fixed savings rate assumption, the increased income implies increased investment in steady state. Similarly, this price signal will also induce additional investment under an endogenous savings rate assumption. Assuming a declining economywide marginal product of capital (an assumption violated for interior equilibria in the Heckscher–Ohlin–Samuelson model), both savings behaviours imply an expansion of the capital-intensive sector. With endogenous savings rates, this expansion will continue until the returns to investment fall back to steady-state levels. This adjustment process will move the economy from point 2 to a new steady-state equilibrium at point 3.

Of course, trade policy shocks are not neutral with regard to factor and goods prices. Rather, they are usually associated with shifting relative price signals. In other words, characterizing the income and investment effects of a trade policy shock in terms of a shock to the aggregate GDP function is not fully satisfactory. Consider, for example, the same economy in steady state, but with a tariff on imports of good $X1$. This is represented in Figure 12.3 by the tariff-distorted production point 1, with the world price line intersecting

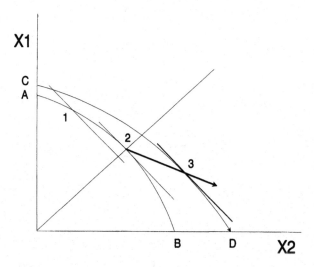

Figure 12.3. *Output expansion in a two-sector model following a capital-friendly trade liberalization*

the PPF. Trade liberalization, in the short run, implies a shift in production from point 1 to point 2, with an expansion of capital-intensive production and a contraction of labour-intensive production. Again, the results are an increase in the return to capital and investment and an induced expansion of the capital stock under both savings behaviours (fixed and endogenous savings rates). The result is continued expansion of production of $X2$, as the PPF expands from AB to CD. The new steady state is at point 3. Alternatively, the income and/or factor price effects of trade liberalization may also signal a draw-down of the capital stock. We shall refer to liberalizations that induce capital accumulation effects, through factor price effects, as *capital friendly*. Baldwin (1992) demonstrates that, when the social rate of return to capital exceeds the private rate of return, induced capital formation following a capital-friendly liberalization will enhance welfare. It should be emphasized that, in an applied trade model with policy variables interacting across primary goods sectors and factor markets, the social return to investment may exceed or understate the private return.

Beyond the second-best implications of underlying policy variables embedded in the GDP function, further complications can relate to terms-of-trade effects following induced investment. In particular, once we drop the small country assumption, the implications of capital accumulation effects will hinge on terms-of-trade effects, in addition to the profile of intertemporal social and private preferences and the rate of adjustment from one steady state to another. The mechanisms and linkages will of course become even more complex as we introduce such elements as capital mobility, scale economies and imperfect competition, endogenous innovation, or sector-specific resources.

III.3 Welfare Comparisons

In general, a policy change that forces changes in steady-state capital may or may not have welfare implications at the margin. Whether or not a steady-state gain in income from such a policy change generates greater welfare depends on the existence of a wedge between the private and social rates of return to capital. Scale economies and endogenous growth mechanisms can, of course, point to such a wedge. At a more basic level, however, even in standard models, trade policies, almost by definition, create such wedges. In essence, with trade policy simulations, we are not dealing with indirect policies directed at capital accumulation, but rather directly with the policies that drive a wedge between private and social returns to investment.

Welfare comparisons must also take into account the cost of increased capital accumulation. One option in steady-state models is to focus on consumption paths. However, consumption changes in the steady state may or may not reflect consumption effects during the transition to a new steady state. This is because of the cost of accumulating capital to reach the new steady-state level with higher capital. In models with variable savings rates, consumption may rise or fall during the transition to a new steady state. Under fixed savings rates, investment and consumption increase in tandem, and the preceding concern will not apply as new capital is paid for out of income gains. Alternatively, it may be best to model adjustment path dynamics formally (see Chapter 13) and to calculate changes in the present value of future income streams. However, in relatively large multi-region models, the implicit dynamic optimization problem can prove quite problematic.

IV A Numerical Application

We now turn to the introduction of capital accumulation effects to a CGE model. We work with the same Korea-focused model employed in Chapters 9 and 11, focusing on the full Uruguay Round scenario detailed in Chapter 9. To highlight capital accumulation effects, we adopt three alternative closure rules for the capital market. In the first, regional capital stocks are assumed to be fixed. In the other two, steady-state accumulation effects are included, under alternative assumptions of fixed savings rates and fixed real returns to investment. Variations of these closure rules have been employed by Ho and Jorgenson (1994), Haaland and Tollefson (1994), and Francois et al. (1994). In this application, we do not model changes in international financial capital flows induced by trade policy changes. Rather our capital market closure involves fixed net capital inflows and outflows. This corresponds to the joint assumptions that we have: (i) minimal cross-ownership of capital and (ii) restricted substitutability between foreign and domestic assets (Goulder and Eichengreen, 1992).

IV.1 Fixed Capital Stock Closure

The standard static capital market closure involves a fixed aggregate capital stock. We assume that, given the supply of capital, the stock of capital is allocated across the sectors of a region to equalize returns. With a fixed capital stock, we have the supply of capital defined for each period as follows:

$$K_1 = K_0 = \overline{K} \tag{12.6}$$

Trade liberalization will induce changes in the sectoral allocation of capital, but *not* in the total capital stock, under this assumption.

IV.2 Fixed Savings Rate Closure

Alternatively, under the assumption of fixed savings rates, the change in steady-state capital stocks, following a shock to the GDP function, will be proportionate to the change in the steady-state value of the GDP function itself, controlling for any changes in the price of capital. In terms of an economy that produces a composite good Y that is devoted to consumption or investment, we have

$$K_1 = K_0 \left(\frac{Y_1}{Y_0} \right) \tag{12.7}$$

where K_0 and K_1 refer to steady-state capital stocks under the initial steady-state benchmark and under the counterfactual steady state. By making the assumption that we are working with an initial steady-state equilibrium, we can solve explicitly for steady-state capital stock values. The steady-state capital stock is allocated across sectors so that returns are equalized. We do not allow for international capital movements. Changes in steady-state investment will be related to the change in the capital stock as follows:

$$I_1 = I_0\left(\frac{K_1}{K_0}\right) \qquad (12.8)$$

We may want to drop the assumption that the same composite good is either produced or invested, and explicitly model the production of capital goods. This can involve a simple transformation function between the composite good when used for consumption and alternatively when used for investment. Depending on the availability of appropriate social accounting data, this may also involve an explicit capital goods production or import function. When capital goods prices change relative to GDP, equation (12.7) must be modified. In particular, if we drop the assumption of a composite good used for consumption or investment, and explicitly model the production and/or trade of capital goods, steady-state capital would be defined as follows:

$$K_1 = K_0\left(\frac{Y_1}{Y_0}\right) \times \left(\frac{P_0}{P_1}\right) \qquad (12.7')$$

where P is an index of the relative price of investment goods.

In implementing this closure rule, we endogenize the capital stock, dropping the condition represented by equation (12.6) and replacing it with equation (12.7'). Investment is determined by equation (12.8).

IV.3 Endogenous Savings Rate Closure

When shifts in trading conditions shift the real price of capital and labour, incentives may be realized for further investment. We allow for such effects under an alternative approach that involves steady-state comparisons with endogenous capital stocks and endogenous savings rates. We again assume an initial steady state in the benchmark equilibrium. Under this closure, investment and the capital stock adjust so that the real return of capital is held, in the long run, at the benchmark level. (Operationally, this is similar to fixing the real price of labour, though the cost of increased investment must also be accounted for in the system of equations.) Underlying this condition, we are implicitly assuming that the stock of capital is at its steady-state level in the benchmark equilibrium, and that the stock adjusts in the counterfactual to return the rate of return to its steady-state level. The steady-state rate of return to capital is therefore inferred from benchmark social accounting data.

Formally, a number of strong assumptions about households are required. Households have perfect foresight (identical in this case to rational expectations). In each period, they make decisions about how much to save or consume. Households can borrow or lend freely in their regional market, and the no-Ponzi game condition is imposed (the inter-temporal budget constraint must be met). In each period s each household maximizes the following objective function:

$$U_s = \int_s^\infty u(c_t)e^{-\rho(t-s)}dt \qquad (12.9)$$

where ρ is the (constant) rate of time discount, c_t is additive in consumption of Y, and $u(.)$ exhibits a constant elasticity of substitution (i.e., it is a constant relative risk aversion [CRRA] function). Under these conditions, equation (12.9) implies that the return on investment (net of depreciation) will be $r=\rho+n$, where n is the rate of population growth. For simplicity, if we ignore population growth, the steady-state real return to capital will be constant and equal to $\bar{r}=\rho$. The discussion here is closely based on Blanchard and Fischer (1989, Chapter 2). The capital market closure rule adopted is also common in the recent endogenous growth literature (Grossman and Helpman, 1991) and is followed by Baldwin (1992).

As under the fixed savings rate closure, the result that the rate of return on capital is equal, in steady state, to a constant rate of interest ρ is a direct result of specifying a composite good model, where Y is used for consumption and investment. When capital goods production is specified explicitly, so that the price of the capital good varies relative to the price of the composite consumption good, then our closure rule must be modified so that the expected return to investment equals ρ, allowing for relative price changes between investment and consumption goods. We have the following condition:

$$r_1 = r_0 \times \left(\frac{P_1}{P_0}\right) \qquad (12.10)$$

In implementing this closure rule, we endogenize the capital stock and fix the return to capital, dropping the condition represented by equation (12.6) and replacing it with equation (12.10). Investment is determined by equation (12.8). Under this closure, a *capital-friendly* liberalization will tend to lead to accumulation effects, while alternatively one that forces down the return to capital may force decumulation effects.

V Results

Tables 12.1 through 12.5 present estimates of the welfare and macroeconomic effects of the Uruguay Round, under the assumptions of (i) a fixed

Table 12.1. *GDP quantity index (percentage change)*

	fixed capital fixed savings rate	endogenous capital fixed savings rate	endogenous capital endogenous savings rate
Korea	2.1	2.7	9.2
Japan	0.4	0.4	0.9
Other Asia	0.8	1.3	1.8
North America	0.1	0.1	0.4
Europe, Australia, and New Zealand	0.1	0.3	0.5
Rest of World	0.1	0.2	0.5

Table 12.2. *Welfare (per capita utility from private expenditure, percentage change)*

	fixed capital fixed savings rate	endogenous capital fixed savings rate	endogenous capital endogenous savings rate
Korea	2.5	2.9	3.3
Japan	0.6	0.6	0.8
Other Asia	0.6	1.1	1.3
North America	0.2	0.3	0.5
Europe, Australia, and New Zealand	0.3	0.4	0.6
Rest of World	-0.1	-0.0	0.2

capital stock, (ii) a fixed savings rate, and (iii) a fixed real price of capital. Welfare effects are proxied by a comparison of steady-state utility derived from consumption. The most striking result is the general increase in GDP and consumption-based welfare effects as capital accumulation is introduced (Tables 12.1 and 12.2). The fixed savings rate column provides some indication of the implications of income-induced investment increases for medium-run effects. At the same time, the generally larger increases under the endogenous savings rate closure suggest that the Uruguay Round is capital friendly. Hence, while static income gains imply increased savings and investment (compare column 1 and column 2 of Table 12.1), the increased return to capital induces a further increase in investment, as suggested by column 3. This is confirmed in Table

Table 12.3. *Percentage change in real investment returns, by region*

	fixed capital fixed savings rate	endogenous capital fixed savings rate	endogenous capital endogenous savings rate
Korea	7.6	6.9	0.0
Japan	1.1	1.0	0.0
Other Asia	1.2	0.6	0.0
North America	0.8	0.7	0.0
Europe, Australia, and New Zealand	1.2	0.7	0.0
Rest of World	0.7	0.5	0.0

Table 12.4. *Regional capital stocks (percentage change)*

	fixed capital fixed savings rate	endogenous capital fixed savings rate	endogenous capital endogenous savings rate
Korea	0.0	1.2	15.8
Japan	0.0	0.0	1.4
Other Asia	0.0	1.1	2.2
North America	0.0	0.2	1.1
Europe, Australia, and New Zealand	0.0	0.4	1.2
Rest of World	0.0	0.4	1.0

12.3, where the real return to investment increases even with induced investment based on rising real incomes. This leads to further capital accumulation, as indicated in Table 12.4. An important qualitative result is the reversal in the sign of welfare effects for the Rest-of-World region when savings rates are endogenous. This illustrates an important feature of fixed and endogenous savings closures – they can lead to qualitatively different results.

Another important effect illustrated in the tables relates to large expansion of small economies. Adopting a steady-state closure rule with dynamic optimization and a fixed rate of time discount pegging the interest rate in steady state, as in equation (12.10), can lead to relatively large adjustments in savings and steady-state capital stocks. In particular, with regional aggre-

Table 12.5. *Volume of merchandise exports (percentage change by region)*

	fixed capital fixed savings rate	endogenous capital fixed savings rate	endogenous capital endogenous savings rate
Korea	12.9	13.6	21.6
Japan	4.6	4.6	5.2
Other Asia	5.4	6.0	6.6
North America	3.3	3.4	3.9
Europe, Australia, and New Zealand	4.0	4.2	4.6
Rest of World	2.8	3.0	3.4

gation schemes that involve relatively "small" regions, where internal prices are strongly linked to external prices and trade policy wedges, massive adjustments in capital stocks may be necessary to reach a new steady state following a policy shock.[3] A mild example of this process is illustrated by Korea in the present application. In this aggregation, Korea is the smallest region. Not coincidentally, under the endogenous savings rate closure, it also realizes the largest capital stock expansion. The mechanisms linking large internal expansion to changes in external prices are also manifested by a very large expansion in export quantities (Table 12.5). This is another case where alternative closure rules lead to conflicting qualitative results.

VI Extensions

The implications of trade and trade policy relate not only to static resource allocation efficiencies, but also to accumulation of capital (human, knowledge, and physical) and negative accumulation (i.e., depletion) of natural resources. As the older and more recent growth literatures have emphasized, such effects have dynamic implications for the level and the growth of income. Empirical evidence also points (Levine and Renelt, 1992) to an important linkage among trade policy, investment, and the path of income. In this chapter we have emphasized the more basic of these effects related to

3 For example, we leave it to the reader to verify that, in a Heckscher–Ohlin–Samuelson model of a small country with an interior equilibrium (i.e., where both goods are produced), if we assume an initial steady state, then any shock that drives up the return to capital will force the economy onto a dynamic path that leads either to specializing in the capital intensive good or to becoming a large country. This is because world prices alone determine factor prices in such a model.

investment and the accumulation of capital. Trade and investment linkages have been explored in the context of simple steady-state closure rules linking trade to consumption, production, and investment. We have modeled explicit linkages between investment and income levels, and between investment incentives (i.e., real factor prices) and capital accumulation. When policy shocks are *capital friendly*, induced investment may be greater than that suggested by current savings rates. Of course, the importance of this effect will hinge on the sensitivity of savings rates with respect to real returns. Empirical evidence points to a sensitivity of savings to income, such that income shocks can be magnified by induced savings (see Carroll and Weil, 1993). However, it is not clear to us that we should expect trade policy shocks to induce discernible first-order changes in the *rate* of savings (see Kotlikoff, 1989).

An obvious direction for extension relates to cross-border investment flows. The closure rules developed here are extensions of a standard CGE assumption, regional capital markets. In a small country context, international capital can be introduced with rules similar to the fixed real return closure developed here (see Sobarzo, 1994). In a large country context, the rules implementation is more complex (see Goulder and Eichengreen, 1992). Ideally, in the context of steady-state analysis such efforts should be motivated by a belief that long-run capital flows are variant to trade policy changes. However, in our view the empirical evidence on global capital mobility is mixed at best (Feldstein and Horioka, 1980; Obstfeld, 1985). On net, it points to a strong long-run correlation between regional savings rates and regional investment rates, which is a "standard" CGE assumption. Even so, CGE-based work on capital flows under NAFTA indicates that such effects, when they do occur, may swamp direct trade effects, at least in the short run (Brown et al., 1992; Brown, 1994).

References

Baldwin, R.E. 1989. "The growth effects of 1992." *Economic Policy* 4:247–283.
Baldwin, R.E. 1992. "Measurable dynamic gains from trade." *Journal of Political Economy* 100:162–174.
Baldwin, R.E. and P. Krugman. 1988a. "Industrial policy and international competition in wide-bodied jet aircraft." In *Trade Policy Issues and Empirical Analysis*, edited by R.E. Baldwin. Chicago: University of Chicago Press.
Baldwin, R.E. and P. Krugman. 1988b. "Market access and international competition: A simulation study of 16K random access memories." In *Empirical Methods for International Trade*, edited by R.C. Feenstra. Cambridge, Massachusetts: MIT Press.

Baldwin, R.E. and A.J. Venables 1995. "Regional economic integration." In *Handbook of International Economics*, Vol. III, edited by G.M. Grossman and K. Rogoff. Amsterdam: North-Holland/Elsevier.

Barro, R.J. 1991. "Economic growth in a cross section of countries." *Quarterly Journal of Economics* 106:407–444.

Blanchard, O.J. and S. Fischer. 1989. *Lectures on Macroeconomics*. Cambridge, Massachusetts: MIT Press.

Brown, D. 1994. "Properties of applied general equilibrium trade models with monopolistic competition and foreign direct investment." In *Modelling Trade Policy: AGE Models of North American Free Trade,* edited by J.F. Francois and C.R. Shiells. Cambridge: Cambridge University Press.

Brown, D.K., A.V. Deardorff, and R.M. Stern. 1992. "A North-American free trade agreement: Analytical issues and a computational assessment." *World Economy* 15:11–29.

Carroll, C.D. and D.N. Weil. 1993. "Saving and growth: A reinterpretation." NBER working paper 4470, September.

De Melo, J.M. and A. Panagariya. 1992. "Regional integration: An analytical and empirical overview." Presented at the World Bank and CEPR Conference on New Dimensions in Regional Integration, Washington, D.C.

Feldstein, M. and C. Horioka. 1980. "Domestic savings and international capital flows." *Economic Journal* 90:314–329.

Francois, J.F., B. McDonald, and H. Nordström. 1996. "Trade liberalization and the capital stock in a multilateral framework." Centre for Economic Policy Research discussion paper.

Francois, J.F., H. Nordström, and C. Shiells. 1996. "Transition dynamics and trade policy reform in developing countries." Centre for Economic Policy Research discussion paper.

Francois, J.F., B. McDonald, and H. Nordström. 1994. "The Uruguay Round: A global general equilibrium assessment." Centre for Economic Policy Research Discussion Paper 1067.

Francois, J.F., B. McDonald, and H. Nordström. 1995. "Assessing the Uruguay Round." Paper 6, World Bank Conference, The Uruguay Round and the Developing Economies.

Francois, J.F. and C.R. Shiells. 1994. *Modelling Trade Policy: AGE Assessments of North American Free Trade*. Cambridge: Cambridge University Press.

Goldin, I., O. Knudsen, and D. van der Mansbrugghe. 1993. *Trade Liberalisation: Global Economic Implications*. Paris: OECD and World Bank.

Goulder, L.H. and B. Eichengreen. 1992. "Trade liberalization in general equilibrium: Intertemporal and inter-industry effects." *Canadian Journal of Economics* 25:253–280.

Grossman, G.M. and E. Helpman. 1991. *Innovation and Growth in the Global Economy*. Cambridge, Massachusetts: MIT Press.

Grossman, G.M. and E. Helpman. 1995. "Technology and trade." Centre for Economic Policy Research Discussion Paper No. 1134.

Haaland, Jan and T.C. Tollefsen. 1994. "The Uruguay Round and trade in manufactures and services: General equilibrium simulations of production, trade and welfare effects of liberalization." Centre for Economic Policy Research Discussion Paper No. 1008.

Harrison, A. 1993. "Openness and growth: A time-series, cross-country analysis for developing countries." World Bank, mimeo.

Ho, M.S. and D.W. Jorgenson. 1994. "Trade policy and U.S. economic growth." *Journal of Policy Modeling* 16:119–146.

Kotlikoff, L.J. 1989. *What Determines Savings?* Cambridge, Massachusetts: MIT Press.

Levine, R. and D. Renelt. 1992. "A sensitivity analysis of cross-country growth regressions." *American Economic Review* 82:942–963.

Obstefeld, M. 1985. "Capital mobility in the world economy: Theory and measurement." NBER Working Paper No. 1692.

Reynolds, L.G. 1993. "The spread of economic growth to the Third World." *Journal of Economic Literature* 21:941–980.

Samuelson, P. 1975. "Trade pattern reversals in time-phased Ricardian systems and intertemporal efficiencies." *Journal of International Economics* 5:209–364.

Smith, M.A.M. 1976. "Trade, growth and consumption in alternative models of capital accumulation." *Journal of International Economics* 6:385–388.

Smith, M.A.M. 1977. "Capital accumulation in the open two-sector economy." *Economic Journal* 87:273–282.

Sobarzo. H.E. 1994. "The gains for Mexico from a North American free trade arrangement: An applied general equilibrium assessment." In *Modelling Trade Policy: AGE Models of North American Free Trade,* edited by J.F. Francois and C.R. Shiells. Cambridge: Cambridge University Press.

Srinivasan, T.N. and J.N. Bhagwati. 1980. "Trade and welfare in a steady state." In *Flexible Exchange Rates and the Balance of Payments*, edited by J.S. Chipman and C.P. Kindleberger. Amsterdam: North-Holland.

13

Dynamics of Trade Liberalization

Christian Keuschnigg and Wilhelm Kohler

1 Introduction

Why should we bother about making computable general equilibrium (CGE) trade policy models dynamic? After all, the theory of commercial policy is largely static in nature, focusing on the welfare consequences of production and consumption distortions attendant upon various trade policy measures. These concerns, one might argue, are adequately captured in static CGE models and, therefore, little can be gained by imposing dynamic machinery on our CGE models, which are sometimes quite hard to digest anyway.

Our response to this question is that any treatment of trade liberalization on the basis of static theory potentially misses an important part of the story. Suppose we know that the static efficiency gains of some proposed measure of trade liberalization (or integration) amount to a 2 percent increase of gross domestic product (GDP). Should we conclude that welfare of all individuals will increase by this percentage amount? Trade theorists are quick to point out that we should not. For one thing, there may be consumption gains in addition to production gains, ultimately leading to a larger than 2 percent *equivalent income variation*. Moreover, depending on their factor ownership position, individuals may be affected in perhaps dramatically different ways by the policy shift in question. In other words, efficiency gains are likely to have *distributional implications* which should not be ignored in careful policy evaluation. These are the concerns that static CGE models are geared to capture in a rigorous way, and they are addressed in other chapters of this book. But suppose our policy also increases investment and thus the capital stock. Without going into details at this stage, our intuition tells us

We should like to thank the Austrian Ministry of Science for financial support. Christian Keuschnigg also gratefully acknowledges support through the Erwin Schrödinger Foundation for a visiting research fellowship at Princeton University.

that the 2 percent static efficiency gain may easily be dwarfed by *accumulated growth effects*. This, at any rate, seems to be a presumption very often alluded to in the rhetoric of trade liberalization, and it is in striking contrast to the absence of growth effects in many numerical treatments of commercial policy. But how are we to evaluate such growth effects in welfare terms? Growth requires investment, and thus forgone consumption or increased foreign indebtedness (if the economy has access to world capital markets). While adding a simple mechanism of capital accumulation to a static CGE model may enable us to capture some of the *positive aspects* of growth (see Chapter 12), it is quite clear that a satisfactory *welfare analysis* requires introducing intertemporal preferences of households (who decide on savings), as well as intertemporal optimization of firms (who decide on investment). Indeed, one might argue that extending the model structure in this way is necessary in the first place to identify precisely why a given commercial policy should have growth effects at all, in addition to the static distortionary effects emphasized by traditional theory. Extending CGE models to such intertemporal optimization is the major theme of this chapter. In addition to a general motivation and a brief survey of the relevant literature we present a specific CGE model featuring full intertemporal optimization and overlapping generations which allows us to treat important growth implications of commercial policy. We illustrate this by applying our model, which is calibrated to the Austrian economy, to various commercial policy scenarios.

In addition to giving precise meaning to the notion of *dynamic gains from trade*, intertemporal models allow one to address adequately *current account effects* of commercial policy, which invariably command a high level of attention in practical policy debates. Trade theory has a longstanding tradition of putting current account effects into the realm of macroeconomic analysis. This explains why they have for such a long time largely remained outside the scope of CGE trade policy analysis, which is firmly rooted in the microeconomics of exchange. Specifically, current account effects are either assumed away or else are not subject to any intertemporal resource constraint in static CGE models. Traditional macroeconomics of commercial policy, on the other hand, is largely based on models with distinctly Keynesian features, such as price rigidities and unemployed resources, with relatively simple savings and investment hypotheses and hardly any model structure pertaining to reallocation and distribution, which are so crucial to both the analytical theory of commercial policy and CGE trade policy experiments.[1] However, more recently a whole strand of analytical studies

---

1 For a survey of traditional macroeconomics of protection, see Krugman (1982).

has emerged which address current account adjustment to commercial policies (or analogous "shocks," such as terms of trade changes) within a framework of intertemporal optimization, featuring complete price flexibility and due emphasis on reallocation and distribution aspects.[2] This work has identified a number of interesting channels through which commercial policy, though not primarily aimed at intertemporal decision making, is likely to have important intertemporal effects which show up in a certain pattern of current account dynamics and a long-run change in the level of foreign indebtedness. Hence, incorporating intertemporal optimization in CGE models allows us to demonstrate, numerically, how the pattern of savings and investment which lies behind growth effects translates into a certain pattern of current account dynamics, and to separate these from welfare issues in a rigorous way. This is very important in view of the fact that policy debates in practice very often tend to identify a short-run current account improvement as something which is desirable per se.

An additional point relates to the inherent dynamics which typically characterizes commercial policy. Thus, trade liberalization is very often *anticipated* as being phased in over several periods, rather than taking agents by surprise in a once-and-for-all manner. Moreover, some protectionist measures may be *temporary* in nature, because of certain legal restrictions, such as envisaged by certain General Agreement on Tariffs and Trade (GATT) provisions (countervailing duties, safeguard protection, or antidumping). In either case, it is to be expected that such commercial policy scenarios generate interesting time profiles of adjustment which may be identified with the aid of an intertemporal CGE model. The preference, often revealed by policymakers, for a certain degree of gradualism in policy implementation probably has to do with some vague notion of minimization of adjustment costs. Such costs can be (and usually are) made explicit in intertemporal models, allowing the modeler to evaluate alternative adjustment paths in welfare terms, where static models to a large extent have to be agnostic.

The chapter is organized as follows. In Section II, we present more details as to the advantages of adding intertemporal optimization to large-scale CGE models, and we provide a brief survey of the relevant literature. As illustration, in Section III, we present the structure of our own model and comment on some of the methods that we have employed when calibrating the model to an Austrian data set. Section IV turns to an application of this model to certain tariff policy scenarios, featuring both gradual liberalization across the board and transitory protection of individual sectors. Section V concludes the chapter with a general summary.

---

2 A selective list of references includes Matsuyama (1988), Gavin (1990, 1991), Sen and Turnovsky (1989), and Engel and Kletzer (1990).

II Dynamic Effects of Commercial Policy

For the sake of a clear focus, we begin by stating precisely what we mean by dynamic effects of commercial policy. One of the most important questions that come up here is whether or not trade policy is allowed to affect the (long-run) *rate of growth*. Traditional growth theory of the Solow type does not allow for any systematic influence of this kind. The long-run rate of growth in GDP is essentially regarded as being exogenous and equal to the rate of growth of effective labor units, or determined by innovation, which is, in turn, similarly treated as an exogenous influence. Recent developments of growth theory, however, have in various different ways endogenized the technology factor, and this has also served to identify channels through which commercial policy may influence the long-run growth rate. The incorporation of endogenous growth channels in CGE models is still in its infancy and, therefore, remains outside the scope of this chapter.[3]

But even if the policy in question is not allowed to have any lasting influence on the *rate of growth*, it may importantly affect the long-run *levels* of income per capita. This is what Baldwin (1989) has called the *medium-term growth bonus*. The easiest way to capture this bonus numerically is to specify some aggregate production function and to postulate a Solow-type savings and investment relationship which says that a constant fraction of periodic output is saved and invested in physical capital. The static efficiency gain then shifts both the output and the savings-and-investment schedules upward and, with unchanged population growth and depreciation, initiates accumulation. The long-run increase in GDP, then, is clearly larger than the static efficiency gain. By exactly how much depends on the extent of external scale effects that one wishes to incorporate into the production function. Such external scale effects may, in fact, even generate an endogenous growth model where the policy in question affects the long-run growth rate (long-run growth bonus). This is the knife edge case in which the accumulated factor exhibits a constant overall marginal productivity, due to its external effect on the state of technology.[4] Baldwin (1989, 1993) uses a Cobb–Douglas production function and resorts to econometric evidence on the relevant parameters (including an externality parameter) to compare the growth effects of the European internal market program to the static gain

---

3 For a general survey of various relationships between trade and growth, see Francois and Shiells (1993).

4 The case where the accumulated factor exhibits increasing marginal productivity involves explosive behavior (and is unreasonable on this account), whereas the remaining case of diminishing marginal productivity brings us back to the traditional Solow model. See the discussion by Romer (1994), Solow (1994), Grossman and Helpman (1994), and Pack (1994).

reported by the European Commission. He obtains a medium-term growth bonus which is between 30 percent and 136 percent of the static gain, depending on the parameter values for the externality involved and the country considered. If accumulation of human capital is considered in addition to accumulation of physical capital, then the static efficiency gain is tripled by the growth effect. These numbers serve as a first indication as to the magnitude of the dynamic effects involved.

Suppose we have numbers like these that we believe in. What, then, are the welfare implications of our policy? Intuition tells us that the extra welfare resulting from accumulation is much lower than the extra output that it generates, for accumulation requires forgone consumption. We have already emphasized in the introduction that any satisfactory treatment of welfare issues requires introducing intertemporal preferences. One way to do this is to stipulate a representative, infinitely lived household with an additively separable intertemporal utility function. We may briefly explore the implications of this for the aggregate approach considered previously. If households choose an intertemporal allocation of their lifetime resources so as to maximize such a utility function, the steady-state capital stock is governed by the condition that the marginal private rate return to capital be equal to the rate of time preference plus the rate of depreciation. Knowing these parameters, one can then calculate long-run accumulation effects and medium-run growth bonuses exactly as before, but it turns out (as expected) that such an accumulation per se does not guarantee a welfare increase. Indeed, Baldwin (1992) shows that if there is no divergence between the social and private return to capital the welfare effect of a small trade liberalization is entirely determined by the static efficiency gain. The future increase in consumption facilitated by growth is exactly offset, in welfare terms, by the necessary forgone consumption. This is a very important point which tends to be overlooked in policy oriented debates where growth bonuses are sometimes equated with extra welfare. There are, of course, many ways in which a divergence may arise between the social and private returns to capital. In this regard, a distinction may be drawn between the type of externalities emphasized by the new growth literature and distortions due to taxes/subsidies which may similarly drive a wedge between the social and private returns to capital. Baldwin (1992) calibrates a specific model of the former type and calculates that the implied dynamic gains from trade are significant, though still small relative to the static gains from trade. As to the divergences caused by taxes/subsidies, this is where we might hope for help from CGE models, since a detailed representation of a whole system of taxation has traditionally been a prime concern in applied general equilibrium modeling. In a further step, one might then merge the two aspects by incorporating "new growth" externalities also in large-scale CGE models, but we have already indicated that this is still part of a future agenda, and we shall restrict this chapter to the dynamic implications of the type of tax imposed divergences that are at the core of conventional CGE models.

Whether there will be dynamic gains or losses from trade liberalization depends on the direction of the divergence, and on whether liberalization will actually increase or reduce the marginal return to the accumulated factor. The aggregate production function approach outlined relies on some external estimate for the static efficiency gain and identifies this as a Hicks-neutral productivity boost. A dynamic welfare gain would then materialize if the social marginal rate of return to capital were to exceed the rate of time preference plus rate of depreciation, and vice versa. However, from a trade theory perspective an increase in the marginal productivity of capital seems far from certain. Thus, in the two-commodity world of the Heckscher–Ohlin–Samuelson model the marginal productivity of capital is governed by the Stolper–Samuelson effect, while in the Ricardo–Viner model the rate of return is industry specific, defying a general conclusion for the economy as a whole. Again, CGE analysis seems the appropriate way to identify the precise way in which sectoral marginal productivities of capital (or the single marginal productivity if capital is assumed mobile, as between sectors) respond to a given commercial policy scenario. We may also add that a CGE approach allows one to consider large policy changes, in which case accumulation has welfare implications even without any divergence of the sort indicated.

Equating investment with savings, as in all the approaches discussed so far, ignores the possibility of international borrowing, or mobility of financial capital, which is such an important feature of the present day world economy. This is of particular relevance if the focus of the analysis is on a single country or a subgroup of countries. The appropriate way to allow for international capital mobility is to model investment independently of savings. A convincing way to accomplish this is to assume that installation of new capital is costly. Specifically, if we assume that it is subject to some form of convex adjustment cost, we may view investment as being governed by the kind of intertemporal optimization by forward looking agents that we have already encountered on the household side. With investment thus being divorced from the savings decision, absorption is also divorced from income. As a consequence, current account dynamics are endogenously determined by intertemporal optimization and, therefore, are also subject to an intertemporal resource constraint.

The first study of this kind was Goulder and Eichengreen (1989), where the focus is on savings and investment promotion. In Eichengreen and Goulder (1991) and Goulder and Eichengreen (1992), the same model (called GE model in what follows) is applied to commercial policy.[5] We shall abstain from discussing any model details at this stage. We focus, instead, on the broad characteristics and the issues on which the GE model and other models of this kind have been brought to bear. Details will more conveniently be discussed in connection with the relevant parts of our own model in the following section. The GE model is a two-country model (the United States and the rest of the world), featuring a representative, infinitely lived household with exogenous labor supply. A unique feature which proves of crucial importance in almost all model applications is an assumed preference of households for domestic assets (corporate debt and equity) in their portfolio decisions. This gives rise to diverging interest rates for the two countries. Moreover, it allows the model to capture varying degrees of international mobility of (financial) capital. Households allocate expenditure across time so as to maximize lifetime utility subject to a dynamic budget constraint. The production side of both countries features maximization of sectoral firm values which are determined in a forward looking way by a no-arbitrage condition incorporating risk adjustment and a rich structure of taxation. Physical capital is sector-specific and its accumulation is subject to convex adjustment costs. The model covers ten different sectors with conventional utility nests. Solution of the model underlies the assumption of perfect foresight.

In Goulder and Eichengreen (1989) the model is used to evaluate two different savings and investment promoting tax policies in terms of their effect on the capital intensity of production, export performance (taken to proxy international competitiveness), and trade balance. The two policies considered are a reduction in the marginal income tax rate, balanced in a revenue neutral way by increased indirect commodity taxation (savings promotion), and an increase in investment tax credits (investment promotion). It turns out that in the presence of international capital mobility the outcome is significantly different for the two policies, although both imply a medium-term growth bonus. Savings promotion increases exports (and the trade balance) in the short run but hurts export performance in the long run, while the reverse is true with respect to exports (but not the trade balance) for investment promotion. These results are driven by the capital account reactions to the two types of policies, and the resulting interest rate effects.

---

5 The model is also discussed in Bovenberg and Goulder (1991), which, in addition, also contains more general observations on the desirability of extending CGE models to intertemporal optimization.

The GE model compares the counterfactual growth path of the model economy to a benchmark steady-state growth path with zero foreign indebtedness and, therefore, balanced trade and current account. Eichengreen and Goulder (1991) generate a growth path with an initial trade (and current account) deficit (by an assumed increase in households' time preference and an exogenous increase in public expenditure, respectively), and then investigate what the model can tell us about the effects of certain policies that are sometimes proposed to cure trade deficits. It is important to see that a model of this kind would never view a trade deficit at any point in time as undesirable per se; hence the motivation of the exercise is entirely based on the fact that measures to reduce a given trade deficit are often proposed in practical policy debates, in particular in the United States. Given the intertemporal constraint on the trade balance, it is clear that such measures can only change the time profile of the trade balance, with its present value remaining the same in each case. The results are as expected: Both a temporary and a permanent import surcharge reduce the trade deficit in early periods and reduce the trade surplus in later periods. Again, the degree of international capital mobility is quite important, in particular for the short-run trade balance effect. Both policies also entail a medium-term growth bonus. Two important further aspects of this model application are noteworthy. Since the trade deficit is introduced via an exogenous shock, it is possible to discriminate between the effects of import surcharges under different assumptions about the cause of the initial trade deficit. Moreover, since the model is rigorously based on optimization, it also gives the welfare consequences of the policies in question, in addition to their trade balance effects. An import surcharge is revealed to increase welfare, measured by an equivalent wealth variation (discussed later), but this effect is larger for a permanent than for a temporary surcharge. It should be noted, however, that this is due to favorable terms of trade effects, not to the short-run improvement of the trade balance as such. Hence U.S. welfare increase is at the expense of the rest of the world.

In Goulder and Eichengreen (1992), the GE model is used to evaluate the positive and normative consequences of U.S. tariffs and some non-tariff trade barriers. As with the import surcharge, the results are importantly driven by terms of trade effects. The terms of trade deteriorate when a unilateral tariff removal occurs, and this causes a U.S. welfare loss. We also observe a negative medium-run growth "bonus," but in light of what we have said we should be cautious in equating this with a negative dynamic gain which aggravates the terms of trade effect. By way of contrast, eliminating quantitative restrictions increases U.S. welfare, because the quota rents are modeled so as to accrue to the foreign country. Also, in this case the medium-run growth bonus is positive. International capital mobility lowers the welfare loss in the case of tariff removal and increases the welfare gain of eliminating quotas. If one assumes that the foreign country has the same system of tariffs and quotas, multilateral liberalization is a Pareto improvement. Finally, we observe a temporary deterioration of the trade balance at the tariff removal, whereas the trade balance improves on impact if we eliminate quotas. In the long run, both policies lead to a trade surplus and increased foreign indebtedness.[6]

The GE model assumes an exogenous effective labor supply which grows at an exponential rate. Endogenizing labor supply introduces a further important channel through which medium-term growth effects might emerge. Cheaper commodities may induce households to substitute commodity consumption for leisure and, thus, to increase their labor supply.[7] This exerts a downward pressure on wages and initiates capital accumulation. An important CGE model capturing such a mechanism has been presented by Jorgensen and Wilcoxen (1990), where it is used to evaluate environmental policies. In Jorgensen and Ho (1993), the model (henceforth called the JWH model) is applied to a trade policy scenario. The JWH model is unique in several respects, only some of which can be mentioned here. It imposes exogenous time trends at various places in order to take into account important developments not explained by the model itself. Thus, there is an exogenous productivity growth which operates differently as between industries and which also depends on factor prices. To make the model consistent with a steady-state equilibrium, however, productivity growth is assumed to take a logistic time trend, so that it peters out in the long run. A further point worth mentioning is that the JWH model, like the GE model, assumes that imports are imperfect substitutes for home produced goods, but it incorporates a time trend of (price independent) import penetration. As with the other time trends, this effect must eventually disappear for the economy to reach a well defined steady state. On the consumption side, the model allows for non-homothetic preferences and, again, some boundary has to be im-

---

6 Apparently, in this model, a long-run increase in foreign indebtedness does not require any trade deficit along the adjustment path. This contrasts with our own model presented later, but the difference is easily explained. In the GE model, domestic wealth as well as the net foreign asset position are denominated in domestic currency, whereas in our model all assets are denominated in terms of import goods whose prices are all normalized to unity and remain constant throughout any counterfactual exercise. In the GE model, the exchange rate plays an important role in commodity market clearing since it enters the relative price of domestic to foreign commodities. It will, therefore, typically change on impact, and this has revaluation effects on wealth components. The net foreign asset position may thus change on impact, which is impossible in our model.

7 See Sen and Turnovsky (1989) for an analytical study emphasizing this mechanism.

posed on the exogenous projection of the aggregate household size (in terms of time endowment) to allow for a steady state. Finally, the model assumes an independent time trend for foreign income (determining export demand), which is similarly assumed to decline to zero in the long run. Household behavior evolves around the notion of full consumption, comprising both commodity consumption and leisure. Intertemporal allocation of full consumption is determined by forward looking optimization of infinitely lived households, and within period allocation of expenditures follows a largely conventional system of nests, except for the fact that households also consume capital and labor services (e.g., housing, consumer durables). The model also features a rich structure of demographic characteristics which influence household behavior. Producers are similarly assumed to be forward looking when deciding on accumulating an economywide physical capital stock, which, by assumption, is malleable and completely mobile across all uses (including household use).[8] Unlike the GE model, the JWH model does not extend to a symmetric treatment of the foreign economy (rest of the world). Instead, import prices are assumed to be given whereas export demand is governed by a constant price elasticity and a time trend (through foreign income). In this regard, the JWH model is comparable to our own model, except for the fact that JWH use domestic labor instead of imports as the numéraire.[9] While the GE model endogenizes the composition of household portfolios, the JWH model imposes an exogenous allocation of household savings to the three assets involved: firm equity, government bonds, and foreign assets. Accordingly interest rates are assumed exogenous, rather than being determined by the model as in the GE case. Moreover, assuming an exogenous projection for the current account, the JWH model unfortunately does not allow one to address issues of current account adjustment. Further important differences between the GE and the JWH model lie in the sectoral disaggregation, which is much higher in the case of JWH (thirty-five sectors, as opposed to ten), and in the method of empirical implementation: While the GE model is calibrated to a single data point, JWH use econometric models based on duality theory to estimate their coefficients from time series.

Looking at the results obtained by Jorgensen and Ho (1993) for a multilateral tariff liberalization scenario, we observe that the effects are rather modest, as with all previous experiments that disregard scale economies and

---

8 This contrasts with the assumption of sector specificity employed in both the GE model and our own model to be presented later.

9 This implies that another variable must enter the picture since JWH fix the nominal values of two prices: imported goods *and* the domestic wage rate. This is a sort of exchange rate, or terms of trade variable, determining the price of home goods relative to imports.

imperfect competition, but the medium-term growth bonus as such is quite substantial. Thus, while the impact effect on commodity consumption is 0.16 percent, it increases by as much as 0.82 percent in the long run. If quantitative restrictions are lifted as well, the corresponding figures are 0.36 and 1.08 percent, respectively. By way of comparison, the GE model reveals a comparable long-run effect, but a much higher impact effect, so the implied growth bonus is much lower. This may be due to the fact that the GE model does not capture labor supply effects, which figure importantly in the JWH model. It is also quite illuminating to see that sizable medium-term growth bonuses are achieved by very modest differences in average annual growth rates of output. These differences are, in fact, well below one-tenth of a percentage point.

A further example of intertemporal CGE analysis is Mercenier and Akitoby (1993) (henceforth MA), who investigate the importance of accumulation effects of the European internal market program. Unlike the calculations presented by Baldwin (1989, 1992, and 1993), MA do not rely on an external estimate of the static gain, such as the commission's own estimate in the case of Baldwin, but instead deal with static and dynamic effects in a unified framework. In addition, their model is disaggregated into nine sectors, and it covers six regions, including non–European Community (EC) countries. As to the dynamic part of the MA model, it aggregates an underlying infinite time dimension of the type considered previously to two periods. The principal reason for this is that it allows one to "apprehend dynamic features for which adjustment mechanisms and speed are not fully understood." These features relate to the labor market and industrial organization. Thus, MA assume different labor market mechanisms in the two periods to capture short-run real wage rigidity and elements of hysteresis.[10] As to industrial organization, the assumption is that firm entries/exits do not take place in the first period so that non-zero profits may emerge, while profits are competed away even in differentiated sectors in the second period. Investment and savings are modeled in an integrated way such that a representative household maximizes intertemporal utility (specified in the usual way as earlier) subject to an acccumulation relationship for physical capital and an intertemporal budget constraint.[11] The scenario simulated is a

10 The interesting point to note here is that their setting implies that first period real wage rigidity is conducive to employment in the second period. Higher productivity as brought about by integration is not absorbed by higher wages but, instead, by higher employment in the first period. And in the second period wages are flexible to ensure the increased employment inherited from the first period (this is the hysteresis element).

11 Even though investment and savings are modeled in an integrated way, there is no restriction that investment has to equal savings; hence current account effects may emerge. These matters are, however, not addressed in Mercenier and Akitoby (1993).

disappearance of all non-tariff trade barriers that may enable firms to price discriminate between different national markets within Europe. This is simply captured by setting all perceived price elasticities equal to the average perceived elasticity observed initially in a static Cournot–Nash game. Mercenier and Akitoby (1993) find that there is a medium-term growth bonus in the amount of a 1 percent increase in the capital stock. While this is far from being insignificant, the overall gain concluded by MA is well below the commission estimate of 2 to 6 percent. Moreover, as a result of the specific treatment of industrial organization aspects in the two periods smaller (larger) European countries observe a lower (higher) second period welfare, while all European countries experience a higher first period welfare. If the labor market is modeled differently in the two periods as well (see previous note), then there are unambiguous gains for all European countries in the second period labor market.

Growth implications and issues of adjustment through time have also played a significant role in the recent debate on the North American Free Trade Area (NAFTA), in particular as regards trade and capital movements between the United States and Mexico. Again, a number of researchers have pointed out that static models may underestimate the gains from liberalization, and various attempts have been made to address the issue in a growth oriented context. Among the studies surveyed in Francois and Shiells (1994), the study that is closest to a fully specified growth model is Young and Romero (1994) (henceforth YR).[12] Like Jorgensen and Ho, YR conduct econometric investigations based on duality theory, instead of implementing their model by means of calibration to a single data point. As with the model to be presented later, a crucial channel through which liberalization affects capital accumulation is the price of capital goods. Thus, the precise composition of the capital stock is made explicit in the model, and steady-state

12 Other studies involving dynamic aspects are Kehoe (1994), Levy and van Wijnbergen (1994), and McCleery (1994). Kehoe analyzes endogenous growth channels in an aggregate econometric approach. Levy and van Wijnbergen address issues of agricultural liberalization and income distribution in a CGE model which is basically static in nature, but amended by certain assumptions regarding the evolution through time of some key exogenous (including policy) variables. McCleery focuses on international capital movements and aspects of learning by doing. In his model, capital accumulation in Mexico and in the United States is driven by net savings available for investment in the two countries, and these are assumed to be certain fractions of GDP which are, in turn, made dependent in an ad hoc way on the rates of return. In addition, Mexico receives additional investment financing through direct foreign investment from the United States. This comes about because of an exogenous reduction in the risk premium that investors require for holding Mexican equity, the underlying assumption being that NAFTA increases investor confidence. Finally, McCleery captures endogenous growth mechanisms by assuming that productivity growth is driven by investment rates and capital goods production (United States) and capital inflow (Mexico). Plausible as all of these assumptions may be, the crucial difference between the McCleery model and our concern in this chapter is that dynamic effects of trade liberalization are not generated by an extension of optimization to intertemporal dimensions.

accumulation effects are determined by the familiar condition that the steady-state user cost of capital (which is importantly determined by the acquisition cost for capital goods) equals the rate of return on capital in production. Having determined steady-state effects, YR then exogenously specify a given point in time at which the economy is assumed to reach its steady state and calculate adjustment paths that maximize the transition period GDP, evaluated at domestic prices. Under these assumptions YR calculate substantial dynamic "gains from trade": first period GDP is about 1.8 percent higher under liberalization than with tariffs in place, while after eleven periods, when the steady state is assumed to be reached, the difference amounts to 3.3 percent. This holds for a 10 percent real interest rate, but if the real interest rate is reduced to 7.5 percent, then first period GDP is somewhat lower under liberalization than with tariffs, but in the final steady state the difference jumps up to 6.4 percent.

All the approaches considered so far rely on the notion, explicit or implicit, of an infinitely lived household when addressing welfare issues. This dynastic view of preferences is obviously a very extreme one. It disregards the simple fact that the generations who save in early periods to facilitate accumulation are different from those who harvest the returns of accumulation in the long run. If we treat welfare on a generation-specific basis, then, of course, the welfare neutrality theorem of Baldwin (1992) is no longer available, and we must expect serious welfare implications of accumulation quite irrespective of any divergence between the social and private marginal returns to the accumulated factor. These implications are largely distributional in nature; the principal question is simply (in somewhat simplified form) whether dynamic gains from trade accrue to older or younger generations. The model that we shall turn to in detail incorporates this type of distributional dimension by specifying an overlapping generations structure on the household side, and we shall see that this has quite important implications for commercial policy scenarios.

III A Computational Model

We now move on to illustrate the usefulness of intertemporal CGE analysis by turning to the details of a specific model. The following model presentation as well as the specific policy scenarios that it is applied to are intended to be complementary to our earlier work (see Keuschnigg and Kohler [1994, 1995]). In particular, we shall place more emphasis on household dynamics and generational welfare analysis than we did in our previous presentations. As regards the policy scenarios, we include multilateral (in addition to unilateral) tariff liberalization, and we extend the application to temporary tariff protection targeted toward individual sectors, as well as investment promotion by means of a selective removal of all tariffs on investment demand.

III.1 Household Behavior

Determining Overall Consumption Our model exhibits exogenous trends in both labor productivity (at rate x) and population (at rate n). The number of efficiency units, therefore, increases at a rate $\bar{g} = (1+x)(1+n)$. For a clear separation of endogenous dynamics from exogenous trends, we present all variables in detrended form through division by $(1+\bar{g})$. The economy is populated by an infinite number of overlapping generations with lifetime uncertainty.[13] In each period, individuals of different ages choose a certain amount of commodity consumption and labor supply and face a constant probability θ of dying thereafter ($1-\theta$ is the probability of surviving into the next period). For each generation, we postulate a von Neumann–Morgenstern intertemporal utility function which is additively time separable and which features a constant intertemporal elasticity of substitution. Felicity is Cobb–Douglas in commodity consumption C and leisure $1-L^s$ (where the time endowment is normalized to unity and L^s denotes labor supply).[14] We simplify our notation by writing $v_{.,t}$ for full consumption (i.e., consumption of commodities and leisure) as of period t of an arbitrary generation (and analogously for other generation-specific variables). Aggregate consumption is denoted by v_t. A typical generation maximizes

$$\sum_{s=t}^{\infty}\left[(1-\theta)\beta\right]^{s-t} u(v_{.,s}) \tag{13.1}$$

subject to an intertemporal budget constraint of the form

$$A_{.,t} = \frac{1+r_t}{1-\theta}\frac{A_{.,t-1}}{1+x} + y_{.,t} - p_t^v v_{.,t} \tag{13.2}$$

$v_{.,t}$ is already detrended from productivity growth; hence the discount factor β includes both the subjective discount rate and the rate of exogenous productivity growth x. Lifetime uncertainty effectively increases the rate of

---

13 We follow Blanchard (1985), Frenkel and Razin (1987), Buiter (1988), and Weil (1989) in specifying the household side of our model.

14 Cobb–Douglas is, admittedly, a restrictive parameterization, but given our exogenous trends it is necessary for the model to possess a well defined steady state. For more details, an appendix is available from the authors upon request.

individual discounting, and it increases the effective rate of interest paid on financial assets A, which are denominated in imported goods and detrended from productivity growth. r denotes the (net of tax) real interest rate in terms of imported goods, and we assume that this is given exogenously from the rest of the world. Thus, the stock of financial assets at the end of period t is determined by financial assets inherited from the previous period, scaled down according to productivity growth and augmented by effective interest, plus savings out of period t full disposable wage income $y_{,t}.^{15}$ p_t^v is a price index dual to the full consumption aggregate, and we shall henceforth write $M_{,t} \overset{\text{def}}{=} p_t^v v_{,t}$ for full consumption expenditure. Note that this is real expenditure in terms of imported goods whose prices are all normalized to unity and held constant throughout the chapter. Analogous interpretations hold for financial assets and wage income.[16]

Lagrangian methods may be employed to solve this problem, from which we obtain the following determination of generational consumption:

$$(a) \quad p_t^v v_{,t} = \Omega_t^{-1} w_{,t} \qquad \Omega_t \overset{\text{def}}{=} \sum_{s=t}^{\infty} \left[(1-\theta)\beta \right]^{\gamma(s-t)} \left[\frac{p_s^v}{p_t^v} R_{t+1,s} \right]^{1-\gamma}$$

$$(b) \quad w_{,t} \overset{\text{def}}{=} \frac{1+r_t}{(1-\theta)} \frac{A_{,t-1}}{(1+x)} + y_{,t} + H_{,t} \qquad H_{,t} \overset{\text{def}}{=} \sum_{s=t+1}^{\infty} y_{,s} R_{t+1,s}$$

$$(c) \quad R_{t,s} \overset{\text{def}}{=} \prod_{u=t}^{s} \frac{(1+x)(1-\theta)}{(1+r_u)} \qquad R_{t,t-1} \overset{\text{def}}{=} 1 \qquad (13.3)$$

Here, γ is the constant intertemporal elasticity of substitution. As usual, real consumption expenditure is determined by total wealth w via a marginal propensity to consume, Ω^{-1}, which is in turn determined by the utility discount factor and the consumption based real interest rate. Total wealth is composed of (updated) financial assets inherited from the past, plus current period real wage income and human capital H, which is the discounted future stream of real wage income.

We can now aggregate over all generations to obtain aggregate consumption. If generations are sufficiently large we can invoke the law of large numbers to equate the proportion of a generation surviving any given period with θ. Given a population growth rate of n, this implies a constant gross birth rate of $n+\theta$, and an age distribution of the population according to

---

15 y is nothing but the value of time endowment augmented by lump-sum government transfers.
16 The appearance of life uncertainty in the dynamic budget constraint is motivated by the existence of a competitive insurance industry, as in Blanchard and Fischer (1989). See our appendix for more details.

$$\omega_a = \omega_0 \left(\frac{1-\theta}{1+n} \right)^a \qquad \omega_0 \overset{\text{def}}{=} \left(\frac{n+\theta}{1+n} \right) \tag{13.4}$$

where ω_a is the weight of a generation of age a. It is easily seen that aggregate full consumption per efficiency unit can be written as

$$v_t = \sum_{a=0}^{\infty} \omega_a v_{t-a,t} \tag{13.5}$$

Assuming (1) that wage income (inclusive of government transfers) is age independent and (2) that successive new generations always enter without any financial wealth (no bequests), and realizing that all generations face identical prices and life expectancies, aggregate consumption can be described by the following set of equations:[17]

$$(a) \quad M_t \overset{\text{def}}{=} p_t^v v_t = \Omega_t^{-1} \mathcal{w}_t$$

$$(b) \quad \mathcal{w}_t \overset{\text{def}}{=} \frac{1+r_t}{1+\bar{g}} A_{t-1} + l_t + y_t + H_t$$

$$(c) \quad A_t = \frac{1+r_t}{1+\bar{g}} A_{t-1} + y_t - p_t^v v_t$$

$$(d) \quad H_{t-1} = \left(\frac{1+\bar{g}}{1+r_t} \right) \left(\frac{1-\theta}{1+n} \right) [y_t + H_t]$$

$$(e) \quad \Omega_{t-1} = 1 + (1-\theta)\beta^{\gamma} \left[\left(\frac{1+x}{1+r_t} \right) \frac{p_t^v}{p_{t-1}^v} \right]^{1-\gamma} \Omega_t \tag{13.6}$$

It is important to note that individual life uncertainty is cancelling out in the evolution of aggregate financial wealth (c), while it does show up in the equation of motion for the aggregate human capital stock (d) and the marginal propensity to consume (e).

Dynamics of Aggregate Consumption and Wealth To develop a deeper understanding of the complex mechanism determining our model behavior, we offer a brief investigation into the dynamics of aggregate consumption and wealth under the simplifying assumption of a constant price index p^v, in addition to a constant real interest rate r. For the time being, we thus disregard all the sectoral detail behind the price index p^v. These details will be an important ingredient of the story to be told from the subsequent simulation exercise, but the dynamic forces operating on the household side may conveniently be understood, for the time being, by picturing a one-good

17 For details, see again our appendix.

economy. Such an economy will exhibit a constant marginal propensity to consume:[18]

$$m \stackrel{\text{def}}{=} \Omega^{-1} = 1 - (1-\theta)\left(\beta\frac{1+r}{1+x}\right)^{\gamma}\frac{1+x}{1+r} \tag{13.7}$$

Given the definition of $\bar{g}$, we may note that

$$1 - m \equiv \frac{(1+\xi)}{\bar{\mu}} \qquad \text{where } \bar{\mu} \stackrel{\text{def}}{=} \left(\frac{1+r}{1+\bar{g}}\right)\left(\frac{1+n}{1-\theta}\right)$$

$$\text{and } (1+\xi) \stackrel{\text{def}}{=} \left(\beta\frac{1+r}{1+x}\right)^{\gamma} \tag{13.8}$$

Note that $\bar{\mu}$ is the effective discount factor for human capital, equation (13.6d).

We show in detail in our Appendix that equations (6a–6d) imply the following system of difference equations for consumption expenditure, M, and financial wealth, A:

$$\begin{bmatrix} M_t \\ A_t \end{bmatrix} = \begin{bmatrix} (1+\xi) & -z_1 \\ -(1+\xi) & \left(\frac{1+r}{1+\bar{g}} + z_1\right) \end{bmatrix}\begin{bmatrix} M_{t-1} \\ A_{t-1} \end{bmatrix} + \begin{bmatrix} 0 \\ y_t \end{bmatrix} \qquad \text{with } z_1 \stackrel{\text{def}}{=} \omega_0 m\bar{\mu} \tag{13.9}$$

It is clear, intuitively, why household behavior as described by the equation system (13.6) should imply such a system of difference equations. For financial wealth this is straightforward: Current assets are previous assets plus savings. But savings are determined by current income and consumption, which, in turn, depend on previous financial assets and current plus future income. Present income and human capital are related to human capital of the previous period, which is, in turn, related to previous consumption. Hence, current financial wealth is determined from previous financial wealth, previous consumption, and current income. Similar reasoning applies to consumption, which is a function of wealth. Wealth is defined as previous financial assets augmented by current income and human capital. Financial assets of the previous period are, in turn, related to previous consumption and previous human capital. But previous human capital is also related to previous consumption, hence the first line in the preceding system

---

18 This will also be the steady-state value of Ω^{-1} in our counterfactual exercises later, but in the present context it should not be confused with the steady state; we have simply imposed it on the model by assuming a constant aggregate price index.

of difference equations, which is nothing but an aggregate version of the Euler equation.

We may now explore the existence of a steady state and stability of the preceding system, given some value for full disposable income. Denoting steady-state values by a subscript ∞, we have

$$M_\infty = \frac{-m\omega_0\bar{\mu}y}{|I-Z|} > 0 \qquad A_\infty = \frac{-\xi y}{|I-Z|} > 0,$$

where Z is the coefficient matrix of the system. The inequalities in these expressions assume that the determinant $|I-Z|$ is strictly negative. This is also necessary for saddle-path stability, which can be seen as follows: The characteristic roots of Z can be shown to be

$$\mu = (1-m)\frac{1+r}{1+\bar{g}} = (1+\xi)\frac{1-\theta}{1+n} \quad \text{and} \quad \bar{\mu} = \frac{1+\xi}{1-m} = \frac{1+r}{1+\bar{g}}\frac{1+n}{1-\theta}$$

Dynamic efficiency requires $\bar{g} < r$ and thus $\bar{\mu} > 1$. Hence, stability requires that $0 < \mu < 1$, which also implies $|I-Z| < 0$.[19] $\mu = 1$ would imply a zero determinant $|I-Z|$, in which case we could not uniquely determine a steady state from y. Being able to compute the steady state independently of initial conditions and the adjustment path is a very convenient property of this type of model from a computational point of view (discussed later). Accordingly, $\mu < 1$ is an important condition to be imposed on the calibration procedure.

We can depict dynamic adjustment of consumption and wealth by the usual phase diagram in the (A, M) space. Taking the Euler equation for consumption first, we can derive a line through the origin with slope $\xi/z_1 > 0$, along which consumption remains stationary. Similarly, financial wealth remains stationary on a line with slope $[1+\xi]/[(1+r)/(1+\bar{g})+z_1-1]$, and intercept $-[(1+r)/(1+\bar{g})+z_1-1]^{-1}y$. Saddle path stability implies that this latter line is steeper than the stationary Euler line, and their intersection determines the steady-state values M_∞ and A_∞. Figure 13.1 depicts the saddle path leading the system to this steady state. An increase in income y shifts the A-schedule. The dynamic behavior, however, crucially depends on whether or not financial wealth has a forward looking component. If it does not, the system jumps horizontally onto a new saddle path leading to the new steady state (not drawn to prevent clutter). But in our case financial wealth includes equity, which is evaluated in a forward looking way. Hence, financial wealth may jump on impact. In addition, disposable wage income

---

19 The reader may wish to check stability by focusing on the eigenvalues of the matrix $Z-I$ instead of the matrix Z. The eigenvalues of this matrix are $1-\mu$ and $1-\bar{\mu}$, respectively. The previous condition then translates into the usual formulation according to which the eigenvalues split into a positive and a negative one.

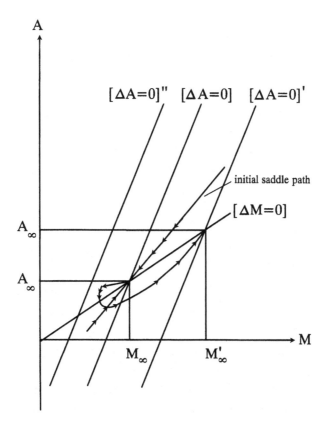

Figure 13.1. *Dynamic adjustment of consumption and financial wealth*

may change gradually because of sticky capital accumulation, thereby shifting the A-schedule in a gradual way and generating more complicated adjustment dynamics (see Keuschnigg [1994]). Figure 13.1 depicts a possible scenario in which disposable income falls on impact (A''-schedule), and then begins to increase to approach its long-run value (A'-schedule), which exceeds the initial steady state. We observe a non-monotonic adjustment path for financial wealth, which will also be borne out by our numerical results later. It must also be emphasized that the adjustment dynamics of Figure 13.1 hold for a constant interest rate and a constant price index p^v. The model dynamics emerging in our counterfactual exercises later are importantly influenced by changes in p^v, so we must be cautious in trying to find too much of the present adjustment pattern in the results to be presented later. But the simplified exposition of this section should nonetheless contribute to a deeper understanding of our results.

Generational Welfare Analysis We have pointed out in the previous section that accumulation may be carried out through savings of present generations who may not benefit from increased future consumption. We now address this issue by means of a full generational welfare analysis, and in doing so we depart from the previous assumption of a constant full consumption price index p^v. Indeed, variations in p^v through time now become an integral part of the story to be told, as are variations in income y.

Before we go into the details, we must point out that demographic change, while being present, is captured in a rather crude way in our model. In particular, the welfare calculations to be presented here do not literally incorporate individuals who actually die during the adjustment period. Instead, we have generations who enter the economy at different points during the transition, or who have entered in the old or will enter in the new steady state, all of which have an *identical life expectancy*.[20] And expected lifetime utility is all that we look at for each generation. In what sense, then, can different generations be affected differently by a given policy? The first crucial point to note here is that different parts of the price and wage income (or transfer) profiles will be relevant for different generations, depending on when they enter the economy. The second point is the simple assumption that each generation enters the economy without any financial wealth. This implies that generations not yet born at the time when new information on some policy change arrives cannot be affected by the resulting impact revaluation of financial wealth, while old generations are, and are so to a different extent, depending on how important these assets are in their overall wealth portfolios.

We now derive a money equivalent measure of utility changes which allows us to quantify the welfare effect of a given policy separately for each generation. Given intertemporal optimization on the household side, this is a wealth equivalent variation, rather than the income equivalent measure discussed in Chapter 3. Equation (13.1) gives expected lifetime utility, as of the beginning of period t, for a generation aged a. We denote this by $EU_{t-a,t}$, and we first look at the generation with age 0, i.e., the generation born at the beginning of period t. We substitute out all future consumption, $v_{t,s}$ for $s>t$, by utilizing the Euler equation and the constant intertemporal elasticity formulation of $u(\cdot)$. As a result, we can write expected lifetime utility as a function of present full consumption and intertemporal prices as embodied in the marginal propensity to consume, Ω:

---

20 This is why models of the present type are sometimes called models of perpetual youth.

$$EU_{t,t} = \Omega_t \frac{\left(v_{t,t}\right)^{1-1/\gamma}}{1-1/\gamma} \tag{13.10}$$

Using the consumption function (13.3a) to replace present (full) consumption, we arrive at the indirect utility function

$$EU\left(\mathcal{P}_t, \mathcal{W}_{t,t}\right) = \frac{\left(\mathcal{W}_{t,t}\right)^{1-1/\gamma}}{1-1/\gamma} \cdot \mathcal{P}_t \qquad \mathcal{P}_t \overset{\text{def}}{=} \Omega_t^{1/\gamma}\left(p_t^v\right)^{(1-\gamma)/\gamma} \tag{13.11}$$

We have introduced a convenient intertemporal price factor $\mathcal{P}_t$, which is the same for all generations alive at the beginning of period t. Inverting the indirect utility functions, we derive an intertemporal expenditure function of the form

$$e\left(\mathcal{P}_t, EU_{t,t}\right) = \left[\left(\frac{1-1}{\gamma}\right)\frac{EU_{t,t}}{\mathcal{P}_t}\right]^{\gamma/(\gamma-1)} \tag{13.12}$$

This is the amount of wealth that our generation would need, given intertemporal prices as embodied in P_t, to achieve an expected lifetime utility equal to $EU_{t,t}$. Suppose that with the initial policy, this generation would have faced intertemporal prices $\mathcal{P}_t^0$ and its wealth would have been $\mathcal{W}_{t,t}^0$, with expected lifetime utility implicitly given by $\mathcal{W}_{t,t}^0 = [(1-1/\gamma) EU_{t,t}^0/\mathcal{P}_t^0]^{\gamma(\gamma-1)}$. Suppose, moreover, that at the beginning of period t new information hits the economy on some policy change, say trade liberalization. As a result, expected lifetime utility changes to $EU_{t,t}^1$, as a result of a variation in both intertemporal prices and period t wage income plus human wealth. Note that this generation does not have any financial wealth at the time of the policy change. The equivalent variation in full wealth for this generation is then defined as

$$EV_{t,t} \overset{\text{def}}{=} 100 \cdot \frac{e\left(\mathcal{P}_t^0, EU_{t,t}^1\right) - \mathcal{W}_{t,t}^0}{\mathcal{W}_{t,t}^0} \tag{13.13}$$

This measure translates the welfare change into a pure wealth change at notionally unchanged prices. A positive value of $EV_{t,t}$ indicates a welfare gain, and vice versa. It is clear that what we have just said about the generation entering the economy at the time of the policy change can be applied by complete analogy to all subsequent generations. We henceforth call generations born at the beginning of period t or later new generations. Successive new generations will have different equivalent variations because their new expected lifetime utility will be different. Thus, a generation born s periods after the policy change would have $EU_{t+s,t+s}^1 = EU(\mathcal{P}_{t+s}^1, \mathcal{W}_{t+s,t+s}^1)$.

The preceding procedure, however, does not fully describe the utility change for generations who were born prior to the policy change (old generations). The reason is that they are affected by a revaluation of their financial wealth, in addition to changes in income and human capital. Note that every old and the first new generation face identical period t incomes and stocks of human wealth: $H_{t-a,t}=H_{t,t}$ and $y_{t-a,t}=y_{t,t}$. Hence, they will all be affected in identical ways in these terms. Without any policy change, total wealth of a generation aged $a>0$ as of the beginning of period t would be equal to $\mathcal{W}_{t-a,t}=y_{t,t}+H_{t,t}+(1+r)/[(1-\theta)(1+x)]A_{t-a,t}$; see equation (13.3b). All financial assets (including equity holdings) would yield a real return of r, because of the no-arbitrage condition which would hold between periods $t-1$ and period t if no new information had been arriving in between. But if such information hits the system, then the no-arbitrage condition is violated for firm values, and dividends plus capital gains (or losses) imply an effective rate of return on equity which is different from the given interest rate r.[21] To obtain equivalent variations for old generations, we calculate an average economywide rate of return for financial wealth between periods $t-1$ and t and apply this to financial wealth of all old generations to obtain generation-specific figures for total wealth, as of period t, under the new policy. This implies that all individuals hold the same economywide portfolios. Moreover, it requires knowledge of the distribution of existing financial wealth across old generations in the initial steady state. Ultimately, we arrive at generation-specific welfare measures $UE_{t-a,t}^1$, which we then use to calculate generation-specific equivalent variations $EV_{t-a,t}$ according to the previous definition.

This approach enables us to provide a full generational welfare analysis of the policy scenarios that we shall address later. We may thus also address the question of intergenerational redistribution, in addition to distributional issues along the sectoral or factoral dimension which have so far been at the center of CGE analysis. In addition to equivalent variations for a large number of old and new generations, we shall report a steady-state welfare equivalent variation in our results later. This is nothing but the preceding definition applied to steady-state values of total wealth and the price factor $\mathcal{P}$.

Linking Households to the Rest of the Economy Financial wealth consists of three types of assets, all of which are perfect substitutes: government debt,

---

21 For details on the no-arbitrage condition for equity, see later discussion. A more detailed account of or procedure to derive equivalent variations for old generations can be found in the appendix.

net foreign assets (which may be negative), and domestic equity.[22] They all earn the same rate of return r, and their supplies evolve according to laws of motion which are completely analogous to equation (16.6c), with the corresponding flows being the primary government deficit, the trade balance, and dividends plus capital gains on equity (see later discussion). This, of course, raises the question of capital market equilibrium: The end-of-period overall financial wealth position that households wish to attain has to be equal to the sum of all asset supplies as determined by their previous values and current period flow magnitudes. We shall return to this question.

In determining full consumption expenditure M, we have assumed a given price index p^v in each period. This is nothing but the unit expenditure function associated with $v(C, 1-L^s)$. Since $v(\cdot)$ is strictly quasi-concave and linearly homogeneous, p^v is a well-behaved, quasi-concave function of a commodity price index p^c and the price of leisure, which is the net wage rate w^n: $p^v(p^c, w^n)$. In turn, p^c is the unit expenditure function corresponding to the commodity aggregate C, which is again strictly quasi-concave and linearly homogeneous in sectoral aggregates C_i. On the bottom level, we employ the so-called Armington assumption, that C_i is composed of an imported good and a domestic good, again using a quasi-concave and linearly homogeneous parameterization. The important point to notice is that this utility nest allows households to employ multistage budgeting: Given expectations on all future prices and future incomes (as embodied in the forward looking variables Ω and H), they determine the intertemporal allocation of full consumption expenditure. On the second stage, they allocate periodic consumption expenditure between overall commodity consumption and leisure, depending on prices p^c and w^n. The next stage allocates overall commodity consumption across different sectors, and so on. The reader will have recognized that within-period decisions follow standard procedures, hence we abstain from any more detailed presentation.[23]

Labor supply and commodity demand determined in this way feed back into market clearing conditions for each period, which, in turn, determine prices for each period. But since household behavior is subject to expectations on future prices (through Ω and H), this raises the question of whether these expectations will be borne out by future prices or, more generally, the

---

22 Goulder and Eichengreen (1989) assume that domestic and foreign assets are imperfect substitutes, so that they need not yield equal rates of return in equilibrium. They model imperfect substitutability by incorporating a portfolio preference index in the felicity.

23 More details may be found in Keuschnigg and Kohler (1994).

question of how expectations are formed. We have employed the assumption of perfect foresight (discussed later).

III.2 Firm Behavior

Firms decide on production and investment. Production is subject to sectoral production functions, which are Leontief in intermediate inputs and a value added product. Intermediate input requirements are in terms of a composite good, according to the Armington assumption mentioned earlier. Value added is generated according to a strictly quasi-concave and linearly homogeneous production function, using intersectorally mobile labor and sector-specific physical capital as inputs. Physical capital within every sector is predetermined by history, while firms determine labor demand L^d so as to equate the marginal productivity of labor with the gross wage rate. Net outputs for every sector are thus determined in the usual way by purely static considerations. Moreover, given constant returns to scale, the number and scale of firms are not determined; nor do they play any role in our model economy.

In static models this is all we would have to say about firm behavior. Intertemporal models, however, now add a dynamic dimension through forward looking investment. Firms are owned by households, who require a net-of-tax rate of return on holding equity which is equal to that obtained for all other assets (government debt and foreign assets).[24] The rate of return on equity is determined by dividend payments χ and capital gains on firm values V. The no-arbitrage condition is

$$V_t = \frac{1+r}{1+\bar{g}} V_{t-1} - \chi_t \qquad (13.14)$$

where we abstain from sector indices to avoid clutter. Forward integration of this equation gives the fundamental ex-dividend value of the firm as

$$V_t = \sum_{s=t+1}^{\infty} \chi_s \prod_{u=t+1}^{s} \frac{1+\bar{g}}{1+r_u} \qquad (13.15)$$

Given the gross wage rate w^g and, therefore, the marginal productivities of labor and capital, dividend payments are determined by how much firms decide to spend on investment, and on how they decide to finance investment expenditure. We assume that all investment is financed internally through retained earnings, so that dividends emerge as

---

24 Alternatively, one may require a larger, risk-adjusted rate of return on equity, as in Goulder and Eichengreen (1989).

$$\chi_t = \left(1 - t_y\right)\left[\tilde{p}_t\left(F\left(\frac{K_{t-1}}{1+\bar{g}}, L_t^d\right) - \Phi_t\right) - w_t^g L_t^d\right] - \left(1 - et_y\right)p_t^I I_t \quad (13.16)$$

where we have again omitted sectoral indices. t_y is the marginal income tax rate, $\tilde{p}$ is the net output (or value added) price,[25] F is the value added product, Φ_t denotes capital installation costs, e is the fraction of investment expenditure allowed as a deduction from the tax base, and I is the quantity of gross investment with an associated price of the capital good p^I.[26] We specify installation costs as $\Phi = \psi[K_{t-1}/(1+\bar{g}) - (\bar{g}+\delta)]\ I_t$, which is linearly homogeneous in the capital stock and gross investment, decreasing in the capital stock, and strictly quasi-convex in investment. The linear homogeneity property allows us to equate marginal and average shadow values of sectoral capital stocks (see Hayashi [1982]). Notice also that the capital input in the value added production function is expressed per efficiency unit of the current period.

Firms are now assumed to maximize firm values as given earlier subject to the usual equation of motion for capital stocks

$$K_t = \left(1 - \delta\right)\frac{K_{t-1}}{1+\bar{g}} + I_t \quad (13.17)$$

All sectors use the same capital good, which is an aggregate commodity. The detailed composition of this commodity is modeled as with the consumption aggregate C. The acquisition price p^I must therefore be seen as a function of all commodity prices. As we show in Keuschnigg and Kohler (1994), this problem may be solved with Lagrangian methods, and we obtain sectoral equations for investment demand which may be written as

$$I_t = I\left(p_t^I, \tilde{p}_t, K_{t-1}, V_t\right) \quad (13.18)$$

Note that in addition to present prices (as embodied in p_t^I and $\tilde{p}_t$) and the predetermined capital stock, investment demand also depends on the forward looking firm value. Hence, firm behavior is subject to expectations on future prices. As with household behavior, we implement the assumption of perfect foresight also with respect to firm values. Having determined investment for every sector, we then translate this into commodity demands by invoking the familiar principle of multistage budgeting.

---

25 With an eye on the effective protection literature, $\tilde{p}$ might also be called the *effective* price.
26 Our modeling of capital taxation is rather simple and is primarily dictated by data restrictions. In particular, our model does not capture the double taxation feature of a separate corporate tax or a capital gains tax in addition to a personal income tax. For comparison, see Goulder and Eichengreen (1989).

III.3 Government and Foreign Sector

Government Our government collects a variety of taxes which it uses for government procurement and a lump-sum transfer to households. There are three types of indirect taxes (value added tax, general excise tax, and tariff), a social security tax, and a general income tax subject to a lump-sum deduction which is intended to capture a progressive income tax schedule. Government procurement is kept constant per efficiency unit in terms of an aggregate commodity. In modeling the allocation of government expenditure across different commodities we follow the principle of multistage budgeting that we have already introduced above. We allow debt financing, but we impose a pre-specified path of government debt, with the base case scenario holding government debt constant in terms of imported goods. Lump-sum transfers are then adjusted in each period to keep the government on this debt path.

Foreign Sector We have already pointed out above that within every sector imported goods are imperfect substitutes for domestic goods (Armington assumption). This allows us to treat prices of imported goods as constants (set to one by implicit scaling) without generating extreme specialization effects in trade policy scenarios. On the export side, we assume downward sloping export demand schedules with constant price elasticities.[27] Being able to endogenously determine the trade balance and the associated path of foreign indebtedness was among the prime motivations for constructing models like the present one (see the introduction). Hence, we do not force the trade balance to be zero or to take on any prespecified value in any period. Instead, domestic households may sell unlimited amounts of domestic assets on world capital markets as long as these assets yield a return equal to the given world interest rate r. Similarly, they may buy unlimited amounts of foreign assets at this interest rate. We thus assume perfect international capital mobility.[28] The trade balance, however, is subject to an intertemporal constraint, so that perfect capital mobility does not constitute the possibility of a free lunch for the domestic economy. This is ensured

---

27 Whalley and Yeung (1984) explore the properties of such external sector closing rules for static models. Given that we endogenously determine the trade balance, however, their results cannot directly be applied to our model. Our treatment of the foreign sector is similar to that of Jorgensen and Ho (1993), but again different from that of Goulder and Eichengreen (1989), who model import supply by a symmetric treatment of foreign production. On the export side, however, Goulder and Eichengreen also resort to the type of demand function that we postulate in our model.

28 Goulder and Eichengreen (1989) implement imperfect capital mobility by specifying portfolio preference functions for domestic and foreign households. In this case, an endogenous risk premium emerges between the foreign and domestic interest rates.

by the intertemporal budget constraint that we have imposed on household behavior. The path of the net foreign asset position evolves according to an equation of motion which is completely analogous to that of financial wealth.

III.4 General Equilibrium

A detailed presentation of equilibrium conditions may be found in Keuschnigg and Kohler (1994), so we are brief here. General equilibrium must be thought of as a sequence of *temporary equilibria* which are interconnected by backward looking and forward looking variables. Each temporary equilibrium requires market clearing for all commodities as well as the labor market. In addition, the government budgetary balance must satisfy the prespecified government debt path, and, finally, overall savings generated by households must equal the sum of investment outlays, the current account, and the government deficit (which may be seen as a flow version of capital market equilibrium). Walras's Law implies that commodity and labor market clearing plus the restriction on the government balance imply equilibrium also on the capital market. Such a temporary equilibrium is connected to all previous equilibria as a result of stocks inherited from the past (physical capital stocks plus net foreign assets and government debt). Moreover, it is conditional on expectations about future prices as embodied in firm values, human capital, and the marginal propensity to consume (discussed previously). As we have repeatedly pointed out, we implement the assumption of perfect foresight. Agents form their expectations such that their own actions, which are subject to these expectations, will prove them right. For instance, investment depends on expectations about the future, but it also determines the future through the capital stock that it accumulates and that forms the basis of future production. Perfect foresight simply implies that the investor entertains expectations which lead him to invest such that his expectations will be borne out by future temporary equilibria. A complete *intertemporal equilibrium* is, therefore, characterized by all laws of motion for backward *and* forward looking variables being satisfied between any two temporary equilibria. The procedure that we use to compute a complete perfect foresight intertemporal equilibrium is due to Wilcoxen (1989) and is described in detail by Keuschnigg (1991). It requires knowledge of terminal values of all forward looking variables. These are generated by an independent computation of the steady-state equilibrium which is characterized by the stationary versions of all laws of motion, in addition to clearing commodity and labor markets.

III.5 Calibration

We have calibrated this model to a 1976 data set for the Austrian economy.[29] Again, we may abstain from details here since we have described these in Keuschnigg and Kohler (1994). We restrict ourselves to pointing out a few special problems which relate to the intertemporal structure of our model. First of all, the calibration procedure is such that the model generates the benchmark data set as a steady-state equilibrium. We do not, of course, intend to say that the Austrian economy was in a steady-state position in 1976. But calibrating a model like this for non-steady-state situations (i.e., for a temporary equilibrium along some adjustment path) raises unresolved issues and would, at any rate, require much more information than is typically available. In our view, then, there is no way to avoid admitting that CGE work along these lines can claim to be empirical work (in the usual interpretation) only to a very limited extent. Perhaps it should better be seen as theory with numbers.

What are the magnitudes that calibration of a dynamic model needs to determine, over and above the parameters of static models? On a general level, the answer is quite easily stated: Take the laws of motion for all dynamic variables plus the optimality conditions from intertemporal optimization, write them in stationary form, and see which of the magnitudes involved are given from the data or some extraneous econometric evidence. It is conceivable that one might end up with too much information in the sense that data plus econometric evidence violate some steady-state restriction. Suppose, for instance, that the data gives us independent information on $y, p^v v, r, \bar{g}$, and the stock of overall financial wealth A. We could then not possibly expect that these values would exactly satisfy the stationary version of equation (16.6c). In this case, we would have to discard the piece of information that we are least comfortable with, and determine the remaining magnitude from (16.6c). The typical case, however, is one where information is much more sparse, and there is ample room to determine various magnitudes so as to ensure steady-state versions of dynamic relationships. We have in this way calibrated all stock variables, in addition to the productivity growth rate x (as embodied in the overall growth factor $\bar{g}$) and the subjective discount rate ρ, which reflects savings behavior, from the flow magnitudes observed in our data set, and econometric evidence and informed guesses on certain intertemporal parameters as listed in Table 13.1. These parameters are intended to capture past trends of the Austrian

29 Thanks are due to Josef Richter, Josef Schwarzl, and Gottfried Tappeiner for generous support on the data side.

Table 13.1. *Basic parameters*

x	productivity growth rate	0.025
n	population growth rate	0.010
θ	probability of death	0.060
ρ	**subjective rate of time preference**	0.006
γ	intertemporal elast. of substitution	0.800
α	**share of commodity cons. in** v	0.722
r	world interest rate	0.055
δ	depreciation rate	0.150
ψ	adjustment cost parameter	10.000
t_y	marginal income tax rate	0.200
e_i	**investment expensing rate**	0.400

Legend: Bold faced parameters have been calibrated; the rest was taken from extraneous sources (see text and appendix).

economy. Notice that in this model the rate of time preference is not dictated by the choice of the interest rate, as is the case for models with a representative infinitely lived household. This is most easily seen by looking at the steady-state version of the Euler equation for full consumption. Moreover, intertemporal parameters also have to satisfy the stability condition for full consumption derived earlier, as well as the condition for dynamic efficiency ($\bar{g}<r$). Table 13.2 gives an overview of some important features of the data set as well as the Armington elasticity parameters taken from outside econometric sources. When reading the value added and trade columns of this table, the unit of measurement should be noted. We have scaled our whole benchmark data such that total labor supply is equal to 100 (with the wage rate normalized to unity). Total value added must thus exceed 100 in the amount of non-labor income. Table 13.2 also gives shorthand expressions for sectors for later use. The foreign tariff rates are industrial countries' average pre–Tokyo Round tariff rates computed from Deardorff and Stern (1986), using Austrian trade shares as weights.

IV Simulation Results

Unfortunately, our data restrictions do not allow us to carry out policy scenarios that are directly related to the present or future trade liberaliza-

Table 13.2. *Sectoral features of benchmark data set and parameters*

Sector		VA	TAR	TAR*	Imports	Exports	σ
1	Agriculture & Forestry	Agr/For	10.579	6.758	1.743	3.120	1.156	1.413
2	Mining	Min/Quar	1.211	1.280	0.501	1.886	0.691	0.551
3	Foodstuff	Food	6.769	5.384	5.856	2.858	2.361	0.797
4	Textiles & Clothing	Tex/Clot	5.238	4.922	3.774	7.131	5.892	1.581
5	Wood & Wood Processing	Wood	4.349	2.648	2.128	1.812	3.684	0.969
6	Paper & Paper Processing	Paper	4.210	3.316	3.622	2.378	3.224	1.905
7	Chemicals (excl. Petroleum)	Chemic	5.708	2.261	5.141	8.296	5.952	1.065
8	Petroleum	Petrol	0.939	1.751	3.282	5.221	0.557	1.046
9	Non-ferrous Minerals	Nonferr	3.916	2.911	3.218	1.409	1.176	1.596
10	Basic Metals	MetProd	5.428	1.720	2.111	4.226	5.604	2.012
11	Metal Processing	MetProc	21.403	2.536	3.972	23.858	18.305	1.712
12	Energy & Water Supply	Energy	6.461	0.000	0.000	0.150	0.660	0.440
13	Construction	Constr	18.145	0.000	0.000	0.000	0.218	1.100
14	Commerce	Trade	27.581	0.000	0.000	1.072	3.864	0.100
15	Hotels & Restaurants	Hot/Cat	5.504	0.000	0.000	0.195	7.837	0.100
16	Transport & Communication	Trans	10.452	0.000	0.000	0.758	2.844	0.100
17	Banking, Insur. & Real Est.	RealEst	17.606	0.000	0.000	0.487	0.902	0.100
18	Other Services	OthSer	11.060	0.000	0.000	1.049	0.520	0.100
19	Public Services	Public	28.152	0.000	0.000	0.000	0.016	0.100

Legend: All flow magnitudes have been scaled down so as to yield a total labor supply of 100. VA is value added, TAR denotes average domestic tariff rates, while TAR* denotes average foreign tariff rates. σ denotes the elasticity of substitution between home goods and imports, taken from extraneous econometric sources (see appendix).

tion agenda. Our scenarios are partly historical, and partly hypothetical; hence the principal purpose of this section is illustration rather than ex ante evaluation of immediately relevant policy proposals. Since our earlier applications featured a complete *unilateral* tariff removal across all sectors (see Keuschnigg and Kohler, 1994; 1995), we now extend the application to *multilateral* liberalization. Given that our benchmark equilibrium is pre–Tokyo Round, it appears natural to contrast a complete multilateral tariff liberalization with the cuts negotiated in the Tokyo Round. These followed the simple harmonizing formula

$$t_1 = \frac{16t_0}{16+t_0} \qquad (13.19)$$

where t_1 and t_0 denote post– and pre–Tokyo Round tariff rates, respectively, expressed in percentage terms. We distinguish between a once-and-for-all tariff cut which takes all agents by surprise (referred to as the instantaneous scenario), and a gradual implementation which is anticipated four periods ahead and which spreads out the tariff cuts in equal steps over seven periods. This corresponds, roughly, to what happened with the Tokyo Round cuts, and we shall subsequently call it the gradual scenario. The second scenario that we want to focus on is *temporary* tariff protection granted to a single sector, such as might occur under the safeguard provision of the General Agreement on Tariffs and Trade (GATT). We take metal processing (sector 11) as the targeted sector on the grounds that it has low initial protection and that it is rather important in terms of both value added and trade volume. We assume, again, that the event is anticipated four years ahead and that it lasts for seven periods. We contrast targeted protection of a single sector with a general import surcharge applied to all sectors. The points of interest here are the dynamic adjustment to temporary protection and the general equilibrium repercussions of targeting individual sectors. A final scenario has tariffs removed only for investment demand. This might be considered a special policy of investment promotion. Again, we are primarily interested in the adjustment dynamics involved, in particular as regards financial wealth and foreign indebtedness.

IV.1 Multilateral Liberalization

Table 13.2 gives pre–Tokyo Round tariff rates for Austria and average tariffs of industrial countries which are computed from Deardorff and Stern (1986). Foreign tariff rates drive a wedge between domestic producer prices and foreign consumer prices for Austrian goods. Austrian and foreign tariffs are now simultaneously removed, or reduced according to the Tokyo Round formula, to compare the Tokyo Round effects with a move to free trade. Using a single-country model in this way to simulate multilateral tariff cuts is, admittedly, less than perfect. In particular, since the model does not extend to a fully symmetric treatment of the rest of the world, we have to ignore possible effects of multilateral liberalization on world prices of traded goods. Instead, we maintain our assumption of given world prices for imports. Moreover, export demand is driven exclusively by changes in domestic prices and foreign tariffs, precluding general equilibrium feedbacks on

Table 13.3. *Long-run macro effects*

Variables, changes in %		UNIL	TOKYO	MULTILAT. BASE	MULTILAT. HIGH	INVESTMENT BASE	INVESTMENT HIGH
p^v	full price index	-2.437	-0.049	0.076	2.126	-0.404	-0.045
p^c	consumption p.i.	-2.506	-0.156	-0.467	1.190	-0.410	-0.118
p^I	investment p.i.	-2.163	0.009	-0.059	1.652	-0.855	-0.556
$\bar{p}$	terms of trade	-2.090	0.066	0.332	2.310	-0.435	-0.091
z	gov. transfers	-6.035	-0.378	-1.577	1.457	-0.921	-0.216
w	wage rate	-2.258	0.228	1.504	4.601	-0.390	0.144
y	disp. wage income	-3.152	0.072	0.706	3.723	-0.514	0.051
C	commodity cons.	-0.662	0.228	1.179	2.504	-0.105	0.169
L^s	labor supply	0.610	0.103	0.524	0.559	0.083	0.062
K	Capital Stock	0.373	0.213	1.438	1.882	0.425	0.639
EV	welfare change	-0.732	0.122	0.629	1.564	-0.110	0.096
A	financial wealth	-3.152	0.072	0.706	3.723	-0.514	0.051
V	firm values	-1.538	0.209	1.318	3.307	-0.326	0.132
D^G	government debt	0.000	0.000	0.000	0.000	0.000	0.000
D^F	net foreign assets	-1.613	-0.137	-0.612	0.416	-0.189	-0.081

Legend: Lower part of table reports changes of variables in percent of initial financial wealth. $\bar{p}$: Terms of Trade variable defined as a weighted average of domestic producer price changes with sectoral export shares serving as weights. EV: Equivalent wealth variation. UNIL: Unilateral removal of all tariff rates. TOKYO: Tokyo-round tariff cuts. MULTILAT.: Multilateral removal of all tariff rates. INVESTMENT: Investment promotion through selective removal of tariffs on investment demand. BASE: Base case elasticities of export demand. HIGH: Base case export price elasticities scaled up by factor of 5.

export demand, such as would occur if foreign countries were to experience expansionary or contractionary effects of the policy on capital stocks or labor supply. These effects are emphasized for the domestic economy, but assumed away for the rest of the world. Limited as no doubt it is, our exercise nevertheless nicely serves to highlight certain intertemporal aspects of multilateral, as opposed to unilateral, tariff reductions.

For easier comparison, Table 13.3 first reproduces the long-run macro effects of a unilateral tariff removal from Keuschnigg and Kohler (1994),

Table 13.4. *Long-run industrial effects: multilateral tariff removal*

Sector	p^d	$\tilde{p}$	V	K	L	C^d	C^m	I^d	I^m	E
1 Agr/For	0.120	0.152	0.400	0.416	-0.522	-0.260	10.235	0.919	13.884	3.122
2 Min/Quar	0.816	1.200	1.762	1.560	0.790	1.796	5.862	0.559	0.000	-0.049
3 Food	0.179	1.073	1.786	1.611	0.417	0.640	5.957	1.197	0.000	3.904
4 Tex/Clot	-0.103	1.233	3.509	3.297	1.764	-0.497	8.477	1.320	11.171	5.614
5 Wood	0.357	1.076	2.579	2.401	1.082	0.381	3.349	1.022	4.769	2.918
6 Paper	0.190	1.113	2.381	2.196	0.855	-0.700	4.022	1.186	0.000	4.161
7 Chemic	0.165	0.996	6.998	6.831	5.491	0.388	4.904	1.206	6.814	14.190
8 Petrol	-0.075	1.017	1.183	1.020	0.252	0.726	9.021	1.401	11.811	0.252
9 Nonferr	0.599	0.974	1.700	1.545	0.018	-1.357	7.647	0.767	8.491	3.724
10 MetProd	0.411	1.196	3.371	3.167	1.469	-0.524	1.992	-0.240	7.012	4.067
11 MetProc	0.306	1.036	3.011	2.841	1.934	-0.845	4.501	-0.078	4.612	5.536
12 Energy	0.416	0.603	1.200	1.122	0.565	0.293	0.476	0.959	0.000	-0.141
13 Constr	0.567	0.914	1.182	1.040	0.541	0.138	0.000	0.807	0.000	-0.845
14 Trade	0.623	0.752	1.338	1.229	-0.264	0.082	0.000	0.751	0.000	-0.927
15 Hot/Cat	0.451	0.733	0.580	0.476	-1.006	0.253	0.000	0.923	0.000	-0.673
16 Trans	0.879	1.257	1.790	1.576	0.089	-0.172	0.000	0.495	0.000	-1.305
17 RealEst	0.514	0.455	1.087	1.040	-0.457	0.191	0.000	0.000	0.000	-0.766
18 OthSer	0.740	0.942	1.351	1.203	-0.285	-0.030	0.043	0.719	0.793	-1.099
19 Public	1.199	1.199	1.465	1.263	-0.220	-0.487	0.000	0.178	0.000	-1.771

Legend: p^d: Domestic prices. $\tilde{p}$: Value added prices. V: Firm values. K: Sectoral capital stock. L: Labor demand. C^d: Consumption demand domestic goods. C^m: Consumption demand for imported goods I^d: Investment demand for domestic goods. I^m: Investment demand for imported goods. E: Exports.

and then reports the results for Tokyo Round cuts and multilateral free trade in columns 2 and 3. The difference between these two is largely a matter of degree, while unilateral liberalization and multilateral liberalization produce a markedly different pattern of results. Perhaps most importantly, under multilateral liberalization increased export demand that is due to lower foreign tariffs causes a terms of trade improvement and, therefore, prevents the welfare loss implied by the unilateral scenario. We observe a positive steady-state equivalent variation in the amount of 0.6 percent.

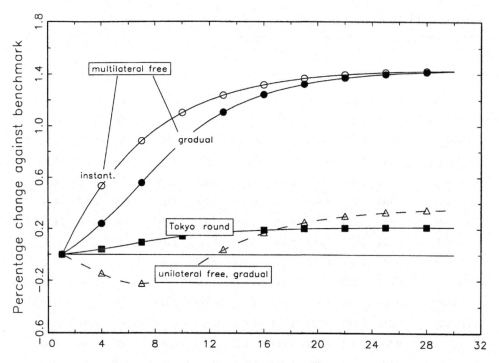

Figure 13.2. *Tariff liberalization and aggregate capital stock*

Greater demand for home goods also causes the wage rate to increase despite increased labor supply. The expansionary effect on labor supply is somewhat lower than under unilateral liberalization, but the medium-term growth bonus due to fixed capital formation is significantly larger. This also expands the tax base, thus requiring a lower cut in household transfers. Together with the higher wage rate, this makes for a significant increase in disposable wage income, both in nominal terms and deflated by the overall price index p^v. Looking at Table 13.4, which contains sectoral information, we realize that capital intensities increase throughout.[30] As a consequence, the marginal productivity of capital falls. However, because of higher output prices this is more than offset by the increase in the shadow value of capital; hence firm values increase, both in the aggregate and in all sectors individually. Notice, however, that capital deepening in some sectors (mostly non-traded goods sectors) is accompanied by a fall in employment.

30 We show in Keuschnigg and Kohler (1994) that this effect depends on the movement of the acquisition price of capital (p') relative to the sectoral effective price $\bar{p}$. In the present case the effective price increases for all sectors, while p' falls, and this implies a higher capital intensity in the new steady state.

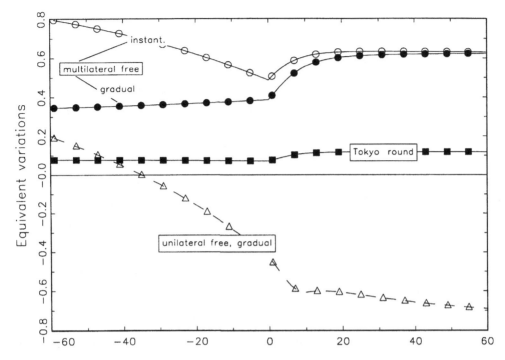

Figure 13.3. *Tariff liberalization and generational welfare*

Figures 13.2 through 13.5 reveal some aspects of dynamic adjustment, again including a comparison with the (gradual) unilateral policy. These figures strongly suggest that the Tokyo Round cuts were a relatively small step toward free trade. There remains a lot to be gained from further liberalization. While the long-run capital stock is determined by the equality between the marginal productivity of capital and its user cost, the short-run behavior is determined by movements in the shadow value of capital and its acquisition cost. Interestingly, the medium-term growth bonus sets in immediately even in the gradual scenario, while a unilateral policy, if implemented in a gradual way, causes capital decumulation during an initial phase in which agents delay investment until tariff cuts and lower home goods prices reduce acquisition costs. With multilateral cuts, domestic prices move in the opposite direction; hence the incentive for intertemporal substitution is much lower and there is no initial capital decumulation, though capital formation does set in somewhat more slowly in the gradual scenario.

Figure 13.3 depicts how expected lifetime utility of individual generations changes as a result of various policies. We know that old generations are affected by windfall profits or losses on their equity holdings, in addition to

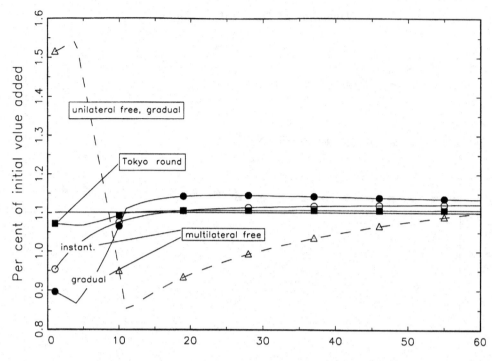

Figure 13.4. *Tariff liberalization and trade balance*

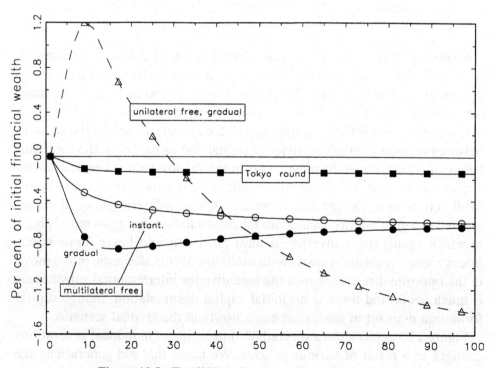

Figure 13.5. *Tariff liberalization and net foreign assets*

human capital and intertemporal price changes.[31] In the unilateral case, we observe a significant welfare loss of all new generations, and a marked redistribution toward old generations. By way of contrast, multilateral liberalization increases welfare for all generations, with hardly any discernible redistributive effect for the Tokyo Round cuts. In the case of complete tariff removals, the gradual scenario implies a very moderate redistribution toward new generations. The instantaneous scenario, on the other hand, favors very old as well as future generations, relative to generations entering at the time of the policy change. Generations born immediately after this change do not gain from equity revaluation, while having to go through initial periods of relatively modest wage increases. The later a generation enters the economy, the more it will gain from an increasing profile of wage income; the more favorably, therefore, will its human capital be affected by the policy.

Figures 13.4 and 13.5 turn to dynamic adjustment of the trade balance and foreign indebtedness. One might perhaps intuitively expect that trade liberalization would cause a temporary worsening of the trade balance and, accordingly, a long-run increase in foreign indebtedness. This is, indeed, what our model shows, but what are the forces at work? First, there is intertemporal smoothing of full consumption carried out by successive generations with differing expected income profiles. The gradual policy implies a rising time profile of disposable income during almost the entire adjustment path, while the instantaneous policy causes a large impact effect in the first period, followed by a slight overshooting and gradual reduction to the long-run income level (the graph of disposable income is not shown because of shortage of space). On this account alone, we would thus expect a temporary worsening of the trade balance in the gradual scenario, while the instantaneous policy may conceivably imply a temporary improvement. There are, however, additional effects which defy any clear-cut presumption. In particular, there are intertemporal substitutions caused by the precise intertemporal pattern of prices, and within-period substitution between home goods and imports, depending on market clearing prices for domestic goods. On the production side, any expansionary effect on the capital stock implies increased investment demand, which precedes the increase of production. This again exerts an influence toward a temporary worsening of the trade balance. Finally, any wealth redistribution from future to presently living generations will – all other factors being equal – increase present expenditure and thus worsen the trade balance in initial periods of adjust-

---

31 In Keuschnigg and Kohler (1994), we have also shown the intersectoral pattern of these windfall gains/losses.

ment.[32] While the early adjustment path is pretty much dominated by intertemporal substitution effects, and is characterized by temporary improvements of the trade balance in the gradual unilateral scenario, such is not the case in the gradual multilateral scenario. One explanation is that lower prices for imported goods, due to tariff removals, are now accompanied by rising prices for domestic goods, due to cuts in foreign tariffs and higher export demand. There is thus much less incentive to postpone expenditure to later periods. Indeed, the intertemporal substitution effects appear to operate in the opposite direction. In the long run, however, the multilateral liberalization scenario causes increased foreign indebtedness, albeit to a lower extent than does a unilateral tariff removal. Moreover, adjustment is much faster for multilateral moves than for a unilateral policy.

Among the set of most important parameters driving these results is the price elasticity of export demand, which we have taken from econometric studies of trade flows, as usual. Column 4 of Table 13.4 presents results for a complete multilateral tariff removal that we have obtained upon scaling up these base case elasticities by a factor of 5. With a higher price elasticity of export demand, foreign tariff removals have a greater effect on export demand, thus tending to raise domestic prices to an even greater extent. At the same time, the movement along free trade export demand schedules which is implied by domestic expansion now entails a much smaller downward pressure on home goods prices. For both reasons, a more favorable picture emerges, more than doubling the equivalent variation of the base case scenario and reducing foreign indebtedness in the long run. As a result of shortage of space, we abstain from presenting the detailed adjustment paths that obtain for higher elasticity values, but we should like briefly to point out a few differences that emerge.[33] The overall capital stock now exhibits a slight overshooting after period 10 for the gradual scenario. The movements in the trade balance are much more pronounced than in the base case, with an impact fall from a surplus down to a deficit in the amount of 0.2 percent of initial value added for the gradual scenario. After a 4 year period of further decline it improves while tariff cuts are phased in, but much more dramatically than in the base case and significantly overshooting its long-run value for an extended period. As regards intergenerational distribution, there is now a clear redistribution in favor of new generations, and this is

---

32 These mechanisms of current account adjustment through intergenerational redistribution are characterized in detail for somewhat different model setups by Engel and Kletzer (1990), Eaton (1989), Matsuyama (1988).
33 The relevant figures can be obtained upon request.

much more pronounced for the gradual than for the instantaneous scenario. We must conclude from all of this that some of our results, including dynamic adjustment patterns, are quite sensitive with respect to the price elasticity of export demand, thus strengthening the need for reliable econometric information on trade elasticities to be used in CGE work.

Our model also allows us to examine adjustment paths on the sectoral level, for instance, for capital stocks and firm values. Available space precludes any such detailed presentation, but we may point out that there is a fair amount of intersectoral diversity as to the pattern of adjustment dynamics, with some sectors running through initial phases of capital decumulation followed by expansion later on. Firm values in some cases very quickly jump to their steady-state values, while adjusting more slowly or overshooting their long-run values in others.

IV.2 Temporary Protection

Temporary import surcharges are a frequently considered form of trade intervention, be it because policymakers are worried by peaking trade deficits, or because individual sectors are seeking relief from import competition which would otherwise supposedly cause serious injury. Temporary protection presumably is attractive also because it allows policymakers to accommodate protectionist concerns, at the same time seemingly maintaining a long-term commitment to free trade. There are many reasons to believe that this may turn out to be an uneasy compromise, but we shall not dwell on these here. Instead, our concern is primarily with how such policies may be modeled. By their very nature, such policies require an intertemporal modeling setup, and for this reason they have so far received relatively little attention in CGE analysis.[34] We intend to show some important dynamic implications that emerge if we look at temporary protection through the lens of our intertemopral CGE model. While the model is not particularly geared toward the concerns that might give rise to temporary protection proposals mentioned, it nonetheless serves a useful purpose in highlighting some of its consequences.

We contrast temporary protection granted to a single sector with a general import surcharge, both of which are anticipated four periods ahead and last for eleven periods. In the first case, we increase tariffs on imported metal processing goods by 15 percentage points, and in the second case we assume a uniform increase of all tariffs by 15 percentage points. Neither of these

---

34 To our knowledge, Eichengreen and Goulder (1991) is the only study of this kind.

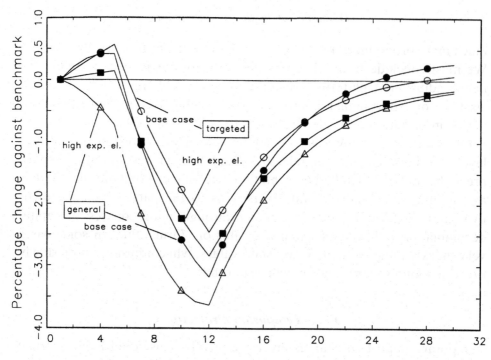

Figure 13.6. *Temporary protection and capital stock: foodstuff*

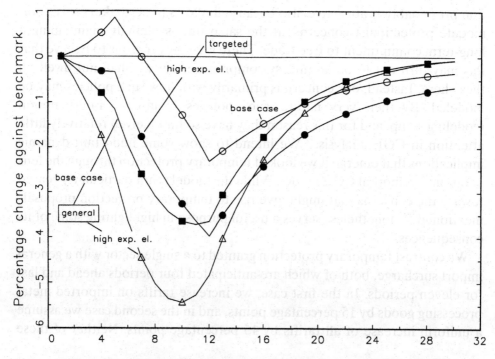

Figure 13.7. *Temporary protection and capital stock: metal processing*

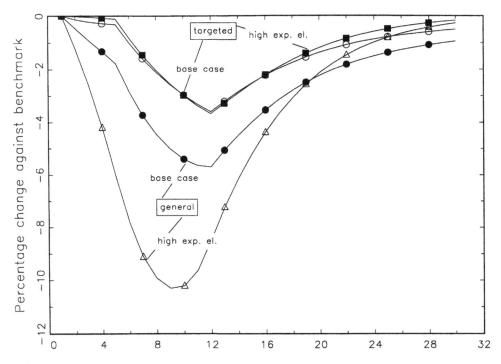

Figure 13.8. *Temporary protection and capital stock: chemicals*

policies has any lasting effects in our model, where the steady state is path-independent. All effects are strictly transitory in nature.

Intuition might lead us to expect that granting protection to a single sector is at the expense of other sectors, where resources are pulled out to be employed in the protected sector. Our results, however, show that inter-temporal effects generate an overall picture where intersectoral differences, though discernible, only play a minor role. Thus, in Figures 13.6 through 13.9 we can see a great deal of similarity between sectors 3 (foodstuff), 7 (chemicals), 11 (metal processing), and 13 (Construction) in the evolution of capital stocks through time.[35] Consider targeted protection with the base case elasticities of export demand first. Sectors 3, 11 and 13 build up physical capital during initial periods, in anticipation of higher acquisition prices for the capital good which will prevail later. Whether or not this type of intertemporal substitution causes initial accumulation also depends on the impact effect on the shadow price of capital, and in sector 7 we observe a very moderate increase which does not suffice to initiate temporary accumu-

---

35 Each of these sectors represents a pattern of adjustment that can also be found for others. More figures may be obtained upon request.

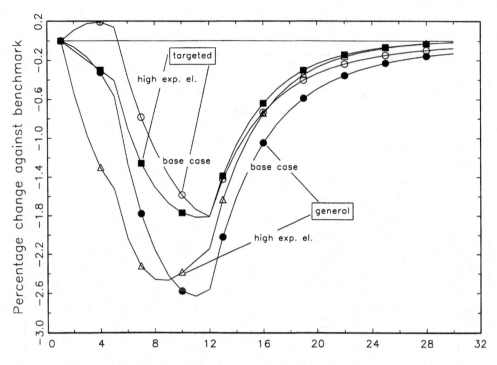

Figure 13.9. *Temporary protection and capital stock: construction*

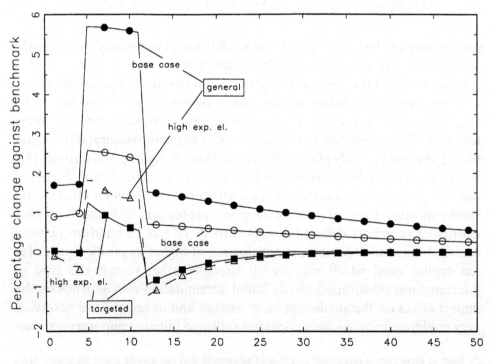

Figure 13.10. *Temporary protection and disposable wage income*

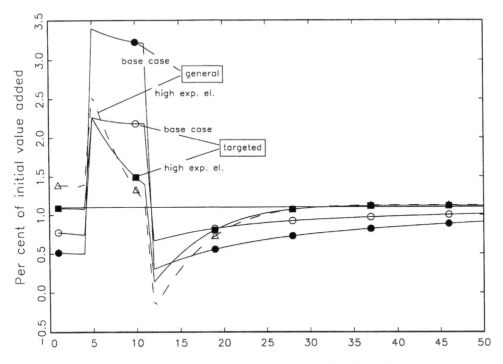

Figure 13.11. *Temporary protection and trade balance*

lation. However, all sectors use the period of protection to run down their capital stocks temporarily and thus delay production to later periods when capital will become cheaper. This holds for both targeted protection and a general surcharge, but it is more pronounced for an overall import surcharge and for high price elasticities of export demand. Although a quick glance might suggest that targeted protection is not much different in result from a general import surcharge, it should be noted that the difference is, indeed, most pronounced for the targeted sector.

Figures 13.10 through 13.13 show certain features of aggregate adjustment and welfare. The most conspicuous result is a significant increase in disposable wage income during the period of higher tariffs, which mainly reflects a terms of trade improvement. The time profile of wage income is clearly reflected in the intergenerational pattern of welfare changes, where the largest equivalent variation is observed for the generation entering in period 5 when the tariff increase becomes effective. The welfare increase of following generations falls dramatically, until the generations born immediately after the return to initial tariff levels face a welfare loss in all scenarios. Old generations are affected by an adverse revaluation (in real terms) of their

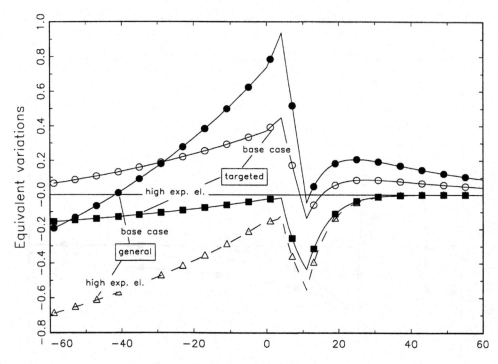

Figure 13.12. *Temporary protection and generational welfare*

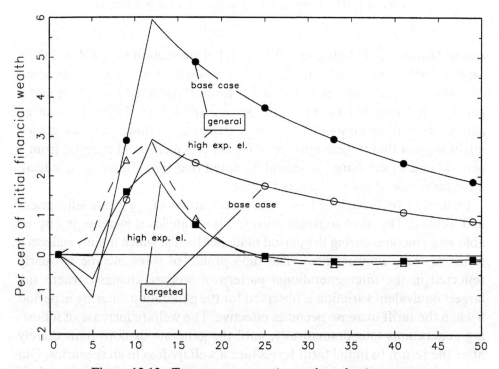

Figure 13.13. *Temporary protection and net foreign assets*

equity, and this effect gains importance with older generations. The welfare gain for most generations is turned into an unambiguous welfare loss if export price elasticities are scaled up by a factor of 5. This, again, testifies to the importance of terms of trade effects as a driving force behind the results. We conclude that temporary protection is associated with a marked pattern of intergenerational redistribution to the disadvantage of those entering the economy shortly after returning to initial tariff levels. As regards the trade balance, all policies show a temporary improvement during the period of protection, followed by a sharp deterioration immediately thereafter, and a lengthy period of lower than initial balance before returning to the new steady-state value. This pattern, which is also found by Eichengreen and Goulder (1991), is explained by expenditure switching during the period of high import prices, and the effect is, of course, more pronounced with a general import surcharge than with targeted import protection.

IV.3 Tariffs on Investment

It is widely recognized that the effect of a tariff crucially depends on whether it is a tariff on intermediate input demand or a tariff on final demand. Trade theory has a long tradition of highlighting this difference. Thus, the so-called theory of effective protection tries to identify the effective protection implicitly granted to different sectors through a given structure of nominal tariffs which are simultaneously applied to final as well as intermediate input demand. However, in a dynamic world with capital accumulation, a similar distinction arises between different types of final demand, i.e., between investment demand and consumption demand. This type of distinction is less widely recognized in empirical trade policy evaluations, since it only arises in a dynamic context. As a final scenario, we therefore eliminate all tariffs on investment demand, while keeping tariffs on other categories of demand in place. The motivation for such a policy might, for instance, lie in the desire to give trade liberalization a touch of investment promotion.

The steady-state results obtained are summarized in the two final columns of Table 13.13, and in Figures 13.14 through 13.17. At first sight, the steady-state macro effects for the base case appear to be simply down-scaled effects of a unilateral elimination of all tariffs (column 1 of Table 13.3). However, closer inspection reveals two important differences. First, the expansionary effect on the capital stock is significantly larger for the investment policy than for general tariff cuts. And the acquisition price for capital now falls, relative to other prices in general, and most importantly relative to value added prices. Both differences are intuitive and need no further comment.

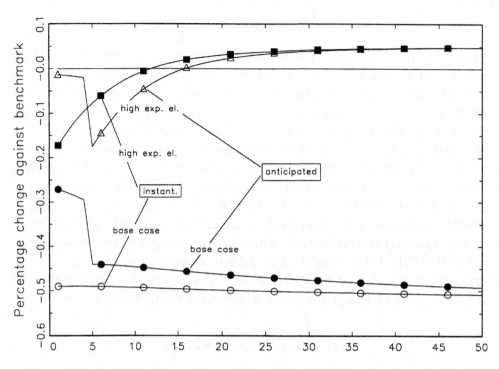

Figure 13.14. *Investment, tariff cut, and disposable wage income*

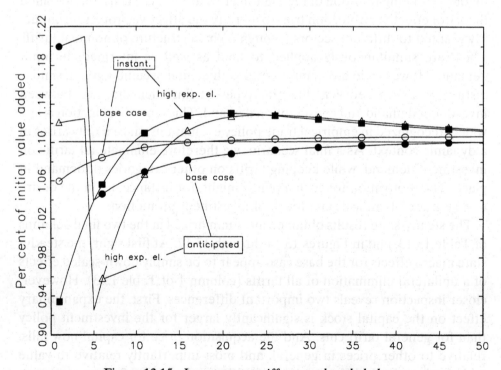

Figure 13.15. *Investment, tariff cut, and trade balance*

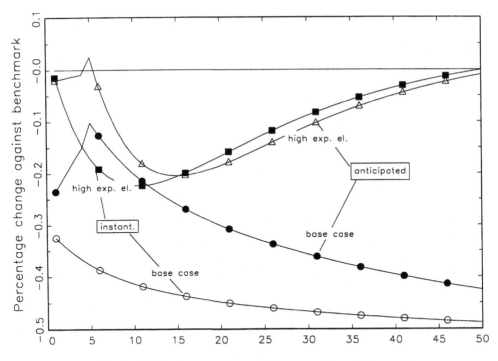

Figure 13.16. *Investment, tariff cut, and financial wealth*

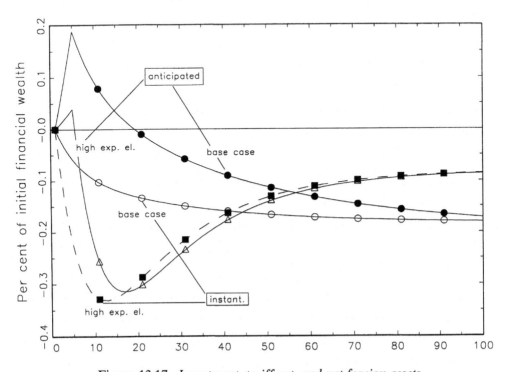

Figure 13.17. *Investment, tariff cut, and net foreign assets*

The same goes for the difference between the base case and high export elasticity values, which is entirely driven by the terms of trade effect. Notice that the terms of trade deterioration which takes place in the base case makes this type of investment promotion welfare reducing in the long run, despite the sizable expansionary effect.[36]

Focusing on the introduction of tariffs on investment, Keuschnigg (1994) notes the possibility of an overshooting adjustment path of financial wealth due to the transitory life-cycle savings motive which is characteristic of Blanchard-type overlapping generations models. In the present case, such a motive only arises in the high elasticity case, since the base case has almost stationary behavior of disposable wage income, apart from an anticipation effect. And for high elasticity values the transitory motive is toward dissavings, rather than savings, since we look at tariff cuts. Hence, households run down their financial wealth well below its new steady-state value. The overshooting adjustment of financial wealth is taking place in an even more pronounced way in its foreign component, as evidenced in Figure 13.17. Figure 13.15 reveals that overshooting also occurs, though to a much lesser extent, in the trade balance. The important point to notice here is that all these overshooting phenomena do not require anticipation or gradualism in the way the tariff cut is implemented. They even arise for a simple once-and-for-all policy which takes agents by surprise.

V. Conclusion

What have we learned from applying our intertemporal CGE model to trade liberalization scenarios? We were able to address, in a quantitative way, a number of important issues that necessarily escape the attention of static models. In addition to the familiar static efficiency effect, tariff liberalization generates incentives for increased investment, spurring economic growth in the medium run, and leading to higher long-run capital stock. Whether or not such a medium-term growth bonus also entails a welfare bonus is uncler a priori. Duly taking into account that investment implies forgone consumption, and emphasizing overlapping generations on the household side, we find that trade liberalization tends to involve redistribution between different generations, mostly favoring future generations and partly also old generations who gain from windfall profits on their equity holdings at the time of policy change. As expected, the effects of liberalization very much depend on whether or not it is reciprocated by our trading partners. Multilateral

---

36 It also reduces welfare for old generations and generations born during the transition. More details can be obtained upon request.

liberalization prevents unfavorable terms of trade effects which we have observed for unilateral tariff cuts and, therefore, delivers a clear welfare gain for all generations, despite the intergenerational redistribution just mentioned. It also implies a markedly different dynamic adjustment, with much less intertemporal substitution than in the case of unilateral tariff cuts, if such cuts are anticipated and phased in gradually.

Dynamic models are particularly well suited to address issues of temporary protection which play an important role in policy debates. We find that such temporary policies imply relatively sharp intergenerational redistribution. Moreover, the intersectoral effect of targeting an individual industry for temporary protection is dominated in magnitude by intertemporal effects which are largely similar for all sectors. We have seen that periods of high temporary protection are mainly characterized by falling capital stocks, as firms try to evade high acquisition costs of capital. Temporary protection may entail positive welfare effects due to terms of trade improvements, but these very quickly vanish if the price elasticity of export demand is increased. Indeed, our results generally reveal that this elasticity is a crucial parameter, not only for welfare, as one would expect from static theory, but also for the details of dynamic adjustment. This is most conspicuous for the case of a tariff cut which is selectively applied to investment demand only. Even absent any anticipation effects, adjustment of financial assets turns out to be highly non-monotonic if the price elasticity of export demand is very high.

A very important potential of this approach, which we have not mentioned so far, is that it allows one to consider alternative budgetary policies to accommodate the revenue consequences of commercial policies, including debt financing. Available space does not permit any detailed analysis in this chapter, so all we can do is simply point out here that our modeling experience suggests that budgetary policies are absolutely crucial for many effects. More details may be found in Keuschnigg and Kohler (1994).

We close this chapter by returning to an important aspect that we have briefly mentioned at the outset: the role of commercial policy in a world of endogenous growth. We have not modeled the type of externalities that the recent literature on the convergence debate has emphasized, nor have we incoporated endogenous growth channels of the neo-Schumpeterian tradition, which emphasizes elements of market power. Neo-Schumpeterian growth models, in particular, point to several entirely new dimensions along which commercial policy may importantly influence the evolution of the world economy (see Grossman and Helpman, 1991). As yet, these dimensions still await empirical quantification on the basis of general equilibrium models. In the meantime, developing models like the one presented and applying these in various contexts may generate a stock of experience and tools of analysis, which will later prove of significant value for quantification of endogenous growth aspects.

References

Baldwin, R. 1989. "The growth effects of 1992." *Economic Policy* 9(2):247–281.
Baldwin, R. 1992. "Measurable dynamic gains from trade." *Journal of Political Economy* 100(1):162–174.
Baldwin, R. 1993. "On the measurement of dynamic effects of integration." *Empirica* 20(2):129–146.
Blanchard, O.J. 1985. "Debt, deficits, and finite horizons." *Journal of Political Economy* 93(2):223–247.
Blanchard, O.J. and S. Fischer. 1989. *Lectures on Macroeconomics.* Cambridge, Massachusetts: MIT Press.
Bovenberg, L.A. and L.H. Goulder. 1991. "Introducing intertemporal and open economy features in applied general equilibrium models." *Economist* 139:186–203.
Brown, D.K. 1992. "The impact of a North American free trade area: Applied general equilibrium models." In *Discussion Paper, Research Forum on International Economics* 311. Ann Arbor: Institute of Public Policy Studies, University of Michigan.
Buiter, W.H. 1988. "Death, birth, productivity growth and debt neutrality." *Economic Journal* 98(1):279–293.
Deardorff, A.V. and R.M. Stern. 1986. *The Michigan Model of World Production and Trade.* Cambridge, Massachusetts: MIT Press.
Eaton, J. 1989. "Monopoly wealth and international debt." *International Economic Review* 30(1):33–48.
Eichengreen, B. and L.H. Goulder. 1991. "The impact of permanent and temporary import surcharges on the U.S. trade deficit." In *Empirical Studies of Commercial Policy,* edited by R.E. Baldwin. Chicago: University of Chicago Press.
Engel, C. and K. Kletzer. 1990. "Tariffs and saving in a model with new generations." *Journal of International Economics* 28(1):71–91.
Francois, J.F. and C. Shiells. 1993. *The Dynamic Effects of Trade Liberalization: A Survey.* USITC Publication 2608. Washington, D.C.: U.S. International Trade Commission.
Francois J.F. and C. Shiells, eds. 1994. *Modeling Trade Policy: Applied General Equilibrium Assessments of North American Free Trade.* Cambridge: Cambridge University Press.
Frenkel J.A. and A. Razin. 1987. *Fiscal Policies and the World Economy.* Cambridge, Massachusetts: MIT Press.
Gavin, M. 1990. "Structural adjustment to a terms of trade disturbance: The role of relative prices." *Journal of International Economics* 28(2):217–243.
Gavin, M. 1991. "Tariffs and the current account: On the macroeconomics of commercial policy." *Journal of Economic Dynamics and Control* 15(1):27–52.
Goulder, L.H. and B. Eichengreen. 1989. "Savings promotion, investment promotion, and international competitiveness." In *Trade Policies for*

International Competitiveness, edited by R. Feenstra. Chicago: University of Chicago Press.

Goulder, L.H. and B. Eichengreen. 1992. "Trade liberalization in general equilibrium: intertemporal and inter-industry effects." *Canadian Journal of Economics* 25(2):253–280.

Grossman, G.M. and E. Helpman. 1991. *Innovation and Growth in the Global Economy.* Cambridge, Massachusetts: MIT Press.

Grossman, G.M. and E. Helpman. 1994. "Endogenous innovation in the theory of growth." *Journal of Economic Perspectives* 8(1):23–54.

Hayashi, F. 1982. "Tobin's marginal q and average q: A neoclassical interpretation." *Econometrica* 50(1):213–224.

Jorgensen, D.W. and M.S. Ho. 1993. "Trade policy and U.S. economic growth." *Harvard Institute of Economic Research, Discussion Paper* No. 1634.

Jorgensen, D.W. and P.J. Wilcoxen. 1990. "Intertemporal general equilibrium modeling of U.S. environmental regulation." *Journal of Policy Modeling* 12(4):715–744.

Kehoe, T.J. 1994. "Modeling the dynamic impact of North American free trade." In *Modeling Trade Policy: Applied General Equilibrium Assessments of North American Free Trade,* edited by J.F. Francois and C. Shiells. Cambridge: Cambridge University Press.

Keuschnigg, C. 1991. "How to compute perfect foresight equilibria." In *University of Bonn, Discussion Paper.* Bonn: Sonderforschungsbereich 303.

Keuschnigg, C. 1994. "Overshooting adjustment to tariff liberalization." In *Research Memorandum No. 321.* Vienna: Institute for Advanced Studies.

Keuschnigg, C. and W. Kohler. 1994. "Modeling intertemporal general equilibrium: An application to Austrian commercial policy." *Empirical Economics* 19(1):131–164.

Keuschnigg, C. and W. Kohler. 1995. "Dynamic effects of tariff liberalization: An intertemporal CGE approach." *Review of International Economics* 3(1):20–35.

Krugman, P.R. 1982. "The macroeconomics of protection with a floating exchange rate." *Carnegie–Rochester Conference Series on Public Policy* 16:141–182.

Levy, S. and S. van Wijnbergen. 1994. "Transition problems in economic reform: Agriculture in the Mexico–U.S. Free Trade Agreement." In *Modeling Trade Policy: Applied General Equilibrium Assessments of North American Free Trade,* edited by J.F. Francois and C. Shiells. Cambridge: Cambridge University Press.

Matsuyama, K. 1988. "Terms-of-trade, factor intensities and the current account in a life-cycle model." *Review of Economic Studies* 55(2):247–262.

McCleery, R.K. 1994. "An intertemporal, linked macroeconomic CGE model of the United States and Mexico focussing on demographic change and factor flows." In *Modeling Trade Policy: Applied General Equilibrium Assessments of North American Free Trade,* edited by J.F. Francois and C. Shiells. Cambridge: Cambridge University Press.

Mercenier, J. and B. Akitoby. 1993. "On intertemporal general equilibrium reallocation effects of Europe's move to a single market." Federal Reserve Bank of Minneapolis, Discussion Paper 87.

Pack, H. 1994. "Endogenous growth theory: Intellectual appeal and empirical shortcomings." *Journal of Economic Perspectives* 8(1):55–72.

Romer, P. 1994. "The origins of endogenous growth." *Journal of Economic Perspectives* 8(1):3–22.

Sen, P. and S. Turnovsky. 1989. "Tariffs, capital accumulation, and the current account in a small open economy."*International Economic Review* 30(4):811–831.

Solow, R.M. 1994. "Perspectives on growth theory." *Journal of Economic Perspectives* 8(1):45–54.

Weil, P. 1989. "Overlapping families of infinitely-lived agents." *Journal of Public Economics* 38(1):183–198.

Whalley, J. and B. Yeung. 1984. "External sector 'closing' rules in applied general equilibrium models." *Journal of International Economics* 16(1):123–138.

Wilcoxen, P.J. 1989. "A fast algorithm for solving rational expectations models." University of Melbourne, Impact Research Centre.

Young, L. and J. Romero. 1994. "Steady growth and transition in a dynamic dual model of the North American Free Trade Agreement." In *Modeling Trade Policy: Applied General Equilibrium Assessments of North American Free Trade,* edited by J.F. Francois and C. Shiells. Cambridge: Cambridge University Press.

14

Trade and Labor Market Behavior

Karen E. Thierfelder and Clinton R. Shiells

I Introduction

It is difficult to reconcile inter-industry wage differentials, which are very persistent empirically, with the neoclassical structure of computable general equilibrium (CGE) models.[1] Studies show that the wage differentials persist even after accounting for the obvious explanations such as differences in human capital or job hazard.[2] This raises an important question for the applied modeler – what is the best way to incorporate the observed wage differentials into a model to represent the base data accurately? In the CGE literature, two approaches have been adopted. Ballard et al. (1985) adjust tax and depreciation rates to equalize factor returns across all sectors in CGE models of tax analysis. Dervis et al. (1982) hold inter-sectoral wage differentials constant in counterfactual policy simulations. This approach is common in CGE models for analysis of tax and trade policy in developing countries and trade policy analysis generally.[3] In the latter class of models, the wage differentials are exogenous, suggesting that factors acquire sector-specific skills upon entry into the sector and lose those skills upon exit.

This research was completed before Mr. Shiells joined the International Monetary Fund. The authors would like to thank Robert Baldwin, Mary E. Burfisher, Shantayanan Devarajan, Joseph Francois, Hafez Ghanem, Kenneth A. Reinert, J. David Richardson, David Tarr and Sherman Robinson for helpful comments.

1 For example, evidence from the March 1987 *Current Population Survey* indicates that, in the United States, managers in agriculture earn 97 percent of the economywide average wage while managers in the mining sector earn over two times the average wage (Thierfelder, 1992).

2 For example, Krueger and Summers (1986) regress the log of wages on human capital and demographic characteristics as well as industry dummy variables for the industry in which the worker is employed. Their analysis suggests that a worker's wage does vary by industry since the industry dummy variables are statistically significant. Katz and Summers (1988, 1989) and Dickens and Lang (1988) reach similar conclusions.

3 See Devarajan et al. in this volume. See also Devarajan and Lewis (1991), Burfisher et al. (1994), Kilkenny and Robinson (1990), and Hanson et al. (1993).

In this chapter, we examine the welfare implications of trade and tax policies when there are sector-specific wage differentials. Furthermore, we explicitly model the behavior that can generate the observed wage differentials. In our analysis, the wage differentials are endogenous and reflect optimizing behavior in the labor market. We consider two types of labor behavior – the need to pay either efficiency wages or a union premium. For comparison, we maintain a version of the model with exogenous wage differentials.

In the efficiency wage version of the model, the wage markup exists because there are differences in production technology between sectors. In the competitive sector, it is costless to monitor workers. However, it is difficult to monitor workers in the efficiency wage sector.[4] Assuming workers get utility from shirking, the producer in the efficiency wage sector must provide a disincentive – a wage differential that workers receive in the efficiency wage sector but lose when they move to the competitive sector. The wage differential elicits effort from the workers in the efficiency wage sector. From the producer's perspective, the desire to reduce turnover costs, to enhance morale among workers, or to eliminate shirking can justify a wage markup.[5]

Following Bulow and Summers's (1986) description of the efficiency wage sector, we consider two types of behavior. First, we assume the efficiency wage payment affects labor behavior at the margin. There is a continuous effort function and effort increases with the wage differential. In effect, each worker internalizes the monitoring function. For comparison, we incorporate a discrete effort function by which workers either work or shirk, and contribute nothing to production. Then, the wage markup represents the payment to an explicit monitor that produces non-shirking labor.

In the union version of the model, the wage markup reflects a union's monopoly power in one sector. The appropriate behavior depends on the union's utility function. We consider two cases: (1) The union maximizes the total wage bill to its members and (2) the union has preferences over both

---

4 Alternatively, one can specify a model in which a worker's motivation, as well as the number of workers hired, affects production in *all sectors*. Unemployment can be incorporated as a discipline device. This is involuntary unemployment, since those unemployed would like to work but are unable to bid down wages. See Shapiro and Stiglitz (1984) for this version of efficiency wage theory. In our CGE model, we can redefine the competitive sector as the sector of unemployed labor. All capital would be employed in the efficiency wage sector.

5 See Salop (1986) for a description of efficiency wage payments based on training costs. Akerlof (1986), in contrast, justifies the efficiency wage markup by using sociological norms that reflect the workers' concept of a fair workday. Bulow and Summers (1986) and Shapiro and Stiglitz (1984) focus on imperfect monitoring technology in the efficiency wage sector and express the wage markup as compensation to eliminate shirking. We follow the shirking approach in the remainder of the chapter.

employment and wages, subject to both being above a minimum acceptable level. In both cases, the union maximizes its utility subject to the derived demand for labor. The wage is higher and the employment lower than in the competitive case.[6]

It is known from trade theory that sectoral wage differentials reduce welfare. There is a suboptimal allocation of resources and, as a result, the production possibilities frontier (PPF) lies below the PPF that exists with competitive labor markets. When the wage differentials are exogenous, policies that move labor out of the high-wage sector may reduce welfare. For example, the second best effects of the labor market distortion may dominate the welfare gain due to tariff elimination.[7]

The welfare analysis becomes more complex when the wage differentials are endogenous. A policy shock may exacerbate the labor market distortion and therefore dampen any expected welfare gain. Likewise, a policy shock that reduces the labor market distortion yields a positive effect on welfare compared to the model with exogenous wage differentials. In our analysis of tax and trade policy shocks, we identify the additional welfare changes due to endogenous wage differentials. We also illustrate the changes in resource allocation between sectors and the income distribution between factors.

An understanding of the welfare effects of endogenous wage differentials is important for a number of reasons. First, CGE models used for policy analysis often maintain exogenous wage differentials. We identify potential shortcomings to these models that disregard labor market behavior and therefore may be misrepresenting both welfare changes and resource allocation following a policy shock.

Second, the existence of inter-industry wage differentials has led some to propose that high-wage sectors be subsidized. For example, Katz and Summers (1988, 1989) identify sectors which pay wage differentials and attribute the payments to efficiency wage arguments such as the need to motivate and retain workers; they advocate subsidies to those sectors. Intuitively, more workers will benefit from the higher wage when those sectors expand. We find these results hold only when wage differentials are exogenous. There are welfare gains as more workers move into the sectors in which the value of the marginal product of labor is higher. However, Katz and Summers do

---

6 See de Melo and Tarr (1990, 1992) for an applied model with union behavior in autos and steel. See Devarajan et al. (1995) for a CGE model of union behavior described by MacDonald and Solow (1981). There, the wage and employment are not determined along the derived demand for labor. Instead, there is a contract curve, the locus of tangency points between the union's indifference curves and the firm's isoprofit curves. Wages and employment depend on the relative bargaining strength of the union and the producer.

7 See for example Devarajan and Lewis (1991).

not incorporate any of the behavior an efficiency wage payment suggests. In particular, they do not capture the links between the endogenous wage differential and output of the efficiency wage sector – as the efficiency wage sector expands, more resources are devoted to monitoring, which reduces welfare. We find that policies that expand the high-wage sectors also increase the wage differentials, exacerbating the labor market distortion.

Bulow and Summers (1986) also advocate expanding efficiency wage sectors. However, they use a simple production structure which does not fully capture the effect of the monitoring cost on the producer's optimal resource choice. They use a linear production possibilities frontier and describe policies which change production along the frontier. We consider a production possibilities frontier that is concave to the origin and therefore has diminishing returns to labor. We find that when the efficiency wage sector expands, monitoring costs increase and therefore drain resources available to the producer. This additional cost changes the quantity of labor and capital demanded and reduces welfare.

The remainder of the chapter is organized as follows: In Section II, we review the general theoretical trade models with factor market distortions. A description of applied models with factor market distortions appears in Section III. We present the stylized CGE model in Section IV. In Section V, we describe how either efficiency wage or union behavior can generate endogenous wage differentials. We consider three policy experiments against each base model: a wage subsidy to the high-wage sector, elimination of tariffs in the high-wage sector, and elimination of tariffs in the low-wage sector. Our results appear in Sections VI and VII, and the conclusions follow.

II Theoretical Trade Models with Factor Market Distortions

To understand the welfare effects of policies such as a wage subsidy and trade reform in a stylized CGE model, we first review theoretical models with factor market distortions. As Johnson (1966) demonstrates, the production possibility frontier shrinks toward the origin when one sector pays a wage differential because there is a suboptimal allocation of resources between sectors. The endpoints, however, do not change since resource allocation is efficient when all of the resources are allocated to one sector. When generating the PPFs he notes that the magnitude of the losses from inefficiency due to factor market distortions is small.[8] Johnson also describes

---

8 Bhagwati and Srinivasan (1971) also describe the shape of the production possibilities frontier when there are exogenous wage differentials, providing the mathematics behind the diagrams.

conditions under which exogenous wage differentials cause the production possibilities frontier to be convex to the origin.[9]

The effect of wage differentials on resource allocation, and hence the PPF, can be seen in Figures 14.1, 14.2, and 14.3. In Figure 14.1, a Heckscher–Ohlin model is represented by an Edgeworth–Bowley diagram. In the box, the dotted line represents allocations of capital and labor in identical proportions between sectors 1 and 2. Sector 1 is assumed to be labor-intensive, so that the curved locus between $O1$ and $O2$ represents efficient allocations of resources between the two sectors in the absence of distortions.

A wedge, γ, has been assumed between sector 1 and sector 2 so that

$$W2 = (1+\gamma)W1 \qquad (14.1)$$

Both sectors are distorted when γ differs from zero. In Figure 14.1, sector 1 is assumed to have higher wages ($\gamma<0$), forcing more capital intensive production in the labor-intensive sector, and more labor-intensive production in sector 2. The result is a set of equilibria like that represented by the intersection of the $X2^0$ and $X1'$ isoquants.

The implications of moving off the efficiency locus in this way are illustrated in Figure 14.2. For a given output $X2^0$, production of $X1$ falls from $X1^0$ to $X1'$ – the production possibilities frontier contracts. There is also a non-tangency between the private returns (market prices) and the social rate of return (the slope of the production possibilities frontier).

Bhagwati and Ramaswami (1963) and Johnson (1984) describe the optimal policy intervention to improve welfare. As given in the first-order conditions of Pareto optimality, welfare is maximized when the marginal rate of substitution equals the domestic rate of transformation, which equals the foreign rate of transformation. When there is a factor price distortion, there is an inefficient allocation of resources, as evident in the PPF shrinking toward the origin. The price of the commodity paying the wage differential exceeds its opportunity cost. As a result, the country will be on a suboptimal point, such as point 1, on the restricted PPF.[10]

The various policy options are illustrated in Figure 14.3. The first best option is a wage subsidy in sector 1 that moves the economy from point 1 to point 3. The second best option is a production subsidy that moves the economy to point 2. Trade taxes (or subsidies) are the third best option;

---

9 Johnson (1966) also finds that one needs extreme differences in capital–labor ratios between two sectors to generate PPFs that are concave to the origin in the absence of factor market distortions. Thierfelder (1992) finds a similar result when using a stylized CGE model to generate PPFs with and without factor market distortions.

10 See Bhagwati and Srinivasan (1969) for a discussion of the optimal intervention when a country has non-economic objectives such as maintaining factor employment in certain activities.

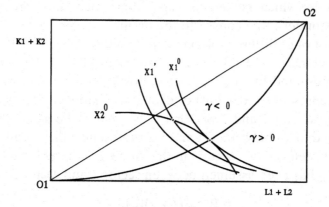

Figure 14.1. *Wage differentials in Heckscher–Ohlin framework*

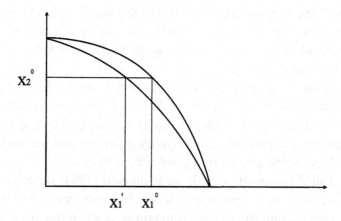

Figure 14.2. *The efficiency effects of wage differentials*

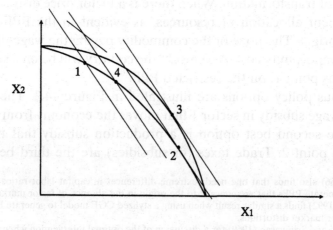

Figure 14.3. *Policy intervention with wage differentials*

welfare will not improve as much as under the optimal production taxes or subsidies because of the underlying consumption distortions implied by trade taxes. Assuming $X1$ is the comparative advantage good, partial correction of the labor market distortion through an export subsidy is represented by point 4, with consumption along the tariff-distorted domestic price line.

A number of studies consider the effect of exogenous wage differentials on the results predicted using a general equilibrium trade model. For example, Bhagwati and Srinivasan (1971) find that factor price equalization does not necessarily hold when there are wage differentials. Magee (1971) describes conditions under which factor price distortions change the factor intensities of sectors. Jones (1971) considers the effects of wage differentials on the links between output prices and both output levels and factor returns, using the classic $2 \times 2 \times 2$ trade algebra. When there are factor payment differentials by sector, a sector that is capital intensive in terms of the endowment allocation (in the physical sense) may be labor intensive in the value sense if the wage differential is large enough that labor receives a higher share of the revenue. As a result, there may be perverse relationships between output and prices. The ranking of sectors according to physical factor intensity controls the relationship between commodity outputs and factor endowments. The ranking of sectors according to the value of revenue paid to labor and capital affects the relationship between factor returns and commodity prices. Consider an industry that is capital intensive in the physical sense but pays a high differential to labor, making it labor intensive in the value sense. An increase in the price of the commodity that is labor intensive in the value sense must increase the wage–rental ratio. Both sectors use capital more intensively. To maintain full employment, the sector that is relatively capital intensive in the physical sense must decline to release labor. As a result, the supply curve is negatively sloped.

Jones also describes the effects of a change in the wage differential on factor returns. He notes that an increase in the wage differential in one sector has the same effect on factor returns as a decline in the relative output price of that good. For example, if labor in the labor intensive sector (in the value sense) receives an increase in the wage differential, the return to labor relative to capital declines, at constant commodity prices. The analysis becomes more complex when both commodity prices and wage differentials change. For example, consider a policy shock that reduces the relative price of the labor intensive good (in the value sense) and reduces the wage differential in that sector. The net effect on relative factor returns is ambiguous. Jones notes that when the demand elasticities are high, the effect of the wage differential dominates.

In this chapter, we address the implications of sectoral wage differentials. We are interested in wage differentials that arise because the same labor input receives a different wage, depending on the sector in which it is employed. Recently there has be a debate over a different kind of wage differential, the one between skilled and unskilled wages in developed countries.[11] Both labor and trade economists conclude that the gap can be attributable to a number of factors: (1) increased imports of unskilled labor intensive imports from developing countries, (2) technological progress, and (3) labor supply changes or skill upgrading. However, there is considerable disagreement over the importance of each.

Richardson (1995) presents a trade economist's perspective.[12] Referring to the Heckscher–Ohlin model, Richardson notes that only changes in the relative price of outputs and sectoral factor productivity affect relative wages. Other changes such as changes in the factor supply or factor augmenting technological progress do not change factor returns. Similarly, Leamer (1995) presents an empirical model in which he considers the relationship between factor returns and output prices and total factor productivity. He finds a large role for trade in explaining the wage gap.

Labor economists take a partial-equilibrium view and focus on changes in labor supply and demand.[13] For example, Borjas et al. (1991) evaluate the factor content of imports and exports and translate this into changes in labor supply. They also consider the effects of immigration, another change in labor supply. They find that both trade and immigration flows contributed substantially to the decline in the relative earnings of less skilled workers in the 1980s. Wood (1995) presents a more detailed factor content approach. He concludes that trade is largely responsible for the widening wage gap. In addition to accounting for changes in labor demand due to trade, he accounts for the role of non-competing imports.[14] With this correction, he finds

11 As Sachs and Shatz (1994) note, the wage ratio of nonproduction to production workers rose from 1.53 in 1981 to 1.64 in 1991. They used data from the Annual Survey of Manufactures, which divides labor into productive and non-productive workers. Productive workers are defined as unskilled and non-productive workers are defined as skilled workers. There is disagreement over this definition of unskilled and skilled workers (for example, see Freeman, 1995).

12 See Baldwin (1995) for another trade economist's views, presented in a detailed survey of the literature. He evaluates studies of trade and employment, direct foreign investment and employment, and trade and other factors on wages. He concludes other domestic forces are important for determining employment and wages. However, one cannot dismiss the role of trade.

13 Note that endowment changes will not cause relative factor prices to change in the Heckscher–Ohlin model when there is a small country and commodity prices are constant (Rybczynski Theorem). As Richardson (1995) notes, studies of changes in labor supply and labor demand as sources of wage inequality were misleading in the long run. See Robinson and Thierfelder (1996) for a trade model with non-traded goods which does allow endowment changes to affect factor returns regardless of the changes in commodity prices.

14 Wood (1995) notes that in manufacturing sectors, less developed countries produce low skill intensive imports which are no longer produced in developed countries. As a result factor content calculations understate the number of workers needed, in the absence of trade, to meet the demand for goods currently imported.

a larger role for trade than do other factor content studies. Freeman (1995), in contrast, reviews the literature and concludes that trade matters, but it is not the primary cause of the wage differential between skilled and unskilled workers.[15]

In the analysis presented in this chapter, one can also consider the effects of trade and tax policies on the average wage of skilled and unskilled labor. Relabel the inputs so that capital refers to skilled labor and labor refers to unskilled labor.

III Applied Models with Factor Market Distortions

Given the extensive theoretical literature on general equilibrium models with factor payment differentials, a number of applied models have been used to explore the effect of wage differentials on the economy following a policy shock. De Melo (1977) provides one of the first CGE models used in this regard. Following the theoretical literature, he considers the effects of removing exogenous sectoral wage differentials. He finds significant welfare gains due to the efficient resource allocations. His general equilibrium specification yields bigger welfare gains than do previous partial equilibrium studies. Since he uses a general equilibrium model, he illustrates the linkages among factor returns, production, trade, and the relative price of tradable to non-tradable goods.

De Melo and Tarr (1992) consider the effects of trade policy reform when there are sectoral wage differentials. They focus on the auto and steel sectors in the United States, two sectors in which wages are above the economywide average wage. First, they eliminate the exogenous wage distortions through a wage subsidy and find that there are welfare gains and a reallocation of labor from other sectors into the auto and steel sector. Then, they eliminate quantity restrictions in autos and steel when there are exogenous wage differentials. There are two offsetting welfare effects – the welfare gain of eliminating the quota and the cost of moving labor out of sectors where their marginal product is highest. They find that wage distortions do reduce the welfare gains of quota elimination, but the effect is small.

To elaborate on the role of wage differentials, de Melo and Tarr then consider the effect of unions, which can generate the observed wage differentials in autos and steel. In their model, the union's utility function depends on the wage and employment levels, subject to these being above a mini-

---

15 Other studies, such as Krugman and Lawrence (1993) and Lawrence and Slaughter (1993), conclude that technological progress is responsible for the wage gap. See Baldwin (1995) for a critical analysis of each.

mum acceptable amount. The union chooses the wage markup that maximizes its utility subject to the derived demand for labor. De Melo and Tarr find that policies that shift the derived demand for labor inward, such as removing auto quotas, will reduce the wage differential and therefore reduce the distortions in the economy. This provides an additional welfare gain, compared to the same policy shock with exogenous wage differentials. However, the additional welfare gain is not dramatic – equivalent variation is 9.74 rather than 9.62 when the wage differential declines from 1.31 to 1.19.

Thierfelder (1992) considers the effects of efficiency wage payments, another source of endogenous wage differentials, in a CGE model of the U.S. economy. She finds that policies to expand high-wage sectors result in lower welfare gains than when the wage differentials are endogenous. As in de Melo and Tarr's analysis, an increase in the wage differentials has a slight negative effect on welfare.

A number of CGE models for trade policy analysis include exogenous wage differentials by sector.[16] However, they typically do not focus on the second best effects these distortions introduce.

IV A Stylized CGE Model

We use a stylized CGE model to focus on the effects of labor market behavior in response to a policy shock.[17] The model is a modified version of the classic Jones model used in trade theory.[18] There are two factors, labor and capital, used to produce two commodities, a low-wage and a high-wage good. Both factors are mobile across sectors. Output is produced according to a constant elasticity of substitution (CES) production function over labor and capital.

Departing from the standard theoretical trade model, we assume imports and domestic commodities are not perfect substitutes. Instead, we use the Armington assumption and distinguish commodities by country of origin. Consumers purchase a composite good which is a CES aggregate of the imported and the domestic variety. Likewise, on the output side, we assume that output for the domestic market is different from output sold on the

---

16 See for example Hanson et al. (1993), Kilkenny and Robinson (1990), Burfisher et al. (1994), Benjamin et al. (1989).

17 This model specification follows the tradition of the 1–2–3 CGE model; see Devarajan et al. in this volume.

18 Other studies have evaluated wage differentials in a theoretical context, using Jones's $2 \times 2 \times 2$ trade model. See Jones (1971) for an analysis of trade with exogenous wage differentials, Thierfelder (1992) for an analysis of trade with an endogenous wage differential corresponding to efficiency wage payments, and Hill (1984) for an analysis of trade with an endogenous wage differential corresponding to union strength in one sector. Each of these models provides a comparative static analysis.

export market. There is a constant elasticity of transformation function describing the relationship between exports and goods for domestic consumption. The Armington specification dampens the price transmission following a trade policy shock. When tariffs are eliminated, for example, domestic prices do not experience the full price change – the changes depend on the degree of substitutability between the imported and the domestic good. A well-known feature of this specification is that in an applied model, trade liberalization is unlikely to yield a corner solution.[19]

We develop a single country model in which one country trades with the rest of the world at constant prices. The trade balance is held constant and both the relative price of imports to the domestic competing variety and the relative price of exports to the domestic competing variety adjust.[20] The domestic price index is the numéraire. Consistent with theoretical trade models, all tariff revenue is redistributed to the consumer in a lump sum fashion. Likewise, the revenue needed to pay for the wage subsidy is collected as a lump sum tax.

The stylized model is summarized in Tables 14.1 through 14.5 and in the Appendix. Tables 14.1 through 14.3 identify the variables in the model and their base values. Table 14.4 indicates the changes necessary to allow either efficiency wage or union behavior. In both cases, the wage differential becomes endogenous. The parameters appear in Table 14.5, and the model equations appear in the Appendix.[21]

V Labor Market Behavior

V.1 Exogenous Wage Differentials

As a reference case, we maintain the exogenous wage differentials evident in the base data. These factor payment differentials affect the producer's hiring decision. For example, when the factor payment differential, $WD_{i,f}$ (where the i refers to the sector and f refers to the factor), exceeds 1, fewer workers will be hired than when the worker receives the economywide average wage. However, since the factor payment differentials are exogenous, once

---

19 To approach Jones's model, we can increase the elasticity of substitution in our specification. In the simulations we assume that the elasticity of substitution between the imported and domestic variety of each good is 1.5.

20 Others identify the exchange rate as the relative price that adjusts to maintain the constant trade balance. See Devarajan et al. (1993) for a discussion of the real exchange rates in this class of models. We avoid this terminology in the text because the model has no money. In the model code, the variable, ER, can be thought of as a trade weighted average of the relative price of imports to the domestic competing good and the relative price of exports to the domestic competing good.

21 GAMS versions of the models used in this paper are available from the authors upon request.

Table 14.1. *Base values for model variables, by sector*

		Low-wage sector	High-wage sector
Quantity variables			
E_i	Exports	10	10
DD_i	Domestic Demand	90	90
M_i	Imports	15	25
X_i	Production of the composite good	100	100
Q_i	Composite consumption good	105	115
Price variables			
PX_i	Producer price	1	1
PQ_i	Composite good price	1	1
PWE_i	World export price	1	1
PWM_i	World import price	1	0.796
PED_i	Domestic price of exported good	1	1
PMD_i	Domestic price of imported good	1	1
PDT_i	Domestic price of domestic variety including tax	1	1
PD_i	Domestic price of domestic variety net of tax	1	1
Sector tax variables			
td_i	Domestic good tax	0	0
te_i	Export subsidy	0	0
tm_i	Import tariff [a]	0	0.3

[a] The import tariff level depends on the policy shock considered. In the wage subsidy experiments, the import tariff is zero in both sectors. When the low-wage tariff is eliminated, the tariff for the low-wage sector is 0.3 and the tariff for the high-wage sector is 0.0 in the base. The reverse is true when the high-wage tariff is eliminated.

established in the base model, it is the change in the economywide average wage that affects resource allocation, as in the case with competitive labor markets.

Since we have a single input, labor, we may be overstating the wage distortion in the model. As Jones (1971) notes, a model with more detailed labor categories will have smaller wage differentials by labor type. For example, the high-wage sector may require more skilled labor than does the low-wage sector. The observed wage differential may reflect payment for human capital which we do not capture in a model with a single labor category.[22]

22 See Burfisher et al. (1994) for a model with segmented labor markets and four labor categories.

Table 14.2. *Base values for aggregate model variables*

Welfare variables

CLIV	Cost of living index in current prices	1
UTIL	Utility	110.114
YN	New income in equivalent variation calculation	NA[a]
EV	Equivalent variation	NA[a]

Macroeconomic variables

PINDEX	Domestic price index	1
Y	Gross national product	220
GR	Government net revenue	3.462
WALRAS	Walras law variable	0
OBJ	Objective function value	0
ER	Exchange rate	1
FSAV	Foreign savings	16.538

[a] These values only become known in the counterfactual scenarios.

Table 14.3. *Base values for model variables, inputs by sector and factor*

		Labor		Capital	
		Low-wage sector	High-wage sector	Low-wage sector	High-wage sector
$FDSC_{i,f}$	Factor demand	30	20	20	40
$FCTRY_{i,f}$	Factor income	40	71.429	60	28.571
$wsub_{i,f}$	Wage subsidy	0.00	0.00	NA	NA
WF_f	Economy-wide average wage	2.23	2.23	1.48	1.48
$WD_{i,f}$	Factor payment differential	0.598	1.603	2.032	0.484

V.2 Efficiency Wage Sector

One can further modify the CGE model by treating the sectoral wage differential, $WD_{ew,l}$, as a variable and incorporating an additional equation to specify the behavior that generates the wage differential. Efficiency wage theory can explain a profit maximizing firm's decision to pay more than the

Table 14.4. *Base values for the model variables and parameters needed for endogenous wage differentials*

		Labor in high-wage sector
Efficiency wage variables		
$MONITOR_{i,f}$	Total monitoring fees	26.857
$WD_{i,f}$	Endogenous wage differentials, monitoring fees at the margin	1.603
Efficiency wage parameters		
$D1_{i,f}$	Probability of being falsely accused of shirking	0.1
$D2_{i,f}$	Probability a shirker will be caught	0.3
$QR_{i,f}$	Exogenous quit rate	0.05
$\Gamma_{i,f}$	Utility from shirking	0.402
R	Discount rate	0.05
Union variables		
$WD_{i,f}$	Endogenous wage differential, union premium	1.603
$UNUTIL_{i,f}$	Union utility, low weight on wages in union's utility function	6.111
Union parameters		
μ_i	Weight on wages in union's utility function, low value	0.3
μ_i	Weight on wages in union's utility function, high value	0.9
η_i	Elasticity of the derived demand for labor with respect to the wage	0.67

competitive wage. In the efficiency wage sector, labor has the opportunity to shirk, an action assumed to increase labor's utility. The production technology in that sector makes it difficult for producers to monitor workers and thereby ensure that they do not shirk. Instead, the firm pays a wage differential which affects the payoff from shirking. If caught, workers are fired and move into the competitive sector, where they do not receive a wage differential. In equilibrium, no one shirks because producers pay the appropriate

Table 14.5. *Base level parameters*

		Low-wage sector	High-wage sector
σ_i	CES trade substitution elasticity	1.5	1.5
Ω_i	CET export transformation elasticity	2.0	2.0
Π_{ci}	CES production substitution elasticity	0.67	0.67
ρ_{ci}	CES import aggregation parameter	-0.33	-0.33
ρ_{ti}	CET export transformation parameter	-1.5	-1.5
ρ_{pi}	CES production function parameter	0.5	0.5
β_i	CES trade share parameter	0.232	0.299
α_i	CET export share parameter	0.75	0.75
δ_i	CES production labor share parameter	0.449	0.639
A1$_i$	CES trade constant	1.625	1.775
A2$_i$	CET export constant	2.610	2.610
A3$_i$	CES production constant	4.209	3.998
cs$_i$	Consumption expenditure shares	0.477	0.523
pwts$_i$	Weights for the domestic goods price index	0.5	0.5

wage markup that compensates workers for their expected utility from shirking.

We consider two specifications of the monitor in the model. First, we assume a continuous effort function and self-monitoring. Effort increases as the wage differential increases. The wage differential to eliminate shirking affects behavior at the margin. The worker in the efficiency wage sector is more productive than his counterpart in the non-efficiency wage sector since the value of the marginal product of labor is higher. Then we consider a discrete effort function by which the laborer either works or shirks and contributes zero to production.[23] The worker receives the economywide average wage – there is no wage differential to affect his behavior at the margin. Instead, there is an explicit monitor that earns the additional payment and produces non-shirking labor. The difference between the two

23 This approach is closest to Bulow and Summers's (1986) description of shirking behavior. In their model, a worker contributes the same amount to production, regardless of the sector in which he is employed. An additional payment is required in the efficiency wage sector to ensure that the worker actually does contribute to production.

specifications is the degree of distortion in the labor market. The first approach is more distorting.

Both Bulow and Summers (1986) and Copeland (1989) define the optimal wage differential needed to eliminate shirking. In the efficiency wage sector, labor has the option of shirking, an activity which increases utility by Γ. When shirking, a worker faces the probability, D_2, that he will be caught and therefore fired. It is also possible, with probability D_1, that a non-shirking worker will be falsely accused of shirking and fired (note that D_1 is assumed less than D_2 since shirking behavior makes a worker more likely to be caught). Finally, workers in the efficiency wage sector quit at a rate Q, which is assumed to be exogenous. In any case, when the worker leaves the efficiency wage sector, he loses the wage differential and receives the competitive wage. In the competitive sector, it is assumed to be easy to monitor workers so there is no opportunity to shirk.

Consider the expected lifetime utility a worker receives under each of the two options, shirking and not shirking, where r is the common discount rate. When a worker shirks, the return on his asset equals the flow return (current utility) plus the expected capital loss:[24]

$$rU_{ew}^s = WF_l \cdot WD_{ew,l}(1+\Gamma) - (Q+D_2)(U_{ew}^s - U_c) \qquad (14.2)$$

The subscript refers to the sector: ew for efficiency wage and c for competitive. The superscript refers to behavior in the efficiency wage sector. A worker has the option to shirk (s) or not shirk (n). There are no superscripts for the competitive sector because workers do not have the option to shirk in the competitive sector; it is costless to monitor them. WF_l is the economywide average wage; $WD_{ew,l}$ is the wage markup in the efficiency wage sector.

When a worker in the efficiency wage sector does not shirk, he does not get the immediate utility of shirking, but he is less likely to leave the efficiency wage sector, so he earns the wage differential in the future. The expected utility of a non-shirker is

$$rU_{ew}^n = WF_l \cdot WD_{ew,l} - (Q+D_1)(U_{ew}^n - U_c) \qquad (14.3)$$

A worker in the competitive sector does not have the option to shirk, but he does have the possibility of moving into the efficiency wage sector in the future. The expected number of jobs available is

---

24 See Copeland (1989) for a more detailed discussion of this derivation, particularly the indirect utility function when the effort level exerted affects the probability of receiving the lower, competitive wage in the future.

$$(Q + D_1)L_{ew} \tag{14.4}$$

L_{ew} indicates the number hired in the efficiency wage sector; likewise, a subscript, c, indicates the number hired in the competitive sector. The total labor supply, L, is

$$L_{ew} + L_c = \overline{L} \tag{14.5}$$

Assuming all competitive workers are equally likely to move into the efficiency wage sector, the expected utility of a worker in the competitive sector is

$$rU_c = WF_l + (Q + D_1)\left(\frac{L_{ew}}{L_c}\right)\left(U_{ew}^n - U_c\right) \tag{14.6}$$

In equilibrium, the optimal wage differential ensures that the utility from not shirking is greater than or equal to the utility from shirking:

$$U_{ew}^n - U_{ew}^s \geq 0 \tag{14.7}$$

Given the expressions for expected utility for shirkers and non-shirkers in the efficiency wage sector, this can be expressed as

$$(D_2 - D_1)(U_{ew}^N - U_c) \geq \Gamma WF_l \cdot WD_{ew,l} \tag{14.8}$$

The expected utility gain of not shirking must exceed the immediate utility gain of shirking if shirking is to be eliminated.

Substituting in the expressions for the expected utility of a non-shirking worker in the efficiency wage sector and the expected utility of a worker in the competitive sector, one can identify the additional payment at which the worker is indifferent between shirking and not shirking (and chooses not to shirk by assumption). This additional payment is the "no shirking condition," NSC_{ew}, where the subscript ew refers to the efficiency wage sector. It is defined as follows:

$$NSC_{ew} = \frac{\Gamma r}{(D_2 - D_1)} + \frac{\Gamma(D_1 + Q)\overline{L}}{(D_2 - D_1)(\overline{L} - L_{ew})} \tag{14.9}$$

The no shirking cost is a percentage increase over the economywide average wage. It can be converted to a wage differential, the specification in the stylized CGE model, as follows:

$$WD_{ew,l} = (1 + NSC_{ew}) \tag{14.10}$$

Note that the wage markup is an increasing function of the labor employed in the efficiency wage sector. When there are more efficiency wage jobs, a worker is more likely to move out of the competitive sector. The increased probability of leaving the competitive sector reduces the penalty of shirking because the punishment – working in the competitive sector at a lower wage – becomes less likely. To offset the decrease in the likelihood of remaining in the competitive sector, producers in the efficiency wage sector must increase the financial cost of shirking, the wage differential. The competitive sector serves as the residual; all workers not allocated to sector 1 are hired in the competitive sector and receive the competitive wage.

Our stylized model is more general than Bulow and Summers's model, which uses a single input, labor, and a constant marginal product of labor, thereby generating a linear production possibilities frontier. In Bulow and Summers's specification, a wage subsidy reallocates labor and therefore changes the equilibrium point on the linear production possibilities frontier. In the CGE model, the production possibilities frontier is concave to the origin. There is a CES production function over the inputs, labor and capital; the marginal product of labor changes along the derived labor demand curve. With this specification, the wage differential to eliminate shirking acts as a distortion because it affects the producer's choice of labor along the labor demand curve. When the wage differential increases, there is a welfare cost to the economy because resources are not allocated efficiently. In terms of the theoretical trade diagrams, the PPF shrinks further toward the origin. In a model with an efficiency wage sector, the wage distortion changes following a policy shock. This additional change affects both factor allocation and welfare.

One can also view the wage markup as a fee that does not affect behavior at the margin. Consider a model with three inputs to production: labor, capital, and monitors. The monitors, M, produce non-shirking labor, L^*, the same input used in the competitive sector, which does not require a monitor. Output is a function of capital and non-shirking labor:

$$X_{ew} = f(L^*, K) \tag{14.11}$$

and labor (possibly shirking) and monitors are needed to produce non-shirking labor:

$$L^* = f(M, L_{ew}) \tag{14.12}$$

Following Bulow and Summers's description of a discrete effort function, L^* is equal to L, the number of workers hired, if a monitor is hired. Otherwise, labor shirks and there is zero productive labor as an input. We assume that labor acts both as a monitor and as an input to production; it receives income for both services. The income for monitoring is determined from the "no shirking" equation while the income labor receives for its contribution to production is the economywide average wage. With this specification, the value of the marginal product of labor is the same in both sectors – the monitoring fee does not affect the worker's behavior at the margin.

To incorporate this version of efficiency wage behavior into the CGE model, the wage differential $WD_{ew,l}$, which affects the derived demand for labor, is set equal to 1. There is an additional monitoring fee which reduces the revenue available to pay productive inputs, labor and capital. The derived demand for labor becomes

$$WF_l = \left(PX_{ew} - \frac{MONITOR}{X_{ew}} \right) f_L(L, K) \qquad (14.13)$$

where MONITOR, the total monitoring costs, can be calculated as

$$MONITOR = (1 + NSC_{ew}) \cdot WF_l \cdot L_{ew} \qquad (14.14)$$

V.3 Union Model

The wage differentials evident in the base data can also represent union behavior. There are many views of union behavior, depending on the specification of the union's utility function.[25] We consider two views of union behavior. In both cases the union is passive; it maximizes utility, taking the derived demand for labor as given. For a discussion of aggressive union behavior, in which the union negotiates for employment as well as wages, see MacDonald and Solow (1981). In their model, the equilibrium wage and employment are determined from the contract curve, the locus of tangency points between the union's utility curves and the firm's isoprofit curves. The position on the contract curve depends on the bargaining strength of the union relative to the firm. Since producers are not hiring along the derived demand for labor, excess workers are hired.[26]

First, we assume the union maximizes the wage bill of its members, recognizing that a reduction in employment will induce firms to pay a higher wage. In essence, the wage differential reflects monopoly power in the labor mar-

---

25 See Farber (1986) for a discussion of union behavior.
26 See Devarajan et al. (1996) for a CGE model with this version of union behavior. De Melo and Tarr (1992) consider the merits of both approaches to union behavior in autos and steel in the United States and conclude that there is no evidence to suggest that producers are not hiring along the derived demand for labor.

ket. Suppose, for example, that there are two sectors in the economy and that output in each sector is produced by using labor and capital, with labor homogenous, perfectly mobile between sectors; the endowment fixed; but capital is sector-specific. Further, assume that sector 1 is unionized while sector 2 is not. Given these conditions, labor can be drawn into sector 1 but under increasing cost so that the labor supply curve for sector 1 is upward sloping. The union is able to restrict all entry by new workers into its membership and maximizes total labor income to its members by setting the wage according to standard monopoly pricing theory, offering that amount of labor at which marginal revenue, determined by the firm's value marginal product of labor in sector 1, equals marginal cost (determined by the labor supply in sector 1). In equilibrium, the wage in sector 1 will exceed the wage in sector 2 because of the existence of a union in sector 1.[27] Analogous to the monopoly markup, the optimal wage differential depends on the wage elasticity of demand for labor in the unionized sector.

To modify the stylized model, the wage differential in the unionized sector is endogenous and is determined as follows:

$$WD_{u,l} = \frac{\eta_u}{\eta_u - 1} \tag{14.15}$$

where the subscript u refers to the unionized sector and η_u is the elasticity of labor demand in the unionized sector.

In the CGE model, we use a CES production function, by which the elasticity of labor demand curve with respect to the wage is constant. As a result, this form of union behavior is identical to the model with exogenous wage differentials. However, the wage differential would be endogenous with a different functional form for production. Then, policy shocks would change the labor market distortion. Furthermore, policy changes that change the degree of competitiveness in the domestic market, for example by flattening the demand curve, also flatten the derived demand for labor. As the elasticity of the derived demand for labor increases, union strength, as represented by the wage differential, declines.

For comparison, we consider a different specification of the union's utility function. In this version, the union has both a minimum acceptable wage, presumably the economywide average wage (which the producer views as exogenous), and a minimum acceptable level of employment. When the sector contracts, for example as a result of increased import competition, the

---

27 This is analogous to the union model Hill (1984) uses to demonstrate comparative statics in a trade model with endogenous wage differentials.

decline in the wage differential can dampen the reduction in employment. This specification follows from de Melo and Tarr's (1990, 1992) union model. The union takes the demand for labor as given and chooses the wage differential that maximizes its utility, *UNUTIL*:

$$UNUTIL = \left(WF_l \cdot WD_{u,l} - WF_l\right)^{\mu}\left(L_u - L_{\min}\right)^{(1-\mu)} \tag{14.16}$$

Given a CES production function (see equation [A14.10] in the Appendix), the optimal labor demand in the union sector is:

$$L_u = \left(\frac{PX_u \cdot X_u \delta_l}{WF_l \cdot WD_u}\right)^{1/(\rho_{p,u}+1)}\left(\frac{X}{A3_u}\right)^{\rho_{p,u}/(1+\rho_{p,u})} \tag{14.17}$$

Substituting this value for labor into the union's utility function and choosing the wage differential to maximize utility, the optimal wage differential is

$$\frac{WD_{u,l}-1}{WD_{u,l}} = \left(\frac{L_u - L_{\min}}{L_u}\right)\left(\frac{\mu}{1-\mu}\right)(1+\rho_{p,u}) \tag{14.18}$$

for

$$\mu \neq 1$$

When the weight on the wage markup in the union's utility function is 1, the union maximizes the wage payment subject to the derived demand for labor.

A policy such as protection in the high-wage sector will shift the demand for labor to the right and increase both the number hired and the wage differential. Conversely, reducing protection will lower the wage differential. Furthermore, the weights on the wage markup in the union's utility function affect the magnitude of the changes in wages and employment following a shift in the labor demand curve.[28] When there is a high weight on wages in the utility function, wages bear a larger percent of the labor demand shift. If the sector expands, wages increase by a larger proportion than if there is a low weight on wages in utility. Likewise, if the sector contracts, wages decline by a larger proportion than if there is a low weight on wages in utility. This seemingly counterintuitive result – that a union that cares about wages will sacrifice wages more than a union that does not care about wages, following a decline in the demand for labor – reflects the existence of

---

28 The authors would like to thank Shantayanan Devarajan and Hafez Ghanem for useful discussions which led to the following analysis. See Devarajan et al. (1996) for discussion of union behavior in Bangladesh and Indonesia.

the minimal acceptable wage and employment level in the union's utility function. As the weight on wages increases, there is more discretion over the minimum acceptable wage so there will be more adjustment in wages.

VI Results

Our stylized model represents the theoretical models described in Section II. To illustrate concepts from the theoretical models, we consider a series of sensitivity analyses in a model with exogenous wage differentials. First, we remove the wage differentials to describe the effects of exogenous wage differentials on welfare and resource allocation in the model. Then, we evaluate the links between price shocks and factor returns for various elasticities in the version of the model with neoclassical labor markets. We find that the Stolper–Samuelson Theorem does not hold when elasticities are low. Finally, we consider trade liberalization and a change in the wage differential. The two changes offset each other in terms of the impact on production. We find that the wage differential change dominates the relative price change. In this scenario, the change in the wage differential is arbitrary. However, the results suggest that endogenous wage differentials can be important when analyzing policy changes.

As presented in Figure 14.3, wage differentials cause the PPF to shrink toward the origin. The price line is not tangent to the new PPF, further reducing welfare. To explore the welfare effects of the wage distortion, we eliminate the wage differentials, restoring neoclassical labor markets, moving to point 3 on Figure 14.3. There are substantial welfare gains – equivalent variation is 25.9, measured in units of the numéraire good (not tabulated).[29] Furthermore, the physical factor intensity of production changes as labor moves into the formerly high-wage sector and capital moves into the formerly low-wage sector (which has a high factor payment differential for capital in the initial model). Initially, the high-wage sector was capital intensive (in the physical sense), with a capital–labor ratio of 2.0 and the low-wage sector was labor intensive (in the physical sense), with a capital–labor ratio of 0.7 (see Table 14.3). When wage differentials are removed, the high-wage sector becomes labor intensive (in the physical sense), with a capital–labor ratio of .9 and the low-wage sector becomes capital intensive (in the physical sense), with a capital–labor ratio of 1.5 (see Table 14.6).

In a model with neoclassical labor markets, theory indicates that trade liberalization will improve welfare. According to the Stolper–Samuelson

---

29 We change the sign when reporting equivalent variation. In the text and tables, a positive value for equivalent variation indicates that welfare has improved.

Table 14.6. *Factor allocations in the different base models used in sensitivity analysis*

	Low-wage sector $WD_f = 1$ $\Pi = 0.67$ $\Omega = 2.0$ $\sigma = 1.5$	High-wage sector $WD_f = 1$ $\Pi = 0.67$ $\Omega = 2.0$ $\sigma = 1.5$	Low-wage sector $WD_f = 1$ $\Pi = 1.7$ $\Omega = 2.0$ $\sigma = 1.5$	High-wage sector $WD_f = 1$ $\Pi = 1.7$ $\Omega = 2.0$ $\sigma = 1.5$	Low-wage sector $WD_f = 1$ $\Pi = 2.0$ $\Omega = 4.0$ $\sigma = 4.0$	High-wage sector $WD_f = 1$ $\Pi = 2.0$ $\Omega = 4.0$ $\sigma = 4.0$
Capital-labor ratio	1.54	0.92	4.55	0.24	6.21	0.15
Share of capital endowment	0.58	0.42	0.84	0.16	0.90	0.10
Share of labor endowment	0.45	0.54	0.22	0.78	1.70	0.83
Share of revenue to capital	0.50	0.37	0.76	0.15	0.82	0.10
Share of revenue to labor	0.50	0.63	0.24	0.85	0.18	0.90

The low-wage sector is capital intensive in the physical sense if its share of the labor endowment minus its share of the capital endowment is less than zero. The low-wage sector is capital intensive in the value sense if the share of revenue paid to labor in the low-wage sector minus the share of revenue to labor in the high-wage sector is less than zero   (Jones, 1971).

Theorem, the real return to the formerly protected sector will decrease, and the real return to the other factor will increase. To identify the standard trade theory results, we use a version of the model with neoclassical factor markets and liberalize trade in the formerly high-wage sector (there are no tariffs in the other sector). Our results appear in Table 14.7. We find that trade liberalization improves welfare; equivalent variation is 0.8. While the output of the labor intensive good declines as it faces increased foreign competition, the real return to both factors increases and the return to labor relative to the return to capital declines. However, there is no magnification. To explain this unanticipated result, we consider the sensitivity of our results to the parameter values in the model. First, we increase the elasticity of substitution between labor and capital production to 1.7 from 0.7. While this change does result in a smaller real wage increase and a larger increase in the real return to capital following trade liberalization, the real returns to both factors still increase. Finally, we consider the sensitivity of our results to the trade elasticities in the model. We increase the elasticity of substitution between imports and the domestic variety of each good in consumption, σ_i, from a value of 1.5 to 4.0. Likewise, we increase the elasticity of transformation between exports and the domestic variety of each good in production, Ω_i, from a value of 2.0 to a value of 4.0. The model more closely resembles the trade models in which the domestic and either the imported variety or the exported variety are perfect substitutes. We do find the Stolper–Samuelson results in this scenario. The real return to labor decreases by 1.3 percent and the real return to capital increases by 4.5 percent.

In all of the sensitivity analysis, we find that the PPF is not convex. Instead, as the price of the high-wage good decreases as a result of trade liberalization, output also decreases. However, we find the output response is stronger in the third simulation, which most closely replicates the theoretical trade model.

Jones also describes the changes in the relationship between the relative factor price and the relative output price when there are factor payment differentials. When the payments are exogenous, the relationship is identical to the relationship under neoclassical labor markets. However, when there are endogenous wage differentials, an increase in the relative factor distortion in one sector operates as a decline in the relative price of that good. To illustrate this effect, we eliminate the tariff in the formerly high-wage sector and then we consider the same trade policy shock with a reduction in the wage differential in the formerly high-wage sector. The formerly high-wage sector is labor intensive in the value sense so trade liberalization reduces the real return to labor and increases the real return to capital (see Table 14.8).

Table 14.7. *The effects of a 30 percent tariff elimination in the high-wage sector under alternative parameter values*

	Low-wage sector $WD_f = 1$ $\Pi = 0.67$ $\Omega = 2.0$ $\sigma = 1.5$	High-wage sector $WD_f = 1$ $\Pi = 0.67$ $\Omega = 2.0$ $\sigma = 1.5$	Low-wage sector $WD_f = 1$ $\Pi = 1.7$ $\Omega = 2.0$ $\sigma = 1.5$	High-wage sector $WD_f = 1$ $\Pi = 1.7$ $\Omega = 2.0$ $\sigma = 1.5$	Low-wage sector $WD_f = 1$ $\Pi = 2.0$ $\Omega = 4.0$ $\sigma = 4.0$	High-wage sector $WD_f = 1$ $\Pi = 2.0$ $\Omega = 4.0$ $\sigma = 4.0$
			(percent change from base levels)			
Labor	1.86	-1.55	2.69	-0.77	13.76	-2.89
Capital	1.42	-1.97	0.53	-2.86	1.51	-13.37
Wage	0.69	0.69	0.43	0.43	-1.28	-1.28
Return to capital	1.35	1.35	1.71	1.71	4.51	4.51
Wage differential	0.00	0.00	0.00	0.00	0.00	0.00
Output	1.64	-1.71	1.04	-1.08	3.65	-3.95
Composite good consumption	-2.28	2.80	-2.63	3.12	-3.94	5.28
Domestic good consumption	-0.59	-3.35	-1.07	-2.91	-0.64	-9.49
Exports	17.58	13.89	15.56	14.93	33.18	45.48
Imports	-12.35	26.67	-11.95	26.82	-25.88	60.82
			(measured in units of the numeraire good)			
Equivalent variation [a]	0.84		0.96		2.29	

[a] A positive value for equivalent variation indicates a welfare gain.

Table 14.8. *The effects of a 30 percent tariff elimination in the high-wage sector with and without a change in the wage differential in the high-wage sector*

	Low-wage sector	High-wage sector	Low-wage sector	High-wage sector
	$WD_f = 1$ $\Pi = 0.67$ $\Omega = 4.0$ $\sigma = 4.0$	$WD_f = 1$ $\Pi = 0.67$ $\Omega = 4.0$ $\sigma = 4.0$	$WD_f = 1$ $\Pi = 0.67$ $\Omega = 4.0$ $\sigma = 4.0$	$WD_K = 1$ $WD_L = 0.7$ $\Pi = 0.67$ $\Omega = 4.0$ $\sigma = 4.0$
	(percent change from base levels)			
Labor	10.53	-9.27	-21.20	18.68
Capital	7.81	-11.51	-7.04	10.38
Wage	-0.30	-0.30	1.89	1.89
Return to capital	3.50	3.50	-1.92	-1.92
Wage differential	0.00	0.00	0.00	-0.30
Output	9.16	-10.11	-14.59	15.48
Composite good consumption	-2.06	3.64	-12.14	11.45
Domestic good consumption	2.36	-13.86	-13.42	4.07
Exports	53.52	28.82	-22.76	127.74
Imports	-31.75	64.51	-2.95	35.84
	(measured in units of the numeraire good)			
Equivalent variation[a]	2.17		-1.25	

[a] A positive value for equivalent variation indicates a welfare gain.

There are welfare gains as tariffs are eliminated; equivalent variation is 2.17, measured in units of the numéraire good. The output and trade variables change in the expected direction.

The results change dramatically when there is a decline in the wage differential as well as trade liberalization. The wage differential operates as an increase in the relative price of the labor intensive good. Output of the formerly protected sector increases by 15.5 percent. The real return to labor increases 1.9 percent and the real return to capital decreases by 1.9 percent. There is a welfare loss as the distortion in the labor market increases. These results suggest that an endogenous wage differential can offset both the Stolper–Samuelson and the welfare results anticipated from trade liberalization.

VII Endogenous Wage Differentials and Policy Shocks

To analyze the impact of expanding the high-wage sectors we consider three policy shocks: (1) a wage subsidy to the high-wage sector, (2) trade liberalization in the high-wage sector, and (3) trade liberalization in the low-wage sector. A wage subsidy targets the wage differential directly while trade liberalization affects output and therefore derived demand for inputs. We consider trade liberalization in one sector and assume that the other sector does not receive protection. This allows us to focus on the effects of a single policy shock. The representative consumer pays for the wage subsidy through a lump sum tax and receives tariff revenue as a lump sum transfer.

To illustrate the effects of labor market behavior under each policy shock, we use five different base models: (1) exogenous wage differentials, (2) efficiency wage behavior that affects productivity at the margin, (3) efficiency wage behavior that affects the average wage, (4) a union that maximizes the wage bill to its members, and (5) a union that has a minimum acceptable wage and level of employment. Under each specification of labor behavior, the base model is calibrated to the factor price differentials shown in Table 14.3. We vary behavior for labor in the high-wage sector. The assumed factor payment differentials for labor in the low-wage sector and capital in both sectors are held constant in the analysis.

VII.1 Wage Subsidy

Exogenous Wage Differentials First, we consider the effects of a 10 percent wage subsidy when the wage differential is exogenous. Labor in the high-wage sector increases by 7.4 percent (see Table 14.9). The capital used in the high-wage sector also increases, by 1.7 percent. This reflects a low elasticity of substitution between labor and capital. Output increases by 5.7 percent, reflecting the increased input use. The equivalent variation welfare improvement is 1.53 (measured in units of the numéraire good).

Efficiency Wage Behavior When efficiency wages are assumed to generate the wage differential, the magnitude of the results changes. Consider the case in which the wage differential affects behavior at the margin. The cost to eliminate shirking increases as the sector expands and employs more

Table 14.9. The effects of a 10 percent wage subsidy to the high-wage sector under efficiency wage behavior

	Exogenous Wage Differential		Efficiency Wage		Efficiency Wage, Monitor	
	Low-wage sector	High-wage sector	Low-wage sector	High-wage sector	Low-wage sector	High-wage sector
	(percent change from base levels)					
Labor	-4.93	7.40	-4.28	6.42	-2.91	4.37
Capital	-3.42	1.71	-2.98	1.49	-0.14	0.07
Wage	7.96	7.96	7.87	7.87	3.04	3.04
Return to capital	0.59	0.59	0.53	0.53	-1.26	-1.26
Wage Differential	0.00	0.00	0.00	1.4	0.0	0.94
Output	-4.03	5.73	-3.50	4.97	-2.00	2.66
Composite Good Consumption	-2.50	3.71	-2.17	3.22	-1.26	1.70
Domestic Good Consumption	-3.32	4.93	-2.88	4.28	-1.65	2.29
Exports	-10.56	12.79	-9.21	11.09	-5.21	5.94
Imports	2.50	-0.61	2.16	-0.54	1.11	-0.37
	(measured in units of the numeraire good)					
Equivalent Variation*	1.53		1.35		0.61	

In all scenarios the base level capital-labor ratio is 0.67 and 2.0 in the low-wage and high-wage sectors, respectively; Π = 0.67 in both sectors; Ω = 2.0 in both sectors; σ = 1.5 in both sectors.

* A positive value for equivalent variation indicates a welfare gain.

labor – the wage differential increases by 1.4 percent. As the cost of labor increases, the quantity of labor demanded expands by a smaller amount than when there are exogenous wage differentials. The demand for labor increases 6.4 percent rather than 7.4 percent. The increase in capital usage is also smaller than when wage differentials are exogenous. The real returns to labor and capital both increase, but by a smaller amount.

The increase in the wage differential further distorts the labor market. The value of the marginal product of labor increases further in the high-wage sector. As a result, labor is allocated less efficiently across sectors and there is less of a welfare gain – equivalent variation is 1.35 rather than 1.53 under the assumption of exogenous wage differentials.

When there is an explicit monitor, there is even less factor movement in response to the wage subsidy. The lump sum monitoring fee increases as the sector expands, draining the amount of revenue that the producer has left over to hire labor and capital. The increase in demand for inputs is smaller, labor increases by 4.4 percent and capital increases by 0.1 percent. As a result of the small increase in the demand for capital in the high-wage sector and the decline in demand as the low-wage sector contracts, the real return to capital declines.

With this specification of the monitor, the welfare gains are lower than in the model in which monitoring fees affect behavior at the margin. Equivalent variation is 0.61, rather than 1.35. Workers drawn into the high-wage sector are not more productive than workers in the low-wage sector, an implication of the first specification of the efficiency wage sector. In that case, the value of the marginal product of labor is higher at the margin.

Union Behavior Union behavior may also be assumed to account for wage differentials evident in the base data. We consider changes in the economy when the high-wage sector pays a union premium. As in the case with efficiency wages, we consider two specifications of the union's utility function. First, we consider the union that has utility over both employment and the wage differential, or union premium extracted. We also consider two different specifications of the union utility function – a low weight of 0.3 on the wage markup and then a high weight of 0.9 on the wage markup. Then, we consider the case in which the union is concerned about the wage differential and acts as a monopolist. This is of course a special case with a weight of 1 on the wage differential in the union's utility function. The results are identical to those from the model with exogenous wage distortions.

Our results for a wage subsidy when union behavior generates the wage differential appear in Table 14.10. As in the efficiency wage case, the pres-

Table 14.10. The effects of a 10 percent wage subsidy to the high-wage sector under union behavior

	Exogenous Wage Differential		Union μ = 0.3		Union μ = 0.9	
	Low-wage sector	High-wage sector	Low-wage sector	High-wage sector	Low-wage sector	High-wage sector
	(percent change from base level)					
Labor	-4.93	7.40	-3.83	5.74	-0.30	0.45
Capital	-3.42	1.71	-2.67	1.34	-0.21	0.11
Wage	7.96	7.96	7.81	7.81	7.18	7.18
Return to capital	0.59	0.59	0.49	0.49	0.05	0.05
Wage Differential	0.00	0.00	0.00	2.38	0.00	10.40
Output	-4.03	5.73	-3.14	4.46	-0.25	0.35
Composite Good Consumption	-2.50	3.71	-1.94	2.89	-0.15	0.23
Domestic Good Consumption	-3.32	4.93	-2.58	3.84	-0.20	0.30
Exports	-10.56	12.79	-8.27	9.92	-0.66	0.77
Imports	2.50	-0.61	1.92	-0.50	0.15	-0.04
			(measured in units of the numeraire good)			
Equivalent Variation[a]	1.53		1.22		0.10	

In all scenarios the base level capital-labor ratio is 0.67 and 2.0 in the low-wage and high-wage sectors, respectively; Π = 0.67 in both sectors; Ω = 2.0 in both sectors; σ = 1.5 in both sectors.
[a] A positive value for equivalent variation indicates a welfare gain.

ence of a union reduces the magnitude of resource changes following a wage subsidy. When the union puts a low weight on the wage differential, labor in the subsidized sector increases by 5.7 percent, rather than 7.4 percent, when the wage differential is exogenous. Likewise, the capital in the subsidized sector increases by 1.3 percent, rather than 1.7 percent. When the union puts a high weight on the wage differential, the result is even more dramatic – labor increases by only 0.5 percent and capital by 0.1 percent. The wage differential increases by 10.4 percent when the union has a high weight on wages, as opposed to 2.4 percent when the union has a low weight on wages in its utility function. With a high weight on wages, the benefits of expanding the sector appear as a high wage differential with little increase in employment. As a result, the economywide average wage increases by a smaller amount with the union compared to the same policy shock in a model with exogenous wage differentials.

The welfare gains are smaller with union behavior. Equivalent variation is 1.22 when the union has a low weight and 0.1 when the union has a high weight on the wage markup in its utility function. In both cases, the reduced welfare increase results from an increase in the wage differential – the latter increases 2.4 and 10.4 percent in the low and high weight cases, respectively. When the union has a high weight on the wage markup, the effect of a wage subsidy is primarily felt as an increase in the wage differential. This further distorts the economy, dampening the welfare gain by an order of magnitude, compared to that found in the model with exogenous wage differentials.

VII.2 Trade Liberalization in the High-Wage Sector

Exogenous Wage Differentials Trade liberalization provides an indirect instrument for changing employment in the high-wage sector. Consider the elimination of a 30 percent tariff applied to imports in the high-wage sector under the assumption of exogenous wage differentials. The direct effect of trade liberalization is to increase imports of the high-wage good by 26.6 percent and to decrease domestic production by 1.5 percent (see Table 14.11). Exports of the high-wage good expand by 14.0 percent. This reflects the increase in the relative price of exports to the domestically produced variety. Given the assumed exogenous trade balance, the increase in imports of the formerly protected good must be offset with an increase in exports. The decline in low-wage imports also reflects the changes in relative prices. There are welfare gains from eliminating protection; equivalent variation is 0.85 (measured in units of the numéraire good). Furthermore, the positive

Table 14.11. *The effects of a 30 percent tariff elimination in the high-wage sector under efficiency wage behavior*

	Exogenous Wage Differential		Efficiency Wage		Efficiency Wage, Monitor	
	Low-wage sector	High-wage sector	Low-wage sector	High-wage sector	Low-wage sector	High-wage sector
	(percent change from base levels)					
Labor	1.16	-1.74	1.01	-1.51	0.91	-1.37
Capital	1.95	-0.98	1.83	-0.91	1.53	-0.77
Wage	0.76	0.76	0.79	0.79	1.37	1.37
Return to Capital	1.31	1.31	1.33	1.33	0.92	0.92
Wage Differential	0.00	0.00	0.00	-0.31	0.00	-0.28
Output	1.63	-1.52	1.50	-1.34	1.12	-1.13
Composite Good Consumption	-2.13	2.74	-2.20	2.85	-2.47	2.95
Domestic Good Consumption	-0.33	-3.32	-0.43	-3.17	-0.75	-3.02
Exports	18.52	14.00	18.12	14.45	17.18	15.09
Imports	-12.47	26.64	-12.40	26.61	-12.37	26.43
	(measured in units of the numeraire good)					
Equivalent Variation [a]	0.85		0.90		0.72	

In all scenarios the base level capital-labor ratio is 0.67 and 2.0 in the low-wage and high-wage sectors, respectively; $\Pi = 0.67$ in both sectors; $\Omega = 2.0$ in both sectors; $\sigma = 1.5$ in both sectors.
[a] A positive value for equivalent variation indicates a welfare gain.

welfare effects of trade liberalization offset the effects of moving labor out of the high-wage sector, where its marginal product of labor is higher.

As evident in the base data (Tables 14.1–14.3), the high-wage sector is capital intensive in the physical sense, as determined by the endowment shares allocated to each sector. However, because of the pattern of factor payment differentials, the high-wage sector is labor intensive in the value sense. As Jones notes, factor intensity in the value sense determines the link between output price changes and relative factor returns. We find that the return to labor relative to the return to capital declines. This is consistent with the Stolper–Samuelson Theorem and the factor intensity in the value sense. As noted in the previous section, when the model has high trade elasticities, the results are more consistent with trade theory. In a version of the model with high trade elasticities (both σ_i and Ω_i equal 4.0), the magnification effects hold as well and the real return to labor declines (not tabulated).[30]

Efficiency Wage Behavior Given the structure of protection, we expect a bigger welfare gain from trade liberalization when the protected sector pays efficiency wages. As the number of efficiency wage jobs declines, the monitoring costs at the margin decline by 0.3 percent (see Table 14.11). There is a slight increase in the welfare effects due to the change in the wage differential; equivalent variation is 0.9 rather than 0.85. The change in resource allocation following the policy shock is also slightly smaller, because of the decline in the wage differential. Labor in the high-wage sector contracts less than when the wage differential is exogenous – it declines by 1.5 percent rather than 1.7 percent, respectively.

When the efficiency wage sector is represented by an explicit monitor in production, monitoring costs also decline as the high-wage sector contracts. In this case, the lump sum monitoring fee declines and so the producer has more revenue left over to pay both labor and capital. As a result, the decline in resource use output in the high-wage sector is smallest under this scenario. The welfare gain is also the smallest because of second best effects. Capital is more productive in the low-wage sector. In this case, fewer units of capital move to the low-wage sector so there is less of a productivity gain.

Union Behavior When the protected sector is unionized, additional welfare gains from trade liberalization would be expected, compared to the gains under assumed exogenous wage differentials. As the high-wage sector contracts, the number employed will fall. The union's strength will decline and the wage differential will fall.

We find that the wage differential declines by 2.2 percent when the union places a high weight on wages, and it declines by 0.6 percent when the union places a low weight on wages (Table 14.12). The welfare changes reflect the additional benefit of reducing the distortion in the labor market. Equivalent variation is higher in the union case than in the case of trade liberalization with exogenous wage differentials; it is 1.2 when the union places a high weight on wages and 0.94 when the union places a high weight on employment, compared to 0.85 when the wage differentials are exogenous.

Interestingly, when the union cares more about wages (i.e., it places a high weight on wages in its utility function), the wage differential declines further

---

30 A complete set of tables for policy shocks with high trade elasticities is available from Thierfelder upon request.

Table 14.12. *The effects of a 30 percent tariff elimination in the high-wage sector under union behavior*

	Exogenous Wage Differential		Union μ = 0.3		Union μ = 0.9	
	Low-wage sector	High-wage sector	Low-wage sector	High-wage sector	Low-wage sector	High-wage sector
	(percent change from base level)					
Labor	1.16	-1.74	0.88	-0.32	0.07	-0.11
Capital	1.95	-0.98	1.73	-0.87	1.10	-0.55
Wage	0.76	0.76	0.82	0.82	0.97	0.97
Return to Capital	1.31	1.31	1.35	1.35	1.45	1.45
Wage Differential	0.00	0.00	0.00	-0.57	0.00	-2.18
Output	1.63	-1.52	1.39	-1.19	0.69	-0.23
Composite Good Consumption	-2.13	2.74	-2.27	2.95	-2.67	3.57
Domestic Good Consumption	-0.33	-3.32	-0.51	-3.05	-1.05	-2.26
Exports	18.52	14.00	17.79	14.82	15.70	17.17
Imports	-12.47	26.64	-12.35	26.59	-12.00	26.45
	(measured in units of the numeraire good)					
Equivalent Variation [*]	0.85		0.94		1.20	

In all scenarios, the base level capital-labor ratio is 0.67 and 2.0 in the low-wage and high-wage sectors, respectively; Π = 0.67 in both sectors; Ω = 2.0 in both sectors; σ = 1.5 in both sectors.

[*] A positive value for equivalent variation indicates a welfare gain.

when the sector contracts than when the union cares more about employment. In effect, the union has a bigger premium to lose when it cares more about wages and the derived demand for labor shifts further to the left.[31] Also, the union has more discretion over wages and it must meet the minimum acceptable employment and wage.

VII.3 Trade Liberalization in the Low-Wage Sector

Exogenous Wage Differentials When tariffs in the low-wage sector are eliminated, the results parallel those obtained in the case where tariffs in the high-wage sector were eliminated and exogenous wage differentials were assumed (see Table 14.13). Imports of the low-wage good increase and competing domestic production decreases. Exports of both goods increase and imports of the high-wage good decrease, reflecting the change in relative prices needed to maintain the assumed exogenous trade balance. Factors move out of the low-wage sector and into the high-wage sector. The wage relative to the return to capital increases, reflecting the fact that the low-wage sector is capital intensive in the value sense. Welfare increases as the trade distortion is removed.

Efficiency Wage Behavior When there are endogenous wage differentials, whether due to efficiency wages or to union behavior, the effects of tariff elimination in the low-wage sector are similar to those of a wage subsidy to the high-wage sector, in terms of changes in the wage differential (Table 14.14). As tariffs are removed in the low-wage sector, production in the low-wage sector decreases, effectively increasing the supply of labor to the high-wage sector. The effect is similar to a wage subsidy in the high-wage sector, at least on the production side of the economy. Of course, the tariff decrease also reduces the consumption distortion. In terms of changes in the factor markets, however, there are subtle differences between the two policies. A wage subsidy targets employment, causing producers to substitute labor for capital as output expands. When tariffs are removed in the low-wage sector, output and factor demand in the high-wage sector expand without a bias toward either input.

The change in the wage differential reflects labor market behavior. As the number of competitive sector jobs declines, the penalty of shirking – being sent to the competitive sector at a lower wage – becomes less likely. To

---

31 This result is consistent with de Melo and Tarr (1992), who eliminate protection in the auto sector with different weights on wages in the union's utility function. See Devarajan et al. (1996) for a discussion of the model calibration which contributes to this result.

Table 14.13. *The effects of a 30 percent tariff elimination in the low-wage sector under efficiency wage behavior*

	Exogenous Wage Differential		Efficiency Wage		Efficiency Wage, Monitor	
	Low-wage sector	High-wage sector	Low-wage sector	High-wage sector	Low-wage sector	High-wage sector
	(percent change from base levels)					
Labor	-0.95	1.43	-0.83	1.24	-0.75	1.13
Capital	-1.58	0.79	-1.49	0.74	-1.25	0.63
Wage	0.72	0.72	0.70	0.70	0.23	0.23
Return to Capital	0.28	0.28	0.26	0.26	0.60	0.60
Wage Differential	0.00	0.00	0.00	0.26	0.00	0.24
Output	-1.33	1.25	-1.22	1.10	-0.92	0.93
Composite Good Consumption	2.32	-1.68	2.39	-1.77	2.61	-1.85
Domestic Good Consumption	-2.41	0.07	-2.32	-0.06	-2.07	-0.19
Exports	8.11	11.6	8.41	11.25	9.12	10.75
Imports	33.96	-7.79	33.88	-7.78	33.84	-7.67
	(measured in units of the numeraire good)					
Equivalent Variation [a]	0.47		0.42		0.56	

In all scenarios the base level capital-labor ratio is 0.67 and 2.0 in the low-wage and high-wage sectors, respectively; $\Pi = 0.67$ in both sectors; $\Omega = 2.0$ in both sectors; $\sigma = 1.5$ in both sectors.
[a] A positive value for equivalent variation indicates a welfare gain.

compensate, the wage differential increases 0.3 percent. This increased distortion slightly dampens the welfare gain evident in the model with exogenous wage differentials. Interestingly, when a monitor represents efficiency wage behavior, welfare increases despite the increase in the monitoring cost. This reflects second best effects that arise from the exogenous factor payments for inputs other than labor in the high-wage sector. The decline in capital use in the low-wage sector is the lowest in this scenario. Since capital earns a high exogenous factor payment differential in the low-wage sector, there are some positive effects on welfare.

Union Behavior The output and trade results follow the direction of the changes that occur when the wage differentials are assumed to be

Table 14.14. *The effects of a 30 percent tariff elimination in the low-wage sector under union behavior*

	Exogenous Wage Differential		Union μ = 0.3		Union μ = 0.9	
	Low-wage sector	High-wage sector	Low-wage sector	High-wage sector	Low-wage sector	High-wage sector
	(percent change from base levels)					
Labor	-0.95	1.43	-0.73	1.09	-0.06	0.09
Capital	-1.58	0.79	-1.41	0.71	-0.92	0.46
Wage	0.72	0.72	0.97	0.97	0.56	0.56
Return to Capital	0.28	0.28	1.45	1.45	0.15	0.15
Wage Differential	0.00	0.00	0.00	0.47	0.00	1.87
Output	-1.33	1.25	-1.14	0.98	-0.57	0.19
Composite Good Consumption	2.32	-1.68	2.44	-1.84	2.78	-2.34
Domestic Good Consumption	-2.41	0.07	-2.26	-0.16	-1.81	-0.82
Exports	8.11	11.6	8.65	10.97	10.26	9.10
Imports	33.96	-7.79	33.82	-7.67	33.40	-7.76
	(measured in units of the numeraire good)					
Equivalent Variation [a]	0.47		0.39		0.16	

In all scenarios the base level capital-labor ratio is 0.67 and 2.0 in the low-wage and high-wage sectors, respectively; Π = 0.67 in both sectors; Ω = 2.0 in both sectors; σ = 1.5 in both sectors.

[a] A positive value for equivalent variation indicates a welfare gain.

exogenous. There are differences in factor returns that reflect the endogenous wage differential. As the wage differential increases, the welfare gains decline as the labor market becomes more distorted. In all cases, the return to labor increases relative to the return to capital since the low-wage sector is capital intensive in the value sense. We do not find the magnification effect, because of the relatively low trade elasticities, as discussed in the sensitivity section. However, when we consider the same series of policy shocks in a model with high trade elasticities (not tabulated), the magnification effects hold; the real return to capital decreases, and the real return to labor increases. Furthermore, when the union has a high weight on wages, the wage differential increases 9.4 percent and welfare actually declines following trade liberalization. This suggests that for certain parameter values, labor behavior can change the welfare analysis found in models with exogenous wage differentials.

VIII Conclusions

In this analysis, we explore the welfare and resource allocation effects of trade and tax policy shocks when there are endogenous wage differentials. We find lessons for both CGE modelers who ignore the underlying labor behavior when they maintain exogenous wage differentials, and industrial policy advocates who urge subsidies to the high-wage sectors. When the high-wage sector expands, the labor market distortions increase, dampening any welfare gains that may arise from the policy shock. Likewise, there is a positive effect on welfare when the high-wage sector declines. In general, endogenous wage differential effects do not reverse the sign of equivalent variation following a policy shock, compared to the same policy shock in a model with exogenous wage differentials. However, they do affect the magnitude of the welfare gains, particularly for the union model with a high weight on wages. For the policy shocks and parameters in the labor behavior equations considered in this chapter, the welfare effects of endogenous distortions are often small. However, for certain parameter values (i.e., the union with a high weight on wages in its utility function) the endogenous wage differential dampens the welfare results considerably. Furthermore, when there are trade liberalization in the low-wage sectors and high trade elasticities, the presence of such a union actually reverses the welfare results. From these simulations, we conclude that exogenous wage differentials can be used as a proxy for the underlying labor behavior, but at some cost to the welfare calculation.

We also find that an endogenous wage differential affects resource movements following a policy shock. For example, when the high-wage sector expands, the wage differential increases as well. This additional factor cost dampens the increase in labor demand, compared to the exogenous wage differential case. While the direction of resource flows is the same as when the wage differential is exogenous, the magnitude is smaller. This also explains the slight difference in factor returns for the same policy shock with different labor market specifications. Our results suggest that labor market behavior can affect the income distribution following a policy shock such as trade liberalization.

Finally, our results suggest that labor behavior should be an important consideration when arguments to subsidize the high-wage sectors are made. When the wage differential is endogenous, one must take into account the general equilibrium effects of the increased wage differential on the resource allocation in the economy. Policies to expand the high-wage sector yield welfare gains due to the nature of the policy shock (trade liberalization) or the existence of other exogenous wage distortions (as in the wage subsidy). The gains are not due to the endogenous wage differential, which increases as the sector expands. Indeed, the endogenous wage differential reduces welfare when the high-wage sector expands.

Appendix 14.1

Model Equations

Price Equations

$$PX_i \cdot X_i = PED_i \cdot E_i + PDD_i \cdot DD_i \tag{A14.1}$$

$$PMD_i = PWM_i \cdot ER \cdot (1 + tm_i) \tag{A14.2}$$

$$PQ_i \cdot Q_i = PDT_i \cdot DD_i + PMD_i \cdot M_i \tag{A14.3}$$

$$PDT_i = PD_i \cdot (1 + td_i) \tag{A14.4}$$

$$PINDEX = \Sigma_i pwts_i \cdot PD_i \tag{A14.5}$$

$$PX_i \cdot X_i = \Sigma_f WF_f \cdot WFIST_{i,f} \cdot FDSC_{i,f} + MONITOR_{i,f} \tag{A14.6}$$

Elasticity Equations

$$\Pi_i = \frac{1}{(1 + \rho_{p,i})} \tag{A14.7}$$

$$\sigma_i = \frac{1}{\left(1 + \rho_{c,i}\right)} \tag{A14.8}$$

$$\Omega_i = \frac{-1}{\left(1 + \rho_{t,i}\right)} \tag{A14.9}$$

Production, Factor Demand and Final Demand Equations

$$X_i = A3_i \cdot \left(\Sigma_f \delta_{i,f} \cdot FDSC_{i,f}^{-\rho_{p,i}}\right)^{-1/\rho_{p,i}} \tag{A14.10}$$

$$WF_f \cdot WFDIST_{i,f} \cdot \left(1 - wsub_{i,f}\right) =$$
$$\left(PX_i - \frac{MONITOR_{i,f}}{X_i}\right) \cdot A3 \cdot \left(\Sigma_f \delta_{i,f} \cdot FDSC_{i,f}^{\rho_{p,i}}\right)^{\left[\left(-1/\rho_{p,i}\right)-1\right]} \cdot FDSC_{i,f}^{\left(-\rho_{p,i}-1\right)} \tag{A14.11}$$

$$X_i = A2_i \cdot \left(\alpha_i \cdot E_i^{-\rho_{t,i}} + \left(1 - \alpha_i\right) \cdot DD_i^{-\rho_{t,i}}\right)^{-1/\rho_{t,i}} \tag{A14.12}$$

$$Q_i = A1_i \cdot \left(\beta \cdot M_i^{-\rho_{c,i}} + \left(1 - \beta_i\right) \cdot DD_i^{-\rho_{c,i}}\right)^{-1/\rho_{c,i}} \tag{A14.13}$$

$$PQ_i \cdot Q_i = cs_i \cdot Y \tag{A14.14}$$

Trade Equations

$$E_i = DD_i \left(\frac{PD_i}{PED_i} \cdot \frac{\alpha_i}{\left(1 - \alpha_i\right)}\right)^{1/\left(1 + \rho_{t,i}\right)} \tag{A14.15}$$

$$M_i = DD_i \cdot \left(\frac{PDT_i}{PMD_i} \frac{\beta_i}{\left(1 - \beta_i\right)}\right)^{1/\left(1 + \rho_{c,i}\right)} \tag{A14.16}$$

$$FSAV = \Sigma_i PWM_i \cdot M_i - \Sigma_i PWE_i \cdot E_i \tag{A14.17}$$

Welfare Equations

$$CLIV = \Pi_i PQ_i^{cs_i} \tag{A14.18}$$

$$UTIL = \Pi_i Q_i^{cs_i} \tag{A14.19}$$

$$UTIL = \Pi_i \left(\frac{cs_i \cdot YN}{PQ0_i}\right)^{cs_i} \tag{A14.20}$$

$$EV = Y0 - YN \tag{A14.21}$$

Income and Objective Equations

$$GR = \Sigma_i tm_i \cdot ER \cdot PWM_i \cdot M_i + \Sigma_i td_i \cdot PD_i \cdot DD_i$$
$$- \Sigma_i te_i \cdot ER \cdot PWE_i \cdot E_i - \Sigma_{i,f} WF_f \cdot WFDIST_{i,f} \cdot FDSC_{i,f} \cdot wsub_{i,f} \tag{A14.22}$$

$$FCTRY_f = \Sigma_i WF_f \cdot WFDIST_{i,f} \cdot FDSC_{i,f} \qquad \text{(A14.23)}$$

$$Y = \Sigma_{i,f}\left(FCTRY_{i,f} + MONITOR_{i,f}\right) + ER \cdot FSAV + GR \qquad \text{(A14.24)}$$

$$Y = \Sigma_i\left(PQ_i \cdot Q_i\right) + WALRAS \qquad \text{(A14.25)}$$

$$OBJ = WALRAS \cdot WALRAS \qquad \text{(A14.26)}$$

Market Clearing Equations

$$\overline{FS}_f = \Sigma_i FDSC_{i,f} \qquad \text{(A14.27)}$$

Efficiency Wage Equations

$$NSC_{i,f} = \frac{\Gamma_{i,f} \cdot R}{\left(D2_{i,f} - D1_{i,f}\right)} + \frac{\Gamma_{i,f} \cdot \left(D1_{i,f} + QR_{i,f}\right) \cdot FS_f}{\left(D2_{i,f} - D1_{i,f}\right) \cdot \left(FS_f - FDSC_{i,f}\right)} \qquad \text{(A14.28)}$$

$$WFDIST_{i,f} = 1 + NSC_{i,f} \qquad \text{(A14.29)}$$

$$MONITOR_{i,f} = NSC_{i,f} \cdot WF_f \cdot WFDIST_{i,f} \qquad \text{(14.30)}$$

Union Equations

$$UNUTIL = \left(WFDIST_{i,f} \cdot WF_f - WF_f\right)^{\mu_{i,f}} \cdot \left(FDSC_{i,f} - LBAR_{i,f}\right)^{\left(1 - \mu_{i,f}\right)} \qquad \text{(A14.31)}$$

$$\left(WFDIST_{i,f} - 1\right) = WFDIST_{i,f} \cdot \frac{\mu_{i,f}}{\left(1 - \mu_{i,f}\right) \cdot \sigma_{p,i}} \cdot \frac{\left(FDSC_{i,f} - LBAR_{i,f}\right)}{FDSC_{i,f}} \qquad \text{(A14.32)}$$

$$WD_{u,i} = \frac{\eta_u}{\left(\eta_u - 1\right)} \qquad \text{(A14.33)}$$

References

Akerlof, G.A. 1986. "Labor contracts as partial gift exchange." In *Efficiency Wage Models of the Labor Market*, edited by George A. Akerlof and Janet L. Yellen. Cambridge: Cambridge University Press.

Akerlof, G.A. and J.L. Yellen. 1990. "The fair wage–effort hypothesis and unemployment." *Quarterly Journal of Economics* 70:254–283.

Akerlof, G.A. and J.L. Yellen, eds. 1986. *Efficiency Wage Models of the Labor Market*. New York: Cambridge University Press.

Baldwin, R.E. 1995. "The effect of trade and foreign direct investment on employment and relative wages." National Bureau of Economic Research, Working Paper No. 5037.

Ballard, C.L., D. Fullerton, J.B. Shoven, and J. Whalley. 1985. *A General Equilibrium Model for Tax Policy and Evaluation*. Chicago: University of Chicago Press.

Benjamin, N.C., S. Devarajan, and R.J. Weiner. 1989. "The 'Dutch' disease in a developing country: Oil reserves in Cameroon." *Journal of Development Economics* 30:71–92.

Bhagwati, J. and V.K. Ramaswami. 1963. "Domestic distortions, tariffs and the theory of optimum subsidy." *Journal of Political Economy* 71:44–50.

Bhagwati, J. and T.N. Srinivasan. 1969. "Optimal intervention to achieve non-economic objectives." *Review of Economic Studies* 36:27–38.

Bhagwati, J. and T.N. Srinivasan. 1971. "The theory of wage differentials: Production response and factor price equalisation." *Journal of International Economics* 1:19–35.

Borjas, G.J., R.B. Freeman, and L.F. Katz. 1991. "On the labor market effects of immigration and trade." In *Immigration, Trade and the Labor Market,* edited by John M. Abowd and Richard B. Freeman. Chicago: University of Chicago Press.

Brecher, R.A. 1992. "An efficiency-wage model with explicit monitoring, unemployment and welfare in an open economy." *Journal of International Economics* 32:179–191.

Bulow, J. and L. Summers. 1986. "A theory of dual labor markets with application to industrial policy, discrimination, and Keynesian unemployment." *Journal of Labor Economics* 4:376–414.

Burfisher, M.E., S. Robinson, and K.E. Thierfelder. 1994. "Wage changes in a U.S.–Mexico free trade area: Migration versus Stolper–Samuelson effects." In *Modeling Trade Policy: Applied General Equilibrium Assessments of North American Free Trade*, edited by Joseph F. Francois and Clinton R. Shiells. Cambridge: Cambridge University Press.

Copeland, B.R. 1989. "Efficiency wages in a Ricardian model of international trade." *Journal of International Economics* 27:221–244.

De Melo, J. 1977. "Distortions in the factor market: Some general equilibrium estimates." *Review of Economics and Statistics* 59:398–405.

De Melo, J. and David Tarr. 1990. "Industrial policy in the presence of wage distortions: The case of the U.S. auto and steel industries." *International Economic Review* 34:833–851.

De Melo, J. and David Tarr. 1992. *A General Equilibrium Analysis of U.S. Foreign Trade Policy*. Cambridge, Massachusetts: MIT Press.

Dervis, K., J. de Melo, and S. Robinson. 1982. *General Equilibrium Models for Development Policy*. Cambridge: Cambridge University Press.

Devarajan, S., H. Ghanem, and K. Thierfelder. 1994. "Labor market regulation, trade and the distribution of income in Bangladesh." Unpublished manuscript.

Devarajan, S., H. Ghanem, and Karen Thierfelder. 1996. "Trade reform and labor unions: A general-equilibrium analysis applied to Bangladesh and Indonesia." Unpublished manuscript.

Devarajan, S. and J.D. Lewis. 1991. "Structural adjustment and economic reform in Indonesia." In *Reform in Economic Systems in Developing Countries,* edited by Dwight H. Perkins and Michael Romer. Cambridge, Massachusetts: Harvard University Press.

Devarajan, S., J.D. Lewis, and S. Robinson. 1991. "From stylized to applied models: Building multisector CGE models for policy analysis." Department of Agricultural and Resource Economics, University of California at Berkeley Working Paper No. 616.

Devarajan, S., J.D. Lewis, and S. Robinson. 1993. "External shocks, purchasing power parity and the equilibrium real exchange rate." *World Bank Economic Review* 7:45–63.

Dickens, W.T. 1990. "Does it matter what we trade? Trade and industrial policies when labor markets don't clear." *NBER Working Paper 3285.*

Dickens, W.T. and L.F. Katz. 1987. "Inter-industry wage differences and industry characteristics." In *Unemployment and the Structure of Labor Markets*, edited by Kevin Land and Jonathan S. Leonard. New York: Basil Blackwell.

Dickens, W.T. and K. Lang. 1985. "A test of dual labor market theory." *American Economic Review* 75:792–805.

Dickens, W.T. and K. Lang. 1988. "Why it matters what we trade." In *The Dynamics of Trade and Employment*, edited by William T. Dickens et al. Cambridge, Massachusetts: MIT Press, 1986.

Farber, H. 1986. "The analysis of union behavior." In *Handbook of Labor Economics*, edited by O. Ashenfelter and R. Layard. Amsterdam: North-Holland.

Freeman, R.B. 1995. "Are your wages set in Beijing?" *Journal of Economic Perspectives* 9:15–32.

Hamermesh, D.S. 1986. "The demand for labor in the long run." In *Handbook of Labor Economics,* edited by O. Ashenfelter and R. Layard. Amsterdam: North-Holland.

Hanson, K., S. Robinson, and S. Tokarick. 1993. "U.S. adjustment in the 1990s: A CGE analysis of alternative trade strategies." *International Economic Journal* 7:27–49.

Herberg, H. and M.C. Kemp. 1971. "Factor market distortions, the shape of the locus of competitive outputs, and the relation between product prices and equilibrium outputs." In *Trade, Balance of Payments and Growth, Papers in International Economics in Honor of Charles P. Kindleberger*, edited by Jagdish Bhagwati, Ronald Jones, Robert Mundell, and Jaroslav Vanek. New York: American Elsevier.

Hill, J.K. 1984. "Comparative statics in general equilibrium models with a unionized sector." *Journal of International Economics* 16:345–356.

Johnson, H. 1966. "Factor market distortions and the shape of the transformation curve." *Econometrica* 34:686–698.

Johnson, H. 1984. "Optimal trade intervention in the presence of domestic distortions." In *International Trade: Selected Readings*, edited by Jagdish Bhagwati. Cambridge, Massachusetts: MIT Press.

Jones, R.W. 1965. "The structure of simple general equilibrium models." *Journal of Political Economy* 73:557–572.

Jones, R.W. 1971. "Distortions in factor markets and the general equilibrium model of production." *Journal of Political Economy* 79:437–459.

Katz, L.F. and L.H. Summers. 1988. "Can inter-industry wage differentials justify strategic trade policy?" *NBER Working Paper 2739.*

Katz, L.F. and L.H. Summers. 1989. "Industry rents: Evidence and implications." *Brookings Papers on Economic Activity* 0:209–290.

Kilkenny, M. and S. Robinson. 1990. "Computable general equilibrium analysis of agricultural liberalization: Factor mobility and macro closure." *Journal of Policy Modeling* 12:527–556.

Krueger, A.B. and L.H. Summers. 1986. "Efficiency wages and the inter-industry wage structure." *Econometrica* 56:259–293.

Krugman, P. and R. Lawrence. 1993. "Trade, jobs, and wages." *National Bureau of Economic Research, Working Paper No. 4478.*

Lawrence, R.Z. and M.J. Slaughter. 1993. "International trade and American wages in the 1980s: Giant sucking sound or small hiccup?" *Brookings Papers on Microeconomic Activity* 2:161–226.

Leamer, E.E. 1995. "A trade economist's view of U.S. wages and 'globalization.'" Unpublished manuscript.

MacDonald, I.M. and R.M. Solow. 1981. "Wage bargaining and employment." *American Economic Review* 71:896–908.

Magee, S.P. 1971. "Factor market distortions, production, distribution, and the pure theory of international trade." *Quarterly Journal of Economics* 85:623–463.

Magee, S.P. 1973. "Factor market distortions, production, and trade: A survey." *Oxford Economic Papers* 25:1–43.

Richardson, J.D. 1995. "Income inequality and trade: How to think, what to conclude." *Journal of Economic Perspectives* 9:33–55.

Robinson, S. and K. Thierfelder. 1996. "The trade–wage debate in a model with nontraded goods: Making room for labor economists in trade theory." *Trade and Macroeconomics Division Discussion Paper No. 9*, International Food Policy Research Institute.

Sachs, J.D. and H.J. Shatz. 1994. "Trade and jobs in U.S. manufacturing." *Brookings Papers on Economic Activity* 1:1–84.

Salop, S.C. 1986. "A model of the natural rate of unemployment." In *Efficiency Wage Models of the Labor Market*, edited by George A. Akerlof and Janet L. Yellen. Cambridge: Cambridge University Press.

Shapiro, C. and J.E. Stiglitz. 1984. "Equilibrium unemployment as a worker discipline device." *American Economic Review* 74:433–444.

Thierfelder, K.E. 1992. "Efficiency wages, trade theory, and policy implications: A computable general equilibrium analysis." Ph.D. dissertation, University of Wisconsin.

Wood, A. 1995. "How trade hurt unskilled workers." *Journal of Economic Perspectives* 9:57–80.

Yellen, J. 1984. "Efficiency wage models of unemployment." *American Economic Review* 74:200–205.

15

Labor Market Structure and Conduct

Andréa M. Maechler and David W. Roland-Holst

I Introduction

In an era of globalization, linkages between international trade and labor markets are receiving intensified scrutiny. Many Organization for Economic Cooperation and Development (OECD) countries are preoccupied with the implications of expanded trade for employment growth and employment diversion (referred to in Europe as *delocalisation*). At the same time, more and more developing countries are concerned with how best to facilitate human resource development for trade-driven expansion. With increasing capital mobility and technology diffusion, the quantity and quality of domestic labor forces are ever more important determinants of comparative advantage. Structure and conduct in domestic labor markets can be just as important in this regard as labor endowments, however. As expanding trade has imbued commodity markets with greater competitiveness and flexibility, trade-induced domestic growth is placing new adaptive pressures on labor markets. Increasingly, labor market rigidities are being viewed as impediments to more effective participation in the global economy, as well as to more sustainable growth in output, employment, and average living standards.

While government and labor groups are understandably reluctant to abandon the social priorities which underlie many labor market interventions and distortions, the efficiency costs these confer upon their economies are often significant and usually not well understood. Despite a vast body of labor market research which has emerged in the last two decades, only a small part focuses on trade or empirical estimates of efficiency effects. The main objective of this paper is to review and synthesize the new labor market

This chapter was written as part of an OECD Development Centre research programme on the employment implications of the Uruguay Round. We would like to thank Dominique van der Mensbrugghe for indispensable technical advice and Maurizio Bussolo for excellent research assistance.

theories, embedding them in an empirical general equilibrium framework so they can be used to answer policy concerns about trade and employment linkages.

Rather than exhaustively testing competing labor market specifications and evaluating real cases, our present purpose is expository and pedagogical. In the following sections, we provide a rational menu of generic labor market specifications, with relatively parsimonious numerical examples of how each can be implemented in a single prototype computable general equilibrium (CGE) model. The CGE model is a real one, based on a complete dataset for Mexico, but its application in this chapter is more methodological than empirical. From the basic tool kit presented here, it is hoped that other practitioners will join us to enlarge the very incomplete basis of empirical evidence on how international trade and domestic labor markets interact.

Each section covers different genera of labor market theory with the same three-part structure: conceptual motivation, literature survey, and numerical example. No attempt has been made to cover every contending story, contributor, or alternative specification. The sample here is intended to represent the main streams of this rapidly growing research area, cite their leading contributors, and offer simple entry points for empirical simulation work.

II Exogenous Wage Rigidity

One of the most common sources of wage rigidity is a broad spectrum of government policies which legislate minimum wage levels directly or support reservation wages via social insurance programs. Although these policies use economic instruments and have pervasive economic effects, they are rarely implemented with economic efficiency criteria in mind. In this section, we conduct a variety of simulation experiments to see how minimum wage policies can affect the adjustment process ensuing from trade liberalization.

The first major contribution to the analysis of minimum wage is presented in Stigler (1946), who demonstrates that the imposition of a minimum wage above the equilibrium wage reduces employment. An alternative version recognizes that minimum wage regulations may apply only to a covered sector, with an uncovered sector in which workers displaced by the higher minimum wage could find jobs. This approach can also be extended to allow for job queuing at the minimum wage, either by those earning the lower wage in the uncovered sector, or by those dropping out of the labor force.[1]

---

1 See Mincer (1976) for a standard model of queuing.

Holzer, Katz and Krueger (1991) demonstrate that jobs paying around the minimum wage have a greater number of applicants than other jobs, suggesting the presence of significant rents.[2] Edwards and Edwards (1990) provide an excellent analytical survey of a number of international trade models with wage rigidities. For further discussions on the theory underlying the economic impact of minimum wage policy, see Riveros (1990) and Fiszbein (1992). Econometric evidence on minimum wage policies includes Riveros and Paredes (1988) and Lopez and Riveros (1988). Using a time-series approach, Santiago (1989) estimates labor market effects of higher effective minimum wage levels.

In this set of simulations, we shall examine four alternative types of minimum wage policy. Each represents different target groups or different social insurance objectives, and together they cover the main policy alternatives and generic types of distortionary effects.

II.1 Minimum Wage by Occupation

In this case, the government attempts to guarantee a nominal hourly minimum to one or more specific labor categories. We assume fixed labor supplies throughout, and in the event that the minimum wage is binding, unemployment will be created in the target occupation groups. We assume that these workers respond by entering the informal labor market and finding jobs there, putting downward pressure on the informal wage. The wage equation for a given target occupational group (l) is modified from the prototype to take the form

$$w_l \geq \overline{w}_l \tag{15.1}$$

Some observations about this specification are in order. First, note that we assume the minimum applies to occupational average wages, rather than to individual wages of workers. Distributional effects within occupations are ignored. Second, inter-sectoral wage differentials are also ignored, so the incidence of the minimum wage policy will be distorted; i.e., sectors with low values of ω_{li} may still pay below the target minimum on average. Third, note that the preceding inequality makes the prototype model under-determined. To eliminate the extra degree of freedom, we add an orthogonality condition

$$\left(w_l - \overline{w}_l \right) \left(L_l^S - L_l^D \right) = 0 \tag{15.2}$$

---

2 See also Hamermesh (1993, pp. 182–191) for a stylized version of labor market effects of minimum wages and a brief survey of relevant empirical work.

Finally, we modify the labor supply equation for the informal occupational group (*I*) to allow for spillover of unemployed workers in the minimum wage target group, i.e.,

$$L_I^S = L_I^S + \left(L_l^S - L_l^D\right) \tag{15.3}$$

II.2 Minimum Real Wage by Occupation

Although most minimum wage policies are enunciated in terms of nominal hourly rates, some have escalation clauses to reflect the social objectives of real purchasing power maintenance. In the case of an occupational target group, such a policy can be simply specified as

$$w_l \geq \overline{w}_l P_l \tag{15.4}$$

where P_l represents an endogenous price index. This might be an aggregate gross domestic product (GDP) deflator or an index more focused on the needs of the target group, such as a consumption-weighted purchaser price index. In any case this simple modification may increase or decrease the distortionary effects of the wage minimum, depending upon whether the external shock under consideration is deflationary or inflationary.

II.3 Minimum Wage by Sector

In some instances, minimum wage policies are targeted at workers in specific occupations and sectors. This more focused approach may be designed to correct severe inter-sectoral differentials or could be the result of sector-specific political forces. In this case, the wage determination equation takes the form

$$\omega_{li} w_l \geq \overline{w}_{li} \tag{15.5}$$

which binds the combined occupational wage and sectoral wage premium. The other modifications are unchanged.

II.4 Minimum Real Wage by Sector

A final variation concerns real wage maintenance in a specific sector. This kind of policy is especially common in public sector employment, where wages are normally legislated in any case and often indexed. Here the wage constraint takes the form

$$\omega_{li} w_l \geq \overline{w}_l P_l \tag{15.6}$$

II.5 Simulation Experiments

We now compare the results of the reference simulation with those obtained under a variety of minimum wage specifications. The first experiment is the reference case used throughout this exercise, a trade liberalization scenario entailing abolition of Mexican tariffs and nontariff barriers (NTBs) on all imports.[3] Five alternative experiments then follow, including a minimum fixed at the observed wage for unskilled workers, a real (GDP deflated) minimum for the same group, sectoral minimum wages for export-intensive (Energy) and import-intensive (Durables) sectors, respectively, and a minimum real wage for service sector workers.

The reference experiment is typical of CGE trade liberalization scenarios, with modest aggregate GDP growth arising from sectoral productivity gains in this fixed employment setting (Table 15.1). Removing import protection, all else equal, will induce real exchange rate and domestic price depreciation, exerting downward pressure on wages in most occupational groups. When labor markets are competitive, as in experiment 1, unskilled workers take most of the brunt of this.

Assuming instead that unskilled wages are protected by official minimum wage policy, nominally in experiment 2 and in real terms in experiment 3, changes the results significantly. The results in the two differ only in the magnitude of the adjustment necessary to offset unskilled wage rigidity, but are otherwise identical in qualitative terms. Because of the factor market rigidity, the real exchange rate must depreciate even further to align domestic and international resource costs.[4] Consumer prices also fall further, this time because of the significant wage repression in the residual, informal labor market, which receives a significant influx of newly unemployed unskilled formal workers. This result clearly illustrates the regressive nature of minimum wage policies, which has been emphasized by many authors.[5] In per capita terms, however, the fixed nominal wage policy is less wage repressive than the reference, while the fixed real wage policy is more so.

Finally, one might first be startled by the increase in aggregate efficiency for two distortionary policies. Upon reflection, however, one must recall that this is a second-best situation where we have assumed inter-sectoral labor productivity differences and calibrated these into a fixed wage distribution. This means that reallocating labor can raise aggregate productivity per unit

---

3 See Reinert, Roland-Holst and Shiells (1995) for a more detailed discussion of such liberalization experiments.

4 This point is omitted by Edwards and Edwards (1990) in their otherwise detailed treatment of this subject.

5 Compare, e.g., Devarajan, Ghanem and Thierfelder (1994).

Table 15.1. *Minimum wage scenarios (percentage changes)*

	Experiment					
Selected Aggregates	*1*	*2*	*3*	*4*	*5*	*6*
Real GDP	.8	3.0	2.3	.9	1.2	3.7
Real Exchange Rate	-5.7	-7.8	-7.2	-5.9	-6.8	-7.6
Consumer Price Index	-9.3	-9.8	-9.9	-9.4	-9.8	-8.5
Real Wages						
Unskilled	-10.2	9.8	.0	-9.8	-11.0	-16.6
Skilled	-3.6	-10.1	-9.2	-3.2	-1.2	-11.6
Informal	-.5	-38.9	-33.5	-.1	3.4	.7
Val. Added Wgt. Ave.	-5.5	-8.3	-10.6	-5.1	-4.0	-11.0
Employment Wgt. Ave.	-7.0	-4.9	-9.8	-6.7	-6.3	-11.5

Premia for Sectoral Real Wage Maintenance				*Energy*	*Durables*	*Services*
Unskilled	.0	.0	.0	23.7	26.3	23.2
Skilled	.0	.0	.0	14.4	12.4	15.6

Experiment 1: Mexican tariff and NTB abolition with competitive labor markets.
Experiment 2: Experiment 1 with a nominal minimum wage for unskilled labor.
Experiment 3: Experiment 1 with a real minimum wage for unskilled labor.
Experiment 4: Experiment 1 with minimum nominal wages for formal workers in Energy.
Experiment 5: Experiment 1 with minimum nominal wages for formal workers in Durables.
Experiment 6: Experiment 1 with minimum real wages for formal workers in Services.

of resource cost, and especially so if the labor is induced to migrate from higher to lower wage categories. Like economies of scale, then, labor market distortions appear to have the potential to amplify efficiency gains, but of course subject to other economic and social costs which may not be incorporated in this model.

Sectoral fixed wages have smaller absolute and distributional effects, except for the large and relatively low wage service sector. Efficiency effects vary with the skill and productivity composition of the target sectors. Real exchange rate depreciation is smaller when the distortion is on the income (export) side (Energy) of the trade balance than on the expenditure (import) side (Durables), but is highest when the distortion is in the large, relatively nontradable service sector (reverse Dutch disease).

Table 15.2 gives an overview of sectoral results associated with the reference and minimum wage experiments. As is typical, sectoral adjustments to liberalization and with respect to different labor market policies are generally more dramatic than aggregate results. In all cases, however, they follow intuitively from the economic structure, pattern of prior protection, and occupational composition of sectoral employment.

The uniformity of weighted average adjustments across experiments is striking but logical, being the result of the macroeconomic components of

Table 15.2. *Sectoral changes resulting from trade liberalization*
(percentages)

Output		Output Exp 1	Exp 2	Exp 3	Exp 4	Exp 5	Exp 6
1	Agriculture	-9	-12	-11	-8	-7	-7
2	Energy	9	5	6	3	11	11
3	NonDurables	-2	-4	-4	-2	-1	-1
4	Durables	6	9	7	6	0	8
5	Services	2	4	3	2	2	1
	Weighted Ave.	1	1	1	1	0	1
Exports							
1	Agriculture	50	30	35	51	57	56
2	Energy	18	11	13	9	21	21
3	NonDurables	48	38	41	49	54	52
4	Durables	50	57	53	51	38	55
5	Services	32	44	43	32	35	22
	Weighted Ave.	40	44	43	40	39	39
Demand for Dom. Goods							
1	Agriculture	-11	-14	-13	-11	-10	-10
2	Energy	-4	-5	-4	-5	-5	-3
3	NonDurables	-6	-7	-7	-6	-5	-5
4	Durables	-10	-8	-9	-10	-13	-9
5	Services	0	1	1	0	0	-1
	Weighted Ave.	-4	-3	-3	-4	-4	-3
Imports							
1	Agriculture	138	156	151	137	132	134
2	Energy	217	232	228	239	205	215
3	NonDurables	52	58	56	52	48	51
4	Durables	27	28	29	27	28	26
5	Services	-24	-29	-29	-24	-26	-19
	Weighted Ave.	38	42	41	38	37	37

the model such as fixed aggregate factor supplies and constant external policy. Individual sectoral differences are significant across experiments, however, indicating that important differences in comparative advantage can emerge under different labor market specifications.

III Endogenous Wage Rigidity

III.1 Simple Rent Sharing

By definition, wage rigidities arise when wages do not move fast enough to reflect the changing value of labor productivity. One of the simplest cases of this arises when firm-level excess profits exist and labor takes a share of these in addition to its competitive wages. This rent sharing partially decouples wages from the first order relationship characteristic of neoclassical labor markets. Before looking at more complex bargaining models, we extend the prototype model with a simple rent sharing rule to see how it may compromise economic efficiency.

The idea that the behavior of labor markets could be represented satisfactorily by standard competitive models was first criticized by Schlichter (1950). He argued that competitive models failed to account for the empirically tested significant wage differentials among observationally homogeneous types of workers. Recent empirical work supports these results (see Dickens and Katz 1987; Krueger and Summers, 1987, 1988; Katz and Summers, 1989a, 1989b; Christofides and Oswald, 1992; Abowd et al., 1994). Several authors advanced the hypothesis that rent-sharing behavior can significantly affect the wage determination process.[6] For a discussion on the implications of industry rents, refer to the excellent work by Katz and Summers (1989), who present an insightful literature review and relevant empirical evidence on the subject.[7] While Blanchflower and Oswald (1989, 1992) present empirical evidence on the negative relationship between workers' earnings and local unemployment level, Blanchflower, Oswald and Sanfey (1992) find that the real wage is an increasing function of employers' past profitability.[8] Christofides and Oswald (1989, 1992) support both of these results, which are consistent with rent-sharing theory.[9]

Assume that, in a given sector, a given occupational group has bargaining power for rent sharing, which can be represented by a simple index β whose value lies between zero and unity. In this case, a premium ω above the competitive wage w will accrue to these workers, given by the rent-sharing rule

$$\omega_l = 1 + \frac{\beta_{li}}{1 - \beta_{li}} \frac{r}{w_l L_{li}^D} \tag{15.7}$$

where r represents firm operating rents.[10] As a practical matter in this implementation, we calibrated the parameter β and rents r equal to the total wage premium and labor value added in the sector under consideration.

---

6 The observed wedge between the marginal productivities of factors in different uses is a type of market imperfection which is likely to cause certain factors to earn rents. In the present context of rent sharing, the idea is that workers are able to capture a large part of the rents earned by firms.

7 Their empirical results find that a large portion of monopoly rents earned by product markets may be captured by workers rather than shareholders.

8 The argument is that workers benefit from higher wages when the firm or industry is booming. Local unemployment, however, tends to weaken workers' bargaining power, producing a negative relationship between wages and unemployment.

9 A standard competitive framework would expect factor prices to be equalized across sectors and firms to hire factors of production up to the point where their marginal productivity equals their cost. Consequently, wages should be affected by labor supply forces rather than by unemployment and the profitability of a firm or industry should not prevent employers from paying exactly the "competitive" wage.

10 Compare to Blanchflower, Oswald, and Sanfey (1992) for details.

III.2 Wage Bargaining

A more elaborate view of endogenous wage determination recognizes the existence of labor unions as explicit bargaining agents. When labor is organized to negotiate the terms of employment, wages may be above and employment below their competitive levels. In this and the next subsection, two cases are considered. Here, we look at the case where unions bargain over wages only and firms choose the level of employment to maximize profits. Next, we shall examine joint wage–employment contracts.

Unions can be viewed as instruments used by employees to extract rents from firms. There exist two broad categories of wage bargaining models, namely, the *monopoly union model* and the *efficient bargaining model.*[11] Essentially, there is a trade-off between wages and employment. The monopoly union model is a special case where the firm has no bargaining power in wage setting and the union has no power in employment. The wage is set unilaterally by the union. However, bargaining over the wage alone will generally not permit an efficient outcome.[12] For a simplified presentation of standard wage bargaining models, see Blanchard and Fischer (1989).[13] An extensive survey of work on the economic theory of union behavior is found in Oswald (1985). Pencavel (1985) reviews microeconomic research on union models and extends them to the macroeconomic level.[14] Excellent empirical work for Britain is presented in Layard and Nickell (1986). Blanchflower, Oswald and Garrett (1990) estimate the relative importance of inside power enjoyed by unionized workers in the wage determination process.[15]

Extending the prototype model to incorporate labor negotiation requires a specification of the union's objective function. Assume that union members are homogeneous, with individual utility represented by $U(\omega_{li}w_l)$, and that their group utility can be represented by

$$V\left(\omega_{li}w_l, L_{li}^D\right) = \left(\frac{L_{li}^D}{L_{li}^0}\right)U\left(\omega_{li}w_l\right) + \left(1 - \frac{L_{li}^D}{L_{li}^0}\right)U\left(w_l\right) \tag{15.8}$$

---

11 This latter category of models is also referred to as the right-to-manage model.
12 Generally, most of the existing applied work assumes that unions bargain over wages and employers select the employment level.
13 See Blanchard and Fischer (1989), Chapter 9, pp. 438–546.
14 See also Calmfors (1985) for discussion on trade union behavior and its macroeconomic implications.
15 The "inside power" hypothesis is also discussed in Solow (1985) and Lindbeck and Snower (1986, 1987) in the context of efficiency wages.

where we assume that employment in the base situation, L_{li}^0, represents maximum union membership.[16] Thus the welfare of the union is a convex combination of utilities for those who remain in the sector, earning the negotiated wage, and those who find employment elsewhere, assumed to earn the average wage. Note now that

$$V\left(\omega_{li}w_l, L_{li}^D\right) - V\left(\omega_{li}w_l, L_{li}^D\right) = \frac{L_{li}^D}{L_{li}^0}\left[U\left(\omega_{li}w_l\right) - U\left(\omega_{li}w_l\right)\right] \qquad (15.9)$$

so that, in a wage-only contract, the net gain for the members retaining employment is independent of the utility of unemployed members. The bargaining problem facing the union is then given by the Lagrangian

$$\text{Max}_\omega L_{li}^D\left[U\left(\omega w_l\right) - U\left(w_l\right)\right] + \lambda\left[L_{li}^0 - L_{li}^D\right] \qquad (15.10)$$

whose interior (i.e., $\lambda=0$) solution is obtained by solving the expression

$$\frac{U_\omega\left(\omega w_l\right)}{\sigma} = \frac{U\left(\omega w_l\right) - U\left(w_l\right)}{\omega} \qquad (15.11)$$

where σ denotes endogenous wage elasticity of labor demand in the prototype CES specification of production. Intuitively, this expression represents an equivalence of ratios for marginal (subjective and technical) substitution rates and values. By using the Extended Linear Expenditure System in the prototype model, this specification can be implemented without difficulty.

III.3 Efficient Contracts

Most anecdotal evidence indicates that unions bargain over wages and firms generally have discretion about employment levels.[17] Despite this, however, wage-only bargaining can produce outcomes which are not on the firm–union, wage–employment contract curve and are therefore inefficient. To remedy this, we extend the prototype model below to incorporate simultaneous bargaining over both wages and employment levels.

Under efficient bargaining models, firms and unions share equal bargaining powers in wage and employment setting. In their seminal paper, McDonald and Solow (1981) argue that a contract is efficient when it lies at a point of tangency between an indifference curve and an isoprofit locus,

---

16 A number of authors (e.g., de Melo and Tarr, 1990) use a single utility function for the union, but this is more difficult to motivate from principles of demand theory. See Oswald (1985) for more on this point.
17 See Oswald (1985) for discussion.

that is, at a point on the contract curve. Which point is chosen on the contract curve will depend on the relative bargaining power of the firm and of the union. If the union is relatively weak, the outcome may be close to the competitive equilibrium; if the union is relatively powerful, it may be close to the firm's zero profit point.[18] In terms of efficient contracts, the bargaining outcomes are most likely going to lie off the demand curve. This occurs because at the bargained wage level, employers would prefer to cheat by reducing the level of employment. Abowd and Lemieux (1993) estimate a simple model of efficient wage setting. Espinosa and Rhee (1989) extend standard bargaining models to allow for repeated bargaining.[19] Empirical evidence supporting efficient bargaining models includes MaCurdy and Pencavel (1986) and Brown and Ashenfelter (1986).[20]

The basic implementation for wage–employment bargaining relies on a Nash solution to the following joint optimization problem:

$$\text{Max}_{\omega,L} L\big[U(\omega w_l) - U(w_l)\big]\big[F_i(L;\cdot) - \omega w_l L - C_i(\cdot)\big] + \lambda\big[L_{li}^0 - L\big] \quad (15.12)$$

where F_i and C_i denote the production and (nonlabor) cost functions in sector i, respectively. Omitting second-order cost effects, the solutions to this problem can be approximated with the following two expressions

$$\omega = \frac{\alpha_E}{2w_l}\left[\frac{F}{L} + F_L\right] \quad (15.13)$$

$$F_L L_\omega - \omega w_l = -\beta_E\left(\frac{U(\omega w_l) - U(w_l)}{U_\omega(\omega w_l)}\right) \quad (15.14)$$

where α_E and β_E are calibrated parameters. These two equations are easily interpreted. The first represents a rent-sharing rule like that in the Simple Rent Sharing section. It states that the wage premium equals an arithmetic mean of the average and marginal products of labor.[21] The second expression is the equation representing the locus of efficient wage–employment bargains, the firm–union contract curve. The right-hand side represents the firm's isoprofit loci, the left-hand side the union's indifference curve.[22]

---

18 See also Pencavel (1985) and Oswald (1985) for further discussion.
19 The authors show that when choosing the level of employment, firms may often give up short-term profits (i.e., cheating on the level of employment) for better contracts in the future.
20 For different point of views, see Layard and Nickell (1990), who show that employment may not be always higher under efficient bargaining than under monopoly union models, and Alogoskoufis and Manning (1991), who reject both the monopoly union model and the efficient bargaining model in favor of a generalized model of inefficient bargaining for wages and employment.
21 More on rent sharing can be found in Abowd and Lemieux (1993).
22 For more details, see MacDonald and Solow (1981) and Oswald (1985).

Table 15.3. *Endogenous wage rigidity experiments*
(percentage changes)

Selected Aggregates	Experiment 1	7	8	9
Real GDP	.8	.7	.8	.8
Real Exchange Rate	-5.7	-5.5	-5.8	-5.5
Consumer Price Index	-9.3	-9.1	-9.3	-9.2
Real Wages				
Unskilled	-10.2	-11.2	-9.9	-11.5
Skilled	-3.6	-1.6	-4.1	-2.9
Informal	-.5	-.7	-.4	-1.0
Val. Added Wgt. Ave.	-5.5	-5.1	-5.6	-5.8
Employment Wgt. Ave.	-7.0	-7.6	-6.8	-8.0
Sectoral Wage Premium and Employment				
WP.Skilled.Durables	.0	-10.9	3.6	1.6
LD.Unskilled.Durables	29.5	18.1	32.7	19.8
LD.Skilled.Durables	-16.1	18.2	-25.3	1.7
LD.Informal.Durables	-30.8	-40.3	-28.0	-39.1
LD.Durables	7.7	9.2	7.3	9.0
Output.Durables	5.8	6.9	5.5	6.8

Experiment 7: Experiment 1 with rent sharing by skilled labor in Durables.
Experiment 8: Experiment 1 with wage bargaining by skilled labor in Durables.
Experiment 9: Experiment 1 with wage and employment bargaining
in Durables.

The results of three endogenous wage experiments are presented in Table 15.3, accompanied by the reference simulation. Since each of these experiments is confined to a single occupational group (skilled labor) and sector (durables), aggregate differences are negligible.

Wage and employment results are affected in significant and revealing ways, however. In the rent-sharing scenario (experiment 7), skilled labor takes a significant, -10.9-1.6=-12.5 percent wage cut, thereby reversing a 16.1 percent employment loss to an 18.1 percent gain. This permits output and total employment expansion in the durables sector, but still comes at the expense of unskilled and informal workers. The latter suffer less than under minimum wage policies, however, in part because we assume no crossover from skilled to informal labor markets.

When the same group bargains over wages only, their sectoral gain in wage premium (3.6 percent) is only just offset by a 4.1 percent decline for skilled workers across the economy, implying they achieve significant own-wage protection. This occurs at the price of job security, however, when 25.3

percent of skilled workers in this sector are laid off.[23] As has been observed in some long-term union bargaining situations, labor shedding induced by wage escalation contributes to the economywide wage losses, ultimately undermining the original group's bargaining power. Despite this mixed result, however, skilled workers better their lot vis-à-vis the reference case in terms of the target variable, wages.

When both wages and employment are negotiated, skilled workers gain job increases of 1.7 percent and wage premia in Durables rise slightly. As a group, skilled workers in Durables still see slight (1.6−2.9=−1.3 percent) wage depreciation, resulting mainly from competition with unskilled workers. All in all, however, it appears that combined wage and employment bargaining yields significant improvement in the latter (1.7 against −16.1 percent) without much sacrifice in the former (−1.3 against −0.5 percent), particularly with respect to the reference case.

IV Efficiency Wage Models

IV.1 Incentive Wages and Fair Wages

Traditional neoclassical production theory views wages as determined by prices and labor productivity, which in turn are determined by exogenously given technologies and economic conditions outside the worker–employer contract. In reality, compensation has complex incentive properties, and there are causal links running not just from productivity to wages, but from wages to productivity. In modern labor market theory, such issues come under the rubrics of efficiency wages and fair wages. These theories recognize that a worker's productivity depends not only on human endowments, but on the perceived reward for effort. This section derives a basic specification where worker effort depends upon wages, and we give indications about how such behavior might qualify the conclusions drawn from the prototype model.

At first, the efficiency wage hypothesis was formulated by Leibenstein (1957) to highlight linkages among wages, nutrition, and health in less-developed countries. Then, Solow (1979) transferred the efficiency wage concept to developed economies with a model in which increased wages improve morale and thus directly affect productivity through an increase in

---

23 The laid-off workers join the rest of the skilled labor pool and, on average, experience greater wage losses than their former co-workers. This and the minimum wage effect on informal workers illustrate two important effects of wage distortions, own-regressive (within occupational group) and cross-regressive (spilt over to another occupational group) wage linkages. These are among the most complex and interesting aspects of incidents which can be analyzed with labor-oriented CGE models, but detailed analysis extends beyond the scope of the present exposition.

worker effort. Akerlof (1984) develops a "gift exchange" model in which firms can raise effort by offering a "gift" of higher wages in return for higher individual effort. Another school of thought emphasizes sociological evidence supporting the view that workers' effort level may significantly depend on the perceived fairness of their wage.[24] Excellent surveys of works on efficiency wage theories are presented in Katz (1986) and Blanchard and Fischer (1989).[25] Efficiency wage models have been advanced as providing a coherent explanation for empirically observed "noncompetitive" wage differentials across firms and workers with similar productive characteristics.[26] Bulow and Summers (1986) introduce a model of dual labor markets based on employers' need to motivate workers. Gibbons and Katz (1992) present evidence that wage differentials reflect unmeasured differences in workers' productive abilities.[27]

Assume that worker effort can be represented by a twice continuously differentiable increasing function of the wage premium, denoted by $e(\omega)$ and satisfying $0 \le e(\omega) \le 1$. This function will then enter the firm production function multiplicatively; e.g., $F(L)$ is replaced by $F(e(\omega)L)$ to represent effective labor input. For firms facing a market wage then, the optimal employment level is that where the marginal product of an additional worker equals the wage, taking account of effort as determined exogenously by wage levels.

To implement this specification, we choose a general functional form

$$e\left(\omega_{li}w_{l}\right) = \frac{\omega_{li}w_{l}}{\omega_{li}w_{l} + \alpha_{w}e^{-\beta_{w}\omega_{li}w_{l}}} \tag{15.15}$$

where the parameters α_{w} and β_{w} are calibrated to exogenously specified base effort levels and wage elasticity of effort, σ_{ew}, satisfying

$$\sigma_{ew} = \frac{\partial e}{\partial w}\frac{w}{e} = \alpha_{w}e^{-\beta_{w}w}\frac{1 + \beta_{w}w}{w + \alpha_{w}e^{-\beta_{w}w}} \tag{15.16}$$

where, for the sake of brevity, $w = \omega_{li}w_{l}$.

24 See Akerlof and Yellen (1990), who introduce the "fair-wage–effort" hypothesis and explore its implication. For an alternative specification of the effort function, see Wadhavani and Wall (1991).
25 See Yellen (1984) and Murphy and Topel (1990) for an additional survey on the theory and evidence of efficiency wages.
26 Recent empirical studies indicate that large and substantial wage differentials remain even after controlling for observed worker and job characteristics. See, for example, Dickens and Katz (1987), Krueger and Summers (1988), Katz and Summers (1989), Blanchflower and Oswald (1992), and Abowd, Kramarz and Margolis (1994). The theory of equalizing differences in the labor market reflects an alternative explanation for the existence of true wage differentials across industries. For a comprehensive review of the theory of compensating differentials, see Rosen (1986).
27 A number of empirical studies suggest the existence of wage differentials, focusing on specific aspects. See Bishop (1987) for employee's performance, Brown and Medoff (1989) for plant size, and Groshen (1991) for establishment type.

IV.2 Principal–Agent Relations (Shirking and Monitoring)

A significant component of labor productivity is thought to be governed by pecuniary incentives and worker supervisory mechanisms. Wage premia might be offered to bias recruitment in favor of higher productivity workers and motivate workers already on the job. Monitoring may be a complement to or substitute for this, a means of overcoming moral hazard and seeing to it that workers perform as expected. Both these approaches entail costs which exceed those which would be incurred by a firm with perfect information which could perfectly discriminate in the labor market, but the degree to which these second best approaches compromise efficiency is an empirical question.

When shirking detection is uncertain, the firm attempts to pay wages in excess of market clearing to induce workers not to shirk.[28] Then, if a worker is caught shirking and is fired, he will pay a penalty. Considering the threat of firing a worker as a method of discipline is not novel. The works of Calvo (1979) and Shapiro and Stiglitz (1984) have highlighted the moral hazard problem underlying the employer and wage–earner relationship.[29] However, the equilibrium unemployment rate must be sufficiently large that it pays workers to work rather than to take the risk of being caught shirking. Shapiro and Stiglitz (1984) develop a model introducing a "non-shirking constraint."[30] For a formal discussion on the reasons why firms monitor their workers, see Dickens, Katz, Lang and Summers (1990). For empirical evidence on the substantial resources devoted to monitoring workers, see Dickens, Katz and Lang (1986). Empirical evidence that efficiency wages are paid to elicit effort includes Raff and Summers's (1987) examination of Henry Ford's five dollar day, Bulow and Summers's (1986) analysis of the impact of sectoral wage declines on employment and Cappelli and Chauvin's (1991) finding of a negative relationship between wage premiums and dismissal rates.

In this section, the prototype model is extended to incorporate a simple shirking and monitoring specification, giving an indication of how principal–agent relations might affect empirical conclusions from general equilibrium

28 Models of this type have been recently analyzed by Bulow and Summers (1986), Calvo (1985), Eaton and White (1983) and Shapiro and Stiglitz (1984).

29 In this type of model, unemployment is involuntary, in the sense that workers without jobs would be happy to work at the market-clearing wage, but cannot credibly signal not to shirk at this wage. For further discussion on this issue, see also Nalebuff, Rodriguez and Stiglitz (1993), and Akerlof and Katz (1987, 1989).

30 It has been argued that up-front performance bonds could provide incentives for adequate employee productivity. Bulow and Summers (1986), Dickens, Katz, Lang and Summers (1990), and Shapiro and Stiglitz (1984) provide detailed discussions of why firms may be limited in requiring workers to exhibit performance bonds, pay fines or charge entrance fees.

models. Consider a given sector (i) and labor category (l), and assume that workers in this sector have an exogenously defined quit rate (q) and, if they shirk, a probability (f) of being fired. In a steady state, it can be shown that the wage premium necessary to make workers just indifferent between shirking and not doing so is given by

$$\omega_{li} = 1 + \alpha_N \frac{N_l}{N_l - L_l^D} \frac{q}{f} \tag{15.17}$$

where N_l and L_l^D denote total labor supply and labor demand for occupational group l, respectively.[31] The parameter α_N is calibrated from base data on sectoral wage differentials and f may be exogenous or endogenous, depending upon whether the firm uses monitoring in an effort to influence worker productivity. In a relatively simple case, such a firm would choose monitoring resources M to impose firing risk $f(M)$ on shirking workers. Assume, as is common in this literature, that $f(M)$ is twice continuously differentiable and $f_M > 0$ and $f_{MM} < 0$ in the relevant range. Then the firm will use monitoring inputs just until their marginal cost equals the marginal benefit they occasion in terms of reduced wage premia, i.e.,

$$c_M = -\frac{\partial \omega_{li} w_l L_l^D}{\partial M} = \frac{f_M}{f} (\omega_{li} - 1) w_l L_l^D \tag{15.18}$$

In other words, the marginal cost of the last unit of monitoring inputs should equal the percentage change in monitoring effectiveness, times the premium component of the wage bill.

To implement this specification, we assume that workers in another occupational category (k) are monitors, and unit monitoring costs equal their wage (i.e., $c_M = w_k$). We then choose a generalized logistic function to represent how the monotone and bounded ($0 < f < 1$) risk of firing depends upon the level of monitoring. Thus $f(M)$ takes the general form

$$f(M) = \frac{M}{M + \alpha_M e^{-\beta_M M}} \tag{15.19}$$

where the parameters α_M and β_M are calibrated from an exogenously specified number of supervisory workers M and elasticity of firing risk with respect to monitoring inputs, $\sigma_{f,M}$. Table 15.4 presents the results of four experiments, which are compared to the reference case as usual. Again, activity is largely confined to sector and occupational groups and aggregate effects are relatively small.

---

31 See, e.g., Bulow and Summers (1986) for a discussion of no shirking constraints.

Table 15.4. *Incentive wage and monitoring experiments*
(percentage changes)

	Experiment				
Selected Aggregates	*1*	*10*	*11*	*12*	*13*
Real GDP	.8	.3	.6	1.1	.8
Real Exchange Rate	-5.7	-6.7	-5.8	-6.5	-5.6
Consumer Price Index	-9.3	-10.1	-9.4	-9.7	-9.2
Real Wages					
Unskilled	-10.2	-10.2	-9.6	-12.0	-10.0
Skilled	-3.6	10.5	-1.1	1.2	-4.0
Unformal	-.5	10.5	1.5	3.1	-.7
Val. Added Wgt. Ave.	-5.5	2.5	-3.8	-3.4	-5.6
Employment Wgt. Ave.	-7.0	-3.0	-5.9	-6.8	-7.0
Sectoral Wage Premium and Employment					
WP.Unskilled.Durables	.0	.0	.0	27.6	-2.2
LD.Unskilled.Durables	29.5	-53.2	19.2	-17.8	34.0
LD.Skilled.Durables	-16.1	105.0	4.8	33.4	-20.4
LD.Informal.Durables	-30.8	104.2	-10.1	19.5	-34.8
LD.Durables	7.7	-7.2	4.7	1.1	8.4
Output.Durables	5.8	-5.4	3.7	1.0	6.3
Effort.Unskilled.Durables	.0	-45.7	-9.0	.0	.0
Firing Risk	.0	.0	.0	.0	3.4
Monitors	.0	.0	.0	.0	9.1

Experiment 10: Experiment 1 with basic effort function, elasticity = 2.0.
Experiment 11: Experiment 1 with basic effort function, elasticity = 0.5.
Experiment 12: Experiment 1 with constant effort, endogenous wage premium.
Experiment 13: Experiment 1 with monitoring.

Experiments 10 and 11 use two simple specifications of the effort function to evaluate efficiency or incentive wage effects for unskilled workers in Durables, one with a wage elasticity of effort of 2.0 and the other with $\sigma_{ew}=0.5$. In these simulations, declining incentive wages generally lead to falling effort (depending in magnitude on the relevant elasticity), falling efficiency, and a competitive disadvantage for the sector of employment. Where effort falls faster than wages (experiment 10), Durables employers substitute away from unskilled labor. If the wage elasticity of effort is less than unity, an employment shift in favor of this group occurs.

Experiment 12 poses the question, What wage premium in Durables would be necessary to maintain constant effort in the face of declining economywide unskilled wages, and what would be its ultimate effect on the rest of the adjustment process? The answer in this case is 27.6 percent, driving many unskilled workers (17.8 percent) out of Durables employment, but keeping sectoral output relatively constant. Thus a significant own-regressive effect emerges, where firms are induced by the incentive problem to choose a new occupational mix, including fewer unskilled worker who receive higher wages to maintain their effort levels, but shedding a significant number of them to face unemployment or sharply lower wages in new jobs. Vis-à-vis the reference case, unskilled employment in Durables reverses a 29.5 percent gain to a −17.8 percent layoff, while skilled workers switch from −16.1 percent laid off to 33.4 percent more employed.

A final simulation implements our simple monitoring specification, with the result that both durables employment and output can exceed reference levels by employing more monitors. Under trade liberalization, the opportunity cost of monitors (skilled workers) falls, making it economic to have (9.1 percent) mode of them, thereby raising the firing risk for unskilled shirkers 3.4 percent (from 80 percent in the base) and lowering the sector's unskilled, constant effort wage premium by 2.2 percent.

V Transaction Costs

The prototype model assumes that the process of job creation and destruction is costless for workers and firms, but in general both parties may incur significant expenses from labor market participation. Workers may engage in costly search activities and purchase goods and services designed to increase their search effectiveness. For firms, labor market transaction costs fall into four broad categories: (1) recruitment, (2) training, (3) severance, (4) costs arising from labor relations. Although some of these costs might affect a worker's ultimate productivity, they must be factored into firm profits in addition to basic wage compensation.[32] For this reason, transaction costs drive a wedge between labor productivity in the firm's production function and the hiring–firing decision, with a commensurably detrimental effect on efficiency.

The role of labor turnover costs in the efficiency wage mechanism is analyzed in Salop (1979) and Stiglitz (1985). Turnover is costly to firms in terms of search for new workers, lost production during vacancies, and loss of specific training. If firms must bear part of the costs of turnover and if quit rates are a decreasing function of wages paid, firms will attempt to pay above market clearing wages in order to reduce costly labor turnover costs.[33] However, the same wage may not clear simultaneously the market for new hires

---

32 Training costs can in some cases be amortized into the wage.
33 In most types of efficiency wage models, firms' willingness to pay higher relative wages leads to involuntary unemployment equilibrium, mainly because the wage is unable to clear the labor market when it must simultaneously allocate labor and provide adequate incentives. See Krueger and Summers (1988) for discussion.

and the market for trained workers.[34] There are almost no available data on the size or breakdown of labor market transaction costs. While few surveys have attempted to analyze the costs of firing and hiring, even fewer have tried to infer the accounting costs of turnover within particular firms. Taken together, the diversity of the reported estimates illustrates the difficulty of clearly identifying and measuring these costs.[35] Given these constraints, turnover models predict high wages where hiring and training costs are substantial. Empirical studies indicate that industry wage premiums reduce voluntary turnover (Brown and Medoff, 1978; Dickens and Katz, 1987; Krueger and Summers, 1988).[36] These results provide additional evidence that wage premiums may not reflect compensating differences.[37]

Because of their symmetry and complexity, transaction costs can lead to a broad array of distortions on both sides of labor markets, including under-employment or overemployment, wage premia or wage discounts, excessive worker retention and employment stability or excessive layoffs and employment volatility. Higher costs and more limited information both confer strategic disadvantage on those who possess them. Ultimately, qualitative results will depend upon relative recruitment–severance cost and information quality for firms and workers, while magnitudes can only be assessed empirically.

To illustrate the role of labor market transaction costs, we extend the prototype model with a simple specification for both workers and firms. For workers, it is assumed that employment is associated with a cost equal to a fixed proportion of their entry wage representing turnover costs.[38] For firms, we assume that both recruitment and severance are associated with a cost in fixed proportion to wages. In a competitive labor market, one might expect these costs to be passed through equilibrium wages, while in a bargaining or rent-sharing environment they might be shifted from strategically stronger to weaker agents.

34 The dual role of wages causes a type of market failure which induces a non-unique market-clearing wage equilibrium for workers with different quit functions (Salop 1979). Following this line of thought, Stiglitz (1985) provides a rationale for wage distributions within an industry for similar workers.

35 Penclavel (1972) presents a general discussion on training and labor turnover in U.S. manufacturing industries and Hamermesh (1993) reports available data on this issue.

36 Krueger and Summers (1988) find a positive and statistically significant effect of industry wage premiums on job tenure, and a negative but statistically insignificant effect on quit rates. Moreover, Brown and Medoff (1978) estimate a mean elasticity of quits with respect to the wage premium of about −0.3. Dickens and Katz (1987) find qualitatively the same results for non-union workers. See also Freeman (1980) and Leonard and Jacobson (1990).

37 See also Gavin (1986) and Lazear (1990a, 1990b) for a discussion and econometric results concerning severance pay.

38 For convenience only, we assume the payment is made to the government. In general, this turnover cost would appear as worker demand for goods and services associated with employment. We assume there is no direct worker cost associated with a layoff.

Table 15.5. *Transaction costs, selection, and search/matching experiments (percentage changes)*

Selected Aggregates	Experiment 1	14	15	16	17	18	19	20	21
Real GDP	.8	.6	.8	.0	1.0	.7	1.0	.7	.7
Real Exchange Rate	-5.7	-5.9	-5.6	-5.6	-5.6	-5.7	-5.7	-5.7	-5.6
Consumer Price Index	-9.3	-9.5	-9.2	-9.3	-9.2	-9.3	-9.2	-9.3	-9.3
Real Wages									
Unskilled	-10.2	-11.7	-9.9	4.3	-14.3	-9.8	-13.0	-9.9	-11.5
Skilled	-3.6	-4.5	-3.0	5.3	-6.0	-3.4	-5.0	-3.4	-4.5
Unformal	-.5	-1.4	-.2	6.2	-2.5	-.4	-1.6	-.4	-1.4
Val. Added Wgt. Ave.	-5.5	-6.6	-5.1	5.1	-8.5	-5.3	-7.4	-5.3	-6.6
Employment Wgt. Ave.	-7.0	-8.3	-6.7	4.9	-10.5	-6.8	-9.3	-6.8	-8.2
Sectoral Wage Premium and Employment									
LD.Unskilled.Durables	29.5	19.0	30.0	7.0	35.8	28.1	34.4	28.2	29.9
LD.Skilled.Durables	-16.1	-18.4	-10.3	1.4	-20.9	-14.1	-20.1	-14.3	-15.2
LD.Informal.Durables	-30.8	-32.9	-30.6	-3.6	-36.4	-28.7	-35.5	-28.8	-29.9
LD.Durables	7.7	8.2	7.6	3.9	8.5	7.5	8.3	7.5	7.7
Output.Durables	5.8	6.1	5.8	3.8	6.1	5.7	6.1	5.7	5.7

Experiment 14: Experiment 1 with unskilled *ad valorem* Hiring cost of 10 percent.
Experiment 15: Experiment 1 with unskilled *ad valorem* Firing cost of 10 percent.
Experiment 16: Experiment 1 with selection via labor-embodied productivity.
Experiment 17: Experiment 1 with matching function in unskilled labor, $\beta = \{5,5,5\}$.
Experiment 18: Experiment 1 with matching function in unskilled labor, $\beta = \{.2,.2,.2\}$.
Experiment 19: Experiment 1 with matching function in unskilled labor, $\beta = \{5,.2,.2\}$.
Experiment 20: Experiment 1 with matching function in unskilled labor, $\beta = \{.2,5,.2\}$.
Experiment 21: Experiment 1 with matching function in unskilled labor, $\beta = \{.2,.2,5\}$.

Transaction costs can be incorporated into all the endogenous wage determination models discussed in the previous section, but for illustrative purposes we only evaluate them in the competitive labor market setting. To do this, the labor demand and supply equations for the prototype must be amended to include the parameters δ_h and δ_f, denoting coefficients for transaction costs for employment (from the worker perspective), hiring, and firing (both from the firm perspective), represented as unit costs discounted over the expected term of employment.[39] It is also a simple matter to incorporate search costs from the worker perspective, but this is omitted in the interest of brevity. The results of these experiments are given in Table 15.5 and discussed in Section VII.

---

39 This discounting is necessary in a comparative static framework, where there is only one wage bill during the term of labor market clearing.

VI Selection Models

A large component of modern labor market theory focuses attention upon the process of employee selection by firms. In a simplified neoclassical setting, firms and workers are each homogeneous populations with perfect information, making costless contracts in a frictionless labor market. In reality, of course, both employers and candidates are very diverse and considerable uncertainty governs their interactions. These practical limitations will undermine the efficiency of the labor market and can lead to behavior which has complex incentive properties. In this section, we consider a representative example which indicates how the standard neoclassical model and information set must be expanded to account for these phenomena.

Imperfect information by firms about the quality of workers provides a selection rationale for efficiency wage payments. If workers are heterogeneous in ability and if ability and reservation wages are positively correlated, firms that offer higher wages will attract higher-quality job applicants. The simplest reason for the dependence of productivity on wages is adverse selection (Stiglitz, 1987; Weiss, 1980; Greenwald, 1986). With a continuum of worker types, steepening the wage profile will be a profitable strategy for selecting a subset of types.[40] Some rents will exist because it is not worthwhile to achieve perfect sorting. Nalebuff, Rodriguez and Stiglitz (1993) present a model with asymmetric information in which wages serve as an effective screening device. For an excellent overview of the theory of contracts, see Hart and Holmström (1987). See also Nalebuff and Stiglitz (1983) for a presentation on the role of compensation in economies with imperfect information.[41] Weiss (1980) and Malcomson (1981) apply the efficiency wage concept in the context of a pool of heterogeneous workers, where firms can only roughly estimate the quality of each applicant.

To illustrate how different assumptions about the underlying labor market selection process can affect empirical simulation results, consider two alternative explanations of inter-sectoral wage differentials. In both cases, we assume that the wage differences reflect equilibrium differences in sectoral labor productivity. The first scenario is used in the prototype and is standard in most CGE models. Here one assumes that productivity differences are specific to the firm, and workers who enter a sector "inherit" that sector's productivity and wage premium. Thus workers moving from high to low productivity sectors experience a corresponding drop in their individual

---

40 See Stiglitz (1985) for the implications of imperfect information on the equilibrium wage distribution.
41 The implications of imperfect information in competitive markets are discussed in the seminal paper of Rotschild and Stiglitz (1976).

productivity. At the other extreme, we assume that labor productivity is specific to workers, and the existing wage distribution reflects equilibrium differences in recruitment which place more productive workers in higher wage sectors. In this case, workers take their productivity levels with them when they change jobs. As usual, the truth probably lies somewhere between these two extremes, but their implications for the adjustment process are very different.

To implement the second scenario in the prototype model is a simple matter. We need only to convert the base sectoral employment levels from worker units to efficiency units. This is accomplished by simply rescaling employment in each sector and occupation by the observed wage differential, then setting the latter to unity. The results are presented and discussed in the next section.

VII Labor Market Search and Matching

The prototype neoclassical model represents an extreme simplification of the process by which workers seek employment and firms seek recruits. The true underlying dynamics of labor market search and matching is of course very complex, and an extensive theoretical and econometric literature has developed to elucidate it. Most of this work simplifies this task considerably, representing the underlying process by a functional form which, while parsimonious in most cases, has enough structure to capture the essential behavioral features of search and matching.[42] We incorporate one such functional form in the prototype to give an indication of how its general properties are affected and as an example of how more empirical work might be done in this area.

It is the large literature on the Unemployment–Vacancy (UV) curve which has fueled new interest in the analysis of structural change in the labor market.[43] Search theory has emerged from the idea that trade in the labor market is an economic activity which yields crucial implications for unemployment.[44] Mortensen (1986) presents a useful survey of the literature on

---

42 At the microeconomic level, the work of Pissarides (1984, 1985b, 1986, 1987) is representative, while the work of Blanchard and Diamond (1990) on the Beveridge curve shows how search and matching are approached from a macroeconomic perspective.

43 Early studies on vacancy–unemployment interactions were motivated by the desire to find a way of measuring the excess labor demand discussed in Phillips curve studies. For recent empirical work on the *UV* curve, see Jackman, Layard and Pissarides (1989) for Britain, and Blanchard and Diamond (1989) for the United States.

44 Lucas and Prescott (1974) present a theoretical paper in which the theory of job search is used to develop an equilibrium theory of employment.

job search.[45] Stochastic job matching functions were first developed by Jovanovic (1979).[46] Standard references in the matching literature include Diamond (1981, 1982a,b), Mortensen (1982b), and Pissarides (1985b, 1987, 1990). For an insightful discussion on the methodology and empirical evidence of search and matching models, see Eckstein and Wolpin (1990) and Stern (1990).[47] In these models, the labor market is characterized by unemployed workers searching for jobs and firms recruiting workers to fill their vacancies. The potential trading partners are brought together pairwise by a given stochastic matching technology and the probability of matching a worker–firm pair depends on the number of active searching workers and recruiting firms. A number of authors have examined the (in)efficiency of search equilibria.[48] Pissarides (1984) presents a model with endogenous demand for labor, later extended to include a dynamic dimension (1985a, 1987, 1990). Mortensen (1982a) and Howitt and McAfee (1987) introduce models with variable search intensities.[49] Jackman, Layard and Pissarides (1989) present empirical evidence on variable intensities and Pissarides (1986) provides a search model with interesting econometric results for Britain.

Assume as in the prototype that notional labor demand is given by the number of vacant jobs v, number employed is given by L, and number of employable workers equals N. In a neoclassical labor market, efficiency would prevail and these notional levels would be realized at some equilibrium wage rate. Assume instead that labor market pairing of prospective workers $(u=N-L)$ with vacant jobs (v) is inefficient and can be modeled by a generalized function or matching technology of the form

$$m(v,u,w) = v\left(1 + \alpha_m e^{-(\beta_u v + \beta_i u + \beta_w w)}\right)^{-1} \tag{15.20}$$

where the $\beta_i > 0$ are elasticities of effective job creation with respect to each explanatory variable and α is a calibrated scale parameter. This multinomial logistic function is a generalized version of a variety of specifications discussed and estimated in the literature on this subject.[50]

---

45 See also Layard and Pissarides (1991) for various theoretical extensions and empirical evidence on job search theory.

46 In the context of matching-bargaining models, Howitt's (1985) model of transaction should also be noted. Empirical studies on the probability of leaving include Lancaster (1979), Nickell (1979), Yoon (1981), Flinn and Heckman (1982), Narendreanathan and Nickell (1985) and McKenna (1987).

47 See also Pissarides and Wadsworth's evidence (1994) of on-the-job search for Britain.

48 Mortensen (1982b) argues that agents' search and recruitment expenditures are generally inefficient because no agent internalizes the value of his increased search activity to other searchers. See also Diamond (1982a) and Pissarides (1984, 1985b, 1987).

49 Extending Hosios's work (1990), Pissarides (1990) considers variable intensities as input-augmenting technical progress.

50 See, e.g., Hosios (1990) for more discussion.

Since the matching function is asymptotic to the number of vacancies, the labor market will never clear completely, and this underemployment plus a wage premium are likely to emerge among the efficiency costs of imperfect matching. The matching function is calibrated to an assumed 10 percent and two different hypothetical elasticity regimes.

Table 15.5 presents the results of illustrative experiments with transactions costs, labor market selection, and a search–matching specification. The direct adjustments ensuing under transaction costs are completely intuitive, with hiring costs (experiment 14) increasing unskilled unemployment and reducing wages and firing costs reducing layoffs and wage declines. A 10 percent hiring premium depresses new employment by almost an equal amount ($29.5-19.0=10.5$ percent), but firing costs cannot be compared directly since this requires a reference case with layoffs.

Also significant, and much less obvious, are the spillover effects on other occupational groups. Even though the latter labor markets have been assumed to be competitive, they move with the unskilled group in ways which would be difficult to predict from simple rules of thumb. Of particular interest is experiment 15, where, despite that fact that firing costs are not incurred directly, their presence induces a distortion which reduces wage and employment losses for the other groups.

Experiment 16 represents the simple but illuminating labor market selection experiment. Assuming that labor productivity is embodied in those workers employed in the base equilibrium, removing trade distortions confers no efficiency gains in the presence of resource constraints. This is because worker reallocation cannot raise average efficiency levels. Assuming that base wages and employment reflect worker-specific productivity differentials has very different implications for structural adjustments within the economy, however. The reference simulation indicates that the 1990 Mexican system of prior import protection may have been relatively "worker friendly" in the sense that all three occupation groups' real wages decline as a result of liberalization. When productivity is embodied in those workers, however, they benefit from removing distortions, since they can allocate their skills more "efficiently" (in terms of factor rewards) when distortions are removed. Since we now assume that any sector can pay premium wages to premium workers, and Durables had relatively superior average wages in the base case, they expand less than other sectors which are, for example, more export competitive and can bid away high quality workers.

The final two simulations indicate how more general labor market inefficiencies, captured by a generic matching function, can affect adjustment to trade liberalization. Among a three-dimensional continuum of cases, we chose only two regimes for the three elasticity values in expression (15.20), corresponding to β's = 5.0 and 0.2, respectively. In between these hypothetical extremes, we consider three cases, one where each β equals 5.0 while the other two equal 0.2, thereby imputing most of the new matching to each of the three constituent influences, vacancies, unemployment, and wages. While the results do differ at the sectoral and occupational levels, it is difficult to generalize from these experiments. Apparently, greater sensitivity of the matching function to vacancies (experiments 17 and 19) leads to more job creation for unskilled workers, in part because the declining wage permits firms to recruit more. This does not imply, however, that wage sensitivity (experiment 21) leads to the smallest unskilled wage decline. While the qualitative results are comparable in all cases, and the three intermediate elasticity specifications yield intermediate outcomes, more intensive investigation of this specification is obviously needed. In particular, some detailed econometric work could do much more to narrow the acceptable range of functional forms and parameter values.

VIII Conclusions and Extensions

This chapter offers a practical taxonomy of more recent labor market theories, combined with a menu of specifications to implement them in empirical simulation modeling. After reviewing an extensive theoretical literature and providing guidelines for using these ideas empirically, the task ahead is very clear. Even the focused and parsimonious examples used here show how challenging is the task of understanding trade and employment linkages, particularly when taking account of labor market imperfections. The universe of discourse is an essentially general equilibrium one, where second-best properties are endemic. Thus policymakers cannot reasonably rely only on simple theoretical intuition or rules of thumb.

We have seen how social insurance policies, such as minimum wages, can be regressive; how the same policy applied to different sectors or occupational groups can have very different direct and indirect effects; how the same distortions can hinder efficiency in one case and promote it in another; and how behavioral information unlikely to be available to the average policymaker can undermine or even reverse intended outcomes. Given these varied results, in a relatively aggregated single country application, generalizaton to more detailed interactions or across countries would be even more tenuous. While theoretical work can produce and has produced important insights, only detailed, case by case, empirical work will elucidate the workings of real labor market structures, conduct, and policy interventions.

Appendix 15.1

Specification of the Prototype Mexican CGE Model

For all the experiments reported, a single Mexican CGE model was used. Although the labor market specifications differ between experiments, all are based upon the same set of equations for other economic structure and conduct, as well as the same underlying database. This section provides a more complete description of the model, but it must be emphasized at the outset that our objective in using it is pedagogical and it is not intended to represent empirical analysis of the Mexican economy per se. None of our conclusions or inferences should be construed as applying to this country in isolation.

The Mexican model is a one-country computable general equilibrium (CGE) model, typical in most respects except for the treatment of labor markets. While Mexican trade is disaggregated among the United States, Canada, and other trading partners, these other economic zones are exogenous to the model itself. The second essential dimension of the model is the commodity (or sectoral) breakdown of economic activities. This version incorporates only five sectors which are aggregated from fifty sectors in the basic dataset for the model, a 1990 social accounting matrix (SAM). The purpose of the commodity decomposition is to capture the essential features of Mexican structural adjustment in terms of domestic output, demand, factor use, and trade flows. To elucidate the structure of the base year economy, Table 15A.1 provides some share calculations from the SAM on a sectoral basis.

A third dimension of the model is factor and household disaggregation, since this is essential to analyze labor market dynamics and trace the incidence of trade and other policies. The current version details five labor categories and ten households. These groups represent the main segments of the Mexican labor market and the principal household groups in terms of factor ownership and policy focus.

Production

As with many applied general equilibrium models, the Mexican model decomposes the production structure into a series of nested decisions allowing for a wide range of substitution possibilities between the various inputs. Figure 15A.1 provides a graphical depiction of the nested production structure.

The top level of the production structure decomposes the production decision between aggregate inputs and an aggregate bundle composed of capital and labor value added. While there is a possibility of allowing some substitution between intermediate inputs and value added, for the purposes of this chapter, it is assumed that the substitution elasticity is zero, or in other words the value added is always mixed in fixed proportions with intermediate inputs. It is also assumed that all the intermediate inputs are consumed in fixed proportion among themselves, though it is possible to substitute between domestic and imported intermediate goods.

Table 15A.1. *Sectoral economic structure of Mexico, 1990 (percentages)*

	Sector	Output	Demand	Exports	Imports	Unskilled	Skilled	Informal	Capital
						Value Added Shares			
1	Agriculture	7.27	7.61	3.18	6.10	12.90	5.04	.31	9.88
2	Energy	1.07	.48	8.06	.14	1.70	1.45	.22	1.72
3	NonDurables	25.86	26.47	18.64	31.54	24.44	12.75	8.04	18.68
4	Durables	15.49	14.03	32.81	54.86	14.45	7.19	4.97	9.20
5	Services	50.31	51.41	37.31	7.36	46.51	73.57	86.46	60.52
	Total	100.00	100.00	100.00	100.00	100.00	100.00	100.00	100.00

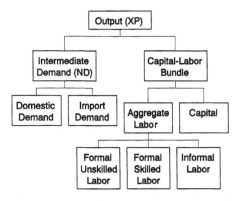

Figure 15A.1. *Production structure*

The next level of the production structure decomposes the value added bundle into aggregate labor demand, on the one hand, and capital on the other. Labor demand is disaggregated into three occupational categories, as shown in the figure. Producers are assumed to choose the optimal mix of labor groups, based on relative wages and the available production technology.

Consumption

For each household, there is a single representative consumer who allocates disposable income across the various commodities. The model uses an extension of the familiar Stone–Geary consumer demand system, known as the extended linear expenditure system (ELES). The ELES has several distinct advantages over other demand systems. It allows for commodity-specific income elasticities which can be either econometrically estimated or derived from literature searches; it is easy to calibrate and implement; and it integrates the household saving decision in the consumer optimization process. In the ELES system, consumption is represented as the sum of two components, a subsistence minimum, and a share of supernumerary income, which is the residual disposable income after subtracting expenditures on the subsistence minimum. Household direct taxation is a fixed proportion of income.

Other Final Demand

There are three other domestic final demand accounts: government expenditures, investment expenditures, and changes in inventory. Aggregate real government expenditure is assumed to be fixed, while aggregate real investment expenditure will depend upon the closure rule. The decomposition into demand for commodities is assumed to use fixed shares in both cases.

Trade

The model uses an extension of the familiar Armington hypothesis to implement trade equations. The principle behind the Armington assumption is that goods are differentiated according to region of origin. In practice this means that each agent specifies demand for a specific *aggregate* good (derived from maximizing utility, for example). This good is a constant elasticity of substitution (CES) aggregate of imports and domestic products in each sector. At this stage of the demand system, agents decompose demand for the aggregate good into its domestic and (aggregate) import components on the basis of relative prices and (calibrated) penetration shares.

Export supply is treated symmetrically to import demand; i.e., domestic producers are assumed to differentiate between domestic and export markets. A rise in export prices (relative to domestic prices) induces producers to shift production resources toward export markets. The model implements a constant elasticity of transformation (CET) curve to capture this assumption.

Equilibrium

Production is modeled with a constant-returns-to-scale technology, which guarantees that supply equals domestic plus external (export) demand for domestic output. Factor prices, wages and capital returns are generally determined by equilibrium conditions. In both markets there is a wide range of possibilities. We assume that aggregate capital is fixed in supply and mobile between sectors. We assume that labor of a specific skill is perfectly mobile across sectors, implying a single economywide average wage rate for each skill, assuming labor markets are competitive. A number of authors have demonstrated, however, that significant and persistent wage differentials exist across sectors for the same occupational groups.[51] To account for this, we calibrate a distribution of inter-sectoral wage differentials which are held constant during the simulations. Explaining the determination of these differentials is one of the main tasks of this chapter.

Closure

There are three key macro closure rules. The first concerns the government revenue–expenditure balance. For the purposes of the simulations, we assume real government saving is fixed in each region. The instrument used to achieve the

---

51 See, e.g., Katz and Summers (1989a, 1989b).

balance is the household tax schedule, which will shift either right or left to guarantee the budget balance holds.[52]

The second closure rule concerns the saving–investment balance. Domestic investment is determined by the stock of domestic private and public saving, plus net foreign saving (which is exogenous).

The third and final closure rule governs the external account, where we assume that the trade balance is equal to the level of foreign saving. If foreign saving were fixed, all adjustment would necessarily be mediated by the real exchange rate, since increased import demands which follow from trade liberalization must be financed by increased exports. At rigid terms of trade, exports can only expand by attracting resources whose relative prices have declined as a result of structural adjustment in other sectors. These include tradables which are being displaced by new imports and nontradables, whose price declines both contribute to falling domestic resource costs or real exchange rate depreciation. When foreign saving is endogenous, as in the present model, net flows of foreign investment will also exert an influence on external adjustment, possibly even driving up the real exchange rate and offsetting the export competitiveness which would otherwise result from trade liberalization.

AI Structural Equations

Consumer Behavior

$$C_i = LES_C\left(P_{Di}, Y\right) = \gamma_i + \frac{\eta_i}{P_{Di}}\left(Y - \sum_{j=1}^{n} P_{Di}\gamma_j\right) \tag{A15.1}$$

Production Technology

$$S_i = \left[CES_S\left(L_{Di}, K_{Di}; \phi\right), \frac{V_{li}}{a_{li}}, \ldots, \frac{V_{ni}}{a_{ni}}\right] \tag{A15.2}$$

$$V_{ij} = a_{ij}S_j \tag{A15.3}$$

Factor Demands $\tag{A15.4}$

$$KD_i = KD_i^d + \sum_f KD_i^f \tag{A15.5}$$

Factor Supplies

$$LS = LES_L\left(w, Y\right) \tag{A15.6}$$

$$KS_i = KS_i^d + \sum_f KS_i^f \tag{A15.7}$$

---

52 This is equivalent to lump sum taxation or rebates.

Commodity Demands, Supplies, and Allocation of Traded Goods

$$D_i = \overline{A}_{Di}\left[\sum_k \beta_i^k \left(D_i^k\right)^{(\sigma_i - 1)/\sigma_i}\right]^{\sigma_i/(\sigma_i - 1)} \tag{A15.8}$$

$$D_i^f / D_i^d = g_D\left(P_{Di}^f / P_{Di}^d; \sigma_i\right) \tag{A15.9}$$

$$S_i = \overline{A}_{Si}\left[\sum_k \delta_i^k \left(S_i^k\right)^{(\tau_i + 1)/\tau_i}\right]^{\tau_i/(\tau_i + 1)} \tag{A15.10}$$

$$S_i^f / S_i^d = g_s\left(\frac{P_{Si}^f}{P_{Si}^d}; \tau_i\right) \tag{A15.11}$$

Composite Domestic Prices

$$P_{Di}D_i = \sum_k P_{Di}^k D_i^k \tag{A15.12}$$

$$P_{Si}S_i = \sum_k P_{Si}^k S_i^k \tag{A15.13}$$

Domestic Market Equilibrium

$$D_i = C_i + \sum_{j=1} V_{ij} \tag{A15.14}$$

$$D_i^d = S_i^d \tag{A15.15}$$

$$LS = \sum_{i=1}^n LD_i \tag{A15.16}$$

$$\sum_{i=1}^n KD_i^d = \sum_{i=1}^n KS_i^d \tag{A15.17}$$

Income and Government Revenue

$$Y = \left(1 - t_L\right)\sum_{i=1}^n wLD_i + \left(1 - t_k\right)\sum_{i=1}^n r_{Di}KD_i + Y_G \tag{A15.18}$$

$$Y_G = t_L\sum_i wLD_i + t_K\sum_i r_{Di}KD_i + \sum_k\sum_i\left(t_{Di}^k P_{Di}^k D_i^k + T_{Si}^k P_{Si}^k S_i^k\right) \tag{A15.19}$$

Balance of Payments

$$B^f = \sum_i\left[PW_{Si}^f S_i^f - PW_{Di}^f D_i^f\right] \tag{A15.20}$$

Foreign Commodity Prices

$$P_{Di}^f = \left(1 + t_{Di}^f\right)ePW_{Di}^f \tag{A15.21}$$

$$P_{Si}^f = \left[\frac{1}{\left(1+t_{Si}^f\right)}\right] e P W_{Si}^f \tag{A15.22}$$

Foreign Demand and Supply Functions

$$D_i^{h,ROW} = \overline{A}_{Mi}\left(PW_{Si}^{h,ROW}\right)^{\varsigma_i} \tag{A15.23}$$

$$S_i^{h,ROW} = \overline{A}_{Ei}\left(PW_{Di}^{h,ROW}\right)^{\xi_i} \tag{A15.24}$$

Numéraire

$$\sum_i \omega_i P_{Di}^d = 1 \tag{A15.25}$$

All Variable and Parameter Definitions

Price Variables

e = Exchange rates (domestic/foreign currency)
P_{Di}^d = Domestic purchaser prices of domestic goods
P_{Di}^f = Domestic purchaser price of imports from region f
P_{Si}^d = Domestic producer price in the domestic market
P_{Si}^f = Domestic producer price for exports to region f
P_{Di} = Purchaser price of composite domestic demand
P_{Si} = Producer price of domestic output
PW_{Di}^f= World price of imports from region f
PW_{Si}^f = World price of exports to region f
r_{Di} = Rental rate on capital
w = Average wage rate

Quantity Variables

C_i = Personal consumption
D_i^d = Domestic demand for domestic goods
D_i^f = Domestic demand for imports from region f
D_i = Composite goods for domestic consumption
KD_i^d= Domestic demand for domestic capital
KS_i^d = Domestic supply of domestic capital
LD_i= Demand for labor
LS = Aggregate labor supply
S_i^d = Domestic production for domestic use
S_i^f = Domestic production for export to region f
S_i = Gross domestic output
V_{ij} = Demand for intermediate good i in sector j

Nominal Variables

B^f =Net foreign borrowing from region f (may be exogenous)
Y =Nominal domestic income
Y_G=Government income

Structural and Policy Parameters

a_{ij} =Intermediate use coefficients (Leontief technology)
γ_i =Subsistence consumption of good i
η_i =Marginal budget share for consumption of good i
ϕ_i =Elasticity of substitution between labor and capital in domestic production
σ_i =Elasticity of substitution between domestic and imported products
τ_i =Elasticity of transformation between domestic and exported products
ζ_i =ROW import supply elasticity
$\underline{\xi_i}$ =ROW export demand elasticity
$\bar{A}_{Di}$=Calibrated intercept parameter for composite product demand
$\bar{A}_{Si}$ =Calibrated intercept parameter for composite product supply
$\bar{A}_{Mi}$=Calibrated intercept parameter for ROW import supply
$\bar{A}_{Ei}$ =Calibrated intercept parameter for ROW export demand
β_i^k =Base share parameter of demand by origin in the composite demand
δ_i^* =Base share parameter of supply by destination in the composite demand
ρ_i^f =Ad valorem equivalent of nontariff barriers on imports from region f
t_{Di}^d =Indirect tax rate on domestic sector production
t_{Di}^f =Ad valorem tariff rate on imports from region f
t_K =Tax rate on capital income
t_L =Tax rate on labor income
t_{Si}^d =Producer tax or subsidy on domestic deliveries
t_{Si}^f =Tax or subsidy on exports to region f
ω_i =Domestic expenditure shares

Indices

i,j=Sectors
d =Mexico
f =Set of foreign trading partners
k =$d \cup f$

References

Abowd, J.A. and T. Lemieux. 1993. "The effects of product market competition on collective bargaining agreements: The case of foreign competition in Canada." *Quarterly Journal of Economics* 108:983–1014.

Abowd, J.M., F. Kramarz, and D.N. Margolis. 1994. "High wage workers and high wage firms." *NBER Working Paper Series*, No. 4917.

Akerlof, G.A. 1984. "Gift exchange and efficiency wage theory: Four views." *American Economic Review* 74:79–83.

Akerlof, G.A. and L.F. Katz. 1987. "Do deferred wages eliminate the need for involuntary unemployment as a worker discipline device?" Harvard Institute of Economic Research, Discussion Paper Number 1325.

Akerlof, G.A. and L.F. Katz. 1989. "Workers' trust funds and the logic of wage profiles." *Quarterly Journal of Economics* 104:525–536.

Akerlof, G.A. and J.L. Yellen. 1990. "The fair wage–effort hypothesis and unemployment." *Quarterly Journal of Economics* 105:255–283.

Alogoskoufis, G. and A. Manning. 1991. "Tests of alternative wage employment bargaining models with an application to the UK aggregate labour market." *European Economic Review* 35:23–37.

Azam, J.-P. 1994. "Efficiency wage and the family: A rationale for the agricultural wage in morocco." Unpublished, CERDI, Clermont-Ferrand, April.

Bentolila, S. and G. Bertola. 1990. "Firing costs and labour demand: How bad is Eurosclerosis?" *Review of Economic Studies* 57:381–402.

Bishop, J. 1987. "The recognition and reward of employee performance." *Journal of Labor Economics* 5:S36–S56.

Blanchard, O.J. and P.A. Diamond. 1989. "The Beveridge curve." *Brookings Papers on Economic Activity* 1:1–60.

Blanchard, O.J. and P.A. Diamond. 1990. "The aggregate matching function." In *Growth, Productivity, and Employment*, edited by P.A. Diamond. Cambridge, Massachusetts: MIT Press.

Blanchard, O.J. and S. Fischer. 1989. *Lectures on Macroeconomics*. Cambridge, Massachusetts: MIT Press.

Blanchflower, D.G. and A.J. Oswald. 1989. "The wage curve." *NBER Working Paper Series*, No. 3181.

Blanchflower, D.G. and A.J. Oswald. 1992. "International wage curves." *NBER Working Paper Series*, No. 4200.

Blanchflower, D.G., A.J. Oswald, and M.D. Garett. 1990. "Insider power in wage determination." *Economica* 57:363–370.

Blanchflower, D.G., A.J. Oswald, and P. Sanfey. 1992. "Wages, profits, and rent-sharing." *NBER Working Paper Series*, No. 4222.

Brown, C., C. Gilroy, and A. Kohen. 1982. "The effect of the minimum wage on employment and unemployment." *Journal of Economic Literature* 20:487–528.

Brown, C. and J. Medoff. 1978. "Trade unions in the production process." *Journal of Political Economy* 86:355–378.

Brown, C. and J. Medoff. 1989. "The employer-size effect." *Journal of Political Economy* 97:1027–1059.

Brown, J.N. and O. Ashenfelter. 1986. "Testing the efficiency of employment contracts." *Journal of Political Economy* 94:S40–S87.

Bulow, J.I. and L.H. Summers. 1986. "A theory of dual labor markets with application to industrial policy, discrimination, and Keynesian unemployment." *Journal of Labor Economics* 4:376–414.

Calmfors, L. 1985. "Trade unions, wage formation and macroeconomic stability: An introduction." *Scandinavian Journal of Economics* 87:143–159.

Calvo, G. 1979. "Quasi-Walrasian theories of unemployment." *American Economic Review* 69:102–106.

Calvo, G. 1985. "The inefficiency of unemployment: The supervision perspective." *Quarterly Journal of Economics* 100:373–387.

Capelli, P. and K. Chauvin. 1991. "An interplant test of the efficiency wage hypothesis." *Quarterly Journal of Economics* 106:769–787.

Christofides, L.N. and A.J. Oswald. 1992. "Real wage determination and rent-sharing in collective bargaining agreements." *Quarterly Journal of Economics* 107:985–1002.

De Melo, J. and D. TW. 1990. *A General Equilibrium Analysis of U.S. Foreign Trade Policy*. Cambridge, Massachusetts: MIT Press.

Devarajan, S., H. Ghanem, and K. Thierfelder. 1994. "Labor market policies, structural adjustment, and the distribution of income in Bangladesh." Unpublished.

Diamond, P.A. 1981. "Mobility costs, frictional unemployment, and efficiency." *Journal of Political Economy* 89:798–812.

Diamond, P.A. 1982a. "Aggregate demand management in search equilibrium." *Journal of Political Economy* 90:881–894.

Diamond, P.A. 1982b. "Wage determination and efficiency in search equilibrium." *Review of Economic Studies* 99:217–227.

Dickens, W.T. and L.F. Katz. 1987. "Inter-industry wage differences and industry characteristics." In *Unemployment and the Structure of Labor Markets*, edited by K. Lang and J.S. Leonard. Oxford: Basil Blackwell.

Dickens, W.T., L.F. Katz, and K. Lang. 1986. "Are efficiency wages efficient?" *NBER Working Paper Series, No. 1670.*

Dickens W.T., L.F. Katz, K. Lang, and L.H. Summers. 1990. "Why Do Firms Monitor Workers?" In *Advances in the Theory and Measurement of Unemployment*, edited by Y. Weiss and G. Fishelson. London: Macmillan.

Eaton, C. and W.D. White. 1983. "The economy of high wages: An agency problem." *Economica* 50:175–181.

Eckstein, Z. and K.I. Wolpin. 1990. "On the estimation of labour force participation, job search and job matching models, using panel data." In *Advances in the Theory and Measurement of Unemployment*, edited by Y. Weiss and G. Fishelson. London: Macmillan.

Edwards, S. and A.C. Edwards. 1990. "Labor market distortions and structural adjustments in developing countries." Working Paper No. 3346, National Bureau of Economic Research.

Espinosa, M.P. and C. Rhee. 1989. "Efficient wage bargaining as a repeated game." *Quarterly Journal of Economics* 104:565–58.

Faini, R. and J. de Melo. 1993. "Trade policy, employment, and migration: Some results from Morocco." Unpublished.

Farber, H.S. 1993. "The analysis of union behavior." In *Handbook of Labor Economics*, Vol. 2, edited by O. Ashenfeld and R. Layard. Amsterdam: North-Holland.

Fiszbein, A. 1992. "Do workers in the informal sector benefit from cuts in the minimum wage?" Policy Research Working Papers, WPS 826, World Bank.

Flinn, C.J. and J.J. Heckman. 1982. "Simultaneous equations models in applied search theory." *Journal of Econometrics* 18:115–168.

Freeman, R.B. 1980. "The exit-voice tradeoff in the labor market: Unionism, job tenure, quits and separations." *Quarterly Journal of Economics* 94:643–673.

Gavin, M.K. 1986. "Labor market rigidities and unemployment: The case of severance costs." Board of Governors of the Federal Reserve Discussion Papers in International Finance.

Gibbons, R. and L.F. Katz. 1992. "Does unmeasured ability explain inter-industry wage differentials?" *Review of Economic Studies* 59:515–535.

Greenwald, B. 1986. "Adverse selection in the labor market." *Review of Economic Studies* 53:325–347.

Groshen, E.L. 1991. "Sources of intra-industry wage dispersion: How much do employers matter?" *Quarterly Journal of Economics* 106:869–884.

Haddad, M. 1991. "The effect of trade liberalization on multi-factor productivity: The case of Morocco." Unpublished.

Hamermesh, D.S. 1993. *Labor Demand.* Princeton, New Jersey: Princeton University Press.

Hart, O. and B. Holmström. 1987. "The theory of contracts." In *Advances in Economic Theory*, edited by T. Bewley. Cambridge: Cambridge University Press.

Holzer, H., L.F. Katz, and A. Krueger. 1991 "Job queues and wages: New evidence on the minimum wage and inter-industry wage structure." *Quarterly Journal of Economics* 106:739–768.

Hosios, A.J. 1990. "On the efficiency of matching and related models of search and unemployment." *Review of Economic Studies* 57:279–298.

Howitt, P. 1985. "Transactions costs in the theory of unemployment." *American Economic Review* 75:88–100.

Howitt P. and P.R. McAfee. 1987. "Costly search and recruiting." *International Economic Review* 28:89–107.

Jackman, R., R. Layard, and C.A. Pissarides. 1989. "On vacancies." *Oxford Bulletin of Economics and Statistics* 51:377–394.

Jovanovic, B. 1979. "Job matching and the theory of turnover." *Journal of Political Economy* 87:972–990.

Katz, L.F. 1986. "Efficiency wage theories: A partial evaluation." In *NBER Macroeconomics Annual 1986*, edited by S. Fischer. Cambridge, Massachusetts: MIT Press.

Katz, L. and L. Summers. 1989a. "Industry rents: Evidence and implications." *Brookings Papers on Economics Activity: Microeconomics* 209–290.

Katz, L.F. and L.H. Summers. 1989b. "Can interindustry wage differentials justify strategic trade policy?" In *Trade Policies for International Competitiveness*, edited by R.C. Freestra. Chicago: NBER.

Krueger, A. and L.H. Summers. 1987. "Reflections on the inter-industry wage structure." In *Unemployment and the Structure of Labor Markets*, edited by K. Lang and J.S. Leonard. Oxford: Basil Blackwell.

Krueger, A. and L.H. Summers. 1988. "Efficiency wages and the inter-industry wage structure." *Econometrica* 56:259–293.

Lancaster, T. 1979. "Econometric models for the duration of unemployment." *Econometrica* 47:939–956.

Layard, R. and S. Nickell. 1986. "Unemployment in Britain." *Economica* 53:S121–S170.

Layard, R. and S. Nickell. 1990. "Is unemployment lower if unions bargain over employment?" In *Advances in the Theory and Measurement of Unemployment*, edited by Y. Weiss and G. Fishelson. London: Macmillan.

Layard, R., S. Nickell, and R. Jackman. 1991. *Unemployment, Macroeconomic Performance and the Labour Market.* New York: Oxford University Press.

Lazear, E.P. 1990a. "Job security and unemployment." In *Advances in the Theory and Measurement of Unemployment*, edited by Y. Weiss and G. Fishelson. London: Macmillan.

Lazear, E.P. 1990b. "Job security provisions and employment." *Quarterly Journal of Economics* 55:699–726.

Leibenstein, H. 1957. "The theory of underdevelopment in densely populated backward areas." In *Economic Backwardness and Economic Growth*, edited by H. Leibenstein. New York: John Wiley.

Leonard, J.S. and L. Jacobson. 1990. "Earning inequality and job turnover." *American Economic Review* 80:298–302.

Lindbeck, A. and D.J. Snower. 1986. "Wage setting, unemployment, and insider-outsider relations." *American Economic Review* 76:235–239.

Lindbeck, A. and D.J. Snower. 1987. "Efficiency wages versus insiders and outsiders." *European Economic Review* 31:417–426.

Lopez, R.E. and L.A. Riveros. 1988. "Wage responsiveness and labor market disequilibrium." PPR Working Papers, WPS 85, World Bank.

Lucas, R.E., Jr. and E.C. Prescott. 1974. "Equilibrium search and unemployment." *Journal of Economic Theory* 7:188–209.

MaCurdy, T.E. and J.H. Pencavel. 1986. "Testing between competing models of wage and employment determination in unionized markets." *Journal of Political Economy* 94:S3–S39.

Malcomson, J.M. 1981. "Unemployment and the efficiency wage hypothesis." *Economic Journal* 91:848–866.

McDonald, I.M. and R.M. Solow. 1981. "Wage bargaining and employment." *American Economic Review* 71:896–908.

McKenna, C.J. 1987. "Labour market participation in matching equilibrium." *Economica* 54:325–333.

Mincer, J. 1976. "Unemployment effects of minimum wages." *Journal of Political Economy* 84:17–35.

Mortensen, D.T. 1982a. "Property rights and efficiency in mating, racing and related games." *American Economic Review* 72:968–979.

Mortensen, D.T. 1982b. "The matching process as a noncooperative bargaining game." In *The Economics of Information and Uncertainty*, edited by J.J. McCall. Chicago: University of Chicago Press and NBER.

Mortensen, D.T. 1986. "Job search and the labor market analysis." In *Handbook of Labor Economics*, Vol. 2, edited by O. Ashenfelter and R. Layard. Amsterdam: North-Holland.

Murphy, K.M. and R.H. Topel. 1990. "Efficiency wages reconsidered: Theory and evidence." In *Advances in the Theory and Measurement of Unemployment*, edited by Y. Weiss and G. Fishelson. London: Macmillan.

Nalebuff, B., A. Rodriguéz, and J.E. Stiglitz. 1993. "Equilibrium unemployment as a worker screening device." *NBER Working Paper Series, No. 4357.*

Nalebuff, B. and J.E. Stiglitz. 1983. "Information, competition and markets." *American Economic Review* 73:278–283.

Narendranathan, W. and S. Nickell. 1985. "Modeling the process of job search." *Journal of Econometrics* 28:29–49.

Nickell, S.J. 1979. "Estimating the probability of leaving unemployment." *Econometrica* 47:1249–1266.

Oswald, A.J. 1985. "The economic theory of trade unions: An introductory survey." *Scandinavian Journal of Economics* 87:197–225.

Pencavel, J.H. 1972. "Wages, specific training, and labor turnover in U.S. manufacturing industries." *International Economic Review* 13:54–63.

Pencavel, J.H. 1985. "Wages and employment under trade unionism: Microeconomic models and macroeconomic applications." *Scandinavian Journal of Economics* 87:197–225.

Pissarides, C.A. 1984. "Efficient job rejection." *Economic Journal* 94:97–107.

Pissarides, C.A. 1985a. "Taxes, subsidies and equilibrium unemployment." *Review of Economic Studies* 52:121–133.

Pissarides, C.A. 1985b. "Short-run equilibrium dynamics of unemployment, vacancies, and real wages." *American Economic Review* 75:676–690.

Pissarides, C.A. 1986. "Unemployment and vacancies in Britain." *Economic Policy* 3:499–559.

Pissarides, C.A. 1987. "Search, wage bargains and cycles." *Review of Economic Studies* 54:473–483.

Pissarides, C.A. 1990. *Equilibrium Unemployment Theory.* Oxford: Basil Blackwell.

Pissarides, C.A. and J. Wadsworth. 1994. "On-the-job search: Some empirical evidence from Britain." *European Economic Review* 38:385–401.

Raff, D.M. and L.H. Summers. 1987. "Did Henry Ford pay efficiency wages?" *Journal of Labor Economics* 5:S56–S86.

Reinert, K.A., D.W. Roland-Holst, and C.R. Shiells. 1995. "North American trade liberalization and the role of nontariff barriers." *North American Journal of Economics and Finance* 5:137–168.

Riveros, L.A. 1990. "Recession, adjustment and the performance of urban labor markets in Latin America." *Canadian Journal of Development Economics* 11:33–59.

Riveros, L.A. and R. Paredes. 1988. "Measuring the impact of minimum wage policies on the economy." PPR Working Paper, WPS 101, World Bank.

Rosen, S. 1986. "The theory of equalizing differences." In *Handbook of Labor Economics,* edited by O. Ashenfelter and R. Layard. Amsterdam: North-Holland.

Rotschild, M. and J.E. Stiglitz. 1976. "Equilibrium in competitive insurance markets: An essay on the economics of imperfect information." *Quarterly Journal of Economics* 90:630–649.

Rutherford, T.F., E.E. Rutström, and D. Tarr. 1993. "Morocco's free trade agreement with the European Community." Working Paper WPS 1173, Policy Research Department, World Bank.

Salop, S. 1979. "A model of the natural rate of unemployment." *American Economic Review* 69:117–125.

Santiago, C.E. 1989. "The dynamics of minimum wage policy in economic development: A multiple time-series approach." *Economic Development and Cultural Change* 38:1–30.

Schlichter, S. 1950. "Notes on the structure of wages." *Review of Economics and Statistics* 32:80–91.

Shapiro, C. and J.E. Stiglitz. 1984. "Equilibrium unemployment as a worker disciplinary device." *American Economic Review* 74:433–444.

Solow, R.M. 1979. "Another possible source of wage stickiness." *Journal of Macroeconomics* 1:1979–1982.

Solow, R.M. 1985. "Insiders and outsiders in wage determination." *Scandinavian Journal of Economics* 87:411–428.

Stern, S. 1990. "Search, applications and vacancies." In *Advances in the Theory and Measurement of Unemployment*, edited by Y. Weiss and G. Fishelson. London: Macmillan.

Stigler, G. 1946. "The economics of minimum wage legislation." *American Economic Review* 36:358–365.

Stiglitz, J.E. 1985. "Equilibrium wage distributions." *Economic Journal* 95:595–618.

Stiglitz, J.E. 1987. "The causes and consequences of the dependence of quality on price." *Journal of Economic Literature* 25:1–48.

Wadhawani, S.B. and M. Wall. 1991. "A direct test of the efficiency wage model using UK micro-data." *Oxford Economic Papers* 43:529–548.

Weiss, A. 1980. "Job queues and layoff in labor markets with flexible wages." *Journal of Political Economy* 88:552–579.

World Bank. 1994. "Kingdom of Morocco, country economic memorandum, issues paper." World Bank.

Yellen, J. 1984. "Efficiency wage models of unemployment." *American Economic Review* 74:200–205.

Yoon, B.J. 1981. "A model of unemployment duration with variable search intensity." *Review of Economics and Statistics* 63:599–609.

16

Trade and the Environment

Hiro Lee and David W. Roland-Holst

I Introduction

The environmental implications of international trade are becoming an important part of multilateral and domestic policy agendas. This is particularly the case for trade relations between developing and developed countries. To what extent developing countries should devote their resources to lowering domestic environmental costs for their own welfare and that of the world as a whole has frequently been debated. The debate stems from the widely held view that a tradeoff between economic growth and environmental quality exists. Many policymakers in developing countries argue that they have the right to pursue the same material aspirations by the same means as did the industrialized world during its developmental stages and are thus willing to spend smaller percentages of their productive resources for pollution abatement than developed countries.

If it is accepted that differing domestic practices yield different environmental effects, how might trade exert its own environmental influence? It is increasingly recognized that the import of goods and services entails an implicit transfer of environmental effects to the exporting country. Given the hierarchical nature of technology in the development process, one might infer that less developed countries would be net losers in the environmental transfer scheme which underlies trade. The data presented in this chapter indicate that trade between Indonesia and Japan has occasioned a large and sustained net transfer of effluents during the 1965–90 period. For example, the implied unit effluent content of Indonesian exports to Japan has been about six times that of its imports from Japan. This appears to suggest that more outward orientation would be harmful to the Indonesian environment.

We thank Sébastien Dessus, David O'Connor, David Turnham, and Dominique van der Mensbrugghe for helpful comments.

517

A number of empirical studies (e.g., Grossman and Krueger, 1992; Hettige et al., 1992; Lucas et al., 1992) have shown an inverse U-shaped relationship between gross domestic product (GDP) per capita and industrial pollution intensity. Birdsall and Wheeler (1992) suggest that the normal good characteristic of environmental quality, relatively high costs of monitoring and enforcing pollution standards, and increase in output shares of manufactures during industrialization are some of the major factors leading to relatively high pollution levels per unit of output in developing countries, while Hettige et al. (1992) and Lucas et al. (1992) indicate that the declining portion in the inverse U relationship is due solely to a shift from industry to services and not a shift toward a less toxic mix of manufacturing output.

Despite an intense pressure from environmentalists and some policy-makers to include environmental standards in recent trade agreements such as North American Free Trade Area (NAFTA) and the Uruguay Round of the General Agreement on Tariffs and Trade (GATT), economists have long argued that trade is not the root cause of environmental degradation. Low and Safadi (1992) suggest that freer trade may provide benefits to the environment through its effects on resource allocation and income levels. Lucas et al. (1992) find that among developing countries, the more closed economies experienced very rapid shifts toward toxic-intensive structures in the 1970s and 1980s. This is because import-substituting industrialization protected mainly capital- and pollution-intensive sectors. Thus, previous studies suggest that trade does not necessarily lead to degradation of national environment and that trade policy should not be used to remedy environmental problems.[1]

We use an applied general equilibrium model which incorporates detailed industrial pollution data to examine the environmental implication of trade and tax policies in Indonesia. Indonesia is well suited to our analysis because it has comparative advantage in pollution-intensive industries and its trade has conferred asymmetric environmental effects. An important empirical result of this chapter is that a combination of trade liberalization and a cost-effective tax policy could raise both the country's welfare and its environmental quality.

In Section II, we review the literature on pollution and appropriate policy instruments, environmental accounting, and recent applied models which link economic activities and the environment. Section III presents some statistics on the embodied pollution service trade between Indonesia and

---

[1] See Beghin, Roland-Holst, and van der Mensbrugghe (1995), Cropper and Oates (1992), and Dean (1992) for a survey of literature on trade and the environment. O'Connor (1994) reviews recent Asian Pacific experience.

Japan during 1965–90. Section IV describes the two-country computable general equilibrium (CGE) model used in this study, followed by the appraisal of the environmental implications of Indonesia's trade liberalization in Section V and the evaluation of the welfare effect of pollution abatement by alternative instruments in Section VI. The chapter closes with general conclusions and remarks about how this work might fruitfully be extended.

II Linkages Between Economic Activities and the Environment

When economic activities generate negative externalities such as environmental degradation, two principal market-oriented instruments which correct external effects are regarded as first-best policies in the absence of other distortions in the economy. The first is corrective effluent taxes, equal to the difference between social and private costs of the activity, as established by Pigou (1920), and the second is a system of tradable emission permits (TEP) suggested by Dales (1968).[2] Trade policy instruments, such as tariffs and export taxes, are inferior to Pigouvian taxes or an assignment of property rights unless trade is the source of externalities. An example of inefficient trade instrument is a pollution abatement and control expenditure (PACE) equalization tax, a U.S. import tax on Mexican exports of "dirty" products designed to equalize expenditures by U.S. and Mexican industries on pollution abatement (Low, 1992).

In the real world, other distortions such as various taxes and imperfectly competitive markets exist. Thus, the first-best instruments may not lead to the most efficient outcome under a second-best setting. For example, Markusen (1975) suggests that although trade is not a source of the environmental problem, for a large country second-best trade taxes could produce an allocation superior to free trade. Krutilla (1991) shows that the optimal environmental tax is greater than the standard Pigouvian tax if the regulating country is large and a net exporter of goods with negative production externality. By contrast, Anderson (1992) suggests that even if a country has comparative advantage in the production of pollution-intensive goods, free trade would still raise welfare unambiguously, so long as an optimal pollution tax is introduced. Thus, theoretical ambiguity exists concerning the welfare impact of trade in the presence of environmental externalities.

---

2 The idea of tradable emission rights is derived from Coase (1960), who viewed externalities as arising from an absence of property rights. These market-based mechanisms have been employed to mitigate pollution in a number of instances. For example, tradable permits have been introduced in the United States for sulfur dioxide, lead additives, and water discharge rights, whereas in Europe emission charges have been used to limit air and water pollution.

Hahn and Stavins (1992) point out that incentive-based instruments such as effluent taxes and TEP are not well suited when there are political and technological constraints. For example, source-specific standards may be more appropriate for highly localized pollution problems with nonlinear damage functions. The polluter-pays principle was recommended by the Organization for Economic Cooperation and Development (OECD) in the early 1970s (OECD, 1975). It represents an allocation of property rights on the environment to consumers, making polluters (producers) pay the social damage. Since it incorporates the internalization of environmental externalities into the production cost, it is consistent with efficient pollution abatement.[3]

When environmental problems transcend national boundaries such as emissions of CO_2 and other greenhouse gases (GHGs), it is usually not possible to implement first-best policy instruments because there is no supra-national agency to enforce them (Anderson and Blackhurst, 1992). In addition, there is a great deal of uncertainty about the impact of global warming on potential damage resulting from a rise in atmospheric concentration of GHGs. Although some attempts have been made to estimate the magnitude of climate change impacts (e.g., Cline, 1992; Mendelsohn, 1995; Nordhaus, 1991), the estimates vary substantially across studies.[4] As a result, many of the previous studies have emphasized cost effectiveness and distributional implications of alternative policies.[5] While different models yield different cost estimates of any given carbon emission reductions relative to the baseline, qualitatively similar results are derived. First, because marginal abatement costs differ substantially across countries, a uniform carbon tax could reduce significantly the global costs of achieving a given emission curtailment target compared with country-specific carbon taxes. Second, because a common emission tax tends to shift the burden of reducing global emissions from developed to developing countries, the likelihood of securing an international cooperation depends upon the level of transfers from the former to the latter. Third, a TEP system will also lead to the equalization of abatement cost across countries. However, compared with TEP for local pollutants, implementation of a global scheme like a uniform carbon tax or TEP for CO_2 may be difficult since it requires substantial preparations

---

3 See Low and Safadi (1992) for a discussion of the polluter-pays principle.
4 Estimates of the impact of global warming on agricultural production also vary significantly depending upon assumptions and are associated with a great deal of uncertainty. See, e.g., IPCC (1990), Mendelsohn et al. (1994), R. and Tobey et al. (1992).
5 See, for example, Burniaux et al. (1992), Coppel and Lee (1996), Jorgenson et al. (1992), Manne and Richels (1992), OECD (1993, 1994), and Perroni and Rutherford (1993). An important exception is a study by Nordhaus (1992), who examines optimal emissions over time using a dynamic integrated climate–economy (DICE) model.

and negotiations between countries on distributional issues, monitoring, and enforcement. Furthermore, as an efficient outcome requires equalization of marginal benefit and marginal cost, these policy instruments designed to minimize global abatement costs are second best.

Estimation of damage associated with externalities is an important direction for future research as economic accounting of environmental costs and benefits would be essential for comprehensive integration of trade and environmental policies. While the new System of National Accounts (SNA) does not recommend modifying the basic flow aggregates in the national accounts to account for environmental damages and changes in the stock of natural resources, it lays out the structure of satellite accounts on the environment which complements the SNA (United Nations, 1993a,b). Satellite accounts combine physical information from environmental statistics and natural resource accounts with conventional national accounts. The UN System of Environmental and Economic Accounting (SEEA) advocates the inclusion of estimated physical and monetary flows associated with the depletion and degradation of natural resources.[6]

The Bureau of Economic Analysis (BEA) of the U.S. Department of Commerce has introduced the framework for integrated economic and environmental satellite accounts (IEESAs), which are fashioned after SEEA and aim to provide interactions between the economy and the environment (U.S. Department of Commerce, 1994). For example, degradation of air and water quality could lead to such economic feedback as lower timber yields and fish harvests, additional cleaning costs, and increased pollution abatement and health expenditures. In IEESAs natural resources and environmental resources are regarded as productive assets, and the depletion of mineral reserves is treated like the depreciation of fixed capital assets. For a measure of sustainable income, the BEA suggests the use of net domestic product, which is GDP less depreciation and depletion. However, many valuation and measurement issues have to be resolved before an IEESA production account can be completed.

Keuning (1992) suggests that the publication of "green GDP" is not advisable because it may create an erroneous impression that it is an appropriate measure for the level of sustainable income. He indicates that there are no proper valuation methods for resource depletion and environmental degradation. Instead, he proposes an environmental module linked to SNA, the National Accounting Matrix including Environmental Accounts (NAMEA). This module is based on the social accounting matrix (SAM),

---

6 See U.S. Department of Commerce (1994) for a detailed discussion of the UN System of Environmental and Economic Accounting.

and two new accounts are added to record emissions and extraction of environmental agents/resources and changes in environmental assets. Because those environmental flows and stocks with no market transactions are valued at a zero price in NAMEA, all accounts present complete balance in both value and volume terms. NAMEA can then be used as the database for a CGE model, where, for example, alternative assumptions on prices for depletion and degradation may be simulated.

An attempt to model interactions between the economy and the environment explicitly has been made by Bergman (1993). He includes an environmental quality measure in his CGE model of the Swedish economy. A household maximizes the utility function over final goods and environmental quality, which is negatively affected by the amount of CO_2 and SO_2 emissions. Since taxes on CO_2 and SO_2 emissions are assumed to reflect marginal damage costs, they are used as proxies for the marginal willingness to pay (MWTP) for emission reductions. It is assumed that SO_2 emissions lower the total factor productivity and that a system of tradable emission permits is implemented to attain different SO_2 abatement targets. The preliminary results indicate that the environmental quality adjusted NNP (denoted ENP) is maximized when SO_2 emissions are reduced by 20–30 percent while the aggregated MWTP and marginal cost for SO_2 abatement are equalized when the emissions are curtailed by 30–35 percent. Bergman attributes the different SO_2 abatement results for the two criteria to the terms of trade losses and suggests that the market clearing price of emission permits does not reflect the true social cost of emission curtailment.

A three-region world CGE model that incorporates local and global environmental externalities is constructed by Perroni and Wigle (1994). It is assumed that private marginal benefits are equal to a constant elasticity of transformation (CET) aggregation of unit local and global emission fees. Unit abatement costs are independent of production levels but rise as sectors reduce the ratios of emissions to output. Environmental quality is the difference between endowments of environmental quality and damage, which enters a CES utility function with per capita consumption. Through payments of emission fees, polluting parties internalize part or all of the external cost. It is shown that while international trade tends to cause some negative effect on environmental quality, changes in trade policies have little impact on the magnitude of the welfare effects of environmental policies. Although the main conclusion is robust to alternative values of many of the parameters, the internalization rate and the elasticity of marginal valuation with respect to damages are found to affect the size of benefits of internalization crucially.

The empirical results of Bergman (1993) and Perroni and Wigle (1994) suggest that while incorporating externalities into the models is possible, additional work is needed to improve the quality of pollution data and consensus values for key elasticity parameters. It is highly unlikely that the issue of social valuation of environmental quality will ever be resolved. Since results derived from the models that include environmental externalities critically depend upon the assumptions of the model structure and parameters, they must be interpreted with caution. Nevertheless, these models provide insights on the linkages between trade and the environment.

III Patterns of Effluent Transfer Between Indonesia and Japan

This section presents some historical evidence on how international trade influences the transfer of environmental effects. We introduce the concept of embodied effluent trade (EET) to capture the idea that traded commodities embody an environmental service: the amount of pollution emitted domestically when goods are produced for export. For example, if countries impose different costs on pollution, the ability to pollute might become a source of comparative advantage. In such a case, one would expect to see a pattern of relatively high EET in exports from countries with low environmental standards and relatively low EET in their imports, while the opposite would prevail in countries with higher environmental standards.

The evidence we have obtained for Indonesia and Japan shows a significant degree of EET imbalance between the two countries. The data indicate that Indonesia's net embodied effluents per unit exported to Japan are over six times the reverse flow and 29 percent higher than for its exports to the rest of the world. For Japan's part, imports from Indonesia have about twice the embodied effluent content per unit of its imports from elsewhere. This trend has remained relatively stable over the 1965–90 period, and the result is a sustained and significant transfer of environmental costs between the two countries.

Before reviewing the detailed results, a few definitions are required to clarify interpretation. To measure the effluent levels embodied in tradable commodities, we began with estimates of unit effluents in domestic production. To measure average effluent levels embodied in tradable commodities, the acute human toxic linear (AHTL) index developed by Wheeler (1992) is used. AHTL is a weighted average of various effluents with weights representing their human health risk. The index of sectoral effluent output is defined as

$$e_i = \frac{\varepsilon_i}{\sum_i \varepsilon_i q_i} \qquad (16.1)$$

where ε_i denotes the sectoral AHTL emission rate per unit of output in U.S. manufacturing and q_i denotes sector i's share in total domestic output.[7] If these indices are multiplied by 1985 U.S. sectoral output shares, they sum to unity. For any other country, such a sum measures the effluent potential of domestic output in units relative to the United States. Thus in 1985, for example, Japanese output shares give a value of $E = \Sigma e_i = 0.86$, indicating that, under the same technologies, the effluent intensity of Japanese domestic production would be 14 percent below that of the United States by this index. The comparable figure for Indonesia is 2.45.[8] Thus E serves as an index of aggregate effluent levels for a given composition of domestic production. If the structure of the economy shifts toward relatively cleaner activities, such as services, E will decrease. E is unaffected by the absolute level of output, but simply allows comparison across countries of one representative unit of domestic product.

This measure can also be used to evaluate the implicit effluent content of trade. The indices

$$E_x^f = \sum_i e_i x_i^f \qquad (16.2)$$

and

$$E_m^f = \sum_i e_i m_i^f \qquad (16.3)$$

measure the embodied effluent content of exports and imports, respectively. x_i^f and m_i^f are the sectoral shares of exports to destination f (f=bilateral partner, rest of the world [ROW]) and the sectoral shares of imports from origin f. If E_x^f exceeds unity, for example, the composition of the country's existing exports represents (in their production) a higher level of pollution per unit than representative output in the United States. Values less than unity mean that the country's overall exports are "cleaner" than overall U.S. domestic output.

---

7 Such detailed emission rates are at the moment only available for U.S. manufacturing sectors, obliging us to apply them to both Japan and Indonesia.
8 In the light of differing environmental standards in the two countries, the disparity is likely to be greater than the indexes would indicate. Japan's effluent controls are more stringent than those of the United States, and thus the compositional index for the former is likely to overstate Japanese effluent levels. Likewise, Indonesia's environmental controls are weaker than those of the reference country, so its actual effluent levels are probably underestimated by E.

Table 16.1. *Trends in embodied effluent content of exports and imports*

	1965	1970	1975	1980	1985	1990	Avg
Indonesia							
Exports to							
Japan	11.32	11.45	15.34	13.43	11.77	10.41	12.29
Rest of World	7.28	6.49	14.14	12.20	10.59	7.23	9.66
Imports from							
Japan	2.10	2.17	2.03	1.80	1.99	1.67	1.96
Rest of World	2.29	2.73	2.79	4.44	4.16	3.34	3.29
Effluent Trade Ratio (Ex/Em)							
Japan	5.38	5.29	7.57	7.47	5.93	6.24	6.31
Rest of World	3.18	2.38	5.06	2.75	2.54	2.17	3.01
Japan							
Exports to							
Indonesia	2.10	2.17	2.03	1.80	1.99	1.67	1.96
Rest of World	1.75	1.62	1.69	1.60	1.52	1.54	1.62
Imports from							
Indonesia	11.32	11.45	15.34	13.43	11.77	10.41	12.29
Rest of World	4.09	3.87	7.63	8.86	7.39	4.78	6.10
Effluent Trade Ratio (Ex/Em)							
Indonesia	0.19	0.19	0.13	0.13	0.17	0.16	0.16
Rest of World	0.43	0.42	0.22	0.18	0.21	0.32	0.30

These indices measure embodied effluent content of exports and imports relative to the emission intensity of overall U.S. domestic output. Values greater than unity imply that the country's overall exports by destination or imports by origin are more pollution-intensive than the U.S. output.

Sources: Wheeler (1992), United Nations' COMTRADE database, and authors' calculations.

The indices E_x and E_m thus measure the embodied effluent trade (EET) for a given composition of exports and imports per unit of trade. E_x and E_m for Indonesia–Japan bilateral trade and their trade with the rest of the world are presented in Table 16.1. These estimates were constructed for the 1965–90 period at five-year intervals, with detailed trade data from the United Nations' COMTRADE tables. The ratios of E_x to E_m are also given in the table.[9]

It is quite apparent from these results that the effluent composition of trade varies from that of domestic output for both countries, but that this

---

9 The pollution content of U.S. exports and imports has been estimated by Walter (1973). He estimated environmental-control loadings entering U.S. trade flows and found that the pollution content of U.S. exports exceeded that of imports in thirty-one of seventy-eight sectors in 1971.

disparity is much greater for Indonesia. Indonesia's export industries appear to be generating three to four times as much effluent as overall domestic output, while Japanese exports are about twice the effluent intensity of domestic product as a whole. One reason for this is the omission of agriculture and services in the effluent database. Although this omission would be unlikely to bias the trade comparisons between the two countries (the two sectors are insignificant in bilateral trade), they do understate the pollution content of production for the domestic market.

The most arresting feature of Table 16.1, however, is the imbalance in direct EET between the two trading partners. This can be seen more clearly in two extreme graphs of Figure 16.1. Over the last two and a half decades, Indonesia's production for export to Japan has been about six times more effluent-intensive than Japanese exports to Indonesia. In a long-term situation of relatively balanced bilateral trade, this implies a sustained and significant transfer of environmental costs from Japan to Indonesia. Although the trend in recent years has reduced this disparity, it is still quite significant.

These results are even more striking when compared to each country's trade with the rest of the world. Indonesia's imports from Japan are about half as effluent-intensive as what Indonesia buys from other countries and its exports to Japan are about 30 percent as effluent-intensive as other countries' exports to Japan. Trade between countries at different stages of modernization has long exhibited hierarchical properties which are correlated with technology levels and environmental effects.

Identification of this problem is only the first step, however, since it has implications for sustainable living standards in both countries. It is often argued that environmental damage at the early stages of industrialization is a transitory phenomenon, and cleaner technologies and resource conservation are inevitably concurrent with rising living standards. The evidence presented here may support a shifting correlation between the level of development and better environmental conditions, but it does nothing to establish a causality in either direction.

Possible explanations of these trends fall into three general categories: institutions, technology, and economic structure. In each of these general respects, the two countries have important differences which might contribute to an explanation of the effluent asymmetry in their trade patterns. The first category, institutions, includes all those influences of private and public rules and behavior, including differences in economic and environmental regulation and enforcement and behavior patterns which exploit them. Examples of this might be protection or taxation patterns which promote domestic or foreign pollution, differing levels of domestic environmental

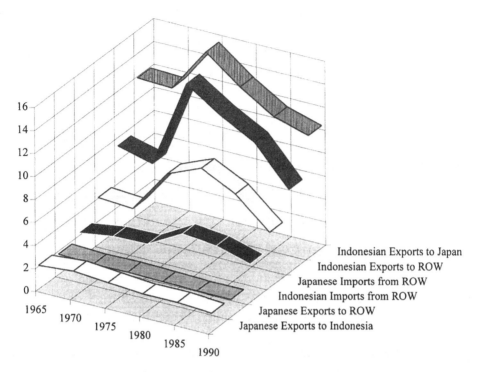

Figure 16.1. *Trends in embodied effluent trade*

stringency, and private or public sector behavior which might facilitate the creation of pollution havens. On the basis of the specific evidence for Indonesia and Japan, as well as the general verdict of economic literature on this subject, we reject institutional factors as decisive in explaining these historical trends. Despite all the public attention and controversy surrounding the pollution haven issue, there is very little evidence to indicate that trade patterns between these two countries can be substantively explained by this phenomenon.[10]

Significant technological disparities between the two countries certainly exist in a variety of industrial activities, and these could reinforce the observed inequality of pollution levels. However, Indonesian–Japanese technology differences have no bearing on the present results, since they were obtained by applying the same (U.S.) effluent coefficients to both countries. Although country-specific data are likely to yield even larger asymmetries, the present results call for and are quite sufficient to justify closer inspection.

10 For a general appraisal of this issue, see Cropper and Oates (1992).

Can economic structure alone explain Indonesia's higher pollution intensities in production, for both domestic and foreign consumption? As will be apparent in a review of the data for the CGE model later, there are indeed significant differences in sectoral and trade structure between the two countries. Moreover, when these differences are compared to sectoral data on effluent intensity, it becomes apparent that, all other things (institutions, technologies, etc.) being equal, the composition of Indonesia's current economic activity is much more pollution-intensive than that of Japan (its export composition even more so). In the next section, a simulation model is developed to examine more closely this structural problem and policies which can mitigate it.

IV A Two-Country CGE Model for Indonesia and Japan

As indicated in Section II, CGE models have increasingly been used as a tool for empirical assessments of the impact of trade and tax policies on economic welfare and environmental quality. While the two-country computable general equilibrium (CGE) model described here is in most respects typical of comparative static, multi-sectoral, economywide models in use today, we incorporate detailed sectoral emission data in the model.[11] Model equations are summarized in Appendix 16.1. An important feature of this model is its endogenous specification of domestic supply, demand, and bilateral trade for the two countries at the sectoral level. This is particularly important for Indonesia as its bilateral trade with Japan as a percentage of the total trade was 47 percent for exports and 21 percent for imports in 1985. While trade between the two countries is modeled endogenously, we assume that their individual trade flows with the rest of the world (ROW) are each governed by the small country assumption.[12] The resulting six sets of sectoral trade flows are then directed by two endogenous price systems (Indonesia–Japan imports and exports) and four exogenous price systems (Indonesia–ROW and Japan–ROW imports and exports).

As has been employed in many other CGE models, a differentiated product specification is used for the demand and supply for tradable commodities. Domestic demand is a CES composite of goods differentiated by origin (domestic goods, imports from the bilateral trading partner, and imports from ROW), while domestic production is a CET composite of goods differ-

---

11 See Chapter 6 of this volume by Devarajan, Go, Lewis, Robinson, and Sinko on simple general equilibrium models.

12 Lee and Roland-Holst (1993) treat Japan as a large country so as to affect prices in the ROW market. For the moderate trade flow adjustments for Japan described in this study, however, the small country assumption makes almost no change in the results of simulation experiments.

entiated by destination (domestic market, exports to bilateral partner, and exports to ROW).[13]

Every sector is characterized by constant returns to scale and perfect competition, and sectoral prices adjust until they are equal to average costs of composite supply.[14] Sectoral emission levels by pollutant and destination of supply are computed as

$$EMI_{ih}^k = \varepsilon_{ih} P_{Si}^k S_i^k \tag{16.4}$$

where ε_{ih} are sectoral effluent intensities of pollutant h, and P_{Si}^k and S_i^k are domestic producer price and production for supply to destination k. Ad valorem domestic production taxes, t_{Si}, are the sum of ad valorem indirect taxes, t_{Di}, and ad valorem effluent taxes

$$t_{Si} = t_{Di} + \sum_h \tau_{ih} \varepsilon_{ih} \tag{16.4}$$

where τ_{ih} are excise taxes on emissions (\$/ton of pollutant h).

We assume both countries have a fixed aggregate stock of domestic productive capital which is mobile between sectors, while the economywide average rental rate adjusts to equate aggregate capital demand to the fixed total supply. We also assume that labor in both countries is mobile between sectors, but the total labor supply is specified as a function of the wage rate and household income. In the product markets, prices are normalized by a fixed numéraire chosen to be the GDP price deflator. Finally, we assume that the real exchange rate is flexible while the current account balances for the two countries are fixed at the baseline values.[15]

The Indonesia–Japan CGE model is calibrated to a 1985 SAM constructed by the authors.[16] The principal data source used to estimate the SAM was a 128-sector input–output table constructed by the Institute of Developing Economies (1991). Structural parameters of the model are obtained by calibration, direct estimation, or imputation from other sources. Calibrated values are obtainable for most share parameters, input–output coefficients, nominal ad valorem taxes, and tariff rates from the SAM itself. Sectoral employment and capital stock data are obtained from official publications of both countries. Elasticity parameters have been obtained from a variety of published and unpublished sources.

---

13 See equations (A16.9) and (A16.11) in Appendix 16.1.

14 While varying returns to scale does affect the magnitude of impact of trade and tax policies, the key results of this chapter are robust and not affected by different specifications on market conduct (e.g., oligopolistic behavior) and returns to scale.

15 Since there are no assets in the model, the real exchange rate is the relative price of tradables to nontradables.

16 See Chapter 4 of this volume by Reinert and Roland-Holst on social accounting matrices.

Table 16.2. *Economic structure of Indonesia and Japan, 1985 (all figures in percentages)*

		(1) S shr	(2) D shr	(3) X shr	(4) M shr	(5) X/S	(6) M/D	(7) Xb/X	(8) Xr/X	(9) Mb/M	(10) Mr/M	(11) tm
	Indonesia											
1	Agriculture	22.8	22.8	9.5	5.3	5.7	2.4	15.3	84.7	0.3	99.7	9.8
2	Petroleum	15.8	8.3	64.2	8.7	55.1	11.1	62.6	37.4	0.3	99.7	5.2
3	Mining	0.8	0.8	1.0	1.4	17.4	18.2	90.1	9.9	9.1	90.9	4.8
4	FoodProc	5.1	5.3	1.2	1.1	3.2	2.1	7.0	93.0	9.5	90.5	20.2
5	Textile	1.9	1.7	2.5	1.0	17.6	5.8	2.0	98.0	40.3	59.7	35.3
6	LumWood	1.4	0.8	4.4	0.0	43.8	0.2	15.2	84.8	15.9	84.1	8.6
7	PulpPaper	0.3	0.4	0.1	1.7	4.7	41.0	3.8	96.2	9.1	90.9	32.0
8	IndChem	0.1	0.7	0.2	6.4	47.0	94.5	10.0	90.0	25.7	74.3	12.8
9	OtherChem	1.5	2.2	0.8	7.4	7.6	35.5	3.1	96.9	19.7	80.3	12.3
10	Plastic	0.4	0.4	0.1	0.3	2.8	7.5	0.6	99.4	47.8	52.2	27.5
11	NonMtMnr	0.9	1.0	0.1	1.4	1.5	13.8	2.8	97.2	62.9	37.1	28.7
12	Steel	0.5	0.9	0.1	3.8	4.1	46.5	45.2	54.8	63.3	36.7	9.0
13	NonferMtl	0.5	0.3	2.6	1.6	70.4	51.4	60.4	39.6	13.3	86.7	10.1
14	MetalProd	0.6	1.2	0.0	5.0	0.4	44.1	1.0	99.0	39.6	60.4	24.0
15	MachPrcIs	0.6	2.7	0.2	19.3	3.2	76.2	1.1	98.9	29.9	70.1	26.6
16	ElecMach	0.4	0.8	0.4	3.6	11.4	48.5	0.1	99.9	31.3	68.7	30.8
17	TranspEq	1.1	2.4	0.2	11.8	2.9	52.8	0.1	99.9	22.8	77.2	25.9
18	OtherMfg	0.9	1.0	0.2	0.7	2.6	7.9	34.4	65.6	39.1	60.9	34.0
19	Services	44.3	46.2	12.1	19.6	3.7	4.5	16.2	83.8	7.4	92.6	5.0
	Total/Wgt Avg	100.0	100.0	100.0	100.0	13.6	10.6	47.1	52.9	20.8	79.2	16.2
	Japan											
1	Agriculture	4.4	5.3	0.3	13.9	0.5	15.6	0.3	99.7	5.5	94.5	4.8
2	Petroleum	1.9	4.0	0.7	34.9	2.6	52.5	0.2	99.8	20.6	79.4	4.7
3	Mining	0.6	1.0	0.1	7.1	1.5	41.1	5.9	94.1	2.4	97.6	0.0
4	FoodProc	3.8	4.0	0.5	2.3	0.9	3.5	1.0	99.0	2.5	97.5	16.2
5	Textile	2.0	2.1	2.3	2.9	8.2	8.4	0.9	99.1	1.5	98.5	6.8
6	LumWood	0.6	0.6	0.0	1.1	0.6	10.5	0.3	99.7	9.4	90.6	1.5
7	PulpPaper	1.3	1.3	0.5	0.9	2.7	4.3	1.6	98.4	0.1	99.9	2.7
8	IndChem	1.2	1.3	1.5	2.1	8.6	9.9	6.5	93.5	0.3	99.7	3.3
9	OtherChem	2.2	2.2	3.1	2.5	10.0	6.9	2.7	97.3	0.6	99.4	3.4
10	Plastic	1.2	1.2	0.6	0.4	3.4	1.9	1.5	98.5	0.2	99.8	2.9
11	NonMtMnr	1.3	1.3	1.2	0.5	6.5	2.4	4.7	95.3	0.1	99.9	2.7
12	Steel	4.1	3.8	6.5	1.2	11.2	1.8	2.3	97.7	0.9	99.1	1.9
13	NonferMtl	0.8	1.0	0.7	5.0	7.0	29.2	1.5	98.5	5.0	95.0	2.3
14	MetalProd	2.0	1.9	2.2	0.4	8.0	1.3	5.6	94.4	0.1	99.9	3.5
15	MachPrcIs	6.6	5.5	19.4	4.5	21.3	4.9	1.7	98.3	0.1	99.9	2.8
16	ElecMach	4.1	3.1	15.2	1.5	26.9	2.9	0.4	99.6	0.0	100.0	2.9
17	TranspEq	5.1	3.5	24.3	2.1	34.3	3.5	0.7	99.3	0.0	100.0	4.2
18	OtherMfg	2.9	2.9	2.9	2.2	7.1	4.6	0.6	99.4	2.4	97.6	4.6
19	Services	53.8	54.1	18.1	14.4	2.4	1.6	0.5	99.5	4.6	95.4	0.0
	Total/Wgt Avg	100.0	100.0	100.0	100.0	7.2	6.0	1.2	98.8	9.3	90.7	3.7

(1) Gross output shares, (2) composite demand shares, (3) export shares, (4) import shares, (5) ratios of exports to gross output, (6) ratios of imports to total demand, (7) ratios of bilateral exports to total exports, (8) ratios of ROW exports to total exports, (9) ratios of bilateral imports to total imports, (10) ratios of ROW imports to total imports, and (12) nominal tariff rates.

The data in Table 16.2 reveal significant structural differences between the two economies. These differences are characteristic of their respective stages of development and arise from three distinct but interdependent sources: endowments, demand, and degree of industrialization. A highly aggregated service sector accounts for a large proportion of total output, but Japan's share is about 10 percentage points higher than Indonesia's. Among the remaining eighteen sectors, the composition of output is considerably more diversified for Japan, which has higher levels of technology and income and is thus less endowment-driven than Indonesia.

The role of demand can be seen in column 2, where lower Indonesian incomes lead to narrower emphasis on subsistence and tertiary goods and services. External demand (column 3) also plays a significant role for Indonesia, and this reinforces the endowment-driven focus on primary products (especially petroleum). Japan's demand for imports is negatively endowment-driven, and thus the two countries settle into a finely delineated relationship of comparative advantage (columns 7 and 9), with Japan supplying a significant portion of Indonesia's advanced manufactures in exchange for Indonesian primary products.

The weighted averages at the bottom of each subtable give general indications about the orientation of each economy. For example, Indonesia's exports (column 3) are 13.6 percent of its gross output, making it almost twice as export-dependent as Japan.[17] Indonesia is also more import-dependent (column 4) than Japan, although the difference here is smaller. The bilateral relationship is also much more important to Indonesia than to Japan, accounting for 47.1 percent of its exports and 20.8 percent of its imports on average, while the corresponding Japanese figures are 1.2 and 9.3 percent, respectively. Finally, Indonesia has higher levels of average nominal tariff protection than Japan (16.2 versus 3.7 percent). This, coupled with the greater trade dependence, indicates that Indonesia has greater potential for efficiency gains and structural change from trade liberalization.

Each sector in the model has effluent coefficients, linear in output, for a variety of pollutants. We have used the database for the Industrial Pollution Projection System of the World Bank to calibrate sectoral effluent coefficients.[18] This database provides emission rates, as a proportion of base-year output value, for seven air pollutants, two water pollutants, and two toxic pollutants at a four-digit SIC level of sectoral detail. The data are then mapped to four-digit output share data for Indonesia and Japan to obtain

17 Total exports as percentages of GDP are 23.0 for Indonesia and 14.9 for Japan.
18 See Martin et al. (1991) and Wheeler (1992).

Table 16.3. *Sectoral effluent intensities (pound/year/$1,000 unless indicated otherwise)*

Indonesia	PARTIC	SO2	NO2	LEAD	VOC	CO	BOD	SS	TOX	METAL
1 Agriculture	n.a.	n.a.	n.a.	n.a.	n.a.	n.a.	n.a.	n.a.	n.a.	n.a.
2 Petroleum	11.90	35.89	7.65	14.41	3.54	1.43	1.06	1.27	2.54	.13
3 Mining	9.29	44.35	3.65	.88	4.53	43.57	18.01	259.35	8.92	6.15
4 FoodProc	1.55	1.40	4.05	.04	.82	1.12	16.64	4.30	.65	.01
5 Textile	1.11	6.23	10.83	.00	2.65	2.05	.04	.07	3.28	.15
6 LumWood	9.26	3.14	6.83	.00	9.25	11.76	.00	.00	4.52	.04
7 PulpPaper	3.06	29.49	11.93	1.51	6.29	17.02	21.82	87.99	6.84	.03
8 IndChem	1.39	9.01	8.71	.07	9.16	12.34	20.75	46.49	29.91	.18
9 OtherChem	1.19	12.12	5.94	.21	5.68	7.28	5.61	1.60	3.74	.04
10 Plastic	.35	3.00	.89	.00	9.97	.26	.00	.01	7.48	.20
11 NonMtMnr	15.72	15.22	16.81	.63	1.18	3.05	.00	.00	3.39	.83
12 Steel	4.12	9.74	4.40	13.47	2.31	33.66	.04	27.35	7.64	4.10
13 NonferMtl	9.12	44.90	3.39	.00	4.59	46.30	19.11	276.09	9.33	6.54
14 MetalProd	.56	.37	1.80	.49	9.33	.21	1.21	25.82	4.59	.66
15 MachPrcIs	1.49	.81	.61	.43	1.82	.22	.00	.00	1.56	.25
16 ElecMach	.12	.38	.22	.33	4.50	.26	.00	.04	1.80	.31
17 TranspEq	.84	.20	.13	.00	1.87	.05	.00	.02	1.11	.05
18 OtherMfg	1.02	.48	.15	.00	9.08	.07	.00	.00	2.71	.60
19 Services	n.a.	n.a.	n.a.	n.a.	n.a.	n.a.	n.a.	n.a.	n.a.	n.a.

Japan										
1 Agriculture	n.a.	n.a.	n.a.	n.a.	n.a.	n.a.	n.a.	n.a.	n.a.	n.a.
2 Petroleum	11.90	35.89	7.65	14.41	3.54	1.43	1.06	1.27	2.54	.13
3 Mining	25.47	121.56	9.99	2.40	12.41	119.43	49.37	710.91	24.45	16.86
4 FoodProc	2.06	1.86	5.39	.05	1.09	1.48	22.12	5.72	.86	.01
5 Textile	1.05	5.89	10.23	.00	2.50	1.94	.04	.07	3.10	.14
6 LumWood	15.48	5.24	11.41	.00	15.46	19.65	.00	.00	7.56	.06
7 PulpPaper	.66	6.37	2.58	.33	1.36	3.68	4.71	19.00	1.48	.01
8 IndChem	.68	4.43	4.29	.04	4.51	6.07	10.21	22.88	14.72	.09
9 OtherChem	1.85	18.82	9.22	.33	8.83	11.30	8.71	2.48	5.81	.05
10 Plastic	.12	1.06	.31	.00	3.52	.09	.00	.00	2.64	.07
11 NonMtMnr	10.90	10.55	11.65	.44	.82	2.11	.00	.00	2.35	.57
12 Steel	4.12	9.74	4.40	13.47	2.31	33.66	.04	27.35	7.64	4.10
13 NonferMtl	9.12	44.90	3.39	.00	4.59	46.30	19.11	276.09	9.33	6.54
14 MetalProd	.56	.37	1.80	.49	9.33	.21	1.21	25.82	4.59	.66
15 MachPrcIs	.20	.11	.08	.06	.24	.03	.00	.00	.21	.03
16 ElecMach	.02	.05	.03	.04	.57	.03	.00	.00	.23	.04
17 TranspEq	.20	.05	.03	.00	.45	.01	.00	.00	.27	.01
18 OtherMfg	1.02	.48	.15	.00	9.08	.07	.00	.00	2.71	.60
19 Services	n.a.	n.a.	n.a.	n.a.	n.a.	n.a.	n.a.	n.a.	n.a.	n.a.

Sources: Martin et al. (1991), Wheeler (1992), and authors' calculations.

Definition of pollutants:

Air pollutants: particulates (PARTIC), sulphur dioxide (SO2), nitrogen dioxide (NO2), lead (pound/year/$billion), volatile organic compounds (VOC), carbon monoxide (CO).

Water pollutants: biochemical oxygen demand (BOD), suspended solids (SS).

Toxic pollutants / all media: total toxic release (TOX), bioaccumulative metals (METAL).

weighted emission coefficients for the nineteen sectors of the model. The results of this conversion are presented in Table 16.3.[19]

Eight of the nineteen sectors could be roughly classified as pollution-intensive, namely, petroleum, mining, lumber and wood, pulp and paper, industrial chemicals, nonmetallic minerals (consisting of cement and stone products), steel, and nonferrous metals.[20] For example, petroleum has high effluent intensities for particulates, SO_2, NO_2, and lead, while mining and nonferrous metals have high pollution coefficients on particulates, SO_2, carbon monoxide, the two water pollutants, and the two toxic pollutants. Indonesia's heavy export dependence on petroleum is the most significant factor explaining the high effluent content of its exports, but relatively high export shares of lumber and wood and nonferrous metals also contributed to high EET in exports. By contrast, except for steel, Japan's exports are concentrated in sectors with low pollution intensities, resulting in low effluents embodied in its exports.

The matrix of effluent intensities by sector and type of pollutant, $\{\varepsilon_{ih}\}$, forms the basis for calculating environmental effects resulting from policy changes, such as tariff liberalization and effluent taxes. A limitation of this approach at the moment is that there is no scope for technical substitution within sectors, and thus emissions are proportional to output regardless of relative prices and differential effluent taxes. The main advantage of this approach over previous modeling with these coefficients is the general equilibrium nature of the simulations, which allow for changing composition of domestic output, a large medium-term source of pollution mitigation.[21]

V Trade and Domestic Pollution in Indonesia

The evidence discussed in Section III suggests that Indonesia may be realizing its export potential at a disadvantage in terms of the environmental costs it absorbs vis-à-vis trading partners. The two-country CGE model is used to assess the linkage between trade and the environment by removing Indonesia's nominal tariffs on all imports. Table 16.4 summarizes the aggregate results. The tariff removal leads to an increase in Indonesia's real GDP by 0.87 percent and economywide employment by 1.87 percent. Equivalent variation (EV) income, which measures the change in real consumer purchasing power, rises by less than the increase in real GDP because of a fall

19 We aggregated emission coefficients for suspended particulates and fine particulates.
20 Of the remaining eleven sectors, other chemicals and plastics are relatively more pollution intensive than the other sectors.
21 Compare to, e.g., Anderson (1992) and Ten Kate (1993).

Table 16.4. *Aggregate results of Indonesia's tariff liberalization (percentage changes)*

	Indonesia	Japan
Real GDP	0.87	0.00
EV Income	0.53	0.03
Wage Rate	1.10	0.05
Employment	1.87	0.00
Rental Rate on Capital	3.31	0.04
Real Exchange Rate	5.26	-0.07
Total Imports	5.81	0.14
Total Exports	5.72	-0.07

in the bilateral terms of trade with Japan.[22] The wage rate and the rental rate on capital both increase, but the latter increases more because an increase in labor supply in response to higher wages raises the marginal productivity of capital. Indonesia's tariff removal induces real depreciation of rupiah and the subsequent increase in its exports. It has a negligible effect on the Japanese economy, with all aggregate measures changing by a small fraction of 1 percent.

As is usual with trade policy, relatively small aggregate adjustments can mask dramatic shifts in the composition of sectoral trade and output. Table 16.5 gives a more detailed picture of the consequences of Indonesian tariff removal. Although the data on Indonesian tariffs (Table 16.2) do not differentiate between Japan and the rest of the world, the import adjustments vary significantly for two reasons. First, the initial trade flows from the two sources are quite different (Table 16.2, columns 9 and 10), leading to different proportional adjustments to domestic demand changes. Second, because Indonesia is assumed to be a small country with respect to ROW, it imports from this source at fixed prices, while terms of trade with respect to Japan are endogenous. Thus, Japanese exporters benefit less in relative terms from Indonesian liberalization than do Indonesia's other trading partners taken as a group. A similar effect can be detected in the composition of Indonesian exports, but the exchange rate depreciation is large enough to offset most terms of trade effects.

---

22 The terms of trade with the rest of the world are unaffected because of the small country assumption.

Table 16.5. *Sectoral results for Indonesia's tariff liberalization (percentage changes)*

	Indonesia	Output	Total exports	Exp to Japan	Total Imports	Imp from Japan	Labor demand	Capital demand
1	Agriculture	-0.04	5.99	2.91	10.11	5.43	2.01	-0.60
2	Petroleum	4.11	5.64	4.80	1.65	0.45	6.72	3.98
3	Mining	1.56	3.68	3.53	1.96	0.52	2.93	0.29
4	FoodProc	-0.26	2.42	1.49	15.29	6.27	1.79	-0.82
5	Textile	0.06	3.35	2.47	28.50	9.37	1.70	-0.91
6	LumWood	4.33	9.31	6.15	3.24	1.19	6.31	3.58
7	PulpPaper	-18.25	-11.56	-8.38	13.39	3.89	-16.69	-18.82
8	IndChem	33.53	41.12	28.21	0.10	0.05	34.62	31.17
9	OtherChem	-2.44	1.00	0.73	5.81	1.89	-0.27	-2.83
10	Plastic	-1.20	2.41	1.75	20.94	7.84	0.88	-1.71
11	NonMtMnr	-3.11	-1.11	-0.90	19.49	6.66	-1.32	-3.85
12	Steel	-5.69	-3.38	-3.02	1.56	0.50	-3.35	-5.83
13	NonferMtl	9.01	11.16	10.18	-5.58	-1.36	10.92	8.08
14	MetalProd	-9.89	-6.83	-5.15	11.59	3.80	-8.28	-10.64
15	MachPrcIs	4.67	18.64	12.85	6.39	2.23	6.65	3.91
16	ElecMach	-6.54	0.68	0.51	11.33	4.21	-4.78	-7.22
17	TranspEq	-7.27	3.94	2.52	10.53	4.24	-5.71	-8.13
18	OtherMfg	-1.56	1.67	1.36	29.91	9.59	-0.03	-2.60
19	Services	0.28	4.39	2.27	0.58	0.28	1.69	-0.92

	Japan	Output	Total exports	Exp to Indonesia	Total Imports	Imp from Indonesia	Labor demand	Capital demand
1	Agriculture	-0.02	-0.16	5.43	0.14	2.91	-0.03	-0.02
2	Petroleum	-0.22	-0.02	0.45	0.14	4.80	-0.22	-0.21
3	Mining	-0.07	-0.05	0.52	0.03	3.53	-0.08	-0.06
4	FoodProc	0.02	0.03	6.27	0.11	1.49	0.02	0.03
5	Textile	0.02	0.07	9.37	0.12	2.47	0.02	0.03
6	LumWood	-0.07	-0.16	1.19	0.58	6.15	-0.07	-0.05
7	PulpPaper	0.00	0.01	3.89	0.11	-8.38	-0.01	0.01
8	IndChem	0.00	0.02	0.05	0.00	28.21	0.00	0.01
9	OtherChem	0.00	0.02	1.89	0.08	0.73	0.00	0.01
10	Plastic	-0.01	0.07	7.84	0.10	1.75	-0.01	0.00
11	NonMtMnr	0.03	0.33	6.66	0.01	-0.90	0.03	0.04
12	Steel	-0.03	-0.05	0.50	0.14	-3.02	-0.03	-0.02
13	NonferMtl	-0.23	-0.27	-1.36	0.29	10.18	-0.24	-0.22
14	MetalProd	0.03	0.20	3.80	0.10	-5.15	0.02	0.03
15	MachPrcIs	0.00	-0.02	2.23	0.15	12.85	-0.01	0.00
16	ElecMach	-0.02	-0.06	4.21	0.16	0.51	-0.03	-0.01
17	TranspEq	-0.12	-0.20	4.24	0.18	2.52	-0.12	-0.11
18	OtherMfg	0.00	0.01	9.59	0.13	1.36	0.00	0.01
19	Services	0.01	-0.08	0.28	0.13	2.27	0.01	0.02

Domestic structural adjustments in Indonesia are driven by a combination of import penetration and export expansion. These two effects generally promote expansion of primary and basic industries such as petroleum and mining, lumber, chemicals and nonferrous metals, with contractions in many of the manufacturing sectors (Table 16.5, column 1). Those sectors with the largest percentage output adjustments (e.g., pulp and paper, industrial chemicals) are quite small in the economy (Table 16.2, column 1), but petroleum accounts for 16 percent of real domestic output and its expansion may have serious implications for the environment in Indonesia. Given the assumption of an upward-sloping labor supply schedule, the adjustment to trade liberalization entails a substitution of labor for capital across most sectors. Results for Japan are again very small, except for the bilateral trade adjustments. There is some shift of resources toward Japanese export sectors and a slight diversion of import demand in response to the rupiah depreciation.

These results indicate that Indonesian tariff removal can induce significant changes in the composition of domestic production, which can in turn be expected to influence the level and composition of domestic effluent emissions. While removing tariff protection leads to expanded trade and greater economywide efficiency, in the absence of new technologies it entails an increase in the total emission levels. Table 16.6 reports the effects on emission levels of each pollutant embodied in domestic output supplied to different destinations (domestic market, bilateral partner, and ROW). Emissions from the production of goods supplied domestically increase for three pollutants (particulates, SO_2, and lead) while those decrease for the other pollutants. Trade expansion would, however, increase emissions quite substantially from the production of goods that are exported to both Japan and the rest of the world for all pollution categories included in the study. The net effect is an increase in the emission level of all the pollutants generated from total output. The right panel of Table 16.6 reports the effects on emissions from output produced in Japan resulting from Indonesia's tariff removal, which are significantly smaller than those in Indonesia in percentage terms.

The result that trade liberalization leads to higher pollution levels is not surprising because it leads to an increase in real output. A more interesting result is that it leads to an increase in the relative output shares of dirty industries, causing higher average pollution intensities for almost all major pollution categories. The only exception is biochemical oxygen demand (water pollution), whose emission level rises by a smaller percentage (0.51 percent) than the increase in real output. For all other pollutants, the per-

Table 16.6. *Emission levels by destination of supply (percentage changes)*

	Indonesia				Japan			
	Domestic	Japan	ROW	Total	Domestic	Indonesia	ROW	Total
PARTIC	0.89	4.94	7.40	3.27	-0.08	2.82	-0.07	-0.08
SO2	1.04	5.01	7.23	3.41	-0.10	1.58	-0.07	-0.09
NO2	-0.24	4.89	6.96	2.04	-0.03	2.97	-0.04	-0.03
LEAD	1.57	4.79	7.02	3.73	-0.09	0.70	-0.06	-0.09
VOC	-1.15	5.07	7.80	1.47	-0.03	2.77	-0.06	-0.03
CO	-1.20	6.71	9.49	1.73	-0.06	0.67	-0.08	-0.06
BOD	-0.83	6.43	8.66	0.51	-0.02	1.05	-0.07	-0.02
SS	-0.76	7.66	11.71	2.55	-0.09	0.75	-0.12	-0.09
TOX	-0.89	5.46	9.38	1.95	-0.04	1.45	-0.06	-0.03
METAL	-0.91	6.99	9.80	1.83	-0.06	1.00	-0.08	-0.06
AHTL Index	-0.16	5.16	8.76	2.64	-0.03	1.11	-0.05	-0.03

Percentage changes in emission levels of pollutants embodied in output supplied to different destinations resulting from unilateral tariff liberalization by Indonesia. See Table 16.3 for the definition of pollutants.

centage change in emission levels (1.47–3.73 percent) exceeds the percentage change in real output, resulting in higher emission intensities. Thus, it is reasonable to conclude that the historical asymmetry in the effluent content of trade is not a result of the existing pattern of Indonesian protection because the asymmetry only intensifies with the removal of Indonesian tariffs.

VI Trade and Tax Policy Instruments for Improving Environmental Quality

For Indonesia, the results of the previous section amplify the policy challenge of addressing the environmental consequences of trade-based economic growth. In light of the trade-off between outward-oriented industrialization and the environment, we evaluate relative effectiveness of alternative instruments to curtail pollution. Since the uncertainties on marginal benefits of pollution abatement would make the calculation of an optimal tax rate impossible, our approach is to set a particular level of emission target and assess empirically the relative cost of alternative instruments that achieve the target.[23] In the first three experiments, we

---

23 An optimal rate of effluent tax would equalize marginal damage and marginal abatement cost of 1 ton of pollutant. On the cost side, Hartman, Wheeler, and Singh (1994) provide comprehensive estimates on abatement of seven air pollutants for thirty-seven US manufacturing industries.

evaluate the cost of mitigating emissions of various pollutants by 5 percent using three policy instruments: an export tax, sector-specific effluent taxes, and a uniform effluent tax.[24] No taxes are levied on the agricultural or service sector because no emission data are incorporated for these sectors. An AHTL tax is equivalent to a set of taxes on the major air pollutants (particulates, SO_2, NO_2, lead, volatile organic compounds, and carbon monoxide) which act to reduce AHTL by 5 percent. In the fourth experiment, the combination of a uniform effluent tax and tariff removal is simulated to evaluate whether it is possible to increase real output and reduce emissions at the same time. While these experiments were conducted for each pollutant, for simplicity we only report the aggregate results for SO_2 and the AHTL index in Tables 16.7 and 16.8.[25]

In the first experiment, an export tax is chosen as a policy instrument because in Indonesia exports are on average considerably more pollution-intensive than goods supplied domestically (Section III). Since the root cause of the pollution problem is production (regardless of destination), however, the imposition of a tax only on exports would be less efficient than a tax on output supplied domestically and exported. Column (1) in both Tables 16.7 and 16.8 indicates that the cost of achieving the emission target with an export tax, in terms of lost real GDP or EV income, is highest among the three policy instruments. The reduction in total exports is partly offset by a large real depreciation of the rupiah but is still over 10 percent of the baseline quantity. The sharp contraction of trade causes additional reduction in real GDP and EV.

A neoclassical economist would naturally argue that an export tax is an inefficient instrument to control pollution decisions at the producer level. In experiment 2, sector-specific effluent taxes are levied to lower SO_2 emissions or the AHTL index by 5 percent in every sector.[26] While effluent taxes are imposed on all output regardless of destination, an enforcement of the same abatement target in all industrial sectors imposes an extremely high cost on some. This is because SO_2 abatement costs in some sectors, such as metal products, transport equipment, and other manufactures, are significantly higher than those in industrial chemicals, nonferrous metals, pulp

---

24 Different abatement targets have also been tried, but the relative efficiency of these instruments was not affected by the choice of abatement targets.

25 SO_2 is chosen because it is a pollutant that is known to affect local environmental conditions adversely, including acidification of soils and water and corrosion of materials.

26 Sector-specific taxes required to mitigate emissions by 5 percent will lead to the same results regardless of the pollutant chosen except for the effluent tax results, which depend upon the effluent intensities of the pollutant in different sectors.

Table 16.7. *Aggregate results for alternative trade and tax policies to reduce SO₂ emissions (percentage changes)*

Indonesia	(1) Export tax	(2) Sec-specific effluent taxes	(3) Uniform effluent tax	(4) Uniform tax and liberaliz
Real GDP	-1.65	-1.22	-0.56	0.30
EV Income	-1.18	-1.14	-0.34	0.25
Employment	-3.07	-2.46	-0.15	1.82
Wage Rate	-2.53	-2.16	-1.15	0.03
Rental Rate on Capital	-5.75	-5.46	-2.49	0.80
Real Exchange Rate	17.67	4.81	3.61	9.02
Total Imports	-11.87	-1.94	-1.45	4.20
Total Exports	-10.87	-2.26	-2.15	3.31
SO2 Emissions	-5.00	-5.00	-5.00	-2.03

Table 16.8. *Aggregate results for alternative trade and tax policies to lower the AHTL index (percentage changes)*

Indonesia	(1) Export tax	(2) Sec-specific effluent taxes	(3) Uniform effluent tax	(4) Uniform tax and liberaliz
Real GDP	-2.26	-1.22	-0.54	0.33
EV Income	-1.67	-1.14	-0.45	0.14
Employment	-3.99	-2.46	-0.97	0.92
Wage Rate	-3.57	-2.16	-1.09	0.14
Rental Rate on Capital	-7.68	-5.46	-2.78	0.56
Real Exchange Rate	24.70	4.81	3.54	9.03
Total Imports	-15.58	-1.94	-1.47	4.09
Total Exports	-14.25	-2.26	-1.64	3.81
AHTL Index	-5.00	-5.00	-5.00	-3.07

and paper, petroleum and mining.[27] Thus, regulation which would require every sector to cut emissions by the same proportion would also be highly inefficient.

Given the large disparity in marginal abatement costs, a uniform effluent tax would significantly reduce the costs of achieving a given emission curtailment target (experiment 3). The cost of cutting SO₂ emissions by 5 percent

27 SO₂ tax rates are computed under alternative emission targets. It is found that some high-cost sectors would have to spend more than 100 times as much in curtailing SO₂ by the same percentage compared with such low-cost sectors as industrial chemicals and nonferrous metals.

in terms of a loss in real GDP under a uniform tax is less than half (0.56 vs. 1.22 percent) compared with sector-specific taxes (Table 16.7, columns 2 and 3). Under this scheme each sector will abate SO_2 until the marginal abatement cost is equal to the uniform tax rate. Many high abatement cost sectors will not abate any SO_2 emissions at all.

While a uniform effluent tax will tend to minimize the cost of a given mitigation target, those sectors with low marginal abatement cost would bear much of the cost in terms of loss in real output. A system of tradable emission permits is an alternative cost-effective instrument to a uniform tax, but can be more supportive to equity issues. Under this system a fixed number of permits to emit a specified quantity of the pollutant is issued to emitters. Those firms or sectors with low abatement cost can sell permits to those with high abatement cost at a market-clearing permit price, thereby receiving compensation for further abatement in emissions. The equilibrium permit price is determined by demand and supply of permits, which should equal the uniform tax rate required to achieve the same emission curtailment target. In the absence of transaction costs and regulatory distortions, a uniform tax and tradable emission permits would both achieve a given level of environmental quality at minimum cost.

In the final experiment, the same uniform tax scheme implemented in the third experiment is combined with the removal of all tariffs. This experiment is conducted to illustrate a critical point, that the combination of trade liberalization and a cost-effective emission abatement instrument can lead to both an improvement in welfare (in terms of real GDP or EV) and a reduction in pollution (Tables 16.7 and 16.8, column 4). This is possible because the benefits of tariff removal are greater than the cost of cutting pollution by the magnitude which more than offsets pollution induced by trade liberalization. The twin objectives of a welfare improvement and an emission curtailment can be achieved under a range of ex ante abatement targets for each pollutant. It should be recalled that no pollution externalities have been introduced in our model because of the uncertainties regarding marginal damage. In the presence of externalities, therefore, the net social benefits of the combined policy would be even greater than our estimates would suggest.

Table 16.9 summarizes the output results for the four trade and tax policies to curtail SO_2 emissions. Levying export taxes causes large percentage reductions in the output levels of the sectors with high exports to total supply ratios (petroleum, lumber and wood, industrial chemicals, and nonferrous metals). By design, sector-specific taxes would lower output of all sectors except agriculture and services by 5 percent, while a uniform tax tends to

Table 16.9. *Output results for alternative trade and tax policies to reduce SO₂ emissions (percentage changes)*

Indonesia	(1) Export tax	(2) Sec-specific effluent taxes	(3) Uniform effluent tax	(4) Uniform tax and liberaliz
1 Agriculture	-0.1	1.9	1.8	1.9
2 Petroleum	-5.9	-5.0	-5.1	-1.4
3 Mining	2.8	-5.0	-5.0	-3.9
4 FoodProc	-0.1	-5.0	0.4	0.2
5 Textile	-3.2	-5.0	0.3	0.6
6 LumWood	-7.8	-5.0	4.9	10.4
7 PulpPaper	14.0	-5.0	-4.3	-21.6
8 IndChem	-31.8	-5.0	-4.0	26.9
9 OtherChem	4.9	-5.0	1.3	-1.0
10 Plastic	-0.5	-5.0	-0.1	-1.3
11 NonMtMnr	1.9	-5.0	-0.2	-3.3
12 Steel	14.3	-5.0	2.0	-3.7
13 NonferMtl	-13.9	-5.0	-19.8	-13.7
14 MetalProd	8.2	-5.0	1.4	-8.6
15 MachPrcIs	-2.8	-5.0	0.6	5.7
16 ElecMach	2.0	-5.0	2.2	-4.2
17 TranspEq	6.6	-5.0	2.4	-4.9
18 OtherMfg	0.3	-5.0	0.2	-1.2
19 Services	-0.4	-0.5	0.0	0.4

reduce output of the sectors with low abatement cost. When a cost-effective tax policy is combined with tariff liberalization, the agricultural and service sectors, which together account for two-thirds of Indonesia's total output, both expand. The percentage reduction in petroleum output is small compared with other policy scenarios, but the overall SO₂ emission level is lower than in the baseline case.

VII Conclusions and Extensions

The ability of international trade to alter the composition of domestic production activities allows it to exert an important influence on the environment. Export-oriented growth could cause high and unsustainable pollution levels, especially when the country has comparative advantage in dirty industries. This chapter has used data on the economy of Indonesia to appraise the environmental risks of its trade orientation and to evaluate some alternative policy instruments for reducing these risks, including export taxes, sector-specific effluent taxes, and uniform effluent taxes. In addition, a combination of uniform tax and tariff removal is simulated to examine the possibility of lowering domestic emissions and raising material welfare simultaneously.

Four principal conclusions emerge from this preliminary research. First of all, Indonesia's historical trade orientation has been environmentally asymmetric in the sense that it occasioned significant transfers of pollution services from its trading partners, particularly from Japan, to the domestic economy. Second, although trade liberalization would improve Indonesian real income, it would also raise the emission level of major industrial pollutants. Third, our results indicate that a uniform effluent tax is the most cost-effective instrument in abating SO_2 emissions. This result holds for abatement of other industrial pollutants and for different abatement targets. Neither the imposition of an export tax nor uniform emission reduction with sector-specific taxes is recommended as an alternative policy. Pollution abatement using these instruments would result in a loss of real GDP that is significantly greater than achievement of the same target using a uniform effluent tax. Last but not least, it is possible to abate industrial pollution while maintaining or even increasing real output when uniform taxation is combined with trade liberalization. In other words, trade liberalization should not be discouraged because of its environmental effects, and environmental taxation need not be contractionary if distortions can be removed elsewhere.

Much work remains to be done with the data and analytical resources developed in this research. The following areas should be given priority:

1 Broadening the model specifications to include possibilities for technical substitution.
2 Taking account of pollution arising from consumption activities, such as vehicular emissions and fertilizer use.
3 Incorporating direct foreign investment into the model to allow firms to relocate to different regions.
4 Disaggregating domestic institutions to facilitate more clear understanding of the real incidence of economic and environmental effects.
5 Including emissions from agriculture and service activities in the pollution database.
6 Estimating country-specific pollution intensities and abatement costs.

As this family of more extended models is developed, they should be subjected to exhaustive policy experimentation to elucidate the complex environmental role of individual and combined economic instruments. The importance of all this work is to strengthen the empirical foundation for research on the environmental implications of commercial policy and the trade implications of environmental policy, two essential steps to secure the basis for sustainable development.

Appendix 16.1

Structural Equations for the Indonesia–Japan CGE Model

I Country-Specific Equations

Emission Levels by Destination of Supply

$$EMI_h^k = \sum_{i=1}^{n} \varepsilon_{ih} P_{Si}^k S_i^k \tag{A16.1}$$

$k=\{d,b,r\}$, where d=domestic, b=bilateral partner, and r=ROW
$h=\{$PARTIC, SO$_2$, NO$_2$, LEAD, VOD, CO, BOD, SS, TOX, METAL, AHTL$\}$

Consumer Behavior

$$C_i = LES_C\left(P_{Di}, Y\right) = \gamma_i + \frac{\eta_i}{P_{Di}}\left(Y - \sum_{j=1}^{n} P_{Dj}\gamma_j\right) \tag{A16.2}$$

Production Technology

$$S_i = \min\left[CES_S\left(L_{Di}, K_{Di}; \phi_i\right), \frac{V_{li}}{a_{li}}, \ldots, \frac{V_{ni}}{a_{ni}}\right] \tag{A16.3}$$

$$V_{ij} = a_{ij} S_j \tag{A16.4}$$

Factor Demands

$$\frac{LD_i}{KD_i} = \Psi\left(\frac{w}{r_{Di}; \Phi_i}\right) \tag{A16.5}$$

$$KD_i = KD_i^d + \sum_f KD_i^f \tag{A16.6}$$

Factor Supplies

$$LS = LES_L\left(w, Y\right) \tag{A16.7}$$

$$KS_i = KS_i^d + \sum_f KS_i^f \tag{A16.8}$$

Commodity Demands, Supplies, and Allocation of Traded Goods

$$D_i = \overline{A}_{Di} \left[\sum_k \beta_i^k \left(D_i^k \right)^{(\sigma_i - 1)/\sigma_i} \right]^{\sigma_i/(\sigma_i - 1)} \tag{A16.9}$$

$$\frac{D_i^f}{D_i^d} = g_D \left(\frac{P_{Di}^f}{P_{Di}^d}; \sigma_i \right) \tag{A16.10}$$

$$S_i = \overline{A}_{Si} \left[\sum_k \delta_i^k \left(S_i^k \right)^{(\lambda_i + 1)/\lambda_i} \right]^{\lambda_i/(\lambda_i + 1)} \tag{A16.11}$$

$$\frac{S_i^f}{S_i^d} = g_S \left(\frac{P_{Si}^f}{P_{Si}^d}; \lambda_i \right) \tag{A16.12}$$

Composite Domestic Prices

$$P_{Di} D_i = \sum_k P_{Di}^k D_i^k \tag{A16.13}$$

$$P_{Si} S_i = \sum_k P_{Si}^k S_i^k \tag{A16.14}$$

Indirect and Effluent Taxes

$$t_{Si}^d = t_{Di}^d + \sum_h \tau_{ih} \varepsilon_{ih} \tag{A16.15}$$

Domestic Market Equilibrium

$$D_i = C_i + \sum_{j=1}^n V_{ij} \tag{A16.16}$$

$$D_i^d = S_i^d \tag{A16.17}$$

$$LS = \sum_{i=1}^n LD_i \tag{A16.18}$$

$$\sum_{i=1}^n KD_i^d = \sum_{i=1}^n KS_i^d \tag{A16.19}$$

Income and Government Revenue

$$Y = \left(1 - t_L \right) \sum_{i=1}^n w LD_i + \left(1 - t_K \right) \sum_{i=1}^n r_{Di} KD_i + Y_G \tag{A16.20}$$

$$Y_G = t_L \sum_i w LD_i + t_k \sum_i r_{Di} KD_i + \sum_k \sum_i \left(t_{Di}^k P_{Di}^k D_i^k + t_{Si}^k P_{Si}^k S_i^k \right) \tag{A16.21}$$

Balance of Payments

$$B^f = \sum_t \left[PW_{Si}^f S_i^f - PW_{Di}^f D_i^f \right]$$ (A16.22)

Foreign Commodity Prices

$$P_{Di}^f = \left(1 + t_{Di}^f\right) e PW_{Di}^f$$ (A16.23)

$$P_{Si}^f = \left[\frac{1}{\left(1 + t_{Si}^f\right)} \right] e PW_{Si}^f$$ (A16.24)

Foreign Demand and Supply Functions

$$D_i^{h,ROW} = \overline{A}_{Mi} \left(PW_{Si}^{h,ROW} \right)^{\zeta_i}$$ (A16.25)

$$S_i^{h,ROW} = \overline{A}_{Ei} \left(PW_{Di}^{h,ROW} \right)^{\xi_i}$$ (A16.26)

Trade Flow and Price Equivalence

$$D_i^{h,f} = S_i^{f,h}$$ (A16.27)
$$P_{Di}^{h,f} = P_{Si}^{f,h}$$ (A16.28)

Numéraire

$$\sum_i \omega_i P_{Di}^d = 1$$ (A16.29)

II Variable and Parameter Definitions

Price Variables

e = Exchange rates (domestic/foreign currency)
$P_{Di}^{h,f}$ = Demand price by destination (h) and origin (f)
$P_{Si}^{h,f}$ = Supply price by origin (h) and destination (f)
P_{Di}^d = Domestic purchaser prices of domestic goods
P_{Di}^f = Domestic purchaser price of imports from region f (equivalent to $P_{Di}^{d,f}$)
P_{Si}^d = Domestic producer price in the domestic market
P_{Si}^f = Domestic producer price for exports to region f (equivalent to $P_{Si}^{d,f}$)
P_{Di} = Purchaser price of composite domestic demand
P_{Si} = Producer price of domestic output
$PW_{Di}^{h,f}$ = World demand price by destination (h) and origin (f)
$PW_{Si}^{h,f}$ = World supply price by origin (h) and destination (f)
PW_{Di}^f = World price of imports from region f

PW_{Si}^f = World price of exports to region f
r_{Di} = Rental rate on capital
w = Average wage rate

Quantity Variables

C_i = Personal consumption
$D_i^{h,f}$ = Demand by destination (h) and origin (f)
D_i^d = Domestic demand for domestic goods
D_i^f = Domestic demand for imports from region f (equivalent to $D_i^{d,f}$)
D_i = Composite goods for domestic consumption
EMI_h^k = Domestic emission levels by destination of supply (domestic market, bilateral country, ROW) for pollutant h
KD_i^d = Domestic demand for domestic capital
KD_i^f = Domestic demand for imported capital (inward direct foreign investment stock) from region f (exogenous)
KS_i^d = Domestic supply of domestic capital
KS_i^f = Outward direct foreign investment stock in region f (exogenous)
LD_i = Demand for labor
LS = Aggregate labor supply
$S_i^{h,f}$ = Supply by origin (h) and destination (f)
S_i^d = Domestic production for domestic use
S_i^f = Domestic production for export to region f (equivalent to $S_i^{d,f}$)
S_i = Gross domestic output
V_{ij} = Demand for intermediate good i in sector j

Nominal Variables

B^f = Net foreign borrowing from region f (exogenous)
Y = Nominal domestic income
Y_G = Government income

Structural and Policy Parameters

a_{ij} = Intermediate use coefficients (Leontief technology)
$\varepsilon_{i,h}$ = Sectoral effluent intensities of pollutant h
γ_i = Subsistence consumption of good i
η_i = Marginal budget share for consumption of good i
ϕ_i = Elasticity of substitution between labor and capital in domestic production
σ_i = Elasticity of substitution between domestic and imported products
λ_i = Elasticity of transformation between domestic and exported products
ζ_i = ROW import supply elasticity
ξ_i = ROW export demand elasticity
$\overline{A}_{Di}$ = Calibrated intercept parameter for composite product demand
$\overline{A}_{Si}$ = Calibrated intercept parameter for composite product supply
$\overline{A}_{Mi}$ = Calibrated intercept parameter for ROW import supply
$\overline{A}_{Ei}$ = Calibrated intercept parameter for ROW export demand
β_i^k = Base share parameter of demand by origin in the composite demand

δ_i^k = Base share parameter of supply by destination in the composite demand

τ_{ih} = Excise taxes on emissions (\$/pound of pollutant h)

t_{Di}^d = Indirect tax rate on domestic sector production

t_{Di}^f = Ad valorem tariff rate on imports from region f

t_K = Tax rate on capital income

t_L = Tax rate on labor income

t_{Si}^d = Producer tax or subsidy on domestic deliveries

t_{Si}^f = Tax or subsidy on exports to region f

ω_i = Domestic expenditure shares

References

Anderson, K. 1992. "The standard welfare economics of policies affecting trade and the environment." In *The Greening of World Trade Issues*, edited by K. Anderson and R. Blackhurst. Ann Arbor: University of Michigan Press.

Anderson, K. and R. Blackhurst. 1992. "Trade, the environment and public policy." In *The Greening of World Trade Issues*, edited by K. Anderson and R. Blackhurst. Ann Arbor: University of Michigan Press.

Barde, J.-P. 1994. "Economic instruments in environmental policy: Lessons from OECD experience and their relevance to developing economies." Technical Paper No. 92, Paris: OECD Development Centre.

Beghin, J., D.W. Roland-Holst, and D. van der Mensbrugghe. 1995. "A survey of the trade and environment nexus: Global dimensions." *OECD Economic Studies* 23:167–192.

Bergman, L. 1993. "General equilibrium costs and benefits of environmental policies: Some preliminary results based on Swedish data." Stockholm School of Economics, Mimeograph.

Birdsall, N. and D. Wheeler. 1992. "Trade policy and industrial pollution in Latin America: Where are the pollution havens?" In *International Trade and the Environment*, edited by P. Low. Discussion Paper No. 159, Washington, D.C.: World Bank.

Burniaux, J.-M., G. Nicoletti, and J. Oliveira Martins. 1992. "GREEN: A global model for quantifying the costs of policies to curb CO_2 emissions." *OECD Economic Studies* 19:49–92.

Chichilnisky, G. and G.M. Heal. 1994. "Markets for tradeable CO_2 emission quotas: Principles and practice." Graduate School of Business, Columbia University, Mimeograph.

Cline, W.R. 1992. *The Economics of Global Warming*. Washington, D.C.: Institute of International Economics.

Coase, R.H. 1960. "The problem of social costs." *Journal of Law and Economics* 3:1–44.

Coppel, J. and H. Lee. 1996. "The framework convention and climate change policy in Asia." In *The Economics of Pollution Control in the Asian Pacific*, edited by R. Mendelsohn and D. Shaw. London: Edward Elgar.

Cropper, M.L. and W.E. Oates. 1992. "Environmental economics: A survey." *Journal of Economic Literature* 30:675–740.

Dales, J.H. 1968. *Pollution, Property and Prices*. Toronto: University of Toronto Press.

Dean, J.M. 1992. "Trade and the environment: A survey of the literature." In *International Trade and the Environment*, edited by P. Low. Discussion Paper No. 159, Washington, D.C.: World Bank.

Devarajan, S. Delfin Go, J.D. Lewis, S. Robinson, and P. Sinko. 1995. "Simple general equilibrium modeling." In *Applied Methods for Trade Policy Analysis*, edited by J.F. Francois and K.A. Reinert. Cambridge: Cambridge University Press.

Grossman, G.M. and A.O. Krueger. 1992. "Environmental aspects of a North American free trade agreement." Working Paper No. 644, London: Centre for Economic Policy Research.

Hahn, R.W. and R.N. Stavins. 1992. "Economic incentives for environmental protection: Integrating theory and practice." *American Economic Review* 82:464–468.

Hamilton, K. 1994. "Environmental accounting for decision-making." Paper presented at the OECD Seminar on Environmental Accounting for Decision-Making, 27–28 September, Paris.

Hartman, R.S., D. Wheeler, and M. Singh. 1994. "The cost of air pollution abatement." Policy Research Department, Washington, D.C., World Bank, Mimeograph.

Hettige, H., R.E.B. Lucas, and D. Wheeler. 1992. "The toxic intensity of industrial production: Global patterns, trends, and trade policy." *American Economic Review* 82:478–481.

Institute of Developing Economies. 1991. *International Input–Output Table: Indonesia-Japan, 1985*. Statistical Data Series No. 57, Tokyo: IDE.

Intergovernmental Panel on Climate Change. 1990. *Climate Change: The IPCC Scientific Assessment*, edited by J.T. Houghton, G.J. Jenkins, and J.J. Ephraums. Cambridge: Cambridge University Press.

Jorgenson, D.W., D.T. Slesnick, and P.J. Wilcoxen. 1992. "Carbon taxes and economic welfare." *Brookings Papers on Economic Activity: Microeconomics*: 393–431.

Keuning, S.J. 1992. "National accounts and the environment: The case for a systems approach." Occasional Paper No. NA-053. Amsterdam: Netherlands Central Bureau of Statistics.

Krutilla, K. 1991. "Environmental regulation in an open economy." *Journal of Environmental Economics and Management* 20:127–142.

Lee, H. and D.W. Roland-Holst. 1993. "Cooperation or confrontation in US-Japan trade? Some general equilibrium estimates." Irvine Economics Paper No. 92-93-08, University of California, Irvine.

Lloyd, P.J. 1992. "The problem of optimal environmental policy choice." In *The Greening of World Trade Issues*, edited by K. Anderson and R. Blackhurst. Ann Arbor: University of Michigan Press.

Low, P. 1992. "Trade measures and environmental quality: The implications for Mexico's exports." In *International Trade and the Environment*, edited by P. Low. Discussion Paper No. 159, Washington, D.C.: World Bank.

Low, P. and R. Safadi. 1992. "Trade policy and pollution." In *International Trade and the Environment*, edited by P. Low. Discussion Paper No. 159, Washington, D.C.: World Bank.

Lucas, R.E.B., D. Wheeler, and H. Hettige. 1992. "Economic development, environmental regulation and the international migration of toxic industrial pollution: 1960–1988." In *International Trade and the Environment*, edited by P. Low. Discussion Paper No. 159, Washington, D.C.: World Bank.

Manne, A.S. and R.G. Richels. 1992. *Buying Greenhouse Insurance: The Economic Costs of CO₂ Emission Limits*. Cambridge; Massachusetts: MIT Press.

Markusen, J.R. 1975. "International Externalities and Optimal Tax Structures." *Journal of International Economics* 5:15–29.

Martin, P., D. Wheeler, H. Hettige, and R. Stengren. 1991. "The industrial pollution projection system: Concept, initial development, and critical assessment." Washington, D.C.: World Bank, Mimeograph.

Mendelsohn, R. 1996. "The impact of global warming on Pacific rim countries." In *The Economics of Pollution Control in the Asian Pacific*, edited by R. Mendelsohn and D. Shaw. London: Edward Elgar.

Mendelsohn, R., W.D. Nordhaus, and D. Shaw. 1994. "The impact of global warming on agriculture: A Ricardian analysis." *American Economic Review* 84:753–771.

Nordhaus, W.D. 1991. "To slow or not to slow: The economics of the greenhouse effect." *Economic Journal* 101:920–937.

Nordhaus, W.D. 1992. "Rolling the 'DICE': An optimal transition path for controlling greenhouse gases." *Science* 258:1315–1319.

O'Connor, D. 1992. "Measuring the costs of environmental damage: A review of methodological approaches with an application to Bangkok, Thailand." Paris: OECD Development Centre, Mimeograph.

O'Connor, D. 1994. "The use of economic instruments in environmental management: The experience of East Asia." In *Economic Instruments for Environmental Management in Developing Countries*. Paris: OECD.

OECD. 1975. *The Polluter Pays Principle*. Paris: OECD.

OECD. 1993. *The Costs of Cutting Carbon Emissions: Results from Global Models*. Paris: OECD.

OECD. 1994. *Policy Response to the Threat of Global Warming*. Working Party No. 1 Report of the Economic Policy Committee, ECO/CPE/WP1(94)5, Paris: OECD.

Perroni, C. and T. Rutherford. 1993. "International trade in carbon emission rights and basic materials: General equilibrium calculations for 2020." *Scandinavian Journal of Economics* 95:257–278.

Perroni, C. and R.M. Wigle. 1994. "International trade and environmental quality: How important are the links?" *Canadian Journal of Economics* 27:551–567.

Pigou, A.C. 1920. *The Economics of Welfare*. London: Macmillan.

Radetzki, M. 1992. "Economic growth and the environment." In *International Trade and the Environment*, edited by P. Low. Discussion Paper No. 159, Washington, D.C.: World Bank.

Reinert, K.A. and D.W. Roland-Holst. 1995. "Social accounting matrices." In *Applied Methods for Trade Policy Analysis*, edited by J.F. Francois and K.A. Reinert. Cambridge: Cambridge University Press.

Roland-Holst, D.W. 1992. "Stabilization and structural adjustment in Indonesia: An intertemporal general equilibrium analysis." Technical Paper No. 83, Paris: OECD Development Centre.

Ten Kate, A. 1993. "Industrial development and the environment in Mexico." Working Paper No. 1125, Policy Research Department. Washington, D.C.: World Bank.

Tobey, J., J. Reilly, and S. Kane. 1992. "Economic implications of global climate change for world agriculture." *Journal of Agricultural and Resource Economics* 17:195–204.

United Nations. 1993a. *System of National Accounts 1993*. New York: United Nations.

United Nations. 1993b. *Integrated Environmental and Economic Accounting*, Series F, No. 61. New York: United Nations.

U.S. Department of Commerce, Bureau of Census. 1988. *Manufacturers' Pollution Abatement Capital Expenditures and Operations Costs*. Washington, D.C.: U.S. Government Printing Office.

U.S. Department of Commerce, Bureau of Economic Analysis. 1994. "Integrated economic environmental satellite accounts." *Survey of Current Business* 74:33–49.

Walter, I. 1973. "The pollution content of American trade." *Western Economic Journal* 11:61–70.

Wheeler, D. 1992. "The economics of industrial pollution control." Industry Series Paper No. 60, Industry and Energy Department. Washington, D.C.: World Bank.

World Bank, 1992. *Development and the Environment: World Bank Development Report, 1992*. Washington, D.C.: World Bank.

Author Index

Subject Index

accounting, economic, 95; *see also* social accounting matrix (SAM)

ad valorem equivalent, 31

agricultural sector: analytical problems related to reform in, 233; policy reform under Uruguay Round Agreements, 232; subsidies for production, 69

Almost Ideal Demand System (AIDS), 91–2

anti-dumping duties: chilling or harassment effect, 47; effect on price, 39

applied general equilibrium (AGE) model. *See* general equilibrium models

Armington assumption, 7–8, 60, 158; of exogeneity, 260–1; of product differentiation, 272, 311, 343

Armington models: log-linear specification, 135–9; market power in, 343–46; measurement of product similarity in, 343; nonlinear specification, 139–42; sensitivity of results from, 145–6

Atkinson measure, 308

Balance of Trade Function: in evaluation of welfare change, 76–81, 91–2; modified, 82–3

Baldwin multiplier effect of trade liberalization, 369

benchmark equilibrium datasets: CGE models calibrated to, 94; compilation of, 94, 111

CADIC dumping model, 135

calibration: defined, 114; dirty, 274; SAMs in CGE model, 114–15

capital stock accumulation: basic theory, 367–73; model applications with alternative closure rules, 373–6

CGE model. *See* general equilibrium models

closure: capital market, 374–6; defined, 115; labor market, 438–43, 480–2; macroeconomic, 266; use of SAMs in building CGE model, 115–17

Cobb–Douglas demand system, 91–2

commercial policy: dynamics effects of, 385; flexible aggregation approach to analysing, 189–205, 222–3; Goulder–Eichengreen model of savings and investment, 389–92; tools for exact modeling of, 189; using CGE model to estimate, 205–6; using CGE model to examine effects of, 205–22

Commercial Policy Analysis System (COMPAS) model, 135, 147

Compensating Variation: in direct welfare evaluation, 81, 83; measure under Balance of Trade Function of welfare change, 79–81; for single-tariff increase, 85–7; for world price change, 87–9

compensation measures of welfare change, 79–89

competition, imperfect: applied trade policy models with, 15; effects of trade policy instruments under, 333–4; partial equilibrium models with, 135–46; scale economies under, 353–60; trade gains in static models with, 365

competition, perfect: general equilibrium using Armington assumption, 8, 262–70; partial equilibrium models under, 129–35, 142–6; trade gains under, 364–5

computable general equilibrium (CGE) model. *See* general equilibrium models

Constant Difference of Elasticities (CDE), 91–2, 287

Constant Elasticity of Substitution (CES), 91–2

555

Printed in the United States
By Bookmasters